About Access Archaeology

Access Archaeology offers a different publishing model for specialist academic material that might traditionally prove commercially unviable, perhaps due to its sheer extent or volume of colour content, or simply due to its relatively niche field of interest.

All *Access Archaeology* publications are available in open-access e-pdf format and in (on-demand) print format. The open-access model supports dissemination in areas of the world where budgets are more severely limited, and also allows individual academics from all over the world the chance to access the material privately, rather than relying solely on their university or public library. Print copies, nevertheless, remain available to individuals and institutions who need or prefer them.

The material is professionally refereed, but not peer reviewed. Copy-editing takes place prior to submission of the work for publication and is the responsibility of the author. Academics who are able to supply print-ready material are not charged any fee to publish (including making the material available in open-access). In some instances the material is type-set in-house and in these cases a small charge is passed on for layout work.

This model works for us as a publisher because we are able to publish specialist work with relatively little editorial investment. Our core effort goes into promoting the material, both in open-access and print, where *Access Archaeology* books get the same level of attention as our core peer-reviewed imprint by being included in marketing e-alerts, print catalogues, displays at academic conferences and more, supported by professional distribution worldwide.

Open-access allows for greater dissemination of the academic work than traditional print models, even lithographic printing, could ever hope to support. It is common for a new open-access e-pdf to be downloaded several hundred times in its first month since appearing on our website. Print sales of such specialist material would take years to match this figure, if indeed it ever would.

By printing 'on-demand', meanwhile, (or, as is generally the case, maintaining minimum stock quantities as small as two), we are able to ensure orders for print copies can be fulfilled without having to invest in great quantities of stock in advance. The quality of such printing has moved forward radically, even in the last few years, vastly increasing the fidelity of images (highly important in archaeology) and making colour printing more economical.

Access Archaeology is a vehicle that allows us to publish useful research, be it a PhD thesis, a catalogue of archaeological material or data, in a model that does not cost more than the income it generates.

This model may well evolve over time, but its ambition will always remain to publish archaeological material that would prove commercially unviable in traditional publishing models, without passing the expense on to the academic (author or reader).

Visualizing cityscapes of Classical antiquity:
from early modern reconstruction drawings to digital 3D models

With a case study from the ancient town of Koroneia, in Boeotia, Greece

Chiara Piccoli

Access Archaeology

Archaeopress Publishing Ltd
Summertown Pavilion
18-24 Middle Way
Summertown
Oxford OX2 7LG

www.archaeopress.com

ISBN 978 1 78491 889 7
ISBN 978 1 78491 890 3 (e-Pdf)

© Archaeopress and C Piccoli 2018

All rights reserved. No part of this book may be reproduced or transmitted, in any form or by any means, electronic, mechanical, photocopying or otherwise, without the prior written permission of the copyright owners.

Contents

List of Figures v

Acknowledgements xiii

1. Introduction 1

Chapter overview 3

2. Reconstructing past cityscapes before the digital age: A view on Greek and Roman towns 6

2.1 Introduction 6

2.2 The 14th and 15th centuries 7

2.3 The 16th century 13

2.4 The 17th century 24

2.5 The 18th century 29

2.6 The 19th and 20th centuries 34

2.7 Conclusions 47

3. Three-dimensional visualizations in archaeology: An additional tool in the archaeologist's toolbox 49

3.1 Introduction 49

3.2 Creating computer-aided 3D models 53

    3.2.1 Manual 3D modelling 53

    3.2.2 Procedural modelling 55

3.3 Interactive environment: virtual and augmented reality 60

3.4 The scientific value of 3D reconstructions 67

    3.4.1 Rules for 'intellectually transparent' 3D visualisations in archaeology 67

    3.4.2 3D reconstructions as analytical tools 74

        Visibility analysis in a 3D GIS 77

        Analysis of visibility and the use of space using computer graphics methods 78

        Simulation of lighting conditions 80

        Analysis of construction techniques and structural behaviour 82

        Simulation of acoustics 83

        Simulation of human behaviour 83

3.5 Discussion 84

4. The ancient town of Koroneia: Geographical context, historical background and synthesis of the preliminary results by the Boeotia survey 88

4.1. Introduction 88

4.2. Koroneia: Geographical context and historical background 88

4.3 Previous research at Koroneia 97

    4.3.1 Attested cults during the Classical, Hellenistic and Roman times 101

        The temple of Athena Itonia 103

4.4. Preliminary results of the 'Ancient Cities of Boeotia' project 105
    4.4.1 Acropolis 112
        Architecture 112
        Pottery 115
        Stone finds 115
        Discussion 117
    4.4.2 Northern slope 118
        Architecture 118
        Pottery 120
        Stone finds 121
        Geophysics 121
        Water infrastructures 121
        Discussion 121
    4.4.3 Eastern slope 123
        Architecture 123
        Pottery 127
        Stone finds 129
        Geophysics 130
        Water infrastructures 131
        Discussion 131
    4.4.4 Southern slope 134
        Architecture 134
        Pottery 134
        Stone finds 136
        Geophysics 136
        Discussion 137
    4.3.5 Western slope 137
        Architecture 137
        Pottery 137
        Stone finds 138
        Discussion 139
4.5. Conclusions 139

5. The Graeco-Roman town as a physical entity: Sources for a comparison 142

5.1. Introduction 142
5.2 A brief overview of Greek town planning 144
    5.2.1 Archaic period (end of the 8th century – 480 BC) 146
    5.2.2 Classical period (480 – 323 BC) 149
    5.2.3 Hellenistic period (323 – 31 BC) 150
    5.2.4 Roman period (31 BC – ca. 330 AD) 153
    5.2.5 Late Antiquity (330 – 650 AD) 154

5.3 The topography of Graeco-Roman towns: changes and continuities from the Archaic Period to Late Antiquity 157
    5.3.1 Religious foci 158
        Sanctuaries: Diachronic case studies 170
    5.3.2 Agora 174
    5.3.3 Theatres 184
    5.3.4 Houses 190
        Archaic period 192
        Classical period 194
        Hellenistic period 200
        Roman period 204
        Late antiquity 207
    5.3.5 Training spaces 209
    5.3.6 Industrial spaces 212
    5.3.7 Urban fortifications 216
    5.3.8 Trees, groves and gardens 220
5.4 Discussion 223

6. Enhancing Koroneia's GIS survey data with the third dimension: A procedural modelling approach 225
6.1 Introduction 225
6.2 Workflow 227
    6.2.1 A rule-based 3D GIS of architectural survey data 230
        Interpretative visualization for intuitive insights into data clusters 230
    6.2.2 Reconstruction of the ancient terrain morphology and urban layout 232
        Map layers 233
        Street network 236
    6.2.3 Rule based modelling of Koroneia's 3D reconstruction 239
        Domestic architecture 240
        Agora 242
        Theatre 245
        Temple architecture 245
        City walls 245
        Slope dependency 249
        Level of Detail 250
        Sampling points on buildings' surfaces 251
6.3. Results 251
    6.3.1 Visibility analysis in a 3D GIS 251
    6.3.2 Estimating number of houses and population figures 253
    6.3.4 Exporting procedurally modelled Koroneia 259
        Online publication 261
        Interactive navigation and Virtual Reality 261

- 6.4. Discussion 264
  - 6.4.1. Koroneia's 3D reconstruction: Intellectual transparency and reusability 265
  - 6.4.2. Rule-based modelling: challenges and work-arounds 266
- 6.5. Conclusions and future work 270
- **7. Conclusions** 274
- **Bibliography** 280
  - Abbreviations 280
  - Bibliographical references 280

List of Figures

Figure 2.1 Page (13r) from the autograph copy of the Historia Imperialis by the antiquarian and historian from Verona, Giovanni de Matociis. This volume represents an early example of text that is accompanied with drawings, in this case of coins and of a schematic Roman circus (top right corner). The manuscript is kept at the Vatican Library (Ms. Chig. I. VII. 259). [source: https://www.ibiblio.org/expo/vatican.exhibit/exhibit/b-archeology/images/arch01.jpg]..................9

Figure 2.2 Drawing of Rome in a 15th century copy of Fazio degli Uberti's Dittamondo (fol. 18r). [source: copy digitized by Bibliothèque National de France, http://gallica.bnf.fr/ark:/12148/btv1b8426808j/f41.image]......9

Figure 2.3 'Forum' from Giovanni Marcanova's Collectio Antiquitatum (Estense Ms. Lat. 992, fol. 27R, 1465). [source: copy digitized by Princeton University library http://libweb5.princeton.edu/visual_materials/garrett/garrett_ms_158.final.pdf]..................10

Figure 2.4 Left: Reconstruction of the Mausoleum of Hadrian, copy from a drawing by Cyriac of Ancona. Codex Ashmolensis, Bodleian Library, fol. 63r [source: http://bodley30.bodley.ox.ac.uk:8180/luna/servlet]. Right: The imaginary map of Rome in the forgery by Annius of Viterbo: De Aureo Saeculo et de Origine Urbis Romae eiusque Descriptione (1498) [source: http://www.brynmawr.edu/library/exhibits/antiquity/use4c.htm]. 13

Figure 2.5 Map of ancient Nola (engraved by Girolamo Micetto) in the De Nola by Ambrogio Leone (copy from the John Adams Library at Boston Public Library digitised by Internet archive and available at https://archive.org/details/denolaopusculumd00leon)..................14

Figure 2.6 Reconstruction drawings of Rome in Fabio Calvo's Antiquae Urbis Romae cum Regionibus Simulachrum. Top: Romulus' square city, bottom: Rome in Pliny's time (from the digitised copy available at http://arachne.uni-koeln.de/books/FabioCalvo1532)..................17

Figure 2.7 Reconstruction drawing of a Naumachia from Panvinio's De Ludis Circensibus (1600) [source: http://movio.beniculturali.it/bupd/lemusetrailibri/it/159/lapparato-iconografico]..................21

Figure 2.8 The imaginative reconstruction drawing of the temple of Artemis in Ephesos by the Dutch painter Maarten van Heemskerck (1572) [source: https://commons.wikimedia.org/wiki/File:Temple_of_Artemis.jpg]..................22

Figure 2.9 Reconstruction drawing of the siege of Plataea in Justus Lipsius' Poliorceticωn (1596), 66 [digitized by ECHO – Cultural Heritage Online]..................23

Figure 2.10 Hans Gross and a group of German tourists depicted next to the reconstruction of the Meta Sudans in Lauro's Antiquae Urbis Splendor, pl. 90. [source: http://www.harvardartmuseums.org/collections/object/176002]..................27

Figure 2.11 Piranesi's drawing on the construction technique adopted for the funerary monument of Caecilia Metella, in Le Antichità Romane: Divisa in Quattro Tomi: Contenente gli Avanzi de' Monvmenti Sepolcrali di Roma e dell'Agro Romano, vol. III, pl. LIII..................32

Figure 2.12 Left: Restored view of Assos, in de Choiseul 1809, pl. 10; Right: Le Roy's reconstruction of the Temple of Athena in Les Ruines des Plus Beaux Monuments de la Grèce (plate XIII)..................34

Figure 2.13 Restored view of Athens by C. R. Cockerell in Williams 1829..................36

Figure 2.14 Reconstruction of one of the city gates of Pompeii (Gell 1852, pl. XIX)..................38

Figure 2.15 Reconstruction of the 'Queen's Megaron' at Knossos for the Herakleion Museum made by Piet de Jong (after Papadopoulos 2007, Figure 1, p. 3)..................39

Figure 2.16 Gatteschi's reconstruction and photograph of the area of the Via Sacra and the Temple of Jupiter Stator (Gatteschi 1924, 29-30)..................40

Figure 2.17 Top, left: View of Athens, reconstruction drawing by P. Connolly (in Connolly and Dodge 1998). Top, right: The Roman town of Silchester by Alan Sorrel; Bottom: Preparatory stage for the reconstruction drawing of the temple area at Caerwent, Wales by Alan Sorrell with his annotations on the margin (after Catling 2013, 34 and 37)..................41

Figure 2.18 The 3D physical model of Pompeii at the National Archaeological Museum of Naples (source: https://it.wikipedia.org/wiki/File:Plastico_di_Pompei_1.JPG). 43

Figure 2.19 Paul Bigot and his 3D model of Rome in 1911 (after Royo 2006, Figure 95, p. 165). 43

Figure 2.20 Scene from the movie QuoVadis (1951) in which Nero illustrates his plan for his new Rome in front of Gismondi's plaster model (from Wyke 1997, 141). 46

Figure 3.1 Example of reconstructive drawings of elements of the Mater Matuta's temple (Satricum) by P. Lulof (after Ratto 2009). 52

Figure 3.2 L-systems applied to plants and architecture. Left: picture from Prusinkiewicz et al., 2000, 397; Right: picture from CityEngine 2010.3 user manual. 57

Figure 3.3 Example of a CGA rule for the creation of a building. Numerical values are stored as attributes at the beginning of the rule to control them more easily. In this case, buildings are assigned a random height between 6 and 8 meters (line 1). The 2D initial shape "Lot" is turned into a 3D building shell by extrusion (line 4). Next, a component split is used to separate the obtained 3D geometry in individual faces (line 5). A split rule along the y axis is used to divide horizontally the selected face corresponding to the building facade to create two floors (line 6). The first floor is then recursively split along the x axis to create a series of windows (line 7), which are substituted by an OBJ file containing a more detailed window frame (line 8).. 57

Figure 3.4 Table from Koehl and Roussel 2015, 144 highlighting strengths and weaknesses of the CityEngine software. 59

Figure 3.5 Process of creating a CGA rule from existing architecture using an inverse procedural modelling approach. Left: A 3D point cloud is evaluated to extract plane surfaces; Centre: detection of architectural elements and assessment of their size; Right: The reconstruction of the temple of Poseidon, Paestum, obtained with the above mentioned procedure (after Weissenberg 2014, figs. 7.1, 7.4 and 7.5). 60

Figure 3.6 Two of Heilig's inventions: (left) the 'Sensorama Simulator' and (right) the 'Telesphere Mask' (source: http://www.mortonheilig.com/InventorVR.html). 61

Figure 3.7 Schematic diagram of the sources that are generally used for a 3D model of archaeological evidence (after Hermon 2008). 68

Figure 3.8 Screenshots from the virtual environment elaborated by Kensek et al. Left: Hyperlinks point to additional information regarding the different confidence levels of the reconstruction and alternative hypotheses; Right: the interface that allows the user to choose different types of columns, capitals and shafts to be displayed (Kensek et al. 2004, 181 and 182). 71

Figure 3.9 Screenshots from the navigation through the virtual reality application of the Villa of Livia by CNR-ITABC, which used to be available at http://www.vhlab.itabc.cnr.it/flaminia/. The avatar that guides the user through the exploration of the Villa encounters icons that display extra content when triggered. 71

Figure 3.10 Left: Laser scanning session inside the Regolini-Galassi Tomb at the Sorbo necropolis, near Cerveteri (CNR-ITABC); Right: The installation of the virtual reconstruction at the archaeological museum in Leiden (RMO) (images from http://regolinigalassi.wordpress.com/) 72

Figure 3.11 Archaeological site of Carnuntum, Austria. A perspex panel allows the viewer to see the Heidentor gate in its restored appearance (picture by Jan Madaras on panoramio). 75

Figure 4.1 Koroneia's hill viewed from south-west (top: from Bintliff et al. 2009, 18; bottom: photo taken by D. Grosman during an exploratory flight in 2009). 89

Figure 4.2 The large plain once occupied by Lake Copais, north of Koroneia's hill (picture taken by the author on Koroneia's acropolis). 90

Figure 4.3 Topographical map showing the location of ancient Koroneia in respect to Greece, its territory (bordered by a yellow dashed line), and surrounding sites (modified after Farinetti 2009, Appendix I.1, 1). Sites mentioned in the text: 4) Palaia Koroneia North – Spyropoulos' excavations; 5) Thymari; 6) Mamoura/Alalkomenai; 7) Agoriani/Agia Paraskevi; 8) Alalkomenai; 21-22) Sanctuary of Herakles Charops; 22) Pontza – Agioi Taxiarchoi; 30) Butsurati. 91

Figure 4.4 The Frankish tower on the small eminence north-east of Koroneia's hill (picture taken by the author from the lower northern slope of the hill looking south-east). 96

Figure 4.5 Map of Koroneia's hill as published in Maier 1959, 129. 100

Figure 4.6 Sketch of Koroneia's hill and surrounding by Lauffer (1986, Figure 86, p. 77). Note the drawing of the theatre, the Frankish tower, a spring at the eastern foot of the hill and a temple on a lower terrace from the acropolis. 100

Figure 4.7 Stele found at Koroneia depicting a ritual connected to the worship of Sabazios (Bonanno 2008). 102

Figure 4.8 Top left: Remains of one of the excavated building (A in Spyropoulos' report) as photographed by the author in August 2013. Note the visual connection with Koroneia's hill (the Frankish tower is visible in the background); Bottom left: The original position of the reused tripod bases blocks as recorded by P. Amandry (1978, Figure 2), viewed from west; Top right: View of building B (now covered by overgrown vegetation) from building A (Spyropoulos 1973, Figure 225, b). 105

Figure 4.9 General overview of Koroneia's hill, showing the survey units and the location of some classes of finds that will be discussed in this section, such as architectural remains (both in situ and erratic), funerary and honorific elements, miniature vases, kantharoi and column drums. Pappadakis' excavations at the supposed Itonion are marked with A. 107

Figure 4.10 Overview of water infrastructures on the hill: 1) modern fountain constructed by reusing parapet blocks; 2) water channel built with the same technique as the Frankish tower situated in its proximity; 3) sewer with EW orientation (probably flanking a street); 4) underground spring covered by a large fig tree; 5) seasonal stream; 6) cistern (perhaps corresponding to the well excavated by Pappadakis in which the headless statue of Hadrian was found); 7) GPR results possibly indicating a stretch of the Hadrianic aqueduct. 108

Figure 4.11 Geology of the hill (as mapped in the field by K. Wilkinson). 108

Figure 4.12 Overview of the in situ wall lines recorded during the survey and extended to better show their orientation (map made by B. Noordervliet). 110

Figure 4.13 Location of the areas in which the hill has been divided for the discussion of survey finds. 111

Figure 4.14 Examples of some of the fragments of vaulted ceilings recorded on the acropolis (pictures by I. Uytterhoeven). 113

Figure 4.15 Overview of architectural finds on the acropolis. 114

Figure 4.16 Map showing the location of millstone types (made by B. Noordervliet, in Brasser 2013, 46). 116

Figure 4.17 Modern quarry located on the north-western side of the hill (see Figure 4.9 for its position). 118

Figure 4.18 Overview of the finds on the northern slope 119

Figure 4.19 Architectural survey at Koroneia: Inge Uytterhoeven recording some large blocks between grids 709-710 and 704-707 (photo: author). 120

Figure 4.20 Results and interpretation of the magnetic survey conducted by Eastern Atlas on the lower northern slope 122

Figure 4.21 Overview of the finds on the eastern slope where the theatre (grid 377) and the agora (grids 98-128) were located. 124

Figure 4.22 The depression on the slope of the hill once occupied by Koroneia's theatre (picture taken by the author inside the supposed cavea looking north-west). 125

Figure 4.23 The Hellenistic – Roman Ionic capital reused as a press weight probably in Late Antiquity (photos by I. Uytterhoeven). 125

Figure 4.24 Eastern slope, southern part. 127

Figure 4.25 The Roman tomb with arcosolium illegally excavated on the eastern side of the hill. Broken slabs were found in its proximity (picture by the author). 128

Figure 4.26 Sample of finds from the Archaic-Classical cemetery, the figurines highlighted (Bintliff et al. 2010, 39). 129

Figure 4.27 Detail of the interpretation of the magnetometry survey's results (by Eastern Atlas) on the eastern slope of the hill. The raster image of the results in this area is shown in Figure 4.29... 131

Figure 4.28 Overview of the areas on the eastern and southern slopes that have been covered by geophysical survey. The features interpreted as roads (in light pink) and the remains of foundations and walls (in brown) show a regular lay out on the plateau and on part of the southern slope, while at the foot of the latter the orientation shifts, probably to adapt to the terrain. Two large anomalies at the foot of the southern slope (A and B) have been interpreted as the city wall circuit. C identifies the supposed path of the Hadrianic aqueduct resulting from the GPR survey by L. Verdonck.. 133

Figure 4.29 Results of the magnetometry survey on the hill's plateau and southern slope (by Eastern Atlas)..... 134

Figure 4.30 Overview of the finds on the southern slope 135

Figure 4.31 Western slope with surveyed towers (A and B). 138

Figure 4.32 Reconstruction hypothesis of the path followed by the acropolis and lower city wall circuits based on the hill's contour lines, geophysical results and related finds such as funerary elements and stamped rooftiles bearing the city mark Koppa (Ϙ). 139

Figure 5.1 Lato: general plan of the site (Kalpaxis in Greco 1999, 120 after Hadjimichali 1971, 168)..................... 147

Figure 5.2 Plan of Halieis abandoned around 300 BC (Ault 2005, Figure 1). 148

Figure 5.3 Megara Hyblaea: general plan of the site (after Tréziny 2005, Figure 2, p. 58). 148

Figure 5.4 Knidos: general plan of the site (after Love 1973, 414). 150

Figure 5.5 Kastro Kallithea: site map on contour lines (Haagsma et al. 2014, 198). 152

Figure 5.6 Petres of Florina: general plan and detail of the excavated areas (modified after Adam Veleni 2000). 152

Figure 5.7 Ephesos's grid in Hellenistic (left) and Roman (right) times (Groh 2006, 55 and 73). 154

Figure 5.8 Corinth: The extent of the Late Antique settlement revised according to recent investigations (Slane and Sanders 2005, 245)... 156

Figure 5.9 The results of geophysical prospections at Tanagra show that what was initially thought as the Classical fortification, marks instead the perimeter of the Late Roman town, while the Hellenistic town occupied a larger area, here hypothetically mapped with the red line by J. Bintliff on map 1621-101 contained in the report by Eastern Atlas (Meyer et al. 2017). 157

Figure 5.10 Map of Delos' excavated areas (modified after Moretti et al. 2015, pl. 7).. 161

Figure 5.11 Top: Map of the sanctuary of Zeus at Nemea showing the facilities around the sanctuary such as the Xenon, highlighted in red (modified after Miller 1990, 34); bottom: Reconstruction drawing of the Xenon at Nemea (Kraynak 1992, 121). 163

Figure 5.12 The sanctuary of Zeus at Dodona around 400 BC (top) and in the 3rd century BC (bottom) [source: http://ancient-greece.org/archaeology/dodona.html]... 165

Figure 5.13 Plans of a Greek, an Etruscan and a Roman temple. 1) Podium or base; 2) engaged column; 3) freestanding column 4) entrance steps; 5) porch and 6) cella (from Cunningham et al. 2014, 132). 167

Figure 5.14 Reconstruction drawing of the nymphaeum of Herodes Atticus and Regilla at the sanctuary of Zeus in Olympia (after Longfellow 2009, 230). 168

Figure 5.15 The sanctuary of Demeter and Kore from 500 BC to the Roman period (modified after Bookidis and Strout 1997).. 171

Figure 5.16 Top: Plan of the sanctuary of Artemis Orthia in Sparta at the end of the excavations in 1910 where the excavated temples, the altars and the Roman theatre are visible (Dawkins 1929, pl. 1); bottom: Reconstruction drawing of the Roman theatre (from Pausanias Project at http://www.pausanias-footsteps.nl/english/sparta-eng.html). 173

Figure 5.17 Plan of the agora of Kastro Kallithea and 3D reconstructions of the excavated buildings: Building 1 (stoa), Building 4 and Building 5 (Temple) (Haagsma et al. 2014, figs. 2 and 9; 3D modelling by R. C. Lee). 179

Figure 5.18 Top, left: The agora of Kos during the 4th century BC; Top, centre: The modifications of the 2nd century BC; Top, right: The substantial changes during the 2nd century AD including the creation of a monumental access to the square (Rocco and Livadiotti 2011, 387; 397; 407); Bottom: Reconstruction drawing of the monumental access to the square by arch. G. Campanile, G. Carella, E. Cappilli, D. D'Oria, M. Fumarola, S. Valentini, based on the study of G. Rocco and M. Livadiotti (Rocco and Livadiotti 2011, 404). 182

Figure 5.19 The agora of Thasos (Grandjean and Salviat 2000, Figure 21). 183

Table 1 Audience orientation in a sample of 123 preserved theatres across the Greek world (after Ashby 1999, 104). .. 185

Figure 5.20 Reconstruction (a) and cross section (b) of the theatre of Delos at the beginning of the second half of the third century BC (Moretti 2014b, 122); c) Detail of the last phase of the skene in an aquarelle by Th. Fournet (Fraisse and Moretti 2007, Figure 425). 187

Figure 5.21 Left: Examples of Archaic house plans (a-b) Emporios, Chios; c) Thorikos, Attica; d) Eretria, Euboea; e) Aigina; f) Limenas, Thasos; g) Dreros, Crete; h) Koukounaries, Paros; i) Onythe, Crete; j) Vroulia, Rhodes; k) Kopanaki, Messenia, from Lang 2005, 16. Right: Phases of the Archaic house in Lemnos (Caruso 2011, 190). 193

Figure 5.22 Olynthos. Left: Plan of the town (Cahill 2002, 26); Right, top: reconstruction drawing of a domestic insula (Carroll-Spillecke 1989, Figure 3, p. 18); Rigth, bottom: reconstruction drawing of a house's courtyard and pastas (in Hoepfner 2009, 176). 195

Figure 5.23 Left: Plan of the excavated houses around the agora in Lato; right: Detailed plan of House Δ (Westgate 2007, 429-30). 196

Figure 5.24 Plan (left) and reconstruction (right) of House 7 at Halieis. The entrance is characterized by a roofed vestibule (prothyron) (Ault 2005, Figure7 and 9). 197

Figure 5.25 Plan and reconstruction of House II at Eretria (Ducrey 2004, 161 and 163). 197

Figure 5.26 Plan of an insula of 'normal houses' in Delos (Trümper 2003, plate 1). 202

Figure 5.27 Delos: Plan of the excavated quarters near the theatre with the distribution of houses, shops and workshops (Trümper 2003, plate 4). 202

Figure 5.28 Delos: Architectural development of Houses IC and ID (Zarmakoupi 2014, 562). 203

Figure 5.29 Left: Reconstruction drawing of three houses at Petres with hagiati-like roofed open area (Adam-Veleni 2000, 57); Right: Characteristic hagiati in a house at Livadeia, Boeotia (Sigalos 2004, Figure 97, p. 282). .. 203

Figure 5.30 Examples of masonry techniques for stone socles in Late Classical and Hellenistic domestic architecture: (Right) Eretria (Ducrey 2004, 160) and (left) Knidos (Love 1970, Figure 11). 204

Figure 5.31 Plan of the Roman house at Kos with the three representational spaces in color (Albertocchi 2010, 41). 206

Figure 5.32 Reconstructed court and peristyle of the Roman house at Kos after recent restoration (Sideris 2015, 80-1). 207

Figure 5.33 Left: Plan of the excavated house at Hephaisteia, Lemnos (Papi et al. 2008, Figure 44, p. 982); rooms 10, 12 and 13 correspond to the Late Antique house-shop; Right: Reconstruction hypothesis of the house-shop (Piccoli 2008, 244). 209

Figure 5.34 Plan of the south side of the Athenian agora in ca. 400 BC with the area occupied by the race track (Camp 2003, 24). 210

Figure 5.35 Plan and reconstruction model of the palaistra-gymnasion complex at Delphi (ca. 330 BC) (plan: Scott 2013, Map 19.1; picture from http://davidgilmanromano.org/courses/ancient-athletics/lecture-images/24). 210

Figure 5.36 Pottery factory in Messenia in the 1940s (Stillwell 1948, pl. 4b). 212

Figure 5.37 Plan and reconstruction drawing of the Archaic workshop of Mandra di Gipari, Crete (Rizza et al. 1992, 17 and 155).. 215

Figure 5.38 Examples of (top, left) courtyard gate; (top, right) overlapping gate and (bottom) postern gate with overlooking tower at Kastro Kallithea (created by R.C. Lee, source: http://people.tamu.edu/~ryanlee/kallithea.html)... 218

Figure 5.39 Typical Late Antique gates in the Roman East: a) the North Gate of Blaundos; b) a smaller gate at Selge; c) the North Gate of Zenobia and d) the East Gate of Resafa (drawings by I. Jacobs, in Jacobs 2009, 199)............ 220

Figure 5.40 Left: Plan of the Hephaisteion; on the left, the rows of cutting in the bedrock to host trees and flower pots; Right: Flower pots from Olynthos (Burr Thompson 1937, 399; 406; 409)...................................... 222

Figure 6.1 The workflow for the creation of Koroneia's 3D visualization... 226

Figure 6.2 Left: Part of the procedural rule written in CityEngine which evaluates the information contained in the specified columns in the architectural pieces' shapefile (e.g. LengthFIN, HeightFIN sand WidthFIN) to modulate size and appearance of the architectural finds based on their characteristics as recorded in the field................... 228

Figure 6.3 An example of some data layers of Koroneia's 3D GIS: the DEM with overlaid grid of the areas that were accessible during the survey, the terraces mapped during the geomorphological survey, the provisional results of the ongoing geophysical prospections, and the architectural finds. The latter are scaled according to their dimensions (here multiplied by a factor of 10 for visualization purposes) as recorded in the field, and categorized per stone type with a procedural rule that was written in CityEngine and imported in ArcGIS. In this way, clusters of stones, the relationship between the dimension of the blocks and the stone type, and special finds (of which 3D models are automatically imported as OBJ files) become immediately apparent. 229

Figure 6.4 Top: Examples of historical aerial imagery that was used together with the terraces mapped by age (overlaid on the DGPS points representing the current terrain morphology) as guides to create a reconstruction hypothesis of the terrain in antiquity. Green lines represent ancient terraces, red lines modern terraces, yellow lines terraces of uncertain age. Points were added to (represented in blue) or subtracted from those originally recorded on the hill during the microtopographic survey. As a result, a new DEM was created by interpolating the points in ArcGIS using a Kriging interpolation method (see prediction error map). This DEM was then stylized as a grey scale image and exported in TIFF format to be used as a terrain heightmap in CityEngine. 231

Figure 6.5 A TIFF image of the geophysical results and the in situ walls (in red) is imported as map layer in CityEngine, thus allowing the retention of the visual and spatial relationship between the original data and the reconstructed street network. 232

Figure 6.6 The two obstacle maps that limit the generation of the 3D environment only within the white area. Left: the obstacle map covers the largest town extent with the northern stretch at the foot of the slope according to the surveyed architectural remains; right: obstacle map covering the town extent when the geophysical features are considered (for the discussion of the available archaeological evidence, see chapter 4)......................................233

Figure 6.7 Left: TIFF image loaded as attribute layer in CityEngine to guide the creation of different land uses; Right: Window menu that allows the creation of an attribute (i.e. 'Zoning') associated with the land use map.................. 234

Figure 6.8 Rule file that guides the mapping of different land uses according to the input image represented in Figure 6.7.. 234

Figure 6.9 Screenshot from the CityEngine viewport showing the results of the application of the attribute map (visualized as the black and grey image underneath the reconstructed town). This map assigns the rule for the creation of buildings to the light grey area and the rule for the generation of vegetation to the darker grey area. In this way, it is possible to quickly create two reconstruction hypotheses that show the northern area of the town as either sparely or more densely built up.. 235

Figure 6.10 Left: Screenshot from ArcMap's workspace displaying the geophysical results and the in situ wall stretches which have informed the reconstruction of the street network (in blue, the lines that were stored in a shapefile and imported as input data into CityEngine); Right: The reconstructed urban grid adapted to the terrain in one of the proposed hypotheses. 236

Figure 6.11 Screenshot from CityEngine showing the overlap between the terrain heightmap and the layer with streets and blocks. 237

Figure 6.12 Example of the parameters that I have set as attributes in the rule for domestic architecture. Note the addition of explanatory comments preceded in this case by a double slash (//) to exclude them from the parsed code. 238

Figure 6.13 Lines from the rule of domestic architecture which categorize the houses according to their size. Note the insertion of comments, which explain the modelling choices that are recorded in the rule files. In this case the multi-line explanation is excluded by the processed script by adding /* and */ at its beginning and end (cf. other scripting languages such as C). 238

Figure 6.14 Examples of the procedurally modelled house shapes: Type 2 (top, left); Type 3 (top, right); Type 4, in this instance with closed ground floor (bottom, left), and type 5 (bottom, right). Scan the QR code to view a 3D model of one of the houses on SketchFab. 239

Figure 6.15 Example of how an attribute (in this case 'porch') is used to guide the random, yet controlled generation of 3D geometry. In this case, 70% of the instances will be created with a porch, while the rest will be assigned a closed ground floor. 239

Figure 6.16 Top: Examples of the images that I have created for texturing and bump mapping (texture/ bump image for doors; texture for the outer walls). Bottom: Example of rendering (in e-on VUE Infinite 2015 PLE) of the procedurally modelled town with textures applied. 240

Figure 6.17 The procedurally modelled agora area which is occupied by a long stoa on the eastern side and scattered trees and altars on the open space. 241

Figure 6.18 The 3D model of the theatre (in OBJ format) that I have created in Blender and imported into the CityEngine using an ad hoc rule. To create some vegetation around the theatre, I have used a scatter operation which randomly places on the surface a set number of 3D models of trees according to a Gaussian distribution. Left: The original 3D model of the theatre as modelled in Blender; right: screenshot from the CityEngine viewport showing the result of the application of the CGA rule file (with vegetation displayed with a high LoD). 242

Figure 6.19 Lines added in the rule file for temple architecture to be able to visualize two possible reconstruction hypotheses of the supposed Itonion. 242

Figure 6.20 Left: Screenshot from the CE inspector with highlighted the Boolean attribute 'amphiprostyle' defining whether columns are only at the front or also at the back of the temple. Right: Visualization of the two reconstruction hypotheses that can be swopped in real time by switching the attribute 'amphiprostyle' on or off. 243

Figure 6.21 The shapefile containing the remains of the temple as recorded in the field (grey lines) is imported into CityEngine and the procedurally generated 3D reconstruction of the temple (here in wireframe mode) is created on top of it, thus making clear the spatial relation between the original data and the reconstruction. 243

Figure 6.22 Textures of the city wall circuit of the lower town and screenshot from the CityEngine workspace displaying a rule based modelled stretch of the walls. The rule allows the creation of towers at crossing points with streets by inserting 'Crossing' in the inspector's field 'Start Rule'. 244

Figure 6.23 Beginning of the annotated rule file for the modelling of Koroneia's houses, showing the lines that allow setting the pivot of the initial shape to a defined location (see section 6.2.3 for a more detailed explanation of this work-around). In this case I chose the north-east corner of the shape's scope as target pivot to be able to orient the courtyards towards south and east. The rule includes moreover the function to calculate the slope, which informs the generation of the 3D environment and has been used to calculate the number of houses in relation to different slope input values (see below, § 6.3.2). 246

Figure 6.24 Beginning lines of the CGA rule file that is applied to streets. The file starts with commented out references to the dimensions of streets in other 4th century BC sites that have been excavated or surveyed in Boeotia and elsewhere. The proper rule starts at @StartRule and includes the formula to calculate the slope degrees and the conditional rule (case ... else) that guides the creation of a street or different types of steps within the set range of slope degrees. For reference, I have included as a comment the indications from modern construction guidelines. 247

Figure 6.25 Screenshot from the CityEngine workspace where only the street network is selected, to show the dynamic rendering of streets and steps according to the slope degree by applying the rule file written for this project. 248

Figure 6.26 A city block generated by the procedural rule for domestic architecture; in a) one of the possible different configurations of space that are encoded in the rule file are represented (HighLOD = true); b) displays the low Level of Detail scene, which generates geometries as coloured volumes (HighLOD = false); c) shows the panels and points that can be exported and used to perform visibility analysis in ArcGIS, as shown in Figure 6.29. 248

Figure 6.27 The procedure of sampling points and panels on the building's walls and roofs is triggered by switching between the options of the attribute Panels-Generate in the inspector. 249

Figure 6.28 Screenshot from ArcScene workspace showing the overlay between the architectural data displayed using the procedural rule described above and the procedurally modelled reconstruction hypothesis (in low LoD) imported as gdb. 250

Figure 6.29 The application of the possibility to sample points on the buildings' facades. Top: the results of the Line of Sight analysis that was run in ArcScene on a portion of the procedurally modelled environment in CityEngine to map which parts of the temple are visible from the observer points that were located on the agora, on the theatre and in other parts of the lower town. Bottom: A close-up of the temple which shows the sight lines coded according to the target points' visibility from the observers. 252

Figure 6.30 Hypothesis 1: The threshold for the terrain suitable for buildings is up to 9°. This scenario returns a total amount of 321 houses (automatically calculated by including the report operation in the rule). 255

Figure 6.31 Hypothesis 2: The threshold for the terrain suitable for buildings is up to 12°. This scenario returns a total amount of 615 houses. 256

Figure 6.32 Hypothesis 3: The threshold for the terrain suitable for buildings is up to 13°. In this case, the total amount of houses is 765. 256

Figure 6.33 Hypothesis 4: The threshold for the terrain suitable for buildings is up to 14°, which allows 965 houses. 257

Figure 6.34 Hypothesis 5: The threshold for the terrain suitable for buildings is up to 24°, which allows 1883 houses. 257

Figure 6.35 Koroneia's 3D visualization exported in the *.3ws format and viewed in the CityEngine Web Viewer: a) Alternative scenarios can be compared using the swipe view; b) buildings can be tagged so that they are easily searchable, and as shown in c) the lighting conditions can be changed to see their impact on the 3D scene. 260

Figure 6.36 Screenshot from Unity3D showing the 3D reconstruction of Koroneia both from a bird-eye view and as it would appear as a first person navigation. 262

Figure 6.37 A screenshot of the VR experience with a smartphone and a cardboard VR viewer. 262

Figure 6.38 The main layers that compose Koroneia's 3D GIS environment. Bottom: terrain layer; middle: survey data (for the moment limited to architecture and geophysical prospections) and survey grids; top: one of Koroneia's procedurally modelled reconstruction hypotheses based on the current state of the data. 264

Figure 6.39 A screenshot from CityEngine showing the reference system of the initial lot, which consists of an oriented bounding box ('scope') governing all the operations that are performed on the shape. 266

Figure 6.40 Lines of the CGA rule for domestic architecture which allows a more robust control on the reference system of the initial lot. 267

Figure 6.41 The problematic treatment of building facades in default L-shapes: using CityEngine's standard syntax faces 1 and 3 cannot be distinguished and neither can 2 and 4, which makes it challenging to assign a different texture to facades facing the courtyard with respect to those that face the street. The adopted solution is given below. 268

Figure 6.42 Lines of rule that allow a consistent indexing of the L-shaped building's facades 268

Figure 6.43 Results of the test analysis on global (top) and local (bottom) integration values of Koroneia's reconstructed street network. 271

Acknowledgements

This work results from the research that I conducted for my PhD at the Faculty of Archaeology, Leiden University. The successful completion of this book would not have been possible without the support, encouragement and feedback of many people that I would like to thank from the bottom of my heart.

First of all, I would like to thank my supervisor John Bintliff for his guidance and support during these years. I could have not imagined what path my life would have taken after we first met by chance at the Tijdschrift voor Mediterrane Archaeologie Jubileumdag in Groningen when I had just moved to the Netherlands in 2008. His breath of knowledge has always been a source of inspiration and I am grateful that he has trusted me in developing this research in the direction I wanted, while giving me at the same time the necessary feedback. I must thank him also for his genuine interest in my professional development, and for offering me numerous opportunities to teach and give workshops on my research topics. Secondly, I would like to thank my co-supervisor Karsten Lambers for his thorough feedback on my research, which has greatly improved the content of my dissertation. I would like also to thank him for giving me the chance to continue with research and teaching within the Digital Archaeology Research Group, an opportunity which I took with much enthusiasm and commitment. Next, I would like to thank Hans Kamermans, who has been always a constant reference point over the years in Leiden and helped me to develop a critical view on 3D modelling in archaeology. I owe a big thanks also to Hanna Stöger, with whom I have shared the office at the faculty for many years. She has been a constant and trusted support, help and a source of inspiration and advice. Thank you to the PhD committee for taking the time to read the manuscript and send their feedback. I would like to express my gratitude especially to Eleftheria Paliou for her useful comments on chapters 3 and 6.

I consider myself lucky to have conducted my research at the Faculty of Archaeology in Leiden. This faculty offers a vibrant research environment which allowed me to broaden my knowledge about the wide spectrum of archaeologies that are carried out by faculty members covering a broad spatial and temporal range. The large PhD and postdoc community provides always occasions to listen to and discuss about interesting topics. I would like to single out Anita Casarotto, Gianluca Cantoro, Marike van Aerde and Mark Locicero. The time I spent at the faculty would not have been the same without their presence and the chats, coffees and meals that we shared. The support of the Graduate School has been crucial for the completion of this PhD; for this I would like to thank especially the director Miguel John Versluys and the coordinator Roswitha Manning.

My research would not have been possible without the work of the many dedicated members of the Boeotia survey team. First of all, I would like to thank Janneke van Zwienen and Bart Noordervliet for having shared their knowledge on Koroneia with me, for their technical support during fieldwork, and their genuine interest in my research. Next, I would like to thank Inge Uytterhoeven with whom I spent many pleasant hours in the field recording, and learning a lot from her about, the architectural remains at Koroneia and Hyettos. My experience of the Boeotia survey would not have been the same without the company of Athanasios Vionis, whom I also would like to thank for entrusting me with the recording and 3D modelling of the Byzantine churches in Boeotia, which allowed me to expand my knowledge of this phase of Greek history. Chrystalla Loizou has been a great companion during numerous fieldwork seasons, not least during our adventurous recording of the Haliartos tower. I thank Emeri Farinetti, for her support and precious advice in many occasions during my PhD, and Keith Wilkinson, Cornelius Meyer and Dana Pilz for their approachability in discussing the Koroneia's dataset. The work Yannick Boswinkel has done on the architectural finds at Koroneia has been an important data source for this research, so I would like to thank him for his availability in discussing numerous topics about Koroneia's architectural remains. Many thanks also to Fabienne Marchant for providing us with her synopsis on inscriptions related to Koroneia and to the pottery specialists Kalliope Sarri, Mark van Der Enden, Philip Bes and Vladimir Stissi, who have always been available when I had some questions.

I would not have been able to carry out this work without the financial support of the CEEDS project, for which I worked as a researcher for 4 years. Working together with computer scientists, engineers and psychologists has been an enriching experience from many points of view, not least as it challenged my perspective on how we communicate archaeology outside our circle of peers. The scholarships offered by the Dutch Institute at Athens have greatly facilitated my research. I would like to thank the former director Christiane Tytgat and the secretary Emmy Mestropian-Makri for their hospitality and help. The scholarship that I obtained in 2012 at the Virtual Heritage lab of the Italian Institute for Technologies applied to Cultural Heritage (CNR-ITABC) in Rome has been a crucial experience for the development of this work. I learned a lot from every person working in the lab while I was there: Sofia Pescarin, Eva Pietroni, Augusto Palombini, Ivana Cerato, Emanuel Demetrescu, Francesco Vallecoccia, Cécile Thevenin, Andrea Adami, Sara Zanni, Guido Lucci Baldassari, Bruno Fanini and Bartolomeo Trabassi. In particular, I would like to single out Daniele Ferdani and thank him for his feedback on procedural modelling in an early stage of this research. During my stay I have been lucky to find Paola Spataro as my flat mate, I cannot thank her enough for having warmly welcomed me in her Rome.

In the Netherlands, the meetings with the group of Henk Scholten about CityEngine have been particularly helpful, especially in a time when I felt 'like an island' in working with CityEngine. I wish to thank in particular Maurice De Kleijn for the fruitful discussions about 3D in archaeology. The year I spent studying for the Master in Book and Digital Media Studies in Leiden has been enriching and rewarding in so many ways. Not only I got to deepen myself in the history of the beautiful city of Leiden, discovering gems that were previously unknown to me, but I also met wonderful people with whom I shared unforgettable moments. The content of chapter 2 is inspired by the research I carried out during this time, for which I am most indebt to my former thesis supervisor Paul Hoftijzer who introduced me to the world of book history, printing and publishing in the early modern period.

I most certainly would not have finished the writing of my thesis without the help of my parents. Being so distant is difficult, more than ever now that you have become grandparents, but your support and trust in my choices throughout the years have been always reassuring and encouraging for me. I am also lucky to have the best friends one could possibly ask for, who I can always turn to for advice, a laugh and a hug: Giulia Raffaelli, Fabrizia Faes, Cinzia Staltari, Valentina Bellavia, Raffaela Militello, Teresa Sicà and Eleonora Bernardoni, thank you for being part of my life. Finally, I would like to thank my life companion, Jan, for being always at my side. I could not think of a better partner to share this adventure called life with. You are my best friend and my greatest support, as well as a wonderful father. You understand my struggles and my aspirations better than anyone else. We've come so far and we continue to grow together.

This work is dedicated to our daughters, Aurora and Alice, who encourage me to become a better version of myself every day. I wish them to always keep their eagerness to learn new things, and to never doubt what they are capable of.

1. Introduction

It was 1519 when Raphael, together with the humanist Baldassarre Castiglione, wrote his famous letter to Pope Leo X in which he explained his method of architectural representation. He was about to endeavour on an ambitious plan, which Leo X had commissioned him to carry out, to draw the first visual reconstruction of Imperial Rome. This project, which was interrupted by Raphael's death in 1520, aimed to preserve and restore the city which had been ruined by the passing of time, the incursion of barbarian tribes, spoliations and neglect under the Popes. As we learn from the letter, Raphael was convinced that he could in all truthfulness ('per vero argomento') and unerringly ('infallibilmente') reconstruct the buildings in ruins by accurately and systematically documenting the still standing examples, using them as comparison to infer the missing elements, and studying the principles of ancient Roman architecture in the works of Latin authors.

Along with the development of a scientific method of archaeological inquiry, Raphael's self-assurance in the possibility of reconstructing accurately ruined buildings has been progressively substituted for by the awareness of the limitations in our ability to understand the past, and of the necessity to rely on conjectures when trying to reconstruct it. In recent years, the introduction of digital techniques has brought about a revolution in the speed and accuracy with which archaeological evidence can be recorded, and has offered new tools to visualize and analyse complex archaeological datasets. In particular, the use of 3D models in archaeology has increased dramatically in the last few years.[1] Two major topics can be identified, one related to the application of 3D recording techniques to obtain digital replicas of extant remains (which represents the majority of the papers), the other regarding the use of 3D modelling techniques in order to create virtual reconstructions of lost artefacts (which makes up only about 20% of the sample of papers in a survey by Münster).[2] These two branches are conceptually and practically very different, even though they are often subsumed under the common label of 3D modelling.

The ever-growing use of computer-based visualizations and the ubiquitous presence of digital 3D reconstructions have created a new set of challenges for archaeologists working in this field and has made more apparent the conflictual relationship that many archaeologists have with visual representations. While the written word allows an in-depth discussion of the available data and the exploration of the possible alternative interpretations, the visual language calls in fact for more simplified and immediate ways of representation, thus making it challenging to account for the fragmentary nature of the archaeological data and the existence of equally plausible alternative hypotheses in a (on paper or digital) reconstruction drawing. For these reasons, images are traditionally not equated to authoritative interpretations and, as Smiles and Moser put it, 'as a result archaeologists have tended to overlook images or, at best, to consider their existence as an adventitious phenomenon, divorced from the work of 'real' archaeology.'[3]

This unsolved tension between scholarly production and popular culture in archaeology has been reinvigorated by the introduction of 3D modelling techniques, especially in regard to the use of digital archaeological reconstructions. The problematic aspects related to the validation of virtual archaeology have been evidenced by scholars soon after its inception,[4] and the term 'reconstruction' itself has

---

[1] According to a recent survey conducted by Olson *et al.*, among the works that were published in the *Journal of Archaeological Science* those concerning 3D models have increased by 300% in the last decade (Olson *et al.* 2014, 162).
[2] Münster 2013, 198.
[3] Smiles and Moser 2005, 6; cf. also Favro 2006, 325-6, who cites the 'scholarly discomfort with visual representations of ideas'.
[4] E.g. Miller and Richards 1995; Gillings 2000; Forte 2000; Ryan 2001.

been under debate for its implying a certain degree of certainty in the way archaeologists are able to interpret the past through the surviving artefacts. Some scholars have indeed suggested to avoid to use this term completely, and to opt instead for the use of other definitions such as 're-presentation',[5] 'simulation',[6] 'visualization',[7] or 'construction'[8], which reflects the postmodern view that these models are our construction of the past, mediated by our present culture – contrary to the term reconstruction, which conveys a 'false sense of knowledge'.[9]

The implementation of methods for intellectual transparency in relation to the original data and interpretations to ensure a philologically correct 3D reconstruction have indeed received much attention by scholars working in this field and the debate that has sparked for best practices resulted in the publication of documents such as the London Charter and the Seville principles.[10] Despite this progress made in setting standards for computer-based visualizations in archaeology, a recent survey analysing papers presented at major conferences in 2012 has shown that still only a very small percentage of published papers on 3D models in archaeology (1% of 686 papers) included methods to integrate information on the modelling choices and to validate their results.[11] Moreover, since usually the 3D reconstruction is still seen as an accessory phase for the communication of the results to the public, research has been rarely directed to developing a methodology to embed the creation of the 3D model within the cycle of knowledge generation. Advances in computer graphics and 3D GIS, greater accessibility of computer power and 3D modelling software have resulted in an increased knowledge of dedicated programmes by archaeologists allowing them nowadays to experiment more broadly than what was possible before with the use of 3D modelling as a research tool to formulate new hypotheses and analyse complex datasets. Yet in the last decades, there have been only a few examples of 3D visualizations that are exploited for research purposes before (or instead of) being used for public outreach,[12] this latter field comprising still the vast majority of the applications of 3D reconstructions.

The impression one gets is indeed that 3D reconstructions still mainly follow the path that was set since their first popularization in archaeology, when few archaeologists were practically involved in their creation. Especially in early projects related with 3D reconstructions, the quest for realism and for spectacular renderings or interactive experiences could not be fulfilled by archaeologists themselves, who were lacking the computer skills and infrastructure necessary to obtain such results. For this reason, the creation of virtual past environments was often passed over to computer graphics designers or to people that were not directly involved in the data collection and interpretation. Being the focus on delivering the end product, the process of creating the reconstruction and its use as an integral part of research was therefore most of the time overlooked. Except for a few cases (some of which I will discuss in chapter 3), these 3D models are still mostly used as digital counterparts of traditional 2D drawings and as presentation aids for knowledge that is already acquired, namely when the process of data gathering, comparison and interpretation is completed. In doing so, these tools are excluded from the process of hypothesis generation.

This research aims to contribute to current debate on the implementation and use of 3D digital reconstructions in archaeology by developing an intellectually transparent, replicable 3D visualization

---

[5] Kolb 1997.
[6] Forte 1997, 12-3.
[7] Pletinckx 2007, 4.
[8] Clark 2010, 66.
[9] Clark 2010, 66.
[10] http://www.londoncharter.org/; http://smartheritage.com/seville-principles/seville-principles (last accessed Sept. 2016).
[11] Cerato and Pescarin 2013, 290.
[12] A selection of these projects using 3D reconstructions as research tools is discussed in chapter 3 (§ 3.4.2). It must be noted that in other branches of 3D modelling in archaeology such as DEM based regional research, analytical or research uses are much more common (e.g. for visibility studies or optimal path analysis).

that uses advanced methods for the quantitative analysis of the built environment. The approach that I follow in this work is inspired by the use and definition of models in science, namely as dynamic representations of complex systems and phenomena, which are employed as tools for reasoning and continuously evaluated, adapted and updated.[13]

The starting point of this study has been the archaeological survey of the multi-period site of Koroneia, which is located on a hill on the spurs of Mount Helikon in Boeotia, Central Greece. This site has been investigated since 2006 by an international and multidisciplinary team (under the directorship of John Bintliff), which I joined in 2009. The survey research methodology includes a combination of methods such as pottery collection, recording of architectural remains, geophysical prospections and geomorphological analysis, with the aim of shedding light on Koroneia's urban development. The application of such non-destructive methods allows the study of large areas and the collection of a vast quantity of data in a reasonable amount of time. Such investigations add key elements to the comprehension of regional historical development, creating also new narratives for local communities as testimony of their own neighbouring heritage.[14] The sites that are investigated exclusively with such methods continue however to be invisible, which poses challenges for their protection, preservation and valorisation. The use of 3D reconstructions, therefore, is helpful in visualizing the archaeologists' interpretations of the site, both as a way to look at the data from another point of view and as a way to present it to a larger public.[15] The creation of 3D visualizations of past cityscapes, however, presents challenges in itself and therefore the methodology should be chosen carefully to be able both to handle the complex dataset and to enable further engagement with the data and the re-elaboration of the 3D reconstruction.

Koroneia shares the common destiny of 'invisible' town with many other ancient Graeco-Roman settlements, and therefore offers a case study to test methodologies that can be applied also to other contexts. Specifically, the methodology we propose uses in an innovative way tools that are targeted to geo-design and modern urban planning to create a 3D visualization of Koroneia in a GIS environment. With a strong focus on the automation and iteration of the reconstruction process, our visualization allows an intuitive insight into hidden relationships and associations among data and can be used not only as a visualization aid, but also as a platform for generating hypothesis and performing analysis of the townscape.

Chapter overview

The structure of this book is as follows. In **chapter 2**, I will discuss a selection of archaeological reconstructions (both drawings and 3D plaster models) of Roman and Greek cities from the 15th to the 20th century, focussing especially on the motivations, the aims and the methods that guided such endeavours. The attempt to 'reconstruct' ancient urban sites, in fact, is not a novelty of the digital age and, although little research has been done so far in this direction, much can be learned on the role, potential and pitfalls of 3D visualizations in archaeology by taking an historical perspective on reconstructions of archaeological evidence before the introduction of digital techniques. This chapter will shed light on how much the process of reconstruction resulted in a 'construction' of a past that was in fact the re-elaboration of present needs, thoughts and beliefs. The progressive development of a method based on first-hand experience and critical assessment of previous sources led to an increased awareness for the problematic aspects related to 'reconstructing' the past, which can offer food for thoughts to the present day 3D modeller.

---

[13] See the concept of Model-Based reasoning as explored in Magnani *et al.* 2002 and Magnani and Nersessian 2002.
[14] Bintliff 2013b.
[15] Examples of townscapes surveyed with an integrated approach and visualized in 3D are discussed in Corsi and Vermeulen 2012 and Vermeulen forthcoming.

Chapter 3 continues the discussion taking in consideration the use of 3D modelling in the digital age. The various methodologies available to obtain 3D models in archaeology will be presented, and their use, including applications such as Virtual and Augmented Reality, will be discussed from an historical point of view. Attention will be given to the progress made so far towards the creation of more intellectually transparent 3D visualizations, a key element to assess their reliability and their scientific value. I will moreover investigate in more detail what has been done so far to use 3D visualizations as research tools in archaeology and discuss some of the projects that have successfully proven that the potential of 3D goes beyond accurate documentation and public outreach.

After these two introductory chapters, **chapter 4** focusses on the site of Koroneia itself, by presenting its geographical and historical context and discussing both previous research and the currently available preliminary results of the survey on the hill. The combination of old data coming from 19th century travellers' accounts and 20th century excavation reports with the new insights of the survey, will allow us to formulate new hypotheses on the function of some of the surveyed architectural elements and on the urban organization of the hill, which will be further explored and elaborated on in chapter 6.

To offer comparisons to interpret the survey data from Koroneia, in **chapter 5** I shall consider the topographical development of Graeco-Roman towns over the centuries by relying on published material from Boeotia and elsewhere in Greece. In this chapter I will discuss general trends in urban planning in Greece from the Archaic to the Late Roman period, and select specific case studies showing changes or continuities in the architecture and use of public and private spaces (e.g. *agorai*, sanctuaries, theatres and houses). The study of the ancient city has a long tradition, starting from the pioneering work of the French historian Numa Denis Foustel de Coulanges (*La Cité Ancienne*, 1864). The body of literature dealing with aspects of the ancient Greek city (religious, economic, political) and with the development of individual buildings within the city (e.g. *stoas*) has grown immensely over the years. These approaches, however, have often interpreted the ancient city under the light of a dominant socio-economic framework, and presented it as a disjointed ensemble of discrete entities instead of a unified, layered, and ever-changing system. Similarly to the modern city, for which models describing urban growth have been developed since the 20th century (such as the concentric zone model by the Chicago school, or the sector model devised by the economist Homer Hoyt at the end of the 1930s),[16] models have been proposed to explain the origin and development of ancient urban sites. The study of cities has been approached from very different angles and the analytical instruments of various disciplines, such as geography, history, social science, anthropology and economy, have been deployed to investigate urban environments. These models, although complementing each other in partially explaining some aspects of urban developments, focus however on only one element of ancient urban life, such as economic aspects which predominate in the Weber-Finley 'consumer' city and in the 'service' city model proposed by Engels.[17] By simplifying the dynamics of urban life and overemphasizing some aspects over the others, these models evidence the complexity of the city as an entity whose development is difficult to grasp, analyse and predict. The aim of chapter 5 is therefore specifically to reconnect the various phases of the life of Greek urban sites that are often dissected in smaller units, either physical or chronological, due to constraints in the extent of excavation or the deliberate choice of focussing on the best attested phase of occupation, thus offering the background information needed to integrate Koroneia's data and suggest a 3D reconstruction of this site in one of its historical phases.

Finally, in **chapter 6**, the methodology that I have adopted to create a 3D GIS of Koroneia is presented. The workflow is mainly based on the exploitation of procedural modelling techniques and GIS with the

---

[16] For a discussion on the most influential models that have been developed to explain the growth of cities, see Marcus and Sabloff 2008, 3-12.
[17] Engels 1990.

additional assistance of manual modelling software packages. The chapter will focus on the practical implementation of a 3D visualization both of Koroneia's surveyed architectural elements, and of alternative reconstructions of the 4th century BC urban layout. The aim of this work is to provide an intuitive insight into types and concentrations of the recorded architectural pieces, and to create different models that explore a range of possible solutions for building on slope and their impact on urban population size. Our methodology is centred on the exploitation of a rule-based modelling approach, which enables the automation of the 3D modelling process in order to allow for an easy update of the survey data, the iterative display of different reconstruction hypotheses in a time efficient manner, and the creation of a 3D GIS in order to exploit this platform for a quantitative analysis of the built environment. This book concludes with **chapter 7**, in which I summarize the main points that I have explored in this research, discuss the results of the proposed approach, and provide a future outlook for the use of scientific 3D visualizations in archaeology. The rules that I have created for this project are distributed via github for research and educational purposes.[18]

---

[18] https://github.com/cpiccoli/rules.

2. Reconstructing past cityscapes before the digital age: A view on Greek and Roman towns

'The past remains integral to us all, individually and collectively. We must concede the ancients their place...But their place is not simply back there, in a separate and foreign country; it is assimilated in ourselves, and resurrected into an ever-changing present.' (Lowenthal 1985, 412)

2.1 Introduction*

Over the centuries, ancient buildings in ruin have excited the imagination of viewers. Their being fragmentary has triggered artists' creativity and often caused the fabrication of legends to explain their existence. Depending on the sentiment of the beholder, ruins have become a symbol of the transience of life or of the desperate attempt to survive from the oblivion of time.[19] Legends and histories connected with ancient buildings in ruin started to appear in medieval times, in the popular genre of *Mirabilia*. One of the most famous was the *Mirabilia Urbis Romae* (1143) that included a catalogue of monuments of Rome in Classical times, stories connected to the most important ancient buildings, and a suggested itinerary through the city. Despite containing many errors (such as the interpretation of the remains of Roman baths as ruins of palaces), this description, with later modifications and additions, remained a companion for the visitors that came to Rome until the 15th century when it was superseded by a broader knowledge of antiquities by contemporary humanists.[20]

Even more imbued with meanings that transcend their physical appearance has been the creation of reconstruction drawings of these past relics of architecture. Similar to digital 3D reconstructions, these visual restorations are the expressions of the mind-set and cultural milieu of their creators, thus offering us a vivid documentation of the way in which the past was understood, perceived and represented at the time of their realization. As much as the archaeological evidence that they depict, reconstruction drawings also are historical products, as they are the result of the combination of several factors that need to be contextualized to ensure their correct reception.[21] Such factors include the state of the knowledge on the evidence represented, the drawing and survey techniques available at the moment of their creation, and the background and cultural milieu of both the reconstruction maker and the viewer.[22]

As this chapter will show, this type of information is crucial to be able to appreciate reconstruction drawings, and plaster models, however incorrect they appear today, as important sources of documentation not only about the subjects they depict, but more importantly about who made them, and the historical period in which they were produced.[23] One may consider how naïve and fictitious some early reconstruction drawings appear nowadays since a deeper knowledge of the archaeological site under investigation has been acquired, or how outdated some of the first digital visualizations look

---

* An earlier version of this chapter has been published as Piccoli 2017.
[19] For an overview of the fascination for ruins and their use in literature see e.g. Woodward 2001. For the tension between old and new and the consideration of the past as an artefact of the present, see Lowenthal 1985.
[20] Stinger 1998, 67; Benson 2009, 147-182.
[21] Cf. Favro 1999, 366; Smiles and Moser 2005, 6.
[22] See in this respect also Favro 1999, 366.
[23] The decoding of such symbolic values as elements specific of a certain period and cultural milieu belongs to the field of perception studies and has been treated extensively in art history, starting with the pioneering works by Erwin Panofsky (Panofsky 1939). In this regard, see also the works by Pierre Bourdieu, who identifies art perception as a mediate deciphering operation (e.g. Bourdieu 1984, especially chapter 8 – Outline of a Sociological Theory of Art Perception).

to the eye of the present-day viewer whose expectations are high in terms of engagement, realism and interaction. Often, reconstruction drawings or images of plaster models are still being used in presentations and articles without citing the author and the correct period in which they were made, thus leading to the transmission of obsolete ideas, or to the underestimation of works that were instead ahead of their time. Little research has been done so far on this type of visual representations, although they are valuable sources of information for the history of archaeological research. Every drawing entails in fact a process of interpretation of reality, since, as well expressed by the art historian Sir Ernst Gombrich, a drawing 'is not a faithful record of a visual experience but the faithful construction of a relational model (...). The form of a representation cannot be divorced from its purpose and the requirements of the society in which the given visual language gains currency'.[24]

In the next sections, I shall present a selection of archaeological reconstructions depicting Roman and Greek cities and buildings in Europe from the 15th to the 20th century.[25] I will briefly sketch the historical framework in which such representations have been created to provide the contextual information to assess their aims and their novelty. The case studies presented will offer an insight into the variety of functions that reconstructions have fulfilled within the period taken into consideration, which provides the basis for a reflection on the use, purpose and legacy of computer-aided 3D models that have nowadays become ubiquitous in the archaeological domain. This chapter will in fact shed light on the purpose and use of reconstructions, showing the role of reconstruction drawings as functional aids to stir emotional responses, and to support political agendas before being used as a means to present historical information. Moreover, this overview will serve also to investigate the winding path towards the formation of a scientific method of archaeological inquiry, which includes the introduction of personal observations of the extant remains as an integral part of research and the development of a critical appraisal of earlier sources.

2.2 The 14th and 15th centuries

In this period, works describing antiquities rarely used visual representations to integrate or explain the text. One of the early examples of drawings included in a manuscript is to be found in the autograph copy of the *Historia Imperialis* by the antiquarian and historian from Verona, Giovanni de Matociis (or Mansionario), who started to work on it from about 1310. On the side of some pages, he drew a number of coins and a schematic representation of a Roman circus (Figure 2.1). Although Giovanni could have easily inspected directly the architecture of a Roman circus by looking at the specimen still standing in his hometown (the famous Arena of Verona), thus comparing and integrating the textual sources with his personal observations, he relied completely on the encyclopaedia of Isidore of Seville as the primary source for his historical account.[26] As will be discussed in the course of this chapter, the reverence for

---

[24] Cited in Piggott 1978, 7. Piggott was the first scholar who started to critically analyse the history of archaeological illustrations (1965; 1978). In more recent years, Moser has delved deeply into the subject of archaeological representations and their reflections of cultural conceptions and political or nationalistic agendas (Moser 1992; 1998; 2001; 2012; 2014; 2015); Perry has critically analysed the relationship between archaeologists and images (Perry 2009a; 2009b; 2013), stressing the deductive power of reconstructions for example for gaining information about the behaviour and habitat of prehistoric animals (Perry 2013, esp. 293).
[25] The scope of this chapter has been limited to Greek and Roman cities in Europe to provide a context for the case study presented in this work, the Graeco-Roman town of Koroneia in Greece. There are obviously several other instances that show how the past has been 're-constructed' over the centuries in different ways in compliance with the current cultural and political contexts. Examples include other cities (e.g. Babylon, to which the Louvre has dedicated an exhibition in 2008, see http://www.louvre.fr/en/expositions/babylon, last accessed February 2015), archaeological structures (e.g. Stonehenge, to which the travelling exhibition 'Stonehenge belongs to you and me' has been dedicated, see Bender 1998; Hodgson 2004, 140-74) and countries (e.g. Egypt, see Moser 2015).
[26] Weiss 1969, 23.

classical authors and the related general preference for textual documents as seen as more authoritative than knowledge gained by first-hand experience will be long time companions of antiquarian studies.

Most of the examples that I will mention in this section relate not surprisingly to Rome since this city has attracted many humanists that were fascinated by Roman ruins and were trying to preserve the memory of its still obscure ancient past. The humanists' engagement for architectural theory shaped a renewed interest for Roman buildings, which were studied to derive rules of construction, as exemplified by Leon Battista Alberti's De Re Aedificatoria.[27] During this period, the approaches of the antiquarians drawing and reconstructing ancient ruins greatly vary: some of them tried to critically look at earlier sources and treated sceptically the medieval Memorabilia and previous accounts that explained with mythical legends the origins of cities.[28] Generally, however, the interpretations and reconstruction drawings of this period are still mostly based on reproducing the content of earlier textual sources and on creating fantastic explanations and depictions arising from the fascination for these otherwise inexplicable monumental buildings. The Colosseum was for example thought to have been the biggest temple of Rome dedicated to Jupiter and its original shape was reconstructed as being surmounted by a golden dome with a golden statue on top.[29] A similar representation of the Colosseum is to be found in a depiction of the city of Rome that appears in an illuminated 15th century copy of the poem Dittamondo by the 14th century Florentine poet Fazio degli Uberti (1305?-1367) describing in its verses an imagined journey around the world (Figure 2.2).[30] In Rome, the poet imagined meeting the personification of the city, that tells him her story and shows him some of her ancient monuments in ruin, the description of which remains grounded in the traditional view of Rome and draws on the sources that were known by that time, such as the Mirabilia and the chronicle of the 13th century Dominican Martinus **Polonus**.[31]

Rome had severely declined during the ten years' exile of Pope Eugenius IV (1383-1447), who had been forced to leave his episcopal see to escape from the unfavourable political situation in the city. Any visitor coming to Rome in those years could witness a striking contrast between the monumental ancient ruins and the humble 15th century dwellings. In a letter dated March 1443 and addressed to Giovanni de' Medici, Alberto degli Alberti gives us a testimony of this situation, writing that contemporary masonry houses were many but in bad condition, while actually the nicest things to see in Rome were the ruins.[32] Among the scholars that lamented the deplorable state of the eternal city, the name of the Italian humanist Flavio Biondo (ca. 1388-1463) stands out for his innovative approach to antiquities. In his *Roma Instaurata* (1444-46), Biondo assembled his first-hand observations on the ancient topography of Rome with the information that he took from ancient texts such as Pliny, Tacitus, Livy and Suetonius. Although his account is not exempt from errors, Biondo treated ancient texts, medieval sources and hagiographical accounts with a critical approach.[33] Biondo's aim was to collect enough sources for an antiquarian reconstruction of Rome, in order to better inform his contemporaries, who were showing great ignorance about what the city had been like. As appears clear in the preface of the *Roma Instaurata*,[34]

---

[27] Stinger 1998, 66.
[28] See for example Elia Caprioli's *Chronica de rebus Brixianorum ad Senatum Populumque Brixianum (published in* 1505) where he refuses to explain the origins of his hometown Brescia with the tradition that connected them with the myths of Hercules.
[29] Günther 1997, 382.
[30] Fazio degli Uberti, *Il Dittamondo, avec le commentaire d' Andrea Morena da Lodi*, 1447, [Paris, BnF, MSS italien 81], fol. 18r.
[31] Weiss 1969, 47.
[32] 'Le case moderne, cioè in muratura, sono molte ma guaste; il bello di Roma sono le rovine..', Günther 1997, 380.
[33] Günther 1997, 384.
[34] Excerpt from the preface of Roma Instaurata dedicated to Pope Eugenius IV, predecessor of Nicholas V (based on the translation in Warwick 2016, 94, modified by the author): 'Most holy Pope Eugenius, many things persuade me to renew as much as I could the fame of the ruins - more than of the buildings that still can be recognized - of the city of Rome, the mistress of things, but this one thing compelled me the most: there has been so much ignorance of the study of the humanities in previous generations that, since few of the structures of this very city which once existed are understood in their single parts not only by the inexperienced multitude but also by those who are more learned with respect to doctrine, we then see many,

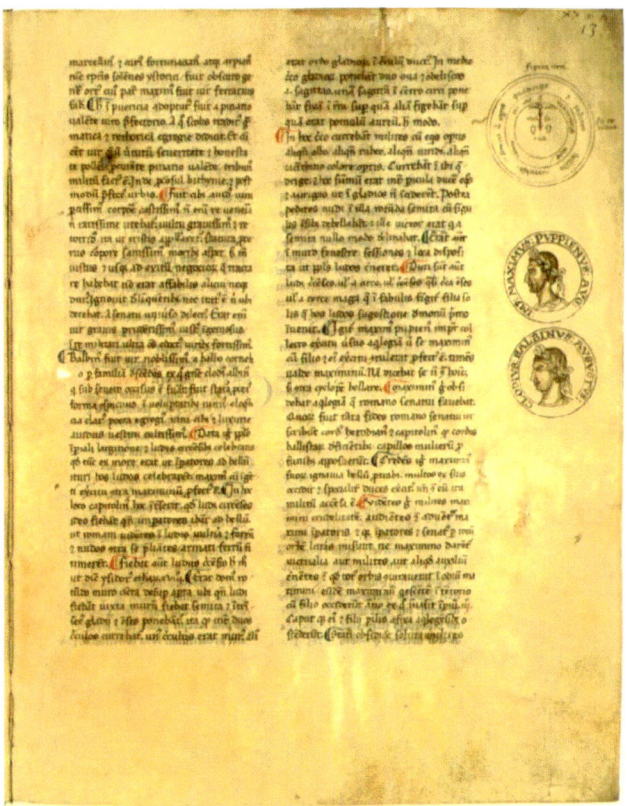

Figure 2.1 Page (13r) from the autograph copy of the Historia Imperialis by the antiquarian and historian from Verona, Giovanni de Matociis. This volume represents an early example of text that is accompanied with drawings, in this case of coins and of a schematic Roman circus (top right corner). The manuscript is kept at the Vatican Library (Ms. Chig. I. VII. 259). [source: https://www.ibiblio.org/expo/vatican.exhibit/exhibit/b-archeology/images/arch01.jpg].

Figure 2.2 Drawing of Rome in a 15th century copy of Fazio degli Uberti's Dittamondo *(fol. 18r). [source: copy digitized by Bibliothèque National de France, http://gallica.bnf.fr/ark:/12148/btv1b8426808j/f41.image].*

the interest of Biondo was however not much focused on the ruins as historical artefacts, but rather on their contribution in a programme of renewing 15th century Rome, with Pope Eugenius IV playing the principal role as its initiator. As McCahill pointed out, through his texts Biondo was indeed 'determined to remind his readers, including Eugenius, that Rome's ancient grandeur is not an irrevocably distant reality but something that has been revived before and can be revived again'.[35]

---

nearly all things fouled, or rather defamed, by false and barbarous names. (...) The return of your pontificate onto its seat confirmed our resolution to write, a return so useful and necessary for its conservation that it is evident that, being already destroyed by calamity and decline, it would be completely lost if you had been absent another ten years. Not only do you nurture Romans with the presence of your accompanying curia, a thing which has always benefited the opulence of the city, but also in many locations you restore and remake fallen, misshapen buildings at the greatest cost. (...) As I owe everything I have to your holiness, why shouldn't I strive to renew Rome with the literary monuments of my small talent likewise you do with the labor of stone workers or carpenters. The renewed account of the works of the Roman Popes who came before you is added to this restoration of our city, which would suit the sanctity of your merit and especially increase your glory (...).'
[35] McCahill 2009, 191.

Figure 2.3 'Forum' from Giovanni Marcanova's Collectio Antiquitatum *(Estense Ms. Lat. 992, fol. 27R, 1465). [source: copy digitized by Princeton University library http://libweb5.princeton. edu/visual_materials/garrett/garrett_ms_158.final.pdf].*

The reconstruction of Rome that Biondo presents is textual, there being no maps or drawings that accompany the verbal descriptions. To find drawings of ancient Rome during the Quattrocento, one has to turn to the *Collectio Antiquitatum* by the Paduan doctor and antiquarian Giovanni Marcanova (1410/18-1467). Several manuscripts of the *Collectio* survive, the earliest being dated to 1465 and kept at the Estense library in Modena.[36] The text, which included copies of Latin and Greek inscriptions, was composed by Marcanova, while the visual representations of ancient monuments and places of ancient Rome have been identified as copies of the drawings of Cyriac of Ancona (1391-about 1455), which were reinterpreted by the painter Marco Zoppo. This manuscript, defined as 'the most lavishly illustrated antiquarian manuscript produced in the Renaissance',[37] contains in fact 18 drawings depicting reconstructed views of ancient Rome and everyday life scenes in the city. Such drawings include, for example, the city gate with towers guarded by armed soldiers, the Monte Testaccio with broken fragments of urns on the ground, the Forum crowded by sellers and buyers and with a circular temple in the centre (Figure 2.3), the Arch of Titus during a triumph, the Diocletian's Baths, and scenes of sacrifices and games, all populated by people in 15th century clothing.

The *Collectio* has received contrasting reviews from contemporary and modern scholars,[38] and although most have dismissed it as a production with low archaeological value, others have tried to contextualize this work within the spirit of the time in which it was produced. As Hülsen noted in his 1907 publication, which discussed the drawings in the *Collectio* for the first time, the reconstructed architecture is a mixture of ancient, Medieval, Renaissance and imaginary elements. Some drawings, in fact, seem to be derived from observations on the spot (such as the equestrian statue of the Emperor Marcus Aurelius, which is reproduced in accurate detail), while others are made by enlarging decorations on cinerary urns (such as in the depiction of the *Vivarium*), or inspired by the contemporary architecture of Bologna, the city in which the *Collectio* was written.[39] The temple in the Forum (Figure 2.3), which has a circular plan instead of the more common rectangular one, is indicative of the early state of the

---

[36] Estense Ms. Lat. 992. Other copies are known, such as the earlier Bern codex (MS. B42) held at the Stadt- und Universitätsbibliothek and the Garrett MS. 158 held at Princeton University Library. While the former has no illustrations, the latter begins with 15 full page drawings with the same representations as the Estense manuscript. A digitized copy of the Garrett manuscript is available at libweb5.princeton.edu/visual_materials/garrett/garrett_ms_158.final.pdf

[37] Trippe 2010, 767-799.

[38] Trippe 2010, 767.

[39] Hülsen 1907.

knowledge on Roman architecture, but also of the preference for circular shapes in sacred architecture during the Renaissance, as exemplified by the theories and works of Leon Battista Alberti.[40] As usual for any depiction of antiquity during this period, these drawings had no intention to reproduce an archaeologically accurate reality; their aim was instead evocative, according to the humanist spirit of 'recollection' that used images as a means to trigger the memories of the viewers, related to a specific place or experience.[41] As Mitchell observed, 'antiquity was in fact becoming an ideal of life, rather than an object of inquiry.'[42]

The contribution of Cyriac of Ancona (1391-about 1455) to the study of antiquities deserves to be explored further as his first-hand recording of Greek and Roman buildings earned him the title of father of modern classical archaeology.[43] Contrary to his contemporaries, who had gained acquaintance with the subject by consulting books in libraries, Cyriac travelled extensively in Greece and Italy, where he recorded and drew in his notes several ancient monuments that he had personally seen. Cyriac was in fact accustomed to travel since an early age, when he used to accompany his uncle, a merchant, in his trade; later on in his life, he became one of the diplomats of Pope Eugenius IV, which took him to several countries, thus allowing him to visit remote places and monuments. Cyriac's first encounter with ancient ruins had been the arch of Trajan in his home town, which, according to Weiss, 'made him realize more and more that what still remained of the ancient world was doomed to perish sooner or later, and that it was therefore his imperative duty to try to rescue, or at any rate record, its relics for posterity before it was too late.'[44] According to Ashmole, although the drawing style of Cyriac is not sophisticated, he paid great attention to reproducing the reliefs or monuments he saw with accurate detail.[45] Probably the most famous of Cyriac's drawings are those that document Hadrian's temple in Cyzicus, which represent an important documentation of this monument that he could visit in 1431 and that would have been almost completely destroyed by 1444 for its intensive use as a quarry.[46]

Besides drawing extant remains, Cyriac drew also reconstructions of the buildings that he recorded. While his documentation drawings are considered fairly accurate, his reconstructions were on the other hand imaginative, giving again confirmation of the fascination that surrounded ancient ruins and the commonly shared intention of reconstructing them 'not to deceive, but as a light-hearted fantasy'.[47] Unfortunately, Cyriac's autograph manuscripts have not survived, his Commentaries probably being lost in a fire that burned down the library of Alessandro and Costanzo Sforza in Pesaro where they were kept. Cyriac's notes and drawings have been transmitted in excerpts and copies in other manuscripts, thus leading to problems of their attribution to Cyriac or to some other draughtsmen.[48] In some cases, however, the copies still give us an idea about the type of reconstructions that Cyriac would have drawn, as in the case of the reconstruction of the Mausoleum of Hadrian (present-day Castel Sant'Angelo). The image of the reconstructed building appears on the folio 63r of the *Liber Monumentorum Romanae Urbis et Aliorum Locorum*[49] that was published at the end of the 15th century and compiled by Bartolomeus Fontius (1445-1513), an important Florentine humanist (Figure 2.4, left).[50]

---

[40] Hülsen 1907, 38.
[41] Trippe 2010, *passim*.
[42] Mitchell 1960, 478.
[43] Bodnar and Foss 2003, ix.
[44] Weiss 1969, 138.
[45] Ashmole 1959, 25-6.
[46] Burrel 2002/3, 36.
[47] Ashmole 1959, 27.
[48] Ashmole 1959, 28.
[49] Codex Ashmolensis, MS. Lat. misc. d. 85, kept at the Bodleian Library.
[50] On this text, see Saxl 1940-41, 19-46, who contextualized it within the role that Roman inscriptions played in the 15th century political panorama. For the contacts between Fontius and Cyriac of Ancona, see especially pp. 29-37.

In other cases, imaginative reconstructions were created on purpose, the lack of a critical approach in analysing texts in this and later periods ensuring their fortune for several centuries. One of the most famous fabricators of stories of this time is the Dominican Annius of Viterbo (1432?-1502), who claimed to publish in his *Antiquitatum* or *Commentaria* (1498) a collection of passages of ancient chronicles and documents, which had been considered previously lost, and that retraced the colonization of Europe to Noah and his grandchildren after the Flood. These texts, to which Annius added his erudite commentaries citing authoritative sources, were skilfully invented by him to reconstruct the history of the Etruscans and ultimately to prove the historical importance of his home town Viterbo as the oldest city in Europe.[51] This work will be published in several editions and will have a great influence on European historiography of the 15th and 16th century, as it provided suitable stories to legitimate the national monarchies that were growing in Spain, France and England.[52] The fortune of Annius' stories is due not only to the fact that they presented Europeans with 'what they wanted to hear about their past',[53] but also that they were convincingly written mimicking the techniques and format of historical scholarship and philology, which immediately evoked scholarly respect.[54]

Other texts that Annius forged are collected in the *Auctores Vetustissimi* printed in Rome in 1489. Among them, there is the *De Aureo Saeculo et de Origine Urbis Romae eiusque Descriptione* by Quintus Fabius Pictor, a 3rd century BC Roman historiographer whose works have not survived. The chronicle describes the early urban developments of Rome on its seven hills and highlights the Etruscan contribution to the early development of the city. Archaic Rome is said to have had the shape of a bow, with the Tiber river as its rope. In one of the editions, a large woodcut view was inserted which represents the city in this way, surrounded by walls in a typically medieval fashion, and features the 'Vicus Tuscus', Viterbo, in a prominent location closed to the city (Figure 2.4, right). This urban configuration of Rome was still taken as authentic into the 18th century.[55]

As the examples discussed in this section show, in this century illustrations of ancient ruins and reconstruction drawings were used sparsely and, when they were inserted, there was no intention or interest to create a historically accurate representation. Generally, antiquarians found satisfaction in an approach to the past based on describing, collecting and comparing ancient relics, where no analytical attempts were made to view the archaeological remains in an historical perspective.[56] Contributions such as Flavio Biondo's and Cyriac of Ancona's stand out for their innovative approach, which included a critical view of previous scholarship and personal surveys. However, this changing attitude does not translate into a different approach towards visual reconstructions. In fact, if present, these are generally an exercise of fantasy, expressing the fascination for the relics of ancient buildings and a means of recollecting memories, in which contemporary elements are mixed together lacking any attempt at historical veracity. In some cases, as shown by Biondo's *Roma Instaurata*, and by Annius' forgeries, furthermore, antiquities and reconstructions become instruments for political propaganda, a metaphor of a past grandeur that could be revived, or threads to weave deceiving narratives of local pride.

---

[51] Weiss 1969, 125-6; Hiatt 2004, 10-1. One of the 16th century detractors of Annius, the Archbishop of Tarragona Antonio Augustín, reports a story according to which Annius, after the discovery of some inscriptions that he had forged and buried in a vineyard in the vicinity of Viterbo, claimed that they matched with a passage in one of his books, confirming that there lay the oldest temple in the world and were the proof that Viterbo had been founded by Isis and Osiris (Stephens 2004, S207).
[52] For the reception of Annius' *Antiquities* and its outreach among European scholars, see Stephens 2013, 277-89; Stephens 2004, S201–S223. The influence of Annius' work on Spanish historiography has been investigated in Caballero López 2002, 101-120.
[53] Allen 1949, 114 cited in Stephens 2004, S203.
[54] Stephens 2004, S216-7.
[55] Weiss 1969, 94.
[56] Stinger 1998, 69.

Figure 2.4 Left: Reconstruction of the Mausoleum of Hadrian, copy from a drawing by Cyriac of Ancona. Codex Ashmolensis, Bodleian Library, fol. 63r [source: http://bodley30.bodley.ox.ac.uk:8180/luna/servlet]. Right: The imaginary map of Rome in the forgery by Annius of Viterbo: De Aureo Saeculo et de Origine Urbis Romae eiusque Descriptione (1498) [source: http://www.brynmawr.edu/library/exhibits/antiquity/use4c.htm].

2.3 The 16th century

During the Renaissance, a new approach towards urban design and planning was developed. While until Medieval times there was the tendency to build a new construction by reusing an existing one,[57] Renaissance architects and commissioners were more prone to razing the old buildings to the ground and using the stones to construct new ones.[58] This situation had a great impact on the urban appearance of Rome, that started more and more to comply with the Popes' agenda of using architecture to create a visually strong impression of their power. Construction works caused accidental discoveries of ancient buildings and sculptures. Especially these latter excited Renaissance antiquarians and led to the production of copies or triggered their imagination in creating tentative restorations of the fragmentary sculptures to their original entirety.[59] This combination of factors prompted an increased interest for antiquities, along with growing complaints by antiquarians against the unscrupulous destruction of ancient buildings and the call for more efforts to document and reconstruct these quickly disappearing testimonies of the past. 'Roma quanta fuit ipsa ruina docet' (how great Rome was, its very ruins tell), a

---

[57] An early example of this practice is the Church of Santo Stefano Rotondo on the Celian Hill that was built on top of a section of the *Castra Peregrina*, on a Mithreaeum.
[58] Weiss 1969, 99.
[59] Barkan 1999, 119–69.

phrase that was written on a drawing depicting the ruins of the Septizodium attributed either to the Dutch painter Marteen van Heemskerck or to Herman Posthumous is the maxim that best summarizes the attitudes towards ancient ruins in this period.[60]

During the 16th century, the amount of visual representations that were used to integrate textual descriptions progressively increases. When antiquarians based their works on classical texts and earlier accounts, a verbal description would be the easiest and most suitable way to transmit this knowledge. However, as was evident already with works such as Cyriac of Ancona's, when a greater attention was paid to the extant remains and their documentation, the use of drawings became the most appropriate technique to record the material evidence that had been personally inspected. This trend of including more visual material in scientific publications as a reflection of an increased reliance on personal observations can be noticed also in other fields such as natural history and the hard sciences.[61] Telling examples are the richly illustrated *De Humani Corporis Fabrica* (1543) by the Belgian Andreas Vesalius (1514-1564) in the field of human anatomy, and the *De Historia Stirpium Commentarii Insignes* by Leonhart Fuchs (1501-1566) in the field of botany. This latter is especially interesting since it breaks with the traditional representations of plants that are found in earlier herbal books and presents instead drawings (made by Albrecht Meyer) based on first hand observations of the plants and seeds that Fuchs had acquired.

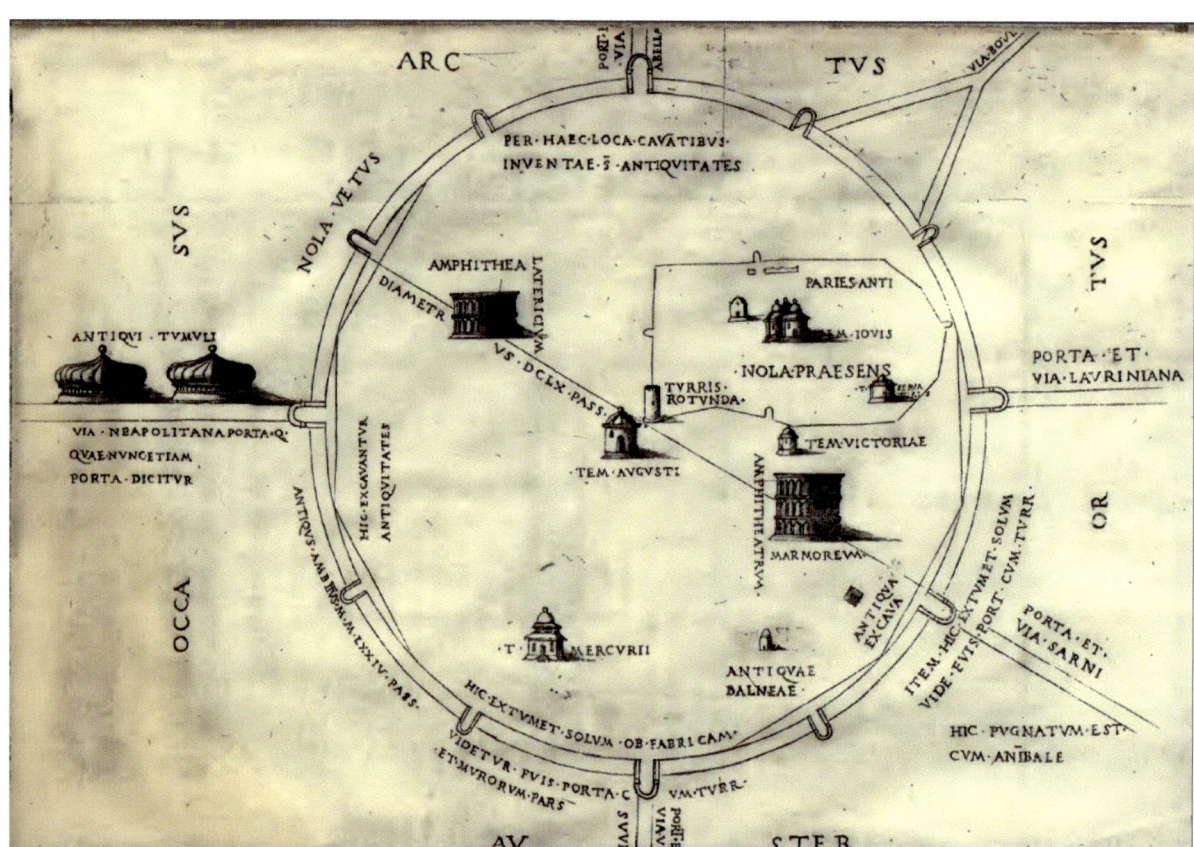

Figure 2.5 Map of ancient Nola (engraved by Girolamo Micetto) in the De Nola by Ambrogio Leone (copy from the John Adams Library at Boston Public Library digitised by Internet archive and available at https://archive.org/details/denolaopusculumd00leon).

---

[60] The coinage of this sentence has been attributed to Francesco Albertini, who wrote it in his *Opusculum de Mirabilibus Novae et Veteris Urbis Romae* (Rome, 1510); after its use for the Septizodium's drawing, the sentence appears again on the frontispiece of Sebastiano Serlio's *Third Book on Architecture* (1544). See Curran 2012, 37. For a contextualization of the first generation of Dutch artists who travelled to Rome in the 1630s such as Herman Posthumous, Lambert Sustris and Maarten van Heemskerck, see Dacos 2004.

[61] Stenhouse 2012, 248.

Fuchs' attitude matches a change of approach in an increasing number of contemporary historians and antiquarians, who dedicated their efforts to survey ancient architectural remains and to provide related documentation based on their personal examination. In Britain, the contribution of William Camden (1551-1623) stands out as a milestone in European antiquarian studies.[62] His *Britannia*, which was published for the first time in 1586 and would be revised and enlarged in the following editions until the 19th century, contained his observations on the places he visited and his study of the material he inspected (such as inscriptions and coins) during his journeys. This topographic work is well situated within the late 16th century and 17th century English Renaissance, in which the study of history underwent a revolution in methodology and scope and contributed significantly to the formation of the 'Englishness' typical of the Elizabethan age.[63] This autoptic approach to antiquities will become more widespread in the course of the 17th century, promoted by the development of a new scientific method that encouraged empirical research over reliance on the authority of Classical authors.

Regarding Roman antiquities, a noteworthy work of the early decades of this century is the *De Nola*, compiled by the physician Ambrogio Leone (1458-1525), friend to the publisher Aldo Manuzio and to Erasmus of Rotterdam. In this work, published in 1514 in Venice, Leone combines the themes of the *descriptio Urbis* and the *laudatio Urbis*, which are typical of humanistic culture, aiming to praise his hometown Nola, near Naples, that he had to leave. Among the engravings that Leone included in the text, we find a reconstruction of Nola in Classical times, which represents the first archaeological plan of a city outside Rome that is known to us (Figure 2.5).[64] In line with the cartographic tradition that depicted Rome as a circular town,[65] the drawing represents Roman Nola as having a circular plan, extending much beyond the town in Leone's time and surrounded by a fortification with twelve regularly spaced gates. A temple of Augustus stands in the middle of the circle, on the same axis as two amphitheatres, one of marble and one of brick. Leone describes the buildings of which the ruins were still visible at his time ('gli avanzi dell'antica città che tuttora si vedono'), providing fanciful reconstructions for the extant remains, again in line with the traditional way of depicting Roman monuments at that time.[66] Noteworthy, moreover, is the effort to contextualize Nola in its territory ('De Agro Nolano' is discussed in the first chapter of the book and presented with an engraving), although the fact that this work is mainly based on inscriptions and ancient texts led Leone to suggest various wrong identifications in attempting to relate ancient names with modern topography.

Around the same years, a project of a much larger scale was designed by the painter and architect Raphael (1483-1520). Pope Leo X (1475-1521), son of Lorenzo the Magnificent, had in fact commissioned him to prepare the first visual reconstruction of Rome in antiquity, which had to be created from measuring and recording the ancient buildings. Although Raphael died before having completed his plan, a surviving letter that he and his friend, the humanist Baldassarre Castiglione, wrote to the Pope in 1519 gives an insight about his view on antiquities, on their destruction and on the method that he was applying to complete the project.[67] In this letter, Raphael blames the time, the Vandals, the Goths, but more than these, he holds the predecessors of Pope Leo X accountable for the destruction of the ancient buildings in Rome, since they allowed the pillage of ancient temples and sculptures to produce mortar for the construction of new buildings.[68] He says that he has been measuring with great

---

[62] See chapter III 'William Camden and the *Britannia*' in Piggott 1978, 33-55.
[63] Richardson 2004, 108-23, esp. 112 and 120.
[64] Weiss 1969, 129.
[65] For the fashion of depicting Rome with a circular or ellipsoidal plan, see Cesarano 2011, 69.
[66] Cf. below Fabio Calvo's plans of Rome. For an analysis of the *De Nola* and its legacy, see Cesarano 2011.
[67] A transcription of the letter is published in Golzio 1936, 78-92. For the surviving manuscripts and a translation of the letter in English, see Hart and Hicks 2006, 177-92.
[68] 'Ma perchè ci doleremo noi de' Gotti, de' Vandalli et d'altri perfidi inimici del nome latino, se quelli che, come padri et tutori dovevano difendere queste povere reliquie di Roma, essi medesimi hanno atteso con ogni studio lungamente a distrugerle et

care the ancient buildings, reading 'good writers' (Vitruvius among others) and comparing the ancient texts with the structures, which gave him a good knowledge of ancient architecture.[69] Moreover, he is convinced that he can unerringly relate the ruins to their original shape, by integrating the missing information with the knowledge of the still standing examples.[70] A long section of the letter is filled with the description of the instruments that he intended to use in order to precisely measure and draw sections and perspective views of the buildings, and gives specific indications on how to operate them.[71] Raphael's attitude is characteristic of this period in which scholars never doubted their capability of reconstructing ancient remains without making mistakes ('infallibilmente', unerringly, to use Raphael's words). Until this period, the reliance on ancient authoritative authors, the collection of several sources, and personal surveys among the ruins were deemed enough to provide an accurate reconstruction of ancient ruins. This approach will start to be put into question in the 17th century, when the scientific methods of Galileo and Descartes spread a new awareness that started to influence also the study of antiquities, and scholars became more conscious of all the unknowns that had to be catered for through conjectures.

Some of the artists that were part of Raphael's circle attempted to finish his project, but the results were not comparable to the extent of Raphael's vision. Among the works that were published with this intention, there were the *Antiquitates Urbis* (1527) by Andrea Fulvio, who used to accompany Raphael in his surveys and showed him the buildings in ruins that were worthy to be documented, and the *Antiquae Urbis Romae cum Regionibus Simulachrum* (1527) by Marco Fabio Calvo, who had translated Vitruvius' *De Architectura* for him. Calvo's book contains a brief text and a series of woodcuts depicting, among others, views of Rome's ancient plan, regions and landmarks, which are randomly mapped and imaginatively reconstructed. The drawings show the urban development of the city, changing its plan in different geometric shapes: a square with four gates when it was founded by Romulus, an octagon under Servius Tullius, a circle divided in sixteen regions with a matching number of portals under Augustus, and a larger urban fabric cut by the Tiber in Pliny's time (Figure 2.6).[72] Calvo was inspired by the descriptions of classical authors, such as Livy, Dionysius of Halicarnassus, Pliny the Elder, and Vitruvius, and by the images of buildings appearing on Imperial coins, but he drew also on Late Antique land-survey treatises such as the 6th century *Codex Arcerianus*, depicting Roman military colonies as geometrically planned settlements.[73]

Later scholarship has judged negatively Calvo's imaginative reconstructions, which were labelled 'une barbarie incroyable!' at the end of the 19th century,[74] and more recently 'so naive as to be little more valuable than the plan invented by Annius of Viterbo'.[75] Similarly to the reconstructions in Marcanova's *Collectio*, these drawings are surely not historically accurate representations of Roman architecture and city planning, but as Jacks showed they offer instead a great testimony of both the attitude towards Classical antiquities that permeated the Renaissance, and of the state of the knowledge in this

---

a spegnerle?', Golzio 1936, 82-3.
[69] 'Onde essendo io stato assai studioso di queste tali antiquitati, et havendo posto non piccola cura in cercarle minutamente et in misurarle con diligentia, e leggendo di continuo di buoni auctori et conferendo l'opere con le loro scripture, penso aver conseguito qualche notitia di quell'antiqua architettura.', Golzio 1936, 82.
[70] '(...) Havendomi Vostra Santità comandato che io ponessi in disegno Roma anticha, quanto cognoscier si può per quello, che oggi dì si vede, con gli edificii, che di sè dimostrano tali reliquie, che per vero argumento si possono infallibilmente ridurre nel termine proprio come stavano, facendo quelli membri, che sono in tutto ruinati nè si veggono punto, corrispondenti a quelli che restano in piedi e che si veggono.', Golzio 1936, 84.
[71] Golzio 1936, 87-92.
[72] For a detailed discussion about each of Calvo's drawings see Jacks 1990, 453-81.
[73] Jacks 1990, 459.
[74] Muentz 1880, 306-7, cited in Jacks 1990, 463.
[75] Weiss 1969, 96-7.

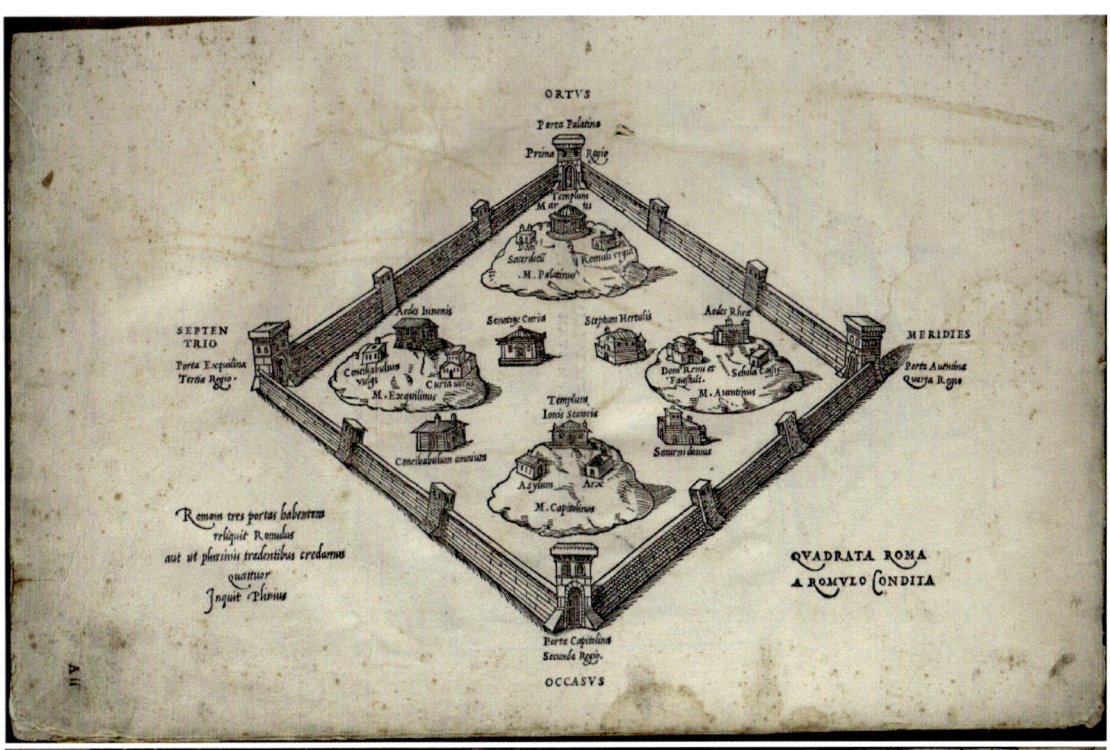
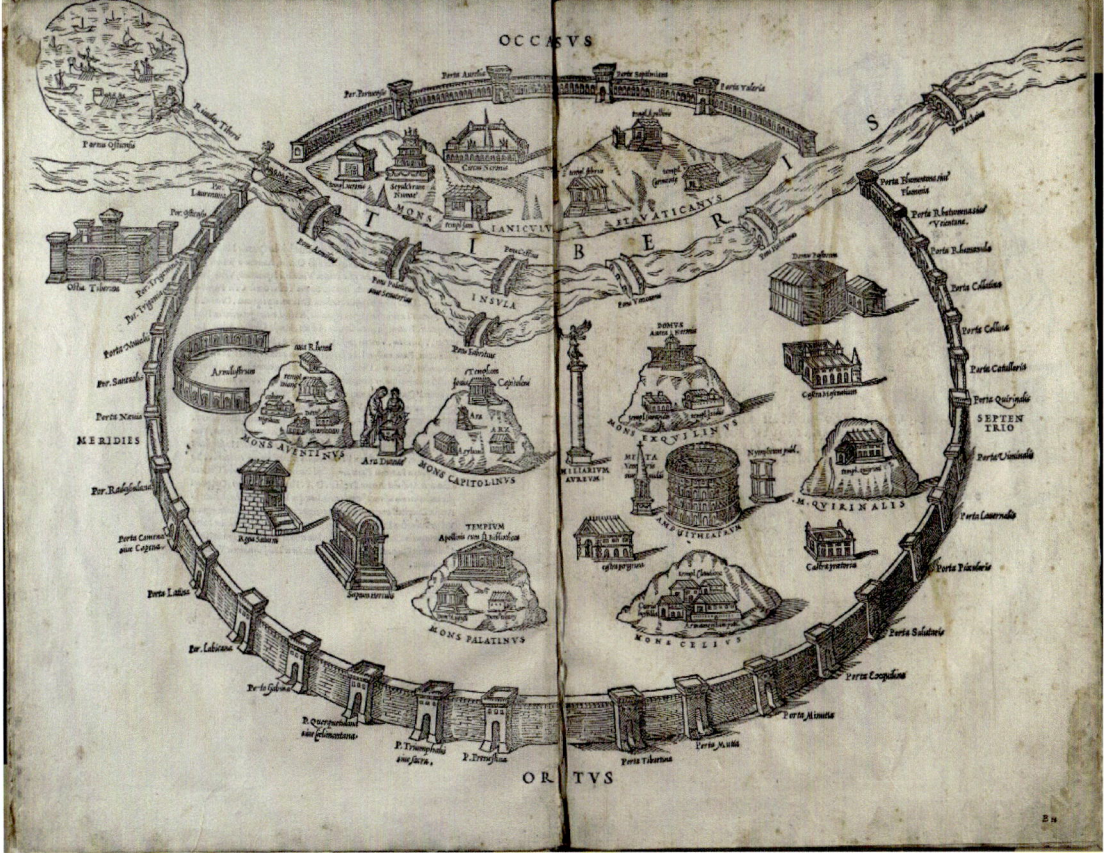

Figure 2.6 Reconstruction drawings of Rome in Fabio Calvo's Antiquae Urbis Romae cum Regionibus Simulachrum. *Top: Romulus' square city, bottom: Rome in Pliny's time (from the digitised copy available at http://arachne.uni-koeln.de/books/FabioCalvo1532).*

domain by scholars of the time.[76] Calvo's reconstructions are indeed a blend of his interpretations of both archaeological evidence and the current architecture 'all'antica', which had found new forms of expression reinterpreting classical authors and monuments.[77]

In 1527, the same year in which Calvo's and Fulvio's works were published, Rome was attacked by Charles V and suffered the pillage and ravages of his troops. Many people lost their lives, among them also Calvo.[78] The sack of Rome and the consequent plague inflicted a grievous blow to the life of the city, in such a way that this year traditionally signs the end of the Roman Renaissance.[79] In a couple of years political stability in Rome recovered and antiquarians and men of letters could continue to reconstruct the city's topography. Among the works that were given to print in the following years was the *Urbis Romae Topographia* by Bartolomeo Marliani (1488-1566),[80] who well embodies the spirit of the antiquarians of this period. The *Topographia*'s second edition, which was published in 1544 and supplied with engravings of monuments in ruins and reconstructions, obtained great success both in Italy and abroad and was reprinted in several editions and translated in other languages. In the preface of the 1588 edition printed in Venice, the editor Geronimo Francino tells us that Marliani had engraved on his sarcophagus the epitaph 'Urbis instaurator', so as to underline his role in the renovation of Rome and in its restoration to its past glories.[81]

In this period, a critical appraisal of earlier and contemporary works starts to be more common in the antiquarians' publications. Inconsistencies and inaccuracies in epigraphic transcriptions and monuments' identifications were found in the works written by Fulvio, Flavio and Marliani himself and denounced by a number of scholars. Among them was the architect Pirro Ligorio, who was born in Naples in about 1513 and moved to Rome some twenty years later. He was in charge of several construction works in Rome and, after the death of Michelangelo, was appointed supervisor of the works at St. Peter's for a short period. In 1549, cardinal Ippolito d'Este gave him the responsibility to carry out some excavations at Hadrian's villa at Tivoli.[82] His interest in antiquities led to the publication in 1553 of his *Libro delle Antichità di Roma*,[83] which was composed of two treatises, one where he described the chief antiquities of Rome focusing on circuses, theatres and amphitheatres, and the other (the *Paradosse*) where he contradicted some of the identifications that previous scholars had suggested.[84] Ligorio, who was also trained as a painter, drew several reconstruction drawings of the structures that he had included in the book.

---

[76] Jacks 1990.
[77] Jacks 1990, 474.
[78] Gualdo 1993, 723-7.
[79] Traditionally, the beginning of the Roman Renaissance corresponds to the election of Pope Nicholas V (1397-1455). The Holy Year of 1450, which fell during his pontificate, brought in fact to Rome an immense number of pilgrims and consequently major earnings for the papal treasury, which the Pope partly invested to restore some churches and to fortify the city for the benefit and protection of himself and his successors (Pade 2007, 318; Miglio 2000, 644-58). For the description and the interpretation of the Sack of Rome by humanists and men of letters, see e.g. Corabi 2005, 81-96.
[80] Among other contributions, Marliani is remembered for the first publication of the *Fasti Consulares* that had been discovered in the Roman Forum in 1546. His description of the *Fasti* was published in the *Consulum, Dictatorum Censorumque Romanorum Series una cum Ipsorum Triumphis, quae Marmoribus Scalpta in Foro Reperta est, atque in Capitolium Translata* (Rome, 1549). As Enenkel noted, this discovery gave impetus to the fast development of the study of antiquity since for the first time a relation could be established between the ancient monuments and the organization of the calendar according to Roman historiography (Enenkel 2008, 36).
[81] Bartholomeus Marliani, *Urbis Romae Topographia*, Venice 1588, fol. 4r.
[82] For a biography of Pirro Ligorio see Coffin 2004.
[83] Full title: *Libro di M. Pyrrho Ligori Napolitano, delle Antichità di Roma, nel quale si tratta de' Circi, Theatri, & Anfitheatri, con le Paradosse del medesimo auttore, quai confutano la commune opinione sopra varii luoghi della città di Roma*, Venezia: Per Michele Tramezino, 1553.
[84] This work, as we learn from the preface that was written by the editor Michele Tramezzino, was dedicated to Ippolito d'Este and was meant to be just an extract of a much greater undertaking that Ligorio was carrying out, namely a treatise in 40 volumes on the antiquities of Rome. Tramezzino and Ligorio hoped that the cardinal was willing to sponsor and finance the work, but this ambitious project was never accomplished, see Daly Davis 2008, 5-6.

2. Reconstructing past cityscapes before the digital age

In the *Paradosse*, he points out that his predecessors have made many mistakes in their interpretations and identifications, like people who walk blindly and stumble into false impressions because they have not spent sufficient time in making acquaintance with the words of the ancient authors.[85] Particularly interesting for our purposes is Ligorio's exposition of his method of investigation. His conclusions were largely based on his surveys in which he carefully observed and measured the remains, integrated them with what he knew from classical authors, and compared them with similar structures that were still standing. The section describing the Circus Flaminius is particularly telling about Ligorio's purpose and methods: his aims were to keep the memory of antiquities alive and to satisfy those that were interested in them; to do so, he says to have tried 'with every possible care' to show the original shape of the circus by studying and measuring each portion of the surviving structure and comparing them with what other authors have written about Roman circuses. Later on, Ligorio explained that often he had to make use of 'conjectures' to integrate the parts that were missing, in order to visually reconstruct the building in its original shape. These integrations, however, were always based on comparisons with other structures, and on the opinions that he exchanged with other scholars.[86] For this reason, Ligorio hopes for the good disposition of his readers, since he underlines that he has been the first person who has undertaken such a cumbersome work.[87]

Ligorio's studies led him to complete Raphael's project forty years after its conception: in 1561 he drew a map of Rome that the brothers Michele e Francesco Tramezzino published in six sheets in 1561 with the name *Antiquae Urbis Imago Accuratissime ex Vetusteis Monumenteis Formata*.[88] This map served as the example for many other 16th century antiquarians that followed Ligorio in his representations and reconstructions of ancient monuments. One of the architects that collaborated with Ligorio and was inspired by his drawings, was the French architect Étienne Dupérac (Stephanus Duperac Parisiensis in its Latin version). Dupérac created many drawings and plans of Rome, such as a map that was published in 1574 with the title *Urbis Romae Sciographia ex Antiquis Monumentis Accuratissime Delineata*,[89] and probably also the *Disegni de le Ruine di Roma e Come Anticamente Erono* ('drawings of the ruins of Rome and their past appearance'), of which only the drawings and a small part of the accompanying text survive. The drawings depict views of Rome in his time and the reconstruction drawings of the same section of the city as it used to be in antiquity.[90] The importance of Dupérac's drawings lies in his effort

---

[85] *Paradosse*, 25v: '(…) ne con la diligenza, che si ricerca leggendo & essaminado le parole, e i sentimenti de gli antichi scrittori, ne' quali si conserva anchor viva in buona parte la memoria di Roma; ma andando à guisa di ciechi, & quando in una, & quando in un'altra falsa apparenza inciampando, sono caduti infiniti, & grandissimi errori'.
[86] *Libro di M. Pyrrho Ligori Napolitano, delle Antichità di Roma*, 18r: 'Desiderando io à tutto mio potere di rinfrescare, & di conservare la memoria delle cose antiche, & insieme di sodisfare à quelli, che d'esse si dilettano, mi sono con ogni possibile cura, & diligentia sforzato, & ingegnato, tra gli altri nobili edificij di dimostare anco la pianta intiera di questo Circo; & per ciò fare sono andato non senza grandissima fatica ricercando minutamente ogni luogo, & parte di esso; non lasciando pezzo alcuno di muro, per minimo che fusse, senza vederlo, & considerarlo sottilissimamente, accompagnandovi sempre la lettione di quelli auttori, che hanno scritto de i Circi alcuna cosa piu particolare; & valendomi bene spesso della coniettura, dove le ruine, che poche sono, mancavano; & pigliando l'essempio de gli altri Circi, che sono più intieri in quelle parti, che in questo erano affatto ruinate; & in somma il tutto di parte in parte conferendo, & communicando con huomini non meno per dottrina, che per giudicio rari, & eccellenti. Tanto che tra per li vestigij, & per l'auttorità, & per le conietture, & per gli essempij, & per le consulte, ne habbiamo alla fine ritratta la presente forma.'
[87] *Libro di M. Pyrrho Ligori Napolitano, delle Antichità di Roma*, 18v: 'Se però alla bontà loro parerà, che io lo meriti, essendo stato il primo che mi sono messo à tanto pericolo, accertandoli che ne havrò loro obligo grande, & che non mi sarà mai discaro l'imparare da chi ne sa più di me.'
[88] A reprint of the 1561 original can be viewed online in the digital collections of the British School at Rome http://www.bsrdigitalcollections.it/details.aspx?ID=3&ST=BS.
[89] A 1661 edition is available online on the digital collections of the Bibliothèque Nationale de France (http://gallica.bnf.fr/ark:/12148/btv1b85290368).
[90] For a re-contextualization of this work and the authorship of the drawings, see Zerner 1965, 507-12.

to be archaeologically accurate, unlike other Northern European artists (such as the Flemish painter Hieronimus Cock), who depicted the ruins of Rome from an artistic point of view.[91]

Another antiquarian that would leave his mark on this century was the Augustinian Onofrio Panvinio (1529-1568), who become librarian of Cardinal Alessandro Farnese and had at his disposal the vast collection of books of the Vatican Library for consultation. Cardinal Farnese had involved Panvinio in his plans to decorate his Villa Caprarola, near Viterbo with iconographic motifs, which triggered his interest in visual representations of ancient monuments and scenes.[92] In fact, Panvinio became very famous for his knowledge of antiquities and published in 1571 the *De Triumpho Commentarius*, a description of how triumphs were celebrated in ancient Rome, with illustrations that depicted reconstruction drawings of the processions. Panvinio underlined the accuracy of his work ('monumentis accuratissima descriptio') and clearly cited the sources that he used, namely the extant remains, coins and ancient authors ('ex vetustis lapidum, nummorum et librorum').[93] Another work of Panvinio which provides insights in his methods and in his aims is the *De Ludis Circensibus Libri II*, which was printed posthumously in Venice in 1600. In these volumes, Panvinio inserted a number of drawings (made by Dupérac) of coins, reliefs, and several reconstructions depicting, among others, the Circus Maximus, a scene of a sacrifice and a *naumachia* (Figure 2.7), which he drew based on ancient stones and coins ('ex vetusteis lapidum, nummorum monumenteis graphica deformatio'). Moreover, Panvinio included what he defined a 'very accurate' map of ancient Rome,[94] which was largely based on Ligorio's.[95] The chapter of the first book, which relates to the Circus of St. Sebastianus on the Via Appia, gives us a glimpse of Panvinio's target audience and purpose for including visual representations in his text: he writes in fact that he included the topography of the circus, a reconstruction and a drawing of the current state of the ruins in the two plates depicting the circus, in order to increase the understanding of the building and to follow his habit of satisfying the interest of eager scholars, who are passionate about Roman antiquities.[96]

As one might expect, antiquarians, architects and artists looked at the ruins and created reconstructions with different purposes in mind. While antiquarians were progressively sharpening their intellectual tools of scientific inquiry, artists were more engaged in creating powerful and appealing scenes that responded to the current fascination for the past, paying little attention to the archaeological documentation. This perception of the past is visible in the set of imaginative drawings depicting the Seven Wonders of the World plus the Colosseum in ruin made by the already mentioned Dutch painter Maarten van Heemskerck and printed by the Dutch publisher and engraver Philip Galle in 1572. These drawings show the artistic intention to create an imaginative interpretation of ancient monuments. The reconstruction of the temple of Artemis in Ephesos, for example, far from being an archaeologically accurate attempt, is inspired by the canon of Renaissance architecture (Figure 2.8). Architects, on the other hand, were interested in studying ancient architecture for the knowledge that they could gain about ancient construction techniques and proportions, which they could then apply to their contemporary projects. During the Renaissance, in fact, ancient architecture was seen as a source of inspiration and comparison for the creation of modern pieces.[97] This last purpose is well expressed in the preface of the *Livre des Edifices Antiques Romains* (1584), a collection of reconstruction drawings of

---

[91] Grafica Antica, Catalogo 46, Antiquarius, 40, available online at www.antiquarius-sb.com/Files/Catalogo%2046.pdf.
[92] Stenhouse 2012, 244.
[93] Stenhouse 2012, 241.
[94] Titled: 'Antiquae Urbis Imago / accuratissime, ex vetusteis monumenteis, et heis quae supersunt reliquieis et parietineis / delineata Onuphri Panvinii Veronensis fratris Eremitae Augustiniani / autoris impensa et aeneis formeis (...).'
[95] Bajard 1992, 579. Panvinio and Ligorio shared in fact a publisher (which made the engravings that Ligorio had used for his work accessible also to Panvinio) and also the collaboration with Dupérac (Stenhouse 2012, 246-7).
[96] 'Haec ut facilius intellegantur , & morem meum sequar in satisfaciendo avidis antiquitatum studiosis Romanarum rerum, duabus tabellis huius Circi topographiam, delineationem, & post ruinam quomodo nunc cernitur adiunxi.' *De Ludis Circensibus Libri II*, 55-6.
[97] Curran 2012, 37.

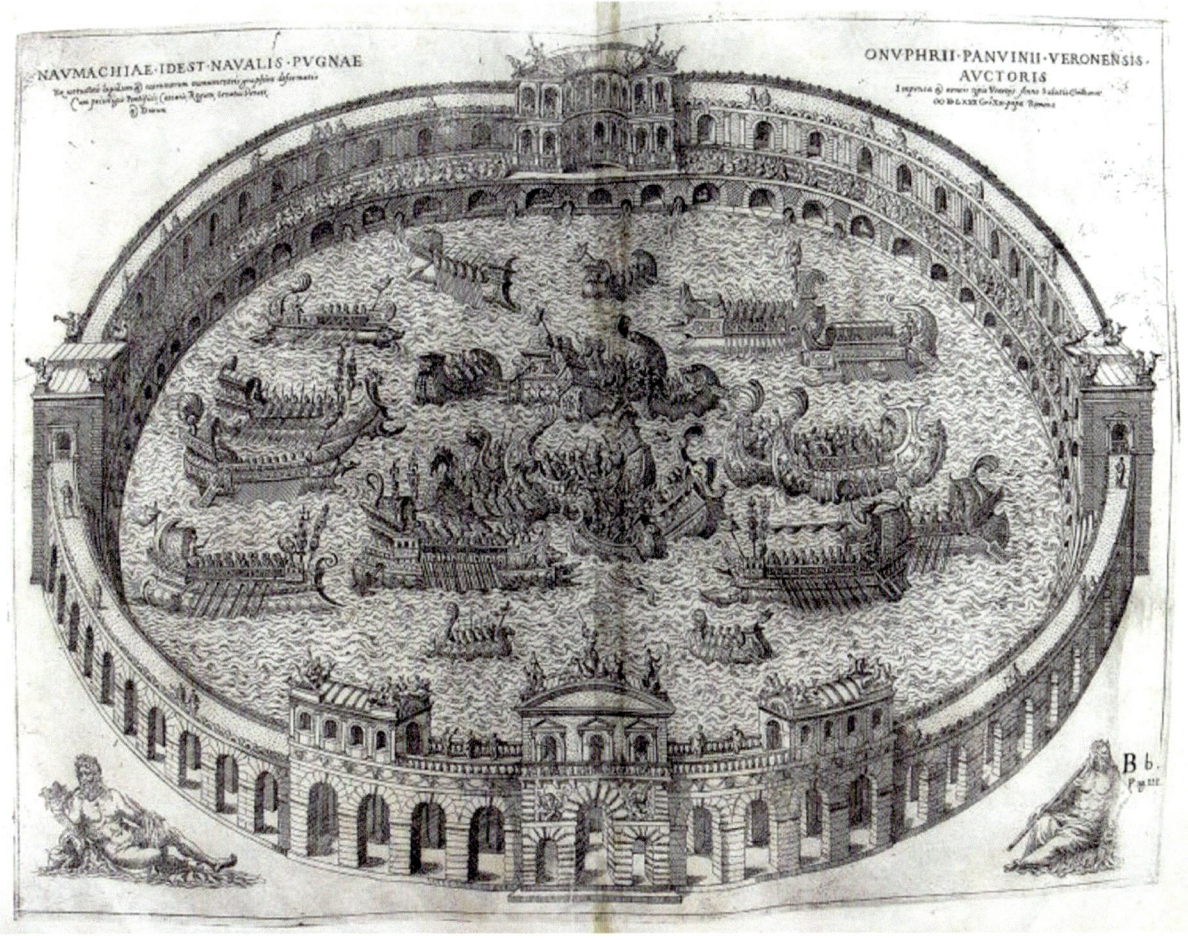

Figure 2.7 Reconstruction drawing of a Naumachia from Panvinio's De Ludis Circensibus *(1600) [source: http://movio. beniculturali.it/bupd/lemusetrailibri/it/159/lapparato-iconografico].*

several buildings in Rome written by the French architect Jacques Androuet du Cerceau, the founder of an important family of artists.[98] In Cerceau's intention, the book could be useful to those that are curious about antiquities and even more to the architects that could be inspired by them.[99]

Over this period, illustrations start progressively to be seen as pleasant additions to texts and publishers pushed for their insertion in books to embellish them and make them more appealing to buyers. Some scholars were however very cautious about which illustrations they wanted to insert in their books, such as the Dutch philologist and antiquarian Justus Lipsius (1547-1606), who applied the same philological approach he used to interpret and reconstruct texts to the study of ancient ruins. Lipsius stayed in Rome from 1568 to 1570 where he worked as secretary to Cardinal Antoine Perrenot de Granvelle and 'diligently sought out many libraries, statues, inscriptions, coins, and whatever was relevant to the understanding of antiquity'.[100] He walked in Rome, admiring and making notes of the ruins with the

---

[98] For a contextualization of the Du Cerceau family see Blomfield 1911, 140-156.
[99] '(...) qui pourra servir à ceux qui sont curieux de l'antiquité, & encore plus (à mon jugement) à ceux qui sont maistres en l'Architecture, lesquels y pourront trouver plusieurs beaux traits & enrichissements pour aider leurs inventions.' *Livre des Edifices Antiques Romains* (1584), letter of dedication.
[100] Papy 2004, 103.

Figure 2.8 The imaginative reconstruction drawing of the temple of Artemis in Ephesos by the Dutch painter Maarten van Heemskerck (1572) [source: https://commons.wikimedia.org/wiki/File:Temple_of_Artemis.jpg].

company and guide of the historian and antiquarian Fulvio Orsini, who had built up a vast knowledge of Roman history together with a collection of antiquities and a well-furnished library.[101]

A passage of Lipsius' second edition of the *Poliorceticωn sive de Machinis, Tormentis, Telis Libri Quinque* (1599), in which reconstruction drawings of *ballistae* were inserted to better convey the textual explanation on the functioning and appearance of this Roman weapon, is particularly interesting for our purpose to investigate the role and development of reconstruction drawings over the centuries. The reason why visual representations are important in Lipsius's view is clearly expressed in a dialogue with his friend, the Flemish humanist, poet and painter Dominicus Lampsonius that he reports in the *Poliorceticωn*: 'Lamps.: Forgive me, Lipsius, but we shall accomplish little, if you present information about these machines to the ears only. Lips.: What can we do further? Lamps.: You should present it to the eyes as well. These can understand and judge more quickly at a single glance, than the ears can after much listening.'[102] Lipsius, however, was a severe judge of the accuracy of the illustrations that he included in his texts, to the point that in the opening of the second edition of his *Saturnalium Sermonum Libri Duo* (1585) he alerts the reader that he did not agree with the insertion of the illustrations that were included by the publisher. Likewise, in another passage of the second book, he notes that the drawing of the gladiatorial games contained some invented elements that are the product of artistic license and not historical truth.[103] However, one has to keep in mind that the 'veritas' that Lipsius advocates in his illustrations corresponds to the state of knowledge of his time, with the result that anachronisms can be

---

[101] Papy 2004, 104-5.
[102] Lipsius, *Poliorceticωn*, I, cap. 6 (p. 37) in the translation by J. Papy (Papy 2004, 116).
[103] 'Insere figuram in qua tu, Lector, scito quaedam à pictore esse ad rem subiiciendam oculis, non à veritate. ut ostiolum ante Editorem, gradus in arenam: quia revera per alios interiores aditus delati gladij & arma in Orchestram.', Lipsius 1585. *Saturnalium Sermonum Libri Duo* II, cap. XIX (p. 150).

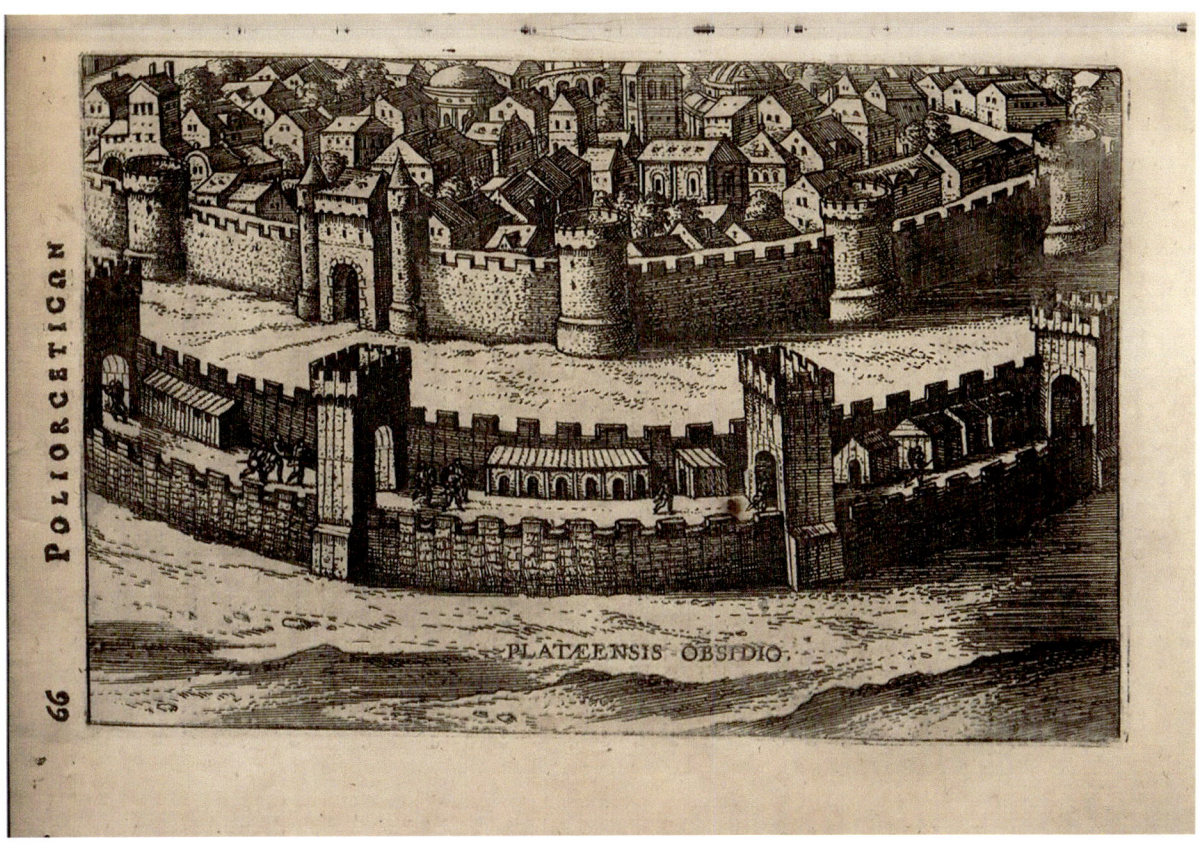

Figure 2.9 Reconstruction drawing of the siege of Plataea in Justus Lipsius' Poliorceticωn (1596), 66 [digitized by ECHO – Cultural Heritage Online].

found, such as the presence of typically Medieval walls protecting the Boeotian city of Plataea depicted under siege in the *Poliorceticωn* (Figure 2.9).

As this overview has showed, in this period scholars had not yet developed what could be called a scientific method in modern terms and their approaches towards the study of antiquities and the making of reconstruction drawings of ruins greatly vary in relation to their personality, interests and background. There are however some elements that emerge as common shared values among scholars, which include a more marked reliance on personal surveys, and hence on primary sources, a more critical approach towards previous scholarship, a conscious use of conjectural integrations based on comparisons and exchange with peers, and a more defined idea about the role of reconstruction drawings in explaining and clarifying concepts otherwise difficult to grasp. These considerations contribute to a reassessment of the antiquarians' approaches to antiquities in line with recent scholarship which has aimed to re-contextualize them in their historical and cultural period.[104]

---

[104] The first work that positioned antiquarians in their historical and cultural context is the essay 'Ancient History and the Antiquarian' by A. Momigliano, which was presented as a paper at the Warburg Institute in 1949 and reprinted twice (in 1955 and 1966) after its first publication in the *Journal of the Warburg and Courtauld Institutes* in 1950. This essay has been influential in setting the framework for the understanding of the relationship between antiquarians and ancient history, and of the development of a historical method. A recent re-contextualization of Momigliano's work is given in Miller 2007. Another important contribution to the field has been given by Piggott 1976, which focusses on the history of antiquarian studies in England and Scotland from the 16th to the 17th centuries. Recent re-assessments of the antiquarian contributions are given by Sweet 2004, Murray 2007, 14-21, and Murray 2014, 189-201.

The traditional rendering of antiquarian endeavours as amateurish and unscientific has been in large part overemphasized and generalized to underline the contrast with the scientific and modern approach of the developing discipline of archaeology in the 19th century.[105] In this view, antiquarianism was therefore dismissed as a 'wrong-turning on the pathway to archaeological enlightenment'.[106] As the next section will further confirm, the reinterpretation of antiquarian production of the 16th and 17th century means that it should not be discarded as naïve, as it in fact sets the basis for the revolution of the historical method that will impact modern day archaeology, and ultimately its analysis enriches the discussion about the roots and methodologies of this discipline.

2.4 The 17th century

In the 17th century wars, pestilences and famine invested Europe. Especially devastating was the Thirty Years' War (1618-1648) which ended with the peace of Westphalia, but had long term repercussions on the social and political balance of the European powers. Against this background, the cultural panorama was very dynamic and the conceptual and practical developments, which were maturing in the last decades of the previous century, consolidated. Philosophers such as Francis Bacon (1561-1626), Thomas Hobbes (1588-1679), René Descartes (1596-1650), and Benedict Spinoza (1632-77) all contributed to create a vibrant intellectual scene; science made important advances thanks to the observations and theories by Galileo Galilei (1564-1642), Johannes Kepler (1571-1630), Blaise Pascal (1623-1662), and Isaac Newton (1642-1727); art and architecture flourished in the Baroque style with the achievements of artists and architects such as Caravaggio (1571-1610), Gian Lorenzo Bernini (1598-1680), and Francesco Borromini (1599-1667).

During this period, a new way of researching is conceived, which originated primarily from relying on empirical observation and on the use of reason, as expressed in the ideas and writings of Bacon, Galileo and Descartes. In 1637, Descartes published his *Discours de la Méthode* where he explained his view on the method that he thought necessary to be applied to study and research. The key elements were a rational and critical approach towards traditionally accepted knowledge: everything had to be doubted, while the only certainty was the existence of the being who conceives the doubt, which is summarized in his famous proposition 'cogito ergo sum': I think, therefore I am. These principles and the broader philosophical view of Descartes inspired philosophers such as Spinoza and Leibniz and found opposition and criticism from others, such as Hobbes.[107] Empiricism and rationalism promoted the development of a scientific method based on original observations and first-hand experience, and on a deductive reasoning to reach knowledge. Especially towards the end of the century, these principles would start to impact more profoundly also the study of antiquities, by reinforcing the emphasis on the self-inspection of ruins and on a critical approach towards tradition, both in the form of Classical authors and of previous generations of scholars.

The interest in antiquities and the collection of small finds, coins and inscriptions continued to rise in the course of this century. The antiquary became a figure which was enough defined to be satirised in 1628 in the collection of characters by the British bishop John Earle as a man 'that hath that unnaturall disease to bee enamour'd of old age, and wrinckles, and loves all things, (as Dutchmen doe cheese) the better for being mouldy and worme–eatern'.[108] In his caricature, Earle presents the antiquarian as a

---

[105] Marchand 2007, 248-85.
[106] Murray 2007, 14. Murray focuses in particular on the construction of British prehistory during the 16th and 17th centuries, discussing what he defines the 'interactionist methodology' that antiquarians adopted to reconcile new sources of information, such as ruins, coins and inscriptions with 'authorities' such as the Bible and the histories of Classical authors such as Tacitus (Murray 2014, 189-201; Murray 2007, 14-9).
[107] For an overview and placement of Descartes in respect to his contemporaries, see Abbagnano 1993, *passim*.
[108] Excerpt from section n. 7 ('The Antiquary') of John Earle's *Microsmographie* (1628).

great admirer of past relics, which he seeks, inspects and collects with much passion, to the point that he disdains all his contemporary products, even printed books which 'he contemnes, as a novelty of this latter age'. This tension between those who sustained the supremacy of the ancients and those who instead considered the inventions of modern times as the proof of the cultural superiority of their age is a recurrent theme in the Renaissance thought, starting with Petrarca.[109] In 17th century France, this debate peaked with the so called 'Querelle des Anciens et des Modernes', a dispute initiated within the Académie française among scholars sustaining opposing views of artistic inspiration and models. The 'casus belli' was the reading of the poem *Le Siècle de Louis le Grand* that Charles Perrault had composed in 1698 for the King, in which the French author compared the 'siècle de Louis' with that of the Emperor Augustus, stating that the ancients are 'men like us'.[110] This view represents the feelings of the 'Modernes', who praised the accomplishments of their contemporary artists under Louis XIV, as opposed to the 'Classiques', who instead considered Greek and Roman achievements as unparalleled and therefore promoted imitation as the only way to replicate the artistic perfection of the Classical works.[111]

In Italy, the fascination for Rome continued to inspire antiquarian works, one of the most famous being the *Antiquae Urbis Splendor* by Giacomo Lauro. Lauro, born most likely in Rome at an unknown date in the second half of the 16th century, started to work on the *Antiquae Urbis Splendor* probably around 1586. The four volumes came out between 1610 and 1628, after which they were reprinted in several editions until the very end of the 17th century. As the title promises, Lauro's aim was not to create an accurate reconstruction of Rome; instead, he wanted to represent the glory and splendour of the ancient city, which he conveys through a series of reconstruction drawings of monuments and views of ancient Rome and nearby places of interest, such as Portus, the ancient harbour of Ostia. These representations were appreciated by artists such as Bernini and Borromini as models and source of inspiration,[112] and were popular among travellers and visitors that came to Rome, serving as a sort of tourist guide. In the 1625 edition, in fact, descriptions of the represented buildings in Italian, German and French were added to the original Latin text to make this work more appealing for a broader audience.[113] The editions published in 1637 and 1641, moreover, were sponsored by the Swiss Guard Hans Gross (under the pseudonym of Giovanni Alto), who was working in his spare time as a tourist guide in Rome.

As we can gather from Alto's dedication to the reader, 17th century tourists, especially German and French, wanted to better understand the buildings in ruins and to have some visual souvenirs to take home. Lauro's reconstruction drawings were therefore meant to serve this very purpose by providing those visiting Rome with a visual memory of the monuments they saw, that they could show to relatives and friends at home. Gross is himself portrayed in one of the drawings, while he is showing the reconstruction of the *Meta Sudans* between the Colosseum and the Arch of Constantine to a group of German nobles (Figure 2.10). The explanatory text under this drawing well illustrates the idea that these encounters with the distant past held an educational value. They were perceived not only as an honest and recreational way to spend the time, but also as an opportunity to reflect upon the 'vicissitudes of all things, on how now lies what previously had flourished.'[114]

---

[109] Boruchoff 2012, 133-164; Fumaroli 2001, 7-220.
[110] 'La belle Antiquité fut toujours vénérable,/ Mais je ne crus jamais qu'elle fut adorable./ Je vois les Anciens, sans plier les genoux./ Ils sont grands, il est vrai, mais hommes comme nous;/ Et l'on peut comparer, sans craindre d'être injuste,/ Le siècle de Louis au beau siècle d'Auguste (...)' cited in Mortier 1982, 51.
[111] This opposition was however not only limited to literature, but was the expression of different political orientations as discussed in Fumaroli 2001, 167-8.
[112] Del Pesco 1984, 418-9; Di Calisto 2005.
[113] For an analysis of this work, its context and its dedications, see Del Pesco 1984.
[114] *Antiquae Urbis Splendor* (1641), pl. 90: 'Vides hic praeterea Ioannem Grossum Heluetium pro more suo nobilibus Germanis antiquitates ostendentem Romanas, cuius ipsi ut etiam nobiles Galli, sunt inspectores curiosissimi et merito quidem, nam praeter quam quod decet honestos uiros huiusmodi honesta occupatio ad ponendum tempus utiliter et cum voluptate

The dedication to the reader at the beginning of the volume and the explanations of the drawings give us also an indication of the method and sources that had been used to create such representations: accurate recording of the extant remains that were compared to the buildings engraved in medals, marbles and metals, ancient writers (most notably Vitruvius, Varro, Livy, Suetonius), and modern authors such as Ligorio, Dupérac,[115] Biondo, Marliani, Fulvio, Panvinio and Lipsius.[116] It must be noted, however, that Lauro was mainly an engraver and had little knowledge of architecture. He therefore relied much on the visual models that were known at the time, supplying with coherent fantastic elements the missing pieces in his reconstructions.[117] As previously noted, the expertise of the drawing-maker has a great influence on the drawing method, the choices about which elements to draw and the final aim of the work.

This difference is clearly visible when comparing the reconstructions included in Lauro's work, which were mainly aimed at tourists visiting Rome, with the drawings made by the French architect Antoine Babuty Desgodetz (1653–1728) and published in *Les Edifices Antiques de Rome: Dessinés et Mesurés Très Exactement* (1682), which were meant instead to create a reliable documentation of the buildings for French architects interested in Roman architecture. Desgodetz's treatise, which remained a reference work on Roman antiquities in the following century, is organized in chapters, each one describing one monument (mainly temples, arches, and theatres) that was illustrated with plans, sections, details, and reconstruction drawings. The reconstruction drawings are purely geometric and report accurately the measurements of each part of the structures. Buildings are drawn either from the front or from one

---

interim dum alij illud impendunt pecuniasque profundunt in res cum honestate pugnantis et in plurima mala quae secum solet afferre otium malorum omnium origo, proficiunt etiam hac cognitione ad cognoscendam rerum omnium uicissitudinem quomodo plurima nunc iaceant quae olim floruerunt, adde quod multum facit haec cognitio antiquitatis ad intelligendos et interpretandos profanos auctores.'

[115] In the explanation related to the reconstruction drawing of Portus, the ancient harbour of Ostia (pl. 119), Lauro in fact stated that the depiction was taken from the description of Ligorio, from antiquities, medals and from ancient and modern authors: '(...) come in questa descrizione si vede, cavata da quella di Pirro Ligorio, delle antichità, e medaglie, e da gl'Autori antichi, e moderni.'

[116] Transcription of the dedication to the reader opening the 1641 edition: 'Gio. Ridolfo Alto / Svizzero a chi leggerà / La città di Roma, si come, per la vastità dell'Imperio non ebbe mai altro popolo, o Natione, che l'agguagliasse, così ha lanciato nelle sue Rovine sì alti vestigi dell'antica maestà, e grandezza, che è forza, da' soli avanzi, che se ne veggono, (tutto che le reliquie miserabili del tempo, e dell'hostilità de' Barbari) ammirarla per Capo del Mondo, e trionfatrice dell'Universo, E perchè essendo questi monumenti, non solamente venerati; ma con estraordinaria curiosità, e diligenza da tutte le genti continuamente ricercati; poichè (spinte dal rimbombo della Fama) sin da gli ultimi confini della Terra, qua si trasferiscono a posta per vederli, e contemplarli dappresso: nè essendo poi lor possibile descriverne, ritornati alle lor case, così esattamente le maraviglie, che, & essi, e gli ascoltanti ne restino pienamente sodisfatti.; ho voluto servire in quella parte al godimento universale, rappresentandole nuovamente in queste carte delineate al naturale dalla dotta mano di Giacomo Lauro; e da penne sublimi vivamente descritte in varie lingue; Opera veramente di grandissima spesa, e fatica; già che per darle la perfettione, che si poteva maggiore, oltre all'essersi esattissimamente ricercate le piante delle Antichità nelle macerie stesse; & investigate le forme vere delle fabbriche, nelle Medaglie, Bassi rilievi, Marmi, Metalli, & altre cose tali de' secoli passati, si sono anche rivoltati con sommo studio gli Autori più celebri, e rinomati, come Pollione Vitruvio, M. Varrone, Tito Livio, Svetonio, Tacito, l'uno, e l'altro Plinio, Plutarco, Dione, Appiano Alessandrino, Diodoro Siciliano, Herodiano, Dionisio Alicarnaseo, Ammiano Marcellino, Sesto Rufo, Giulio Capitolino, Elio, Lampridio, Flavio Vopisco, Elio Spartiano, Flavio Eutropio, Flavio Gioseffo: & oltre a questi Giovanni Zonara, Gio. Boemo, Fenestella, Pomponio Leto, Andrea Alciato, il Biondo, l'Albertino, il Boccaccio, Guido Pancirolo, Alessandro de Alessandri, Gugiielmo di Choul, il Marliano, & il Fauno, e L. Mauro, Andrea Fulvio, Carlo Sigonio, Honofrio Panvinio, il Lipsio, e tutti gli altri finalmente, da' quali si poteva aver notitia, sì degli edificij notabili publici, e privati, come delle Attioni Sacre, Civili, e Militari de' Romani, più degne di memoria; che sono state per colmo aggiunte, parimenti delineate al vivo in questo Libro. Ricevi (amico Lettore) queste fatiche, qualunque sieno: e pascendo in esse la tua virtuosa curiosità, gradisci l'animo di coloro, e mio, che per servire in uno stesso tempo all'utilità, e dilettatione commune, ci siamo volentieri adoperati in metterle insieme e pubblicarle; riputandoci non indegni della tua affettione, se non per altro, per havere impiegato le nostre industrie nel rappresentarti, quasi in maestosissimo Teatro, quelle cose, che sono state sempre l'oggetto della maraviglia, lo stupor de' secoli, e 'l miracolo del mondo: E vivi contento.'

[117] Del Pesco 1984, 426.

Figure 2.10 Hans Gross and a group of German tourists depicted next to the reconstruction of the Meta Sudans *in Lauro's* Antiquae Urbis Splendor, *pl. 90. [source: http://www.harvardartmuseums.org/collections/object/176002].*

side, without a perspective view or any attempt to insert vegetation or people, to make them more engaging to the viewers as Lauro had done in his drawings.

The predominance of works on Roman antiquities in the previous paragraphs is a reflection not only of the prevalent interest of antiquarians and tourists in the 17th century, but also of the options of travellers in that period. Greek antiquities were in fact more challenging to visit, as the Ottoman conquest of Greece in the 15th century had closed the frontiers of the empire, making Greece difficult to enter from this period onwards. Cyriac of Ancona was indeed one of the last travellers that could freely move in Greece, at least until 1687 when the Venetians invaded Greece and took possession of Athens even if only for a short period. In the meantime, sparse information over Greek antiquities was coming from diplomats, traders or missionaries who came back also with some ancient artefacts.[118]

The political situation in Greece has had an impact also on the state of the scholarship on Greek antiquities. The isolation of Greece and the reduced accessibility of its monuments made the books on this subject an appealing reading for both scholars and non-specialists. Given the difficulty to reach the

---

[118] Sánchez Hernández 2010, 11.

country, publications on Greek antiquities were mainly based on descriptions offered in ancient sources, such as the 2nd century AD Greek traveller Pausanias. For example, the Dutch Johannes Meursius (1579-1639), professor of Greek and History in Leiden in the second decade of the 17th century, wrote his *Athenae Atticae* (1624) without having ever visited Athens, but by relying on the material he found in the well-furnished Leiden University library.[119] The inaccessibility of Greek antiquities made moreover possible the circulations of unverified information and allowed publications such as Guillet de la Gulletière's book *Athènes Ancienne et Nouvelle* (Paris, 1674), that were not substantiated by any personal encounter with the ruins described and reconstructed. Although the frontispiece of the second edition of this book (1675) promises that the treatise was 'augmentée en plusieurs endroits, sur les memoires de l'auteur', de la Gulletière, historiographer of the Royal Academy at Paris, had never been to Greece himself and had based his work on Meursius' and on the information that he could access because of his appointment at the Royal Academy. The book contained a map of ancient Athens that was completely fanciful. De la Gulletière's forgery was disproved some years later when the French doctor Jacob Spon wrote the accounts of his journeys in his *Voyage de l'Italie, de Dalmatie, de Grèce et du Levant* (1678) and was able to prove the unreliability of Guillet's map and correct also some of the inaccuracies and errors in Meursius' text.[120]

At the turn of the century, the signs of a changing approach towards the study of antiquities can be seen in the work of the Florentine antiquarian Filippo Buonarroti (1661-1733). In 1698 Buonarroti published his *Osservazioni Istoriche Sopra Alcuni Medaglioni Antichi* ('historical observations over some ancient medallions'), a treatise on the coins and medals from the collection of cardinal Gasparo di Carpegna, which he illustrated with several drawings of his study material. Although this iconographic work does not contain any reconstructions, it is worth mentioning since it is quite telling on a changed perception towards the study of antiquities that will become more marked in the 18th century.[121] In the preface of his work, Buonarroti confesses the many doubts that he felt in studying this material, insomuch as to define his treatise a 'stodgy collection of doubts, instead of one of certain and digested observations'.[122] Casting doubt on his observations is quite remarkable and stands out from the prevalent approach of antiquarians claiming to present 'accuratissimae descriptiones' of the documented and reconstructed antiquities. Buonarroti explains the reasons for his doubts, saying that the study of antiquities greatly differs from any other, and requires a more complex method of investigation. Its premise was a sincere confession that one does not know what ancient painters and sculptors have had in their minds ('il confesar sinceramente di non sapere tuttociò che ha potuto venir' in capo a tanti pittori e scultori antichi'),[123] and the acknowledgment of the challenging task that is set out for a scholar studying

---

[119] For Meursius' scholarship and his contacts with several scholars who sent him materials, see Sánchez Hernández 2010, 9-11.
[120] Sánchez Hernández 2010, 11.
[121] Gallo defines this treatise as the 'manifesto of a new antiquarianism' that was influenced by the establishment in 1657 of the Accademia del Cimento, a Florentine scientific society that followed Galileo and his experimental method, and by the Newtonian approach (Gallo 1999, 828). In Buonarroti's reasoning one can also recognize the influence of 'Cartesian doubt', Descartes' method of investigating the truth by starting with the assumption that the only certainty is uncertainty.
[122] '(...) Indigesta collezione di dubbi, che d'osservazioni certe, ben digerite, & esaminate.'
[123] '(...)Benchè io sappia, che per contentare il gusto presente, ci volevano altre cose che queste, messe giù senz'ordine e alla rinfusa, e con tal' incertezza e dubbio della mia opinione e sentimento, che meriteranno forse d'esser'avute piuttosto per un'indigesta raccolta di dubbi, che d'osservazioni certe, ben digerite, & esaminate. Egli è ben vero però, che in quanto a questa seconda parte, io ci sono caduto volontariamente, sperandone anche l'approvazione di tutti coloro, i quali faranno riflessione, che lo studio dell'antichità e dell'erudizioni è differente da molti altri, ne' quali non pare che in rigor di metodo si ricerchi, che l'adattare le conclusioni a quel solo principio, da cui dependono; dovecchè in questo non si può sperare di seguitare un metodo così semplice; posciachè vi sono, per così dire, infiniti principii, e le conietture dipendono da favole, istorie, riti, & altre cose divise e disparate fra di loro: e conseguentemente dovrà giudicarli per effetto d'una certa cognizione delle forze dell'arte, il confesar sinceramente di non sapere (per pigliare un esempio da una sola parte, che potrebbe sembrare la più facile) tuttociò che ha potuto venir'in capo a tanti pittori e scultori antichi, i quali ci hanno lasciato i monumenti dell'opere loro, circa l'aggiungere, & ancora mutar'affatto i simboli, & i suggetti delle favole e delle Deità: poichè per regolati che si fossero nel seguitare la pubblica erudizione, più di quello che sieno adesso i nostri, gli artefici antichi; potevano nondimeno essere

antiquities, facing the difficulty to identify the correct information in the many previous works on this topic instead of simply reporting what others had written before, thus behaving 'like sheep that leave a closed space, one following the others'.[124]

2.5 The 18th century

The beginning of the systematic excavations at Herculaneum in 1738 is traditionally taken as the starting date of the discipline of Classical archaeology. In previous years, excavations had been carried out on the Aventine (1705), on the Domus Flavia on the Palatine (1720) and on the graves along the Via Appia (1726) directed by the antiquarian from Verona Francesco Bianchini.[125] These, and the excavations that started in 1748 in Pompeii,[126] gave a great impetus to a widespread interest in Roman antiquities in the 18th century that was nourished by young savants visiting the ruins during their *Grand Tour*.[127] Even the models and vocabulary of the French Revolution came from the classics, and Rome, Greece and Egypt were seen as the cradle of civilisation.[128] Illustrations were by now seen as an integral part in the study of antiquities, as confirmed by the words of the British antiquarian William Stukeley, who stated that 'without drawing or designing the Study of Antiquities or any other Science is lame and imperfect'.[129] The new discoveries created an even more pronounced need to document and represent the monuments and their decorations in their context, with a visual language that was appropriate for presenting them to the public.[130] The first musea of antiquities started to be established growing out the antiquarians' private collections and opened to visitors, the first being the Capitoline Museums in Rome (1733) that was followed by other similar initiatives all over Europe, such as the British Museum (1759) and the Louvre (1793).[131] After the mid-18th century, an interest for landscape started to increase, encouraged by the ideas on nature by Jean-Jacques Rousseau.[132] This new way of looking at landscape was of great importance for the contextualization of ancient buildings, that started to be seen not in isolation any more, but as part of their surroundings.

Works on antiquities started to be systematically collected in larger publications such as the *Thesaurus Antiquitatum*. At the turn of the 17th century, the famous *Thesaurus Antiquitatum Romanarum* (Utrecht/Leiden, 1694-1699) edited by the German scholar Johannes Georgius Graevius in twelve volumes and the *Thesaurus Antiquitatum Graecarum* (Leiden, 1697-1702) by the Dutch Jacobus Gronovius appeared in print in The Netherlands.[133] The aim of these collections was to reprint and make available to a wider

---

costretti per fatti e favole particolari delle Città (che ora per la scarsezza degli Scrittori, i quali sogliono per lo più parlare delle generali e ricevute da tutti) sovente ancora per servire a' privati sentimenti di coloro, che facevano ad essi fare i simulacri, di dare agli Dei figure e simboli differentissimi da quelli, dava a' medesimi il comune dell'altre nazioni (…)', Buonarroti 1698, ii-iii.

[124] 'E se veruna scienza ha bisogno d'un sì fatto preparamento d'intelletto e cautela, lo studio dell'erudizione e dell'antichità è quello che ne ha una necessità particolare, non solo per le cagioni addotte, ma ancora per il gran numero degli scrittori, e per la varietà delle opinioni che ci sono; onde è molto difficile in una strada tanto frequentata da ogni sorta di ingegni seguitare le vestigie, che conducono alla verità, e non piuttosto, a guisa delle pecorelle che escon dal chiuso, E ciò che fa la prima l'altre fanno, quelle che vanno a finire in falsità e menzogne (…).', Buonarroti 1698, v.

[125] Bianchini is remembered as an important name in the dawn of archaeology as a scientific discipline for his scrupulous method that he applied during the excavation and in the process of publication of the results (Gallo 1999, 833).

[126] See e.g. the published excavations diaries by Francesco and Pietro La Vega in Pagano 1997.

[127] The *Grand Tour* started to include also sites in South of Italy, such as Paestum, which was properly 'rediscovered' only during this century (Villani 2011, 85-98).

[128] Díaz-Andreu 2007, 67-78.

[129] From the first minute-book of the Society of Antiquaries of London in 1717, of which William Stukeley was first Secretary, cited in Piggott 1978, 7.

[130] Barbanera 2010, 33-4.

[131] Díaz-Andreu 2007, 46-7; Halbertsma 2003, 22.

[132] Dubbini 2002.

[133] For the third, less successful, *Thesaurus* on Italian antiquities published by the Leiden publisher Pieter van der Aa between 1704 and 1725 see Piccoli 2013, 61-82.

audience works that had been previously published or that were difficult to access. However, the works that were published or republished in these years varied greatly in terms of the accuracy and reliability of the material presented. In one of the 1712 issues of the *Giornale de' Letterati d'Italia*, an important literary journal founded in 1710, an article by the intellectuals Pietro Caterino Zeno, Scipione Maffei and Giusto Fontanini criticized the fact that many histories of Italian cities were still being published even though they were not based on historical documentation but on myths and legends.[134]

In the second half of the century, in Germany Johann Winckelmann published his *Geschichte der Kunst des Alterthums* (1764) where he considered ancient artistic productions from the point of view of their style to establish their chronology and not only from the point of view of their iconographic motifs, as was the prevalent approach in the circles of antiquarians.[135] Winckelmann is considered the founding father of art history and had a great impact on the development of German Hellenism with his studies on Greek art. The German scholar, in fact, sustained the superiority of Greek art over Roman, which he saw as always attempted at imitating the Greek original,[136] and was one of the leading intellectuals who saw the roots of European identity in Greece.[137] The influence of Winckelmann's writings impacted in various degrees on the study of antiquities in the other European countries. In Italy, for example, his contribution was not absorbed much by Italian antiquarians, not only because of the linguistic barrier posed by reading the German text, but also for the diffidence of erudite circles towards a foreigner's opinion.[138]

In France, the Comte de Caylus (1692-1765) stands out among his contemporary antiquarians.[139] The mutual antipathy with Diderot and with the 'Encyclopédistes', caused not least by Caylus' aristocratic lineage, resulted in a sort of *damnatio memoriae* of Caylus in France.[140] From the 19th century onwards, however, several studies have reassessed his contribution to the development of a scientific method, to the point that he has been paired with Winkelmann as a founder of Classical archaeology.[141] His most important work, the *Recueil d'Antiquités Égyptiennes, Étrusques, Grecques et Romaines*, was published in six volumes and a supplement between 1752 and 1767, and contained explanations and drawings of the materials that he personally owned and inspected. De Caylus' reliance on the comparative method allowed him to go beyond the taxonomies that had been established by Classical authors (e.g. Varro), thus contributing to the elaboration of the typological method based on his observations and comparisons between the artefacts that were part of his large collection.[142] On the other side of the English Channel, the comprehensive *History of the Decline and Fall of the Roman Empire*, written by the historian Edward Gibbon (1737-1794) and published in six volumes between 1776 and 1788, will influence the historical method of the 19th century for its reliance on primary sources and will become a reference work on the subject for the following generations.[143]

---

[134] Gallo 2007, 111-2. In this regard, it must be noted that the lack of a firm criterion of selection for the works to be inserted in these *Thesauri* depended in some cases purely on the publishers' wish to create huge collections to attract more buyers. This situation is documented for the compilation of the *Thesaurus Antiquitatum et Historiarum Italiae* (Leiden, 1704-1723), which caused disagreements between the publisher Pieter van der Aa and the editor Pieter Burmann (see Piccoli 2013, 6).

[135] For Roman antiquarians, see Gallo 1999, 840.

[136] As he stated: 'A statue by an ancient Roman hand will always stand in the same relationship to a Greek original in the way that Virgil's Dido with her retinue, compared with Diana among the Oreiades, relates to Homer's Nausicaa, which the former attempted to imitate' (cited in Carter 2013, 32).

[137] Morris 2006, 258.

[138] Gallo 1999, 841.

[139] For a discussion of his contributions see Fumaroli 2007, 154-83; Cronk and Peeters 2004.

[140] Fumaroli 2007, 168. For an analysis on Caylus' relationship with Diderot see Massau 2004, 45-57.

[141] Gran-Aymerich 2001, 40. Miller actually sustains that in fact de Caylus was a 'much better historian' than Winckelmann (Miller 2007, 35).

[142] Warin 2011.

[143] Momigliano 1954, 450-63.

In Italy, one of the most controversial figures of this period, not least for his reconstruction drawings, is Giovanni Battista Piranesi (1720-1778), a troubled and restless architect who was fascinated by Roman architecture. Like the architects of the previous century, he was convinced that ancient buildings should be the starting point for the modern architect to 'reshape the good taste in architecture, which was twisted by the barbarian coarse and ill-fated way of construction'.[144] Some of the publications of the archaeologist Bianchini were the starting point for the composition of Piranesi's *Antichità Romane*, a treatise on Roman antiquities that he published in 1756. In the preface of this work in four volumes, he stated clearly the purpose of this publication in trying to preserve the memory of the ancient buildings of Rome with his prints: 'And since I've seen that the remains of the ancient buildings of Rome, that are scattered in gardens and other cultivated fields, are decreasing in number day after day, either because of the harm committed by time, or for the greed of their owners who are surreptitiously digging them up to sell their parts to construct new buildings, I decided to preserve them by means of my prints.'[145] In the same preface, Piranesi complained that he could not rely much on modern works on Roman antiquities since they contained many mistakes, to be attributed either to the fact that their authors did not carefully inspect the ruins, or to their ignorance of architecture, or to the fact that they did not have a complete plan of Rome (such as the famous one that Giovan Battista Nolli had worked on between 1741 and 1743 and was published in 1748).[146] For this reason, Piranesi had to turn to ancient authors, analysing them and comparing them with the extant remains that he carefully recorded.

Piranesi has received much attention with publications and exhibitions devoted to him and to his unusual approach to architecture and antiquities. His style of drawing is characteristic and his interest for ancient building techniques is clear in his publications, in which he supplied etchings representing sections and details of buildings that aimed to illustrate ancient construction methods (Figure 2.11). The composition style that he adopted in many of his drawings was meant to collate all the different sources that he drew on to create the reconstructions, resulting in what Nixon has called 'multi-dimensional images'.[147] In these drawings, Piranesi took into consideration all the elements that compose a structure, such as its foundation, the elevation and its construction technique, contrary to the traditional view which focussed primarily on decoration.[148]

His reconstructions, however, have puzzled contemporary and modern scholars for their mixture of archaeology and invention, their purpose being difficult to grasp. Piranesi possessed in fact a great knowledge of Roman architecture, that he acquired with personal observations of the buildings and by reading modern and ancient authors that he combined with his skills in architectural design; yet, he introduced many elements from his own imagination that made his reconstruction drawings to be discarded by many as mere imaginative depictions. An example of his approach is his reconstruction of the Campus Martius in Rome, titled *Ichnographia Campi Martii* which he published in 1762. In the dedication to the Scottish architect Robert Adam, Piranesi explains his concerns about the reception of this work, especially the fact that his work could be seen as imaginative and false, while he had taken some creative license, likewise, he observed, had ancient architects.[149] This plan seems therefore

---

[144] 'E la semplice esteriore osservazione degli avanzi delle antiche magnificenze di Roma è bastata a riformare negli ultimi tempi l'idea del buon gusto dell'Architettura, depravato per l'innanzi dalle rozze e infelici maniere de' Barbari (...).' Preface of the *Antichità Romane* (Rome, 1756).
[145] '(...) E vedendo io, che gli avanzi delle antiche fabbriche di Roma, sparsi in gran parte per gli orti ed altri luoghi coltivati, vengono a diminuirsi di giorno in giorno o per l'ingiuria de' tempi, o per l'avarizia de' possessori, che con barbara licenza gli vanno clandestinamente atterrando, per venderne i frantumi all'uso degli edifizi modeni; mi sono avvisato di conservarli col mezzo delle stampe (...).'
[146] Leto 2013.
[147] Nixon 2002, 476.
[148] Barbanera 2010, 35.
[149] G. B. Piranesi, preface of *Ichnographia Campus Martius*, Rome, 1762: 'I am rather afraid that some parts of the Campus which I describe should seem figments of the imagination and not based on any evidence: certainly if anyone compares them with the

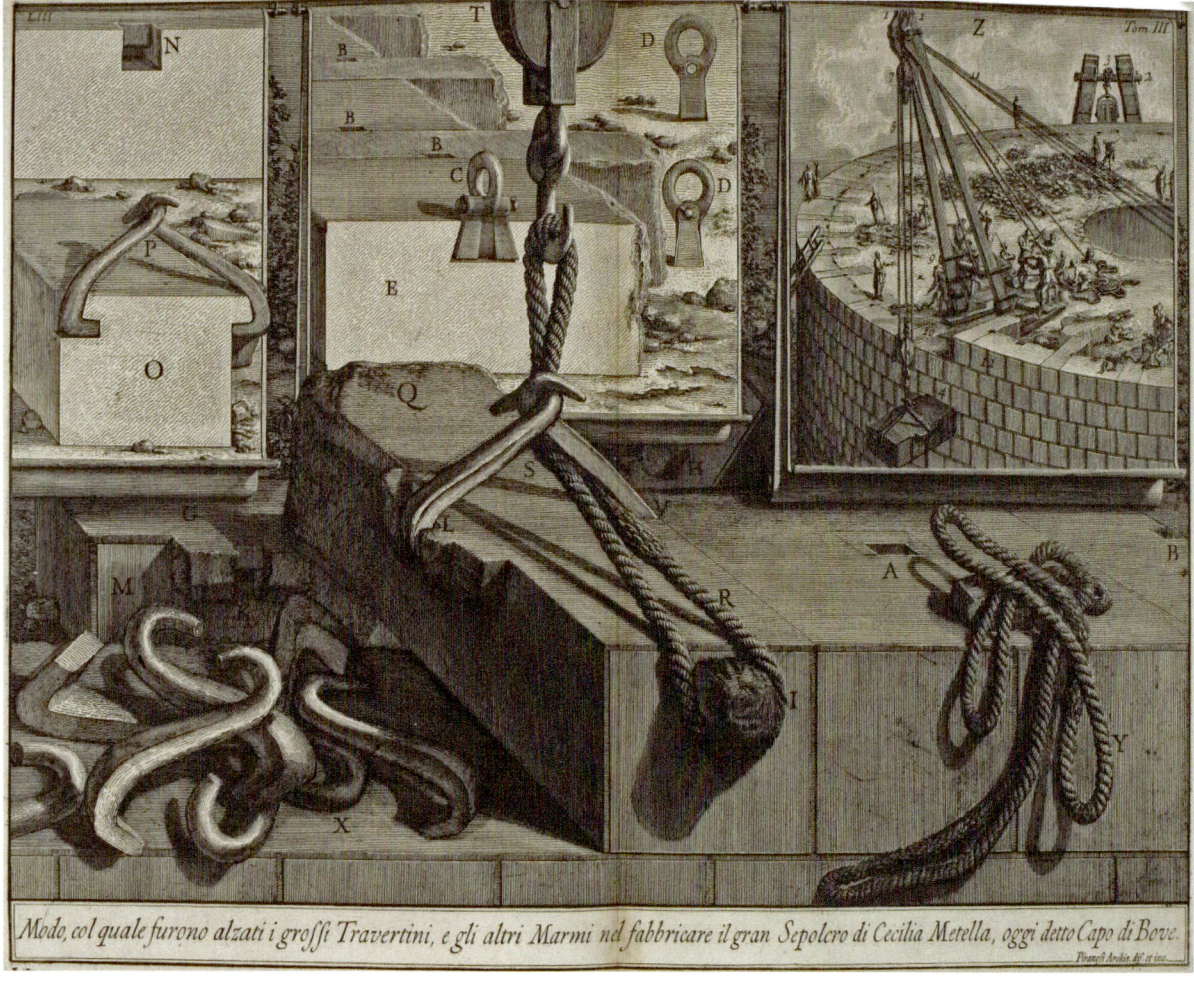

Figure 2.11 Piranesi's drawing on the construction technique adopted for the funerary monument of Caecilia Metella, in Le Antichità Romane: Divisa in Quattro Tomi: Contenente gli Avanzi de' Monvmenti Sepolcrali di Roma e dell'Agro Romano, *vol. III, pl. LIII.*

a conscious attempt to break the rules of architecture and therefore should not be considered as a mere visionary reconstruction; instead, according to Aureli, it needs to be contextualized within the as already noted recurrent theme of the 'instauratio Urbis', the ruins of ancient Rome being used as symbols to convey a message of renovation, as 'attempts to restore the latent vocation of the city: Rome as the capital not only of the ancient world but also of the modern world'.[150]

In the late 18th century, a Greek revival movement started to grow out of the interest in ancient Greek architecture. In Britain, The Society of Dilettanti, which was founded in London around 1734, contributed to make known the deplorable state of ancient monuments in Greece and financed studies and publications on the subject. Notable outcomes of the Society were the surveys of Athenian

---

architectural theory of the ancients, he will see that they differ greatly from it and are actually closer to the usage of our own times. But before anyone accuses me of falsehood, he should, I beg, examine the ancient [Marble] plan of the city (...), he should examine the villas of Latium and that of Hadrian at Tivoli, the baths, the tombs and other ruins outside the Porta Capena and he will find that the ancients transgressed the strict rules of architecture just as much as the moderns. Perhaps it is inevitable and a general rule that the arts on reaching a peak should decline, or perhaps it is part of human nature to demand some license in creative expression as in other things which we sometimes criticise in buildings of our times.'

[150] Aureli 2011, 93; see Aureli 2011, 85-140 for an in-depth contextualization of Piranesi's Campo Marzio within the previous attempts at mapping ancient Rome and the tradition of the *instauratio Urbis*. On 'Il Campo Marzio', see also Dixon 2005, 115-132.

architecture by the artist James Stuart and the architect Nicholas Revett between 1751 and 1754, who produced accurate drawings of monuments that are now lost. The four volumes resulting from their work were published between 1762 and 1816 under the title of *The Antiquities of Athens* and will influence the taste for architectural classicism during the late 18th and 19th centuries.[151]

Greece had become the subject of romantic and idealised writings by many scholars and men of letters, as testified by works such as the *Voyage Pittoresque de la Grèce* (1782) by the French ambassador to the Ottoman Empire and scholar of Greek antiquities Marie-Gabriel-Florent-Auguste de Choiseul-Gouffier (1752-1817).[152] In this collection of his impressions of Greece gathered during his travels, he included numerous reconstruction drawings of the monuments he had seen, such as a reconstructed view of the ancient town of Assos on the coast of Asia Minor (Figure 2.12, left), aiming at conveying 'a faint idea' of the original cityscape. Interestingly, he legitimates his attempts at reconstructions of architecture by making a parallel between the visual reconstruction of ancient monuments and the philologist's restoration of a corrupted ancient text,[153] an analogy that will be used again in recent years to call indeed for a 'new philology' of 3D digital reconstructions, a requirement to ensure the correct assessment of computer-based reconstructions by the academic community.[154]

The arguments among scholars aiming to establish which between Romans and Greeks had the most sophisticated methods of construction continued, as testified to by the dispute between Piranesi, supporter of Roman architecture and the French architect Julien David Le Roy, an exponent of the Greek revival movement. Le Roy published in 1758 his praise to ancient Greek architecture in his *Les Ruines des Plus Beaux Monuments de la Grèce*, where he affirmed the supremacy of Greek monuments over the Roman. This publication was supplied with plans, sections and reconstruction drawings of some of the monuments, which were meant to express his fascination and reverence for Greek antiquities. In the case of the reconstruction of the Propylaea of the temple of Athena (Figure 2.12, right), for example, Le Roy admits that these drawings were meant to give just an 'inadequate idea' about the superb sight that they must have created in antiquity.[155] In reply to Le Roy's publication, Piranesi published in 1761 *Della Magnificenza ed Architettura dei Romani*, in which he ridiculed Le Roy's position, whilst reaffirming the highest achievements of Roman architecture in respect to Greek.[156]

In this period, the separation between the rigorous and archaeologically accurate documentation and a more visionary and artistic way of depicting antiquities starts to become increasingly evident and will become more pronounced from the second half of the 19th century. Piranesi's style of creating composite images remained quite unique and was followed up only for the illustrations of the 'voyages pittoresques', a genre that became popular at the end of the 18th century to describe journeys in thus far unknown destinations.[157] The archaeological documentation, on the other hand, became more and more specialized,

---

[151] Stiebing 1993, 121.
[152] For de Choiseul's biography see Barbier 2010.
[153] 'J'ai osé (...) relever ces belles ruines, recomposer ces édifices, et essayer d'en donner une faible idée. Qu'on daigne juger avec indulgence ce travail, ou, si l'on veut, ce jeu d'une imagination qui, rétrogradant de quelques siècles, se plaît à voir ce qui n'est plus, et admet la fiction à se présenter à la place de la réalité que l'on regrette. C'est la première fois que je me suis permis de montrer ainsi de simples souvenirs, de restaurer des édifices, ainsi qu'on se hasarde à restaurer des statues, ou à rétablir le texte des manuscrits. Ce n'est que tenter pour l'architecture, ce que d'autres ont fait pour Quinte-Curce, et pour Salluste: et pourquoi m'interdirait-on de redresser les colonnes d'un temple abattu, lorsqu'on pardonne aux efforts du savant qui n'a pas tremblé de se mesurer avec Tacite?' (de Choiseul 1809, 87).
[154] Frischer *et al.* 2002, 7-18; see chapter 3, 68.
[155] Le Roy 1758, second part, 13: 'Tous ces choses réunies devoient produire, dis-je, un spectacle superb, digne des éloges des Athéniens, & dont le dessein que j'ai fait, ne donne sans doute qu'une foible idée'.
[156] Nixon 2002, 474.
[157] See for example the illustrations by Jean-Laurent-Pierre Hoüel in his *Voyage Pittoresque des Isles de Sicile, de Malte et de Lipari, ou l'on Traite des Antiquites qui s'y Trouvent Encore; des Principaux Phenomenes que la Nature y Offre; du Costume des Habitans, & de Quelques Usages* (2 vols., 1782 and 1784) that Nixon considers 'the most bold of Piranesi's imitators' (Nixon 2002, 476). Hoüel

Figure 2.12 Left: Restored view of Assos, in de Choiseul 1809, pl. 10; Right: Le Roy's reconstruction of the Temple of Athena in Les Ruines des Plus Beaux Monuments de la Grèce *(plate XIII).*

in a drawing style that aimed to accurately record the evidence and to establish some standard methods to distinguish between documentation and interpretation, and this will become more evident in the course of the 19th century. The gradual increase in knowledge of the subjects depicted resulted in an increased capacity of the draughtsmen to capture the significant details of the archaeological evidence, which helped in the development of typologies to which these drawings gave a critical contribution.

2.6 The 19th and 20th centuries

In the 19th century, archaeology started to gain the status of an academic discipline and was introduced into universities. By the mid-19th century, ten chairs of archaeology existed in Germany and one in France, while in 1851 the first chair was established in Great Britain by John Disney at the University of Cambridge.[158] France and Germany were also the first countries to establish their schools in Athens: the École française in 1846 and the Deutsches Archäologisches Institut in 1874. Italy was struggling to become a truly united country after 1861 and, despite individual bright examples such as Giuseppe Fiorelli, Italian archaeology was lacking experienced personnel able to be in charge of the developing institutions for the new born state.[159] The first professor of 'archaeology and art history' in this country was the Austrian archaeologist Emanuel Löwy, who was appointed in Rome in 1891.[160]

In the first decades of this century, the stratigraphic principle established in geology was introduced to archaeology. Although stratigraphic excavation would still be far from being the standard field methodology, a considerable change is noticeable in excavation practise in the closing decades of the 19th century. In the 1870s, the German scholar Alexander Conze started the large scale and meticulous excavations at Samothrace, which were published in a report that for the first time included photographs;[161] the German Archaeological Institute commenced the excavations at Olympia, under the

---

shares the same attitude towards illustrations as Piranesi and he synthesizes it by stating in the preface of his work: 'J'affirme mes dessins par mes écrits, et je confirme mes écrits par mes dessins' (cited in Nixon 2002, 478).

[158] Leach 2007, 35-39. The world's first professor of archaeology was Caspar Reuvens, appointed at Leiden University in 1818. Reuvens was also appointed director of the university's archaeological cabinet, a rather neglected collection of artefacts that became the first core of the now internationally known Leiden's National Museum of Antiquities, thanks to his crucial contribution (see Halbertsma 2003).

[159] For the Italian situation after unification and the methodological debate between a philological/academic and a more practical approach to archaeology, see Barbanera 2000, *passim*.

[160] Chairs of archaeology had existed in Italian university before the unification, such as the one in Naples where Giuseppe Fiorelli was professor from 1861 (Barbanera 2000, 47).

[161] For an account of the intertwined histories of photography and archaeology, see Bohrer 2011.

directorship of Ernst Curtius, paying great attention to small finds and stratigraphic information.[162] In Britain, Pitt Rivers' careful excavations at his Cranborne Chase estate in Dorset between 1880 and 1900 set the methodological standard for the following generations.[163] Outside the academic environment, local antiquities societies, museums and journals grew exponentially, mirroring the increased participation of the middle class in the study of antiquities.[164]

The fascination for classical literature and Greek and Roman antiquities inspired and promoted narratives of national identity.[165] In Greece, the revolts that had begun in 1821 against the Ottomans fuelled sentiments of Romantic Nationalism in the other European countries. These feelings and calls for action are well embodied by the poem 'Hellas' composed by Percy Bysshe Shelley in 1821, in which he urges the British to support the Greek War of Independence writing that 'We are all Greeks'.[166] The independence obtained led to the formation of the new state, which was rooted in the ancient Greek past, and measures were taken (such as the creation of the Greek Archaeological Society in 1837) to protect the Greek heritage that had already been looted and appropriated by other European countries.[167] As Hamilakis and Yialouri have shown, Greek classical antiquity played a crucial role in the formation of the new state and has been used throughout Greek history as symbolic capital that could be exchanged in the negotiation for power and as an authoritative source that has been used to legitimate or resist a regime.[168]

In Victorian Britain (1837-1901), Latin and Greek held a predominant role in the curriculum at elite schools and universities,[169] with Homer being considered an inspirational and relaxing reading,[170] and the study of Roman Empire being seen in the light of the politics of colonial consolidation of the British Empire. Mythological and historical scenes and atmospheric views of ancient Rome and Greek landscapes appear in the works of several painters, such as William Turner's 'Ancient Rome' exhibited in 1839,[171] and in the many paintings by the Dutch-born artist Sir Lawrence Alma Tadema (1836-1912).[172] In this context, illustrations of ancient monumental architecture took a different route than the drawings of finds, the latter being increasingly employed by archaeologists to create artefacts' typologies.[173]

Roman and Greek architecture continued to be used as training material for young European architects. During the 19th century, numerous French architects came to Rome and visited Greece leaving many drawings of ruins and reconstructions of the monuments. The 'Prix de Rome', a scholarship established in the 17th century and opened to architects in the early 18th, gave in fact the possibility for many

---

[162] Stiebing 1993, 138; Fagan 2016, 92.
[163] Regarding Pitt Rivers and his legacy, Mortimer Wheeler stated: 'Between 1880 and 1900 General Pitt Rivers in Cranborne Chase had brought archaeological digging and recording to a remarkable degree of perfection, and had presented his methods and results meticulously in several imposing volumes. Then what? Nothing. Nobody paid the slightest attention to the old man. One of his assistants had even proceed to dig up a lake-village much as Schliemann had dug up Troy or St. John Hope Silchester: like potatoes' (Wheeler 1958, 55 cited by Lucas 2001, 36). The reality of the facts seems more nuanced than what appears from Wheeler's strong statement as recently pointed out by G. Lucas, as Rivers' methodology was received and applied in other contexts (see Lucas 2001, 36ff).
[164] Marchand 2007, 255.
[165] Murray 2002, 238. Italy for its historical developments represents a different case as elucidated by Barbanera 2000, 42-4.
[166] For a contextualization of this work, see Findlay 1993, 281-6.
[167] However, it must be noted that Greek intellectual circles in Greece started to react against the pillages of Greek antiquities already before independence, founding for example the Society of the Friends of the Muses in Athens in 1813, but stronger reactions took place only after 1821, see Díaz-Andreu 2007, 46 and 82-6.
[168] Hamilakis and Yialouri 1996, 117-129.
[169] See Goldhill 2011.
[170] Wood 1999, 178.
[171] Thomas 2008, 89-90.
[172] For a discussion on the classicizing painters of this period, see Wood 1999, esp. chapter 14 and 15 (176-221).
[173] Lewuillon 2002, 226.

French students to spend some years in Rome, applying their skills to study ancient sculptures and monuments.[174] One of these architects was Augustin-Nicolas Caristie (1783-1862), who won the prize in 1813. After he came back to France he was in charge of the restoration of the Roman arch at Orange which he published in his *Notice sur l'État Actuel de l'Arc d'Orange et des Théâtres Antiques d'Orange et d'Arles* (1839) and his *Monuments Antiques à Orange: Arc de Triomphe et Théâtre* (1856).[175] Later on, others won the prize such as Constant Moyaux (1835-1911) in 1861, Julien Guadet in 1864 and Louise Noguet in 1865, all of them engaging in creating reconstruction watercolours of monuments in Rome, especially in the Forum. To Greece, instead, went Albert Tournaire (1862-1958), who participated in the excavations at Delphi and in 1894 created a restored drawing of the complex of the sanctuary of Apollo, by merging the extant remains that he had surveyed with the information from ancient texts.[176]

Among the British scholars who travelled in Greece and Italy in this period, one of the most famous is the London architect Charles Robert Cockerell (1788-1863), who spent over seven years in his *Grand Tour* around Greece and then Italy studying ancient architecture and participating in excavations. He then applied his taste for classical architecture to design buildings such as the offices of the Bank of England in different cities. Moreover, he expressed his interest for Greek and Roman buildings in several reconstruction drawings, such as of the city of Athens, the Parthenon, the Roman fora and the

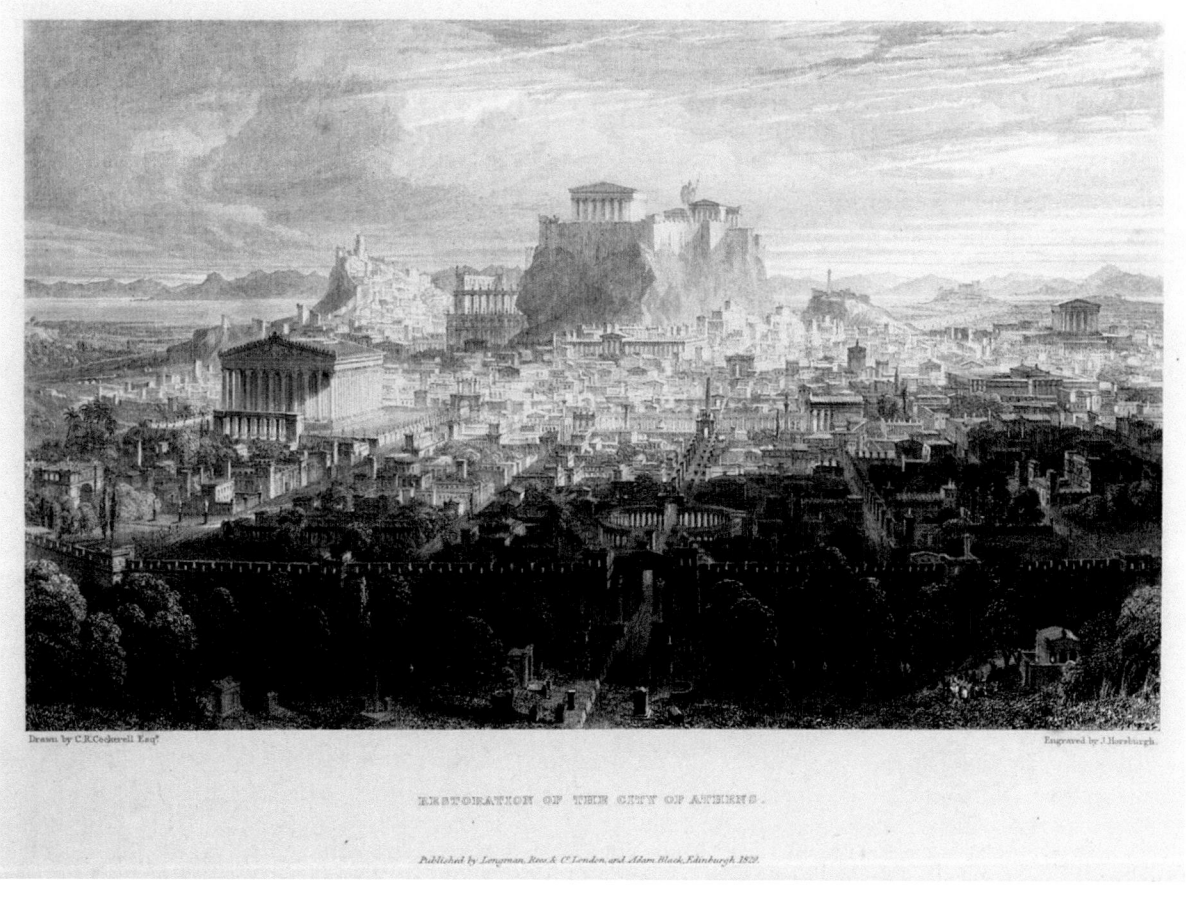

Figure 2.13 Restored view of Athens by C. R. Cockerell in Williams 1829.

---

[174] See Cassanelli *et al.* 2002.
[175] Sturgis 1905, 455.
[176] Ragon 1995, 57.

houses at Pompeii.[177] His restored views were used in other publications, such as his view of Athens (Figure 2.13) which is included in the second volume of H. W. Williams, *Selected Views in Greece* (1829).

In this period, archaeologically informed reconstructions and art productions depicting imaginative scenes of the past developed in increasingly different directions. Scholars in fact started to pay more attention to the choices they made in the reconstruction drawings to be inserted in their publications, thus offering more elements to the reader to assess the reliability of their illustrations, a topic which still generates discussion nowadays among scholars dealing with reconstructions in the digital age. An early example of an attempt to make the reconstruction drawings 'intellectually transparent' comes from the British scholar Sir William Gell (1777-1836). In his *De Pompeiana* (1819) that he wrote in collaboration with the British architect John Peter Gandy (1787-1850), several reconstruction drawings are presented, that were accompanied by explanations to facilitate the reader in understanding the choices made in the restorations. In the preface, the method that was used to create the drawings is elucidated, which consisted of using the 'camera lucida', a device which helped in rendering the correct perspective in the drawings. Each plate is preceded by an introduction that discusses the drawings and the accuracy of the elements that were inserted. For example, for plate XIX (Figure 2.14), the authors state that 'The gateway is restored in the simplest manner possible, but the biga over it is imaginary. Of the walls there can be no question. The pedestal supporting a statue on the left undoubtedly was built for that purpose; but it possibly might have been an equestrian or other group since the plan of the pedestal is not square. The statue is from one found in the city. (...) As a general observation, it may be marked that in this view everything beneath the horizontal line is certain; above it, only partly so'.[178]

In some cases, the drawing of the reconstruction was juxtaposed to the one of the extant remains, as in the case of plate XXIX representing the restored atrium of the house of Sallust, since by comparing the two 'it will be seen how far the restoration is authorised.'[179] Moreover, the text updates the reconstructions when some new discovery would shed new light on the section of the city that was drawn. This is for example the case of the restored view of the temple of Jupiter, where the textual explanation specifies that 'The part to the right had perhaps a second order, as two sizes of columns are found upon the spot; but this restoration was imagined before the excavation had fully laid open the part beyond the building marked 3.'[180]

During the 19th and 20th century, illustrations depicting reconstructions of ancient buildings and sites started to be increasingly made either by archaeologists themselves, or by draughtsmen and architect participating in excavations and being actively engaged in discussions with the archaeologists, in order to visualize the most plausible reconstruction hypotheses in their drawings. One of them was the Dutch Piet de Jong (1887-1967), who is considered 'one of the best-known, most distinctive, and most influential archaeological illustrators of the 20th century'.[181] By the first decades of the 20th century, he was involved in several projects: he worked with Arthur Evans and the British School to make reconstructions of the Palace at Knossos and with Carl Blegen and the American School at Athens for the reconstruction of the Palace at Pylos, and participated for several years in the American excavations in the Athenian Agora. His numerous watercolours, depicting reconstruction of objects, wall paintings and buildings (one example in Figure 2.15), have had a great influence on shaping the image of Aegean prehistory and Classical archaeology. The level of detail and quality in the drawings made these works of art in themselves, as stated by Rachel Hood: 'The archaeologists asked for a restoration of the pictures and patterns on the pottery or a reconstruction of an architectural moulding. What they got were

---

[177] Richardson 2001, 79.
[178] Gell and Gandy 1852, 98.
[179] Gell and Gandy 1852, 125.
[180] Gell and Gandy 1852, 168.
[181] Papadopoulos 2007, 2.

Figure 2.14 Reconstruction of one of the city gates of Pompeii (Gell 1852, pl. XIX).

works of art.'[182] All the scholars that he worked with held a high opinion about him, Blegen for example remembered him as '(...) our artist, whose constructive imagination recreated and brought to vivid perception the lingering aura of the Royal Mycenaean rulers who dwelt in this palace.'[183]

In the same period, in Italy, the archaeologist Giuseppe Gatteschi (1862-1935) was working on a series of reconstruction drawings of ancient Rome. The research related to this study took up thirty-four years of his life (1890-1924) and its publication in 1924 (the '*Restauri*') was endorsed by great archaeologists of the time, specialists in Roman topography such as Rodolfo Lanciani (1845-1929), and Christian Hülsen (1858-1935).[184] Unlike de Jong, Gatteschi is nowadays not well known and sparse information on his life can be derived from his documents and publications, such as the fact that he was born in Alexandria in Egypt and moved to Rome in 1895.[185] Gatteschi based his reconstructions on a variety of sources (ancient authors, coins, the Severan *Forma Urbis Romae*, works of Renaissance architects), on his own personal observations of the buildings, and on the new archaeological discoveries that were made at that time.[186] With the help of a photographer and some artists, such as Ulderico Bellioni, Oreste Betti, Augusto e Guido Trabacchi, he tried to recreate lively scenes of the ancient urban way of living by inserting drawings of people occupied in everyday activities in his reconstructions.

Gatteschi embarked in this work aiming to preserve the memory of the ruins that he was seeing quickly disappearing after the major urban renovation that Rome was undergoing in that period. As Raphael before him, he complained that Rome had been destroyed not so much by the weather, earthquakes

---

[182] Rachel Hood cited by Papadopoulos 2007, 17.
[183] Cited by Papadopoulos 2007, 13.
[184] Gatteschi 1924. See also Capodiferro 2006.
[185] From an autograph document by Gatteschi kept at the Archivio Storico Capitolino di Roma, cited in Cecchini 2007, 400.
[186] This information is found in the preface of Gatteschi's publication (1924) written by Orazio Marucchi.

Figure 2.15 Reconstruction of the 'Queen's Megaron' at Knossos for the Herakleion Museum made by Piet de Jong (after Papadopoulos 2007, Figure 1, p. 3).

and Barbarian invasions, but rather by men, and especially by the 16th century Popes.[187] He wanted to provide the reader with enough information about the reliability of his reconstructions. For this reason, his method was to supply each reconstructed view of ancient Rome with a photograph of the current state of the corresponding place taken from the same perspective of the reconstruction. In this way, one could immediately catch the correspondence between the two and be convinced of Gatteschi's accurate study.[188] Moreover, likewise Lauro's *Antiquae Urbis Splendor*, each drawing is accompanied by a short textual explanation in Latin, Italian, French and German discussing the sources that were used for the reconstruction (Figure 2.16).

A brief note in Italian at the end of another of his work, the *Restauro grafico del Monte Capitolino, Foro Romano e monumenti circostanti nell'anno 300 dopo Cr.*,[189] published in 1897, informs us that 'Gius. Nob. Gatteschi, archaeologist, is recommended to the foreign gentlemen for archaeological excursions to the monuments of ancient Rome and to the Villa at Tivoli'.[190] This can help us to better situate Gatteschi's vision and didactic aims: as the 17th century Swiss guard Hans Gross, he also worked as tourist guide

---

[187] See the introduction in Gatteschi 1924 and their autograph letters which are enclosed at the beginning of the work under the title 'Giudizi di illustri scienziati sull'opera del prof. Gatteschi'.

[188] 'Il Gatteschi, nel presentare agli studiosi i Restauri di questi gloriosi monumenti ha adottato il metodo assai razionale di mettere a confronto con i suoi disegni di restauro le fotografie dello stato attuale, cioè dello stato in cui presentemente si trovano gli avanzi di quei monumenti stessi fra i moderni edifizi; onde se ne veda a colpo d'occhio la corrispondenza. E chiunque potrà persuadersi che i suoi restauri non sono il prodotto di una fervida immaginazione come alcuni ideati da altri, ma che hanno la loro base nello studio accurato di tutto ciò che può sapersi intorno alla vera forma di ogni singolo monumento.' Preface of Gatteschi 1924.

[189] The title continues: 'Conferenza letta al Museo Urbano nell'Orto Botanico l'8 marzo 1897 per invito della commissione archaeologica comunale'.

[190] Gatteschi 1897, last page (unpaginated).

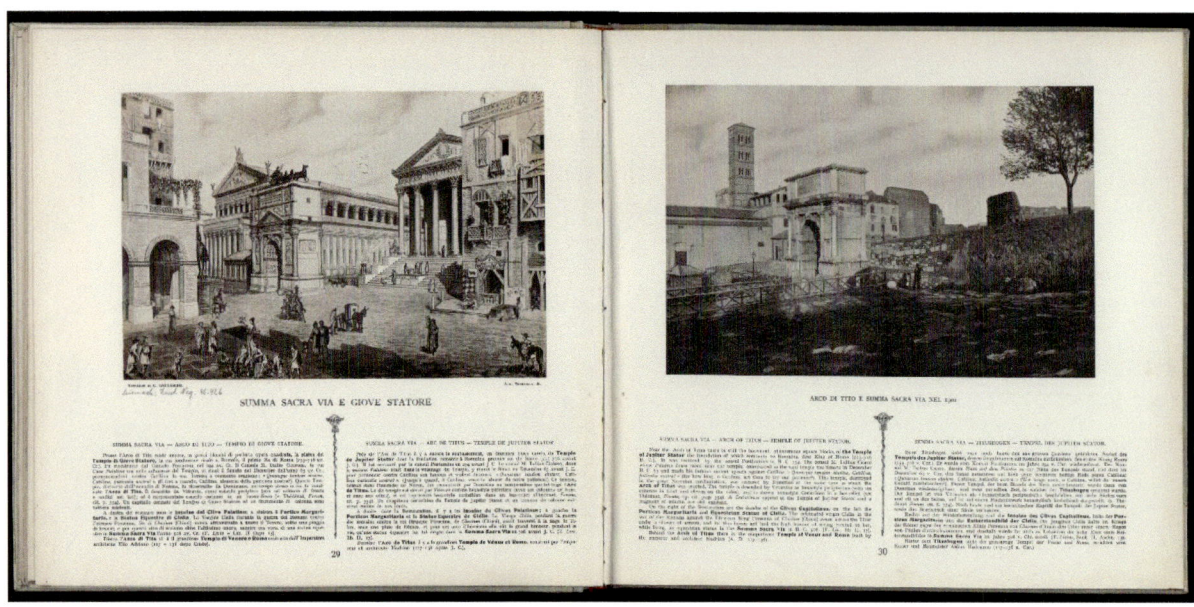

Figure 2.16 Gatteschi's reconstruction and photograph of the area of the Via Sacra and the Temple of Jupiter Stator (Gatteschi 1924, 29-30).

and certainly was confronted by the difficulty of conveying an image of the ruins' past appearance to the interested tourists. Following his will, some of the visual reconstructions that he prepared for the *Restauri* were placed in the area from the Imperial Fora to the Theatre of Marcellus, on the spot of the sites represented on the occasion of the fiftieth anniversary of the unification of Italy in 1911. From an epistolary exchange between Gatteschi and the municipality of Rome, we learn that he saw this as the only way in which 'the great majority of people that look at our glorious ruins without understanding anything about them, will be able to get the right impression of Imperial Rome at its maximum splendour'.[191] This reconstruction of Imperial Rome, which aimed to impress the viewers with a powerful visual image of its past grandeur, is a recurrent topic in the period between the Risorgimento and WWII and was instrumental in the process of construction and legitimation of the role of Rome as the capital of the unified peninsula, and of Italian colonial aspirations.[192]

The didactic use of reconstruction drawings continues also in more recent periods. They appear copiously as illustrations in books and exhibitions to convey a more immediate impression of the everyday life in the ancient world. Examples of influential publications that employed such drawings in the 20th century are Wycherley's *How the Greeks Built Cities* (1949), Paul MacKendrick's *The Greek Stones Speak* (1962) and Peter Connolly's and Hazel Dodge's *The Ancient City, Life in Classical Athens and Rome* (1998), containing, among others, the reconstruction drawing of the acropolis of Athens reproduced in Figure 2.17 (top left). A good example of an artist who was able to inject his artistic flair to archaeologically informed reconstructions, was the Englishman Alan Sorrell (1904-1974).[193] He studied art in England and won in 1928 a Prix de Rome scholarship that allowed him to get acquaintance with antiquities and archaeologists in Rome. Sorrell's unique style has fascinated and inspired generations of archaeologists

---

[191] Letter by Gatteschi addressed to the Ufficio VI di Storia dell'Arte – comune di Roma, cited in Cecchini 2007, 401.
[192] See Giardina and Vauchez 2008, esp. 181-2.
[193] An exhibition of Sorrel's works was held at Sir John Soane's Museum in London from 25 Oct. 2013 to 25 Jan. 2014. For a biography and discussion of his works, Llewellyn and Sorrell 2013.

Figure 2.17 Top, left: View of Athens, reconstruction drawing by P. Connolly (in Connolly and Dodge 1998). Top, right: The Roman town of Silchester by Alan Sorrel; Bottom: Preparatory stage for the reconstruction drawing of the temple area at Caerwent, Wales by Alan Sorrell with his annotations on the margin (after Catling 2013, 34 and 37).

(Figure 2.17, top right). Among the archaeologists whom he worked with, there is Sir Mortimer Wheeler, who involved him in the reconstruction paintings of Ur.[194]

---
[194] Llewellyn and Sorrell 2013, 41.

Although Sorrell was always keen on describing himself as an artist and not as an archaeologist, his drawings helped to trigger new research questions that the archaeologists that he collaborated with had not thought about before. In a preparatory sketch of the temple area at Caerwent, Wales, one could see his drawing method, based on a gridded canvas that allowed him to maintain the correct proportions and perspectives and the presence of many annotations and questions about the rendering of the scene that he wanted to discuss with the excavators. For example, Sorrell wonders about the most likely vegetation cover on the background of the scene and of the temple's courtyard, and makes inquiries on the correct locations of architectural elements (Figure 2.17, bottom).[195]

Other drawings bear traces of the extensive correspondence he engaged with archaeologists to clarify his uncertainties and suggest the inclusion of details in a rigorous and collaborative reconstruction process.[196] When he was asked to create a reconstruction drawing of the Mesolithic archaeological site of Star Carr in Yorkshire, he decided to add a shelter to the scene even if no archaeological evidence could support its presence. The reasonableness of his conjecture was proved when in 2010 the traces of what has been defined 'Britain's oldest house' were discovered at the site.[197]

In the 19th century, physical models also started to be employed as a means to display the extant remains or the reconstruction hypotheses for an archaeological site. One of the earliest three-dimensional models of Italian antiquities is the one of Pompeii that was made in the late 19th – early 20th century (Figure 2.18). This model had a troubled history and was on display again in the early 1990s at the National Archaeological Museum of Naples after restoration work that tried to save this delicate and dusty piece.[198] The streets were made of plywood, while the walls were of cork that was incised to create the different brickworks such as *opus reticolatum* and *incertum*. The frescoes are reproduced on the walls by using at first a base of plaster, and later on decorated paper that was used also for the floors. The vaults and ceilings were made in separate pieces so that it was possible to lift them to inspect the interior of the buildings.[199] The model was of great importance for scholars, since, as the German archaeologist Johannes Overbeck pointed out, it recorded the ancient city, and allowed an overview of the excavations that could not be achieved with the panorama photographs that were available at that time.[200] It is, however, even more important nowadays because, notwithstanding the ravages of time, the model keeps the record of *insulae* and decorations that are now lost, either destroyed during the wars or decayed from negligence.

Several physical 3D models have been created to represent the city of Rome in Imperial times. The first attempt to create a three-dimensional reconstruction of this city was made by the sculptor Giuseppe Marcelliani between 1904 and 1911.[201] This monochromatic model, known as the *Restitutio Urbis* (or 'La Roma di Coccio', since clay is the material that it is made of), aimed to show Rome in the 4th century AD. The result, however, should be considered more as an artistic product than a reliable attempt to create a volumetric reproduction of the ancient urban layout. Marcelliani's artistic background played in fact a relevant role in the realization of the project, which shows little archaeological knowledge of ancient Roman topography and landscape and is mainly based on fantasy.[202]

---

[195] Catling 2013, 32-39.
[196] Perry and Johnson 2014.
[197] Catling 2013, 37.
[198] Sampaolo 1993, 89-91.
[199] Sampaolo 1993, *passim*.
[200] Cited by Sampaolo 1993, 85.
[201] An earlier three-dimensional representation of some key monuments of Rome (among others, the triumphal arches of Titus, Septimius Severus and Constantine that are now lost) is the fountain called 'la Rometta' made by Pirro Ligorio in the gardens of the Villa d'Este. This scenographic monument had a symbolic meaning and embodied in three dimensions Ligorio's interest for Roman antiquities (see Madonna 1991).
[202] Giuliani 2007, 261; Ciancio-Rossetto 1990, 11-15.

Figure 2.18 The 3D physical model of Pompeii at the National Archaeological Museum of Naples (source: https://it.wikipedia.org/wiki/File:Plastico_di_Pompei_1.JPG).

Figure 2.19 Paul Bigot and his 3D model of Rome in 1911 (after Royo 2006, Figure 95, p. 165).

In the same period, the French architect Paul Bigot created his 'Le plan de Rome', a 75 m² model presenting again the city at the time of the emperor Constantine. The model was first displayed during the 1911 exhibition celebrating the fiftieth anniversary of the unification of Italy (Figure 2.19).[203] In order to facilitate the assembling of his model, Bigot divided it into 102 modules that could be easily combined together as pieces of a puzzle. The French architect started to work on this project in 1904 and continued to modify it until his death in 1942, conducting in the meantime research on Roman architecture and city planning.[204] During this period, the urban layout of Rome went through major changes and many archaeological discoveries were made that shed new light on the urban development of the ancient city. For this reason, Bigot devised a workflow that allowed him to quickly update the model when new information needed to be included. He therefore based his work pipeline on the creation of sketched mock-ups made of clay that could be revised several times before being finally plaster casted.[205] Bigot paid also much attention to colours, that nowadays have mostly faded away, and to the contrast that the architecture in travertine and marble would create against the surrounding green vegetation.[206] Moreover, it seems that Bigot had installed several projectors around the model emitting various colours to recreate the effect of light in Rome during different day and night times.[207]

A different celebration, the bi-millenary of Augustus' birthday in 1937, was the occasion to create another plaster-model of Rome, made by the Italian architect Italo Gismondi. The model was displayed during the 'Mostra Augustea della Romanità', an exhibition that Mussolini wanted in order to stress the connection both between the magnificent ancient Rome and the new one that he intended to create, and between Augustus and himself.[208] Gismondi, as previously Bigot, based his model on the fragments of the 'Forma Urbis' that Rodolfo Lanciani had published in 1901 and that reported all the major buildings of ancient Rome that were known at the time of its creation at the beginning of the 3rd century AD. The model was made on a 1:250 scale and it extends over a surface of about 200 m², filling up an entire room of the *Museo della Civiltà Romana* in Rome. While the plaster-model of Rome is Gismondi's best known achievement, he actually created many reconstruction drawings of ancient buildings and other plaster-models, representing for example Hadrian's Villa at Tivoli,[209] the complex of Claudius' and Trajan's harbours, and the ancient city of Ostia, the last two being currently on display at the Museo della Via Ostiense – Porta S. Paolo in Rome.[210] Especially Gismondi's reconstructions of Ostia's apartment complexes (or *insulae* as they have been called by Guido Calza, the director of the excavations in that period) moved beyond the scope of archaeological representation and became ideal models for contemporary urban planning and architecture. According to Kockel, in fact, Gismondi's drawings provided a powerful visual tool to express Calza's view, namely that the *insula* could be seen as the exemplary solution to be emulated in order to resolve the pressing problem of finding accommodations for the increasing population in Rome during the 1920s and 1930s.[211]

Gismondi looked at the ancient structures with the technical eye of an architect, looking especially to materials and construction techniques, but 'he combined a knowledge of the archaeological material which is remarkable for a technician',[212] and the archaeologists trusted him for his accuracy and

---

[203] Pasqualini 2006, 631. The model has been restored and kept at the University of Caen; recently it underwent a process of digitization and a virtual visit has been created, see Fleury and Madeleine 2010, 67-75.
[204] Royo 1992.
[205] Giuliani 2007, 261.
[206] Bigot 1942, 6 cited by Royo 1992, 596.
[207] Royo 1992, 596.
[208] The Istituto Luce recorded a propaganda video that presented the exhibition, see http://www.youtube.com/watch?v=cneYAemeNqU (last accessed Sept. 2016).
[209] Ten 2007, 277-80.
[210] Pellegrino 2007, 275-6.
[211] Kockel 2005.
[212] In the words by archaeologist Giuseppe Lugli, cited in Filippi 2007, 15.

precision in surveying and recording ancient monuments. It is interesting to analyse the methodology that Gismondi applied to the creation of his model of Rome, to see how the Roman architect dealt with challenges that also the modern model-maker is confronted with.[213] The first challenge that Gismondi had to overcome was the necessity of reconstructing the entire city, although many of its parts were not archaeologically documented. This situation called for solving two problems, the first one was to find a way to relatively quickly fill in the empty areas with buildings, and the second one was to distinguish the buildings archaeologically attested from those that were inserted only to create a plausible view of the ancient city. To tackle the first problem, Gismondi created two categories of Roman building types, the *insula* and the *domus*, dividing each of them in three subtypes, thus obtaining six basic types that he could then arrange randomly to generate variety in the urban layout.[214] To solve the second problem, he chose to create buildings with different levels of detail, by moulding only a volumetric outline for the building for which little or nothing was known and adding more details to those that were archaeologically documented. As Tschudi noted, 'these two different approaches to architectural 'unknowns' may be seen to mark a transition from a historicist model of ancient Rome to a modernist one.'[215]

In 1951, Gismondi's plaster model of Rome was used in Mervyn LeRoy's cinematographic adaptation of *Quo Vadis: A Narrative of the Time of Nero*, the epic historical novel by the polish writer Henryk Sienkiewicz (1895). Ironically, the model that was originally commissioned for the 1937 exhibition aiming to connect Mussolini's and Augustus' Rome was now used in the scene where Nero illustrates to his court his megalomaniac project for the new Rome he had envisioned (Figure 2.20).[216] The novel was rendered as a movie adaptation on five different occasions (the Italian silent movies in 1912 and 1925, the Hollywood blockbuster in 1951, the miniseries for Italian television in 1985 and the Polish version in 2001), each of them giving prominence to and interpreting in different ways the various themes of the story such as politics, ethnicity and religion.[217] For example, in the adaptation released in 1951, the aftermath of WWII, the American audience could easily grasp the reference to Hitler and the Nazi's persecution of the Jews in Nero's madness, his destructive effects on Rome and the persecutions against the Christians.[218] The Polish version of the novel focused instead on different aspects (such as the more explicit allusions to Poland and to the pontificate of Pope John Paul II), associating Nero's rule to the communist regime and Saint Peter to the Polish Pope.[219]

Quo Vadis' movies are just an example of how the image of the reconstructed ancient world that has been elaborated and transmitted in movies has always been permeated by contemporary ideas and messages. In recent years, film historians have started to look at historical movies as powerful agents that shaped and popularized a historical narrative of the past, which represented and addressed the needs of the contemporary society.[220] At the beginning of the 20th century, some indeed considered cinema as the new frontier to teach history and reconstruct the past in a way that could surpass in accuracy and capability of engagement any previous attempt.[221] As Wyke has shown, Roman virtues, such as military courage, the Emperors' vices and the rise of Christianity opposed by the cruel Roman Empire have been

---

[213] For a detailed explanation on how Gismondi organized his work through preparatory sketches and drawings, see Giuliani 2007, 261-5.
[214] Tschudi 2012, 391.
[215] Tschudi. 2012, 391.
[216] Wyke 1997, 140-1.
[217] The five adaptations have been analysed in Scodel and Bettenworth 2009.
[218] Scodel and Bettenworth 2009, 93-7; see also Skwara 2013, 166. As Skwara notes, the 1951 version of the movie was received very differently by the Polish audience, which could see it only in the 1980s and could relate less to the allusions suggested in the movie (Skwara 2013, 167-8).
[219] Scodel and Bettenworth 2009, 97.
[220] Wyke 1997, 8-13.
[221] Wyke 1997, 9.

Figure 2.20 Scene from the movie QuoVadis (1951) in which Nero illustrates his plan for his new Rome in front of Gismondi's plaster model (from Wyke 1997, 141).

deployed as recurrent themes in an extensive filmography to support different narratives, including nationalism, imperialism or opposition to tyrannical regimes.[222] In the early years of the introduction of cinema, for example, movies provided the collective experience needed to foster feelings of national identity in the United States and in Italy, two countries struggling to create an internal cohesion. The Italian cinematographic production of *Scipione l'Africano* in 1937, sustained by copious financing by the Fascist regime, was infused with colonial ideology. This movie aimed to contribute to the creation of the ideal Fascist Italy that had to be 'wise, strong, disciplined and imperial', and resurrect the 'immortal spirit of Rome', as envisioned by Mussolini in his speech for the celebration of the foundation of Rome on the 21 April 1922.[223]

The dominant Hollywood style of historical movies that was popular until the 1950s and is well expressed by the colossal productions such as *Ben-Hur* (1959) and *Spartacus* (1960) knew a rapid debacle in the course of the 1960s, culminated in the bankruptcy of the 20th Century Fox caused by the costs that the movie studio had to sustain for *Cleopatra* (1963), the most expensive production of the time, that did not return the expected revenues.[224] During the 1960s, the audience could not identify any more with the clichéd characters and themes that had been proposed until that time in these rather

---

[222] Wyke 1997, 14-33, esp. 20.
[223] Transcript of Mussolini's speech published in his newspaper *Il popolo d'Italia*, cited in Wyke 1997, 21.
[224] Wyke 1997, 184.

standardized productions.[225] In striking contrast with the visual language that characterized Hollywood historical movies, European filmography adopted other schemes and narratives. The change in taste and the different image of the past that is projected in movies in the late 1960s and early 1970s is well represented by Fellini's *Satyricon* (1969), where alien and desecrating Roman characters played in the fragmented narrative that wanted to render in this way 'the potsherds, crumbs and dust of a vanished world.'[226]

2.7 Conclusions

This chapter has attempted to contextualize the reconstructions of Graeco-Roman cities within their historical framework by discussing a selection of case studies from the 15th to the 20th century. Such research aimed to contribute to the still rare studies on the creation and reception of visual reconstructions of antiquities, which add interpretative keys to explore the complex relationship between ancient and modern cultures. The case studies discussed in this chapter have demonstrated the richness of clues in visual reconstructions, which, their often questioned archaeological reliability aside, contribute to the interpretation of the historical context in which they were created. The act of visually representing a reconstruction hypothesis in fact always entails a (more or less conscious) process of selection, interpretation and cultural appropriation. Any type of reconstruction of antiquities, be it a drawing, a plaster model or a cinematographic adaptation, lends itself to be constructed to express and legitimate present ideas and needs, at the same time shaping and aligning itself to the contemporary traditional view of the past.

The ways in which humanists, antiquarians, architects, artists and film makers have looked at the past and what they wanted to express with their renditions have varied considerably: for the humanist historian Biondo, the ancient restored monuments were instrumental to support the papal plans of the architectural renovation of Rome; Annius of Viterbo's forgeries contributed to emphasise the role of his hometown; antiquarians such as Lauro wanted to convey a suggestive impression of ancient Rome that could still transmit the ancient glory of the city and be popular among visitors who came from across the Alps; Gismondi's plaster model visually and physically brought back the magnificence of Imperial Rome that Mussolini wanted to connect to; and finally, the cinematographic images of Rome mirrored contemporary political, ideological and social issues. The attention to this topic is still relevant today, as the selection of specific elements of the past for substantiating a cultural narrative or an ideological discourse can still be seen in how archaeological objects are represented and how the notion of heritage is constructed, as shown by recent research in the field of heritage studies.[227]

The attempt to preserve the vanishing traces of an ancient past that could still hold meaning for the present has been always one of the triggers for surveying and drawing material remains. Many scholars over the centuries have complained about the critical condition of ancient ruins, which have been constantly spoiled not only by time and weather, but also by pillages, commerce and negligence, or indifference. This is well exemplified by the city of Rome, first the capital of the Roman empire and then of the Catholic church, that, soon after the decline of the Roman empire, became a quarry of marble for the construction and embellishment of new buildings and a 'warehouse of ancient sculpture'.[228] Reconstructions, therefore, have become also a valuable source of information on the state of knowledge of the time of their creation and also a visual memory of many structures that nowadays are lost, as the drawings of Cyriac of Ancona or the 3D physical model of Pompeii remind us.

---

[225] Wyke 1997, 184-5.
[226] Fellini 1978, 17 cited in Wyke 1997, 189.
[227] Watson and Waterton 2010, 84-97; Hamilakis 2016.
[228] Weiss 1969, 8.

When the interest for antiquities started to extend outside the limited audience of antiquarian circles, another reason to prepare reconstruction drawings was to present what the ancient buildings looked like to visitors and to engage them in a more popular and approachable vision of antiquities. This is the purpose of the 17th century Swiss Guard Giovanni Alto, but also, more close to us, of many drawings that were commissioned to Piet de Jong and Alan Sorrel to be displayed in musea. Finally, architects have been accustomed to prepare reconstructions of ancient buildings as part of their training, to understand how buildings were constructed and to gain the skills that would allow them to apply ancient construction techniques in their contemporary architectural projects. This is a recurrent theme in the work of Leon Battista Alberti, in Piranesi's engravings and in the European architects that came to Rome and then created many buildings in their own countries following classical taste.

Besides exploring the different functions of reconstructions over the centuries, the case studies discussed have allowed us to follow the development of a scientific methodology to deal with historical sources and archaeological remains. By starting to question the reverence for the authority of the written word, antiquarians began to adopt an empirical approach based on first hand observations and personal surveys as the prime way to gather information. The direct study of the extant remains, starting with Biondo, Cyriac of Ancona and Ligorio, had a clear impact also on the way in which antiquities were represented, as the textual descriptions that had been well suited to replicate the information found in ancient authors fell short in conveying the physicality of the ruins, thus opening to an increasing use of visual representations. A further methodological turning point is moreover represented by the growing awareness of the uncertainty related with any reconstruction of antiquities, as is present in the work of Buonarroti, and the related increased inclusion of explicit information about the reliability of the reconstructed parts, as well exemplified by Gell's *De Pompeiana*.

As a final note, one might find a parallel between the enthusiastic views on the potential benefit offered by the new cinematographic representations of historical narratives and the introduction of computer technology for the creation of digital reconstructions. As the next chapter will show, while the challenges of representing the past remained the same in the digital era, computer-based visualizations can offer some solutions (although some of them still underexploited) to convey the transient nature of reconstructions, which inevitably reflect the state of the knowledge at the time of their creation, and to make explicit the subjectivity of the reconstruction derived from the modeller's interpretation of the available archaeological evidence.

3. Three-dimensional visualizations in archaeology: An additional tool in the archaeologist's toolbox

'Fundamentally a model is understood from the first [i.e. theory] as a simplification for purposes of making sense of complex data-sets, to be set against alternative models for the goodness of it. This is also a procedure to be constantly renewed as new data and new models appear within the discipline.'
(Bintliff 2015, 33, emphasis of the author)

3.1 Introduction

As shown in the previous chapter, drawings of archaeological remains have been used since the 15th century; it is therefore undeniable that these kinds of visual representations are deeply connected with archaeological studies. Outlines of archaeological layers and pottery, plans and sections of buildings were sketched down in order to keep a memory of these remains, to allow comparison and the creation of typologies. Illustrations displaying hypothetical reconstructions of archaeological structures that were created out of a fascination for their distant past have also been employed to facilitate the understanding of the context that is being studied and to get a more vivid impression of what a site or structure might have looked like. These representation modes continue to be used nowadays both to keep a record of all information and hypotheses that arose in the field, and in the post processing phase, and also to communicate the results to the public in a way that is comprehensible also for non-specialists.

The obvious problem with this traditional way of documentation is the lack of the possibility to record the 'z' value, the depth of the recorded entity, being it an artefact, a stratigraphic unit or a building. In order to create a complete documentation, several 2D drawings are therefore needed, representing the archaeological record from different perspectives. Although archaeologists have become familiar with this way of representing archaeological evidence using sections and prospects to account for the three dimensionality of the recorded object, it is undeniable that this process is not ideal. The result is in fact a segmentation of a continuous reality into separate entities, which not only requires a cognitive and interpretative effort to reconcile the different parts, but also limits the amount of recorded information, and constraints the possibilities of further manipulation, exploration and analysis.

It is therefore not surprising that archaeologists have soon become interested in 3D digital recording and modelling techniques. A 3D model can be defined as a mathematical representation of a concrete or abstract entity in which its features are displayed according to the geometry of their real volume. This means that the modelled entity is fully described from any point of view and can be seen from different perspectives with the same level of detail. To create 3D models, dedicated programs are needed that allow the representation of an object as a set of points that are connected to each other by geometric shapes (triangles or polygons). Once the 3D model is created, it can still be rendered as a 2D image, which allows a final photorealistic result, or used in a computer simulation for a real time interaction.

Besides the creation of a complete documentation encompassing all the three dimensions, other advantages of 3D digital models can be highlighted. First of all, many different types of information can be summarised within a single model with a multi-scale approach. A 3D model, in fact, allows us to recreate the complete picture of a landscape from a single unit to the entire territory. Secondly, a 3D model permits further manipulation of data that are not static as notes, sketches drawn on paper or plaster models, but that can be more easily updated and transformed. Thirdly, their digital nature allows an easier circulation within the scientific community, thereby stimulating a more dynamic debate on interpretations and methodologies. 3D models are also important tools of interpretation because the addition of volumetric characteristics allows a deeper understanding of the recorded entity. Moreover, 3D representations are an effective means of communication, since they are appreciated by the public of non-specialists as comprehensible and immediate visions from an ancient past.

During the 1980s, examples of publications concerning archaeological 3D models were appearing, still sporadically, especially in technical journals. One of the first articles concerning a 3D archaeological reconstruction was written by Smith in 1985 and presented the 3D model of a Roman bath.[229] The first researchers that tried to develop complex 3D models of archaeological remains were however faced with many technical limitations. A telling example is the paper presented at the Computer Applications and Quantitative Methods in Archaeology (CAA) conference in 1991 that illustrated a guided-tour through the Sanctuary of Demeter at Eleusis.[230] Since each of the four processors that were used for the project had only between 8 and 32 MB of memory, the authors decided to model only what was visible to the viewer and represented the model with 'as few objects as possible'.[231] This solution is comparable to Gismondi's decision to add details only to the parts of his plaster model of Rome that could be seen by visitors. To save time and costs, only 15% of the Gismondi's model was in fact characterised with doors, windows and other architectural features, while the rest was simply white plastered.[232]

Not only technical problems burdened early archaeological applications of 3D visualizations. A more challenging and long lasting problem was related to the dominant role of technology to the detriment of the actual archaeological content. As Ryan wrote in 1996, many early virtual reality projects were in fact undertaken as 'vehicles for demonstrating advanced graphics techniques with any archaeological considerations playing a less important role'.[233] A telling example is the reconstruction of virtual Pompeii, made by the Simlab of Carnegie Mellon University (Pittsburgh) and shown at De Young Museum in San Francisco in 1995. As Frischer *et al.* wrote, 'Despite the project's financial support by the Archaeological Institute of America, no professional Pompeianists are known to have been consulted when the project was in its inception, nor to have had any major input on the final product (...) [They] were not expected to do anything but admire the results'.[234] As will be discussed later, this is a recurrent problem in 3D archaeology and Ryan's call for archaeologists to 'communicate archaeological and historical information to their colleagues and to the public, not to demonstrate their skills in the latest computer graphics techniques'[235] can be considered still applicable nowadays.

Another problematic aspect of 3D digital visualisations in archaeology was the fact that they were perceived as more truthful than traditional reconstruction drawings, although both are used to suggest reconstruction hypotheses and both imply a process of interpretation by the draftsman/3D modeller.[236] A change in the communication medium alone (from paper to computer-aided

---

[229] Smith 1985, 7-9.
[230] Cornforth *et. al.* 1992.
[231] Cornforth *et. al.* 1992, 220.
[232] This realization hampered Frischer's initial plan to run a miniature robotic camera through Gismondi's model to create a virtual tour, see B. Frischer, 'Beyond Illustration: New Dimensions of 3D Modeling of Cultural Heritage Sites and Monuments', Keynote address to CNI Plenary, 15 Dec., 2009, available at https://www.cni.org/wp-content/uploads/2011/06/cni_beyond_frischer.pdf (last accessed Sept. 2016).
[233] Ryan 1996, 107.
[234] Frischer *et al.* 2002, 7-18.
[235] Frischer *et al.* 2002, 7-18.
[236] Daniels-Dwyer 2004, 261.

drawing) created a shift in the perceived truthfulness of the representation, which was increased by the degree of immersion and realism that 3D visualisations allow the user to experience. As Favro pointed out, 'the use of computers imparts an imprimatur of scientific validity that must be constantly challenged as any reconstruction is only as good as the data and methods used'.[237] Niccolucci et al. paralleled this situation to the introduction of Database Management Systems in archaeology, when it seemed that 'after they have been recorded into a database, archaeological records lose any element of uncertainty and subjectivity and become as trustworthy as the computer itself'.[238]

This problem is typical of any kind of data stored in, and processed by a computer, and lies in the difficulty of dealing with data that are fragmentary, uncertain and subjected to the individual's interpretation. However, it becomes even more visible in the case of reconstructions of archaeological evidence. When documenting finds and architectural pieces, archaeologists usually use dashed lines or a lower level of detail to integrate the missing parts when necessary (see Figure 3.1). For digital 3D reconstructions, researchers have not agreed on a standardized way to visualize the reconstructed parts, although several different methods have been suggested to deal with this aspect.[239] Moreover, early 3D reconstructions were not supplied with additional information on the sources that were used as comparison, which makes it difficult to distinguish the archaeologically documented from the integrated elements. The 3D model appears therefore as a 'closed box', or a monolithic block that leaves the viewer little possibility both to assess the reliability of the reconstruction, and also to re-use the work for different purposes.

Since the mid-1990s, scholars expressed concerns about the misuse and deceptive power of 3D reconstructions. Taking on board these concerns, a fruitful discussion has started from the early 2000s aiming at developing standard methods for the creation and presentation of 3D visualizations of archaeological evidence. As will be discussed in detail later on in this chapter, this debate has converged in issuing guidelines such as the London Charter for the computer-based visualisation of cultural heritage,[240] and the Seville principles for computer-based visualisations in archaeology.[241] These efforts have the merit to have raised the awareness of problems that have afflicted 3D reconstructions in archaeology since its beginning. The sign that this problem is far from exhausted, however, is that a practical implementation of the general guidelines offered by the above mentioned documents is still missing. No standard workflow has been developed about how to deal with and how to present the sources that have been used for the reconstruction and how to account for the modelling choices employed in the process, so that practitioners in this field have come up with *ad hoc* solutions tailored to the needs of their current projects.

When London-charter compliant 3D visualizations are created, it is still rare that the results of these efforts are made publicly available as an interactive experience that could engage the public and foster discussion among the scientific community on the proposed reconstruction hypotheses. The 3D visualizations that are created for museum settings are often not available anymore when the exhibition closes, and those that are made for research purposes remain locked in the creator's computer and are usually published as 2D renderings. This means that all the human and financial resources that have been invested in the project have little impact (or at least not as much as they could have) on society and on the actual progression of hypothesis-generating archaeological inquiry.

---

[237] Favro 2013.
[238] Niccolucci *et al.* 2001, 109.
[239] See below, § 3.4.1.
[240] http://www.londoncharter.org/ (last accessed Sept. 2016).
[241] The Seville principles is available at http://smartheritage.com/seville-principles/seville-principles (last accessed Sept. 2016).

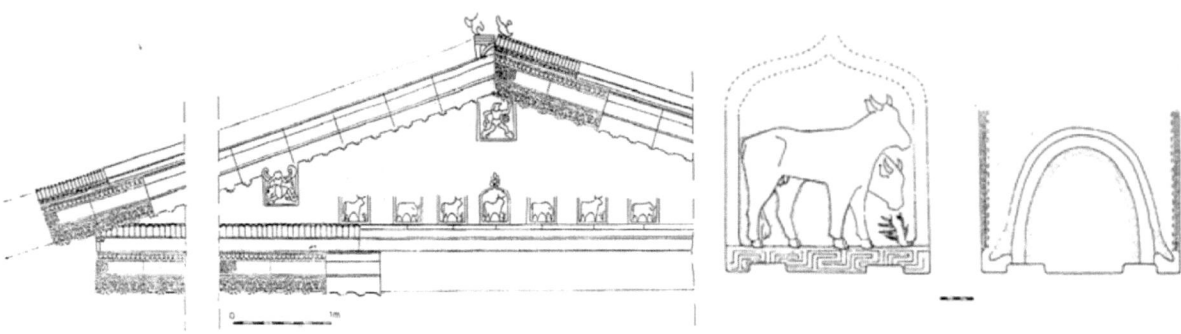

Figure 3.1 Example of reconstructive drawings of elements of the Mater Matuta's temple (Satricum) by P. Lulof (after Ratto 2009).

Technical constraints are usually at the basis of a reluctance of sharing the 3D environment. As for any tool that is made publicly available, one has to ensure the full functionality of every aspect of the navigation in the virtual environment (especially when a free navigation of the user is desired),[242] the compatibility with any computer system, and the development or availability of the right platform to share it. This requires extra expertise, time and costs that are often not within the research team or the available budget.[243] The journal *Digital Applications in Archaeology and Cultural Heritage* was launched in 2014 to promote the online publication and peer-reviewing of 3D models.[244] The high open access fees (3,000 USD) and the technical limitations for the publication of interactive digital models, however, represented a substantial obstacle for researchers in this field. For these reasons, the founding editor of the journal, Bernard Frischer, has recently left the editorial board and launched *Studies in Digital Heritage*, an open access journal with no article processing charge, which uses WebGL technology to publish 3D models online.[245]

In a field that has been since its beginning more practice-driven than theory-laden, the impression is that archaeologists have adopted these visualization techniques as fancier and more sophisticated replacements of traditional drawing tools, instead of exploring the new possibilities that they offer.[246] In recent years, however, a growing number of archaeologists with technical skills in this field is contributing to a methodological discussion on good practises, and are using 3D visualizations with a more mature view both on their limitations and on their analytical potential. In the next section I will present a brief overview of the main modelling techniques that are used to make 3D reconstructions of structures that are now (partially) lost. Next, I will deal with the topic of source documentation and the solutions that have been implemented for the creation of 3D visualizations as intellectually transparent knowledge providers. The following section focuses on the scientific value of 3D reconstructions, by exploring their still underestimated role as analytical instruments in their own right and not only as presentation aids and educational tools. Through a discussion of published case studies, I will argue that 3D reconstructions enable us to generate new insights and hypotheses on ancient construction techniques, and on the use and the social implications of architecturally defined spaces. The chapter closes with some considerations on the past, present and future of 3D visualizations in archaeology, suggesting some practical solutions for an effective use of 3D modelling techniques by archaeologists as both research and presentation tools.

---

[242] See e.g. Fleury *et al.* 2014.
[243] A successful example of such implementation is the online navigation through the 3D virtual environment of Montegrotto, Italy (by CNR-ITABC) available at http://www.aquaepatavinae.it/portale/?page_id=2174 (last accessed 30-11-2015, OSG4WEB plugin required); see also Fanini and Ferdani 2012, 107-15.
[244] http://www.journals.elsevier.com/digital-applications-in-archaeology-and-cultural-heritage (last accessed March 2017).
[245] https://scholarworks.iu.edu/journals/index.php/sdh/index (last accessed March 2017). A blog post at the bottom of the page presents the new journal and the context of its launching.
[246] Gillings 2005.

3.2 Creating computer-aided 3D models

Nowadays, there are several ways in which a computer-aided 3D model can be obtained. The main difference in approach lies between the techniques that are used to *record* archaeological finds (reality-based models) and those that are used to *reconstruct* a site that is now (partially) lost. A digital documentation of objects or still standing buildings can be obtained with so called 'remote sensing' techniques that are based on either image-based or range-based 3D data collection at distance. 3D reconstructions can be manually done with Computer-Aided Design software such as AutoCAD and computer graphics software such as the open source Blender or commercial packages such as 3D Studio Max, Maya or Cinema4D. Alternatively, as will be discussed below, procedural modelling offers a parametric approach to (semi-) automatically generate 3D geometry. These two ways of obtaining digital 3D models are not meant as being part of separate workflows but can be combined, depending on the available dataset and on the purpose of the project in order to achieve the best result. For example, 3D data of extant architectural remains that are acquired by remote sensing techniques, such as laser scanners, can be manipulated and integrated with reconstruction hypotheses by means of CAD or computer graphics software. On a more conceptual level, in both real and non-real approaches the process of obtaining the 3D digital model poses numerous challenges: during the recording of a still standing structure, uncertainties may arise related to e.g. correctly identifying *in situ* remains, or distinguishing contemporary phases from later additions, while creating a digital reconstruction implies the formulation of justified hypotheses about a reality that no longer exists. In this respect, the sources used to integrate the missing data and the thinking process that led to a specific reconstruction need to be documented, in order to offer to the viewer the possibility to assess the value of the archaeological visualization. This topic has been debated since the earliest applications of virtual reconstructions in archaeology and will be treated extensively later on in this chapter. I shall now present the main techniques used in recent years in archaeology, with a particular focus on their application to the built environment. Since the methodology that I will discuss in chapter 6 aims at the reconstruction of a lost site, and since the use of image-based and range based modelling techniques applied to heritage has been extensively treated in numerous publications,[247] in the following sections I will focus only on manual and procedural modelling approaches.

3.2.1 Manual 3D modelling

The software packages that allow the manual creation of a 3D environment can be divided into Computer-Aided Design (CAD) and Computer Graphics (CG) software. These two types of software are targeted to different purposes and users and their differences have to be considered when choosing the most appropriate software to fulfil the requirement of a project. While the roots of CAD software (e.g. Autodesk AutoCAD) lie in prototyping and drafting, CG software packages (e.g. the open source Blender and commercial suites such as 3D Studio Max, Maya and Cinema4D) have been developed with other users in mind, namely game developers and graphics artists. The main characteristics (and limitations) of these software packages reflect therefore their originally intended purposes.

---

[247] Overviews on 3D recording techniques applied to cultural heritage include: Stylianidis and Remondino 2016, Remondino 2011, Remondino and Rizzi 2010. Image-based recording techniques such as photogrammetry and Structure from Motion are extensively used in archaeology. Recent applications for heritage purposes to create a 3D digital documentation of lost or endangered sites include: the digital reconstruction of the big Buddha statue in the valley of Bamiyan (Afghanistan), destroyed by the Taliban in 2001 during a raid of non-Islamic iconoclasm (see Remondino and El-Hakim 2006, 309-10; Grün et al. 2004, 177-99); the Project Mosul (http://projectmosul.org/) initiated by Matthew Vincent, Chance Coughenour, and Marinos Ioannides and partly funded by the 'Initial Training Network for Digital Cultural Heritage: Projecting our Past to the Future' (ITN-DCH); and the 'Million Image Database' project (http://www.millionimage.org.uk/), a collaboration between the Institute of Digital Archaeology at Oxford University and UNESCO, aiming at capturing images of endangered objects and heritage sites in order to create 3D replicas (both digital and physical through 3D printing). For the application of laser scanning techniques for the recording of archaeological artefacts and structures, see e.g. Thuswaldner et al. 2007, 1-27; Salonia et al. 2006, 347-52; Blersch et al. 2006, 389-94; Boochs et al. 2006, 395-400). For urban reconstruction techniques based on imagery and LiDAR data see Musialski et al. 2013, 146-77.

From the 1980s, CAD software started to become more and more used in those fields in which drafting and documentation processes could benefit from digital drawings. This software improved and speeded up two dimensional drawings by offering tools that made almost obsolete the usage of pencil, ruler and compass. Moreover, it also allowed for a 3D documentation of objects that can be manipulated and rotated with ease in the virtual environment. CAD software packages guarantee a high precision in data handling, hence they are very useful when it comes to creating 2D or 3D objects starting from exact measurements. For this reason, CAD software has been widely used also in archaeological documentation where accuracy of drawings is essential.[248]

CG software packages, on the other hand, are able to produce highly realistic scenes, allow an easier modelling of organic shapes, have elaborate settings to accurately recreate the properties of the materials, allow a high control on lighting parameters, and include complex shaders, namely scripts that are attached to the 3D object and govern its rendering effects.[249] These software suites allow moreover the animation of characters by creating a skeleton that controls the mesh (a procedure called *rigging*), which can then be imported into a game engine. While their functionalities are very extensive, traditionally the control on accurate measurements has a low priority given their target market.

Often the use of a single software limits the possibilities; for this reason, a familiarity with different software packages is recommendable when dealing with a complex project, in order to construct a workflow that best exploits the characteristics of each software. In this respect, the major obstacle is related to the limitations in exchanging files between different platforms, which was either impossible for the use of proprietary formats, or risky for the possible loss of information. To this end, the CG industry has agreed on a number of platform independent formats, most notably Wavefront OBJ and DAE Collada, which can be used to exchange files across different software.[250]

Regarding the most common techniques to obtain a 3D model in different software, the most common way is to convert 2D elements into 3D entities by *extrusion*, namely the extension of a 2D surface (that has to be a closed path) perpendicularly into the third dimension. In this way, a cylinder or a tube is obtained by extruding a circle, likewise a box is generated from a square or a rectangle. The process of extrusion can also be made along a curved path, so that a variety of more complex shaped solids can be created. Extrusion was one of the most frequently used techniques in the earliest applications of 3D modelling in archaeology. One of the first examples is the digital model made by J. Eisler *et al.* of the Mortuary Temple of Raneferel at the Unfinished Pyramid at Abusir.[251] The aim of this project was to create a 3D model both of the structure of the Temple and of the terrain behind it that summarised

---

[248] A software that has become quite popular in recent years is Google SketchUp, originally developed by Google to allow an easy creation of 3D assets to be imported in Google Earth. SketchUp allowed in fact the addition of a geolocation to the scene and the export of the created model in kmz format to be used in Google Earth. The availability of a free version, its user friendly interface, the intuitive modelling process and the numerous plug-ins have increased the number of its users over the years. This software has however some limitations, for example in the available options for texture and material mapping, and in the allowed import and export formats in the free version, e.g. the standard CAD formats dwg and dxf among the import options; among the export options only two formats (DAE Collada and kmz) are available, while other formats such as fbx (recommended for the import into a game engine such as Unity3D) is supported only in the Pro version.
[249] An overview is given in Wittur 2013, 219-47.
[250] Both OBJ and Collada are text based formats, the main difference being that while OBJ stores only the geometry information (with an additional file with *.mtl extension needed for materials), Collada is XML based and can store also information on lighting and animation. The downside of using these formats is that being text-based they create potentially very large files. Other formats, such as the Autodesk proprietary fbx, are also supported by many software for its wide use and capabilities. Ideally, the 3D modeller should be able to know the strengths and downsides of each software in order to create a hybrid workflow that is best targeted to the project's needs. For example Blender can be used as an intermediate step to import the DAE Collada created in the free version of SketchUp in order to export fbx. Also, the plan and eventually the building shell which is drafted in AutoCAD can be exported as dxf and then imported to a CG software to create a detailed 3D model.
[251] Eisler *et al.* 1988, 109-32.

the results of the excavations that had been obtained until the end of 1984. While the 3D model of the structure was created mainly by extrusion, the creation of the terrain was based on original methods of digital terrain-modelling developed in Prague in the late 1970s and early 1980s.[252] A slightly later example of the application of extruding techniques is the 3D model of the Hoffman Limekiln at Langliffe, UK created by G. Chapman in the early 1990s.[253] The base of the kiln was formed by two polygons, one that followed the shape of the cross-section of the base and the other one that described the path taken by the outside edge of the kiln viewed in plan. The basic 3D shape was then obtained following the extrusion procedure by 'sweeping' the cross section around the path. The extrusion technique remains a fast and effective way to elaborate the 3D visualisation of an entity, and it is particularly suited to add the elevation to 2D plans of buildings. Additional 3D modelling techniques include the creation of a so-called 'shell' that describes only the surfaces and not the entire geometry of an object. These techniques, which range from the creation of polygonal meshes to Non-uniform rational Basis spline (NURBS) surfaces, are especially useful to create curves and complex geometries.

An additional step in the workflow for the creation of a 3D model is the mapping of textures and materials, which adds both colour information and details without increasing the polygon count, i.e. the complexity of the scene from a geometrical point of view. Textures can be created in a variety of ways. 2D images that are mapped on the 3D object can be created anew in a photo editor programme or by using existing pictures. An alternative approach relies on procedural textures, i.e. computer generated images that allow the creation of randomized patterns replicating realistic characteristics of materials (e.g. wood and stone veining and cracks) or the addition of noise to create more visually interesting results (e.g. stains on surfaces). Materials, instead, simulate properties and behaviours in relation to lighting conditions, such as opacity, reflectivity, and roughness. A useful technique to add detail to the model, while at the same time avoiding distortions and saving rendering time, is *texture baking*. With this technique, the properties and the behaviour of the materials, including the interaction with light sources which are assigned to the 3D model, are pre-calculated and the results are saved into a texture, which is in turn mapped onto the 3D model, thus avoiding the repetition of these calculations in real time during rendering. Techniques such as *bump* and *displacement mapping* allow the user to respectively simulate and create irregularities on the object's surface. Bump maps, in fact, do not affect the geometry of the object, but only how its surface interacts with the lighting conditions, which is useful to add realism to a texture. On the contrary, displacement maps actually modify the object's surface, which makes this technique useful for a variety of purposes such as creating realistic landscapes and waves.

3.2.2 Procedural modelling

In the case of recursive geometry that would be too tedious to be manually modelled, a procedural modelling strategy is the best suited solution. Procedural modelling allows a formal, parametric and hierarchically encoded description of the 3D geometry that is obtained by writing rule files that follow a specific syntax. Such a strategy is particularly useful for the efficient modelling of large scenes and repetitive elements that can be populated from a concise set of rules. Parametric values are used to define the characteristics of the 3D entities. These parameters can be easily modified when needed and the 3D model will update accordingly, thus making this modelling method interesting for archaeological reconstructions to display different hypotheses. In this way the user is able to speed up the modelling process, since it is easy to update the 3D visualisation simply by changing some parameters in the script. The main drawback of a procedural modelling approach is the steep learning curve, since one first needs to learn the shape grammar of the software, which makes the modelling process less intuitive than in computer graphics where one starts the modelling by directly interacting with shapes.

---

[252] Eisler *et al.* 1988, 110.
[253] Chapman 1992, 213-18.

Procedural modelling is particularly suited for the creation of cityscapes, where several domestic neighbourhoods need to be populated by buildings with similar characteristics and yet different from each other for a realistic result.[254] Being quite challenging from a technical point of view, the 3D modelling of cities has triggered the interest of computer scientists to create solutions that simplified and automated this process.[255] Several domains are touched by this demanding task. The game and the movie industries are especially interested in tools that allow the creation of realistic virtual cities from scratch in a reasonable amount of time. Urban planners and geo-designers, on the other hand, are concerned with the creation of a 3D GIS of modern cities where multi-scale information can be stored efficiently in a semantically meaningful, three-dimensional environment and different development scenarios can be visualized in real time to improve the decision making process and to facilitate the involvement of local communities. A general move towards the representation of spatial data in 3D is perceivable in recent years, one of the main signs being the creation of user-generated 3D buildings to insert in Google Earth. This need has inspired the development of tools that allow a (semi-)automatic extraction of information from aerial images and 3D point clouds.[256]

Several tools have been developed over the years to create 3D cities with different target users in mind. For example, ProGen, a procedural tool (not yet available) that is being developed in a collaboration between academia and a computer games studio, is aimed at the game industry.[257] A plugin for Autodesk Maya has been created to enhance the capabilities of this CG software with the procedural generation of buildings' facades.[258] Focussing more on the semantic of 3D cities is CityGML, an XML based format for the storage and exchange of 3D city models, thus enabling their sustainable maintenance and reusability.[259] Among the currently available software packages that are targeted to the creation of 3D cities, we chose to use the procedural modelling tool CityEngine (CE). Since it constitutes one of the main components of our methodology that will be discussed in chapter 6, I will dedicate the next paragraphs to describe the characteristics of this software.

CE, originally developed by Pascal Müller during his PhD at ETH Computer Vision Lab in Zurich, was commercialized in 2008 by Müller's company Procedural. The acquisition of CE by Esri, the developer of ArcGIS, in 2011 has introduced the possibility to work with real world data, thus broadening its possible domains of application. CE handles in fact GIS data, aerial images, 2D building ground plans and a 2D street network that can be either automatically generated by the software or imported directly as a shapefile or in the drawing exchangeable format (dxf). Moreover, it can export the created 3D scene as a geodatabase containing textured multipatches, the Esri format for describing 3D geometry.[260] With the acquisition of CityEngine and the partnership with CyberCity3D, a 3D modelling tool that processes real world data (stereo imagery) to generate high resolution models of buildings,[261] Esri is currently the market leader in the development of a 3D GIS of the built environment.

The procedural generation of buildings in CityEngine follows the CGA (Computer Generated Architecture) shape grammar created by Pascal Müller and Peter Wonka.[262] CE's grammar is based on the so-called

---

[254] In fact, similar problems were already recognized by the makers of physical 3D model, as discussed in chapter 2 (pp. 44-5).
[255] For an overview of modelling techniques, including procedural modelling, that are currently available for urban environments in several domains (e.g. entertainment industry, urban planning and emergency management), see Vanegas et al. 2010, 25-42.
[256] See an overview in Meyer et al. 2008, 217.
[257] http://www.doc.gold.ac.uk/progen/
[258] Zweig 2013.
[259] See http://www.citygml.org/ and http://www.opengeospatial.org/standards/citygml
[260] See 'The Multipatch Geometry Type. An Esri White Paper. December 2008' available at https://www.esri.com/library/whitepapers/pdfs/multipatch-geometry-type.pdf
[261] http://www.cybercity3d.com/
[262] See Müller et al., 2006 for a description of its implementation and previous work.

'L-systems', developed by the Hungarian biologist Aristid Lindermayer in 1968 to describe the growth of plants in a formalised language.[263] Lindermayer observed that plants grow by recursively repeating parts that have a similar shape (see Figure 3.2), according to the principle of self-similarity. L-systems were then adapted to be used in computer graphics in the 1980s by the American engineer Alvy Ray Smith, co-founder of the animation studio Pixar.[264] Initially, L-systems were applied in particular to the generation of fractal-like shapes and the realistic representation of plants, but they were soon translated to describe architectural shapes since the latter also are often composed by repeating similar elements. The CGA grammar is based on a sequence of rules defining steps and parameters for shape creation, which can be further detailed with the insertion of 3D models in OBJ and Collada DAE formats. These imported models can be instantiated or modified according to the procedural rules (for example, it is possible to model a column in a CG software and replicate it several times in CE). An example of a CGA rule file is shown in Figure 3.3.

Apart from creating 3D geometries from scratch, rules can be also used to generate 3D geometries according to the attributes of the GIS data. If aerial pictures and building plans are stored into a geodatabase or a shapefile where the information on the buildings' heights is provided, a straightforward processing of the data is possible: by writing a rule file that contains the instructions to extrude the footprints according to the height that is stored in the attribute table it is possible to automatically create 3D buildings and apply the aerial images as textures for the roofs of the 3D models. This procedure can be handled either within CE, or by importing procedural rules written in CE directly in ArcGIS

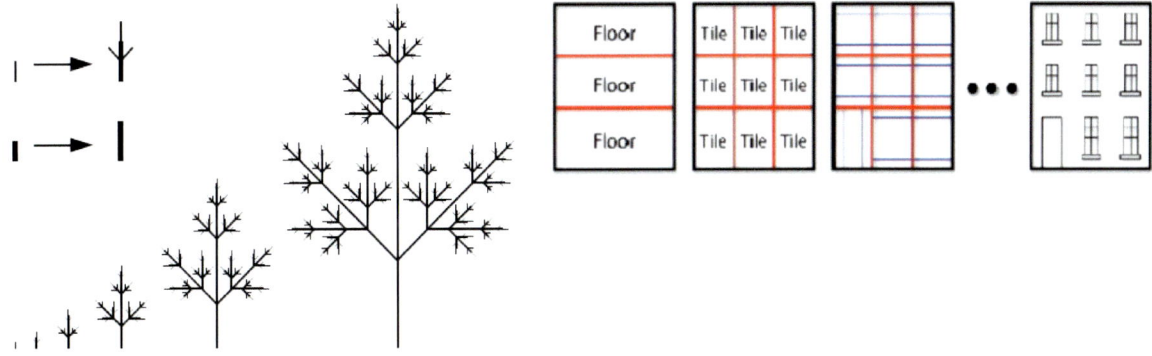

Figure 3.2 L-systems applied to plants and architecture. Left: picture from Prusinkiewicz et al., 2000, 397; Right: picture from CityEngine 2010.3 user manual.

```
1.  attr buildingHeight = rand (6, 8)
2.  attr storeyHeight = 3
3.  attr windowWidth = 2
4.  Lot --> extrude (buildingHeight) building
5.  building --> comp(f) {top : roof | front : facade | side: sideWalls}
6.  facade --> split(y) {storeyHeight : groundFloor | ~1 : upperFloor}
7.  upperFloor --> split(x) {~1 : wall | windowWidth : window}*
8.  window --> i ("window_frame.obj")
9.  groundFloor --> …
```

Figure 3.3 Example of a CGA rule for the creation of a building. Numerical values are stored as attributes at the beginning of the rule to control them more easily. In this case, buildings are assigned a random height between 6 and 8 meters (line 1). The 2D initial shape "Lot" is turned into a 3D building shell by extrusion (line 4). Next, a component split is used to separate the obtained 3D geometry in individual faces (line 5). A split rule along the y axis is used to divide horizontally the selected face corresponding to the building facade to create two floors (line 6). The first floor is then recursively split along the x axis to create a series of windows (line 7), which are substituted by an OBJ file containing a more detailed window frame (line 8).

---

[263] Ochoa 1998.
[264] Smith 1984, 1-10.

using the CityEngine toolbox that was introduced in the 10.1 release. In this way, a rule package (in rpk format) containing both rules and the textures can be applied to the (polygon) features to create the 3D environment. This recently improved interoperability with GIS, although being conceived to address the needs of urban planners and modellers of the modern city, makes CityEngine a valuable tool for archaeologists for the 3D modelling and analysis of past cityscapes starting from fieldwork data. In chapter 6, I will describe how I exploited the possibility of importing rule packages into ArcGIS to enhance the understanding of specific characteristics of the architecture survey data from Koroneia.[265]

From its initial implementation, CityEngine was used for the modelling of archaeologically attested cities and architecture. The procedurally modelled scene of Pompeii and the CGA rule for the Parthenon are part of the examples that are available as training material for CE users. The Parthenon rule offers an interesting example of how the mathematical principles that governed the proportions of Greek temple architecture are well suited to be implemented in a parametric modelling system. In chapter 6, I will describe in more detail the set of CGA rule files that I have developed for Greek architecture and applied to the creation of reconstruction hypotheses of 4th century BC Koroneia. Sets of rules for Roman housing architecture have been created for a variety of Roman cities,[266] including Rome itself,[267] Bononia (Bologna, Italy),[268] Portus[269] and Forum Lepidi (Reggio Emilia, Italy).[270] Other architectural typologies, such as pre-Columbian Maya architecture,[271] and historical cities, such as 19th century Nicosia in Cyprus,[272] have also been formalized in a rule-based approach. Rule based modelling is less suited for less standardized (or less well known) architectural traditions, such as prehistoric contexts and rural areas, although a rule file could be written to efficiently deal with the automatic placement of manually made 3D models on the target locations.[273]

Since the earlier applications of CityEngine to archaeological case studies, the developers have highlighted the usefulness of this approach for the visualization of alternative reconstructions and for the embedding of semantics into the procedurally created 3D models.[274] The parametric modelling approach on which CE is based allows in fact the possibility to change in real time the numerical values that have been declared in the rule files. This possibility is particularly useful to display and test alternative reconstruction hypotheses, e.g. the building's height, the number of windows, slope angle and appearance of the roof. However, the potential of creating procedurally modelled variations to clarify and explore uncertain aspects of the archaeological record has been so far not yet fully exploited in archaeological projects, with the exception of the pioneering work by Earl *et al.* on the Basilica Portuense.[275] The text-based nature of scripting allows moreover the insertion of comments within the lines of code, which increases the intellectual transparency of the modelling process.[276] As I will show more extensively in chapter 6, I made use of this opportunity to include in my rules references to published work that I used as comparative material and if necessary also on the modelling choices that I made.

---

[265] See chapter 6, § 6.2.1.
[266] Müller *et al.* 2006, 287-97; Noghani *et al.* 2012, 41-4; on Roman and Hellenistic architecture: Saldaña 2015, 148-63.
[267] Dylla *et al.* 2010; Saldaña and Johanson 2013.
[268] Pescarin *et al.* 2010.
[269] Harrison *et al.* 2013.
[270] Forte and Danelon 2015.
[271] For the creation of an individual building, see Müller *et al.* 2006, 139-46; for the procedurally modelled reconstruction of a cityscape in Honduras, see Richards-Rissetto and Plessing 2015, 85-8.
[272] Charalambous *et al.* 2012.
[273] This approach is similar to what I have adopted for the automatic distribution of 3D models of special architectural finds in Koroneia's 3D GIS, see chapter 6, § 6.2.1.
[274] Haegler *et al.* 2009.
[275] Earl *et al.* 2013.
[276] Single line comments are preceded by a hash sign (#) or a double slash (//), while multi-line comments start with /* and end with */ (see JavaScript). The same notation can be used to prevent execution of lines of code.

Operation	Efficient use of CityEngine	Comments
Learning time	+	Good documentation, adapted to complete virtual cities
GUI	+	Complete GUI, complex for sample operations
Time for modelling setting-up	+	Allows integration of many different formats
DTM	++	Construction and integration from GIS data
Integration of basic outlines	++	Integration from GIS and CAD datasets
Modelling of basic outlines	++	Extrusion tools, including for complex forms
Modelling of facades / faces	++	To decomposition in horizontal and vertical subsections
Modelling from ortho-images	+	Works well in classical cases
Modelling of curved elements	-	To decompose into polygons
Integration of existing models	++	Use of other modelers for complex details
Export / Interoperability	+	Towards GIS or classical formats
Texture	++	Easy application
Rendering	++	Several renderings available
Efficiency of unique model	-	Writing of a rule for a single operation is not effective in this case
Writing of rules	+	Simple for simple rules, CGI scripts
Re-use of rules	++	Simple but requires a decomposed end structured writing of rules
Creation of rules library	++	Interesting for re-use in case of massive modelling.
Export and web visualization	++	Web service for remote consultation

Figure 3.4 Table from Koehl and Roussel 2015, 144 highlighting strengths and weaknesses of the CityEngine software.

Being conceived to address the need of a fast modelling tool for cityscape creation, the CGA CityEngine shape grammar does not allow one to model elaborate architectural elements in detail. Such components (e.g. column capitals, window/door frames etc.) need to be created in other software packages, such as CG or CAD software, and then imported into CE, either as static models or as assets that can be subjected to procedural rules.[277] For a broader assessment of the main strengths and weaknesses of the CityEngine software, I will refer to Figure 3.4 showing the list compiled by Koehl and Roussel. The main drawback of modelling using procedural rules relates to the modelling of curved shapes, for which no standard rule syntax is available yet and that has to be solved either by importing assets that are created in

---

[277] Koehl and Roussel present for example a workflow that integrates CityEngine, SketchUp and Blender for the modelling of historical monuments at Turckheim, Alsace, France (Koehl and Roussel 2015). As will be discussed in chapter 6, Blender and Sketcup were also used as additional modelling tool for the Koroneia case study.

Figure 3.5 Process of creating a CGA rule from existing architecture using an inverse procedural modelling approach. Left: A 3D point cloud is evaluated to extract plane surfaces; Centre: detection of architectural elements and assessment of their size; Right: The reconstruction of the temple of Poseidon, Paestum, obtained with the above mentioned procedure (after Weissenberg 2014, figs. 7.1, 7.4 and 7.5).

another software, or by 'decomposing' the required shape into sub-polygons that can be handled by CE. Moreover, as already noted for procedural modelling in general, CE is advantageous for the creation of large environments, or, as shown in the case of Portus, for the modelling of parametric variations on one building. For the modelling of one single detailed building, instead, a CG software offers the best performance. Finally, Koehl and Roussel assigned a positive grade on the learning time that is necessary to master the software, but this depends much on the technical expertise of the user. As an experiment in the classroom has shown, in fact, students find the CGA grammar difficult to comprehend and the ESRI documentation not suited for beginners' needs.[278]

The procedural modelling approach discussed above deals with the creation of a synthetic city and can be applied to the reconstruction of past cityscapes that are now lost. The automatic modelling of an existing city – an interesting topic for urban planners, architects and the game and movie industry – remains instead a challenge. A 'Facade Wizard' is included in CityEngine that allows a fast and manual creation of 3D building's facades starting with the image that represents the facade. This procedure, despite offering an intuitive and quick tool to create a CGA rule from an existing building, still implies a high degree of manual intervention. The formalization of the architectural language that would allow the automatic extraction of architectural features from facades and the inference of a set of rules that define their style is particularly complex. This set of tasks is performed using the so called *inverse procedural modelling*, a modelling strategy that allows the derivation of a style grammar of existing buildings. An approach based on the CGA grammar has been proposed by Weissenberg in his PhD dissertation.[279] Starting from a 3D point cloud of a structure, the system performs an estimation of the plane surfaces that compose the structure, detects the architectural elements and assesses their size. This method could have interesting applications also in archaeological cities, such as Pompeii and Ostia, where buildings are conserved to such an extent to justify the application of inverse procedural modelling, and for temple architecture that follows a regular pattern of shapes created according to mathematical proportions. Weissenberg has indeed successfully applied his workflow to the modelling of Doric temple architecture (Figure 3.5).

3.3 Interactive environment: virtual and augmented reality

The term Virtual Reality identifies the computer generated experiences characterized by immersion, interaction and real time navigation. A 'proper' virtual experience, indeed, happens when users feel completely part of the virtual world, and in which their actions are followed by a real time change in the environment. This experience can be mediated by the use of devices such as Head Mounted

---

[278] Chamberlain 2015, 359.
[279] See Weissenberg *et al.* 2013. A comprehensive overview of this method is given in Weissenberg 2014.

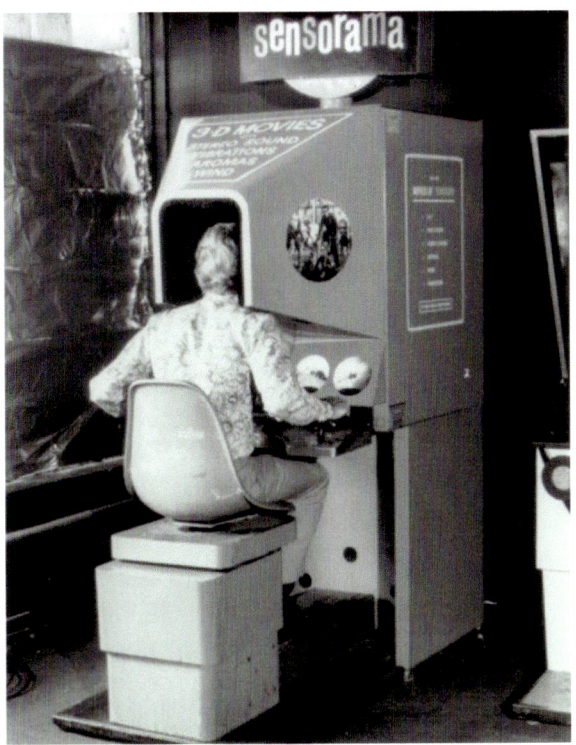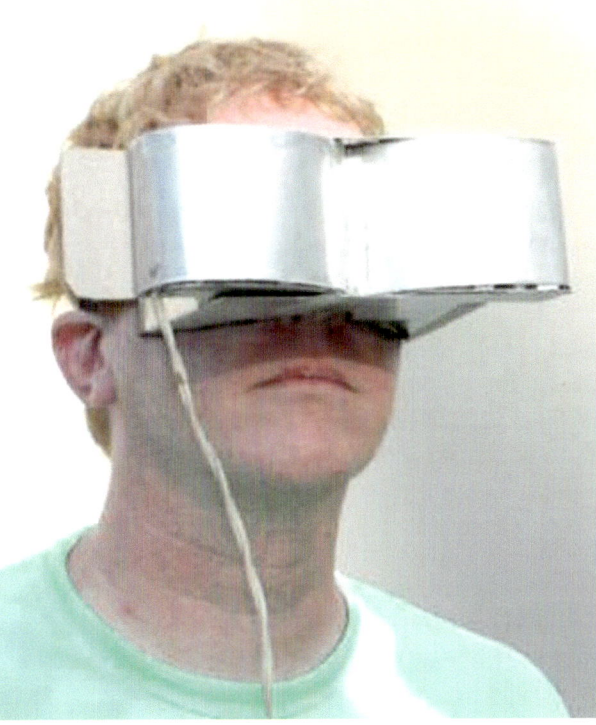

Figure 3.6 Two of Heilig's inventions: (left) the 'Sensorama Simulator' and (right) the 'Telesphere Mask' (source: http://www.mortonheilig.com/InventorVR.html).

Displays (HMDs) and interactive gloves that permit the manipulation of virtual objects, or can be guided by natural movement interaction. An expensive environment for experiencing VR is the CAVE (Cave Automatic Virtual Environment), a room where projectors display the virtual environment on its walls and floor.[280]

The term 'Virtual Reality' (VR) first appeared in the 1980s, popularised by the computer scientist Jaron Leiner who founded 'VPL Research', the first company that sold VR products. The group led by Leiner was a pioneer in this field by implementing 'multi-person virtual worlds', introducing a commercially available HMD, the 'EyePhone' system, and experimenting with the first avatars, virtual characters that represent players in a computer game.[281] Over the years, VR has been used, often inappropriately, to define a wide variety of applications. Two main streams can be recognised, namely Desktop VR and Immersive VR. Desktop VR defines all the 3D visualisations that can be experienced from a personal computer, while Immersive VR identifies all the ways to interact with 3D models, which give also the perception of being *present* in the virtual environment.

The idea of creating an immersive 3D world for entertainment purpose goes back to the mid 1950s when the visionary cinematographer Morton Heilig built a single user theatre called Sensorama Simulator (Figure 3.6), which was patented in 1962. This machine was the first to create a multi-sensory experience and the impression of a full immersion, by showing 3D movies and included stereo-sound, aromas, wind, vibrating seat and handlebars to simulate a motorcyclist's experience on a bumpy road.[282] The display of 3D movies was made possible by two other Heilig inventions, the Sensorama Motion Picture Projector

---

[280] For the use of CAVE's for heritage presentations see Tzortzaki 2001.
[281] A brief biography of Leiner can be found at http://www.jaronlanier.com/general.html (last accessed Sept. 2016).
[282] See http://www.mortonheilig.com/index.html for an impression of the Sensorama experience. An interview with Morton Heilig by Itsuo Sakane is available at https://www.youtube.com/watch?v=vSINEBZNCks (last accessed Sept. 2016).

and the Sensorama 3D Motion Picture Camera that was used to shoot the short movies that were seen by the users. Heilig patented also a multi-user version of the Sensorama machine, the 'Experience Theatre' and the 'Telesphere Mask', the first HMD with stereoscopic TV and stereo-sound. The complexity of the machine, which was ahead of its time for the concept and technological level, resulted in a lack of further investments to go beyond a prototype development.[283]

The conceptualization of Virtual Reality is attributed to the American computer scientist Ivan Sutherland, who published an influential paper in the mid-1960s titled 'The Ultimate Display'.[284] In the period where computers were only able to plot dots and draw lines, Sutherland sets the challenges for the developments in VR hardware and software for the following decades. His 'ultimate display' would be a kinaesthetic and multi-sensory experience, where the computer can track body and eye motion and change the presentation depending on where the user looks. A display connected to a computer, in Sutherland's words, should act as 'a looking-glass into the mathematical wonderland constructed in computer memory', which enables the user to gain familiarity with concepts and simulations that are not realizable in the physical world.[285]

Developing further his vision, Sutherland invented in 1968 the first Head-Mounted-Display, which was tethered to a computer and was able to display images in stereo, thus creating the impression of depth.[286] This system was a very heavy and complex machine that occupied an entire room and needed to be attached to a mechanical arm to be operational. Its imposing architecture overarching the user thus earned it the nickname 'Sword of Damocles'. Sutherland's HMD allowed the viewer to see simultaneously the real environment and virtual images by means of a system of mirrors, and therefore represents the first major step towards the implementation of Augmented (or Enhanced) Reality technology (AR).

Contrary to VR, in AR the virtual world does not *replace*, but it is *merged* into the physical world, which remains an important component of the visualisation.[287] It is possible to 'augment' the reality with a variety of objects (2D images, text or 3D objects) and there is an ever-growing variety of applications on the market that allows the creation of augmented reality experiences in this broader sense. Although AR technologies are quickly progressing, the development of a stable and precise AR application is far from simple. In order to align the superimposed object with the real world, two techniques exist: marker-based and markerless AR. Marker-based AR uses optical tracking of known images to determine the position and orientation of the device, whereas markerless AR uses general feature detection of camera images, often in conjunction with the device's sensory data (accelerometer, gyroscope, compass, GPS).[288] Until recently, marker-based AR has been the only reliable technique to obtain a relatively smooth AR experience. Due to advances in smartphone technology and dedicated software,[289] now, also markerless AR has become possible. Also for HMDs the creation of a smooth AR experience is still a challenge, given the numerous non trivial tasks (e.g. head, gaze and gestures tracking) that are

---

[283] Turi 2014 (online resource).
[284] Sutherland 1965a.
[285] Sutherland 1965a, 506.
[286] Sutherland 1965b.
[287] The idea of combining a reconstructed image of an object with its real entity is not new and was empirically realised for the first time by Brunelleschi in his famous experiments on perspective. The Renaissance architect designed a system that allowed him to superimpose his drawing of the Baptistery in Florence onto the actual building in order to check the correctness of its perspective lines. Brunelleschi depicted the Florentine Baptistery on a wooden panel in which he drilled a small hole that permitted him to see through. With a system of mirrors, he could superimpose the depicted image to the real Baptistery, in such a way that the perspective of his drawing perfectly matched the real building. See Kubovy 1986, 32-33.
[288] For a more detailed explanation of these concepts, see Butchart 2011, 2-4.
[289] Recent developments include the introduction of AR development kits by both Apple and Google (ARKit and ARCore respectively).

necessary to guarantee a reliable and comfortable experience.[290] In the heritage sector, the potential of AR has been early recognised. However, due to technological constraints, high equipment costs and high level of computer skills necessary for the creation of AR applications have, so far, been the main obstacles for its widespread adoption.[291]

Since the time of its conception, VR has been employed in several domains and numerous studies and experiments have been conducted on its applications, benefits and issues.[292] The first application was in military training, especially for flight and combat simulations, to prepare trainees for the real situation and improve their decision making response in stressful circumstances by virtually recreating the latter in a safe environment.[293] Training was the main focus of the development of VR in other fields, as it was employed for example to train medical students and to facilitate the learning of skills in individuals affected by disabilities.[294] In the field of clinical psychology and neuroscience, virtual environments were created for a variety of purposes, including the treatment of phobias and eating disorders, support during a rehabilitation process, and the training and enhancements of skills in children with disabilities.[295]

During the 1990s and early 2000s, VR was surrounded by excitement and high expectations. Futuristic VR applications featuring in movies and novels[296] generated a false impression about what real implementations of VR technology could achieve given the current state of the art of hardware and software. The expectations were therefore soon frustrated, as the promises and envisaged capabilities of VR systems were very different from the products that were made available on the market.[297]

Alongside the growing interest for the envisaged potential of VR across different domains, the concept of 'virtual archaeology' was introduced in 1990 by Paul Reilly, an archaeologist and IBM research scientist.[298] The idea that Reilly presented in his 1991 paper was quite different from the variety of applications that the label of virtual archaeology would encompass in the following decades.[299] His project aimed in fact at creating a simulated, but realistic computer-based 3D archaeological formation that would help novices to familiarize themselves with the concepts that lay at the basis of stratigraphic excavations (such as context, spit, phase, horizon etc). In Reilly's vision, archaeologists could moreover use this platform as a 'controlled dataset' to conceive different excavation scenarios and assess the validity of their excavation procedures. The solid models of the various layers that composed the simulated excavation could then be linked with additional resources that could be accessed by the user via hyperlinks.

---

[290] A recent survey of novel mobile AR interaction techniques is given in Härkänen et al. 2015.
[291] Quattrini et al. 2016, 388.
[292] A list of involved domains can be found in Bowen Loftin et al. 2005, 479-89.
[293] See e.g. Dovey 1994.
[294] Chestnut and Crumpton 1997.
[295] See an overview of applications in Riva et al. 1998.
[296] See e.g. the 'metaverse' coined in Neal Stephenson's science fiction novel *Snow Cash* (1992) and described as the successor of the internet where people would interact as avatars in a 3D virtual world.
[297] A telling example is the video game console Nintendo Virtual Boy that was released in 1995 and advertised as the first affordable console to be able to provide a VR game experience. To keep the cost low, the developers had chosen a monochromatic display based on red shades, which strained the eyes and provoked headaches in the users. Moreover, the absence of a tracking system that could synchronize the user's movements and the display caused nausea. In the eyes of customers, the relatively high pricing of the console (180$) could not be justified in view of its shortcomings, which contributed to its rapid demise.
[298] Reilly 1991, 133-9.
[299] A reflection on virtual reality in archaeology and a comparison between its potential and its real uses are offered in Pujol 2008.

A few years after Reilly's article, the term virtual archaeology was echoed and popularized by the volume *Virtual Archaeology. Recreating Ancient Worlds,* edited by Maurizio Forte and Alberto Siliotti, which was published in 1997 with a foreword by Colin Renfrew.[300] This book was organized in richly illustrated chapters presenting numerous archaeological sites distributed in a wide geographical and chronological span. In the introduction to the volume, Forte describes the potential of computer-generated reconstructions in archaeology: besides having a strong impact on the public, they allow 'the presentation of complex information in a visual way that enables it to be used to test and refine the image or model that has been created'.[301] To emphasize the role of such computer-based visualizations as exploratory means and not as just 'graphic reproductions', Forte suggests to call them 'simulations' as they can be used for the 'objective verification' of possible interpretations of archaeological evidence.[302]

Unfortunately, this use of 3D reconstructions as expressed in the introduction does not shine through the following chapters of the book. The computer-aided reconstructions were used in fact only as illustrations of the text, and were not integral part of the interpretative process of the presented case studies. As Fletcher commented in his review of the volume, the illustrations were no more than 'electronic artworks', similar to 'regular artist's reconstructions'.[303] According to Fletcher, not only the useful outcomes of the use of computer-generated reconstructions that had been envisaged in the introduction of the book were not evident in the rest of the chapters, but their representations also failed to convey in most cases 'the sensual and emotive flavour of a graphic artist', which is instead present in many artistic reconstruction drawings.[304]

The fact that the 3D reconstructions included in the book as printed images were not exploited as interpretative tools by the archaeologists involved in the publication should not surprise. At that time, in fact, only few archaeologists possessed the competence and skills to be able not only to guide the creation of virtual archaeological worlds, but also to understand and take advantage of the potential of such computer-generated visualizations for archaeological interpretation. In fact, the creation of such visualizations was almost exclusively in the hands of computer-savvy programmers and graphics artists, who had also more easily access to the hardware and software needed for this purpose. Indeed, big companies such as Taisei Corporation in Japan, EDF in France, and ENEL in Italy invested in 3D modelling of archaeological sites in the 1990s, as archaeology was seen as an interesting field of application for demonstrating computational capabilities.[305]

As Forte pointed out, the 1990s were the 'wow era' of VR in archaeology.[306] Applications in this field were focused on the achievement of photorealistic results, with a strong prevalence of technology over archaeological content. There were moreover no clear boundaries between 'proper' VR applications as originally defined, and static renderings: all without distinction fell under the broad definition of virtual archaeology, since 'the label is so sexy that we would be foolish not to exploit it'.[307] The first enthusiastic and uncritical approaches to VR in archaeology as a tool to 'bring the past back to life' produced a sceptical reaction in academic settings regarding the contribution of virtual archaeology, which was seen as a field of application with a low interpretative value, in which many additions had to be made

---

[300] This volume was a translation of the original in Italian: Forte and Siliotti 1996.
[301] Forte 1997, 11.
[302] Forte 1997, 12-3.
[303] Fletcher 1998, 57.
[304] Fletcher 1998, 57.
[305] Forte 2015.
[306] Forte 2010.
[307] Fletcher 1998, 56.

to ensure the users' engagement with the reconstructed past, thus ending up creating 'acontextual, stimulating fiction'.[308]

In all fields, the expectations that surrounded the first wave of VR were not met. The long awaited and repeatedly announced revolution that virtual reality promised to bring about in how people lived, experienced the world, and interacted with each other was not realized for a variety of reasons. The costs for the hardware were tremendously high, thus limiting VR to an elitist technology. Moreover, the various types of HMDs that were developed caused nausea and made the VR experience very uncomfortable, while the 360° panorama that was displayed within the CAVE forced the user to unnatural constant movements of the head. VR therefore never became main stream, which resulted in relatively little content that was developed to be experienced with VR technology.

In the last couple of years some new developments have resurrected the idea that VR can eventually mature into a mainstream technology. The most interesting news relates to the commercialization of relatively low cost HMDs, such as the Oculus Rift[309] and the HTC Vive,[310] and of standalone headsets (e.g. Google cardboard and Samsung Gear VR) that transform the current top-end smartphones into VR viewers. The great investments made in the last years by the smartphone industry to improve video and hardware performances has created favourable conditions for VR, which is now more widely accessible, since the main needed components are already contained in the last generation smartphones: a good screen, enough processing power, and most importantly, an accelerometer and compass which are suitable for head tracking.[311] Facebook purchased the Oculus Rift in 2014 in order to develop further the possibilities of creating, sharing and experiencing immersive content.[312] The commitment of the largest social media platform and the integration into the major game engine suggest that important improvements will be made within the next few years that will contribute to a move towards the 'democratization' of VR. Moreover, investments in research and hardware by competing developers, to improve the components (such as eye tracking) that are needed for a comfortable experience will lead to the availability of a more stable and less bulky technology at a lower cost.

In the near future, technological advances will improve immersive VR and make the experience more comfortable and affordable. HMDs will become smaller and lighter than previous models and computer power will better handle the visuals with higher resolution images, while tracking software will be able to create a seamless navigation by synchronizing the user' movements in real life and the perceived movements in VR, one of the major causes of motion sickness. The issue remains however about the content development. For VR to be used beyond the game industry and become main stream, high quality content will have to be developed that exploits the possibilities of immersion and engagement that this technology offers to the fullest, and experiments with new storytelling modes instead of applying the old ways that are proper to traditional media.

In archaeology, the field of VR and AR applications has continued to exist and expand over the years.[313] During the 2000s, a great effort was invested in discussing guidelines for the creation of 'intellectually transparent' 3D reconstructions, a topic that I will treat in more detail in the next section of this chapter.

---

[308] Earl *et al*. 2002.
[309] https://www.oculus.com/rift/ (last accessed March 2017).
[310] https://www.vive.com/ (last accessed March 2017).
[311] Pierce 2015 (online resource).
[312] Facebook has launched already 360° videos (https://www.facebook.com/Facebook360/) and aims at pushing the Oculus to provide an immersive experience.
[313] Recent projects using AR technologies for heritage purposes include for example the AR application developed for the gladiators school at Carnuntum, Austria (using the Wikitude platform, http://www.wikitude.com/showcase/wikitude-brings-roman-history-life-carnuntum/ last accessed Dec. 2016), and the applications for the *in situ* visualization of lost architecture discussed in Pierdicca *et al*. 2015 and Quattrini *et al*. 2016.

Advances in gaming technologies have been continuously adopted in the archaeological domains: Multi-user systems have been developed to promote (at distance) collaboration between different users,[314] interaction by human gesture has been introduced to make the navigation seem more natural.[315] In a process of 'gamification', elements and dynamics that are typical of game playing have been used to create engaging experiences in past environments.

The main target of these types of application has been public outreach and in fact museums have experimented with new ways to attract and engage visitors. The impression is however that we are still in a transitional phase where traditional ways of storytelling are used with new technologies, which instead should require a completely new approach in how a museum display is organized and how the objects are enriched with extra content. An example comes from the recent exhibition 'Museo Glass Beacon: Il Museo del Futuro' at the Museo dei Fori Imperiali nei Mercati di Traiano (Museum of Trajan's Market) in Rome, where Google glasses and Epson Moverio glasses have been used with the aim to provide extra content to visitors.[316] According to a review of the exhibition, the impression is that the additional information, although well presented, could have suited a traditional video guide, which would have been both less expensive and more effective.[317] Therefore, despite the praiseworthy efforts of musea to keep themselves up to date and experiment with technologies that could enrich the visits, we still witness the predominance of technology over content and a difficulty to put the former at the service of the latter in a way that goes beyond a catchy advertisement to attract more visitors. In this sense, not much progress has been made since the similar observations that were raised in relation to the exhibition Building Virtual Rome organized in 2005 at the same museum, where interviews to visitors showed that they 'were retaining more the application than the details of the contents and in general, could not tell if or how technology helped them to better understand the contents'.[318] The creation of professional digital content curators who both understand the technology and their potential, and have the required archaeological knowledge will bridge the gap between disciplinary compartments and offer a more informative and engaging experience to museum visitors.

In recent years, Forte suggested the new definition of 'Cyber-archaeology', to describe the last decade's 'post-virtual' approach in which the interaction with the virtual environment is at the core of the simulation process.[319] Contrary to the static and photorealistic virtual archaeology, in which the creation of 'the' model was the aim of the process and the data had to be transformed from analogue to digital with a possible loss of information, in Forte's view Cyber-archaeology deals with digitally born data and generates new 'affordances' through the interaction between the virtual environment and the user.[320] Using this Gibsonian term in the context of archaeological interpretation, Forte aimed to explain how a single artefact can have several uses that change through time and space. The meaning

---

[314] See e.g. Forte 2007 and Forte *et al.* 2010, 422 with related bibliography.
[315] E.g., the 3D real time application 'Imago Bononiae' presented at the Digital Heritage Conference 2013 http://www.digitalheritage2013.org/imago-bononiae/ (last accessed Sept. 2016).
[316] http://www.mercatiditraiano.it/mostre_ed_eventi/eventi/museo_glass_beacon_il_museo_del_futuro (last accessed Sept. 2016). The extra content was activated by beacon devices (broadcasting messages at specific point of interest using Bluetooth low energy network technology) and image recognition respectively.
[317] See the review of the exhibition by N. Mandarano at https://nicolettemandarano.wordpress.com/2015/11/06/alla-prova-dei-google-glass-e-degli-epson-moverio-ai-mercati-di-traiano/ (last accessed Sept. 2016).
[318] Forte, Pescarin and Pujol Tost 2006, 64-9.
[319] Forte 2010; Forte 2015.
[320] The term 'affordance' was coined by the American psychologist J.J. Gibson from the verb 'to afford', in order to indicate the opportunities and constraints that an environment offers to an animal (more specifically 'terrain, shelters, water, fire, objects, tools, other animals and human displays'), and the complementary relationship that is established between the animal and its environment (see Gibson 1986 (1979), 127). According to Gibson, the theory of affordances 'rescues us from the philosophical muddle of assuming fixed classes of objects, each defined by its common features and then given a name...But this does not mean you cannot learn how to use things and perceive their uses. You do not have to classify and label things in order to perceive what they afford' (Gibson 1986 (1979), 134).

and role of an object changes based on the interaction between the user and the environment. In Forte's view, therefore, the interaction in the simulated environment becomes the key process to disclose new interpretations.

3.4 The scientific value of 3D reconstructions

The benefits of a 3D digital documentation, by means of photogrammetric or laser scanning techniques, are appreciated by archaeologists as they provide a complete and accurate documentation of the geometrical and surface properties of archaeological finds, structures or sites. They are widely used during excavations and surveys and recent examples show that these techniques greatly enhance the comprehension of archaeological structures and are useful to contextualize the site under investigation in its three-dimensional environment, providing a documentation that accounts for the relationship between sloping ground and structures much better than a two-dimensional representation.[321] In contrast, 3D digital reconstructions, in which the missing pieces in our archaeological data are integrated with the most plausible reconstruction hypothesis, struggle to be seen as a valuable research tool. Several reasons, deeply rooted in how 3D reconstructions have been used since their first applications in archaeology, have contributed to this condition. In the next section (3.4.1) I will focus first on two aspects that have undermined the 'academic reputation' of 3D reconstructions, namely the lack of an explicit documentation for the research sources that are used, and the creation of only one reconstruction, which does not account for other equally plausible hypotheses that are possible given the available archaeological dataset. Secondly, in the following section (3.4.2) I will discuss another important aspect of 3D reconstructions that has been largely overlooked, namely their analytical potential to help in formulating hypotheses and observing otherwise oversight phenomena. Specifically, I will focus on the projects that have been successful in exploiting 3D reconstructions as research tools, with the aim to concretely show what kind of archaeological questions can be investigated by using 3D modelling techniques.

3.4.1 Rules for 'intellectually transparent' 3D visualisations in archaeology

Intellectually transparent data are crucial in all academic disciplines, as they are the prerequisite to allow quality control and peer reviewing. Traditional scholarship has developed a standardised way to publish results by including footnotes and references in scientific articles, which allow the reader to assess the scientific value of the results, to evaluate the supporting arguments, and to retrieve additional content for further research. 3D reconstructions that are not intellectually transparent can be paralleled to an article where only the conclusions are expressed, without discussing the sources and reasoning, which would represent an aberration in academic scholarship.[322] This problem was already identified in the 1990s,[323] and can be summarised by Forte's words highlighting that 'noticeable gaps are represented by the fact that the models are not 'transparent' in respect to the initial information (what were the initial data?), and by the use of peremptory single reconstruction without offering alternatives'.[324]

---

[321] See e.g. the analysis of the archaic temple of Hera at Olympia where the photogrammetric recording has allowed the researchers to reconsider the building in relation to the sloping ground which was not taken into account in previous documentation (Sapirstein 2015, 129-139).
[322] For the parallel between scientific articles and 3D reconstructions: H. Denard's lecture 'The London Charter' at the POCOS symposium 'Visualisations and Simulations', 16-17 June 2011, available at https://vimeo.com/26767611 (last accessed March 2017).
[323] E.g. Reilly 1991, 21; at this respect see Denard 2012, 57.
[324] Forte 2000.

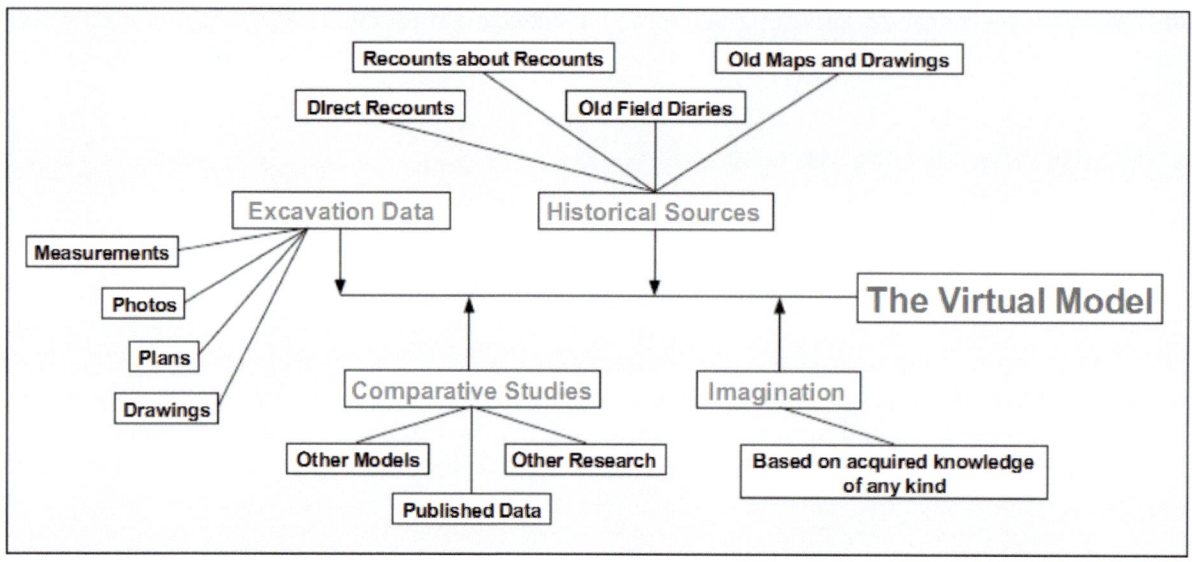

Figure 3.7 Schematic diagram of the sources that are generally used for a 3D model of archaeological evidence (after Hermon 2008).

The necessity of finding ways to provide 3D visualisations with an accurate documentation of the sources that were used, the thinking/interpretation process (the so called *paradata*) and the methodology that was followed has been recognized as a key element for increasing the impact of 3D models as knowledge providers. While this is important for reality-based 3D models, which need to be accompanied by a documentation explaining the methodology followed during the recording and data processing, it becomes even more crucial for 3D reconstructions (see a schematic diagram of the components that flow into the creation of a virtual model according to Hermon in Figure 3.7).[325] In a thoroughly researched 3D reconstruction, in fact, the time that is invested in evaluating and interpreting the sources in most cases exceeds the time that is employed for its actual creation.[326] Too often, however, 3D reconstructions are 'closed boxes' where the demarcation between original data and reconstruction hypotheses is too blurry, thus leaving the viewer puzzled about the reliability of the representation.

During the 1990s, a photorealistic result was sought after as if a realistic rendering was the warranty of the trustworthiness of the 3D reconstruction, thus giving a false perception of authenticity to what in fact was a modern sophisticated looking 'construction' of the past.[327] For this reason, the explicit presentation of the level of reliability of the 3D reconstruction has been deemed a necessary requirement for an intellectually transparent communication. To this end, in 2002 Frischer *et al.* suggested that 3D visualisations needed a 'new philology', making an analogy with how philologists prepare a corrupted text for publication by providing an *apparatus criticus* to explain their integrations.[328] By doing this for 3D reconstructions, other researchers are enabled to assess sources and thinking processes that led them to choose a certain hypothesis over others to be visualised in the virtual environment. It is indeed the complex relationship between the original data and the interpretation that is usually not apparent in 3D reconstructions, as they present an image of the past where all the elements are displayed with the same degree of certainty.[329] The 'different realities' that compose and need to be distinguished in a 3D reconstruction can be summarised in Zubrow's words: '(...) what part is based upon observation, what part is based upon 'connecting the material dots - interpolating', what part is based upon 'extending the

---

[325] Cf. Wittur 2013, 205-18.
[326] See in this respect Pletinckx 2012a, 205.
[327] On the 'authenticity' of VR representations, see Gillings 2002.
[328] Frischer *et al.* 2002.
[329] Early discussions on this topic can be found in Ogleby 1999 and Kensek *et al.* 2004.

material dots - extrapolating', what part is based upon ethnographic analogy, what part is based upon a theoretical stand, and what part is based upon informed speculation'.[330]

To fill the lack of a 'philological *apparatus*' for 3D visualisations, a group of experts in the field of virtual archaeology came together in 2006 to draft the 'London Charter' that aims to ensure a methodological rigour to computer-based visualisations of cultural heritage.[331] The later 'Seville principles' are more precisely focused on the needs and challenges of computer-based visualisations in archaeology.[332] The trigger for the compilation of these guidelines was the need to create a consensus on the best practice for such visualisations and to establish a series of rules to achieve intellectually transparent visualisations. Among the principles listed in the London Charter, some are particularly interesting. The second principle, for example, invites us to assess at first which are the project's aims in order to choose consequently the best approach to address them. 3D visualizations in fact should not be *a priori* considered the best method available, if other strategies can serve the same purpose. The third and fourth principles focus on the need to evaluate and document in a structured way the research sources of any kind that were used to create the visualisation, with the aim to make clear 'the relationship between research sources, implicit knowledge, explicit reasoning, and visualisation-based outcomes'. The last two principles deal with sustainability and access, stressing that it is important to plan a long term preservation of the 3D visualisation, along with the sources and the thinking process that led to its creation.[333]

The London Charter and the Seville principles represent a huge step forward in regulating the creation of 3D models of heritage and archaeological structures, and have set essential standards for their creation, which have been recalled and further specified in following projects and publications.[334] In order to encompass all the different applications of the vast field of 3D in archaeology, in fact, the principles listed in these guidelines are general and theoretical. For this reason, researchers have implemented various solutions to comply with the principles, some of which I will discuss in the next paragraphs. Despite these progresses, a recent survey taking into consideration papers presented at major conferences in 2012 has shown that still only a very small percentage of published papers dealing with 3D models in archaeology included methods to integrate this type of information within their workflow (1% of 686 papers).[335] This shows that this aspect is far from having become the norm, and a greater amount of simple and standardized solutions are needed to facilitate the documentation, analysis and comparison of sources used for 3D reconstructions and to ensure the long-term preservation of 3D visualisations in archaeology.

---

[330] Zubrow 2006, 24.
[331] http://www.londoncharter.org/ (last accessed Sept. 2016).
[332] The Seville Charter is available at http://smartheritage.com/seville-principles/seville-principles (last accessed Sept. 2016).
[333] The London Charter principles are available at http://www.londoncharter.org/principles.html (last accessed Sept. 2016).
[334] A recently closed European project, the Virtual Museum Transnational Network V-MUST (http://www.v-must.net/home) developed case studies where a practical workflow is suggested, tested and evaluated to be able 'to provide the heritage sector with the tools and support to develop virtual museums that are educational, enjoyable, long-lasting and easy to maintain'. Other European projects have been funded over the last years and have produced methodological results and practical tools available for the research community in the field of virtual heritage (see http://cordis.europa.eu/fp7/ict/creativity/digicult-heritage_en.html). Among others, we can note EPOCH (2004-2008) the EU FP6 Network of Excellence on the Applications of ICT to tangible cultural heritage (the webpage of the project, http://www.epoch-net.org/, is no longer supported. Documents related to the project can be found at http://public-repository.epoch-net.org/), 3D COFORM (2007-2013, http://www.3d-coform.eu/), CARARE (2010 -2013, http://carare.eu/eng), and 3D Icons (2012-2015, http://3dicons-project.eu/). The outcomes of 3D COFORM are the development of open source software such as MeshLab (http://meshlab.sourceforge.net/) created by a team of the Italian CNR-ISTI for the processing and editing of unstructured 3D triangular meshes typically produced by 3D scanning. CARARE was dedicated to finding the best option to publish 3D content online, especially to be included in Europeana, the European digital library. The more recently funded 3D Icons aims to take further the results of 3D COFORM and CARARE to bring 3D models of architecture and archaeological structures into Europeana (a European digital library of Cultural Heritage), by using digitisation and 3D scanning techniques (http://3dicons-project.eu/eng/Resources/VSMM-2012). See also the list of rules for the interpretation of sources and hypotheses in Pletinckx 2007, 6.
[335] Cerato and Pescarin 2013, 290.

The inclusion of additional information concerning research sources and thinking process is not only beneficial for assessing the academic standard of a 3D reconstruction, but also creates a more informative platform for the dissemination of cultural heritage to the public. To investigate the visitors' expectations, a survey was carried out during the multi-media exhibition 'Building Virtual Rome: Trajan's Markets in Rome' held in Rome in 2005, in which a virtual reconstruction of Trajan's Markets was presented. The interviews with the visitors showed that they would have liked to be able to access historical information about the meaning and the function of the virtually reconstructed building, and also wanted to be informed about the methodologies followed to create its 3D reconstruction.[336]

In the next paragraphs, I will discuss some of the methods for intellectual transparency that have been used over the years. Some differences in the chosen approaches are noticeable in relation to the final user (academic or general public) of the application, although the boundary can be very blurred and one user does not exclude the other. When 3D reconstructions are meant for museum settings, the choice generally falls either on leaving to the user the possibility to choose whether to access or not the extra content,[337] or on creating external resources (e.g. blogs) where the additional information is presented in a structured way. For the academic user, methods that would be less engaging for the general public, such as databases, XML schemas or simply textual explanations have been chosen for documenting the creation process of 3D reconstructions.

One of the first, pioneering solutions was developed by Kensek *et al.* in 2004 for the sanctuary of the Great Aten Temple at Amarna (Figure 3.8).[338] The 3D reconstruction of the temple was enriched with hyperlinks directing the viewer to additional information (such as the confidence level of the reconstruction or other possible reconstructions) that the user could access without leaving the virtual environment. Moreover, the system was devised in such a way that the user could change the columns, capitals and shafts types of the temple's facade to display equally plausible reconstruction alternatives. To this end, constraints had been added to prevent selection of stylistically incompatible elements. Conceptually, this system is still one of the most complete and elaborate solutions for the representation of the certainty level, the accessibility of research sources, and the possibility offered to the user to intervene in modifying the 3D reconstruction to convey the array of different interpretations.

More specifically developed for museum settings, was the virtual reality application of the Villa of Livia at Prima Porta, created by CNR-ITABC between 2006 and 2008 as part of the Virtual Museum of Ancient Flaminia for the National Roman Museum at the Baths of Diocletian in Rome.[339] Pioneering the possibilities offered by gaming dynamics, a multi-user VR system was developed, which allowed a third-person navigation around and within the Villa (with the possibility to choose between viewing the current state of the digitally documented site or its reconstruction). During the exploration, the user controlled an avatar that triggered icons granting access to extra content. For example, as shown in Figure 3.9, when the avatar walked through the icon 'references', a video started that gave an overview of the architectural comparisons that were used to integrate the parts of the Villa that are now lost. Time and technical expertise are needed to develop such a virtual navigation and the real time interaction, but it represents a successful attempt to make research sources available in a non-obtrusive way and only if the user desires to access them.[340]

---

[336] Forte, Pescarin and Pietroni 2006.
[337] Cerato and Pescarin 2013, 294.
[338] Kensek *et al.* 2004.
[339] Forte 2007.
[340] The assets that were developed for this project have been recently re-used in a VR application based on natural interaction for the Museo Nazionale Romano - Terme di Diocleziano (http://www.itabc.cnr.it/progetti/flaminia-re-loaded-museo-virtuale-della-villa-di-l-000. Last accessed Sept. 2016).

3. Three-dimensional visualizations in archaeology

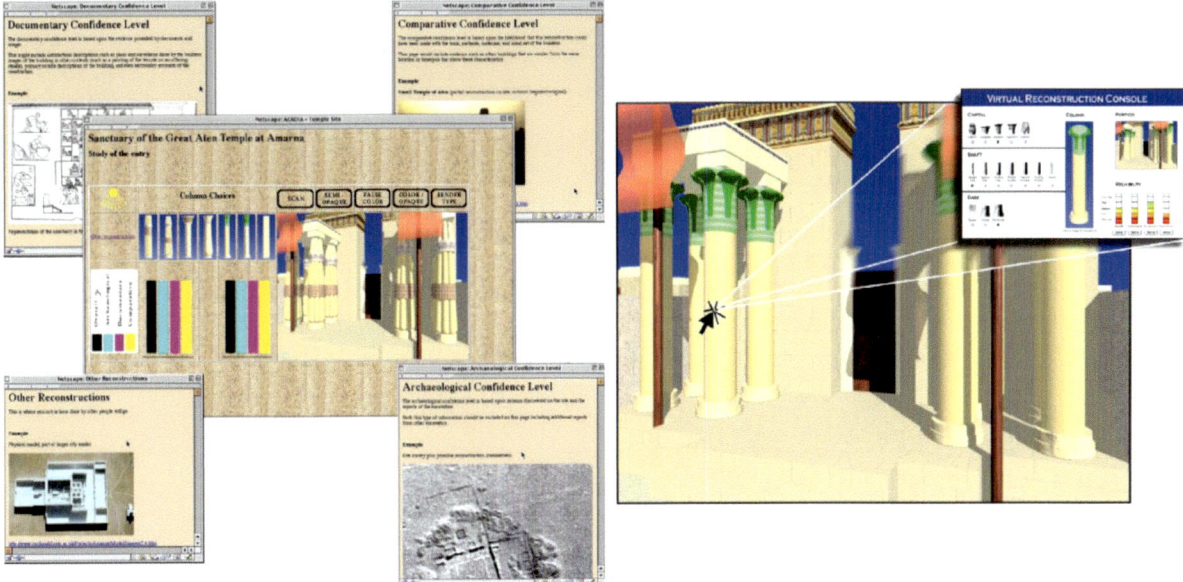

Figure 3.8 Screenshots from the virtual environment elaborated by Kensek et al. Left: Hyperlinks point to additional information regarding the different confidence levels of the reconstruction and alternative hypotheses; Right: the interface that allows the user to choose different types of columns, capitals and shafts to be displayed (Kensek et al. 2004, 181 and 182).

Figure 3.9 Screenshots from the navigation through the virtual reality application of the Villa of Livia by CNR-ITABC, which used to be available at http://www.vhlab.itabc.cnr.it/flaminia/. The avatar that guides the user through the exploration of the Villa encounters icons that display extra content when triggered.

In other cases, the documentation of the creation process has been detached from the 3D visualisation, by exploiting blogs as instruments to present sources, methods and the reasoning behind the final product. This solution has been adopted recently by two visualisation projects, 'Etruscanning' and 'Abbey Theatre, 1904'. Etruscanning was carried out in the framework of the V-MUST by CNR ITABC and the company Visual Dimension with the aim of creating a virtual experience of the Regolini-Galassi Etruscan tomb (Cerveteri, Central Italy) for museum visitors (Figure 3.10). The tomb was discovered in the late 19th century and it is not accessible anymore, while the grave goods are kept in the Vatican museums. The virtual reconstruction was therefore the occasion to re-contextualise the objects and to provide an exploration of the nowadays closed tomb in a virtual environment. During the Etruscanning project, the structure was documented by laser scanning and the objects were photographed and turned

Figure 3.10 Left: Laser scanning session inside the Regolini-Galassi Tomb at the Sorbo necropolis, near Cerveteri (CNR-ITABC); Right: The installation of the virtual reconstruction at the archaeological museum in Leiden (RMO) (images from http://regolinigalassi.wordpress.com/)

into 3D models by applying photogrammetry techniques. All the process of recording the tomb and its content, and the different hypotheses and comparative material were published in a blog.[341]

The Abbey Theatre project aimed to digitally reconstruct this famous theatre in Dublin that was damaged by fire in 1951. Hugh Denard, a King's College historian and one of the initiators of the London Charter, set up a blog to document the phases of the reconstruction of the theatre as it was at the time of its opening in 1904.[342] The blog was chosen as the place to present the sources that were gathered, so that everyone could evaluate the choices made for the reconstruction, which is presented in video clips, one of which held information about the reliability of the reconstructed theatre.[343] One of the reasons for choosing blogs to document the process of creation of 3D visualisation is to stimulate and facilitate the exchange of opinions between researchers working on the same project. It seems, however, that the research community is not yet at ease with these tools, in particular if blogs are public. Observations on the use and reception of the Etruscanning blog proved, in fact, that 'experts are reluctant to contribute on a public blog as they see this as a kind of publication with final conclusions, while the contributions are ongoing research, of a volatile and progressive nature'.[344]

A different approach is based on the creation of standardised ontologies to describe heritage documentation in a formalised way. Such ontologies aim to improve the data integration and exchange among different sources of information and entities, such as libraries, museums and archives. The standardization of definitions and categories encompassing the variety of records is however a very challenging task. The Conceptual Reference Model has been developed with this purpose by the International Committee for Documentation of the International Council of Museums (CIDOC-CRM) and it has officially become ISO standard in 2006.[345] In recent years, progress has been made to integrate archaeological and architectural heritage in CIDOC-CRM to provide a common platform where also 3D models can be documented, exchanged and more easily found in the ever-growing amount of data available on the web.[346]

---

[341] The blog, compiled by D. Pletinckx, can be accessed at http://regolinigalassi.wordpress.com/; see also Hupperetz *et al.* 2012.
[342] http://blog.oldabbeytheatre.net/
[343] http://blog.oldabbeytheatre.net/posts/visualisation
[344] Pletinckx 2012b, 106.
[345] http://www.cidoc-crm.org/index.html
[346] See Niccolucci 2012, 35-6 and M. Doerr's presentation 'New Developments of CIDOC-CRM' given at the 'CIDOC-CRM seminar' (Istituto Centrale per il Catalogo Unico delle Biblioteche Italiane, Rome, 14 Sept. 2012) available at http://www.otebac.it/

Building on this and other existing standards for metadata mapping, the CARARE metadata schema was developed for this purpose within the framework of the 3D ICONS project.[347] Based on the CARARE schema was for example the process of documentation of the Hellenistic-Roman theatre of Paphos, Cyprus.[348] The data acquisition phase was carried out by aerial photogrammetry (aerostatic balloon) and terrestrial laser scanning and a virtual reconstruction was created of the architectural phases of the theatre. The theatre was hierarchically divided into architectural components (e.g. cavea, stage, orchestra etc.) that were then mapped into an XML structure equivalent to the various elements of the CARARE schema. The project dealt also with making explicit the reliability of the reconstruction, which was displayed by mapping RGB and saturation values onto the 3D model: red corresponded to high reliability, green to moderate and blue to low. For each of these colour channels, the saturation value further specified the reliability to create a more nuanced transition between the three categories.

Other approaches to make explicit the level of reliability of a 3D reconstruction have been suggested, ranging from a colour coding of each part of the visualisation, to the 'deconstruction' of the reconstruction process by using charts that show the relationships between the various components of the visualization,[349] to the application of a fuzzy logic approach that defines a scale between '0' (totally unreliable) and '1' (absolutely reliable) for each component of the 3D visualisation.[350] Alternatively, in projects such as in the case of the 'Villa of Livia' and 'Aquae Patavinae' (ITABC-CNR),[351] the online virtual environment makes it possible to switch between a 3D model of the extant remains and their 3D reconstruction. In the latter case, the user could choose among three levels: the *current state* of the archaeological evidence, its *interpretation* (in which the reconstructed buildings are rendered with see-through walls), and the actual *reconstruction*, in which the reconstructed buildings are rendered in their physical appearance. In this way, the user can see the current state of the archaeological evidence and is made aware of the existing relationship between the finds and the interpretation given by the archaeologists.

Besides the explicit presentation of documentation sources and the level of reliability, the second aspect that is rarely explored is the creation of multiple reconstruction hypotheses, which would better represent the range of equally plausible hypotheses that archaeologists formulate to explain archaeological evidence. Before 3D digital reconstructions, this problem was already apparent, even more dramatically, in some of the physical restorations of sites that were carried out in the early decades of the 20th century, the most notable example being the Palace of Knossos in Crete. As is clear from Evans' report, his work of consolidation and reconstitution of the excavated structures was a genuine effort to preserve the Palace and make it more understandable to the visitors.[352] Under the light of modern archaeological methodology, however, Evans' approach resulted in a misleading and heavily conjectural *anastylosis*. Not only the physical reconstruction was done in such a way that it is difficult to distinguish the original parts from the restored elements, but also the correctness of the restoration, including the use of modern materials, has been questioned. Moreover, the reconstitution took into account only one historical phase of the site, hiding the remains of other important periods

---

index.php?it/22/archivio-eventi/229/roma-seminario-cidoc-crm (last accessed Sept. 2016).
[347] The current version of the CARARE metadata schema can be accessed here: http://pro.carare.eu/doku.php?id=support:metadata-schema (last accessed April 2017), where a list of schemas and best practises that the CARARE schema builds upon can also be found.
[348] Georgiou and Hermon 2011.
[349] Ogleby 2007. Demetrescu is developing a framework (Extended Matrix) for the integration of semantics in 3D virtual environments, aiming at documenting the scientific process behind the virtual reconstruction of a (partially) lost building (Demetrescu 2015, Demetrescu and Fanini 2017).
[350] Hermon and Nikodem 2008; Niccolucci and Hermon 2010.
[351] http://www.aquaepatavinae.lettere.unipd.it/portale/?page_id=2174 (last accessed Sept. 2016).
[352] Evans 1927.

(namely the Neolithic, Greek and Roman settlement) both to visitors and experts.[353] As I already noted in the chapter on reconstructions before the digital age, once again the same issues that have been identified for 3D digital reconstructions were already evident in non-digital reconstructions. However, the reflections aroused from these early works, albeit in a different domain, have not been picked up by the early practitioners in the field of virtual archaeology and the possibilities that the digital *medium* offers to tackle this problem have not been fully exploited. For example, while the physical reconstruction obviously does not allow to present several hypotheses, this is actually possible in the digitally reconstructed environments, where alternatives can be created and displayed.

The problem of displaying a single reconstruction has been approached in various ways, since the early demonstration by Roberts and Ryan, who in 1997 suggested a system based on VRML.[354] One of the explanations for the lack of more numerous projects including different reconstruction hypotheses is that the creation of several 3D models is usually unfeasible as too costly and too time consuming. While in the last years a substantial drop in costs of hardware and software is noticeable, early projects had to sustain considerable expenditure for creating and setting up the infrastructure and the 3D environment, not to mention the limitations posed by the graphics hardware that were available.[355] Although this obstacle has been solved, the fact that creating several reconstruction takes up much time is still a problem nowadays, especially for 3D reconstructions created using a manual approach. As already mentioned, procedural modelling offers in this regard a very efficient solution, as the parametric approach allows the user to change in real time the appearance of the reconstruction.

As I will more extensively present in chapter 6, I chose a procedural modelling for Koroneia's case study as this seemed the best methodology not only for the characteristics of the site (an ancient town of which the archaeological investigation is still in process), but also to create an intellectually transparent 3D reconstruction. The text-based formal description of the created geometry allows in fact the introduction of documentation sources as comments; moreover, the parametric approach enables the creation of different reconstruction hypotheses in a time efficient and compact way. In the next section, I will deal with another aspect of 3D reconstructions, namely their underestimated value as research tools.

3.4.2 3D reconstructions as analytical tools

Over the last two decades, we have witnessed a dramatic increase in the number of papers dealing with 3D archaeology in a broad sense, which have been presented at archaeological conferences and have appeared in dedicated journals.[356] As Hermon noted, papers dealing with this subject can be divided in two major groups, namely those using 3D/VR for presenting heritage sites to the public, and those discussing technical advanced in the methods to create 3D/VR applications.[357] 3D models of archaeological artefacts or structures have been in fact traditionally exploited mostly for heritage purposes, with the aim to create convincing visual representations that allowed the preservation and the dissemination of (partially) lost or endangered artefacts or buildings. In some of these cases, however, one might question the actual usefulness and added value of such digital representations, as a creative use of traditional techniques may serve the same purpose in a cheaper and more sustainable way (see for example the solution adopted at Carnuntum in Austria in Figure 3.11). It is therefore reasonable to

---

[353] Papadopoulos 1997, 115-17.
[354] Roberts and Ryan 1997.
[355] See e.g. the reconstruction of the Temple Mount conducted by the Urban Simulation Team at UCLA and the Israel Antiquities Authority that was available on the internet and included pop-up windows with pictures and explanations of the extant remains (Kensek *et al.* 2004, 179-80).
[356] Olson *et al.* 2014, Hermon 2008, 35-6.
[357] Hermon, 2008, 35.

Figure 3.11 Archaeological site of Carnuntum, Austria. A perspex panel allows the viewer to see the Heidentor gate in its restored appearance (picture by Jan Madaras on panoramio).

expect that a digital 3D reconstruction should have a clear added value to justify the effort to create it, such as the possibility to access the reasoning process and sources that led to its creation, view alternative hypotheses, or to use them as tools to aid the archaeological interpretation.

Over the years, archaeologists working in the field of digital visualisations have in fact reflected on their use and on how to shift them from being simply 'pretty pictures' that can mislead the public by conveying a wrong image of the past, to become an instrument in the hand of the research community to answer archaeological questions and communicate archaeology responsibly. The need to ensure an academic standard to 3D visualizations has resulted in guidelines and solutions to present metadata and paradata that I have discussed in the previous section. These improvements, however, still mainly relate to 3D visualizations as presentations of already acquired knowledge, instead of as tools to work with for generating new questions and visualizing hypotheses. The analytical potential of 3D visualizations in archaeological interpretation has been not yet extensively explored. In the era of Cyber-Archaeology as defined by Forte, the interaction and embodiment in the virtual environment promises to generate new insights for the interpretation of archaeological evidence, a task that the dismissed 'Virtual Archaeology' has failed to persuasively fulfil. At present, however, this vision remains largely theoretical, as there is not yet any solid case study showing that the development of such interactive environments has yielded new interpretations that furthered a deeper understanding of our archaeological record.

The advantages related to the use of 3D recording over traditional documentation techniques are self-evident, and a shift from a collection management approach to a research driven agenda has resulted in the inclusion of digital recording techniques in the archaeologist's analytical 'toolbox'. These techniques allow in fact a quick creation of an accurate and complete documentation of extant archaeological remains, which represents an important source of information for monitoring a structure's condition and planning restoration interventions. The 3D models thus obtained become moreover measurable digital replicas that are stored locally or on the cloud, to allow researchers to inspect the recorded entity also when fieldwork is concluded. For artefacts and bone finds, the availability of digital models reproducing precisely their volumetric properties enables the creation of virtual reference collections in which information such as shape, size and texture can be easily retrieved and compared, encouraging the development of techniques for automatic feature extraction.[358]

The position of 3D reconstructions within the field of scientific research is instead more complex. The already recalled quest for realism and the uncritical claims about the potential of VR as a tool to bring the past back to life that have characterized many early applications[359] have distracted from the tangible added value of using them as research tools. Although the heuristic use of 3D modelling to enhance archaeological interpretations has often been highlighted,[360] the number of papers in which 3D reconstructions are used for this purpose are still few in comparison with those presenting methodological advances in 3D recording techniques or 3D reconstructions for heritage preservation. Not accidentally, amongst the papers submitted to the session 'The scientific value of 3D archaeology', organized by Hans Kamermans, Roberto Scopigno and the author at the XVII UISPP World Congress at Burgos, only one focussed on the use of a 3D reconstruction for research purposes, while the majority of the others were dedicated to 3D recording methodologies.[361] In the next paragraphs, I will discuss some examples of analytical visualizations and a set of related case studies that have successfully unlocked the potential of 3D models. In line with the topic of this work, my attention will be especially directed to research aiming at the formulation of hypotheses on past built environments and their social implications. I shall argue that these types of application set the direction for the inclusion of 3D visualizations within the 'toolbox' that archaeologists should be equipped with, to investigate specific archaeological questions.

Gordin has divided visualizations into 'interpretative' and 'expressive':[362] the former encompassing all visualizations that help to clarify complex evidence or abstract concepts, while the latter allows the communication of knowledge in an easier and more intuitive way. Depending on their use and the purpose of their creation, 3D reconstructions and simulations can belong to both groups. They allow for example the contextualization of landmarks into their urban surroundings, show more clearly the relationship between above and under surface archaeological elements, and help a non-expert viewer to comprehend fragmentary remains by offering a summary of the available data and interpretations.[363] A good example of interpretative visualization is the Oplontis project.[364] The 3D model of the Villa A at Oplontis acts as a spatial index for all the data that have been collected during the archaeological campaigns. In doing so, all the pieces of information (both raw data and reconstruction hypotheses) are organized in a structured way following the spatial arrangement of the Villa. Apart from collating all the available data and reconstruction hypotheses, the 3D model allows the reposition of the Villa into the ancient landscape, showing for example that while nowadays the villa is located about half a

---

[358] For artefact analysis, see e.g. Karasik 2008; for palaeosteology, see e.g. the recently funded project VZAP by the Centre for Virtualization and Applied Spatial Technology of the University of Florida led by Professor Herbert Maschner, aiming at creating a virtual 3D osteological reference collection from the Arctic which exploits the functions of 3D PDF to view, rotate and measure the 3D objects (see Betts et al. 2011, available at http://vzap.iri.isu.edu/)
[359] See e.g. Gillings 2002, 232-3.
[360] See e.g. Frischer and Dakouri-Hild 2008 and Wittur (2013, 30-6), who discusses some analytical applications of 3D reconstructions with a series of case studies.
[361] See Kamermans et al. 2016.
[362] Gordin et al. 1996.
[363] See Hermon 2008, 40.
[364] http://oplontisproject.org/ (last accessed Sept. 2016). The project aims to develop 3D models of the Villas A and B at Oplontis that are linked to an online database.

kilometre inland, recent studies have proved that it was originally built on a cliff 13 meters above the sea.[365]

A third category, that we could call *analytical visualizations*, should be added to the two main groups mentioned above. This kind of visualizations consists of 3D models that are created both to turn heterogeneous data into knowledge and to act as proper analytical tools in their own right. The most obvious type of 3D analytical visualization is the creation of a 3D GIS environment. The enhancing of GIS with the 3rd dimension has the advantage of enabling the possibility to store information and conduct analysis in a georeferenced and fully 3D environment. The development of a 3D GIS for modern cities has attracted ever growing attention since the 1990s,[366] but the possibility to work in a 'full' 3D GIS is a recent development as common GIS platforms were either 2D or 2.5D in the past. In the latter case, the z value could in fact be stored as a single attribute of the x and y coordinates (e.g. TINs) and not as a separate entity or as multiple values, thus limiting the analytical capabilities of the system, especially for the built environment. In fact, while the capabilities of 2.5D are sufficient in landscape studies (e.g. for *viewshed* calculation), visibility analysis for buildings was confined only to establishing whether a building could or could not be seen in its entirety. A recent development exploits procedural rules for the quick creation of a uniformly separated grid of points on the buildings' facades, that can be exploited as target or observer points to achieve a more detailed visibility analysis on portions of buildings in ArcGIS.[367] In chapter 6, I will discuss in more detail how I included this possibility in Koroneia's workflow.

A 3D GIS is particularly interesting for municipalities that need to have tools for improving their ability to plan, manage, design and analyse infrastructures, public transportation, alternative development scenarios etc. The creation of 'smart' cities that could exploit digital technologies to achieve a more efficient urban planning and a more effective communication with citizens and stakeholders, has led companies to create targeted software packages that allow an integrated approach for data handling and provide analytical tools for a variety of analyses.[368] A 3D GIS for the modern city allows in fact municipalities to store and interrogate their data in a 3D cadaster, thus solving problematic situations that were common with 2D mapping (e.g. how to represent a bridge that crossed a street in a 2D environment). Besides improving the mapping capacities, a 3D GIS increases also the analytical possibilities, which include visibility analysis, shadow impact, sun exposure and flood modelling.[369]

Visibility analysis in a 3D GIS

In recent years, archaeologists working on past cityscapes have increasingly become familiar with the new capabilities of a 3D GIS environment and have started to use it for both research and dissemination purposes. The 3D reconstruction hypothesis embedded into a georeferenced environment can shed light on topographical choices that were made in antiquity. Moreover, types of documentation that are not usually included in a GIS environment, such as old perspective drawings and landscape views depicting archaeological features that are now lost, can enrich the georeferenced data set with additional data. A 3D GIS was for example created for the Roman city of Tarrago, which was used to compute several views of the Roman city from various perspectives and supported the theory that Tarrago's topography was laid out to be best appreciated by the visitors coming from the sea.[370] The location of a lost stretch of the

---

[365] Clarke 2012.
[366] See e.g. Gruber 1999; Stoter *et al.* 2011; Stoter *et al.* 2013.
[367] Van Maren 2014.
[368] See e.g. the suite of software packages for 3D cities by Bentley https://www.bentley.com/en/solutions/3d-cities.
[369] On 3D urban mapping, see 3D Urban Mapping: From Pretty Pictures to 3D GIS. Esri Whitepaper. December 2014 available at https://www.esri.com/library/whitepapers/pdfs/3d-urban-mapping.pdf (last accessed Sept. 2016).
[370] Orengo and Fiz 2008.

Roman walls was moreover estimated by deriving their location from a 16th century drawing depicting a view of Tarragona from a church's tower.

Focussing on the analytical capabilities of 3D GIS is the recently started project aiming at analysing Insula V 1 in Pompeii, within the framework of the Swedish Pompeii Project carried out by the Swedish Institute in Rome. For their case study, the researchers chose to focus on the house of Caecilius Iucundus that was documented with a laser scanner device. The 3D model obtained was used in a 3D GIS that aimed both at acting as a platform for integrating old and new data and as an analytical tool.[371] The possibility of editing in 3D, which is enabled by the 3D Analyst extension of ArcGIS, allowed the annotation of observations and interpretations that were made in the field directly on the 3D replica of the building. A virtual reconstruction of the house was made in 3D Studio Max by using as reference the 3D model obtained by the laser scanner recording of the extant remains. This 3D interpretation of the structure was then imported into the 3D GIS and used to perform a visibility analysis within the domestic space. As a starting point for further research, two inscriptions of different dimensions and located in different rooms were used as a case study to formulate hypotheses on the symbolic use of space in the Roman house.[372]

In the last few years, several projects have been initiated aiming to develop web-based (2D and 3D) GIS platforms, as the online availability of these tools facilitates data sharing and encourages collaboration between different research groups.[373] Recently, a web-based 3D GIS has been developed for the ancient Maya city of Copan in Honduras as part of the MayaArch3D project. A pilot initiated in 2009 has grown into an international interdisciplinary project that integrates LiDAR data and low resolution 3D reconstructions of buildings made with SketchUp in a WebGIS platform, thus allowing the user to perform spatial analysis (e.g. line of sight) on the 3D landscape and architectural remains.[374] A forerunner of this system is the ARCHAVE, a virtual reality CAVE-based visualization that was created to allow archaeologists to view and query the finds collected from the Great Temple of Petra within their architectural context.[375] The project was initiated in 1999 and represents a successful synergy between computer scientists and archaeologists, in finding a solution for visualizing and better understanding clusters of finds and their relationships in a 3D environment when 3D GIS solutions were not yet available. The finds were spatially distributed and contextualized in the excavated trenches where they came from, thus allowing the archaeologists to perform spatial analysis and to observe patterns in the data that had been not previously identified.[376]

Analysis of visibility and the use of space using computer graphics methods

Alternative methods have been developed to perform visibility analysis on 3D past built environments.[377] A methodology for the visibility analysis in 3D spaces that exploits CG techniques is the approach developed by the Archaeological Computing Research Group at the University of Southampton and presented at the CAA conference in Tomar in 2005.[378] This method is based on the principle that a single light source that casts light in all direction will illuminate or keep in the dark the parts that

---

[371] Dell'Unto *et al.* 2016; Landeschi *et al.* 2015.
[372] Landeschi *et al.* 2015, 356-8.
[373] See e.g. the web GIS created within the Mappa project (University of Pisa), which aims to create an open digital archive of the archaeological data that are produced by Italian municipalities (http://www.mappaproject.org/?lang=en) and the 3D Spatial Data Infrastructure developed for the *Mapping the Via Appia* project (De Kleijn *et al.* 2016).
[374] Von Schwerin *et al.* 2016, 99; Auer *et al.* 2014; Von Schwerin *et al.* 2013.
[375] Vote *et al.* 2000; Acevedo *et al.* 2001.
[376] Acevedo *et al.* 2001, 496.
[377] For a recent discussion on the approaches for visibility analysis in 3D spaces see Paliou 2013.
[378] The paper has been published in the conference proceedings in 2007 (Paliou and Wheatley 2007); on the same technique see also Earl 2005.

are respectively visible or not visible of the structure under investigation. In practise, the 3D model of a building created using a CG software is first illuminated by the light source and then its textures, which conserve the information on the amount of light received, and are extracted using the so called *texture baking* technique. This technique is usually used to speed up the rendering process and to reduce the polygon count of a 3D model. By doing so, all the geometry's characteristics, which derive by the combination of mesh, texture and environment settings, are pre-calculated and saved ('baked') into an image (texture). The approach developed in Southampton exploits this CG technique to quantitatively calculate how many times a part of the 3D model has been seen, by summarizing the information of the extracted textures.[379]

This method has been used for the quantitative assessment of the visibility of wall paintings in a digitally reconstructed building (Xeste 3) in Late Bronze Age Akrotiri, to advance hypotheses on the reception and function of mural decoration in Theran society.[380] The building was interpreted as a ritual centre for the community, where ceremonies took place both on the ground and the first floor.[381] On the walls of rooms 3a and 3b, in particular, famous scenes were depicted such as the 'Adorants', the 'male scene' and the 'Crocus gatherers'. The visibility analysis identified the most seen portions of these paintings from the adjoining spaces, which corresponded to the figures that were visually emphasized also by iconographic attributes such as their position in the scene, their posture, their hairstyle and dress.[382] In another application of this approach the researchers investigated the social implications of the distribution of believers in the Church of San Vitale in Ravenna, showing that the place in which women were allowed to stay were the least visually integrated part of the church, both on the ground floor and in the *matroneum* on the second floor.[383] This approach expanded the analytical limitations of space syntax which is confined to the assessment of degrees of visual integration or seclusion based on a single horizontal or vertical portion of space.[384] Besides providing an analysis based on visual perception, they integrated also acoustic data within their mapping, thus implementing a multi-sensory analysis of the space.[385]

Focussing on the social implications of the visibility of roof architectural terracottas was the project on the virtual reconstruction of a 6th century BC temple dedicated to Mater Matuta at Satricum initiated at the University of Amsterdam in 2003.[386] The 3D visualization created in the CG software Maya was aimed at investigating specific theories about the role that the temple decorations assumed as propaganda means for pre-Roman elites. Details of the temple architecture could be reconstructed, such as the original colour of the decorations, which was derived by the pigments that were still present on the terracotta fragments, and the heavy and low roof, sloping at 17°.[387] With the help of a CAVE, the 3D reconstruction of the temple was inspected in an immersive navigation, which showed that the decorations could not be seen from a distance as previously hypothesised, and thus could not carry a political message for the public.[388]

Interestingly, although being a rare example of a thoroughly researched 3D reconstruction that was used in combination with CAVE technology, with the specific purpose of helping in the archaeological interpretation, this project was met with scepticism by both terracotta specialists and computer

---

[379] Paliou and Knight 2013, 232.
[380] Paliou *et al.* 2011; Paliou 2014.
[381] See e.g. Vlachopoulos 2008.
[382] Paliou *et al.* 2011.
[383] Paliou and Knight 2013, 233-5.
[384] Paliou and Knight 2013, 231.
[385] Paliou and Knight 2013, 233-5.
[386] Lulof 2011, 16.
[387] Lulof 2011, 18.
[388] Lulof 2011, 20.

scientists.[389] The specialists were in fact not convinced by the use of these tools to assess the visibility of the decorative motifs, while computer scientists judged the technology as too old and the visualization as not visually appealing enough. When submitted for the Virtual Reality, Archaeology, and Cultural Heritage conference (VAST 2005), the project was in fact rejected by the reviewers' panel.[390] Ratto identified the contrasting epistemic commitments of the two research groups as one of the causes of the not particularly favourable reception of this project.[391]

Besides the analysis of a single structure, 3D modelling and simulations are useful tools to investigate the relationships between buildings, allowing the testing of theories on the 'grammar of space' underlying choices in urban planning. A reconstruction of the Roman Forum that can be explored in a first-person visit and was developed with the game engine Unity 3D has allowed researchers to simulate the location and the evolution of the space for performance within the Forum during the Republican period.[392] The creation of a multi-period simulation that follows the building phases of the Basilicas in the Roman Forum suggests that the space hosting the games was confined at the beginning to a restricted area and occupied later on a much larger area corresponding to the plaza itself.[393]

Another aspect that can be investigated using 3D models is the dialogue that ancient architects wanted to establish between inner spaces and natural landscape. This was one of the aims of the 3D reconstruction of the 3rd century AD House of the Drinking Contest at Antioch.[394] The house was lavishly decorated with mosaics, which are however dispersed across several museums in the United States and in Turkey. The digital model allowed researchers to restore the mosaics in their original location and to create different reconstruction hypotheses with different possible ceiling and column heights. The presence of large windows in the triclinium and in the courtyard wall was hypothesised based on comparative evidence (e.g. Pompeii, Zeugma), where such windows allowed views to inner courtyards or landscape features. Sight lines were tested using computer modelling which showed that there was an unobstructed view to Mount Casius to the south of the house. Besides visibility analysis, a script in Maya was used to simulate the position of natural sunlight. This simulation showed that low light rays would enter the *triclinium* in the late afternoon, thus illuminating the mosaics of the drinking contest. Moreover, the computer model showed that the portico protected the rooms of the northern side (possibly bedrooms) from direct sunlight, which greatly improved living conditions during the hot summer months.

Simulation of lighting conditions

The simulation of light behaviour in past built environments has been the focus of several 3D modelling projects. Natural or artificially created light sources were crucial elements in defining how space was used, experienced and perceived in antiquity, thus making lighting conditions an important interpretative key to shed light on the type of activities that were carried out in a specific space.[395] The simulation of a physically correct light is not a straightforward task. The light source properties need to be simulated correctly, and at present only a few studies have formally investigated the characteristics of different fuels.[396] Moreover, environmental factors that influence how light is distributed in space (such as dust, smog, and humidity) need to be included as well in the 3D modelling process to ensure a reliable

---

[389] Ratto 2009.
[390] Ratto 2009.
[391] Ratto 2009. Cf. Favro 2006, 329 on how different groups of viewers use opposite criteria to evaluate Virtual Reality models of historical cities.
[392] Saldaña and Johanson 2013, 208-9.
[393] Saldaña and Johanson 2013, 208-9.
[394] Gruber and Dobbins 2013.
[395] Papadopoulos and Earl 2014, 135-65, esp. 135-7.
[396] See e.g. the work by Roussos (2003) and by Devlin *et al.* 2001, 2002 (below).

result.[397] Also, the computation of lighting conditions usually requires long rendering times as both light parameters and their interaction with the environment (i.e. how the geometry and the materials that are assigned to objects in the scene absorb, reflect and refract light) have to be calculated. For this reason, high performance workstations are currently needed to handle such complex calculations.[398]

The simulation of sunlight for investigating the Augustan planning of the Campus Martius in Rome was the aim of the 'Digital Meridian of Augustus Project', commissioned to the IDIA Lab, Ball University by the Virtual World Heritage Laboratory at Indiana University, directed by Bernard Frischer.[399] For the simulation of the correct position and size of the sun, the researchers developed a plug-in for Unity that used the NASA Horizon's system database.[400] The simulation aimed at shedding light on the relationship between the Montecitorio obelisk and the Ara Pacis, two monuments that were both constructed in the previously unbuilt northern part of the Campus Martius under Augustus. The obelisk, with a sphere added to its top, worked as a *gnomon* (indicator) for the nearby meridian and it is therefore known as the *Horologium Augusti*. The simulation was used to test different theories about the role of the obelisk and suggested a different interpretative key for the relationship between the monuments: the most important elements would not have been the obelisk's shadow, nor the date of Augustus' birthday, as originally thought, but the position of the sun which was centred over the obelisk in the late afternoon of 9th October, the annual festival to Apollo, whom Augustus had appropriated as his patron god.[401]

As far as indoor spaces are concerned, pioneering the application of 3D models for the simulation of lighting conditions in such environments was Simon Ellis, whose case study was the *triclinium* of the upper class Late Antique residence, the so called 'Huilerie' in Salamis, Cyprus.[402] The aim of his study was to investigate how Romans controlled and manipulated light sources to reach the required dining 'ambience' and how darkness and shadows were also acceptable in part of the house. Although Ellis' computer reconstruction was not physically accurate (sunlight was approximately located and windows were absent), it confirmed the hypothesis that the apse of the *triclinium*, where the dinner took place, functioned also as a 'light trap' for natural light. Even when artificial light was used by means of pottery, bronze or glass lamps, the apse was the best lit part of the room, while the rest was deliberately left darker.

One of the first projects dealing with a physically correct lighting simulation within an architecturally defined space was carried out in the early 2000s and aimed at producing a computer model of the frescoes of the House of Vetii in Pompeii as lit by olive oil lamps.[403] The researchers recreated a replica of an olive oil lamp flame and gathered its spectral data using a spectroradiometer. These values were then transformed into RGB and simulated using the software *Radiance*,[404] a suite of programs developed at the Lawrence Berkeley National Laboratory in Berkeley and released as an open source platform in 2002. The results show how the red and yellow pigments that were used as main shades in the frescos are considerably warmed-up by the organic fuel, which accentuates also the *trompe l'oeil* that characterised the composition. A similar workflow was used by Sundstedt *et al.* to simulate the interior and exterior lighting conditions at the Egyptian temple of Kalabsha, which was moved from its original location in the early 1960s. The team created a 3D reconstruction of the temple and recorded various

---

[397] See in this regard Gutierrez *et al.* 2008. An early example can be found in Chalmers *et al.* 1995.
[398] The Iridis3 that is used at Southampton has up to 8000 cores (for comparison: a good laptop currently has up to 8 cores).
[399] See http://idialab.org/virtual-meridian-of-augustus-presentation-at-the-vaticans-pontifical-academy-of-archeology/ (accessed Dec. 2015).
[400] http://solarsystem.nasa.gov/
[401] From B. Frischer's opening speech '3D Simulations as Tools of Discovery' at the 2014 CAA conference in Paris.
[402] Ellis 1994.
[403] Devlin and Chalmers 2001; additional case studies are presented in Devlin *et al.* 2002.
[404] Ward Larson and Shakespeare 1998.

organic flame spectra with a spectroradiometer, which were then rendered in *Radiance* to simulate how sunlight entered the building and how the hieroglyphics would have appeared if lit by olive or sesame oil lamps.[405]

A recent paper by Papadopoulos and Earl presents an overview of projects that included physically correct lighting simulation aiming to suggest how illumination may have affected building design and the reception of mosaics or polychromy decorations.[406] In addition, they enriched the number of case studies with their own research on the role of lighting in Minoan architecture, focussing on the burials of the cemetery at Phourni, one house at the harbour of Kommos, and a room that was identified as a pottery workshop at Zominthos. Several reconstruction hypotheses were created for the burials, accounting for different possible roofing arrangements as this was not established with certainty. The reconstruction of the investigated house confirms how light penetration within the building responded to the functions of the rooms: areas that were used for everyday activities were well lit through doors and windows, while the storage unit received little illumination, as the position and small size of the windows allowed air circulation, but not direct contact of the sunlight on the kept food.[407] The most interesting result regards the interpretation of a small room in which the presence of elements such as tools and a potter's wheel had led to its identification as a ceramic workshop. The 3D reconstruction and light simulation showed that this room was poorly lit, in contrast with the typical light conditions that were observed in ethnographic comparisons of pottery workshops.[408] This simulation triggered a reconsideration of the archaeological evidence found in this room, which pointed towards its use as a space to dry and store vessels produced elsewhere in the building.

Analysis of construction techniques and structural behaviour

Furthering their approach on the use of 3D modelling as a research tool, the Amsterdam team focussed on the Temple of Caprifico di Torrecchia, which was chosen because it was well studied and had been also represented in several illustrations.[409] They approached the reconstruction of the temple as a stone by stone process,[410] mimicking its physical building, thus aiming at shedding light on the construction techniques employed for its erection. Interestingly, the 3D modelling process highlighted aspects that had not been seen before, had not been fully investigated or had been ignored in textual descriptions and traditional illustrations, notwithstanding the wealth of publications that had been produced on this structure. New insights into the temple construction could be identified, such as the presence of an interlocking system to allow each *ranking sima* (the pan tiles around the edge of the pediment) to overlap with the following one in order to avoid water percolation on the lower part of the structure. Moreover, a trussed roof appeared to be a better option than the post-and-lintel system (common in Greek temple architecture) as the former guaranteed a better stability to the wooden temple construction.

As illustrated by the example of the Temple of Caprifico, a stone by stone virtual rebuilding can help in shedding light on ancient construction techniques, reaching a deeper understanding of the structure under investigation, but also on the economics behind its construction (e.g. how much material was needed, how many persons, how much did it cost). The use of 3D modelling for such purposes was already evidenced in the 1990s,[411] but was criticised by Gillings, who sustained that the insights that

---

[405] Sundstaet *et al.* 2004.
[406] Papadopoulos and Earl 2014, 135-165. These projects include: Happa *et al.* 2009; Dobbins and Gruber 2013; Callet and Dumazet 2010; Frischer and Fillwalk 2012; Earl *et al.* 2012.
[407] Papadopoulos and Earl 2014, 146.
[408] Papadopoulos and Earl 2014, 148.
[409] Lulof *et al.* 2013.
[410] The models of the architectural components were mostly created using commercial CG software such as Cinema4D, Autodesk 3D Studio Max and Google SketchUp, but obtained also by structural light scanning of original pieces (Lulof *et al.* 2013, 336).
[411] Daniel 1997.

were reached in this way could not be justified by the effort that was put into the creation of the 3D reconstruction.[412] This critique has nowadays lost its value not only for the improved software and hardware availability and capabilities over the last years, but also for the use of 3D reconstructions for a holistic analysis of ancient buildings. Simulation tools such as the ANSYS structural software can for example be used to assess the stability and the design of a structure.[413] A recent project has performed a structural analysis of the Early Bronze Age so called 'corridor house' in Helike (Achaea, Peloponnese). This study has suggested that the house could sustain a second floor and shed light on the type of roof that would allow the structure to stand both in dry and wet weather conditions.[414]

Simulation of acoustics

In the case studies that I discussed so far, sight acted as the central sensory receptor to perceive and simulate space, and indeed a preference towards a visual approach to the past environment has been already recognised and criticised as limiting the broader sensorial experience of people in the past.[415] Among the few projects that have included other senses into their simulations is the ERATO project (2003-2006), which aimed at investigating acoustics in ancient Greek and Roman theatres. The researchers have created virtual reconstructions of both open air and closed theatres (*odeia*), and avatars representing Greek and Roman actors and public to simulate ancient performances.[416] The software that was used for the acoustic simulation was the ODEON Room Acoustics developed at the Technical University of Denmark, which is used by design engineers to predict indoor noise propagation.[417] The software allows the import of the building's 3D model to set the type of audience, the noise receivers and the characteristics of the building materials, to simulate the correct absorption and refraction of sound waves. The analysis confirmed the different uses of the theatres, showing that the acoustic characteristics of open air theatres made them particularly suited for plays and speeches, while *odeia* were more appropriate for musical performances with instruments such as the lyre and cithara.[418]

Simulation of human behaviour

Virtual crowds of avatars have been used in other projects to populate reconstructed archaeological sites. The aim has been not only to integrate the human component into the architectural space, which otherwise would appear as a void shell, but also to simulate human behaviour in closed and open spaces. One project aimed to test the long held assumption that the Colosseum was efficiently planned to guide people's movements via eighty large staircases (*vomitoria*), which could empty the audience in just a few minutes.[419] The researchers used a multi-agent Artificial Intelligence system to study the behaviour of avatars that were instructed with a set of AI algorithms commanding their reactions and movements through the *cavea* of the amphitheatre.[420] The simulation showed some bottlenecks in the structure, which slowed people's movements at critical points, such as at entrances and at the convergence of several paths.[421] Although more tests with different parameters (e.g. higher numbers of avatars, instructed in different ways and with different timings to enter the building) should be made to reach firmer conclusions, this application shows the potential of crowd's simulation for formulating and evaluating hypotheses on how the past built environment was used in a quantitative and controlled way.

---

[412] Gillings 2002, 228.
[413] http://www.ansys.com/
[414] Kormann *et al.* 2016.
[415] Frieman and Gillings 2007.
[416] De Heras Ciechomski *et al.* 2004.
[417] http://www.odeon.dk/
[418] Rindel 2011; Farnetani 2006.
[419] Gutierrez *et al.* 2006. See also Gutierrez, Frischer, Cerezo, Gomez and Sobreviela 2005; Gutierrez, Frischer and Seron 2005.
[420] For a more detailed overview about the components of the system see Gutierrez, Frischer and Seron 2005, 56-7.
[421] Gutierrez *et al.* 2006.

The simulation of social behaviour by means of virtual crowds has been exploited also in modern urban planning to evaluate different development scenarios, in order to envisage the most practical solutions for traffic and pedestrian flows.[422] Besides the technical challenges related to handle a complex environment made both by architectural and human components (especially when it comes to real time navigation), the most difficult part regards the modelling of human behaviour, which is complex and not easy to formalize into a set of rules. This problem, which has already been observed for the simulation of virtual crowds in modern urban settings,[423] is intensified when past behaviour has to be simulated, as different social rules, emotional responses to space and memories have surely influenced the way people moved individually and as a crowd.[424]

This observation is part of a broader set of considerations related to the use of 3D digital reconstructions for analysis and simulations, that I will like to add to conclude this section. Such visualizations have to be used as an aid to formulate and test hypotheses on past built environments and use of space, but the fact that these analyses are calculated by a computer and in a 'quantitative' way should obviously not be taken as a guarantee of their reliability. In archaeology, a high degree of 'educated guesses' that have to be introduced in the reconstruction is inevitable from the very nature of archaeological data, which are by definition fragmentary. However, such hypothetical integrations, as well as the quality of the original data, have a great impact on the reliability of the results. For analyses such as lighting simulations and visibility, for example, the position and size of windows, the presence of lost and movable elements such as curtains, folding wooden screens (the Roman *valvae*) or plants, played a great role in preventing or allowing the view and exposition to direct lighting in parts of a house. It must be noted, however, that these problematic aspects do not belong only to 3D reconstructions, but are intrinsically rooted in archaeological practise and emerge also when other analytical techniques, such as GIS or Space Syntax, are applied. These techniques have been originally developed in domains (geography/military and modern urban planning respectively) that deal with complete datasets, and have therefore to be used with care in archaeological contexts. While on the one hand, dealing with a fragmentary dataset is one of the most challenging aspects of 3D reconstructions, on the other hand the employment of such techniques represents also a great advantage. By creating 3D reconstructions that are intellectually transparent, missing information that would remain implicit are made explicit in the visualization. Moreover, different hypotheses can be created and tested, thus making visible the array of possibilities that matches the available dataset.

3.5 DISCUSSION

The overview that I presented in this chapter gives us the opportunity to elaborate on the role that 3D modelling has had so far and will have in the future of archaeological research. The developments in the field of 3D recording techniques, their increased ease of use and their decreased costs have made them a valuable tool in the hand of archaeologists for the digital documentation and analysis of archaeological evidence. 3D reconstructions, on the other hand, have been traditionally used as the digital counterpart of manual drawing to create computer-based illustrations, especially for heritage purposes. Their use has proved to be successful in communicating the past to a large audience in documentaries, museum applications and archaeological sites, but an unbalance is clearly visible between 3D reconstructions used for heritage purposes and those used to explore possible answers to questions in the archaeological domain. The examples that I discussed in the previous section show however that 3D reconstructions can play an important role in research, acting as 'laboratories' where hypotheses are visually and quantitatively formulated, tested and opened for discussion. In this sense, they can provide the ideal

---

[422] E.g. Aschwanden *et al.* 2009.
[423] Aschwanden 2014, 4.
[424] See at this respect Merlo 2004.

platform to bridge data interpretation and public outreach. They can be in fact used initially as research tools to analyse the available datasets, explore and compare possible models, and then employed as a visual and approachable means to communicate the results of this process to a larger public.

As was shown in this chapter, the critiques related to the authenticity of 3D reconstructions and the lack of instruments to assess their reliability are being dealt with by developing ways to make explicit the initial data and the interpretations. Their impact as research tools has been instead not much explored. With computers having conquered in various degrees even the more conservative archaeologist, the reason why 3D reconstructions of (partially) lost architecture still struggle to be seen as tools that can be used for analytical purposes, besides their value for heritage presentation, cannot be ascribed anymore only to the 'luddism of old-style archaeologists'.[425] In investigating the reasons why the interpretative and analytical value of 3D reconstructions has been so far exploited only in a few projects, I would like to draw the attention to two interrelated aspects that play a crucial role, namely the role of archaeologists in the creation process and the perceived correspondence between realistic renderings and accuracy.

When 3D reconstructions are created for heritage communication, there are few requirements that are usually sought after to meet the public's high expectations, such as a high visual impact and a smooth interactive experience. To reach these goals, the development of these applications is usually assigned to professionals that are called in when the archaeological research and the interpretation of the archaeological evidence are already completed. At this stage, the computer graphics studio entrusted with the creation of the 3D reconstruction (however knowledgeable about archaeology) is rarely in the position to engage deeper with the archaeological evidence, also from the constraints posed by deadlines and production costs. For this reason, questions that arise during the 3D reconstruction process (such as: What was the original colour? Which height should be estimated for the building giving the width of the preserved walls? What are the roofing configurations that are possible for this building? Is this reconstruction feasible? What are possible alternatives?) are therefore often overlooked.

The traditional identification with 3D reconstructions as heritage visualization tools and their creation entrusted to dedicated team of graphics designers have prevented a larger experimentation and exploration of these techniques for research purposes and as heuristic research tools in academia. With few exceptions, little attention has been dedicated to include 3D modelling techniques as topics within university curricula (and in fact many archaeologists-3D modellers are still nowadays self-taught, despite early calls for the creation of a new field of practitioners).[426] Dedicated summer schools and extra-curricular courses include overviews of the main techniques for 3D modelling applied to archaeology, but rarely the analytical possibilities of these tools are explored, as the time available is limited and the focus is usually on heritage valorisation. This combination of factors risks however to perpetuate the situation that was already noted during the 1990s, namely that computer-based visualizations of archaeological sites have been traditionally used as show-cases for technological advances, all too often with little archaeological value.[427] Archaeologists have therefore to play a key role within the team of experts to guarantee the scientific quality of the result.[428] To do so, however, they should be equipped with an adequate general knowledge in the field of digital technologies to guide the creation process and interact in a fruitful way with IT specialists.

As the overview of case studies, that successfully employed 3D reconstructions in formulating archaeologically meaningful hypotheses, shows, 3D modelling cannot be narrowed down to a simple 'press-button' approach. Such applications require in fact both a deep understanding of the possibilities

---

[425] See Ratto 2009, citing Niccolucci 2002, 46.
[426] Frischer *et al.* 2002.
[427] Miller and Richards 1995.
[428] Wittur discusses the often problematic collaboration between archaeologists and technicians (Wittur 2013, 36-7).

and limitations of the currently available software packages (looking also at domains other than strictly archaeology), and the capability to develop new solutions from scratch if necessary in order to develop the most appropriate workflow for the specific project requirements. Moreover, the fast evolving field of digital technologies and the complexity related to the creation of some virtual reconstructions require the inclusion of skilled modellers, programmers and technicians that are specialized in developing *ad hoc* solutions. This is especially true if such virtual experiences are meant for the public and heritage valorisation, as visitors' expectations are high in terms of the quality of visuals and the easiness of interaction.[429]

Only when archaeologists develop competencies in 3D modelling tools, will they be able to assess more profoundly the role that the creation of a 3D model, whether a digital replica, a 3D reconstruction or a 3D GIS, can play within their research and will be able to see beyond their use as a visualization aid, but transform them into effective research tools. In the future, when archaeologists will be more aware of the potential of these techniques, 3D scientific visualizations will find their place as platforms for discussion within archaeology as they do already in other domains. The view by Gordin, that 'Images are useful in that they address the common problem whereby people often 'talk past one another', that is, they disagree but do not have any easy way to resolve their differences because they have no common basis around which to make meaning'[430] can be extended also to 3D reconstructions. To this end, however, archaeologists still need to develop visual literacy and train their spatial thinking, which will allow them to use and effectively interpret 3D models.[431]

In this panorama of fast changing technologies, academia should be the place in which these digital tools are taught and experimented with. This requires certainly an interdisciplinary collaboration with experts in complementary fields to provide an up to date knowledge of techniques and software packages to students. An interesting parallel can be established with the use of GIS, which in 1995, Goodchild lamented was used 'as little more than a mapping system',[432] echoed some years later by Stoter and Zlatanova in relation to the path that 3D GIS was undertaking.[433] Since Goodchild's remark, researchers have become more familiar with the analytical possibilities of GIS, which resulted in an increased use of this environment not only for overlaying different data sources, but also for analysis. Likewise, 3D visualizations will start to be increasingly used not just for visualization purposes, but also as analytical tools.

In this chapter, I hope to have demonstrated that 3D modelling techniques have earned a place as research tools within the archaeologists' toolbox. The future developments of 3D reconstructions in archaeology are however in the hand of researchers. Only through a larger experimentation, can new methodologies be developed or existing methods adapted to help archaeological interpretation. 3D models can become the equivalent of today's databases: an index that organizes in a spatial way the data and related hypotheses on the site, which will be considered as the embodiment of multidisciplinary research and a laboratory where to formulate hypotheses and make explicit one's assumption on the past. More work is to be done however towards content curation and the development of transparent, unobtrusive technologies in order for the content to be fully appreciated.

In this process, a more mature approach to 3D archaeological visualizations will emerge. Researchers will be able to choose the most appropriate tools and the visualization types (e.g. a more realistic look

---

[429] See recent user experience studies on VR museum installations, such as Ray and van der Vaart 2013.
[430] Gordin 1997, 36.
[431] These observations are common in other domains, such as in biochemistry where visual models are used as teaching material (see e.g. Schönborn and Anderson 2009; K.J. Schönborn and Anderson 2010).
[432] Goodchild 1995, 46.
[433] Stoter and Zlatanova 2003.

or a more conceptual rendering) calibrated to the aims of their project. While one may argue that a realistic looking rendering is still to be preferred if the final aim is to present the 3D reconstruction to the public, other, more schematic and simple to achieve visualization types can be more appropriate for analytical purposes. As demonstrated in the project ARCHAVE, for example, the textured model of the surviving architectural ruins was considered to be distracting for the purpose of analysing the finds, and therefore the architecture was instead rendered with grey colour.[434] In this way, the demand for realism, often lamented as being taken as a sign of an accurate and trustworthy 3D reconstruction, will become less cogent.

---

[434] Acevedo *et al.* 2001.

4. The ancient town of Koroneia:
Geographical context, historical background and synthesis of the preliminary results by the Boeotia survey

> 'Now Coroneia is situated on a height near Helicon. The Boeotians took possession of it on their return from the Thessalian Arne after the Trojan War, at which time they also occupied Orchomenus. And when they got the mastery of Coroneia, they built in the plain before the city the temple of the Itonian Athena, bearing the same name as the Thessalian temple; and they called the river which flowed past it Cuarius, giving it the same name as the Thessalian river. But Alcaeus calls it Coralius, when he says, 'Athena, warrior queen, who dost keep watch o'er the cornfields of Coroneia before thy temple on the banks of the Coralius River.' Here, too, the Pan-boeotian Festival used to be celebrated. And for some mystic reason, as they say, a statue of Hades was dedicated along with that of Athena'. (Strabo, 9.2)

4.1. Introduction

In this chapter I discuss the currently available data on the multi-period urban site of Koroneia in Boeotia. First, I will present the geographical and historical background of the site, then all the previous research conducted on the hill and nearby related sites, and lastly an overview of the currently available survey data and of their interpretation. This chapter is closely linked with chapter 5, which discusses the development of Graeco-Roman towns from the Archaic period to Late Antiquity, providing thus the framework for the interpretation of the survey data from Koroneia. The data and interpretations suggested in this chapter will be used to create a 3D GIS of this site, which comprises both the visualization of the raw data and the reconstruction hypotheses as will be described in more detail in chapter 6. Chapter 4 and 5 contribute therefore to the creation of an intellectual transparent 3D visualization, by thoroughly discussing both the data and the comparative material that I used for the reconstruction of the urban layout.

4.2. Koroneia: Geographical context and historical background

Koroneia (Figure 4.1) lies on a hill (ca. 277 msl) on the spurs of Mount Helicon, which is surrounded by two streams, the Phalaros/Pontza river to the west and the Kyarios/Kakaris river to the east. In antiquity Koroneia overlooked former Lake Kopaïs, drained in the 19th century AD to make space for agricultural land (Figure 4.2). The hill on which the settlement was established is situated at a strategical location on the communication axis between northern and southern Greece, and controlled the road between eastern and western Boeotia. The territory of the *polis* extended to about 95 km^2,[435] and according to Ephorus comprised the valley of Hermaion, the fortress of Metachoion situated between Koroneia and Orchomenos and the sanctuary of Athena Itonia.[436] A survey of the findings in the territory around Koroneia, including a boundary inscription (AE1671) between Koroneia and Levadeia found at the north-east foot of the Granitsa/Laphystion, has established the possible extent of Koroneia's *chora* (see Figure 4.3).[437]

---

[435] Fossey 1988, 322.
[436] Ephorus, *FGrHist* 70, fr. 94a in Hansen 1996, 91. For a detailed contextualization of Koroneia in its territory, see Farinetti 2009, 67-88.
[437] Farinetti 2009.

4. THE ANCIENT TOWN OF KORONEIA

Figure 4.1 Koroneia's hill viewed from south-west (top: from Bintliff et al. 2009, 18; bottom: photo taken by D. Grosman during an exploratory flight in 2009).

Figure 4.2 The large plain once occupied by Lake Copais, north of Koroneia's hill (picture taken by the author on Koroneia's acropolis).

The hill shows traces of occupation from Prehistory up to the 14th century AD when the site was abandoned and the nearby village of Agios Georgios was founded. There is no evidence to securely anchor Koroneia's foundation to a certain set of events, nor to identify the first settlers. Textual evidence provides us with some elements in which historical memory, legends and myths intertwine, as usual for foundation stories.[438] Strabo, while listing the names of the towns which are mentioned in Homer's Catalogue of Ships (*Il.* 2.503), recounts the myth that the Boiotoi[439] took possession of Koroneia on their return from Arne, in Thessaly, after the Trojan War (Strabo 9.2.29). Several ancient sources agree that the Boiotoi resided in Thessaly, and especially in the land around Arne, before migrating to the area later called Boeotia.[440] Pausanias, with his usual attention for the mythical past of Greek towns, ascribed the foundation of Koroneia to Koronos, brother of Haliartos (Paus. 34.7-8). Interestingly, an inscription (IG VII 2873 = E.77.83), dated to the 1st century BC and found at the village of Solinari, bears a dedication by Heras Castricius, son or freedman of Aulus Castricius, of a temple and doors to one Koronios, who according to Frazer is indeed to be identified with the supposed founder of Koroneia.[441] If this is the case, this evidence would attest the presence of a monument dedicated to the *oikist* in the town.

---

[438] See the analysis of foundation stories by J. Hall (Hall 2008).
[439] Boiotoi is the tribal name of the Thessalian tribe that took later possession of Boeotia (see Buck 1979, 75).
[440] Buck 1979, 75.
[441] Frazer 1913, 173. This inscription is also a testimony of the presence of the Roman/Italian family of the Castricii, who are attested especially in the region of Thespiai; one Aulus Castricius Aulii filius is mentioned in one of the victors' lists at the Pan-Boeotian festival (*IG* 7.2871), he was a Roman/Italian resident of Boeotia and perhaps even of Koroneia (Schachter 1981, 126).

4. THE ANCIENT TOWN OF KORONEIA

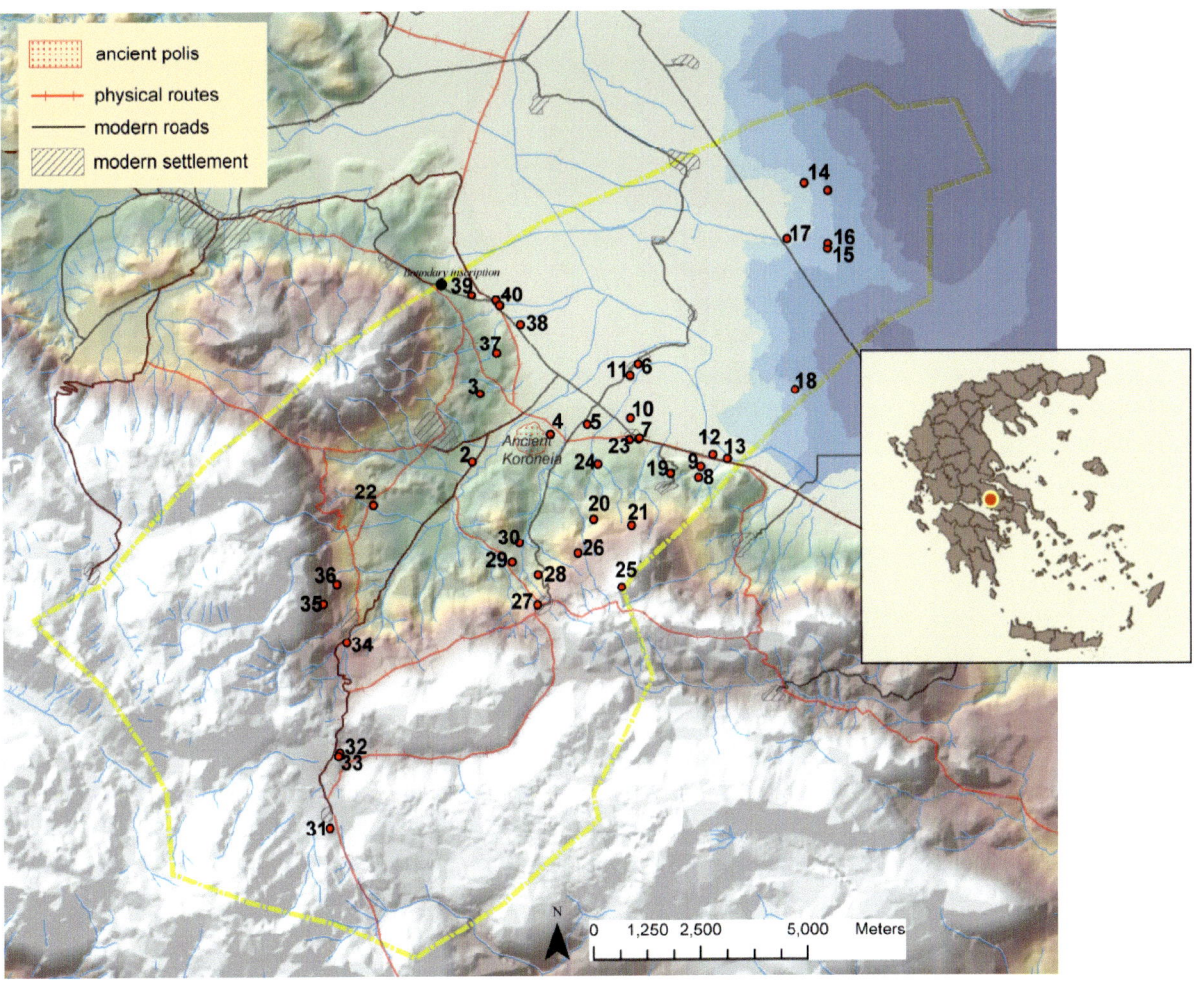

Figure 4.3 Topographical map showing the location of ancient Koroneia in respect to Greece, its territory (bordered by a yellow dashed line), and surrounding sites (modified after Farinetti 2009, Appendix I.1, 1). Sites mentioned in the text: 4) Palaia Koroneia North – Spyropoulos' excavations; 5) Thymari; 6) Mamoura/Alalkomenai; 7) Agoriani/Agia Paraskevi; 8) Alalkomenai; 21-22) Sanctuary of Herakles Charops; 22) Pontza – Agioi Taxiarchoi; 30) Butsurati.

Ancient sources mention Koroneia especially in relation to the sanctuary of Athena Itonia. In this place, the most important Pan-Boeotian festival was celebrated in honour of the goddess (Paus. 34.1) and the representatives of the Boeotian *koinon* (confederacy) met to decide on the League's affairs.[442] The importance of the cult of Athena for the Koroneians is evidenced also by the fact that the civic symbols of Koroneia, chosen to be struck on the reverse of the coins issued by the *polis*, were the bust of Athena with helmet and the apotropaic Gorgoneion that the goddess wore on her chiton. On the obverse, we find the typical eight-shaped Boeotian shield, a common mark of the *poleis* which were part of the Boeotian League.[443]

---

[442] Coins attest the existence of a cooperative coinage in the last quarter of the 6th century by three Boeotian poleis (Thebes, Tanagra, and Hyettos or possibly Haliartos), followed by another four (Akraiphia, Koroneia, Mykalessos, and Pharai) shortly after the first issues, and allow us to follow the evolution of the *koinon* from a power structure that operated mostly regionally during the 5th century (to sustain common expenses related to military operations, ships and temple building), to a cooperation that expanded to comprise a larger compass in the 4th century BC (including Thessaly, Elis, Khalkidiki and Arkadia). See Mackil and van Alfen 2006.

[443] The issuing of coins on the Aeginetan standard bearing these symbols was not continuous at Koroneia, but confined to the following periods: 500-480; during the years ca. 456-46; between the King's Peace in 387 (or earlier) and the Peace of Sparta in

The earliest source on the Itonion is the 7th century BC poet Alcaeus who mentions the location of Athena's temple and her altar 'by the banks of the river Korialios' (fr. 147), testifying to the existence of this cult already in the Archaic period. According to Strabo the sanctuary was built in the plain in front of the city shortly after the Boiotoi from Arne took possession of Koroneia. With the aim to recreate a familiar topography, the new settlers dedicated the temple to Athena Itonia, the goddess to which a sanctuary was dedicated at Arne, and gave the same name of the river in Thessaly to the river flowing alongside the temple (Strabo 9.2.29).[444] As will be discussed in more detail below in a dedicated section, several possible candidates have been suggested, but the location of this sanctuary has not been yet identified with certainty.

A further proof of the strategic importance of Koroneia is the fact that two battles of the Greek city-state wars were fought in the plain to the north of the *polis*, in 447 and in 394 BC, both bringing important consequences for the power balance in Greece. The first battle, fought between the Athenians led by the general Tolmides and the Boeotian forces during the First Peloponnesian War, concluded with the defeat of the Athenians, who left Boeotia and made peace to have their prisoners released (Thuc. 1.113.2-4; Diod. 12.6). The end of the Athenian control in Boeotia boosted Thebes' hegemonic control of the Boeotian *koinon*. The battle of 394 BC was fought during the Corinthian War and saw as main opponents the Thebans and their allies confronting and losing against the Spartans and their allies under King Agesilaus II. The battle was bloody, with many fallen on both sides, as the eye-witness Xenophon recounts (Xen. *Hell.* 4.3.16-21), and a number of soldiers of the Theban forces sought refuge in the sanctuary of Athena, which was near the battlefield according to Xenophon (Xen. *Hell.* 4.3.20).[445]

The fact that Koroneia was positioned near the route that connected southern and northern Greece made this site an appealing conquest for enemies, such as the Phokian general Onomarchos, who succeeded in taking control of Koroneia (together with Orchomenos and Chorsiai) during the Third Sacred War against Thebes (356-346 BC). Diodorus Siculus describes the three cities held by the Phokians as 'strongly fortified' at the moment of their conquest and as the starting point for their pillaging of the Boeotian territory (Diod. 16.58.1). The Phokian stronghold that was established on Koroneia's acropolis did not last long as Philip of Macedon reconquered the city and handed it over to Thebes in 346 BC. It is in relation to this episode that a destruction and subsequent rebuilding of some parts of the *polis* might have occurred. The Thebans in fact punished the town with an *andrapodismos* (Dem. 5.22; 6.13; 19.112, 325), a form of heavy punishment that entails the enslavement of the inhabitants and often the partial destruction of the urban centre.[446] The town, however, must have been resettled quite quickly since a Koroneian citizen is indicated as one of the Boeotian *tamiai* (treasurers) in Delphi in 337/6 (*CID* II 74.50).[447]

After this episode, we find Koroneia mentioned again in Roman sources as one of the Boeotian cities that strongly opposed the Romans. According to Livy, the murder of the anti-Roman Boeotian politician Brachyllas, committed in 196 BC by Zeuxippus and other supporters of the Roman party (with the likely involvement of the Roman commander Flamininus) had been the initial trigger for the tensions and retaliations between Romans and Boeotians (Livy 33.29.1). Livy refers to many murders of Roman soldiers perpetrated by the Boeotians in the Kopaic swamps and to other crimes that had been committed especially at Akraephia and Koroneia (Livy 33.29.6).

---

374 BC; after 338 BC when the battle of Chaeronea signed the defeat of Thebes and a consequent greater poleis autonomy; and in the early Hellenistic period when Demetrios Poliorketes was in control of Boeotia (Hansen 1996, 91; Lagos 2001, 5-6).
[444] On Athena Itonia in Thessaly, see Graninger 2011, 43-86.
[445] For an account of the battle and a discussion on its possible topographical location, see Buckler and Beck 2008, 59-70.
[446] Hansen 2000, 150.
[447] Hansen 1996, 91.

In a following episode, the situation was exacerbated in 191 BC when Livy recounts that Roman soldiers encountered a statue of King Antiochus erected in the sanctuary of Athena Itonia at Koroneia, which stirred the resentment of the soldiers who were then granted permission (however short-lasting) to plunder the land around the sanctuary (Livy 36.20.2-4). Some twenty years later, in 172/171 BC, the Koroneians were punished by the Romans who sacked their town, as they had sided with Perseus of Macedon against the Romans, together with Haliartos and Thisbe, during the Third Macedonian War (172-168 BC). Following the events of 172/1 BC, the Romans dismantled the Boeotian confederacy, which accordingly marked the disappearance of federal magistrates, such as the Boeotarchs, and of the federal assembly.[448] A fragment of a *Senatus Consultum* on Koroneia,[449] inscribed on a broken white marble stele and kept at the Thebes museum, resembles the surviving *Senatus Consultum Thisbaeum* dated to 170 BC, listing the decisions of the Roman senate regarding Thisbe and mentioning Koroneia as having been treated in a similar way.[450] At Thisbe, the decisions include that Thisbe's *chora*, which had become ager public after the city surrendered, was to be returned to the *polis*; that exclusively the members of the pro-Roman party were granted the right to cover magistracies for the next ten years; that the pro-Roman party was given permission to refortify the acropolis and live there; that the decision whether the anti-Roman party had to be held in detention was left to the praetor Q. Maenius.[451] From the surviving remains of the inscription regarding Koroneia, Sherk deduces that the pro-Roman citizens had been forced to leave and all their properties had been confiscated while the city was held by the pro-Macedonian party. The exiled pro-Roman supporters must have sent an embassy to Rome after the Roman victory, thus obtaining this decree. The fragmentary remains bear the Senate's decisions that all of the possessions of the members of the pro-Roman party had to be returned to them and seem to establish the right of the pro-Roman supporters to fortify the acropolis and settle there.[452] From these documents, we can therefore suppose that at Koroneia, similarly to Thisbe, the Romans aimed to protect their supporters and leave the town in their control.

A glimpse of the cultural life of the town a couple of decades after the resettling is offered by a mid-2nd century BC *proxeny* decree in honour of the composer of tragedies and plays Zotion, son of Zotion of Ephesos, which attests two visits that this travelling artist paid to Koroneia.[453] The poet is said to have 'presented recitals of his poetical works, and in commemorating our *polis* and Athena who more than others has ruled the *polis* from its beginning, he has had popular success'.[454] For this reason, he was honoured with 70 drachmas in silver, the concession of the *proxenia* (a formal status of friendship between a non-citizen and the *polis*) to him and his descendants, and a crown of olive. The inscription concludes with the order to the *polemarchs* to inscribe the decree 'in the most prominent place' (*epiphanestatos topos*) of the town. As there is no provision to supply a new stele, but only to inscribe the content of the decree, an existing monument must have been used conforming to the standard procedure. However, since this text was the only one on the stone and the space below was not inscribed, Schachter and Slater suggest that a recently erected monument must have been chosen, perhaps related with the above mentioned fortifications that the Romans allowed on the acropolis in 170 BC.[455] It must be noted, however, that the formula '*epiphanestatos topos*' that is used in this decree and is common in honorific inscriptions, is problematic for the identification of the 'most visible place' in a town. It may indicate

---

[448] The Boeotian confederacy will be restored again under the Romans, but the exact date is still disputed. Recent reinterpretation of the available evidence situates the foundation of a new *koinon* towards the end of the 1st century BC, see Müller 2014.
[449] The transcription and comment can be found in Maier 1959, 130-1 and Sherk 1969, 32.
[450] I have cited these documents also in chapter 5, p. 219.
[451] See Sherk 1969, 30-1.
[452] Maier 1959, 128-9 and Sherk 1969, 32-3.
[453] Further reference to this phenomenon is given in chapter 5, p. 211.
[454] The inscription, found by Pappadakis at the monastery of Agioi Taxiarches (Pontza) and published by him in 1927, has been re-examined and discussed in Schachter and Slater 2007.
[455] Schachter and Slater 2007, 87.

in fact a variety of locations,[456] including a spot on the agora (as the grave of Dionysos of Miletus in the agora of Ephesos),[457] or within a sanctuary. Therefore, the building onto which this inscription was engraved could have been, for example, also a (newly erected) monument in the market place of Koroneia.

The relationship between Koroneia and the Romans improved during the Imperial period. A number of inscribed letters from the emperors to the city testifies in fact to their euergetism in financing the construction of an aqueduct under Hadrian and works to channel the rivers flowing into Lake Kopaïs that were flooding agricultural land, as well as intervening in a boundary dispute with neighbouring Thisbe and in a conflict with Orchomenos.[458] Transcripts of these letters were inscribed on the wall of some major buildings during the second half of the 2nd century AD, the *terminus post quem* being given by the latest inscription, dated to 161 AD.[459] The blocks with inscriptions were reused in modern times to construct the church of Agioi Taxiarkoi at Pontza, north of the modern village of Agios Georgios, where they were discovered in the late 1910s by Pappadakis, but published only in the early 1980s by Fossey.[460]

Among the literary sources that give us a glimpse of ancient Koroneia during the Roman period is the testimony of the Greek traveller Pausanias. Coming from Asia Minor, he recorded in his book *Periegesis Hellados* (Description of Greece) what he deemed 'most worth remembering' (Paus. 3.11.1) of the cities he visited during his journey through mainland Greece in the mid-2nd century AD. While this book has not received much attention in antiquity,[461] it has had a great influence in modern times. It has been in fact extensively used as a topographical account by antiquarian travellers, and it has continued to be used as a proxy to interpret archaeological remains, often guiding the selection of the archaeological remains to be uncovered and presented to the public.[462] Scholars' opinions about the reliability of Pausanias' observations vary, many having focussed more on his limitations than on his merits and questioning his criteria of selection of the elements he chose to write about. Recent studies, however, have analysed Pausanias' work as a description of a cultural (more than an actual) landscape, highlighting its value as a constructed vision mediated by the author.[463] In this view, Pausanias aimed to reconnect the currently Roman ruled Greece with its now perceived distant past, by choosing to remember those elements that were related with religious practises, especially those pre-dating the Roman present, and focusing on the moments in Greek history when the Greeks were united and fought for their freedom, thus emphasizing a sense of Greek identity.[464] As Stewart phrased it, Pausanias' work is therefore 'less a guidebook to Greece than it is a guidebook to Greekness'.[465]

In his description of Koroneia, not surprisingly, Pausanias focuses on religious monuments and rituals. He in fact describes 'two remarkable things' that he had seen in the agora: an altar dedicated to Hermes Epimelius (the keeper of flocks) and an altar of the Winds. The reason why Pausanias considered these two structures remarkable and worth mentioning is not explained. In line with Pausanias' aims that I briefly discussed above, one hypothesis could be that these elements were selected as their appearance made them stand out from other altars that he had previously seen or because they represented important

---

[456] See e.g. Ma 2013, esp. 68-9.
[457] This passage is mentioned in chapter 5, p. 179.
[458] Fossey, 1981-2; Fossey, 1979.
[459] Fossey 1981-2; Fossey 1990, 239-40.
[460] Fossey 1981-82.
[461] The earliest evidence that the book was read is in fact dated 350 years after Pausanias' death, when Stephanus of Byzantium used it to include the name of Greek cities and their ethnics for his geographical dictionary *Ethnika* (Habicht 1998, 1).
[462] Pretzler 2007, 139-40; for a critique on Pausanias' use, see Alcock 1995.
[463] Habicht 1998 (1985); Veyne 1988; Stewart 2013.
[464] Stewart 2013.
[465] Stewart 2013, 245.

elements for the life of the town. In this regard, it might be worth adding that while surveying the hill, we noticed the difference that a northern breeze made to the perceived temperature especially in the hot summer months. It is therefore possible that winds were particularly important for the wellbeing of the town population in antiquity to such an extent to justify the construction of an altar to propitiate them.

Besides the altars on the agora, Pausanias mentions also a sanctuary of Hera which he vaguely located 'a little lower down' (Paus. 9.34.3). It is not clear therefore whether he implied that the sanctuary was located on the lower terrace of the agora, or further downslope. The cult of Hera must long predate Pausanias' visit as he reports that within the sanctuary there was an ancient image, the work of Pythodorus of Thebes, in which the goddess carried Sirens in her hands. According to Pausanias this presence recalls the singing contest that Hera had initiated between the Sirens and the Muses. The association with sirens is related to the chthonic aspect of the cult of Hera, which could hint at a peripheral location of her sanctuary close to the boundary of the (Archaic) city. The archaeological investigations conducted so far have not yielded evidence pointing towards the secure identification of any of the monuments mentioned by Pausanias.

Historical sources do not give us much information about the city in Late Antiquity, but they record that a bishopric was established at Koroneia in the 5th century AD. The first attested bishop of Koroneia, Agathocles, is in fact listed as one of the participants in the Third Ecumenical Council at Ephesos in 431,[466] while Aphobios of Koroneia was one of the signatories of the letter to Emperor Leo in 458, together with other bishops who participated in the Council of Corinth, and was also present at a bishops' council in Constantinople in 459.[467]

In the middle of the 6th century AD, the life of the city may have come to an abrupt end, as Procopius informs us that Koroneia and other cities were destroyed by a number of exceptionally strong earthquakes, which hit Greece in 551 AD.[468] While it is possible that a small community inhabited Koroneia in the Early Byzantine period, the next evidence of habitation on the hill is represented by a halo of Middle and Late Byzantine pottery finds below the remains of the Frankish tower located on a small eminence on its north-eastern side (Figure 4.4).[469] These findings identify the presence of a small village, with the tower aiming at controlling the resident peasants, similarly to the other Frankish towers in Central Greece.[470]

Koroneia is mentioned again as a bishopric in later sources, specifically in the *Notitiae Episcopatuum*, a series of documents shedding light on the Eastern Church's hierarchy. In the list contained in *Notitia* 3 (ca. 754 AD), Koroneia's bishopric appears at the 23rd place as subordinate to the metropolitan of Athens. *Notitiae* 7, 9, 10 and 13 also mentions a bishopric at Koroneia, which was under the jurisdiction of the Athenian metropolis.[471] Kountoura-Galaki, however, warns about the reliability of the list contained in the *Notitiae* 3. The bishoprics seem in fact too many – 39 in total under the metropolitan of

---

[466] Kardaras 2011.
[467] Kardaras 2011.
[468] 'It was at this time that extraordinary earthquakes occurred throughout Greece, both Boeotia and Achaea and the country on the Crisaean Gulf being badly shaken. And countless towns and eight cities were levelled to the ground, among which were Chaeronea and Coronea and Patrae and all of Naupactus, where there was also great loss of life' (Proc., *Bell. Goth.* VIII, 25.17, English translation by H.B. Dewing).
[469] Bintliff *et al.* 2013, 15. The tower is described in Lock 1986, 117.
[470] Lock argued in fact that the towers in Central Greece were located for one reason on the sites of prehistoric or classical settlements, i.e. for the convenience offered by the accessibility to water sources and building materials, and did not have a regional strategic purpose as they were not visually connected with each other, contrary to the Venetian towers on Euboea (see Lock 1986, 102-3).
[471] Kardaras 2011.

Figure 4.4 The Frankish tower on the small eminence north-east of Koroneia's hill (picture taken by the author from the lower northern slope of the hill looking south-east).

Athens, while other evidence suggests that under Michail Choniatis (1182-1204) the metropolis had 10 bishoprics, and the whole of Greece would have had about 25.[472] The numerous spelling mistakes that were made in writing down the name of the Greek bishoprics (e.g. Koroneia was written as 'Κοπονίας', clearly confusing the Greek 'ρ' (rho) for a Latin 'p') suggests that the copyist, who did not possess much knowledge of the region, possibly relied on some Latin catalogue listing the existing Greek cities with (badly translated) Latin names. Given the small community living on the hill, it seems very unlikely that a bishop resided on Koroneia's hill after the 6th century. The title of bishop of Koroneia was however maintained, but his residence was at Granitsa, on the mountain west of Koroneia, as we learn from the accounts of 17th and 18th century travellers.[473]

In modern times, agricultural and construction works have greatly modified the hill and disturbed the archaeological remains. Moreover, worked blocks lying on the hill have been in large parts removed and must have been re-used as readily available material in modern buildings in nearby villages. The ancient remains seen by 19th century antiquarians, such as William Gell and William Martin Leake, on Koroneia's hill were in fact much more abundant than what we have recorded during the several campaigns of the project, as we can gather from the accounts of their journeys. Coming from Kalamachi to the west, where near the mills he supposed to have recognised the stadium of the pan-Boeotian festival in a large hollow, Gell reports for example the existence of two towers, one to his right and one to his left when reaching Koroneia's hill. On the north-east of the hill and above the left tower, he observed the existence of a hollow, perhaps, he says, the site of the theatre.[474] This gives us the

---

[472] Kountoura-Galaki 1996, 35-73, esp. 66.
[473] Wheler and Spon 1689, 7; Leake 1835, 133.
[474] Gell 1819, 150.

indication that besides the Frankish tower, which is nowadays still standing as already mentioned, there was another standing tower on the western side of the hill. Moreover, Gell recounts that he saw 'many marbles and inscriptions' where the supposed theatre lies,[475] a further signal of the numerous archaeological traces that have been removed from the hill.

Also the existence of churches on the hill, now completely lost, is attested to both by Gell, who mentions one ruined chapel near a fountain on the north-east side of the hill where there were also sepulchral inscriptions,[476] and by Leake, who adds another two on the south-east of the hill to the one already mentioned by Gell.[477] According to Leake, these three ruined churches were constructed using ancient blocks. At this stage, there is no evidence to suggest a precise and secure location (but see below in the discussion of the survey results for some possible candidates), and a date for the construction of these churches. Available data from Boeotia and other regions of Greece show that churches were very sparse and erected in and around major centres during the Early Byzantine period, and only a few are attested for the early Middle Byzantine era, while during the 11th, 12th and 13th centuries (the last marking the beginning of the Frankish occupation in Greece) a peak in church architecture is evidenced.[478] The three churches at Koroneia are therefore likely to have been erected during the late Middle Byzantine or Frankish period, and in fact, it is reasonable to conclude that the church that Leake said to have seen below the Frankish tower belonged to the above mentioned nearby Byzantine village. Besides offering further evidence for what was still standing at Koroneia, these accounts testify also to the large amount of architectural elements that have been removed from the hill and dispersed in nearby villages to be reused in other buildings or for the construction of infrastructures.

Nowadays, the name of Koroneia designates a village which is situated some kilometres south from the hill on the northern foot of Helikon mountain. Modern Koroneia was called Koutoumoulas before 1915 when its toponym was changed in the process of Hellenization started soon after the Greek independence. The original name recalls its origin as an Albanian-Arvanitic settlement established around 1400 AD, which had therefore no connection with ancient Koroneia; it is likely that the descendants of ancient Koroneia fled instead to the village of Agios Georgios, which indeed results as one of the few Greek villages in the first Ottoman tax register.[479] The hill where ancient Koroneia used to lie is known in the nearby villages by the name of *Pyrgos* (tower) or *Loutrò* (bath). While the former toponym is easily explained by the presence of the Frankish tower, the latter has been related with the belief of the inhabitants that the remains of the vaulted building on the acropolis belonged to a bathhouse.[480] The surveying of this structure by the Boeotia survey team has disproved the identification with a bathhouse, pointing instead towards an elite mansion (see below). The origin of this toponym might also keep the memory of the presence of water on the hill that was brought from the nearby Butsurati ridge by an aqueduct financed by the Emperor Hadrian (see below, pp. 99-101).

4.3 Previous research at Koroneia

The several inscriptions found around Koroneia soon caught the attention of scholars. In 1916 Nikolaos Pappadakis brought to public attention the numerous manumission decrees that attest to the cult of Herakles Charops at Koroneia and suggested a possible location for its sanctuary in the vicinity of

---

[475] Gell 1819, 150.
[476] Gell 1819, 151.
[477] Leake 1835, 134: 'There are several sources of water on the same side of the hill [i.e. south-east], many pieces of ancient squared stones in two ruined churches, and a third church, just below a ruined tower of lower Greek or Frank construction (...)'.
[478] Bintliff 2012, 391.
[479] Bintliff 2011.
[480] Bintliff 2011.

hot springs at Granitsa, north-west of Koroneia's hill.[481] The excavations carried out in the 1970s by Theodoros Spyropoulos at the supposed Itonion in the plain north of the hill were preceded by other small scale investigations that were made in several locations on the hill itself and on nearby sites in the late 1910s and early 1920s. These *sondages* aimed to investigate what kind of archaeological remains lay underneath the ground, targeting especially Classical and Roman traces and have been briefly or not published at all, thus leaving us with little documentation about what kind of artefacts have been brought to light, their exact findspot and what have been taken away from the hill. Certainly, a thorough investigation at the Thebes museum's and nearby local museums' storerooms will rediscover pieces coming from these excavations.[482]

In the late 1910s and early 1920s Pappadakis carried out some excavations on the acropolis and in nearby sites.[483] The earliest one was conducted in 1917-1919 at the ruins of the monastery of Taxiarchoi by one of the sources of the Pontsa/Phalaros river, where he found Byzantine sgraffito wares, Byzantine and Frankish coins, and *spolia* from the ancient town of Koroneia and its *necropoleis*.[484] The report notifies also the discovery of many inscriptions, mostly funerary, but also honorific (Pappadakis mentions in particular some dedicated to Tyche, Silla, Lollianus and Valerianus), among which was also the one recording the resolution in favour of the already mentioned 2nd century BC tragic writer from Ephesos. During these excavations, the five Imperial inscriptions that will be later published by Fossey under the name of Koroneia's city archive were also found. In his report, Pappadakis singled out the inscription on the hydraulic works that were undertaken in the Kopais' region under Hadrian.[485]

In the early 1920s Pappadakis started excavations on Koroneia's hill itself. According to the report in *BCH* 47, a structure was unearthed on the eastern slope, about two-third from the top, in a place where some columns emerged from the ground. Initially thought as being a temple, the construction was then identified as a Christian church made of reused material; Christian tombs were found in its proximity, to the south.[486] Nearby, on a higher spot that according to the report was frequently exploited by the inhabitants of Agios Georgios, Pappadakis claimed to have found the Roman agora: he could follow a 10 m long foundation, possibly a *stoa*, where he found several Roman architectural pieces and three honorific inscriptions, dedicated to Arcadius, Valentinianus (engraved on a reused inscription originally dedicated to Hadrian) and Carus respectively. In a structure identified as a possible cistern (its location is not given in the report, but the structure of the text leads us to suppose that it was possibly on or nearby the identified Roman agora), Pappadakis found moreover a larger than life marble statue missing the head, which for its characteristics and style was interpreted as being of Hadrian. Other finds listed by the report include a relief (of which the find spot is not specified) depicting on one side a person dressed in the *himation* and on the other side a horse, and some bases and funerary stones with engraved names of Koroneians that were found at Agios Athanasios, which were donated to the Museum of the Church of Agia Triada in the village of Agios Georgios. It is possible that the remains of some (late) Roman buildings on the southern-eastern edge of the acropolis that were built using *spolia* (dubbed the 'Scruffy houses' by the team for an easy identification) were uncovered during these campaigns, but one cannot exclude the possibility that they were part of more recent excavations. Unfortunately, I did not find any publication where they are mentioned.

---

[481] Pappadakis 1916, 256-60.
[482] A work of inventarization and publication of inscriptions at Boeotian museums has been initiated by the 9th Ephorate of Prehistoric and Classical Antiquities of Boeotia and the Greek Epigraphical Society, which has already brought to light much forgotten material, see e.g. Kalliontzis 2014.
[483] These excavations have been briefly published in Pappadakis 1919, 34, in a report in *BCH* 47 (1923), 521-2, and are mentioned also in Woodward 1924, 275.
[484] Pappadakis 1919, 34.
[485] Pappadakis 1919, 34.
[486] BCH 47 (1923), 521-2.

In Pappadakis' excavation reports no plans were published, which makes it difficult to locate precisely the remains he mentions and to relate his findings with subsequent investigations and with the Boeotia survey's data which will be discussed below. The earliest map of the hill and of the location of some structures can be found in Maier (see Figure 4.5).[487] Maier indicates A and B as stretches of a polygonal wall made of well adjoining local limestone blocks with rounded edges. As will be discussed below, both A and B have been recorded during the Boeotia survey as acropolis fortifications and are currently still *in situ*. In Maier's plan, C identifies another stretch of wall, this time made of limestone blocks barely worked, that Maier assigns to either the city wall circuit or a retaining wall and that he tentatively relates to a 'piece of town-wall' that was observed by the Scottish anthropologist James George Frazer;[488] there are a few lines of in situ blocks on the eastern side that can correspond to Maier's feature C and that have been recorded during the Boeotia survey (e.g. record 2010_7). Letter D is assigned to the Frankish tower, from which the inscription *IG* VII 2877 with a fragmentary dedication was found. On the plateau east of the acropolis, Maier observed a foundation (E), a column drum provided with well-made channelling and a smooth marble column, which he tentatively related with what the German philologist Ludwig Ross indicated as the possible ruins of a small Doric temple.[489] Structure E in Maier's plan could correspond to the above mentioned Christian church excavated by Pappadakis in the early 1920s.[490]

Moving to the acropolis, the central part was occupied, according to Maier's account, by two at his time already unrecognizable large structures (elements G and H in his map, Figure 4.5). G is briefly described as bearing traces of 'Gußwerk', which indicates a Roman construction technique that make use of concrete, while H is said to have been made of un-mortared limestone. Cultivated fields on the northern and western side of the acropolis have disturbed the archaeological remains, making it difficult to relate the structures observed by Maier and previous travellers with the Boeotia survey's findings. G is in fact nowadays lost, but from Fossey we can gather some further information about the appearance of the structure, which he described as a large square enclosure of which only the lines could be recognized, and having the same orientation as H.[491] The location of H seems to roughly correspond to the collapsed vaulted building that has been surveyed by the Boeotia team (see below), although it must be noted that the characteristics of the building technique do not match Maier's description. Fossey adds further elements that increase our knowledge of the nowadays heavily modified acropolis' appearance in ancient times. He reports in fact that during recent, unpublished excavations extensive remains of Roman buildings were found *in between* the two structures identified by Meier. These remains, of which nothing has survived, were in well-constructed, mortared work, included some reused column blocks and had at least one tessellated floor.[492]

Other sketches of Koroneia and surroundings were drawn by the German topographer Lauffer during his travels around the Kopaic basin which started in 1938 and were published at the end of the 1980s (see Figure 4.6).[493] Lauffer recognized several traces of a Roman aqueduct that reached the town from the south from the ridge of the Megalo and Mikro Butsurati, south of Koroneia's hill. The aqueduct was composed of a ca. 40 cm width channel surrounded on both sides by large stones, resulting in a 1-1.30 m width infrastructure, and exploited the steady gradient offered by the height difference between the top of the Megalo Butsurati (ca. 400 m) and Koroneia's hill (ca. 277 m).[494] The end point of the

---

[487] Maier 1959, 129.
[488] Frazer 1913, 170.
[489] Ross 1851, 32.
[490] This correspondence is made also by Fossey 1990, 238.
[491] Fossey 1990, 237.
[492] Fossey 1990, 237.
[493] Lauffer 1986, 76-82.
[494] Lauffer 1986, 79.

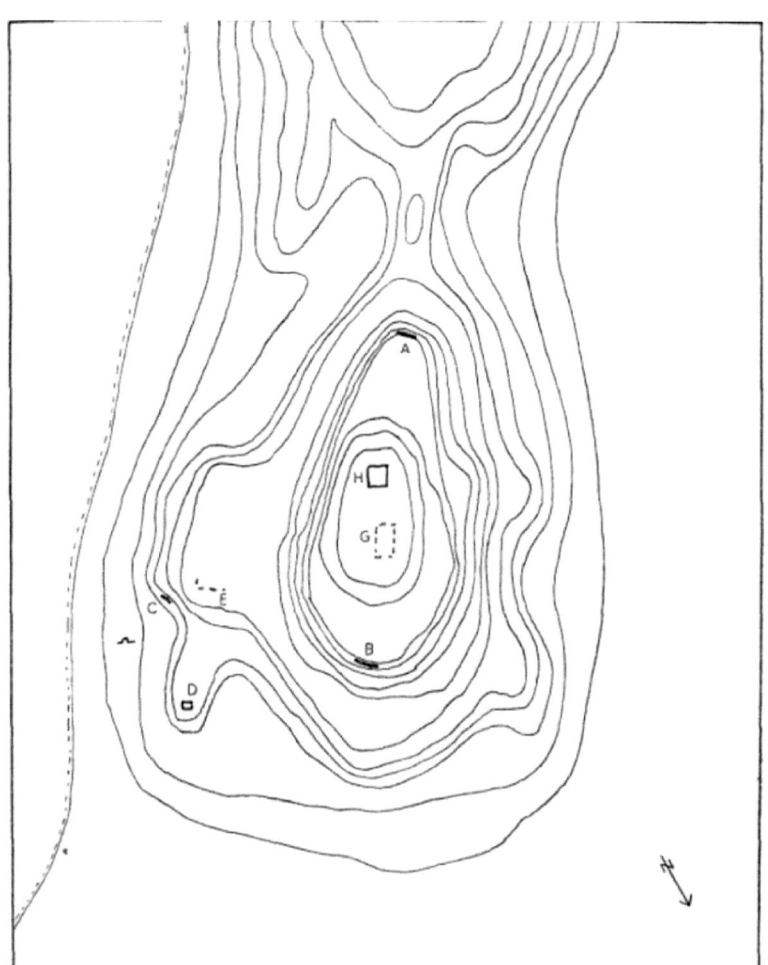

Figure 4.5 Map of Koroneia's hill as published in Maier 1959, 129.

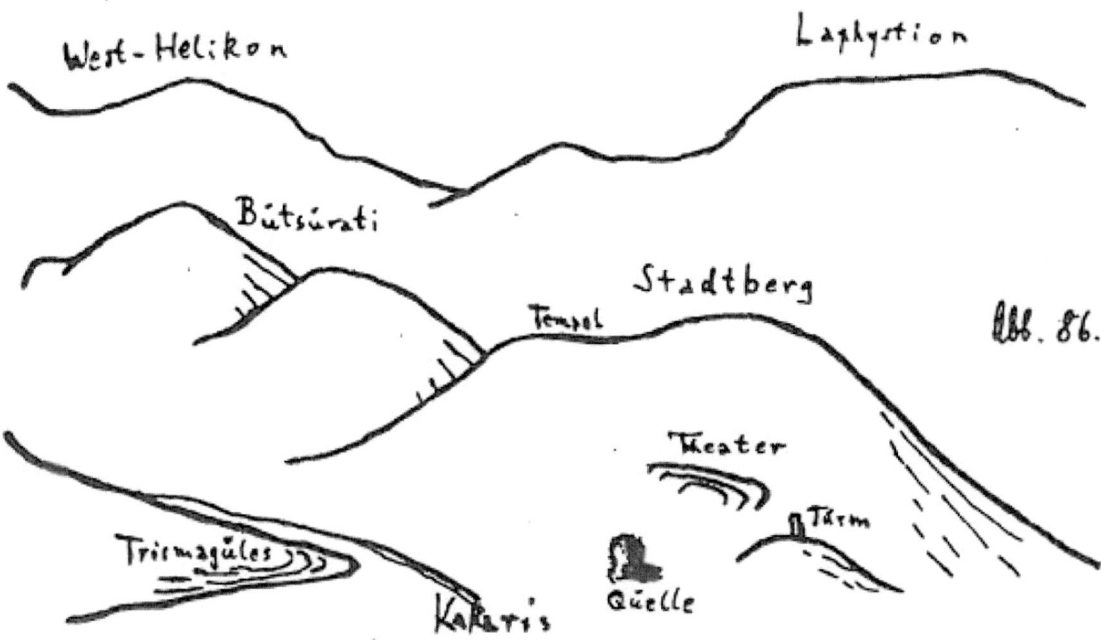

Figure 4.6 Sketch of Koroneia's hill and surrounding by Lauffer (1986, Figure 86, p. 77). Note the drawing of the theatre, the Frankish tower, a spring at the eastern foot of the hill and a temple on a lower terrace from the acropolis.

aqueduct was according to Lauffer the large cistern that Pappadakis discovered on the hill and that contained the larger than life marble statue of Hadrian. All these elements seem therefore to point to the identification of the structure with the aqueduct financed by Hadrian for the town. Furthermore, Lauffer spotted only one water source, a weak spring at the foot of the north-eastern slope, about 150 m south-east from the Frankish tower. Lauffer reported also that many illegal excavations took place on the eastern slope of the hill, resulting in many column pieces, capitals, bases and stelai being exposed and broken. The majority of the diggings, Lauffer recounts, were located between the theatre and the large temple, which he indicates on his sketch as being located on a lower terrace from the acropolis.[495] Unfortunately there is no further description of the temple in the text, which makes it difficult to shed light on Lauffer's identification and on its location, but it is possible that this supposed temple corresponds to Maier's foundation E.

4.3.1 Attested cults during the Classical, Hellenistic and Roman times

As already mentioned, Pausanias records the presence of a sanctuary of Hera and of altars dedicated to Hermes Epimelios and the Winds, none of which have been identified by archaeological investigations. Inscriptions attest the presence of other female cults, such as Demeter Thesmophoros and Arthemis Orthosia during the (Late) Classical – Hellenistic period. Specifically, the inscription *IG* 7.2876 dated to the 4th or 3rd century BC informs us of the repair made by Athanodora, the former priestess of Demeter Thesmophoros, to a *prothyron* (an entrance vestibule) and of her dedication of an *amphithyron* (literally 'having doors on both sides'). Priests and priestesses often funded public buildings, especially in relation to the sanctuaries where they served, and wanted to be commemorated by dedicatory inscriptions remembering their works affixed on public buildings.[496] As Schachter already pointed out, this inscription hints at the existence of a temple dedicated to the goddess and of the celebration of the Thesmophoria at Koroneia.[497] Based on comparisons with other sites where Demeter's sanctuary has been excavated and given the ritual connected with the religious festival of the Thesmophoria, we can suggest a location which was distant and secluded from the town centre. At present, however, there is no archaeological evidence from Koroneia that can tie Demeter's temple to a specific location, and that can therefore justify any speculation.

To Arthemis Orthosia was dedicated a statue of the former priestess Periklia by her father, as inscribed in the inscription E.77.06, dated to the 3rd century BC. Studies on the location of priestly statues during the Hellenistic and Roman times show that generally statues of priestesses were set up within or close to sanctuaries (not inside the temple itself, but close to its entrance or to the entrance of the sanctuary) and not in *agorai*.[498] We can suppose that the statue of Periklia stood therefore in the vicinity of the sanctuary of Artemis, but similarly to Demeter's sanctuary, there is no evidence for the location of the cult of Artemis at Koroneia. As will be discussed in chapter 5, Artemis being the goddess of wilderness and protector of young girls, her sanctuaries were located on boundary zones, either on the border between different *chorai*, or at the edge of the city near the gates.[499] For the relation of female cults and rituals with water, as discussed in chapter 5, we could suggest a place near to a river, and removed from the town's centre.

Oriental cults are also attested at Koroneia, such as Egyptian gods and Sabazios. Egyptian gods were worshiped in the whole Boeotia region from the second half of the 3rd century BC to the 3rd century AD and were part of the official cults of the *poleis*. Despite the majority of the evidence

---
[495] Lauffer 1986, 82.
[496] Meier 2013.
[497] Schachter 1981, 155.
[498] Mylonopoulos 2013, 141-2.
[499] See chapter 5, p. 159.

being manumission decrees, these cults were popular among the Boeotian elites, especially during the Empire.[500] Koroneia has yielded so far two documents attesting the presence of Egyptian cults. A manumission decree dated to the 2nd century BC, which records the consecration by a man and a woman of a slave to Serapis, [Isis and Anubis] (*IG* VII 2872),[501] and an Imperial period inscription that was found by Pappadakis at the church of Taxiarchai at Pontza in the 1920s and recently re-discovered in Thebes' museum. The inscription was carved on a large block of grey limestone and seems to have been joined to another stone, thus giving the impression that it was originally used in a wall.[502] This inscription not only sheds light on the existence of the cult of the Egyptian gods at Koroneia in Roman times, but contains also important information about the topography and life of the town. The complete text is not given, but it is only summarized by the editors: it recorded the transaction of a large property and slaves (10 male slaves and 12 female slaves, whose names are recorded), numerous animals (including oxen, mules, mares, pigs, and sheep), a fully equipped house, and numerous house plots on the acropolis, and in other parts of the town.[503] The content of the inscription at the time of its original discovery was announced in the *Journal of Hellenic Studies* as 'dealing with the sale of a large estate to a sanctuary of the Egyptian gods',[504] but the editors hint that there could be other possible scenarios.

Figure 4.7 Stele found at Koroneia depicting a ritual connected to the worship of Sabazios (Bonanno 2008).

The cult to Sabazios, originally a Thracian-Phrygian god of vegetation whose mystery rituals involved a snake, is attested by the dedication on a stele made of local stone by one Charmokratis. On the stele, a male figure was carved, dressed with the *chiton* and *himation* and bearing on his right hand a *phiale*, towards which a snake reaches out (Figure 4.7). This inscription is the only evidence of the cult of Sabazios in Boeotia, and the only representation in the whole Greece of the deity, of which only 5 documents have been found.[505]

Another god worshipped by the Koroneians was Heracles Charops, whose cult is mentioned in Pausanias (Paus. 9.34.5) and attested by numerous manumission decrees dated from the second half of the 3rd to the second quarter of 2nd century BC and found in Koroneia's territory. A number of these decrees were inscribed on two stone door posts, testifying to the presence of a building connected to the cult, possibly the temple of Heracles.[506] Two possible locations have been suggested for the sanctuary, which supposedly included a cave: one at the ruined monastery of Agioi Taxiarchoi and the other one near the hot springs at Granitsa, to the north-west of Koroneia's hill. According to Schachter, the second location seems more likely for its vicinity with Orchomenos that is connected with Herakles according

---

[500] For a discussion on the presence of Egyptian cults in Boeotia, see Schachter 2007; Bonanno 2008.
[501] Schachter 2007, 372. These finds from Koroneia are discussed also in Bömer 1960, 57-8; 65-7.
[502] Kalliontzis and Papazarkadas 2014, 551.
[503] Kalliontzis and Papazarkadas, 2014, 551.
[504] Wace 1921, 272.
[505] Bonanno 2008, 242-3.
[506] Schachter 1986, 7-8.

to the myth.⁵⁰⁷ Another possible dedication to Herakles is attested by inscription *IG* VII 2874, found at the near village of Agios Georgios and undated, where one Melantichos is said to have dedicated a temple, a *stoa* and 'all the other things' to the *polis* and Herakles, to which 'Palaimon' is added, which can be interpreted either as an epithet of Herakles or as an independent name.⁵⁰⁸ The location of the temple and the *stoa* is not known. Schachter suggests two possible locations, either the *stoa* that Pappadakis identified in what he interpreted as the Roman agora on the slope of Koroneia's hill, or at Pontza where the local *ephoreia* excavated a Roman *stoa*.⁵⁰⁹

The temple of Athena Itonia

Together with the two battles that were fought in its proximity, the sanctuary of Athena Itonia is one of the main reasons why Koroneia is mentioned in ancient sources.⁵¹⁰ From written texts and inscriptions we can gather the importance of this place in which the representatives of the Boeotian *poleis* met to decide on matters that were relevant for the League, where the federal decrees were exposed and where a festival in honour of Athena was celebrated. Evidence points to the existence of the cult since the 7th or 6th century BC. Depictions on 6th century BC vases (provided that the attribution to the cult at the Itonion is correct), and ancient texts (e.g. Pindar) testify in fact to the existence of sacrificial processions and agonistic performances connected to the cult at the Itonion.⁵¹¹ In this period, however, there is no clear indication of a pan-Boeotian character yet, which seems to become instead more defined by the end of the 4th or early 3rd century. From Livy (36.20.2-4) we know that the territory around the sanctuary was pillaged in 191 BC by the Roman army led by the consul Acilius Glabrio, who interpreted as a sign of ingratitude towards the Romans the statue of the Roman enemy King Antiochus that had been erected by the Boeotians in the temple of Athena Itonia. Schachter suggested that the Pan-Boeotian festival was suspended after the dissolution of the Boeotian confederacy in 172 BC, which seems to be confirmed by the currently existing gap in the retrieved inscriptions between the second half of the 3rd and the 1st century BC.⁵¹²

The attributes of Athena Itonia, 'Polemadoke' ('war-sustaining') as defined by Alcaeus, and her traditional depiction with helmet, shield and spear, point towards the character of the goddess at Koroneia as being the patroness of warriors. Not coincidentally, in fact, the festival included competitions aimed at showing military skills, such as the horse races that were held starting from a statue of Ares, the Greek god of War, as evidenced by the inscription *IG* 7.2871 dated to the 1st century BC.⁵¹³ Dedications of team competitions among military troops during the Hellenistic period have been interpreted as evidence that the agonistic performances were the occasion to test the military skills of the various contingents that were part of the federal army.⁵¹⁴

In Roman times, the Itonion becomes again the seat of the resurrected Boeotian *koinon*.⁵¹⁵ An inscription dated to the 1st century AD (*IG* 7.2711) attests that the Pan-Boeotian festival was celebrated in that period and Pausanias informs us that in his times the federal assembly was held at the sanctuary and that rituals were performed by a priestess every day. In his *Periegesis*, Pausanias indeed describes in detail what he saw in the sanctuary, and some of the myths and cults connected with this place. Specifically, Pausanias tells that in the temple there were bronze statues of Athena and Zeus made

---

⁵⁰⁷ Schachter 1986, 4.
⁵⁰⁸ Schachter 1986, 9-10.
⁵⁰⁹ Schachter 1986, 9-10.
⁵¹⁰ A list of ancient sources and literature on the sanctuary is discussed in Schachter 1981, 117-27.
⁵¹¹ Schachter 1981, 122-3.
⁵¹² Schachter 1981, 124.
⁵¹³ Schachter 1981, 91.
⁵¹⁴ Schachter 1981, 124.
⁵¹⁵ Müller 2014, 129.

by the late 5th century BC sculptor Agorakritos, a disciple of Phidias, and that statues of the Charites, patron deities of Orchomenos, were dedicated in his time (Paus. 34.1). These elements testify to the long lasting existence of this cult place. A myth that Pausanias records about the sanctuary informs us that the goddess was served by priestesses. Pausanias was told in fact about the priestess Iodama who was turned into stone at the sight of the Gorgoneion on Athena's *chiton*, when the goddess appeared to her one night within the sacred precinct. In remembrance of this episode, Pausanias continues, every day there is a woman (likely a priestess herself) who lights a fire on an altar dedicated to Iodama, repeating three times in the Boeotian dialect that Iodama is alive and lights the fire (Paus. 34.2). The fact that priestesses served Athena Itonia is confirmed by the inscription *IG* 7.3426 honouring the chief priestess Flavia Laneika with a statue erected by her son, and dated to ca. 200-250 AD.

The location of the sanctuary, as well as the place where the competitions were held, including the *stadion*, are still disputed. Descending from the village of Kranitza (mod. Palea Granitsa) to the mountain west of Koroneia, Sir William Gell believed to have recognised the *stadium* of the Pan-Boeotian festival in an artificial hollow near the (now in ruins) mills of Calamachi,[516] but this identification remains uncertain. Ancient sources give some hints about the setting (e.g. by the banks of the river Korialios, according to Alcaeus; before reaching Koroneia from Alalkomenai in Pausanias), which have been followed since the 19th century by scholars eager to discover the site of the sanctuary. Victors' lists at the Pan-Boeotian festival and other inscriptions containing references to Athena Itonia and the Boeotian *koinon* have been found in several places within Koroneia's *chora*, which tempted scholars to identify these locations as possible candidates for the Itonion. Specifically, Pritchett suggested the area around the village of Mamoura (modern Alalkomenai; n. 6 in Figure 4.3), in particular the chapel of Metamorphosis, on its north-east, where some inscriptions concerning federal decrees were found.[517] The remains in the modern village, according to Pritchett, could relate to the establishments that grew around this important sanctuary.[518] This identification has been supported also by other scholars such as Fossey and Buckler in his reconstruction of Koroneia's battle field.[519] Another location was advanced by Pappadakis and Lauffer who proposed Thymari (n. 5 in Figure 4.3), NW of the Prehistoric mound of Agoriani and NE of Koroneia's hill.[520]

The excavations by Th. Spyropoulos during the 1970s in the plain north-east of Koroneia (n. 4 in Figure 4.3) unearthed three buildings, orientated east-west, and added new elements to the debated identification. The construction of the largest of the buildings, measuring 20 x 10 meters, was dated to the mid-6th century BC, but repairs are attested during the 1st-2nd century AD and 4th-5th century AD. The discovery of finds dated from the archaic to the Imperial period testify to the long use of the site and include a female marble statue head dated to the 4th century BC, two herms bases dated to the Roman period, one of which is inscribed with a dedication to Nike, two tripod bases reused as threshold blocks (see Figure 4.8),[521] and several stamped tiles.[522] One of the inscribed tiles was dated to the Hellenistic period and with a yellowish-white paint on the exterior side bears the stamp [--ΘAN--], which has been interpreted as [A]than[as iera], thus providing the evidence for Spyropoulos' identification of the site with the Itonion. Although this should not be excluded, other restorations are possible, as also at sanctuaries stamps could identify the tiles' maker and not necessarily the name of the deity.[523] Already

---

[516] Gell 1819, 149-50.
[517] Pritchett 1969, 86-7 and plates 57-64.
[518] Pritchett 1969, 87; among the establishments, there must have been for example a *xenon* (hostel) to house the partecipants, see chapter 5, pp. 162-4.
[519] Fossey 1988, 331-2; Buckler 2003, 91-2.
[520] Lauffer 1986, 91-7.
[521] Amandry 1978, 565-69. For a religious biography of tripods in ancient Boeotia see Papalexandrou 2008.
[522] Spyropoulos 1973, 385-92; Spyropoulos 1975, 392-414.
[523] Krentz 1989, 315.

Figure 4.8 Top left: Remains of one of the excavated building (A in Spyropoulos' report) as photographed by the author in August 2013. Note the visual connection with Koroneia's hill (the Frankish tower is visible in the background); Bottom left: The original position of the reused tripod bases blocks as recorded by P. Amandry (1978, Figure 2), viewed from west; Top right: View of building B (now covered by overgrown vegetation) from building A (Spyropoulos 1973, Figure 225, b).

Spyropoulos hinted at the possibility that this area lay within the ancient town's agora,[524] a hypothesis that other scholars too have later sustained.[525] In view of the current state of the survey data that will be discussed below, this hypothesis seems very unlikely. The identification of this complex with the Itonion is moreover problematic. Buckler argued against it in his reconstruction of the battlefield of Koroneia, as these buildings would lie too close to the town thus contradicting Xenophon's account and his personal topographical observations.[526] In any case, there is no doubt that these buildings belonged to a sanctuary that was in use from the Archaic to the Roman period and that occupied a large area, as testified to by a stele with inscribed HO[ROS], the formula to identify the boundary stone of a sacred space, which was found some 200 meters west of the buildings.

4.4. Preliminary results of the 'Ancient Cities of Boeotia' project

The survey of Koroneia is part of the 'Leiden Ancient Cities of Boeotia' fieldwork programme initiated by John Bintliff in 2000 at Leiden University. This project represents the fourth phase of the 'Boeotia survey project' which started in 1979 under the directorship of John Bintliff and Anthony Snodgrass. The overall aim of the Boeotia project is to reconstruct the population history, economy and socio-political development of the region by using non-destructive methods such as surface surveys and geophysical prospections.[527] Boeotia was identified as suitable for setting up an intensive regional survey as the

---

[524] Spyropoulos 1975, 396.
[525] E.g. Moggi and Osanna 2010, 408.
[526] Buckler 1996, 62.
[527] For a presentation of the aims of the Boeotia survey, see Bintliff 1985, 196.

rural character of the region had left large areas unbuilt and therefore accessible for survey. In its first phase (1979 – 1986), the survey focussed on the urban sites of Thespiai and Haliartos and investigated also their countryside, including the Valley of Muses and the small town of Askra. To test the results of this initial phase,[528] a second phase of the survey programme was initiated (1989 – 1992), which concentrated on the urban area and countryside of ancient Hyettos, situated in the northern part of the region. A third phase of the project aimed at recording and studying the medieval and post-medieval evidence of the region, which included the Frankish-Crusader towers, deserted medieval and post-medieval villages, and the domestic architecture that was quickly being demolished to make space for modern constructions. In the fourth phase of the project, the fieldwork included the ancient cities of Tanagra and Koroneia in the regional surveyed sample area.

The archaeological investigation by the Boeotia survey project at Koroneia commenced in 2006. In the framework of her MA thesis, Janneke van Zwienen created a DEM by manually recording points with a DGPS across the site over several survey seasons.[529] The DEM was meant to provide an accurate representation of the shape of the hill to be used for further analysis.[530] The hill has been heavily modified by ancient and more recent terraces, some of which have in the last few years been bulldozed to make space for olive trees. Through past and current maintenance and improvement of these terraces, the architectural elements that were still visible on the surface have been pushed towards the terraces' edges. The terraces have been subsequently investigated to establish whether they were part of the original morphology of the hill or the result of modern bulldozing and documented with a DGPS.[531] Pairing his survey with the information gathered from aerial photographs and geological maps, the team geomorphologist Keith Wilkinson has also mapped the geology of the hill, which appears as being divided across the western edge between a stable high-grade metamorphic mudstone to the east and an unstable low-grade metamorphic mudstone to the north-west.[532] This marked division has affected the morphology of the hill, which presents more sculpted slopes on the west (where two gullies caused by rainwater washing away the slopes are clearly visible), and more gentle slopes on the eastern side; the latter were preferred by the hill's settlers for their suitability for buildings and have returned the higher density of finds (see Figure 4.9 for a general overview of the distribution of finds).

Water supply must have been a concern for Koroneia's inhabitants, as fresh water was available only at the foot of the hill (the water sources are mapped in Figure 4.10). From an Imperial inscription found by Pappadakis at Pontza we know that Hadrian financed the construction of an aqueduct to provide the Koroneians with a more stable water supply.[533] As already mentioned, traces of the aqueduct have been surveyed by Lauffer, who identified it as a channel running from the ridge of the Megalo and Mikro Butsurati, and reaching Koroneia's hill from the south. Geophysical prospections have likely identified the aqueduct in a linear feature running along the street which approaches the hill from the south (Figure 4.10, nr. 7), but at present the endpoint of the aqueduct has not been established with certainty. According to Lauffer, the endpoint of the pipeline was the cistern excavated by Pappadakis where the headless statue of Hadrian was found, but its location is uncertain (perhaps it corresponds with the only excavated cistern found on the hill, nr. 6 in Figure 4.10). Until the construction of the aqueduct and to supply areas of the town far from it once it was constructed, rain water must have been harvested and stored in cisterns and *pithoi*, large jars commonly used for domestic storage and consumption.

---

[528] Published in Bintliff and Snodgrass 1985. The final publication of the Thespiai rural hinterland is Bintliff and Howard 2007; the final publication of the Thespiai city survey is Bintliff *et al.* 2017.
[529] Van Zwienen 2008.
[530] Van Zwienen and Noordervliet 2009.
[531] Wilkinson 2010.
[532] Wilkinson 2010, 50; Bintliff *et al.* 2013, 14.
[533] *BCH* 47 (1923), 522.

4. THE ANCIENT TOWN OF KORONEIA

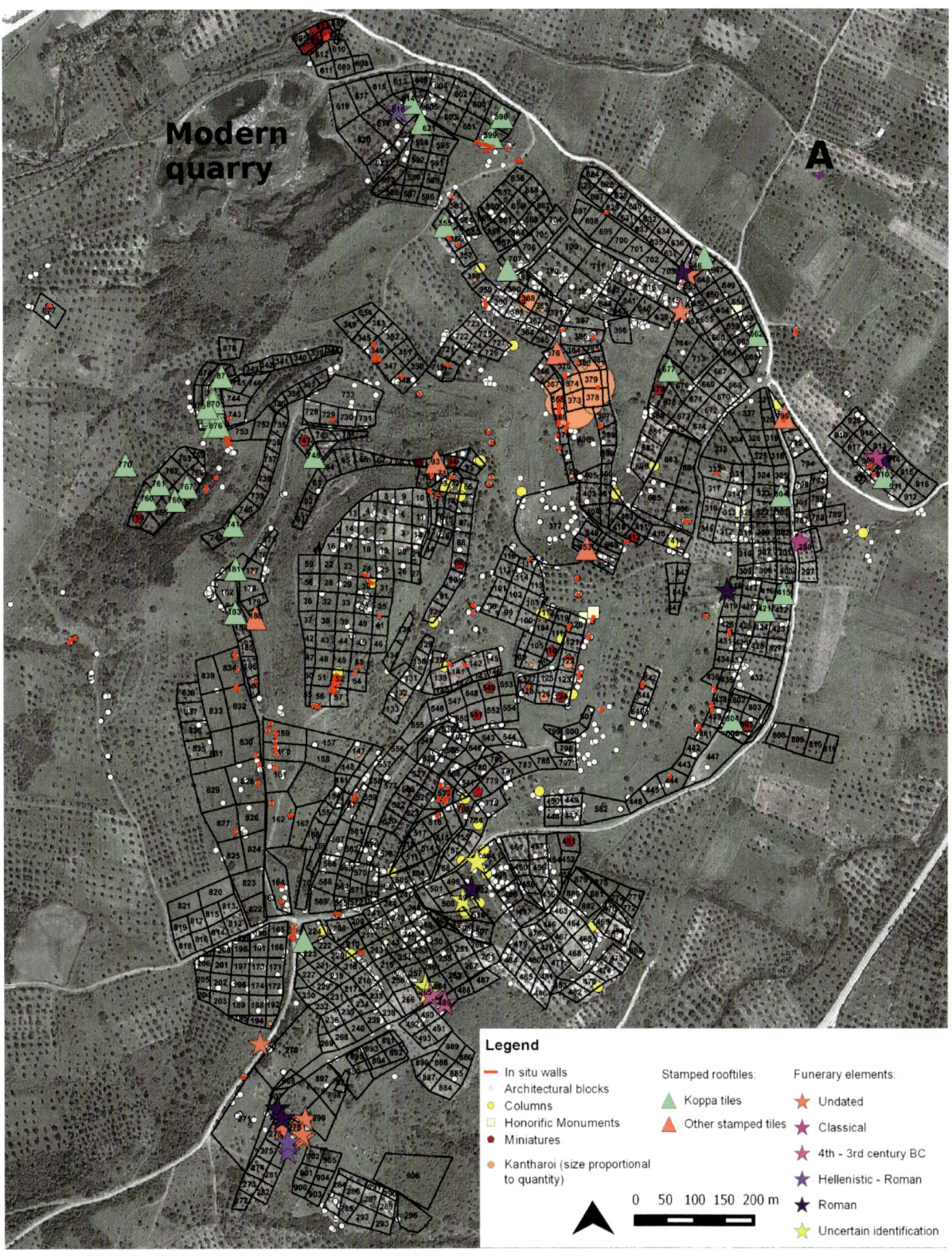

Figure 4.9 General overview of Koroneia's hill, showing the survey units and the location of some classes of finds that will be discussed in this section, such as architectural remains (both in situ and erratic), funerary and honorific elements, miniature vases, kantharoi and column drums. Pappadakis' excavations at the supposed Itonion are marked with A.

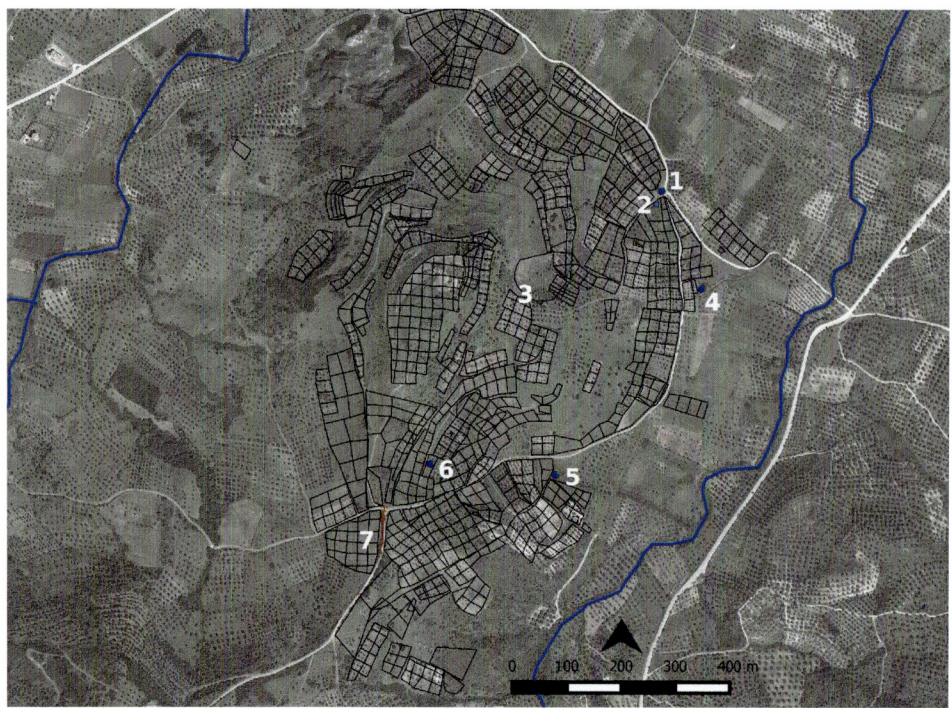

Figure 4.10 Overview of water infrastructures on the hill: 1) modern fountain constructed by reusing parapet blocks; 2) water channel built with the same technique as the Frankish tower situated in its proximity; 3) sewer with EW orientation (probably flanking a street); 4) underground spring covered by a large fig tree; 5) seasonal stream; 6) cistern (perhaps corresponding to the well excavated by Pappadakis in which the headless statue of Hadrian was found); 7) GPR results possibly indicating a stretch of the Hadrianic aqueduct.

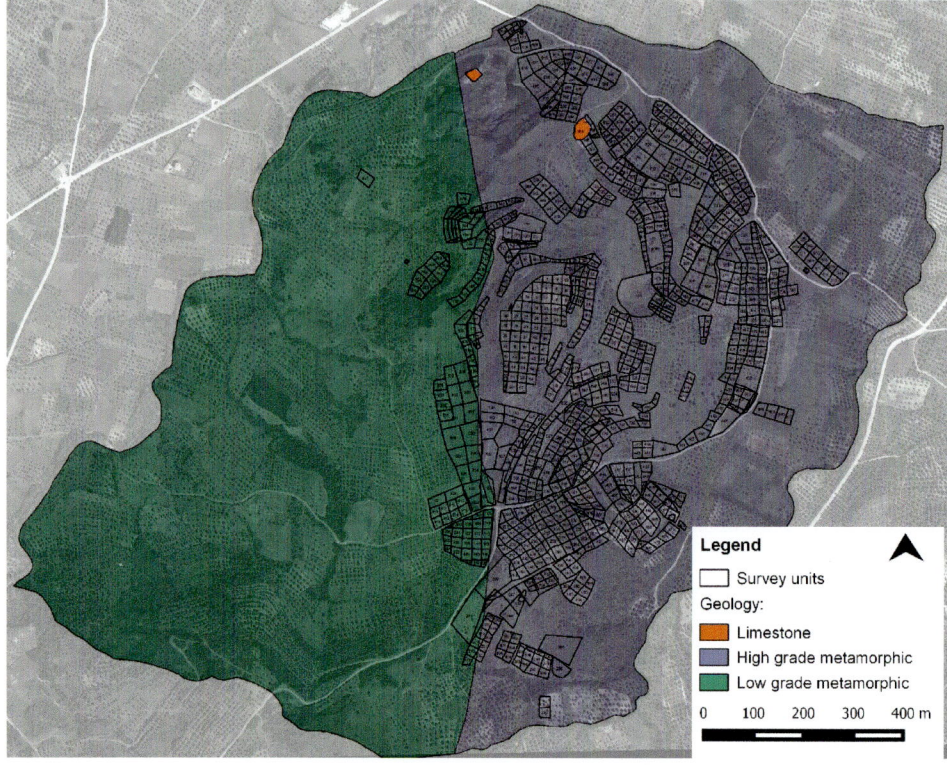

Figure 4.11 Geology of the hill (as mapped in the field by K. Wilkinson).

The hill was divided into grids of approximately 20x20 m (adapted to the terrain) that were recorded by a DGPS and mapped onto a GIS in order to be able to relate the surface finds to their location.[534] An architectural survey was undertaken that resulted in the recording of more than 2000 pieces, using a GPS for the loose blocks and a DGPS for the in situ walls.[535] The majority of the blocks are made of local grey and white-yellowish limestone, of which only rare exposures are visible in the northern slope (see Figure 4.11),[536] but there are also pieces in pink limestone, which is not locally available at Koroneia and therefore possibly hints at a specific purpose for its use.[537] The 145 recorded *in situ* walls show a roughly north-south and east-west orientation in the northern part of the town with a shift of about N25°E in the southern part (Figure 4.12). This arrangement has been confirmed by the ongoing geophysical survey, which has investigated so far some areas of the northern and south-eastern sections of the town, as well as disclosing traces of the lower wall circuit.[538] The pottery sherds that were collected in the field are currently being studied by a team of pottery specialists, yielding a database with an elaborate description of each entry. Within the framework of the European Commission FP7 funded project CEEDS, of which the author was appointed researcher between 2010 and 2014, a pilot project has been initiated in collaboration with the department of Computing at Goldsmiths, University of London and the Centre for Research and Technology (CERTH) in Thessaloniki for experimenting with automatic techniques of pottery classification based on visual feature extraction and profile matching using part of the Koroneia's database as a test case.[539]

The architectural and pottery surveys are completed, but the analysis of the materials and the geophysical investigations are still in progress. For this reason, the overview given below presents some preliminary results based on the materials that were available at the time in which this chapter was written.[540] The study of some of the finds has been assigned to BA and MA students, resulting in dissertations that are cited in the following sections. One outcome of an RMA thesis has been the preparation of an online map of Koroneia's architectural pieces, which can be operated as a WebGIS and fosters the accessibility of this dataset.[541] While all the recorded blocks and wall alignments have been taken into consideration in the dissertation by Boswinkel (2015), it must be stressed that for other find classes, the assemblage studied represents only a portion of the entire dataset, which, as already mentioned, is not entirely processed yet. For example, the 95 textile implements studied by Meens (2011) were found in the material processed by the team of pottery specialists in a three-week campaign in spring 2011. This partial availability of results can create bias in the finds' density; in fact, for example, a high density of loomweights was recorded in some grids west of the acropolis, but this could be related to a coincidental distribution of finds in the sample considered, instead of reflecting a particularly intense activity area. When the amount of finds should be taken as a provisional indication and not as representative of the complete dataset, this will be notified in the related section below.

Finally, it must be noted that, as usual in survey projects, the findspot of the large majority of the finds and architectural blocks that are discussed here does not correspond to their original location. Large architectural blocks are likely to have remained close to the place where they were originally used, but smaller blocks and finds can have been moved for longer distances, either being reused already in

---

[534] Bintliff *et al.* 2009, 19; Van Zwienen and Noordervliet 2010.
[535] Uytterhoeven 2014a and b. The architecture survey team was composed of Bart Noordervliet, Janneke van Zwienen, Yannick Boswinkel, Ipek Dagli and the author under the direction of Inge Uytterhoeven.
[536] Bintliff *et al.* 2013, 14.
[537] Uytterhoeven 2014b, 1.
[538] Verdonck 2013; Meyer and Pilz 2015; Meyer and Pilz 2016.
[539] The methodology and the preliminary results of this study are presented in Piccoli *et al.* 2015.
[540] This overview includes the survey results available by August 2015.
[541] The map was prepared by Y. Boswinkel as one of the results of his RMA thesis and the online publication was managed by B. Noordervliet. The map is currently accessible at http://www.boeotiaproject.org/gis/qgiswebclient.html?map=/home/boeotia/public-www/gis/projects/architecture/Koroneia_OnlineMap.qgs

Visualizing cityscapes of Classical antiquity

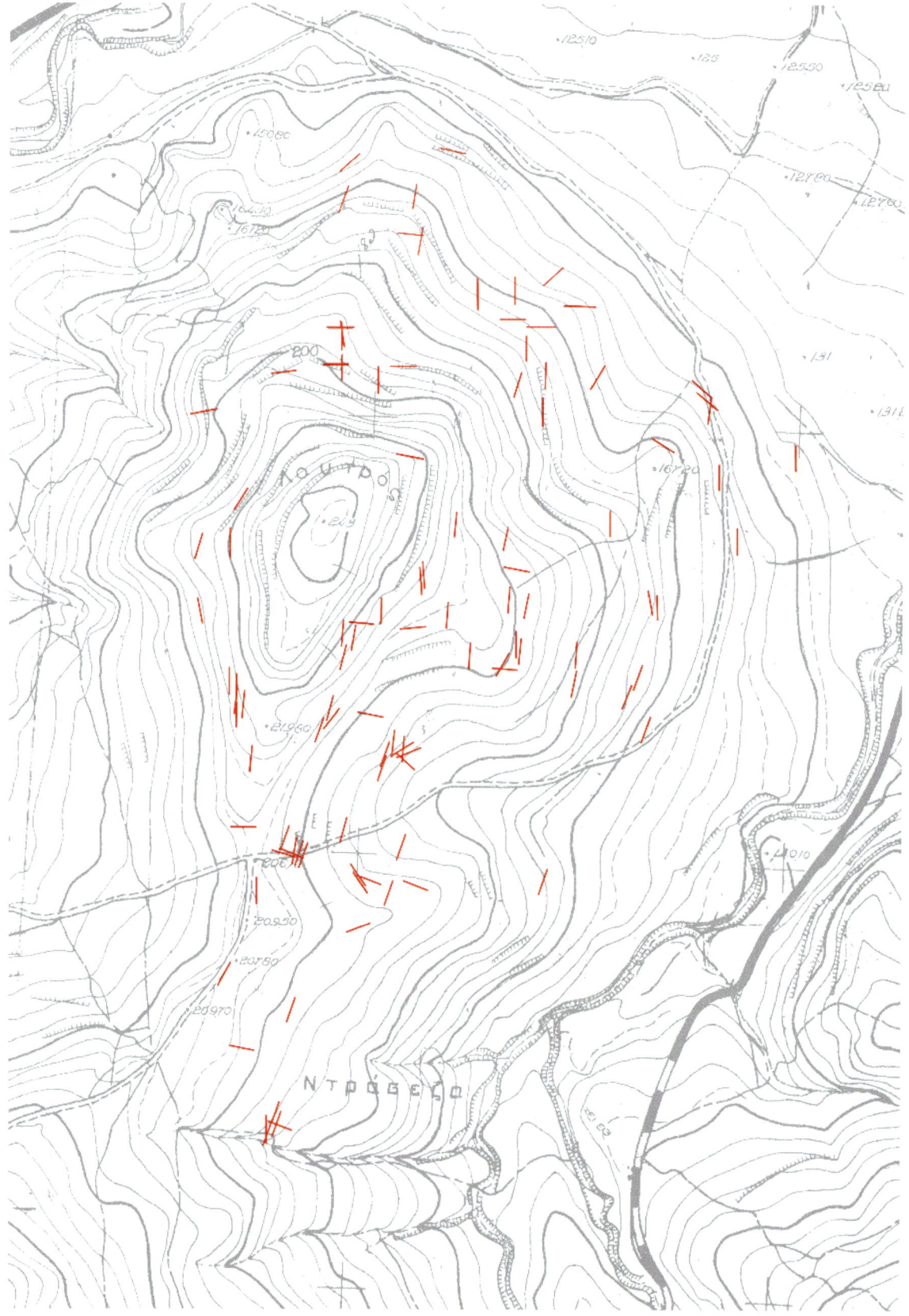

Figure 4.12 Overview of the in situ wall lines recorded during the survey and extended to better show their orientation (map made by B. Noordervliet).

antiquity, or as a result of agricultural work on the hill. In fact, by inspecting the distribution of such finds, one notes concentrations of architectural blocks on the terraces' edges as they have been pushed aside to allow cultivation. As far as ceramic finds, the topography of the hill and its numerous terraces argue for an original deposition not too far from the find grid-unit.

Pottery find classes are dated on a typological and fabric basis to distinguish local production and imported wares, using the published assemblages from excavated sites as comparison. Regarding the architectural pieces, although some of the recorded fragments were chronologically and functionally identified, the majority of them are roughly worked stone blocks, which therefore do not offer many elements for dating. Only when all the material will be processed and studied, will a more refined definition of functions and dates be possible. For the moment the discussion presented below offers some preliminary considerations that will have to be updated and revised under the light of the latest results. The methodology that is presented in chapter 6 was adopted precisely to be able to deal efficiently with further updating of the survey data.

For the above mentioned reasons, I chose to follow a spatial criterion instead of a chronological one in discussing the survey finds. In this way, undated finds are included in the discussion and the association of finds can be more easily retrieved. To this end, I divided Koroneia's hill into five areas (acropolis, northern, eastern, southern and western slope, see Figure 4.13), according to which the finds are analysed in the next sections. For each of these areas, the finds are subdivided into four categories, based on the main data sources that are currently available, namely architecture, pottery, stone finds and geophysics. Moreover, an additional entry on water infrastructures was added. Each area closes

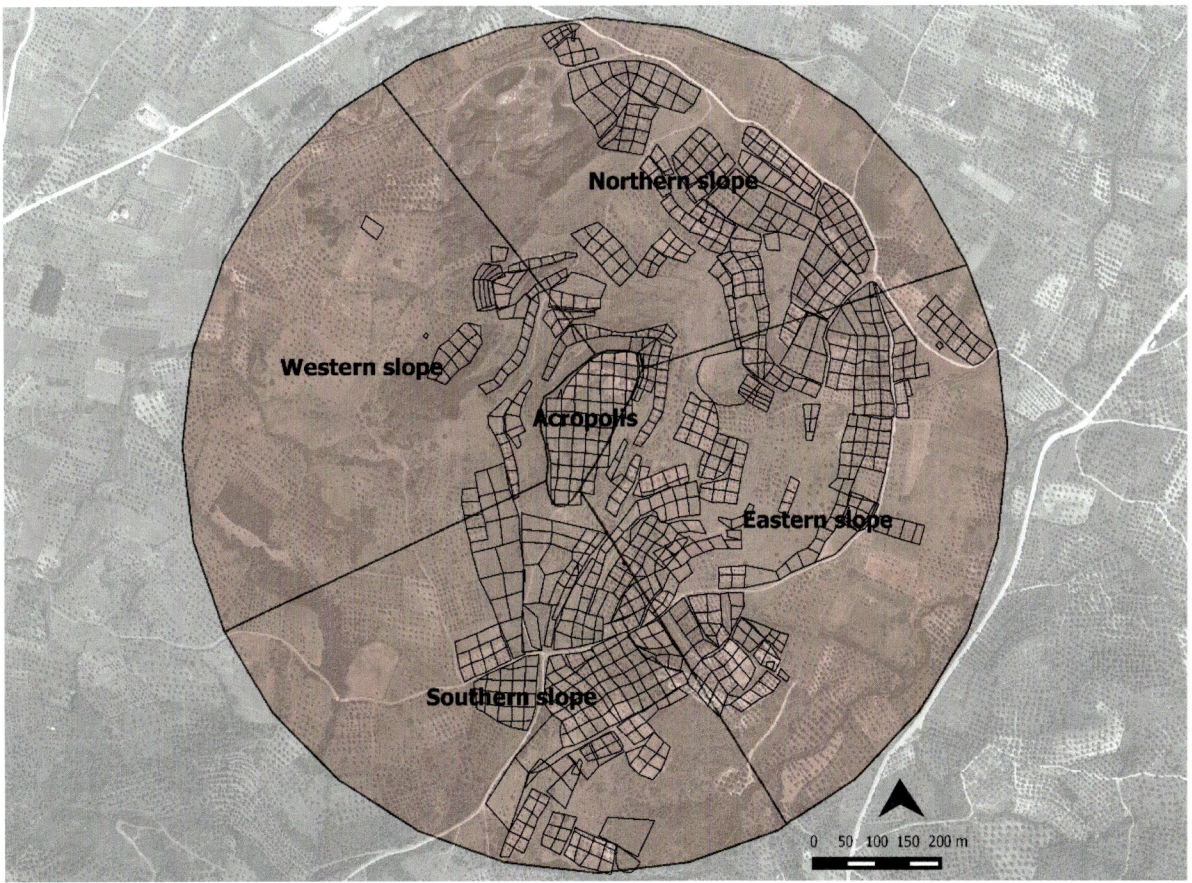

Figure 4.13 Location of the areas in which the hill has been divided for the discussion of survey finds.

with a discussion where the survey finds belonging to each category are summarized, thus providing some provisional considerations on the nature of the area and on possible future investigations.

4.4.1 Acropolis

In its current shape, the acropolis consists of two parts: a lower terrace to the south and a higher area to the north. The geomorphological analysis of the area by K. Wilkinson identified some ancient terraces on the acropolis, although some modifications have been caused by bulldozing works and cultivation. The recorded evidence, both architecture and pottery fragments, belongs for most part to the Late Roman period, thus attesting the occupation and (domestic) use of the acropolis up to the 6th (or even 7th) century AD, although the available data are not conclusive in establishing whether the occupation was continuous or interrupted at some point.

Architecture

The architectural survey has recorded some 70 pieces on the acropolis (see Figure 4.15 for an overview), the majority of which seems to belong to Late Antiquity or the Early Byzantine period and includes *spolia*. Three fragments of unfluted columns (in two cases with *entasis* visible) were recorded; one more than 2 meters long was documented in grid 52 and the other two, both about 1 meter long, were close to each other in grid 30.[542] It seems that in both cases the columns were re-used in walls. As far as fortification walls, stretches of a circuit that surrounded the acropolis are visible in several locations. On the southern and northern edge, the survey team recorded the two *in situ* stretches of large polygonal blocks that had been already identified by previous research on the site;[543] for their construction techniques these walls have been dated to the Classical period, although only a single row is visible while two rows would be expected.[544] On the eastern and western edges of the acropolis, stretches of a Late Antique fortification made of mortared rubble and brick have been also identified during the survey.[545]

The most conspicuous remains that are currently visible on the acropolis belong to a large (barrel?) vaulted structure made of brick and limestone rubble in mortar and are concentrated in grids 30 and 34 (see Figure 4.14). The remains were surveyed in 2009 and have been extensively documented by students in 2011, as part of a summer school organized within the ArcLand project under the supervision of H. Stöger and E. Dullart.[546] Several pieces of the collapsed vaulted ceiling lay on the ground, covering an area of approximately 8 by 10 meters, their thickness suggesting that the structure could support a height up to 5 or 6 meters.[547] A pit that was dug by robbers close to one of the pieces enabled the surveyors to notice that the structure continued underneath the collapsed fragments, the latter belonging indeed only to vaulting pieces.[548] This observation led Terpstra to suggest that the structure collapsed after being hit by an earthquake.[549] For its construction technique the structures has been tentatively dated to Late Antiquity (5th or 6th century AD) and interpreted as a possible elite mansion.[550]

---

[542] The pictures of the discussed finds are stored on a directory of the project's website, see http://www.boeotiaproject.org/files/09-13PDF/2009_003-004.pdf and http://www.boeotiaproject.org/files/09-13PDF/2009_003.pdf.
[543] Maier 1959.
[544] Uytterhoeven 2012, 16.
[545] Bintliff *et al.* 2009, 25.
[546] The analysis of the structure was the subject of D. Terpstra's BA thesis 'Koroneia's 'Bishop's Palace' Investigating Late Antique architectural remains on the acropolis of ancient Koroneia in Central Greece' (2012).
[547] Terpstra 2012, 37.
[548] Terpstra 2012, 38.
[549] Terpstra 2012, 39.
[550] Uytterhoeven 2012, 16; Terpstra 2012, 25-43.

4. The ancient town of Koroneia

Figure 4.14 Examples of some of the fragments of vaulted ceilings recorded on the acropolis (pictures by I. Uytterhoeven).

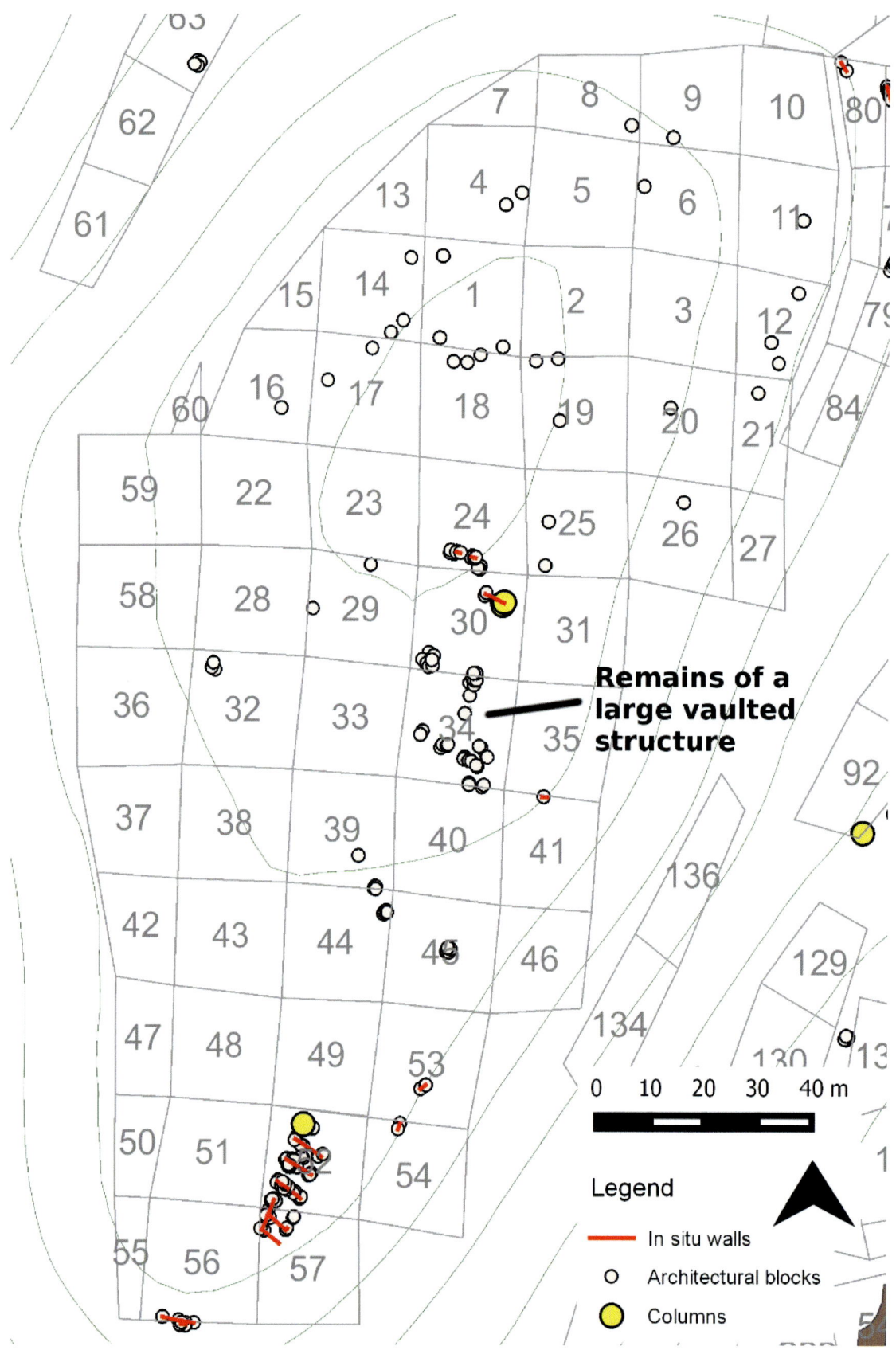

Figure 4.15 Overview of architectural finds on the acropolis.

Other remains that have been dated to the Late Roman period are some *in situ* walls that are located on the southern-east edge of the acropolis (in grids 52 and 57, see Figure 4.15 for location).[551] These wall alignments have been excavated at an unknown date and their discovery has remained unpublished (assuming that we are dealing with official excavations and not with robber trenches). It is not known therefore why this area was chosen for excavating and what kind of artefacts were associated to these walls. Their construction technique using *spolia*, mortared rubble and bricks points towards a Late Roman date and for the space arrangement have been interpreted as (a) domestic structure(s).[552]

Pottery

The acropolis is the only area of the ancient city for which the study of Hellenistic and Roman pottery has been completed.[553] For the Hellenistic period, pottery data show a wide range of domestic functions, with predominance of vessels for drinking and food consumption. Early Roman pottery is represented by 12 fragments of which eleven are for consumption and beverage and one amphora fragment is in local fabric; 7 fragments of Mid-Roman pottery relate to food consumption and 92 fragments of Late Roman pottery represent vessels for consumption/serving of food and beverages, cooking and transport/storage. According to Bes and van der Enden, a few fragments suggest an occupation of the acropolis into the second half of the 6th century AD (even into the 7th century AD). These preliminary results confirm therefore the domestic use of the acropolis for these periods, as we indeed would expect from the Roman documents discussed above.

As for textile implements on the acropolis, their provisional count in 2011 amounted to 3 loomweights and 1 spindle whorl.[554] Two loomweights were located in grid 55, specifically a pyramidal weight dated on a typological basis to the Hellenistic period and a seal stamp weight of uncertain date (possibly Classical-Hellenistic). A discoid weight dated to the Hellenistic period was found in grid 32, while the spindle whorl was collected from grid 1.

Stone finds

A number of stone finds have been recorded on the acropolis, which testify to the presence of food processing activities on the higher part of the hill. Grinding tools have been collected during the survey on the hill and have been studied in the course of a BA dissertation.[555] It must be noted that although the original use of these tools is indeed related with grain grinding, they could have been reused for other purposes when broken, such as building material in later periods, and indeed some of the fragments in the Koroneia's sample bear this kind of trace.[556] Their presence therefore should not be automatically related to grain grinding activities close to their finding spot. On the acropolis, a fragment of the *catillus* of a Hopper-Rubber Mill which belong to the Late Classical – Hellenistic period and two fragments, one of the *catillus* and the other part of the *meta*, of a Pompeian Donkey Mill dated to the Roman period have been collected (in grids 39, 20 and 27 respectively, see Figure 4.16 for the complete overview of millstone types on the hill).[557] While the Hopper-Rubber Mill was found in Olynthian houses,[558] the Pompeian Donkey Mill is usually associated with the production of bread on a commercial basis.[559]

---

[551] Pictures at http://www.boeotiaproject.org/files/09-13PDF/VE2009_004.pdf.
[552] The documentation and re-study of these remains was the subject of Y. Boswinkel's BA thesis (Boswinkel 2012).
[553] Bes and van der Enden 2012.
[554] Meens 2011 (catalogue nrs. 24, 64, 87 and 91).
[555] Brasser 2013.
[556] Brasser 2013, 42.
[557] Brasser 2013, catalogue, stones nrs. 25, 97 and 99.
[558] Robinson and Graham 1938, 208, in Brasser 2013, 30.
[559] Brasser 2013, 45.

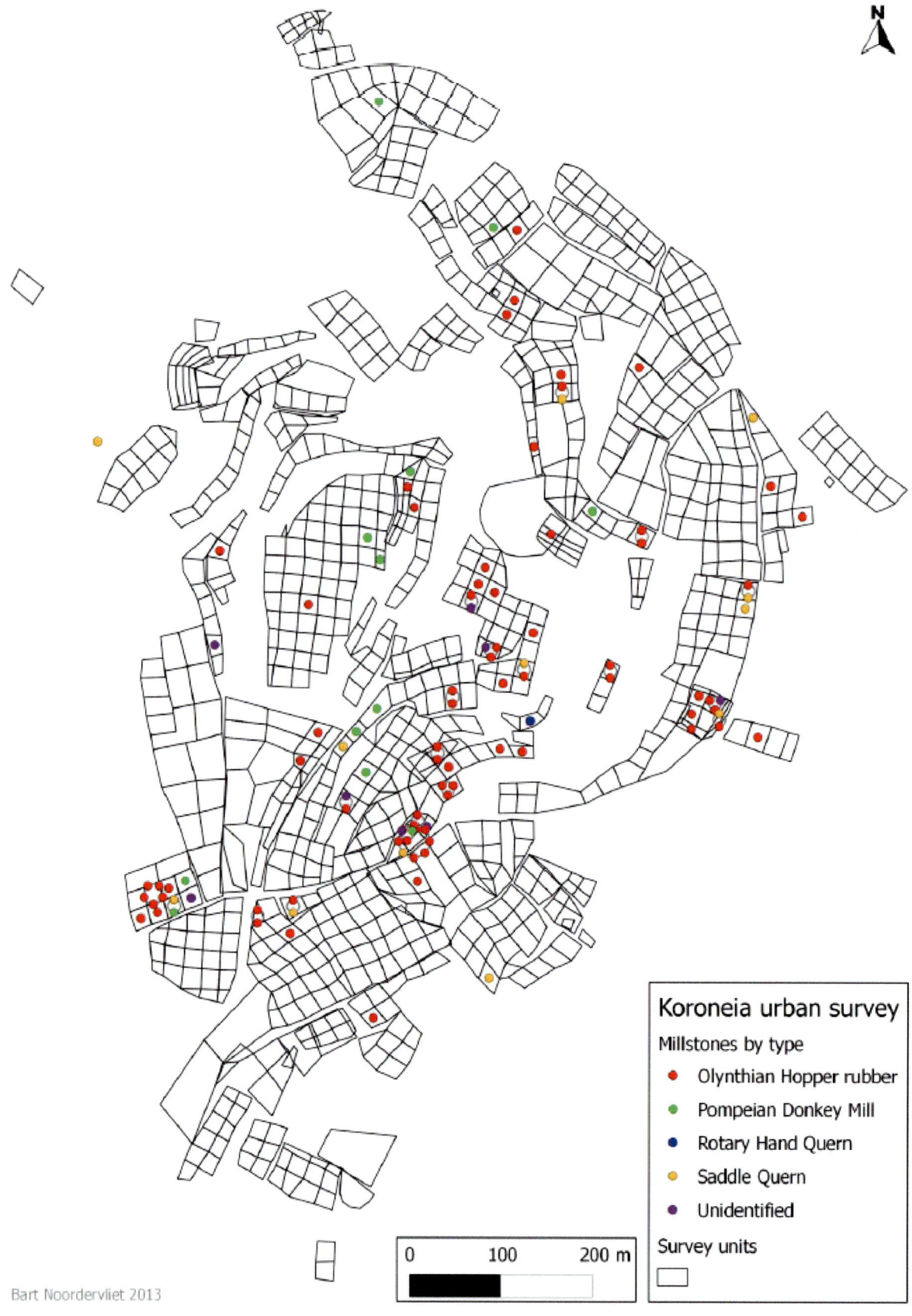

Figure 4.16 Map showing the location of millstone types (made by B. Noordervliet, in Brasser 2013, 46).

Finally, testifying to the industrial activities that took place on the acropolis in Late Antiquity was a large olive press base that was recorded on its western edge (grid 32).[560] This compares to what was observed elsewhere, such as at Thespiai and Tanagra, where industrial activities occupy spaces that were previously central areas of ancient cities.[561]

Discussion

The early stage of pottery study limits our current possibility to define specific functions on the acropolis over the centuries. Stretches of polygonal walls provide us the evidence that the acropolis was surrounded by a fortification wall in the Classical period. Although it is premature to draw conclusion before the complete dataset coming from the survey is processed, the preliminary results seem to point towards a domestic use of the acropolis at least since the Roman period (and perhaps even during the Hellenistic era). Drinking and food consumption are well represented in the pottery dataset and the types of grinding tools that have been found are related to food processing both on a domestic and commercial level. These data match the inscriptions previously discussed that attest indeed to the presence of houses on the acropolis in the Roman times. It is notable that so far no clear evidence of cult practises has emerged from the pottery and architecture dataset. While cultic activities are not necessarily associated with imposing architectural remains, dedicated types of pottery sherds are typical of cult practises,[562] and these seem so far to be missing from the Hellenistic and Roman dataset.

Regarding the (Roman) architectural features that have been observed in previous investigations on the hill, there is a conspicuous number of structures that were not retrieved during the survey. These are the feature marked G in Maier's map, which Fossey wonders if it could be interpreted as the Roman agora that Pappadakis claimed to have found in his excavations,[563] and the well-constructed Roman buildings which according to Fossey were excavated in recent years between Maier's structures G and H and never published.[564] A targeted survey on the acropolis and geophysical prospections could help in finding traces of these structures, if any are left after the perturbation of the geomorphology of the hilltop due to cultivation.

The evidence for the Late Roman period points towards the existence of a community that settled on and fortified the acropolis. The fragments of vaulted ceilings have been in fact interpreted as the remains of an elite mansion, and hypotheses have been suggested that this structure could have been the residence of the bishop or the governor of the Late Antique town.[565] The remains of the excavated walls on the southern part of the acropolis interpreted as houses of Late Roman date give further indication of the small settlement that occupied the acropolis during this period.

There is still an open question regarding the water provisions for the people residing on the acropolis, since so far no traces of water infrastructure have been found there. The water sources at the foot of the hill seem an unpractical solution as the path to reach the acropolis from the lower slopes is very step. Therefore, it is also possible that the collection of water was done using cisterns or *pithoi* (or that other water infrastructures existed that have not been found yet or have in the meantime disappeared), and that the location of the Hadrianic aqueduct facilitated water supply.

---

[560] Bintliff *et al.* 2009, 25. Pictures available at www.boeotiaproject.org/files/09-13PDF/2009_005.pdf.
[561] Bintliff 2013a, 199.
[562] See as a comparison the traces of cultic activities that have been found on Plataiai's acropolis in the Archaic period (Konecny *et. al.* 2013, 288).
[563] Fossey 1990, 238.
[564] Fossey 1990, 237.
[565] Bintliff *et al.* 2013, 17.

4.4.2 Northern slope

On the northern slope, made of stable high grade metamorphic stone, numerous modern terraces were mapped in the geomorphological survey on the hill.[566] As will be discussed in more detail below, these modifications have affected the archaeological record. Moreover, a quarry which is now partly occupied by a water basin, was opened in modern times on the NW side of the hill, probably to provide fill material for dirt road construction and to be used to pave the villages nearby (Figure 4.17). To locate the survey finds discussed in this section, refer to Figure 4.18.

Architecture

In the northern sector of the site, the architectural survey has recorded two stretches of walls running in parallel, which were identified as a possible 3.60 meters wide gate in the city wall (on the southern edge of grid 599),[567] and several wall lines with roughly a NS and EW orientation. About 14 stretches of walls following this alignment were exposed by bulldozing activities in a field (left un-gridded during the survey) which is located between the row of grids 350-354 and that of 355-357. These walls seem

Figure 4.17 Modern quarry located on the north-western side of the hill (see Figure 4.9 for its position)

---

[566] Wilkinson 2010, 50-2.
[567] Uytterhoeven 2014a, 2. Pictures are available at www.boeotiaproject.org/files/09-13PDF/VE2010_015.pdf; www.boeotiaproject.org/files/09-13PDF/VE2012_036.pdf.

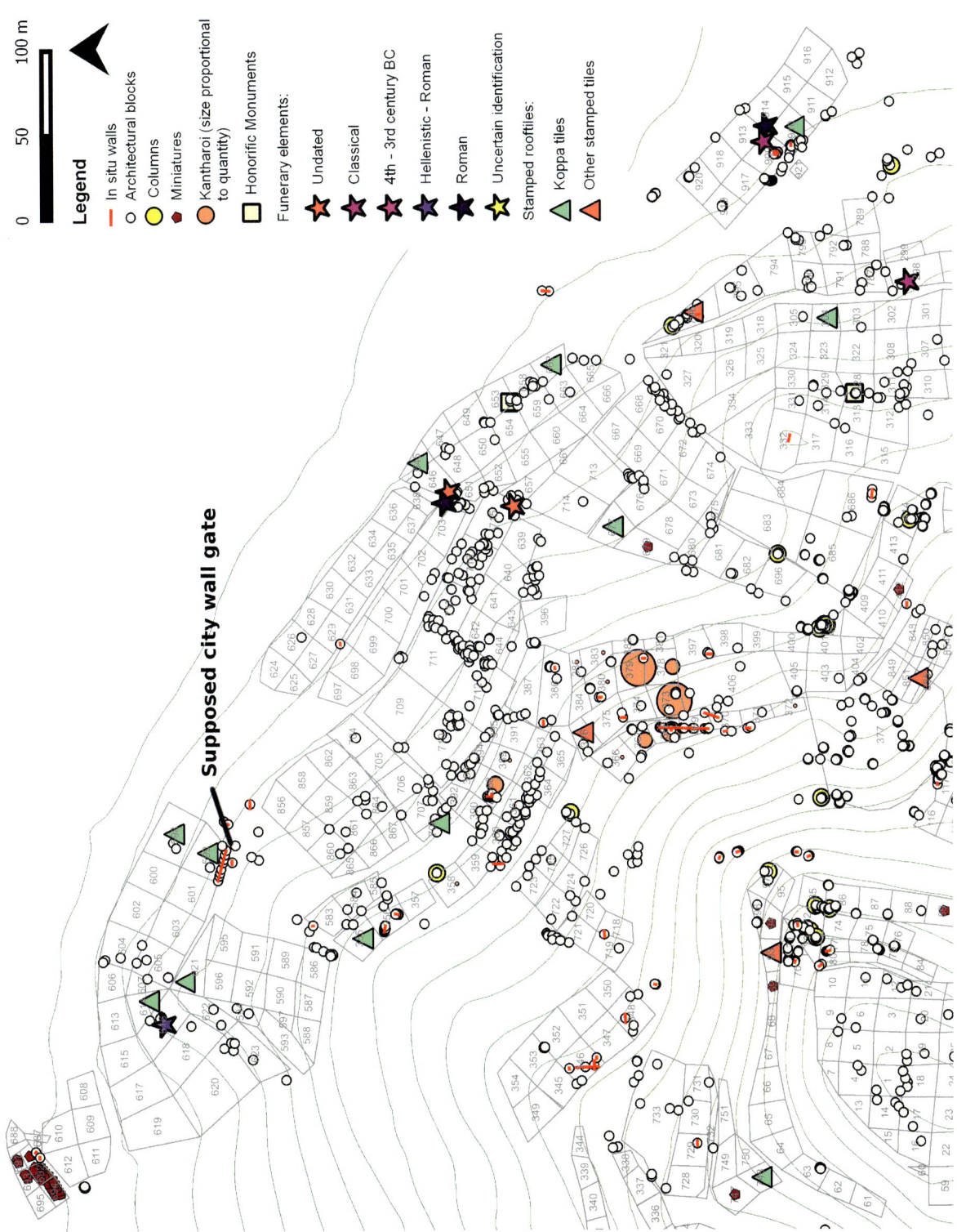

Figure 4.18 Overview of the finds on the northern slope

to be part of a regularly laid down domestic quarter.[568] In the same area, other stretches of *in situ* walls present the same NS-EW orientation, such as in grids 346 and 348, 356 and on the north-west edge of grid

---

[568] Uytterhoeven 2014a, 5.

583. The walls recorded in grid 346, some of which could be followed for more than 13 meters, allowed the identification of an *insula* measuring at least 15 x 15 m.⁵⁶⁹

In grids 360-4, 388-395 and on the border between grids 711-712 and 642, 644 and 717, a high number of large grey limestone building blocks have been recorded. The blocks have been clearly pushed towards the terraces' edges, and their disposition in grids 711 and 712 seems to indicate that they have fallen from above; it seems likely that they come from nearby, given their large dimensions. If we assume that larger blocks were used for more imposing architecture, this concentration could point to the presence of some large structure (see below for the geophysics' results in this area). Large blocks have been recorded also between grids 709-710 and 704-707 (Figure 4.19). Towards east, a large number of roughly cut and finished grey limestone blocks has been recorded west of grids 367 and 368 and an *in situ* wall was followed for about 28 meters across grids 368-369. Three fragments of funerary architecture were found on the lower northern slopes. Notable is a large fragment of

Figure 4.19 Architectural survey at Koroneia: Inge Uytterhoeven recording some large blocks between grids 709-710 and 704-707 (photo: author).

a Roman sarcophagus lid with *acroteria* (database nr. 180) pushed towards the edge of grid 703,⁵⁷⁰ which borders with the path between this grid and grid 651 where an undated funerary slab was recorded. Another funerary slab was found in grid 715.

Pottery

The pottery study is still in progress in this area, however among the available data some clusters stand out that are worth mentioning in this overview. A high number of (Classical) miniature vessels (27) have been collected in grids 690-694, which are located on the north-western edge of the surveyed area, outside the lower city wall circuit and close to a stream. Towards east, a concentration of *kantharoi* was found in the grids 366-385 (peaking in grids 373 and 379 with 11 fragments each) and 388-389.⁵⁷¹ This type of drinking cup was used in the context of (public) dining and is also found in graves. In this area the above mentioned large number of roughly cut and finished grey limestone blocks were also found. A grab sample taken by the author from grids 378-9 has shown the presence of fine pottery that ranged from the Archaic to the Roman period (V. Stissi, pers. comm.), a number of (oysters?) shells and a die of unidentified date.

---

⁵⁶⁹ Uytterhoeven 2014a, 5.
⁵⁷⁰ Recorded twice: nrs. 2011_180 and 2012_521: pictures available at http://www.boeotiaproject.org/files/09-13PDF/2011_180.pdf and http://www.boeotiaproject.org/files/09-13PDF/2012_521.pdf.
⁵⁷¹ Specifically: 366 (1), 367 (4), 368 (6), 372 (1), 373 (11), 376 (2), 378 (4), 379 (11), 380 (1), 383 (1), 385 (1), 389 (1), see Mulder 2012, 38.

Regarding stamped tiles, a piece of a stamped rooftile, dated to the Roman - Late Roman period was found in grid 93, just below the acropolis, and some fragmentary stamps bearing the 'Koppa' mark which identify them as Classical-Hellenistic city stamps were collected on the lower slope.

Stone finds

A funerary inscription provisionally dated to the Hellenistic – Imperial period by F. Marchand was found in grid 616, which is in fact outside of the lower city wall circuit. In the same grid, a fragment of Pompeian Donkey Mill was found.[572] Another fragment of the same mill type was found in grid 864, while in the closeby grid 705, a fragment of the Olynthian Hopper Rubber was collected. This type of grinding tools dated to the (Late) Classical – Hellenistic period is frequently found on the northern slope, as additional pieces were found in the adjacent grids 362 and 389, in grids 378 and 379 and in the lower grid 677 (see Figure 4.16 for the overview of grinding tools studied so far). In 378, a fragment of saddle quern was also found. The saddle quern develops from the Archaic to the Hellenistic period, the fragment found at Koroneia has been therefore dated to this broader time frame.[573]

Geophysics

Some areas of the northern slope were selected to conduct a magnetic survey (see Figure 4.20).[574] Specifically, the lower slope, where we had expected to find further traces of the path of the city wall circuit of which some stretches had been already found to the west, and the area where the cluster of *kantharoi* was found were investigated. The lower slope shows few (faint) traces of walls, ditches or backfills, but none of them is recognizable as belonging to any specific building. It is not clear yet whether this reflects the actual absence of buildings on this slope in antiquity, or if it is the result of bulldozing works which have profoundly modified the hill and the archaeological record. It is noteworthy, however, that a clear anomaly corresponding to a wall runs along grids 360-363 and 386.

In the area where the concentration of *kantharoi* was found, wall alignments following the usual roughly NS/EW orientation are clearly discernible, although highly perturbed. Longer stretches are recognisable running NS, with shorter EW partitions, but it is not possible to identify a specific building, nor distinguish between inside and outside areas. Moreover, the walls running EW seem to be artificially cut on their eastern side by modern terracing. It is therefore possible that they continued towards the east.

Water infrastructures

A modern fountain made of reused blocks is found at the north-eastern foot of the hill (Figure 4.10, nr. 1). This fountain follows the course of a nearby water channel (Figure 4.10, nr. 2), which is constructed with the same building techniques and materials as the Frankish tower and according to the architecture specialist Inge Uytterhoeven was presumably preceded by an ancient channel.[575]

Discussion

Given the NS/EW surviving *in situ* wall alignments and the results of the geophysical analysis, it seems that at least the upper northern slope of the hill was regularly laid down and was occupied by a domestic quarter. These walls share the same orientation as the stretches that were identified in the

---

[572] Brasser 2013, 46 and catalogue nr. 100.
[573] Brasser 2013, 46 and catalogue nr. 104.
[574] Meyer and Pilz 2016.
[575] I. Uytterhoven, database record WRS1.

Figure 4.20 Results and interpretation of the magnetic survey conducted by Eastern Atlas on the lower northern slope.

magnetic survey on the plateau on the eastern slope and on part of the southern slope (see below), thus suggesting that they belong to the same chronological phase. For the lower part of the northern slope, the magnetic survey has shown only faint traces of walls up to grids 360-363 and 386, where a discernible feature, interpreted as a wall structure, could be followed along these grids almost without interruption. It is noteworthy that in these grids and in the area just below the architectural survey has recorded the presence of numerous large building blocks which could hint in fact at the existence of a large structure. It seems possible, therefore, that the anomalies can be identified as (one of) the lower city wall circuit which used to run on the northern slope, indeed along grids 360-363 and 386, and that would then run towards north to reconnect with the supposed city wall gate found in grid 599 (see Figures 4.18 and 4.32 for the projected path of the city wall). For certain, the location of the Hellenistic – Imperial inscribed funerary stele in grid 616 indicates that this area was outside the town extent during the corresponding time frame. Towards the north-east, the limits of Koroneia's urban area in Roman times are marked by the funerary architecture elements dated to the Roman period that were found in grid 703 and nearby. Also the cluster of miniatures found in grids 690-694 indicates an extra urban votive area, associated with a Classical extra urban sanctuary as well as a cemetery. The offering of miniature vessels and the proximity to running water fit a variety of female cults, which makes it possible that this location hosted in fact the sanctuary of Hera, Demetra or Artemis, cults attested at the town in the Classical period. Other possible shrines are located on the upper northern slope, near an area which is used as parking space and on the lower slope where fine pottery has been collected.[576]

As far as the location where the concentration of *kantharoi* was recorded, the wall alignments showed by the results of the magnetic survey cannot be clearly related to a specific building. Further investigation with another instrument (e.g. GPR) could shed light on the spatial arrangement and building structure of this area. Although the limited dataset does not allow more certain interpretations, the presence of grinding tools of large dimensions dated to the Late Classical – Hellenistic period in the same area can indicate that besides drinking, also the preparation of food was carried out in this establishment. A possibility to investigate further is the identification of this area with a sanctuary, which is hinted at also by the above mentioned presence of fine pottery dated from the Archaic to the Roman period and shells.

4.4.3 Eastern slope

The eastern slope is made of stable high grade metamorphic rock and has a plateau projecting towards east. 19th century travellers had already suggested that the core of the ancient town had to be located on the eastern and southern slopes where the majority of pottery and architecture were visible. As already observed, most of what used to lie on the surface was most likely already removed and the remains underneath have been heavily disturbed. Nevertheless, the survey has collected and recorded numerous finds that attest to the high building density of this area in antiquity.

Architecture

The depression on the eastern hill slope (corresponding to grid 377 in Figure 4.21) has been interpreted as the *koilon* of the theatre in the ancient city. Little has survived that can be securely related to it (Figure 4.22). An accurately worked stone piece, which was recorded in nearby grid 850, was initially tentatively identified as a component of the theatre seating system, but according to the theatre architecture expert Marco Germani this piece does not provide any element to reach a secure identification (Germani, pers. comm.).[577] Apart from this piece, numerous architectural blocks have been found in this area, together

---
[576] J. Bintliff, pers. comm.
[577] Pictures are available at http://www.boeotiaproject.org/files/09-13PDF/2013_138.pdf.

VISUALIZING CITYSCAPES OF CLASSICAL ANTIQUITY

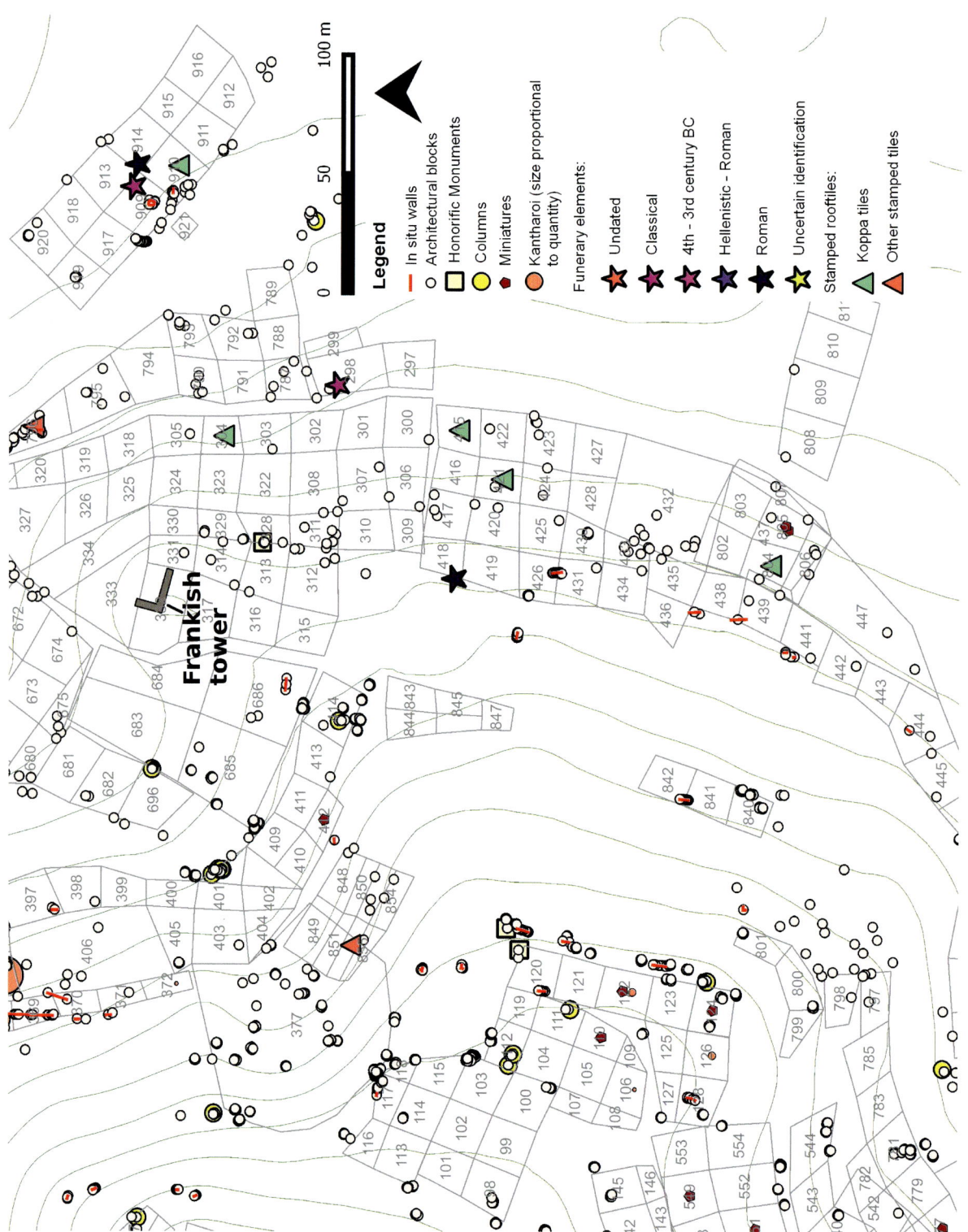

Figure 4.21 Overview of the finds on the eastern slope where the theatre (grid 377) and the agora (grids 98-128) were located.

with a fragment of statue base with a circular dowel hole on its top and mouldings on one face.[578] In grid 407, a little lower than 377, a column capital offers us a glimpse of Koroneia's various historical phases

---

[578] Pictures are available at http://www.boeotiaproject.org/files/09-13PDF/2010_102.pdf.

Figure 4.22 The depression on the slope of the hill once occupied by Koroneia's theatre (picture taken by the author inside the supposed cavea looking north-west).

Figure 4.23 The Hellenistic – Roman Ionic capital reused as a press weight probably in Late Antiquity (photos by I. Uytterhoeven).

and of the recycling of older architectural pieces for new usages: a Hellenistic – Roman Ionic capital (perhaps dated to the 3rd BC, L. Gentili, pers. comm.) was in fact recut and reused as a press weight, probably in Late Antiquity (Figure 4.23).

On the plateau lying just south of the theatre, numerous architectural blocks have been recorded and an illegal dig found during the survey season in May 2015 at its northern side (grid 117) brought to light a brick and mortar wall segment. On the plateau and on its lower terrace (grids 120-124), numerous honorific and architectural elements of a public character have been recorded. Specifically, a pediment block of a freestanding honorific monument (Roman period?) with mouldings,[579] and a fragment of moulded architrave were found north east of grid 120;[580] a not *in situ* large limestone threshold (2.34

---

[579] Pictures are available at http://www.boeotiaproject.org/files/09-13PDF/2011_027.pdf.
[580] Pictures are available at http://www.boeotiaproject.org/files/09-13PDF/2011_028.pdf.

m long) lying upside down was recorded in grid 123, which presumably belonged to a large building;[581] *in situ* walls made of limestone and rubble were recorded following the sloping ground east of grids 120-123;[582] column fragments, some of considerable diameter, were also found in the area: in grid 111 (d=0.63m), 112 (d=0.30m), to the south of grid 124 (d=0.67m); at the north edge of grid 139 (d=0.56m).

The sloping ground east of the plateau is occupied for the large part by dense bushes and has been left to a great extent uncovered by the survey. South of grid 801, however, two lines of *in situ* walls were recorded, meeting at a right angle and made of soft yellowish limestone, which is a similar stone to what was used for some of the recorded city walls' stretches. Another stretch of soft yellowish limestone was found south of grid 840. Lower down towards east, in grids 433-435, several large blocks of light grey and pink limestone have been recorded, which could hint at the presence of a large (public) structure.[583]

Moving towards south, in grid 532, a series of very large collapsed wall fragments of limestone rubble and bricks (for convenience of quick identification dubbed the 'Big Thing' by the survey team), tentatively identified as the foundation or the first floor (this latter hypothesis has been advanced by L. Gentili, pers. comm.) of a large structure was found (see Figure 4.24 for its location). The construction technique is ascribed either to *opus incertum* or *opus vittatum* and the structure can possibly be dated to the late Republic/early Empire.[584] The reasons why these pieces have survived up to today, contrary to other large buildings that we would expect in a Graeco-Roman town, are to be ascribed to the fact that this area was fairly recently bulldozed and that the material that it was made of could not be reused. The function of the building and its context still remain unclear, but its prominent position, central to the extent of the Roman town, leads us to suppose that it was either a public or an elite private building. It must be noted, incidentally, that an *iconostasis* is located just below the lower collapsed stretch, and testifies to worship by nearby villagers. Whether the choice of this location to install an *iconostasis* has or not some relation with this ancient building, marking in the former case a long tradition of cult activities, is impossible to say. One theory is that this structure might have become a church in Late Antiquity – perhaps one of the churches seen by Leake. This would make the hypothesis of it being a temple in the Roman period, perhaps located on the aqueduct route, more likely. In any case, that the area around this structure was not a normal housing quarter seems to be confirmed by the presence of several column fragments, some of which are of considerable diameter, on the grids below and east: in grid 786 (⌀ = 0.3m), 784 (visible ⌀ = 0.42m, but must have been much larger), 756 (⌀ = 0.42m), 494 (preserved ⌀ = 0.56), north-west of grid 450 (⌀ = 0.42m).

Beyond the modern street towards the south, in grids 463, 464 and 465, several large blocks of schist stone and brown-grey conglomerate were documented and in grid 471 several (probably not *in situ*) blocks of the same stone that were used for the city wall (yellow limestone) were recorded. Moreover, fragments of a Late Antique *opus sectile* floor made of square, rectangular and triangular white marble elements was found close to this area (south of grid 469), which according to the architecture specialist I. Uytterhoeven could hint at the presence of a villa or church,[585] testifying to the Late Antique occupation of this area of the hill.

---

[581] Pictures are available at http://www.boeotiaproject.org/files/09-13PDF/2009_038.pdf.
[582] E.g. http://www.boeotiaproject.org/files/09-13PDF/VE2011_010.pdf.
[583] Uytterhoeven 2014b, 3.
[584] F. Vermeulen, pers. comm., in Boswinkel 2015. Images of the structure can be found at: http://www.boeotiaproject.org/files/09-13PDF/VE2010_002.pdf (max length: 5.70m; not *in situ*, fell from above); http://www.boeotiaproject.org/files/09-13PDF/VE2011_016.pdf (not *in situ*); http://www.boeotiaproject.org/files/09-13PDF/VE2011_017.pdf (*in situ*); http://www.boeotiaproject.org/files/09-13PDF/VE2011_018.pdf (not *in situ*); http://www.boeotiaproject.org/files/09-13PDF/VE2011_019.pdf (not *in situ*); http://www.boeotiaproject.org/files/09-13PDF/VE2011_020.pdf (not *in situ*).
[585] Uytterhoeven 2014b, 2.

4. The ancient town of Koroneia

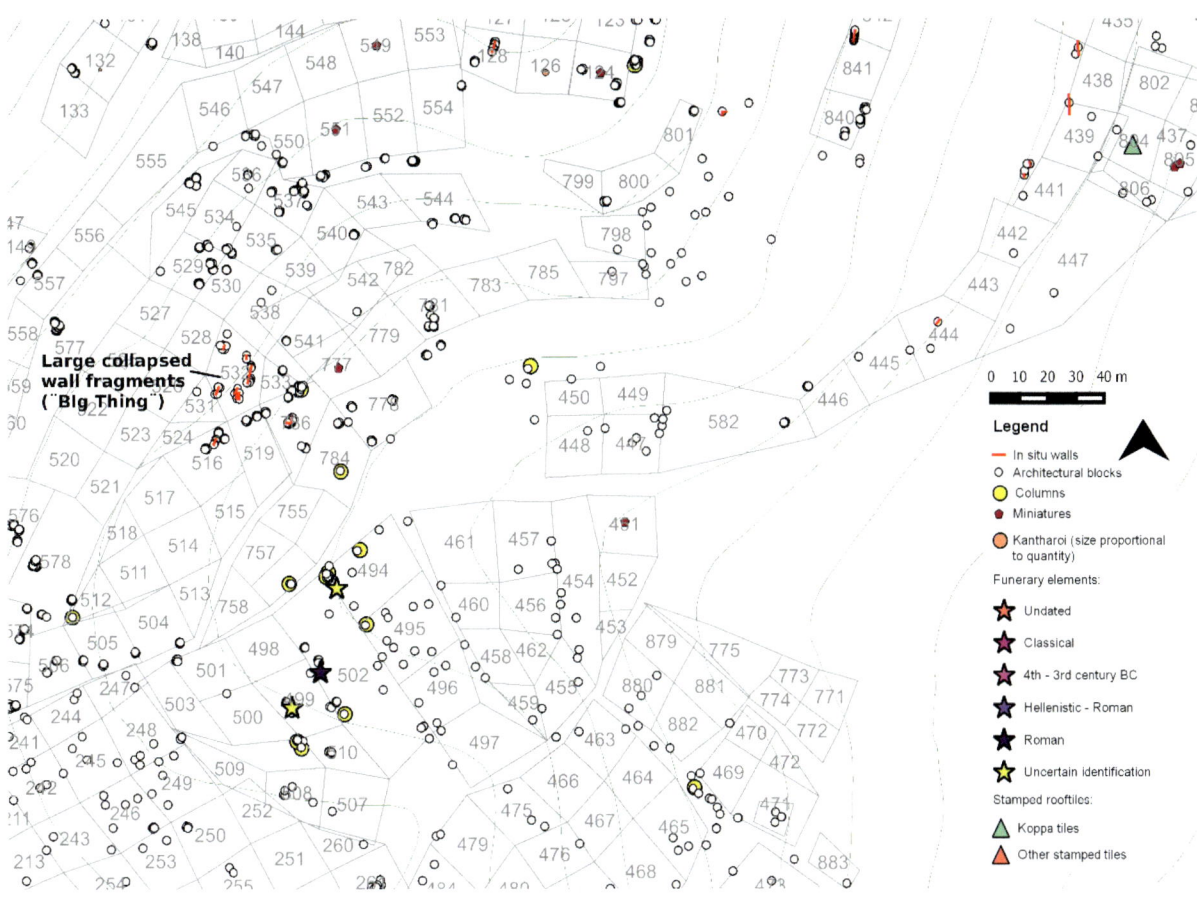

Figure 4.24 Eastern slope, southern part.

Funerary elements have been recorded along the lower eastern slope. On the western edge of grid 418, a (robbed) Roman tomb with *arcosolium* and several fragmentary cover slabs were found (Figure 4.26, location in Figure 4.21). The presence of this tomb can be considered as a marker for the eastern boundary of Roman Koroneia. On the southern side, a possible funerary slab was documented in grid 494. It must be noted that in the nearby grid 499, an inscribed funerary stele was found dated to the Imperial period by F. Marchand, and another possible sarcophagus lid were found. In this area, numerous sarcophagus lids were found along with small columns, but not recorded owing to burial and removal by the farmer of this plot during the survey.[586]

Pottery

In this area, the pottery processing is not yet completed. Grids 803 and 805 show a high density of finds. Among the categories of finds that have been studied so far, a number of loomweights were found, especially concentrated in grids 121-128 and in grids 802-803.[587] Fragments of *kantharoi* were collected in the grids 106 (1), 122 (2), 126 (2); 132 (1) and 141 (1) on the plateau and Classical – Hellenistic miniature vessels in grids 110 (1), 122 (1), 124 (1) and 412 (1), the latter being located on the slope lower than the theatre.

Moreover, fragments of 'Koppa' stamped tile were found in some of the grids in the lower slope (e.g. 404, 415, 421 and 804), while another stamped tile of which only the first or last letter is preserved

---
[586] J. Bintliff, pers. comm.
[587] Meens 2011.

Figure 4.25 The Roman tomb with arcosolium illegally excavated on the eastern side of the hill. Broken slabs were found in its proximity (picture by the author).

was found in grid 853 close to the theatre. The 'Koppa' tiles, defined as such because they bear the city stamp with the letter *Koppa* (Ϙ), used to indicate the /k/ sound in early Greek, are dated to the 5th, 4th and late 3rd or even early 2nd century BC,[588] and give an indication for the location of construction and rebuilding activities that were financed by the city, such as the city walls. The location of the collected city stamped tiles in the above mentioned grid indeed matches well the projected continuation of the city wall circuit whose traces have been found on the SE edge of the hill during the geophysical survey (see below). A fragment of tile dated to the Classical-Hellenistic period was collected in grid 796. The rectangular stamp on this tile has been interpreted by the pottery specialists as possibly bearing the text ']ΤΟΣΙΑ' (']TOSIA'), followed perhaps by another symbol at the end.

During a survey in the first years of the investigations at Koroneia, a concentration of figurines, fine ware and human bones were found in grids 297-298, at the foot of the hill, and outside the supposed city wall circuit in Classical times. These findings point towards the identification of the area as an Archaic – Classical cemetery (Figure 4.26).[589]

The area occupied by grids 754-758 shows a high density of pottery sherds, interpreted as a Roman pottery dump. This area, which was clearly extra urban or in any case peripheral when the sherds were

---

[588] Dated by F. Marchand; their study by Marchand is in progress.
[589] Bintliff *et al.* 2010, 37-9.

Figure 4.26 Sample of finds from the Archaic-Classical cemetery, the figurines highlighted (Bintliff et al. 2010, 39).

discarded here, was included within the Classical – Hellenistic city wall circuit, traces of which have been identified during the magnetic survey beyond the modern road (see below).

During the first orientation survey by the pottery specialists on the hill, numerous traces of misfired pottery sherds and pottery waste have been found on the SE foot of the hill, especially in the area covered by grids 469-472. This zone could therefore be interpreted as an industrial quarter (the evidence pointing towards potters' workshops, but other crafts cannot be excluded as discussed in chapter 5, p. 213) possibly in use both in the Greek and Roman periods right outside the city wall circuit.

Finally, Frankish – Late Byzantine pottery was found to the north of the eminence where the Frankish tower was built, suggesting the presence of a medieval hamlet which seems to have lain north of and below the tower and the northern edges of the cemetery in grids 297-298.[590] It is significant that the water source (located east of grid 298, see Figure 4.10, nr. 4), which is now covered by a large fig tree, is positioned at a convenient location for its supply.

Stone finds

A large amount of fragments of grindstones were found in the agora, mostly belonging to the Olynthian Hopper rubber type (see overview in Figure 4.16). This type of large grindstone is typically dated to

---

[590] Bintliff *et al.* 2010, 39.

the Classical-Hellenistic period and could be related to commercial food processing activities.[591] It is however not clear if those that have been found in the agora can be ascribed to this period or to a secondary later context and purpose of use. Another two fragments of Olynthian Hopper rubber were found in grid 842 and other fragments of the same type of grindstone were collected also in the lower grids 802-807. This type of grinding tool is also the most common toward the south, 797, 785, 779, 780 (2), 778 (3). The highest number of grinding tools' fragments were however collected in the grids interpreted as a pottery dump, especially in grids 756 where 7 fragments of Hopper rubber and 1 of saddle quern were found.[592] Besides the saddle quern, other types of grinding tools found on the eastern slope include a fragment tentatively interpreted as belonging to a Rotary Hand quern, dated to the Roman period, in grid 800.[593] This fragment would represent the only example of this type of grinding tool at Koroneia, but its uncertain identification suggests caution. Evidence of olive or wine press installations that testify to the ruralisation of the urban centre from Late Antiquity onwards has been recorded on the lower eastern slope. Specifically, a fragment of circular press weight made of light grey limestone (architecture database, nr. 2) was recorded south of grid 840 and another, almost square pink limestone weight press (architecture database, nr. 29) was found in the same area. Finally, a fragment of a roughly worked large basin of uncertain function and date was found east of grid 400 (architecture database, nr. 156).

Geophysics

On the plateau, the magnetic survey has identified some wall alignments and streets with a roughly NS/EW orientation (see Figure 4.27). In the northern part, the results show long stretches of walls running NS and shorter EW partitions, which could be identified as a long building, possibly a *stoa*, whose boundaries however are not clear. It must be noted that some of the magnetic anomalies interpreted as wall lay in proximity of the above mentioned brick and mortar wall found during the illegal dig. From the southern edge of the plateau clearer results have instead emerged. The area roughly corresponding to grids 139-144 is occupied by an *insula* measuring about 33 x 33 meters, bordered on its south edge by a street about 3 meters wide crossing grids 547, 548 and 552 (see Figure 4.27). Some of the internal partitions within the *insula* are recognisable, but at this stage it is not possible to clearly identify the spatial arrangement of the structure. South of the street, the wall alignments seem to point to the existence of another building of the same orientation, with another street at about 30 meters from the previous one, but the traces are too faint for any secure interpretation. Further south, across grids 527-529, the magnetic survey evidenced a clearer crossing point of two roads which have the same orientation of the road bordering the above mentioned insula. Interestingly, the distance between the two securely identified roads is about 60 meters, which confirms a recurrent building module of some 30 meters.

The survey has continued the investigation towards the south, around the area where the 'Big Thing' lies (see Figure 4.28 for an overview). The results evidence the presence of stretches of walls with the same orientation as the 'Big Thing', therefore orientated a few degrees off in relation to the *insula* on the plateau, but no clear building shapes can be recognized. A little south, an anomaly interpreted as a street has been identified across grids 514, 515, 757, 755, 754 and, beyond the modern road that surrounds the hill, 461 and 457 where it bifurcates in two segments, one proceeding towards SE, while the other one running towards north. This street is not aligned with the roads that were seen closer to the plateau and it is not possible to establish whether these streets are part of the same network or represent street systems that were laid out in different historical periods. Towards the SE, the road seems to intersect

---

[591] Brasser 2013, 44.
[592] Brasser 2013.
[593] Brasser 2013.

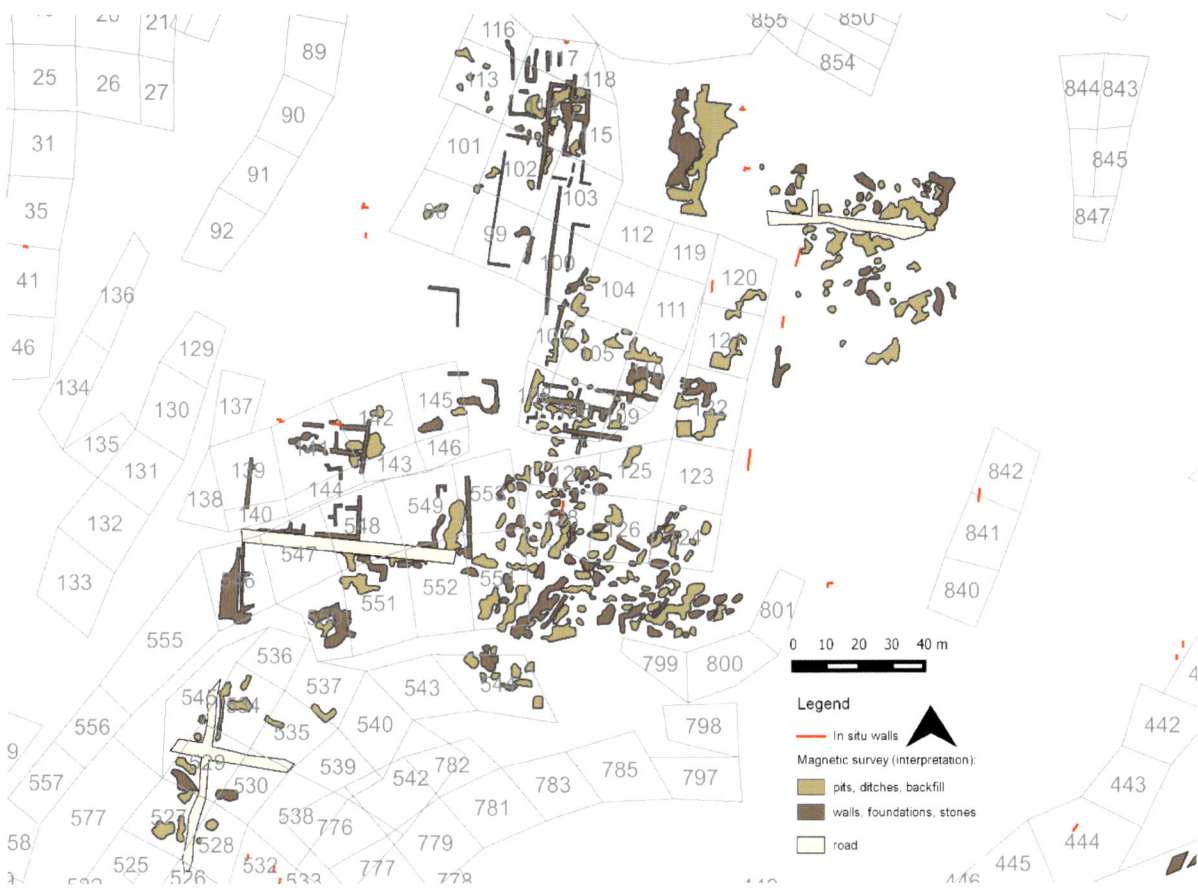

Figure 4.27 Detail of the interpretation of the magnetometry survey's results (by Eastern Atlas) on the eastern slope of the hill. The raster image of the results in this area is shown in Figure 4.29.

the large anomaly that the magnetic survey has identified running from grid 452 until grid 502 (but that continues again towards SW in grid 246, see below *Southern slope*). This anomaly, reaching 20 meters of width as it approaches the modern road, can be identified as the double curtain city wall that enclosed the urban centre on its southern side. The extension of the anomaly, exceeding the typical city wall's width, might be explained as remains of construction debris and limestone fragments.[594] In case the road and the city wall belonged to the same chronological period and were contemporary in use, their position in relation to each other suggest that a gate was located at their intersection.

Water infrastructures

A sewer was recorded just south of grid 377, between the theatre and the plateau, oriented roughly EW and presumably flanking a street (Figure 4.10, nr. 3). At the foot of the hill, some 150 meters SE from the Frankish tower, an underground fountain has been discovered under an overgrown fig tree (Figure 4.10, nr. 4). Another water source was probably located on the SE foot of the hill, near grid 775 (Figure 4.10, nr. 5).

Discussion

The eastern slope has yielded significant traces of occupation of the hill, both in terms of private and public architecture. The ancient theatre of Koroneia was located in the natural depression on the eastern

---

[594] Meyer and Pilz 2016, 12.

slope, close to the plateau where the evidence suggest that the agora/forum of the Graeco-Roman town was located. This proximity is often observed in Boeotian urban centres, where the theatre had usually an important role as a place where festivals and rituals associated with local cults were celebrated, such as the *Agrionia*, a festival in honour of Dionysos, which at Orchomenos took place in the theatre near the temple.[595] The few finds associated with the theatre do not allow us to make hypotheses on its appearance and actual size. The natural depression obviously gives the maximum extent (about 80 meters), but it must be noted that the retaining walls often encompassed a larger area than what was available for the spectators to be seated in.[596] As a comparison, the theatre of Thebes, the largest in Boeotia and dated to the 3rd century BC, had a diameter of ca. 110 meters.[597] Regional comparisons show that Boeotian theatres were often erected directly on the slope, adapting to the natural morphology more than being constructed to follow a preferred orientation.[598]

On and around the plateau, numerous evidences of public and honorific architecture have been found and, for this reason, the area has been identified already in the early years of the survey as the possible agora/forum of the city. The current available data recorded on the northern and eastern parts of the plateau point indeed towards a pronounced public character given the traces of large buildings and honorific monuments. The southern part is instead occupied by *insulae* measuring roughly 30 x 30 meters. The wall alignments recorded on this part of the eastern slope share the same roughly NS/EW orientation as the *in situ* walls documented on the northern slope, which confirms the presence of an orthogonal roughly NS/EW urban layout. This spatial organization can be followed only for some 150 meters towards the south, as the traces of walls identified during the magnetic survey on the lower SE slope have a slightly different orientation (which will become more marked in the wall stretches on the lower southern slope, see below). At this stage of the research we suppose that this is the result of the attempt to negotiate between an orthogonal grid and the natural morphology of the terrain, which has been evidenced in other sites as well such as at Haliartos and Hyettos.[599] The orientation of the *insula* and its bordering street follows indeed the edge of the plateau, while the shift in orientation seems to have been made to adjust the buildings to better fit the sloping ground towards the south (see Figure 4.28).

Regarding the boundaries of the town on the eastern slope, the findspots of the 'Koppa' stamped tiles match well with the projected line of the city wall circuit that the magnetic survey has recognized at the foot of the southern slope (see Figures 4.28 and 4.32 for the hypothetical reconstruction of the path followed by the city wall circuit). The above mentioned funerary elements that have been recorded on the south-eastern slope are located inside the urban area that is marked by the supposed stretch of the city wall identified during the magnetic survey in the south edge of the hill. This is not in contrast with the costume of keeping *necropoleis* outside the urban area. The inscribed stele has been in fact dated to the Imperial period and therefore this area could well have been a Roman cemetery, in use after the destruction or obliteration of the Classical-Hellenistic city wall. The above mentioned Roman pottery dump, located in grids 754-758, is also inside the city wall circuit.

If the identification of the magnetic anomalies will be confirmed, we can suppose the existence of a gate at the intersection of city wall and road, the latter being flanked outside the wall by an industrial quarter, especially in grids 879-882 and 469-472 (in Figure 4.24) where misfired pottery and magnetic anomalies point towards the possible existence of pottery kilns. The location of artisanal quarters at the

---

[595] Germani 2015, 360. See Germani 2012 for an overview of Boeotian festivals and contexts that were held in theatres.
[596] Germani 2012.
[597] Germani 2012.
[598] Germani 2015, 356. See chapter 5, p. 185 for a discussion on Greek theatres' orientation.
[599] See Sarris and Kalayci 2016, 51.

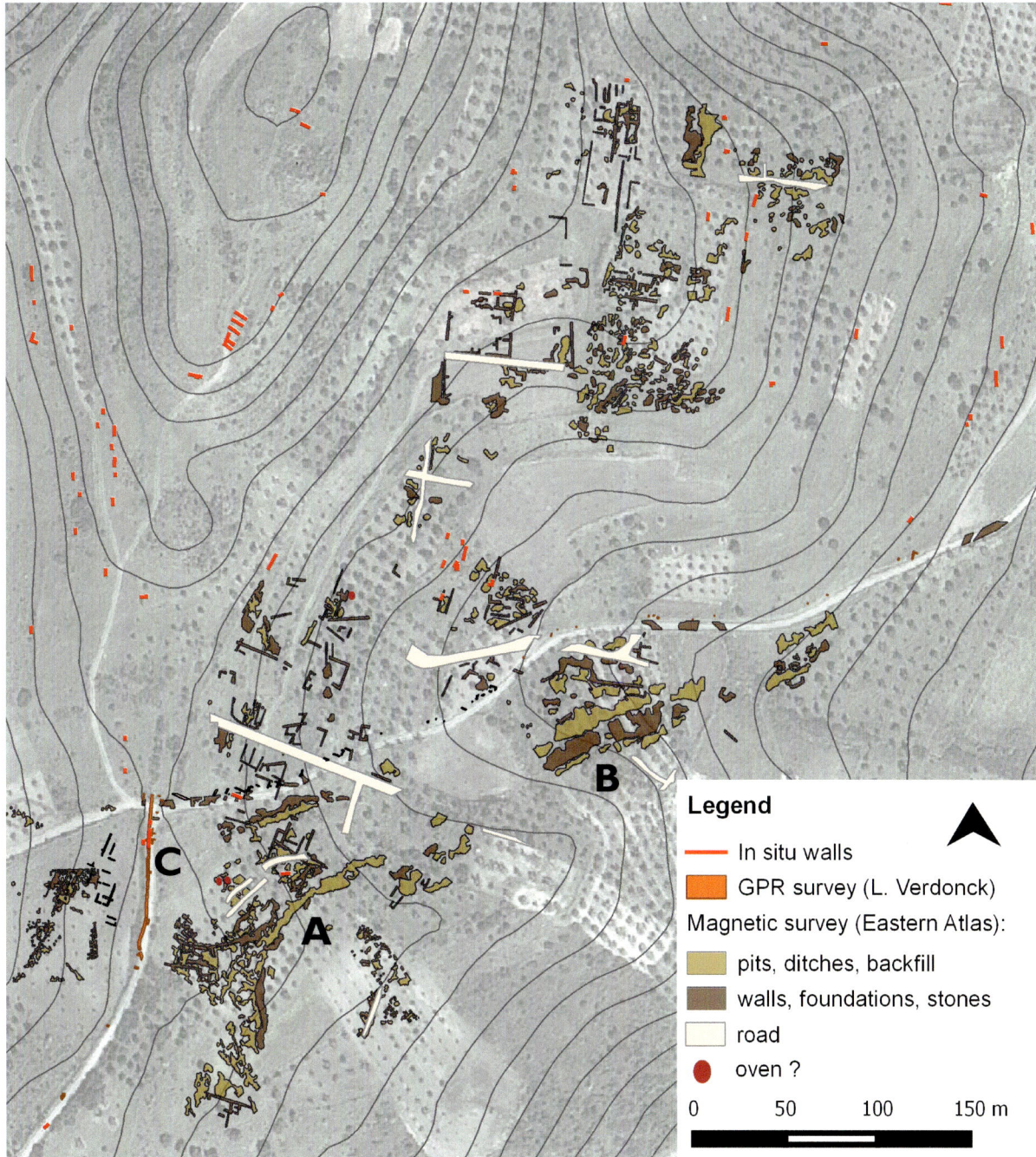

Figure 4.28 Overview of the areas on the eastern and southern slopes that have been covered by geophysical survey. The features interpreted as roads (in light pink) and the remains of foundations and walls (in brown) show a regular lay out on the plateau and on part of the southern slope, while at the foot of the latter the orientation shifts, probably to adapt to the terrain. Two large anomalies at the foot of the southern slope (A and B) have been interpreted as the city wall circuit. C identifies the supposed path of the Hadrianic aqueduct resulting from the GPR survey by L. Verdonck.

foot of the hill can be related also to the presence of water nearby, which represented an indispensable element for the preparation of clay (but see chapter 5, pp. 213-4). In the same area, the finds documented in grids 463-465 and 469, namely large blocks and the *opus sectile* floor testify to the occupation of this area in Late Antiquity, perhaps with a villa or a church.

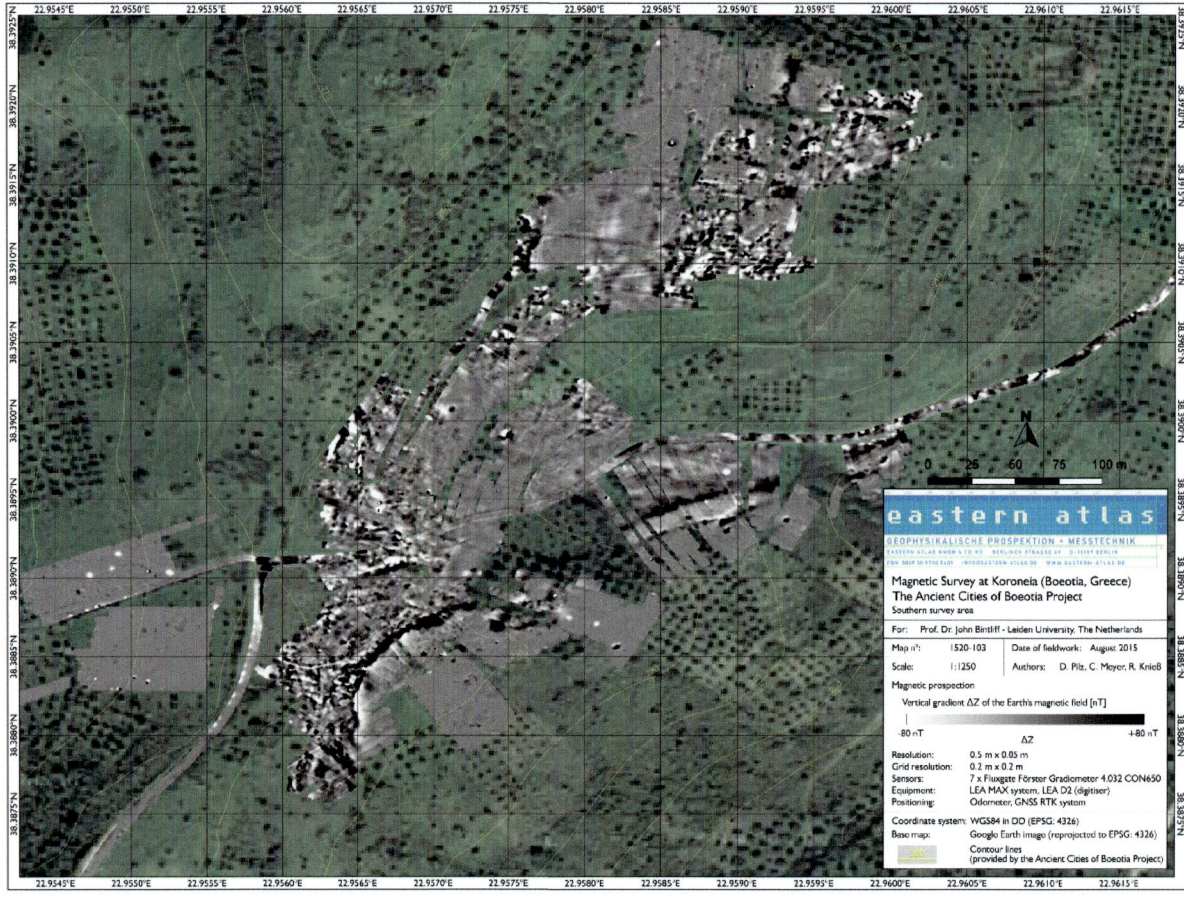

Figure 4.29 Results of the magnetometry survey on the hill's plateau and southern slope (by Eastern Atlas).

4.4.4 Southern slope

Architecture

The overview of the finds are presented in Figure 4.30. On the lower southern slope, a fragment of a Corinthian Byzantine capital decorated with a cross was found west of grid 510.[600] This gives us a clear indication of the presence of a church in this area. The north-east edge of grid 258 is occupied by a cluster of roughly worked grey limestone building blocks, varying in dimension from about 0.40 to 1.8 meter, which have been pushed towards the terrace's edge and could hint at the presence of a large building in the area.[601] Numerous worked stones were documented also on the edge of the terrace occupied by grids 216-224, testifying once again to the intense agricultural works on the hill.

A number of blocks recorded in grid 161 had probably fallen down from the acropolis, similarly to other blocks found on the western slope (see related section).[602]

Pottery

At present, there are only few available pottery data for this area of the town. Some textile implements, mainly discoid loomweights (which reflects the overall situation of the example so far examined), were

---

[600] Pictures available at http://www.boeotiaproject.org/files/09-13PDF/2010_080.pdf
[601] Uytterhoeven 2014a, 2.
[602] Uytterhoeven 2014a, 1.

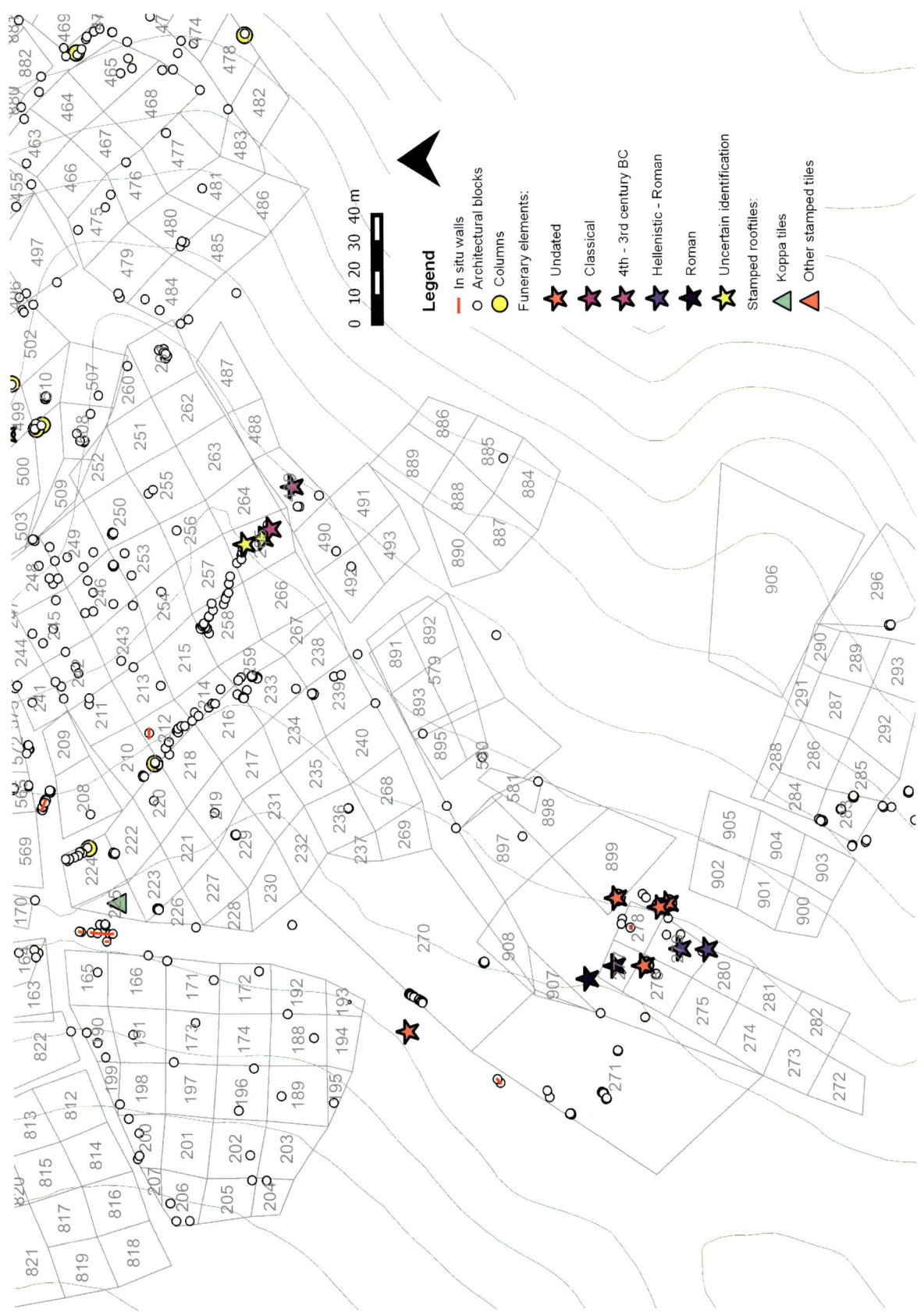

Figure 4.30 Overview of the finds on the southern slope

collected and studied:[603] in grid 165 (nr. 15, conical), 170 (nr. 34, discoid), 171 (nr. 93, spindle whorl), 174 (nr. 10, conical), 188 (nr. 65, discoid), 190 (nr. 42, discoid), 196 (nr. 51, discoid), 220 (nr. 49, discoid). A 'Koppa' stamp that was found in grid 225, which suggests the nearby presence of a structure financed by the town in Classical – Hellenistic time.

Stone finds

Grinding tools collected on the southern slope concentrate in grids 812-819, which are located outside the city wall circuit. Specifically, grids 813 and 814 one fragment of Pompeian Donkey Mill each, in the latter grid a fragment of a Saddle Quern was also found, grids 815 and 816 one fragment of Olynthian Hopper Rubber each, while grid 817 yielded 5 fragments of Olynthian Hopper Rubber. It seems likely therefore that a commercial activity oriented to grain processing and bread making was established in this area from Classical to Roman times. Considering the broader context of Koroneia's *chora*, this area seems in fact to be favourably located for town dwellers returning from their fields.

As far as funerary inscriptions are concerned, two findings in the adjacent grids 265 and 489 are dated to the 4th – 3rd century BC,[604] hinting at the presence of a Late Classical – Hellenistic necropolis in this area, which is in fact outside the supposed city wall circuit on the south. Further south, a Roman *necropolis*, perhaps already in use in late Hellenistic times, can be identified around grids 276-279. Funerary inscriptions dated to the late Hellenistic – (early and late) Imperial period by F. Marchand are in fact concentrated in those grids and in grid 899, where also other pieces of funerary monuments have been found.

Geophysics

A large area on the southern slope has been surveyed by using a GPR[605] and an array of fluxgate gradiometer probes to investigate the magnetic properties of underground anomalies.[606] These investigations showed the continuation of the anomalies, interpreted as the city wall, visible at the foot of the eastern slope, and a regularly laid out sector of the town with a different orientation than what was observed on the northern and eastern slope (ca. N25°E). The street system of this area is comprised of a long street about 3 meters wide that runs diagonally across grids 568, 564, 571, 575, 244, and 248, and continues in grids 507-508 (see overview in Figure 4.28). In between grids 244 and 248, another street, seemingly narrower, departs from the previous one making a 90° turn towards south-west. Another narrow road with the same orientation as the latter was identified further south crossing grids 266 and 492. The magnetic survey has identified several wall alignments which give the impression of a densely built-up area, although no individual building or insula-arrangement can be identified. Three anomalies that could be interpreted as ovens have been recognised in grid 520 (1) and 220 (2).

The GPR survey in this area identified some clearly recognisable traces of walls: wall alignments with the same orientation as the others that were recorded in this area have been found on the field west of the modern road (grids 165, 166, 171). On the modern road, a long stretch of wall, whose remains on surface were also spotted during the architecture survey, was identified (Figure 4.28, C). This feature runs NS for about 80 meters, therefore not sharing the common orientation of the other anomalies recorded in this area and seems to start bending at the end of the GPR-surveyed area (i.e. between grids 172 and 230). The interpretation of this long stretch is not secure, but its width (ca. 1 m) and the fact that it is only one line, which excludes that it can be part of the city wall circuit, leave as the only

---

[603] Meens 2011.
[604] Dated by F. Marchand.
[605] Verdonck 2013.
[606] Meyer and Pilz 2016.

other plausible hypothesis at this stage that these are the remains of the Hadrianic aqueduct that used to bring water to Koroneia. The location matches with the information collected by Lauffer during his survey that the aqueduct's starting point was on the ridge of the Megalo Butsurati, south of Koroneia's hill, and that it reached the town from the south.

Discussion

Since the results of the pottery data for this area are not available yet, we are limited in the hypotheses that we can make on this area of the town. The finds discussed in this section are dated mainly to the Roman and Late Roman period, but this obviously does not exclude an occupation of this area in Classical – Hellenistic times. The southern and eastern slopes seem to have become the focus of the Roman town. The aqueduct (if this identification will be confirmed) passing through this area would have offered a readily available source of water, making this location particularly favourable for housing quarters. As observed by Boswinkel in his analysis of the architectural finds, most of the walls in polygonal masonry are found in the north part of the site, while individual polygonal blocks are found on or near the plateau. This could be explained with the recycling of these blocks in the Roman shrunken town, which indeed occupied the eastern and southern slope leaving the northern part abandoned.[607] A Late Antique presence in this part of the hill is attested by the capital with cross recorded in grid 510, perhaps a trace of one of the churches that we know from 19th century travellers were located on the hill.

4.3.5 Western slope

The western slope is the steepest and made of low grade unstable metamorphic stone, with the exception of the upper terraces, close to the acropolis.[608] The unstable nature of the geology on this side facilitates the creation of gullies, and in fact two of them are present on the slope.

Architecture

On this side of the hill, the survey team identified the most conspicuous traces of fortifications, namely two protruding square towers, one west of grid unit 753 and the other one on the northern edge of grid 832 (located in Figure 4.31). Numerous blocks, most likely fallen from the acropolis wall, have been recorded in grids 176 and 177.[609] At the foot of the slope, in grid 877, 4 *in situ* limestone ashlars belonging to the same structure have been documented, namely two corner blocks and two central pieces lower than the corner blocks, indicating perhaps a threshold. Although at this stage of the research it is difficult to advance any hypotheses given the few surface remains, this structure could be interpreted as a temple.

Pottery

On the western slope, the highest concentration of textile implements was found (6 in grid 177; 5 in 178 and 3 in179; the lower grids 181 returned one loomweight and in 182 a tile which was possibly recut to serve as a loomweight was found).[610] It must be remembered that the studied textile implements represent only a fraction of the total collected pottery finds and therefore should not be used to draw statistical conclusions. On the grids not far from where the remains of one of the towers were recorded, a high concentration of stamped roof tiles were found, peaking with 7 fragments in grid 870. This density confirms the proximity of the city wall circuit running along the western slope.

---

[607] Boswinkel 2015, 202.
[608] Bintliff *et al.* 2013, 137.
[609] Uytterhoeven 2014a.
[610] Meens 2011.

Stone finds

The amount of stone finds on the western slope is very limited. A fragment of Olynthian hopper rubber and another one of an unidentified grinding tool were collected on the terraces below the acropolis (in grid 177 and 186 respectively). On the lower slope (west of grid 761), a fragment of a saddle quern was recorded.[611]

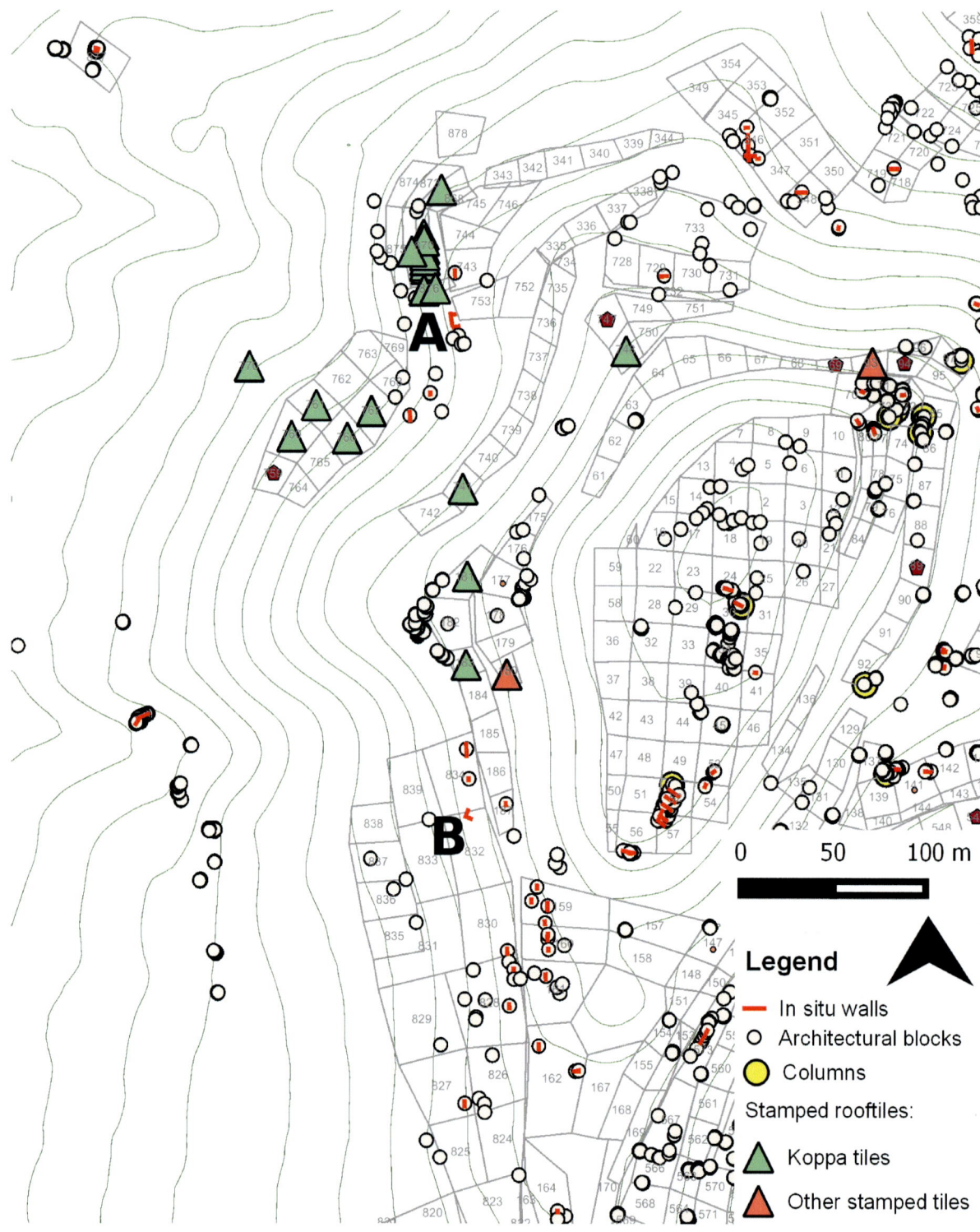

Figure 4.31 Western slope with surveyed towers (A and B).

---

[611] Brasser 2013.

4. THE ANCIENT TOWN OF KORONEIA

Discussion

The fortification line on the western slope can be traced with high likeliness thanks to the remains of two towers, the distribution of the stamped tiles and the morphology of the terrain. The size of the Classical-Hellenistic walled town is therefore either about 34 (yellow line in Figure 4.32) or 37 hectares (orange line in Figure 4.32).

4.5. Conclusions

To sum up, the archaeological record from Koroneia is representative of the typical situation of a multi-period urban site in which building blocks and artefacts have been reused, excavated, removed and dispersed, both in historical and modern times, thus complicating our task of reconstructing its several phases of occupation. Nevertheless, the analysis of the multidisciplinary dataset, including historical

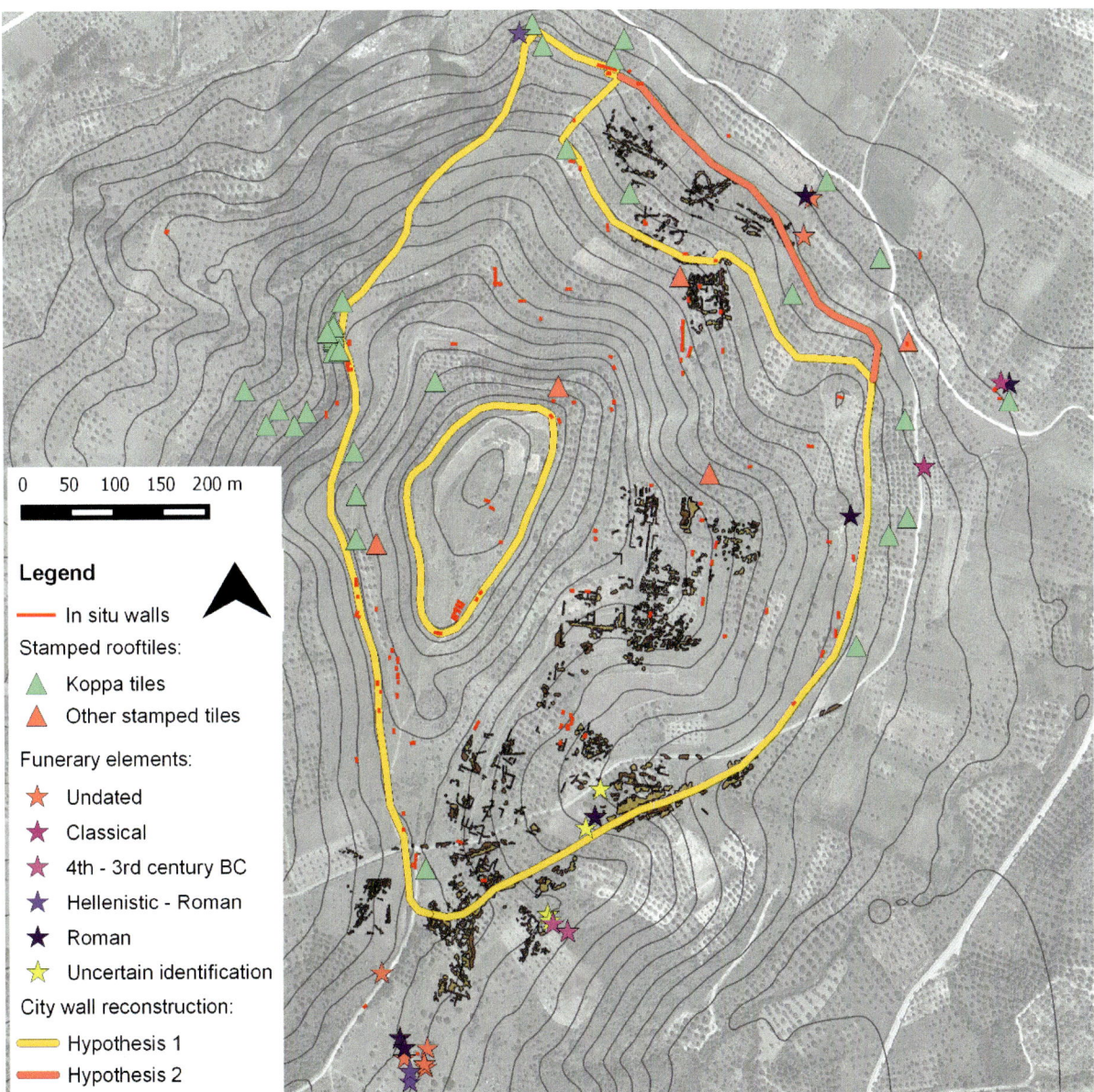

Figure 4.32 Reconstruction hypothesis of the path followed by the acropolis and lower city wall circuits based on the hill's contour lines, geophysical results and related finds such as funerary elements and stamped rooftiles bearing the city mark Koppa (Ϙ).

sources, previous research and the preliminary results of the of non-destructive methods employed by the Boeotia survey team have allowed us so far to: 1) reconstruct parts of the urban layout as regularly laid out with a NS/EW orientation, especially on the upper northern and eastern slope; 2) map provisional functional zones such as housing and public areas and position one area with large public architecture (possibly the agora/forum) on a plateau below and east of the acropolis; 3) establish the path of the lower city wall circuit; and 4) locate several *necropoleis* that marked the boundary between the town and the extra mural areas in Classical, Hellenistic and Roman times, and some possible suburban sanctuaries.

Given that the study of survey finds is still in progress, especially in regard to the pottery sherds, there are some limitations in our current possibilities of following the urban development of the settlement through the centuries. From the integration of the available sources that I discussed in this chapter, however, it is possible to identify some modifications in the settlement's size and location. The Classical-Hellenistic town reached the largest expansion, up to the lower town wall circuit identified during the geophysical and architectural surveys. In Roman times, the urban area shrank considerably, leaving the northern slope abandoned and concentrating on the eastern and southern slope. The Imperial aqueduct, coming from the Butsurati ridge, must have offered a convenient source of water to the southern part of the town, and therefore certainly contributed to the concentration of the settlement in this area. The Late Antique phase features prominently on the acropolis, where some fragments of vaulted ceiling belonging to an imposing building, possibly an elite mansion, still survive, together with the (poorly) excavated remains of some possible houses. The series of strong earthquakes that hit Greece in 551 AD and that, according to Procopius, destroyed Koroneia are probably responsible for the physical destruction of this settlement, but are unlikely to have required abandonment, as other city sites show. Finally, a small community is attested below the Frankish tower during the Middle and Byzantine period outside of the ancient city. Scattered survey finds and the testimonies of 19th century travellers testify to the presence of (three) churches on the lower slopes of the hill, possibly belonging to this period.

The completion of the study of the architectural and pottery finds and the continuation of the geophysical investigations will further refine this provisional information. There will however remain areas that are not accessible for surveying or that have been only partially investigated due to the presence of overgrown vegetation or a steep slope, and features that were shown by the geophysical survey that could be identified securely only by excavating. Moreover, the identification of some of the structures uncovered during previous investigations on the hill remains still obscure. Specifically, the location of the Christian church, the Roman agora and the large cistern excavated by Pappadakis have all not been identified with certainty. The path followed by the aqueduct after entering the town and its endpoint are moreover still unclear.

Regarding the fortifications of the lower town, as discussed above, several *in situ* stretches of a wall built out of rectangular soft yellowish limestone blocks coming from a nearby quarry were recognised in numerous locations.[612] As was ascertained during the survey, the properties of the stone lead to its easy erosion when the blocks are exposed. Uytterhoven has suggested therefore that the choice of such poor quality, yet easily obtainable, stone for fortifying the lower town is a possible sign of an emergency measure in view of a possible military threat for Koroneia after the Classical period.[613] Although the fragmentary historical information that we have discussed above warns caution in advancing hypotheses, it seems possible that a rapid reconstruction of the fortification circuit was needed after the *andrapodismos* that the Koroneians suffered in 346 BC. The speedy recovery of the town, which spanned less than a decade judging from the Delphi inscription dated to 337/6, can be explained by the

---

[612] Uytterhoeven 2014a, 1-2.
[613] Uytterhoeven 2014a, 2.

use of readily available building materials and fits well into the currently available evidence. In this regard, however, further study needs to be done on the 'Koppa' tiles, which have been dated from the 5th to the 2nd century BC by F. Marchand: only when the finds will be plotted on a map and divided by age, will it become more clear if the tiles that have been dated to the 4th century BC can confirm our hypothesis of a rebuilding of the lower city walls in relation to the above mentioned *andrapodismos*. The 2nd century BC tiles, testifying to the final repairs to the city walls, fit well with the historical sources attesting the Roman policy of not allowing the reconstruction of the lower city wall.

As far as Koroneia's urban layout, the architectural and geophysical survey results showed the existence of a regular spatial arrangement, oriented roughly NS/EW, on the higher parts of the northern and eastern slopes. From comparisons with other urban centres in Boeotia and in mainland Greece, it seems likely that this roughly orthogonal organization was laid out in the late Classical – Hellenistic period. Plataiai, for example, received an orthogonal grid upon its re-foundation after Chaironeia in 338 BC,[614] and Tanagra also seems to have assumed its orthogonal plan in the 4th century BC.[615] In both cases, the overall plan was maintained up to Late Antiquity, albeit with some internal modifications that transformed *insulae* that were previously occupied by numerous house plots into large villas and shrinking in size of the town extent (see chapter 5, pp. 155-7). Comparisons with other sites, such as Hyettos and recently at Haliartos, show moreover that the regular grid was adapted to better follow the terrain morphology. This occurred probably also in Koroneia, where the results of both the geophysical and the architectural surveys show a change in wall orientation on the southern and south-eastern slope in respect to the roughly north-south axis which was preferred on the northern and eastern slope. These are therefore the working hypotheses that guided the reconstruction of the urban layout that will be discussed in chapter 6.

As a final point, besides the built environment, also the vegetation that was present in and around the town should be considered. Until now, however, no archaeo-botanical analysis has been made that specifically identifies botanical species at Koroneia.[616] From ancient sources, however, we know that the towns around the Copais had a very peculiar ecology and exploited the vegetation of the marshy areas as a source of income. For example, reeds were used for weaving and a sugary fruit called 'phleos' to make soap powder and as food for children and cattle.[617] Chaironeians especially are said by Pausanias to distil perfumes, which were used as healing unguents, from flowers such as irises that grew in the marsh, lily, roses, and narcissus.[618] Regarding Koroneia, as Fossey has suggested, the inscriptions testifying to the Imperial concern of protecting the agricultural land from flooding point also to the importance of crops as the main resource for the economy of this region.

---

[614] Konecny *et al.* 2013, 32-9.
[615] Slapšak 2012, 53-61. For comparisons with other sites, see also chapter 5, pp. 149-51.
[616] For Boeotia, see Rackham 1983.
[617] Fossey 1990, 220-66, esp. 251.
[618] Paus. 9.41.7; Fossey 1990, 251.

5. The Graeco-Roman town as a physical entity: Sources for a comparison

'Cities are the accumulation of human experience. They are the manufactured containers, the physical expressions, of human culture. In that sense, all cities are planned environments. They are the results of cultural decisions about the most appropriate physical uses of land and the residential distribution of people. Urban form encapsules time and space. At any moment in time, the physical landscape of the city reveals countless decisions of bygone days about the 'best' uses of space – 'best' means those individual or collective values and judgments about the quality of life made by citizens in the past, judgments that affect the lives of those in the present – and the future. Urban forms reveal what was and was not important to their builders in any given historical moment.' (Schultz 1989, xii)

5.1. Introduction

A large amount of books and articles examines the ancient Greek city, dealing either with single buildings,[619] or with aspects of the city in a specific chronological horizon.[620] This situation reflects, and is partially caused by, the piecemeal development of our knowledge of ancient urban sites. In most cases, new findings are encountered when works for the construction of buildings are carried out in the modern town. Alternatively, accidental discoveries are made by farmers while working their land, which could be followed up by systematic excavations in the area. Even when there would be the physical possibility to investigate the city in its entirety, time and cost constraints impose the selection of specific areas, since excavations, bound by fieldwork seasons, will take years to cover such large expanses. In this respect, surface survey and other non-destructive investigation methods such as geophysical analysis, can greatly accelerate the process of gaining a complete overview of the urban area. Indisputably, however, they cannot reach the high resolution data provided by the stratigraphic analysis of structures and finds.

The studies that have dealt with specific aspects or periods of the ancient Greek urban environments have produced and made available a vast amount of knowledge on the subject. This type of approach, however, tends to dissect the ancient city into smaller units, either physical or chronological, that are isolated from their context. This artificial fragmentation risks to overshadow what the city actually is, namely a unified system that developed diachronically as part of a larger regional context. One of the main reasons for why this has happened is that often the best attested phases of occupation of a site have received preference over the others.[621] Classical *poleis* have received much attention, not least by the systematic and in-depth studies of the Copenhagen *Polis* Centre.[622] The urban developments that occur in Roman and, even more, in Late Roman Greece have instead started to be taken into account only in recent years.[623] This is mainly due to a tendency in scholarship that traditionally considered the post-Classical *polis* as a declining urban focus in comparison with the achievements reached during

---

[619] E.g. Coulton 1976 and Miller 1978.
[620] E.g. Mitchell and Rhodes 1997 and Winter 2006.
[621] For example Roman and Late Antique Knossos are less known to the wider public than the Bronze Age phase of the palace (see at this respect Sweetman 2012). Recent systematic and comprehensive surveys aim at filling the gap and are shedding light on all the phases of urban development at Knossos (Whitelaw *et al.* 2006-7). A notable exception is the site of Messene, extensively published by P. Themelis.
[622] See e.g. the volumes of the Acts of the Copenhagen Polis Centre, and Hansen and Nielsen 2004.
[623] For an account of the history of research on Late Roman and Early Byzantine Greece, see Petridis 2014.

Classical times.[624] The upper strata have been often hastily cleaned out to reach the deeper remains of Classical antiquity. Yet, despite the numerous publications that deal with aspects of the Classical *polis*, Morgan and Coulton calculated in 1997 that only 10% of the 800-1000 *poleis* that had been included into the inventory compiled by the Copenhagen *Polis* Centre were investigated to such an extent that would allow generalizations and systematic comparisons between Archaic and Classical towns in Greece.[625]

The uneven distribution of studies relates also to a marked preference for unearthing monumental architecture instead of investigating housing quarters. One may recall Robinson's initially disappointed tone when reporting that 'only houses were found' in the trenches he was excavating at Olynthos.[626] Even when houses captured the interest of scholars, the attention was focussed at first on the most lavishly decorated examples, which allowed the study of decorative elements, most notably mosaics.[627] Besides temples and public buildings, also *necropoleis* received much attention for the aesthetic value of the fine pottery and other grave goods that could be found. A striking example are the 19th century excavations at the Boeotian city of Tanagra that were focussed on the *necropoleis* around the city, after the pillages of thousands of tombs perpetrated by tomb robbers, which had flooded the antiquities market with the famous terracotta figurines.[628] The city itself, however, was never systematically excavated, and only recent investigations have shed light on its urban development.[629]

Moreover, scholars have too often relied on textual evidence alone to create typologies or sustain assumptions that have found little confirmation in the archaeological record. If is true that ancient texts can provide an insight into social-political practices and the use of space that archaeological remains can often not detect, on the other hand their point of view is often ideologically biased and conveys an idealized picture that is far from the reality of their age. Sources that hold an Athenocentric and aristocratic bias are often used to supplement the archaeological evidence at other sites, although the exceptionality of Athens had little to share with other Greek urban realities. Moreover, texts written centuries later have been improperly considered as reliable to describe earlier evidence. Noteworthy is the case of Vitruvius' *De Architectura*. The terminology and observations on Greek architecture that are contained in the text have been often used to label or interpret archaeological evidence, but have proved to be in some cases unreliable.[630]

In recent years, an increasing number of archaeological investigations, both by means of surface surveys and excavations, are approaching the reconstruction of past cityscapes from a different perspective, treating equally every historical phase and filling the gaps in our knowledge of urban developments on a long term perspective and across different social classes.[631] This chapter uses this ever growing scholarship to trace the topographical development of Greek-Roman towns in a diachronic perspective, taking into account at first the city as a whole in the following section and then the typical urban components individually in the second part of the chapter. The aim of this overview is to offer

---

[624] Scholars have read the defeat at Chaironea in 338 BC as a defining moment in the history of the *poleis* that had to resign much of that freedom and autonomy, that they would later have to completely give up with the incorporation into the Roman Empire. This view, however, has been recently challenged not only with increasing data and studies available on Roman Greece (see e.g. Alcock 1993a; Ostenfeld 2002; Scott 2012), but also with a more nuanced perception of the lack of freedom that the *poleis* suffered already under Athens' hegemony (Dickenson 2012, 38).
[625] Morgan and Coulton 1997, 87.
[626] Robinson 1932, 58 cited by Nevett 1999a, 53.
[627] E.g. Akerstrom-Hougen 1974; Charitonidis *et al.* 1970.
[628] Kékulé von Stradonitz 1878; for the history of the looting at the Tanagra's *necropoleis*, see Higgins 1986.
[629] See below, pp. 155-7.
[630] On the caveat of using Vitruvius' nomenclature for Roman houses, see Allison 2001. Below, the examples of the distinction between *prostas* and *pastas* houses and the preferred orientation of theatres will be discussed.
[631] See e.g. Bintliff 2012; Uytterhoeven 2007, 25-6; Bowden *et al.* 2006, with contributions on public civic spaces in Late Antique Mediterranean cities by L. Lavan (Lavan 2006) and on the middle classes houses by S. Ellis (Ellis 2006).

comparisons for the interpretation of Koroneia's multi-period data which have been discussed in chapter 4, and to present the sources that I have relied on for the proposed reconstruction of the urban layout that is discussed in chapter 6.

In this chapter, I have inserted numerous reconstruction drawings and 3D models to give a clearer impression of the possible appearance of the buildings that I discussed in the text. The representations that I chose to include have been created either by the excavators themselves, or have been used to explain the archaeological remains to museum and site visitors. They are therefore authored reconstructions that we suppose have resulted from a scientific process of data collection and interpretation. It must be kept in mind, however, that they represent just one of the possible interpretations of the archaeological record and as such are in line with a traditional use of visual reconstructions that I discussed in previous chapters, when little attention was dedicated to the intellectual transparency of the reconstruction process.

5.2 A brief overview of Greek town planning

'There comes forward now and again some trained architect who, observing the favourable climate and convenient position of the site, first sketches in his own mind wellnigh all the parts of the city that is to be wrought out, temples, gymnasia, town-halls, market-places, harbours, docks, streets, walls to be built, dwelling-houses as well as public buildings to be set up. Thus after having received in his own soul, as it were in wax, the figures of these objects severally, he carries about the image of a city which is the creation of his mind. Then by his innate power of memory, he recalls the images of the various parts of this city, and imprints their types yet more distinctly in it: and like a good craftsman he begins to build the city of stones and timber, keeping his eye upon his pattern and making the visible and tangible objects correspond in each case to the incorporeal ideas.'[632] With these words the Hellenistic philosopher Philo Alexandrinus described how an architect would conceive and construct a newly founded city, giving a glimpse into the types of buildings that were indispensable in a city of the first half of the 1st century AD.

New foundations on empty land could be used to experiment with the layouts that were the most appropriate to the geomorphology of the site and that guaranteed the most efficient pattern of movements. The foundations of colonies in the South of Italy provided a great occasion to implement new solutions that were impossible to apply on the already built-up mother cities. Modifications on the urban layout of cities with a longer history were in fact less likely to occur, although internal rearrangements within *insulae* and changes in the functional use of areas within the city are common. As Lo Sardo pointed out,[633] cities with a long history were populated by myths, legends, deities and heroes and these stratifications of memories and buildings were so deeply connected with the identity of the urban centre that they could not be replaced. Athens is a telling example of a city with a long history that prevented its efficient planning. As reported by the Pseudo Dicaearchus, its intricate streets and the poor planning of water resources made it hard to believe for the ancient writer that what he was looking at was the most important city of Greece.[634]

Destruction following natural disasters, such as earthquakes and flooding, or siege was often the trigger for major urban renovations in old centres. In Old Smyrna, imperial benefactions financed imposing

---

[632] Philo, *De Opificio Mundi* I, 17-18.
[633] Lo Sardo 1999, 85.
[634] "Ἡ δὲ πόλις ξηρὰ πᾶσα, οὐκ εὔυδρος, κακῶς ἐρρυμοτομημένη διὰ τὴν ἀρχαιότητα. Αἱ μὲν πολλαὶ τῶν οἰκιῶν εὐτελεῖς, ὀλίγαι δὲ χρήσιμαι. Ἀπιστηθείη δ' ἂν ἐξαίφνης ὑπὸ τῶν ξένων θεωρουμένη, εἰ αὕτη ἐστιν ἡ προσαγορευομένη τῶν Ἀθηναίων πόλις', *FHG* II, 254.

reconstructions of the city after it was destroyed by an earthquake in 178 AD.[635] The Boeotian city of Plataiai was re-founded by Alexander the Great in 333 BC after its destruction in 373 BC from a Theban attack.[636] The new city was re-planned according to an orthogonal grid and a larger area than needed was included within the urban circuit as the new Plataiai was meant to substitute for Thebes as the leading city in Boeotia in Alexander's plan, which never came true. The inclusion of a larger area than what was actually needed to accommodate the population was not uncommon. Empty spaces could be built upon in later periods if necessity arose,[637] or cut off from the urban grid by means of cross walls (*diateichismata*) as indeed occurred in Plataiai.

Generally, once a convenient urban layout was established that struck a good compromise between the terrain morphology, the most favourable orientation,[638] and an efficient pattern of movement within the city, such an arrangement is likely to have been maintained over the centuries. The position of sanctuaries or other sacred spaces was also usually stable, which therefore contributed to keep on fixed locations the anchor points of the urban layout. Apart from these practical factors, probably one of the greatest obstacles for the re-planning of a city was the ownership of the land, since re-planning would have entailed a redistribution of the land with consequent problems of re-assigning the ownership of the lots.[639]

Sanctuaries were marked off from the rest of space in an early stage of *polis* foundation. For this reason, it is common that the streets' orientation and city layout were structured around the location of early sanctuaries.[640] Streets connected public and sacred spaces and there is evidence that in some sites they were named after the gods whose temples they started from or that they flanked. An epigraph from Thasos that regulates the cleaning of streets gives us the names of the streets that correspond indeed to the sanctuaries they connected.[641] Further evidence comes from Thourii whose foundation is described in exceptional detail by Diodorus Siculus.[642] A major street usually connected important areas of the city with each other and the inner city with the rest of the *chora*. The most important cemetery was also located along this major street outside the city wall.[643]

What follows is a brief overview of the array of possible urban configurations that were adopted from the Archaic period to Late antiquity in Graeco-Roman towns. Case studies are presented that highlight the elements of continuity and discontinuity in the urban layout. The chronological division that is presented below is somewhat artificial, since the development of many of the urban centres that are discussed cross in fact such temporal boundaries, but it has the purpose to situate changes within their historical framework.

---

[635] Beaumont 2006, 666.
[636] Konecny *et al.* 2013.
[637] See e.g. Priene (Wiegand and Schrader 1904), Olynthos (Cahill 2002, 30), Miletus where the empty areas that had been included after its re-foundation in 479 BC were built on only in Hellenistic times (Hölscher 2012, 183).
[638] E.g. courtyards preferably faced south or east, unless other focal points were taken as reference for the urban grid. In Pergamum for example buildings faced west towards the theatre and in Halicarnassus the focal point was the tomb of Mausolus.
[639] Owens 1991, 26-7.
[640] Cole 2004, 52.
[641] Duchene 1992.
[642] Diod. Sic. XII, 10: '(...) They divided the city lengthwise by four streets, the first of which they named Heracleia, the second Aphrodisia, the third Olympias, and the fourth Dionysias, and breadthwise they divided it by three streets, of which the first was named Heroa, the second Thuria, and the last Thurina.' Greco notes that, since the streets' names are derived from deities, it is likely that they were passing by the sanctuaries that gave them their names: Aphrodite, Zeus Olympios and Dionysos (while for Heracleia he gives another possible etymology from the nearby coastal street). See Greco 1999, 419.
[643] Hölscher 2012, 172.

5.2.1 Archaic period (end of the 8th century – 480 BC)

The Archaic period is taken as the starting point of this overview as it marks the establishment of a landscape that was characterized by the *polis*, a centralized entity very different from the sparse nucleated settlements of various sizes that dotted Early Iron Age Greece.[644] These communities had gathered around the residence of the *basileis*, such as at Emborio on Chios, or around ritual areas as attested for Thasos where recent investigations have identified the precursors of the Greek town in two clusters, one around the Artemision and the other around the Herakleion.[645] For a process of synoikism, triggered for a variety of reasons and depending on the specific circumstance of each site, these isolated settlements joined to gradually create what we know as a *polis* in Archaic times.

In this period, the construction of settlements on hilly sites generally followed the morphology of the terrain which resulted most of the time in layouts pivoting around the acropolis and progressing down the slope.[646] Terraces were created following the contours in order to provide more secure spaces to build upon, as shown by evidence from Emborio (Chios)[647] and Cretan settlements such as Azoria, Gortyna,[648] Dreros and Lato.[649] Ultimately, the construction of houses either as single buildings or as agglomerations depended on the social structure of the community.[650] In fact, while at Emborio houses are scattered on the terraces, at Lato the houses were built in rows following the contours, with rooms constructed in a linear sequence (Figure 5.1).[651] In some cases, the morphology of the site and the construction method could lead to a regular appearance of the town layout even if there was not a preconceived master plan. This is for example the case of Zagora (Andros island) where the wall of one house was used to build the next, giving therefore the impression of a regular layout.[652]

The first examples of planning resulting in 'quadrangular' cities are dated to the late Archaic period and come from sites that are located in the Aegean sea of Turkish Mainland, namely Thasos, Samos and Miletos.[653] The earliest example of a regularly planned city in mainland Greece is Halieis in the Argolis (Figure 5.2).[654] The best occasion for experimenting with town planning, however, was given by the colonization of Magna Graecia and the Black Sea.[655] The availability of empty space for construction, especially on the coastal plains, granted the necessary conditions to create cities where the principles of an efficient town planning were implemented that could best respond to the requirements of the site, as is the case at Olbia, Megara Hyblaea and Metapontum.[656] At Megara Hyblaea, for example, the two excavated streets running more or less parallel east-west connected the agora respectively with the temple area and with the Western gate. The crossing north-south streets instead were not kept parallel and resulted in the formation of a trapezoidal area for the agora (see Figure 5.3).[657] At Metapontum, a regular layout was implemented with *insulae* long and narrow (35x190m) and the larger streets of about

---

[644] For a discussion of settlement patterns from Early Iron Age to the Archaic period, see Bintliff 2012, 213-20.
[645] For Archaic Thasos, see Owen 2009.
[646] For an overview of Archaic settlements layout and their social organization, see Lang 1996 and Lang 2007.
[647] Owens 1991, 17.
[648] Caliò 2012, 47.
[649] Owens 1991, 24.
[650] Lang 2007, 189.
[651] The excavated houses are dated to the 4th century, but they correspond to a type that was adopted much earlier and kept over the centuries for its suitability for the sloping terrain (Hadjimichali 1971, 214-5).
[652] Owens 1991, 16.
[653] Caliò 2012, 50.
[654] Ault 2013.
[655] I will use the modern term colonization and colonies even though these definitions are limited in depicting the complex reality of *apoikia* (independent settlement) and *kleroukhia* (dependent settlement), as a discussion on this topic is outside the scope of this chapter. For an introduction on this subject, see De Angelis 2010.
[656] On the topic of Western colonies, see e.g. Mertens 2006; Fischer-Hansen 1996; Owens 1991, 34; Greco 1997, 636.
[657] Gras and Tréziny 1999.

5. The Graeco-Roman town as a physical entity

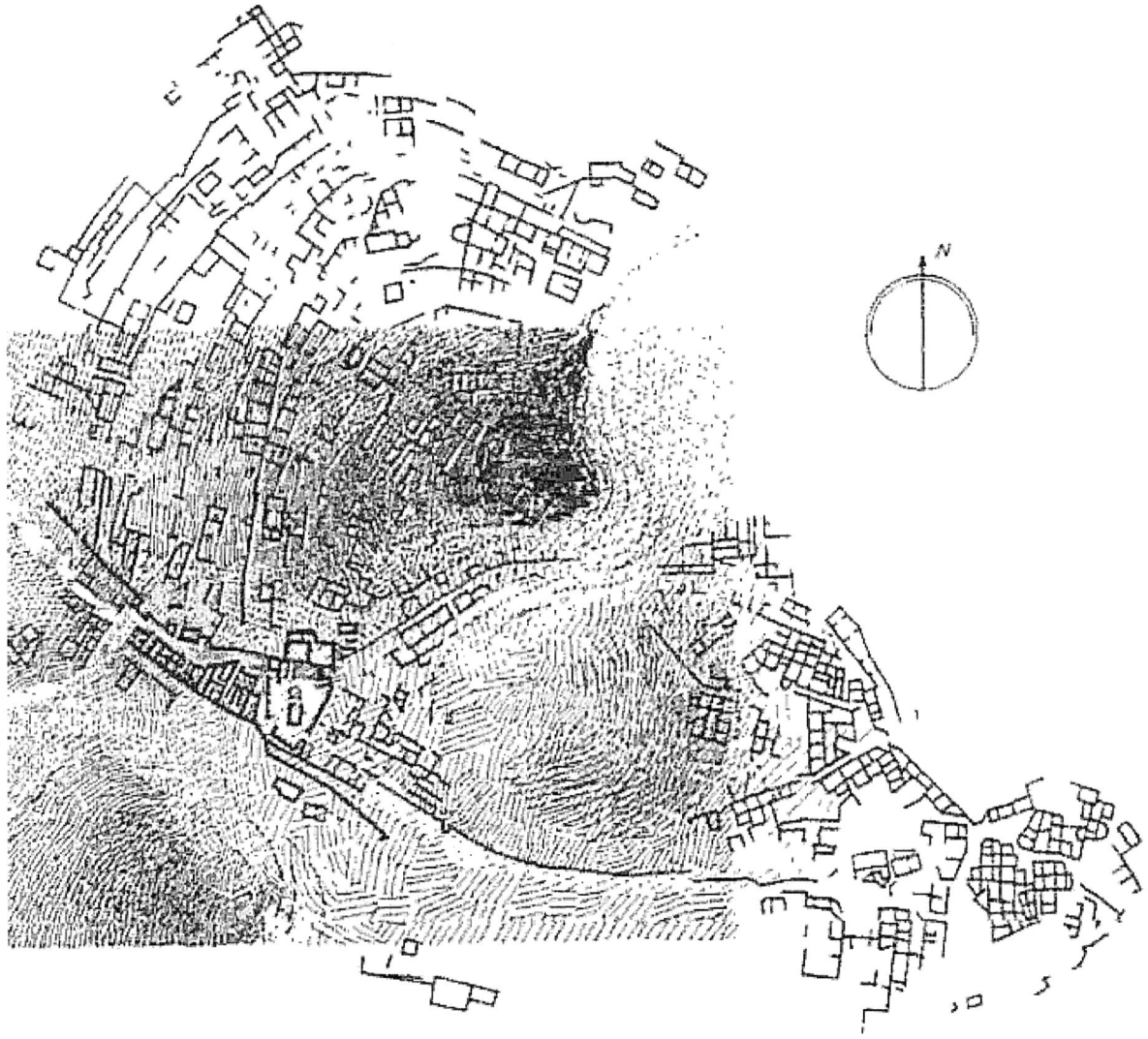

Figure 5.1 Lato: general plan of the site (Kalpaxis in Greco 1999, 120 after Hadjimichali 1971, 168).

12m of width. Interestingly, some of the temples are not aligned to the streets. Among the several factors that have been given to explain this phenomenon practical reasons have been suggested, such as the fact that temples were built in the 7th century, before the remaining plan of the city was laid out, or that this disposition better conformed to the characteristics of the site and the morphological conditions so as to guarantee the drainage of the streets in a location that was subjected to flood.[658] Choices regarding the orientation of temples, however, could have also been dictated by a conscious attempt to distinguish sacred space from the private dwellings, as Greco suggested for Paestum.[659] The Western colonies, being a blank canvas for urban planners, show clearly a particular attention for dividing the city into distinct areas, which was not always possible in cities with a longer history. At Paestum this is particularly visible since a strip in the central portion of the town was set aside and divided into three areas which were occupied by public buildings: the temple of Athena on the Northern part, the temple of Hera to the South and the agora in between the two.

---

[658] Owens 1991, 41.
[659] Lo Sardo 1999, 88.

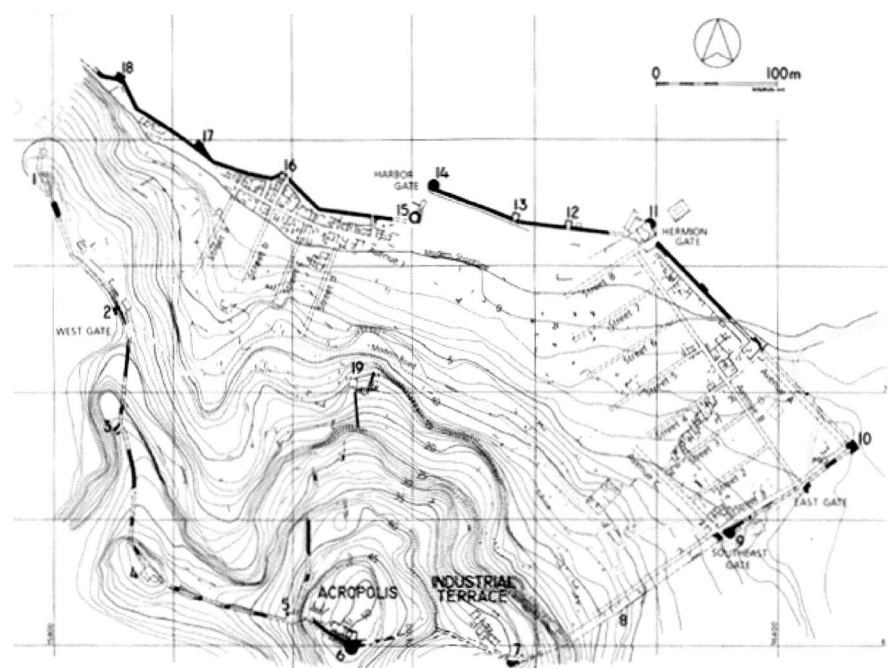

Figure 5.2 Plan of Halieis abandoned around 300 BC (Ault 2005, Figure 1).

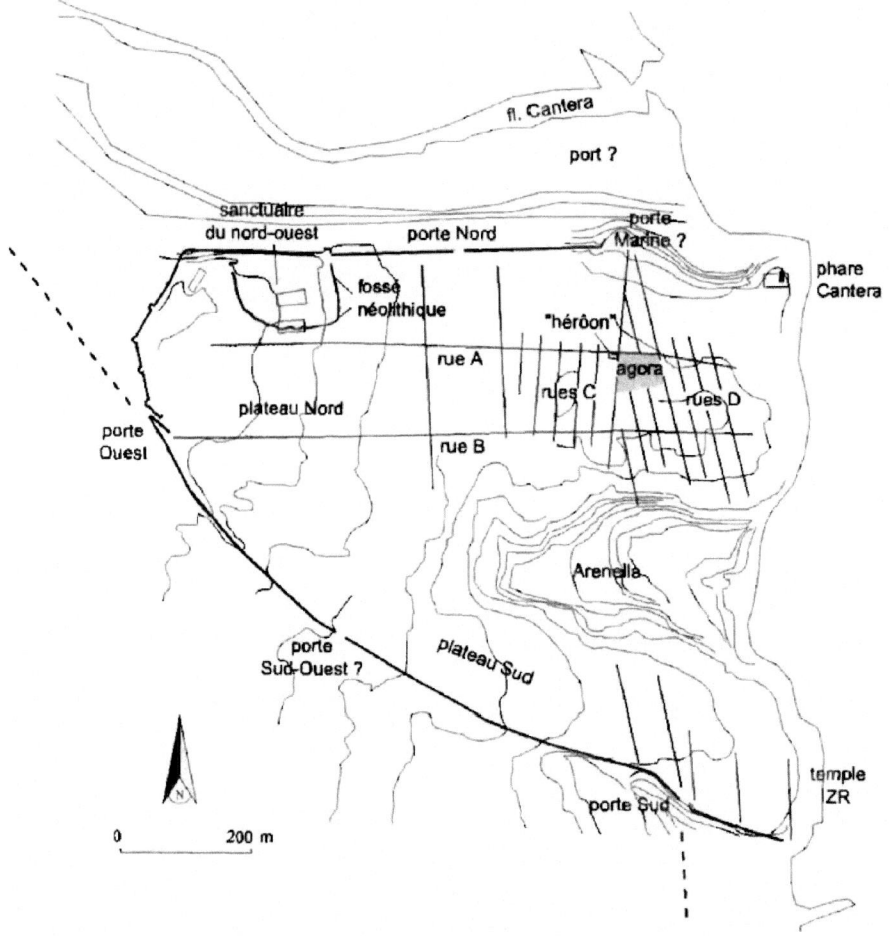

Figure 5.3 Megara Hyblaea: general plan of the site (after Tréziny 2005, Figure 2, p. 58).

5.2.2 Classical period (480 – 323 BC)

During the Classical period orthogonal grid planning was increasingly adopted. Typical examples of this urban arrangement, which would be implemented more broadly in the new foundations of the Hellenistic period, are Rhodes, Piraeus, Thourii and Olynthos. An orthogonal grid was the best suited for regular terrain conditions, but in this period it is also applied to less regular terrains with adaptation and modification of the ideal plan.[660] At Olynthos, for example, the size of the outer *insulae* was reduced to fit the plateau of the Northern district, and avenue B was constructed larger than the others, reducing the width of the bordering *insulae*.[661] In cities that were newly founded in this period on hilly sites, such as Knidos[662] and Priene[663], an orthogonal grid was superimposed on the terrain and steps were created where the slope was too steep for streets. Knidos, founded in the mid-4th century,[664] was laid out with a regular grid on the sloping ground overlooking the Gulf halfway between Kos and Rhodes. The town developed on a series of terraces punctuated by streets running more or less East-West (Figure 5.4). The streets running North-South were instead equipped with flights of steps. A similar situation is visible at Priene, founded in the mid-4th century in a new location down the slopes of Mount Mykale overlooking the Meander River. In this case, however, the implementation of a strict orthogonal grid must have created some obstacles to the movements around the city. Only the long streets running East-West were in fact viable for carts, while the crossing streets in the North-South directions were mostly too steep and had to be substituted for by steps that could be used only by animals and pedestrians.[665] In both sites, while the town plan conformed to the ideal principles of regular town planning, the path of the city walls was instead constructed according to the terrain. By following the contours and exploiting the physical characteristics of the terrain it was possible to create the most efficient defensive barrier against enemies. For this reason, often streets and city gates were not aligned.

Although the orthogonal grid became increasingly popular during the Classical period for its convenience and beauty, cities with a long history maintained their spatial arrangement as already previously discussed. If Athens was haphazardly laid out according to the Pseudo Dicaearchus, in Thucydides' description Sparta resembled in the 5th century BC a cluster of villages more than a densely built up city. This city, according to the Athenian historian, was 'scatteringly inhabited after the ancient manner of Greece', and was of such inconspicuous appearance that it would have misled posterity about its great power and leadership.[666] Moreover, even newly planned cities in Classical times could adopt only roughly regular layouts, as the investigations at Messene have shown. In this case, in fact, sanctuaries and public buildings had different orientations and blocks were of different dimensions. The underlying reasons are probably to be found in the desire to maintain the orientation of the older sanctuaries (possibly the only pre-existing buildings on the area) and in the hasty construction due to the Spartan threat.[667]

---

[660] The famous reconstructions of the urban layout and the housing blocks of Classical cities made by Hoepfner and Schwandner, albeit suggestive for their implications with the principles of *isonomia*, have been criticized. The re-examination of the archaeological records proved that the variations both in the dimension of streets and buildings blocks and within each house were greater than the data that the German architects had presented. For Olynthos, see Cahill 2002, for Pireus see Steinhauer 2007 and Longo 2008.
[661] Martin 1956, 111.
[662] See e.g. Bruns- Özgan 2006; Flensted-Jensen 2004.
[663] Hoepfner and Schwandner 1994.
[664] The results of excavations have however questioned the foundation date of Knidos, see Özgan 1994.
[665] Giuliano 1965; Wycherley, on the contrary, discusses the advantages of the location and access of the agora at Priene, Wycherley 1945.
[666] *Thuc.* I, 10.
[667] Müth 2007, 303-4.

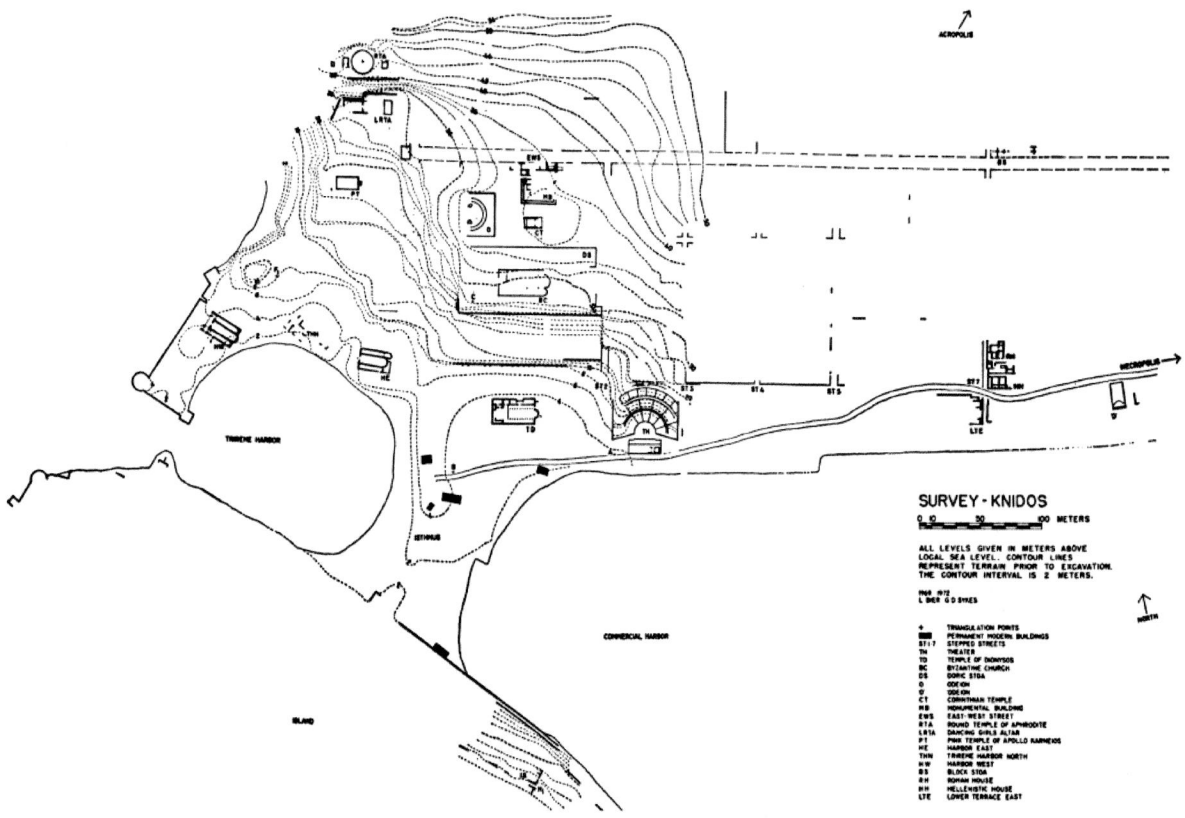

Figure 5.4 Knidos: general plan of the site (after Love 1973, 414).

5.2.3 Hellenistic period (323 – 31 BC)

The Hellenistic period created new occasions for founding cities under the Diadochi and the orthogonal plan became the standard adopted for these new centres where the conditions of the terrain allowed its implementation. Especially during the Early Hellenistic era (323-197 BC), experimentation with town planning was possible in the numerous new foundations. During the following period, conversely, the Roman presence in Greece and the diminishing population decreased both the number of new centres that were created and the urban renovations in old cities.[668] A difference seems to be observable between Northern Greece, where a growth in the number and dimensions of the urban centres is attested, and Southern and insular Greece, where a general decline has been noticed.[669] Construction of public buildings and infrastructures was financed by fundraising among the citizens and by the euvergetism of wealthy families that controlled power and held public and religious offices.[670]

A town founded in the last quarter of the 4th century on Goritsa hill,[671] on the Gulf of Volos, is particularly interesting for the characteristics of its town plan, which combines a regular grid with the necessity to adapt it to the changing terrain. The fact that it was probably abandoned about a century later makes it a suitable case study for this period. The streets, running north-south and east-west and crossing orthogonally, gave shape to elongated *insulae* of various sizes and arranged according to different

---

[668] Signs of renovation in the urban centre have been recorded at Athens, Messene and Thasos. All three of these cities were therefore stable enough to sustain such works (Dickenson 2012, 143ff).
[669] Bintliff 2012, 322.
[670] Bintliff 2012, 322; Meyer 2012.
[671] Bakhuizen 1992.

orientations. The city walls followed the best path along the contour lines and were disconnected from the internal arrangement of the streets that abandoned the regular grid towards the walls, bending their path to meet them at the gates. The fact that the gates are not connected by continuous avenues (as in the case of the main east-west boulevard in Priene) responded to the changing terrain of the city walls, but at the same time served defensive purposes.[672] Goritsa's plan, therefore, fits well Aristotle's description of the best urban layout, namely an arrangement of straight streets with less regularly planned areas to achieve the best combination between beauty and security.[673]

Not far from Goritsa are the remains of Kastro Kallithea that was laid out during the late 4th – early 3rd century on a 600 m high hill and abandoned during the late 2nd – early 1st century BC. Despite the uneven terrain, the town, covering 34 ha, was laid out in an orthogonal grid. The acropolis was fortified by a wall that was constructed earlier than the 2.4 km long lower town's fortifications. The excavators have therefore suggested a first building phase dated probably to the Classical period, where a small fortified settlement on the western part of the acropolis was established, and a second building phase where the lower town was created following an orthogonal arrangement which was protected by a broader city wall.[674] A *diateichisma* was added as a further protection measure for the eastern part of the settlement where the agora and the main residential area were located. The crossing of streets, running north-south, and avenues east-west shaped *insulae* of ca. 38.5 x 45 m.[675] The agora occupied the area of about four *insulae* in the saddle between the two summits of the hill (Figure 5.5).[676] After surface surveys, trial excavations were carried out which clarified the relationships between buildings and the construction strategies that were employed to cope with the sloping terrain, such as the creation of a layer made of stone chips and pebbles packed with red soil that was used to level the sloping terrain before the construction of the stoa.[677] The distribution of finds seems to indicate that the town was reconfigured over time, the agora being abandoned and the eastern sector becoming the only occupied area from the 2nd century BC until its abandonment.[678]

At Petres of Florina in Macedonia a different solution was adopted for the layout of a town on a hilly site. An early settlement of limited extension was founded in the mid-4th century probably by Philip II on a 720 msl hill that had a gradient of 30-45%.[679] In the course of the 3rd century, the town was given a layout organized in *insulae*, but during the 2nd century this organization was suppressed and the settlement, at that time covering almost the entire hill (around 20 ha), was rearranged to better adapt to the slopes.[680] The expansion and rearrangement of the settlement is most likely connected to the construction of the Via Egnatia (140-120 BC) that increased the passage of people and goods in the area and boosted the economy of this previously agriculturally-based centre. The town was then destroyed and abandoned during the Roman civil wars.[681] The areas of the city that were uncovered by excavations show fan-like arrangements where houses were organized in groups of three or four at right angles to the slope and accessed by streets following the contour lines (Figure 5.6). In this case, therefore, a freer arrangement, adapted to the physical characteristics of the site, guaranteed the most efficient occupation of space on the hill.

---

[672] Caliò 2012, 307.
[673] Aristot. *Pol.* 7.1330b.
[674] For the contextualization of the site and the field work carried out by the 15th Ephorate of Prehistoric and Classical Antiquities in Larissa and the University of Alberta, see Tzifalis *et al.* 2006; Surtees 2012.
[675] Haagsma *et al.* 2014, 199.
[676] See below pp. 178-9 for a discussion of the agora at Kastro Kallithea.
[677] Haagsma *et al.* 2014, 200.
[678] Surtees *et al.* 2014, 440-1.
[679] Adam Veleni 2000, 35.
[680] Adam Veleni 2000, 47 and Adam Veleni 1999, 150.
[681] Adam Veleni 1999, 153-6.

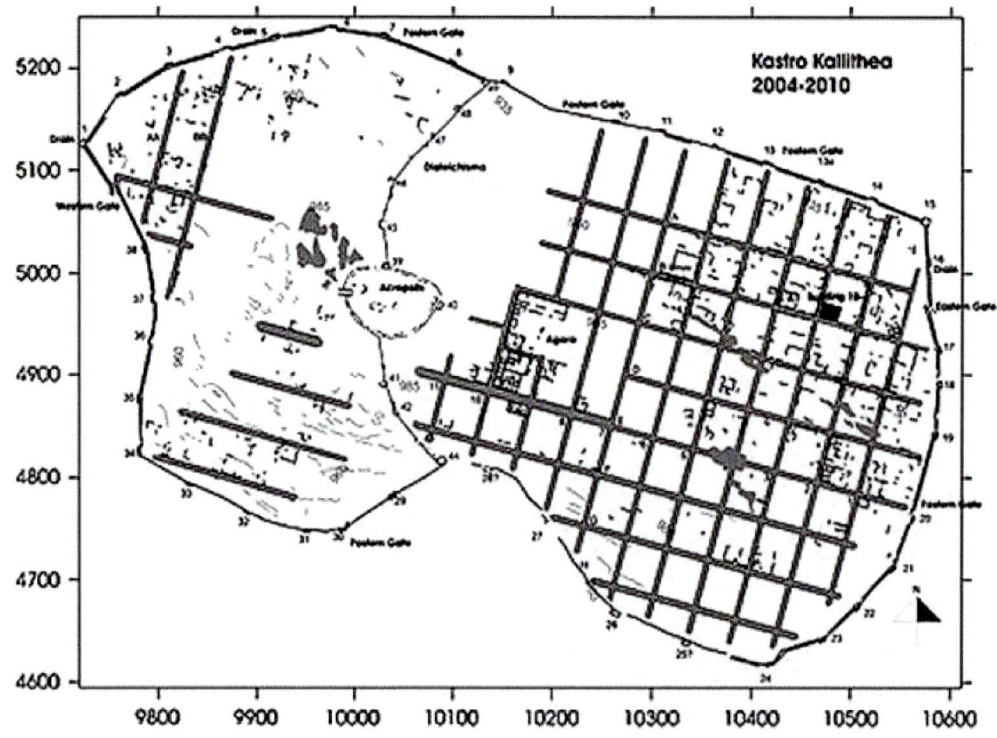

Figure 5.5 Kastro Kallithea: site map on contour lines (Haagsma et al. 2014, 198).

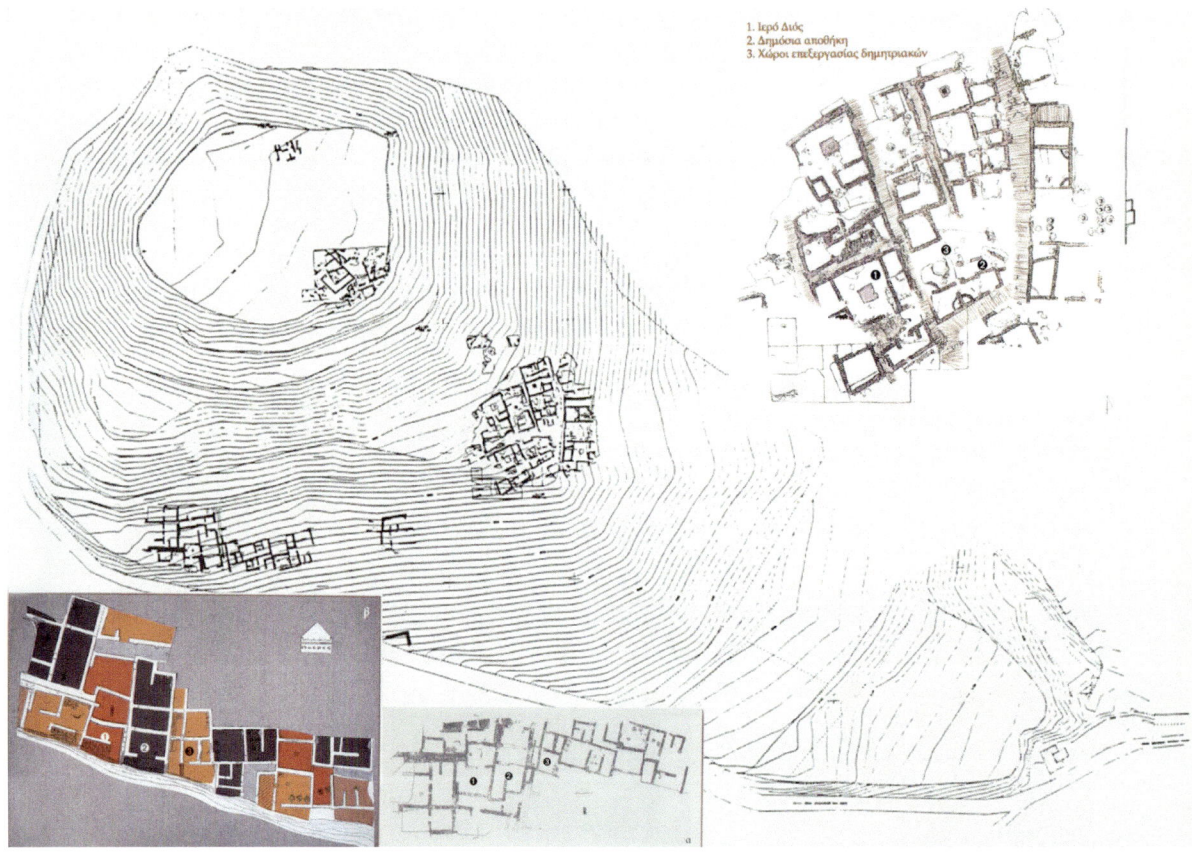

Figure 5.6 Petres of Florina: general plan and detail of the excavated areas (modified after Adam Veleni 2000).

5.2.4 Roman period (31 BC – ca. 330 AD)

As already mentioned, the Late Hellenistic-Early Roman period in many but not all parts of Greece corresponds to a phase of decrease in growth and general decline, due in part to the impact of Roman rule.[682] The 1st century BC corresponds at the same time to a phase of increased number of new foundations and construction works in existing cities.[683] The period from about 50 BC to 50 AD seems to have been especially important for the introduction of typical Roman buildings into provincial cities.[684] As DeLaine pointed out, despite local differences related to a town's specific historical, political and economic circumstances, the Romans created a set of recognizable characteristics which identified a city as Roman, for instance the presence of civic buildings such as the *curia* for the senate meetings, and the *basilica* for the dispute of law cases.[685]

The Romans introduced in Greece new construction methods, materials and building types that gave to Greek cities a typical Roman imprint.[686] The adoption of Roman construction techniques and materials, however, was reinterpreted by the Greeks, resulting in unique solutions, as recent analysis has showed for provinces such as Achaia, e.g. in the baths complex – Asklepieion at Argos,[687] and Macedonia.[688] The renewed attention to public works, in particular the restoration of religious architecture, relates to Augustus' programme that had the concept of *pietas* at its core.[689] Later on, during the 2nd century AD, the renaissance of Greek culture, known as the Second Sophistic, had an impact not only on literature but also on architecture, setting off a period of investment in public architecture that lasted until the 4th century AD.[690] Numerous construction works took place in many cities in the Eastern Roman provinces with more visible outcomes in the rich province of Asia than in Achaia, Epirus and Macedonia. In the latter regions in fact these modifications could be afforded only in major centres.[691] Romans were especially concerned with the creation of public infrastructures, such as roads and aqueducts. In the Greek provinces the Via Egnatia, constructed as a continuation of the Via Appia on the other side of the Adriatic, became in the Imperial period the connection between Rome and the eastern colonies up to Byzantium. Water supply for the increased needs of Roman public infrastructures, most notably baths, was guaranteed by Imperial euergetism, as testified by the aqueducts that Hadrian financed in numerous cities such as Athens, Corinth, Nicopolis,[692] and, as discussed in chapter 4, at Koroneia too.[693]

In the case of newly established Roman colonies on Greek towns, the approach towards the previous layout could vary. The Roman colonists could in fact maintain the urban arrangement of the previous Greek town, as shown in the case of Roman Copiae that was laid out more or less in accordance to the urban grid of its predecessor Thourii.[694] In other cases, the previous layout was given up to the gridded plan, although often elements of the earlier topography were maintained in the Roman town. At Corinth, for example, a different orientation was introduced in the arrangement of the Roman colony, which was established about a hundred years after the destruction of the Greek city. Nevertheless, some

---

[682] Bintliff 2012, 313.
[683] Dickenson 2012, 244. Bintliff discusses the examples of Delos, Thessaloniki, Argos, Sparta and Gortyn (Bintliff 2012, 326).
[684] DeLaine 2008, 104. For the visual impact of Augustus' political program, see Zanker 1988.
[685] DeLaine 2008, 95-6.
[686] Owens 1991, 93; Dickenson 2012, 134.
[687] P. Vitti 2011.
[688] M. Vitti 2011.
[689] Dickenson 2012, 244; DeLaine 2008, 104.
[690] Bintliff 2012, 312; Dickenson 2012, 270-2.
[691] Dickenson 2012, 267-9.
[692] Bonini 2006, 38.
[693] See chapter 4, pp. 94; 99-101; 136-7.
[694] Greco 1997, 646.

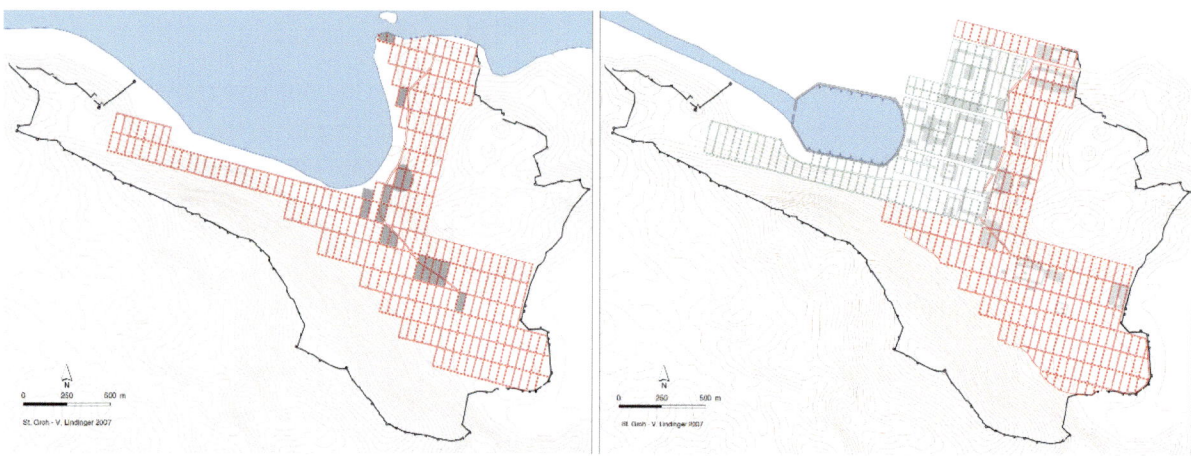

Figure 5.7 Ephesos's grid in Hellenistic (left) and Roman (right) times (Groh 2006, 55 and 73).

important buildings of the Greek city, such as the temple of Apollo, were still in place and conditioned the orientation of new buildings in the forum.[695]

A new element in planning the urban space of Roman cities was the degree of intervention in the natural landscape.[696] As the previous examples have shown, terracing was used in Greek cities to ensure building areas that were stable and large enough. The Romans, however, intervened more profoundly on the landscape with the intention to create monumental cityscapes that were 'dominated by straight lines'.[697] The Roman interventions on a Hellenistic layout are clearly visible in Ephesos that was turned into the capital of the Roman province of Asia under Augustus (Figure 5.7). The Hellenistic city was laid out in *insulae* of about 104 m long divided into 5 m wide *plataiai* oriented east-west, to guarantee the best climate according to Aristotle's 'Politeia', and 3m wide *stenopoi*.[698] During the Hellenistic period, the coastline, which had remained quite stable in Archaic and Classical times, started to be filled by sediments brought by the river and became a marshy area. Starting from the 1st century AD, a programme of levelling the ground around the harbour was therefore initiated to stabilise and enclose the bay into a man-made harbour. Moreover, new buildings in the lower town were constructed. The new street grid followed the same orientation as the Hellenistic one, but with different widths and with *insulae* now 136 m long.[699]

5.2.5 Late Antiquity (330 – 650 AD)

Recent studies on urban developments in Late Antique Greece[700] are shedding light on a period of Greek urban history that was generally neglected with the exception of a few pioneer publications.[701] Whether this was a period of continuity or decline, and the definition of a clear chronology are still matters of

---

[695] Gilman Romano 2005.
[696] DeLaine 2008, 112.
[697] Dickenson 2012, 211.
[698] Groh 2006, 57-61.
[699] Groh 2006, 73-9. For an overview on Ephesos' urban development between Hellenistic and Roman times see also Raja 2012.
[700] See e.g. Jacobs 2013.
[701] E.g. Sodini 1984. Sodini's publication discusses the state of the knowledge until the early 1980s, but later investigations have in some cases greatly modified the interpretations of some of the houses that he discussed. This is for example the case of the 'new praetorium' at Gortyn, where two periods of research (the first between 1989 and 1995 after which the results were published in Di Vita 2000b, and a second phase between 1996 and 2000) have clarified the chronology and better contextualized the building within its neighbourhood (see e.g. Lippolis et al. 2009).

debate.⁷⁰² Emperors promoted reform programmes to reorganize the provinces, making them smaller to achieve a higher control on those areas. In the 3rd century AD, with the reform of Diocletian, the Greek provinces were raised to 6 by reducing Macedonia and Achaia to create new provinces such as the Epirus Nova (Illyricum) and the Aegean islands.⁷⁰³ Despite the long held belief that the Barbarian invasions that started around the mid-3rd century AD have been the chief cause of destruction and decay of urban centres with a consequent demographic decrease, the implications of the raids are not clearly attested archaeologically and signs of a general degradation of urban life are more evident in the following centuries.⁷⁰⁴ A more crucial role seems to have been played by the recurrent outbreaks of the Plague that invested Greece from the mid-6th to the 8th century AD.⁷⁰⁵ These epidemics had devastating consequences for the urban population and economic stability, which in turn led to a weak opposition to the Slavic migrations.⁷⁰⁶

During Late Antiquity, archaeological evidence shows that urban sites shrank considerably in size. At Corinth, for example, the Late Antique circuit wall, which recent studies has identified as Justinian, excluded large sections of the former Roman town such as the Roman forum (see Figure 5.8).⁷⁰⁷ To complicate the assessment of the actual size of urban areas, the actual reduction of the city extension cannot always be established with certainty. It is in fact common that Late Antique city walls encompassed a smaller area than before, but housing quarters were built also outside the urban fortification often to an extent that is not possible to clearly identify for their sporadic character or due to a lack of investigations.⁷⁰⁸ An exception is the Boeotian town of Thespiae, where urban surface survey has been successful in defining the extramural extent.⁷⁰⁹ While the Late Hellenistic- Early Roman town appears to have drastically shrunk in comparison to its Classical predecessor, surface surveys have evidenced a further slight decrease in size in Late Antiquity with the establishment of a *kastron* in the late 4th – early 5th century.⁷¹⁰

The functional areas of the Graeco-Roman town were often re-arranged in this period: areas that previously were central foci of religious or civic activities lose their importance, and others become the new centres of urban life.⁷¹¹ Generally, a tendency towards monumentality is recorded on the city level, especially in relation to the construction of Christian buildings.⁷¹² Numerous churches and monasteries were in fact erected either re-using pagan buildings or employing *spolia* of previous structures.⁷¹³ From a topographical point of view, at some sites such as the Boeotian cities of Plataiai⁷¹⁴ and Tanagra (Figure 5.9),⁷¹⁵ the orthogonal urban grid that was laid out in the 4th century BC was overall maintained, while, as already mentioned, the size of the town decreased considerably. The ongoing geophysical prospections at Tanagra have confirmed, with slight modifications, the path of the city walls that had been recorded in the 1970s by D. W. Roller.⁷¹⁶ These new analyses, however, have shown that what had been previously thought as being the Classical circuit was instead the fortifications of the smaller

---

⁷⁰² For an overview on these topics see Jacobs 2013, 1-7; Waelkens *et al.* 2006.
⁷⁰³ Bonini 2006, 33.
⁷⁰⁴ Bintliff 2012, 363.
⁷⁰⁵ Liebeschuetz (2001, 287) notes a rapid decline in towns in Greece starting from the late 6th century AD.
⁷⁰⁶ Bintliff 2012, 383.
⁷⁰⁷ Slane and Sanders 2005.
⁷⁰⁸ This is the case for example of Late Antique Ephesos, see Foss 1979, 94.
⁷⁰⁹ Bintliff 2013a.
⁷¹⁰ Bintliff pers. comm.
⁷¹¹ Bintliff 2012, 372; Ellis 1988, 573.
⁷¹² Sodini 2007, 331; Bintliff 2012, 360-1.
⁷¹³ Bintliff 2012, 361.
⁷¹⁴ Konecny *et al.* 2013.
⁷¹⁵ Slapšak 2012.
⁷¹⁶ See e.g. Roller 1974.

VISUALIZING CITYSCAPES OF CLASSICAL ANTIQUITY

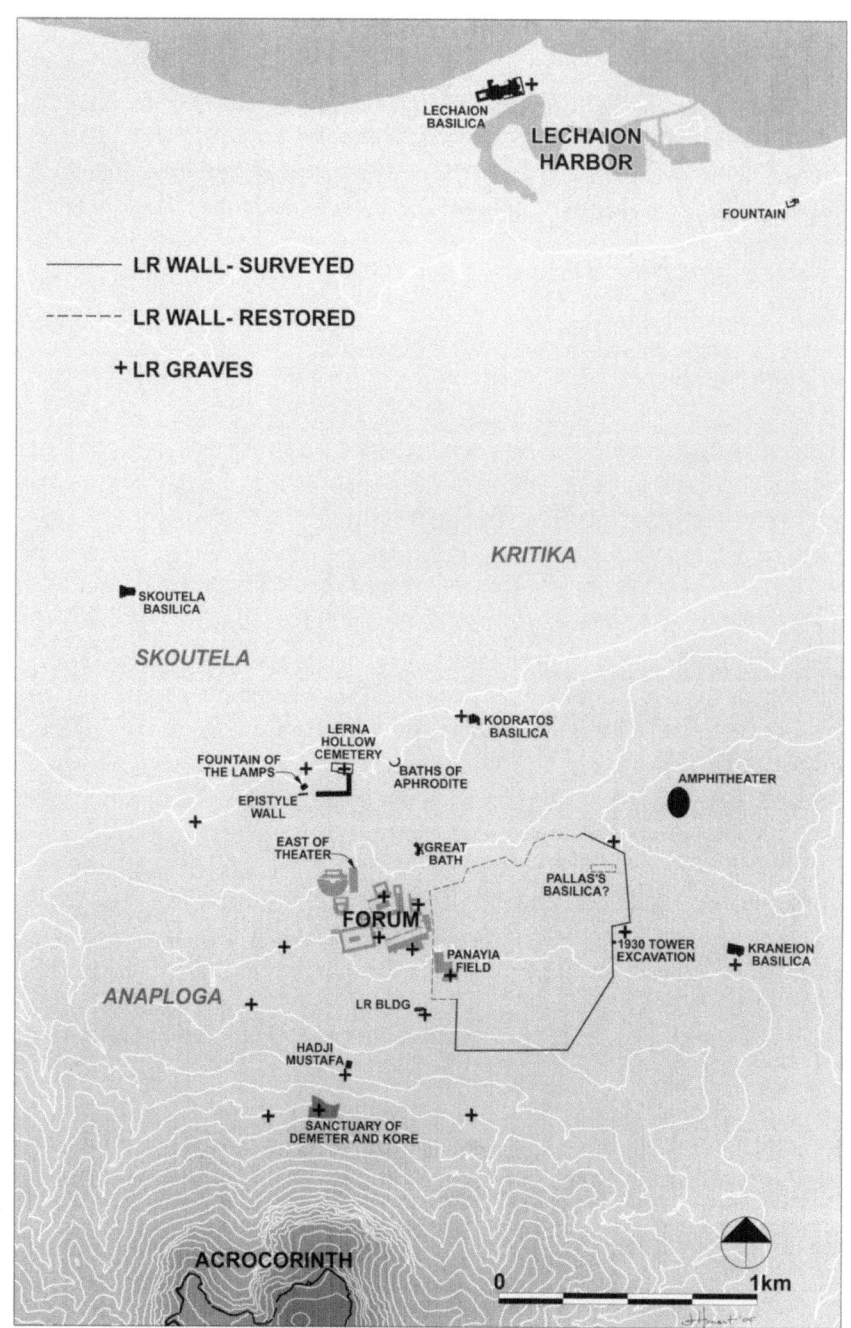

Figure 5.8 Corinth: The extent of the Late Antique settlement revised according to recent investigations (Slane and Sanders 2005, 245).

Late Antique town. Changes were made in the inner configuration of the *insulae* where buildings were adapted or constructed anew to respond to the changed requirements of the town.[717] In other contexts, such as at Messene, instead, the orthogonal grid of the Hellenistic-Roman city was given up, and the new settlement that was established in the first half of the 5th century AD followed an organic pattern with narrow and winding streets.[718]

---

[717] Slapšak *et al.* 2005 (I thank G. Rutar for sending me the paper that was presented at the conference).
[718] P. Themelis, 'Messene. A multiperiod site' available at http://www.academia.edu/12798848/P.Themelis_MESSENE.A_multiperiod_site

5. THE GRAECO-ROMAN TOWN AS A PHYSICAL ENTITY

Figure 5.9 The results of geophysical prospections at Tanagra show that what was initially thought as the Classical fortification, marks instead the perimeter of the Late Roman town, while the Hellenistic town occupied a larger area, here hypothetically mapped with the red line by J. Bintliff on map 1621-101 contained in the report by Eastern Atlas (Meyer et al. 2017).

5.3 The topography of Graeco-Roman towns: changes and continuities from the Archaic Period to Late Antiquity

The aim of this section is to present the transformations that urban centres underwent from the Archaic period to Late Antiquity, highlighting continuities and discontinuities in the ancient topography, by discussing the urban features that typically composed a Graeco-Roman town. This overview will identify the evolution of urban spaces throughout antiquity and how they adapted their form and modified their functions in response to the changed socio-political and economic situation of the town. The overview starts with the architecturally most prominent religious foci of urban centres, the sanctuaries, and continues with the agora, discussing then the role and the evolution of theatres during the period taken into consideration. Domestic architecture is dealt with next, considering also the spaces within houses that were dedicated to workshops and shops. The spaces that were used for training are discussed afterwards, followed by industrial areas (focussing especially on pottery production), and urban fortifications. Finally, the evidence of the types of trees, groves and gardens that were present in town is presented.

5.3.1 Religious foci

The presence of gods permeated every aspect of life in ancient Greece. It is therefore not surprising that sacred and civic spaces were often interlaced within the urban layout of the ancient Greek city.[719] In agorai, where political activities and meetings took place, altars and temples were also present, and often the buildings that hosted political meetings were built close to religious buildings to ensure the divine protection for the decisions that were taken. *Prytaneia* were the seat of the *prytaneis*, the head officials of the *polis*, but in this same building the sacred hearth of Hestia was kept undying as a symbol of *polis* life itself. Houses themselves were the spaces where the *oikos* cult was worshipped by the household with simple rituals that have rarely left archaeological evidence.[720] This section is focused on the most visible traces of the presence of gods in the *poleis*, namely sanctuaries and other sacred buildings.

The development of sanctuaries is parallel to the process of *polis* formation as the community defined itself through these religious foci.[721] Sanctuaries were not only the places in which the gods were worshipped, but also the space in which the city represented itself and constructed its identity, a 'manifestation of power and prestige within the framework of a competitive culture', as Marinatos defined them.[722] This aspect is most visible in the erection of *thesauroi* in the Pan-Hellenic sanctuaries, such as the thirty buildings with this function that dotted the sanctuary of Apollo in Delphi, and in the contests during which athletes from different *poleis* competed against each other.[723] Besides religious and political functions, sanctuaries were also important locations for financial administration in Archaic and Classical *poleis*, as designated buildings within the sacred precinct kept collective economic resources.[724]

The 2nd century AD traveller Pausanias commended the inhabitants of Tanagra for the clear separation that they had established between sanctuaries and people's houses.[725] Pausanias' observations suggest that the urban layout of the Boeotian city was quite exceptional and that a more common arrangement was a shorter physical distance between sanctuaries and houses. The inhabitants had in any case a clear

---

[719] Sourvinou-Inwood 1993, 12-3.
[720] Jameson 1990, 104-5.
[721] For the role played by cult centres in polis formation, see Snodgrass 1980, esp. chapters 1 and 2. This section focusses on intra mural sanctuaries; the extra urban sanctuaries, located in the *polis*' *chora*, were under the *polis*' political influence and were often used as landmark to set the boundaries between different *poleis*' territories. The Pan-Hellenic sanctuaries belong instead to a third category, that of the inter-urban sanctuaries, which were far from major *poleis* and therefore perceived as politically neutral and places to meet, compete and share knowledge, technology and skills (Marinatos 1993, 229-30). See also Bearzot 2009, 64-5.
[722] Marinatos 1993, 229.
[723] The festivals that were organized in the Pan-Hellenic sanctuaries remained places of self-representation of the elites also under the Roman control, see van Nijf 2001.
[724] Sassu 2013.
[725] Paus. 9.22.2: 'I consider that the people of Tanagra have better arrangements for the worship of the gods than any other Greeks. For their houses are in one place, while the sanctuaries are apart beyond the houses in a clear space where no men live'.

perception of the borders existing between areas with different functions. Such borders could be even physically marked by the use of *horoi*, boundary stones that defined the type of space that they enclosed, and consequently informed the passer-by about the necessary behaviour that had to be adopted.[726]

Sanctuaries' locations started to be fixed from the Dark Ages onwards.[727] Their position was not randomly assigned, but the choice followed specific criteria. Scully, in his work *The Earth, The Temple and the Gods*, underlines a strong relationship between landscape and sanctuaries' location.[728] Elements derived from the myths related to the deity, their characteristics or specific aspects of their cults were taken into account to choose the most appropriate location to distribute the cults of the gods within the urban centre. A rock formation, a spring, a tree could be seen as representation of the divine presence and these places were therefore marked off as sacred ground. The availability of water, which was valued as a gift from the gods, is often found in the vicinity of sanctuaries. Water in fact played an important role in purification rituals and in the worship of, among others, Hera, Demeter, Artemis[729] and the Egyptian gods.[730] Often, especially for female cults, a remote area was deemed the most suitable for the rituals that were performed within the sanctuary. This seems the case of the sanctuary of Demeter and Kore in Corinth, which was constructed quite far from natural water supplies, and on the steep, north slope of Acrocorinth, which required a great effort to cut the bedrock in order to create terraces that were suitable for the buildings' construction.[731]

The characteristics of the deities and their related rituals were in fact important factors in deciding their proximity with the core of the urban life. The traditional 'Polias' and 'Polieos' deities, such as Athena, Apollo and Zeus, were usually located in central places, either on the acropolis or in the agora,[732] while deities with a marked chthonic character,[733] and those that were seen as deviating from the canonical behaviour such as Dionysos, where located in the periphery of the urban centre. Demeter, the goddess of agriculture and fertility, had an important place in the Greek pantheon but, being related to female rituals of passage, her sanctuary was usually placed away from the city centre, such as at Corinth, or indeed in transitional places such as at the border of the city, within or just outside its city wall, such as at Thasos and Selinus where her sanctuary was erected near the main gate.[734] Gods representing an 'in-between' state could be placed in different locations according to their most prominent characteristic. The sanctuaries of Artemis, the goddess of wilderness and protector of young girls, for example, are often located on boundary zones, either of different chorai or within the city such as on the agora, at crossroads or at the gate of the city.[735]

Apart from the characteristics of the gods themselves, also the relationships between them as told by myth could have played a role in placing their sanctuaries. In Delos, the earlier religious focus of the *polis* was the sanctuary dedicated to Apollo and Artemis close to the harbour. Scott suggests

---

[726] Caliò 2012, 153-5; Martin 1956, 108. Dickenson sustains however that the practice of marking off the agora with *horoi* is attested only at Athens, Piraeus and Sounio, while it was not a common practice outside Attica (Dickenson 2012, 14-7).
[727] Schachter 1992, 1; see also Sourvinou-Inwood 1993, 1-17.
[728] Scully 1962, 2. Scully received much criticism for this work which was defined an 'imaginative and subjective attempt' by Tomlinson (1980, 372).
[729] Cole 1998, 162.
[730] Mylonopoulos 2008, 64.
[731] See on this matter: Bookidis and Stroud 1997, 423-5.
[732] Hölscher 2012, 174.
[733] A connection can be locally noted between the deities related with the underground world and those related with agriculture, such as Demeter (Fairbanks 1900, 247-8). It must be noted that apart from the typical chthonic gods such as Hades, other deities could have a chthonic epithet, such as Hera in her early cult.
[734] Price 1999, 51; Cole 1994, 211; Osborne 1987, 169; it is interesting to note that at Thasos a precinct dedicated to the Thasian *patriai* (among which was Artemis Orthosia) was close to the sanctuary of Demeter. The *patriai* protected the lineage and Demeter the reproduction and the family (Cole 2004, 52). For the sanctuary of Demeter Malophoros at Selinus see Price 1999, 51.
[735] Cole 2004, 183-4.

that the sanctuary of Hera was on purpose situated halfway up Mount Cynthus, in a difficult to reach position and provided with an entrance facing south which made it spatially separated from the lower religious focus, because of the hostility that Hera nourished towards Apollo and Artemis, born from the adulterous relationship between Zeus and their mother Leto.[736] The natural landscape was once again exploited by the Delians to construct the sanctuary of the Kabiroi, the Great Gods of Samothrace, on the 'terrace of Foreign Deities' that was spatially segregated and therefore invisible from the Apollo sanctuary (Figure 5.10).[737]

The imposing architecture of temples has caused some confusion on the correct assessment of the focal point of the cult, which was the altar in front of them, where sacrifices were offered to the deity, and not the temple itself. In literary sources, altars are often divided into *bomoi* (high structures of various shapes and sizes) and *escharai* (low-lying structures, mounds or simple piles of stones, ashes and bones with an opening into the ground) in relation to the nature of the worshipped god, *ouranic* or *chthonic* respectively. To reach ouranic gods, who inhabited the sky, sacrifices had to be directed upwards and were therefore performed burning the offerings outdoors. Chthonic gods, who populated the underworld, were instead reached by pouring liquids such as water, milk or honey into the *eschara*.[738] This traditional division has been however recently put into question by a re-examination of iconographic and archaeological evidence,[739] which shows that the term *bomos* defines the altar in general, which could be of different sizes and shapes, while *eschara* refers only to the upper part of the altar where the fire was lit, which often consisted of a separate fire-cover protection made of different materials.[740]

An altar, which was erected within a delimited sacred space, the *temenos*, pointing towards east[741] was often the only element of early sanctuaries. During the Archaic and the Classical periods a *peribolos* wall, constructed as either a simple low mud brick wall or as a more elaborate stone wall supplied with an entrance gate giving direct access to the altar area, could border the sacred space of the sanctuary.[742] At the entrance, a basin of water (*perirrhanterion*) was usually placed for ritual purifications.[743] Especially from the 9th – 8th century onwards, a temple could be added within the sacred area, usually oriented towards the altar, with the purpose of housing the cult statue and the votive offerings that were brought to the deity.[744] Early structures were built in perishable materials, therefore the first phases of a cult are often difficult to pinpoint archaeologically.[745] Temples were integrated into the urban layout,[746] and designed according to a system of proportions,[747] which in some cases seems to correlate with the dimensions of the urban grid.[748]

---

[736] Scott 2012, 50-1.
[737] Scott 2012, 62-5.
[738] Pedley 2005, 61; Mikalson 2010, 5.
[739] Ekroth 2001.
[740] Ekroth 2001, 120ff; archaeologically attested materials for altars' fire-protections are serpentine, gneiss and terracotta (Ekroth 2001, 122), but vase depictions show also covers with protruding endings that Ekroth interprets as metal trays on the basis of archaeological evidence (cf. the '*escharas purkaious*' attested in some inscriptions from Delos, Ekroth 2001, 123).
[741] According to some scholars, the orientation of the altar was not strictly towards the east, but could be instead oriented towards important constellations or stars (e.g. the Pleiades and Orion), see Boutsikas and Ruggles 2011.
[742] Mikalson 2010, 17.
[743] Cole 2004, 36.
[744] Sourvinou-Inwood 1993, 8. Important sanctuaries did not include a temple, or the latter was added in a later period, such as that of Apollo Delphinios at Miletos where the temple was built only in Roman times (Sourvinou-Inwood 1993, 16, note 60). See also Price 1999, 47 and Mikalson 2010, 18.
[745] Mazarakis-Ainian (1997) suggested that the early stages which led to the development of temples are to be identified in the communal rituals that were performed in or around elite houses in the Early Iron Age.
[746] Price 1999, 49.
[747] See the studies by J. J. Coulton (e.g. Coulton 1975).
[748] Grupico 2008.

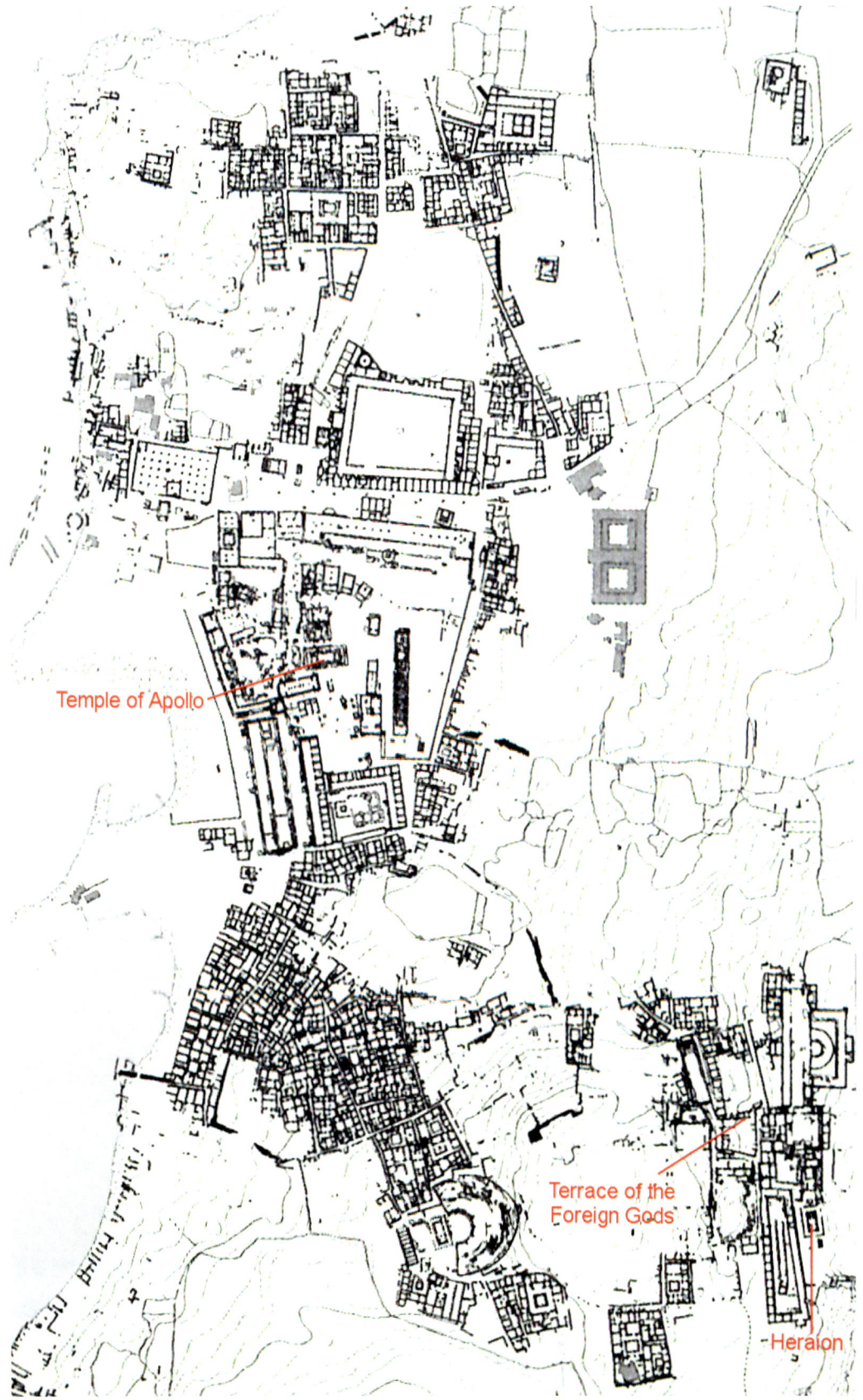

Figure 5.10 Map of Delos' excavated areas (modified after Moretti et al. 2015, pl. 7).

A larger area, defined by Sinn as 'cult-meadow', was part of the sacred space and was separated from the smaller precinct usually by erecting a low wall or by exploiting the natural terraced morphology. In this case, the smaller area was often located higher and separated from the lowest, wider space by a terrace.[749] The meadow was often provided with a water supply through cisterns and wells, which made it suitable to host numerous people in case of need, such as asylum-seekers in search for shelter.[750] In this area ritual dining took place, which was an essential complement of the sacrifices that were performed at the altar. For this reason, findings connected to food preparation and consumption, such as plates, *kantharoi*, bones and other food remains, are commonly found in the area.[751] The monumentalization of sanctuaries is visible also from the creation in later times of *hestiatoria*, additional rooms that were used to host such communal banquets.[752] Several examples of *hestiatoria* have been extensively investigated, such as the dining rooms connected to the sanctuary of Demeter and Kore at Corinth,[753] with the highest number of *hestiatoria* ever discovered in a Greek sanctuary, and the sanctuary of Herakles in Thasos.[754]

Athletics and artistic performances were also closely connected with sanctuaries. Musical, poetry and choreutic contests were performed, and artistic productions were dedicated as votive offerings to the deities.[755] Competitions such as foot or chariot races, wrestling or boxing, attracted the largest amount of visitors during the festivals, especially at Pan-Hellenic (Olympia, Isthmia, Delphi and Nemea[756]) and regional sanctuaries such as the Itonion at Koroneia which was discussed in chapter 4.[757] For this reason spaces that could host these events, such as stadia, are often found in connection with sanctuaries. At Isthmia, given the sloping ground, a great effort was needed to obtain a suitable space to build the first stadium during the second quarter of the 6th century BC, and further expansions were made during the 5th century.[758] In the 4th century the first stadium was substituted for by another, larger stadium which was built following a different orientation that better exploited the natural landscape to accommodate spectators on the adjacent slopes.[759]

The participants to the competitions and the visitors needed a place to stay, hence hotels (*xenon*) were commonly built in the vicinity of sanctuaries and close to main roads. An excavated example is the *xenon* of Nemea that was built at the end of the 4th century BC on the edge of the sacred area of the sanctuary, near to the bath (Figure 5.11). This rectangular building, measuring 85.89 m east-west and 19.78 m north-south, was originally divided into 14 rooms, to which two other rooms were added in a following phase.[760] The southern rooms returned finds associated with dining and food preparation, while the northern rooms were most likely used for sleeping.[761] Hotels of other shapes and sizes are

---

[749] But exceptions exist such as the sanctuary of Hera at Perachora where the opposite was more convenient for the characteristics of the bay.
[750] The inviolability (*asylia*) of (especially extra-urban) sanctuaries, which made them shelters for asylum-seekers is discussed in Sinn 1993 and Schumacher 1993. The Heraion at Perachora offers a clear example of a sanctuary that, lacking natural water sources, was provided by artificially made supplies, among others a large apsidal cistern around 450 BC (Whitley 2001, 295-9).
[751] Some inscriptions from Delos contain information about the types of food that were consumed during the festivals Posideia and Eileithyaia, see Linders 1994.
[752] Marinatos 1993, 228. It has to be noted that, however, *hestiatoria* is not the most attested term for such rooms in epigraphic sources: more often, in fact, the terms *oikos*, *èdrai-èdrana* (benches), *klismòi* (beds) or *exedra* appear (see Livadiotti 2013, 50, citing the study on the epigraphs from Delos by M.-Ch. Hellmann (Hellmann 1992).
[753] Bookidis and Stroud 1997.
[754] Bergquist 1998.
[755] Marinatos 1993, 232-3.
[756] For the early phases of the establishment of these sanctuaries, see Morgan 1993, 18-44, esp. 35.
[757] See pp. 103-5.
[758] The plan of the site is available at https://lucian.uchicago.edu/blogs/isthmia/files/2010/08/fig1_ab.jpg; see Gebhard 1992 and Gebhard 1993, 162-3.
[759] Gebhard 1993, 164.
[760] For a detailed description of this building, see Kraynak 1992.
[761] Miller 1990, 97.

5. The Graeco-Roman town as a physical entity

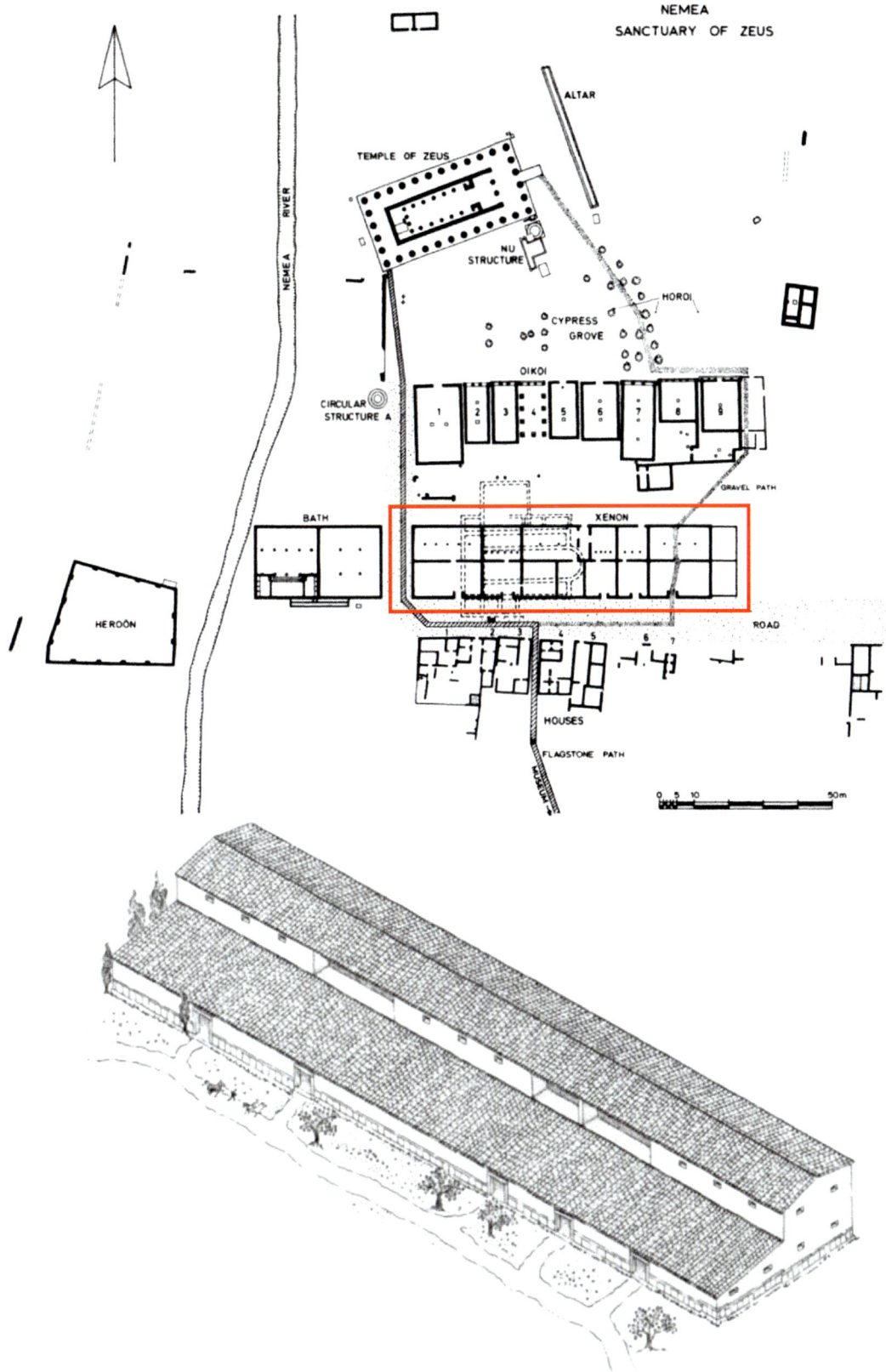

Figure 5.11 Top: Map of the sanctuary of Zeus at Nemea showing the facilities around the sanctuary such as the Xenon, highlighted in red (modified after Miller 1990, 34); bottom: Reconstruction drawing of the Xenon at Nemea (Kraynak 1992, 121).

attested in Greece, such as the Leonidaion at Olympia, the *katagogeion* at Epidaurus and at Eretria.[762] Thucydides mentioned a *katagogeion* that was built in Plataiai, close to the sacred precinct of Hera, after the city was destroyed by the Spartans in the second half of the 5th century BC. The building of 'two hundred feet square, with rooms all round above and below', according to Thucydides was constructed using materials from the buildings that had been knocked down.[763]

During the Hellenistic period, the transformations brought about by the redefinition of powers in Greece and beyond, under Alexander the Great's Diadochi, are reflected in changes in Greek religion.[764] One of the major modifications, as a direct result of an increased mobility of people, is the introduction of new cults, such as that of the Egyptian gods Serapis and Isis, which will become even more widespread during the Roman period.[765] New cults include those of Alexander and his successors, who were honoured with dedications that were usually reserved to gods such as the erection of altars, shrines and statues and with the celebration of festivals.[766] As Mikalson notes, these demonstrations of reverence and gratitude to the Hellenistic rulers can be explained by fact that the Greeks felt that important aspects of their wellbeing, such as peace, safety and the provision of food, depended now on the Hellenistic rulers' as much as on their gods' good will.[767] An increased number of works, including the construction, embellishment or repair of altars, shrines and sanctuaries were financed by the families of landowners and merchants that had gained wealth and social position during this period, with the return of oligarchy encouraged by the new successor states. Their contributions as benefactors of the city were remembered by dedications and inscriptions on statues.[768] As the construction of new temples was now mainly initiated by individual sponsorship, many projects were left unfinished at the death of the benefactor, such as in the case of the temple of Zeus in Lebadeia that was never completed following the death of its financier King Antiochus IV.[769]

From an architectural point of view, more systematic and precise numerical relationships and proportions between individual parts seem to be sought when new temples were erected during the Hellenistic period,[770] and more attention was paid to arrange the architectural elements in order to reach a scenographic and visually pleasing effect.[771] Sanctuaries show signs of monumentalization, which was visible less in temples (that were instead preferably built in rather small dimensions from the 4th century onward),[772] but rather in the addition of propylaia, stoas and altars to existing sanctuaries as a gift from royal and individual patronage.[773] Propylaia were meant to focus attention on the entrance of the sacred area, which was given an inward looking appearance by the addition of stoas. An example of the progressive architectural definition of space around a sacred area is the sanctuary of Zeus at Dodona which was equipped with a propylaion and an Ionic colonnade on three sides during the 3rd century BC (Figure 5.12); the temple itself projected outside the perimeter of the precinct in order to leave enough space for the altar and for the visitor entering the propylaion to appreciate the temple. Altars, although usually proportional to the settings in which they were erected, received a more monumental appearance and more elaborate

---

[762] Winter 2006, 179.
[763] Thuc. 3.68.3. The investigations at Plataiai have not recorded evidence corresponding to Thucydides' description. On this matter see Konecny *et al.* 2013, 150.
[764] For an overview of religion in the Hellenistic world, see Martin 1987.
[765] Mikalson 2010, 188. For a selected bibliography on this topic, see Mylonopoulos 2008, 52.
[766] Mikalson 2010, 190.
[767] Mikalson 2010, 190.
[768] Bintliff 2012, 322.
[769] Winter 2006, 15.
[770] Winter 2006, 10-2.
[771] Winter 2006, 18-9.
[772] Winter 2006, 14.
[773] Winter 2006, 10.

Figure 5.12 The sanctuary of Zeus at Dodona around 400 BC (top) and in the 3rd century BC (bottom) [source: http://ancient-greece.org/archaeology/dodona.html].

decorations during Hellenistic times, peaking with the still exceptionally large Great Altar of Pergamon, which was built under King Eumenes II in the 2nd century BC.[774]

---

[774] Pedley 2005, 62.

Scholars have spoken of a secularization of some aspects of Greek religion during the Hellenistic period, especially in relation to the critical inquiry into traditional gods that was introduced by sophists and philosophers,[775] and to the increased separation of athletics, musical and artistic competitions from religious festivals.[776] It is however difficult to find clear evidence that these changes translated into actual modifications in cult practices. An overview, albeit limited, of terracotta votive offerings from several sanctuaries carried out by B. Alroth did not return any conclusive and widespread sign of a different attitude, but suggested instead a continuity in the types of figurines that were chosen to be offered.[777] It is possible that the changed perception towards religion and a more sceptical approach towards traditional gods and rituals affected more the upper classes than the rest of the population and that therefore these changes are less visible in the material culture that Alroth has examined.[778] On the other hand, as Mylonopoulos observed, the marked increase in the construction of stoas around sanctuaries during the Hellenistic period can be read as a shift towards a spectacularization of the rituals, as spectators needed a sheltered space to observe the performance.[779]

The signs of change that are already visible in Hellenistic times become more pronounced with the advent of the Romans.[780] Space is too limited for an in-depth discussion of the mutual influences between Greek and Roman religion, but some relevant considerations will be made in term of architectural and cult changes that the Romans introduced in Greece. In sacred spaces, as well as in civic buildings, the negotiation between the Romans and Greeks is more evident. As Scott has argued, the introduction of Roman elements in Greek sacred spaces was subtle and respectful, especially at the beginning of the Roman presence in Greece.[781] This attitude can be perceived not only by the preference of reusing existing buildings for the introduction of the Emperor's cult, such as at Cyrene where an existing fountain house was turned into a temple of Augustus,[782] but also by the maintenance of a sacred earlier topography within the city. In Ephesos, for example, this is testified by the progressive embellishment during Roman times of an old processional route that started from the temple of Artemis, the patron deity of the city, and following the natural landscape passed by important sacred places for the city's history.[783]

The assimilation of Greek deities to the Roman pantheon can be considered completed by the 1st century BC.[784] Greek and Roman religious practices and temple architecture, however, were in substance very different. Typically, the Roman temple was raised on a podium, instead of being erected on a low stylobate as the Greek temple, and could be entered only from the front via a flight of steps, a characteristic that was inherited from Etruscan architecture (see Figure 5.13, b). The focus of Roman temples was therefore on the facade, whereas Greek temples were constructed to be seen from all sides and could be amphiprostyle with a portico on both ends (Figure 5.13, a). The frontal character of Roman temples was further accentuated by the presence of lateral, engaged columns that were not functional to the sustainment of the pediment as in Greek temples, but protruded only partially from the wall of the cella (Figure 5.13, c).

---

[775] Alroth 1999.
[776] Mikalson 2010, 190.
[777] Alroth 1999.
[778] See Alroth 1999, 217.
[779] Mylonopoulos 2008, 52-6.
[780] Scott 2012, 163.
[781] Scott 2012, 166.
[782] Scott 2012, 166.
[783] DeLaine 2008, 99-100.
[784] Price 1999, 143.

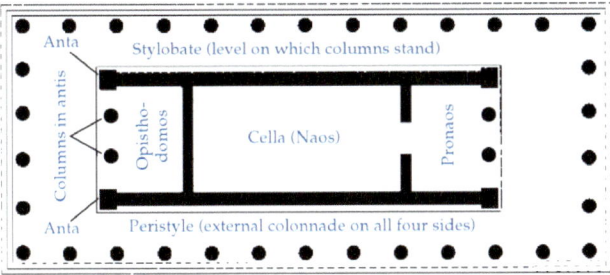

A. Greek Temple Plan

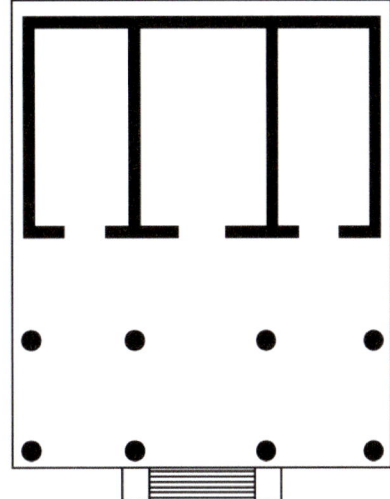

B. Etruscan Temple Plan

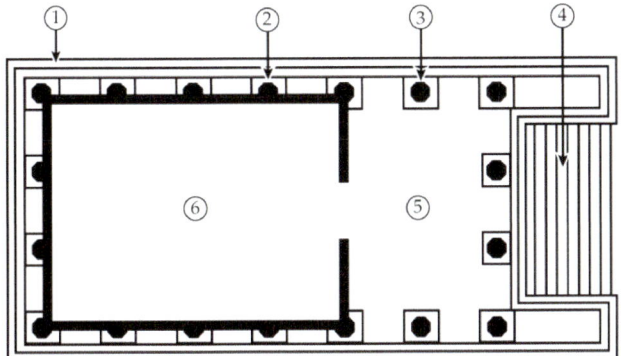

C. Roman Temple Plan

Figure 5.13 Plans of a Greek, an Etruscan and a Roman temple. 1) Podium or base; 2) engaged column; 3) freestanding column 4) entrance steps; 5) porch and 6) cella (from Cunningham et al. 2014, 132).

The reverence for the Emperor and his family could be expressed in various ways, most notably through the dedications of buildings and statues. In some cases, such dedications hint at the institution of an actual cult for the Imperial family members.[785] The Imperial cult was introduced with local adaptations but without problems in Greek cities, as the worship of individuals was part of earlier religious practises, such as the cults of Hellenistic rulers.[786] Emperors were often associated with the traditional gods of the *polis*, which helped to assimilate the Emperor in a more familiar setting.[787] These cults were usually placed in important locations such as on the agora or on the acropolis.[788] The dedication of altars is one of the signs of the institution of an Imperial cult.[789] The remains of a round structure on the Athenian acropolis that have been traditionally interpreted as a small round temple dedicated to Roma and Augustus belong, according to Camp, most likely to an altar.[790] Games in honour of the Emperor could be added to existing festivals (as testified to by the introduction of the *Kaisareia* to the *Isthmia* at Corinth, the *Sebasteia* to the *Nemeia* at Argos, and the competitions of poetry in honour of the Emperor and his family that were added to the *Mouseia* at Thespiae).[791] In addition, priesthoods could be established for the Imperial cult, in some cases associated with the worship of existing deities, such as the *hiereia* of Hestia, Livia and Julia on the acropolis of Athens.[792]

---

[785] Camia 2009, 216. For an analysis of the Imperial cult in Asia Minor, see Price 1984.
[786] Camia 2009, 205.
[787] Camia 2009, 206; Price 1999, 158.
[788] Alcock 1993b, 158.
[789] Camia 2009, 218.
[790] Camp 2001, 187-8.
[791] Camia 2009, 207.
[792] *IG* II-III2 5096, Camia 2009, 209.

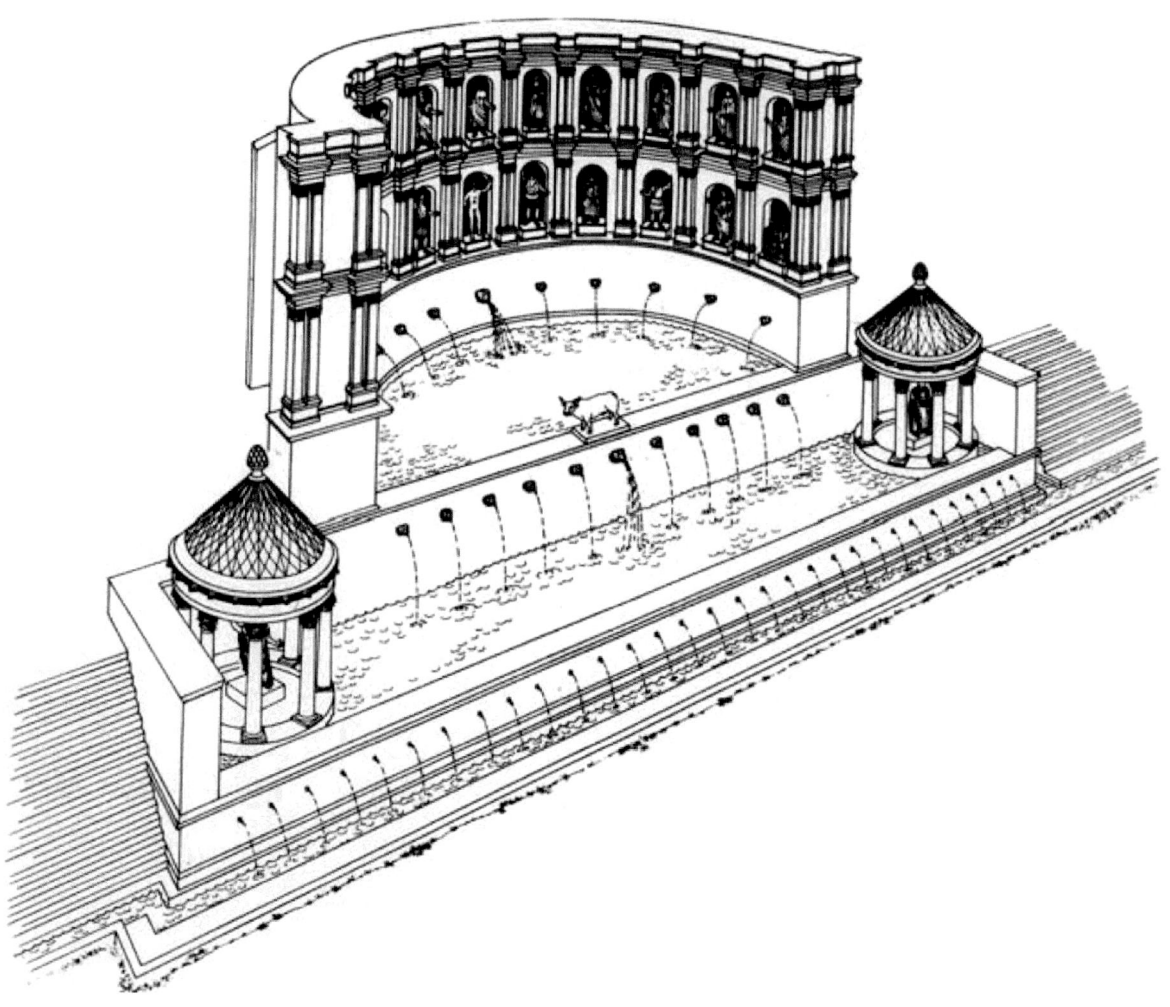

Figure 5.14 Reconstruction drawing of the nymphaeum of Herodes Atticus and Regilla at the sanctuary of Zeus in Olympia (after Longfellow 2009, 230).

Pan-Hellenic sanctuaries maintained their importance in Roman times as the competitions that took place there fitted well into the set of values, among which *virtus* was particularly important, that the Emperors wanted to promote. Wealthy individuals and (more rarely) emperors granted the construction of more infrastructures in sanctuaries, most notably related with water supply, with the addition of baths, cisterns, fountains and aqueducts.[793] These buildings, especially when erected in monumental size, were meant to carry a message and materialize the presence of the financer. It has been in fact noted that new infrastructures were often located on strategic places in order to convey that the benefactor was the protector of the old sacred areas.[794] According to Longfellow, a similar message could be intended with the construction of an imposing, eighteen meters high *nymphaeum* in the sanctuary of Zeus at Olympia, that was financed by the Greek aristocrat and Consul Herodes Atticus and his wife Regilla in the middle of the 2nd century AD (Figure 5.14).[795] In her view, the monument can

---

[793] For the Roman interventions at Pan-Hellenic sanctuaries, see Laurence 2012. For the creation of fountains in Greek sanctuaries, see Longfellow 2012.
[794] Longfellow 2012, 133-55.
[795] Longfellow 2009, 229-32.

be interpreted as 'an appropriation of the emperor's own visual language to glorify a local family and to reclaim, even if in some small measure, the local sacred landscape'.[796]

During the subsequent progressive Christianization of society, sanctuaries were obviously one of the most important terrains of negotiation for religious supremacy in Greece. Constantine gave substantial impetus to the introduction of Christianity in the Empire, becoming himself the first Christian Emperor, but it was Theodosius I who established Christianity as the official religion of the Empire in 380 AD. Recent studies are shedding light on the transition between pagan and Christian cults in Greece.[797] The available patchy dataset points towards a complex process that included both violent disruption of pagan symbols and coexistence with Christian architecture.[798] The overall picture clearly shows a competition for power that is expressed both in literary sources and in the archaeological remains.[799] While in Athens the Asklepeion was turned, not by chance, into the church of the saint physicians Cosma and Damian, and another church was housed inside the Parthenon, in Corinth no temple was converted into a church. Probably, therefore, the Christian worshippers must have gathered in church-houses until the 6th century AD, when a basilica was erected on the east side of the agora.[800] The available archaeological evidence in Delphi demonstrates that the town survived the transition from the pagan cult to Christianity, with a continuity in occupation up to the early 7th century AD.[801] The town was still called *hiera polis* in the first half of the 4th century AD, as attested by two epigraphs dedicated probably posthumously to the Emperor Constantine.[802] The temple of Apollo shows reparation works after being damaged by a fire in the 3rd century AD and it continued to stand into the 6th century AD.[803] A Christian community occupied the area of the sanctuary in the early 5th century AD and at least three basilicas were erected, one in the Gymnasium, another at the entrance to the modern village and a third, whose exact location remains uncertain, perhaps to the east of the Roman agora positioned at the foot of the Sacred Way.[804] The erection of churches on the entrances of the pagan sanctuary that is visible at Delphi, but also at Olympia, Epidauros and Dodona, testifies that the organization of space and the navigation through these pagan sites were maintained, but shows at the same time the Christians' intention to challenge and appropriate the space held by pagan religions.[805]

The tension and competition between pagans and Christians is perceivable also from other actions. Statues displaying pagan gods were moved from their original locations to Constantinople and *spolia* from pagan buildings were re-used to construct new churches as a sign of control and more power of Christianity on pagan cults.[806] Crosses were incised on statues and existing buildings, but the meaning of carving such symbols is still debated.[807] Pagan gods, emptied of their religious value, could still maintain some of their characteristics and become archetype figures in the Christian society, such as of Aphrodite which remained a symbol of love and assumed the role of the temptress in theatrical plays in Late Antique and Medieval Byzantium.[808]

---

[796] Longfellow 2009, 232.
[797] Sweetman has studied the development of churches and the Christianization process in the Peloponnese, highlighting the strategies that led to a smooth adoption of the new religion in this region (Sweetman 2010, 2015).
[798] See Robertson Brown 2006 for an overview of the situation in Panhellenic sanctuaries.
[799] Robertson Brown 2006; Caraher 2003.
[800] Robertson Brown 2008, 121-2.
[801] See Petridis 2009 and 2015, 278-81 for a short review of Late Antique Delphi.
[802] Robertson Brown 2006, 311. See Petridis 2009 and 2015, 278-81 for a short review of Late Antique Delphi.
[803] Robertson Brown 2006, 312.
[804] Petridis 2009, 113.
[805] Robertson Brown 2006, 318.
[806] Robertson Brown 2006, 315-8.
[807] Stirling 2008, 138.
[808] Papagiannaki 2010, 346.

Sanctuaries: Diachronic case studies

The large number of sanctuaries that has been excavated all over Greece allows comparisons with each other, observations on their architectural typology and, where associated finds have been carefully recorded, also hypotheses about the rituals that were performed. Only in a limited subset of such sacred areas, however, have all the various phases of occupation received the same attention by excavators, thus allowing us to reconstruct diachronically the continuity and discontinuity of buildings and religious practices. Especially the Late Antique strata, which provide useful information over the fate of sanctuaries in the period when Christian communities started to become more numerous and edicts were promulgated by the emperors to limit pagan cults, are often overlooked. Corinth is one of the sites that have been thoroughly investigated and provides an exceptional case study to follow the development of the urban centre up to the Christian era. To provide some comparison for the attested cults at Koroneia, I will discuss the evidence from the Sanctuary of Demeter and Kore at Corinth, and of the sanctuary of Arthemis Orthia at Sparta.

The Corinthian sanctuary of Demeter and Kore is located at a distance from the centre of the city, halfway up Acrocorinth, as commonly attested for the two goddess's sanctuaries.[809] The natural morphology has shaped the architectural development of the sanctuary, which was laid out in such way that different activities connected to the ritual were divided across different terraces: the lowest terrace accommodated the dining rooms, small buildings around 4.5 to 5 m long,[810] which offered a wide range of finds shedding light on the foods that were consumed during the ritual meals, such as beans, seeds, nuts, olive pits, honey and possibly fresh or dried fruits.[811] The middle terrace was used for sacrifices (especially pigs that were sacred to the goddesses) and offerings dedicated, which included terracotta figurines, numerous sea shells,[812] and miniature clay models depicting *likna*, baskets containing cakes and bread.[813] On the highest terrace, a small theatre cut into the rock hosted some sort of initiation ceremony.[814] The high presence of oil lamp fragments suggests that (part of) the rituals, which were reserved, although perhaps not exclusively,[815] to women, could be celebrated at night.[816]

The finding of a pan and tile cover type has led the excavators to suggest the presence of a building in the first half of the 7th century BC,[817] although the first *in situ* wall structures are dated to the first half of the 6th century BC and it is during this century that a consistent building activity took place.[818] An interruption in architectural continuity has been detected around the end of the 4th century, where deep debris layers testify to the likely occurrence of a strong earthquake.[819] This event is followed by a phase of renovations and extensions dated around 300 BC, which brought a marked monumental character to the site and changed the pattern of movement between terraces.[820] During the Hellenistic period, the evidence points towards a continuity of structures, without evident signs of new constructions. An

---

[809] Bookidis 1993, 45.
[810] Different users have been suggested for these buildings, consisting of small rooms with kitchen and toilet facilities, see Bookidis and Strout 1997, 411-2.
[811] Bookidis 1993, 55-6.
[812] Bookidis 1993, 54.
[813] Bookidis and Strout 1997, 427. Specifically on *likna* see Brumfield 1997
[814] Bookidis 1993, 47. The presence of a theatre is commonly attested in sanctuaries of Demeter, as in Selinus (dedicated to Demeter Malophoros) where a small rock cut theatre with six steps could accommodate a limited number of people and in Pergamon with a larger theatre of estimated capacity of 800 people (Price 1999, 50).
[815] See Price 1999, 50 regarding the presence of male names in the dedications at the sanctuary of Demeter Malophoros at Selinus.
[816] Bookidis 1993, 47.
[817] Bookidis and Strout 1997, 425.
[818] Bookidis and Strout 1997, 426-7.
[819] Bookidis and Strout 1997, 430-1.
[820] Bookidis and Strout 1997, 431-2.

abrupt interruption occurred in 146 BC when the Roman conquest and destruction affected also the sanctuary, which was left abandoned until the foundation of the Roman colony in 44 BC.

A rebuilding of the sanctuary took place after the colony was established, and followed the same spatial organization over the three terraces of its Greek antecedent.[821] The main focus of the sacred area became however the Upper Terrace, which was slightly re-oriented to follow the Flavian centuriation system.[822] On this area, three parallel prostyle Ionic temples were constructed in the second half of the 1st century AD.[823] The westernmost temple has been identified as dedicated to Demeter as it was provided with a marble statue of the goddess during the second half of the 2nd century AD.[824] The Middle Terrace was then reinforced by a retaining wall and equipped with propylaia and a stoa (Figure 5.15). In the Lower terrace, a large building was constructed using part of the walls of the Hellenistic buildings that were still in place. This structure was used for cult practices that were very different from the previous rituals. There is in fact no evidence for the meals that had been an integral part of the worship in the previous periods, instead, a large number of lead curse tablets, all addressing women, were found.[825] Among the offerings, terracotta figurines and clay models are not numerous anymore, while oil lamps are still attested, thus hinting at the possibility that the rituals were again performed at night.

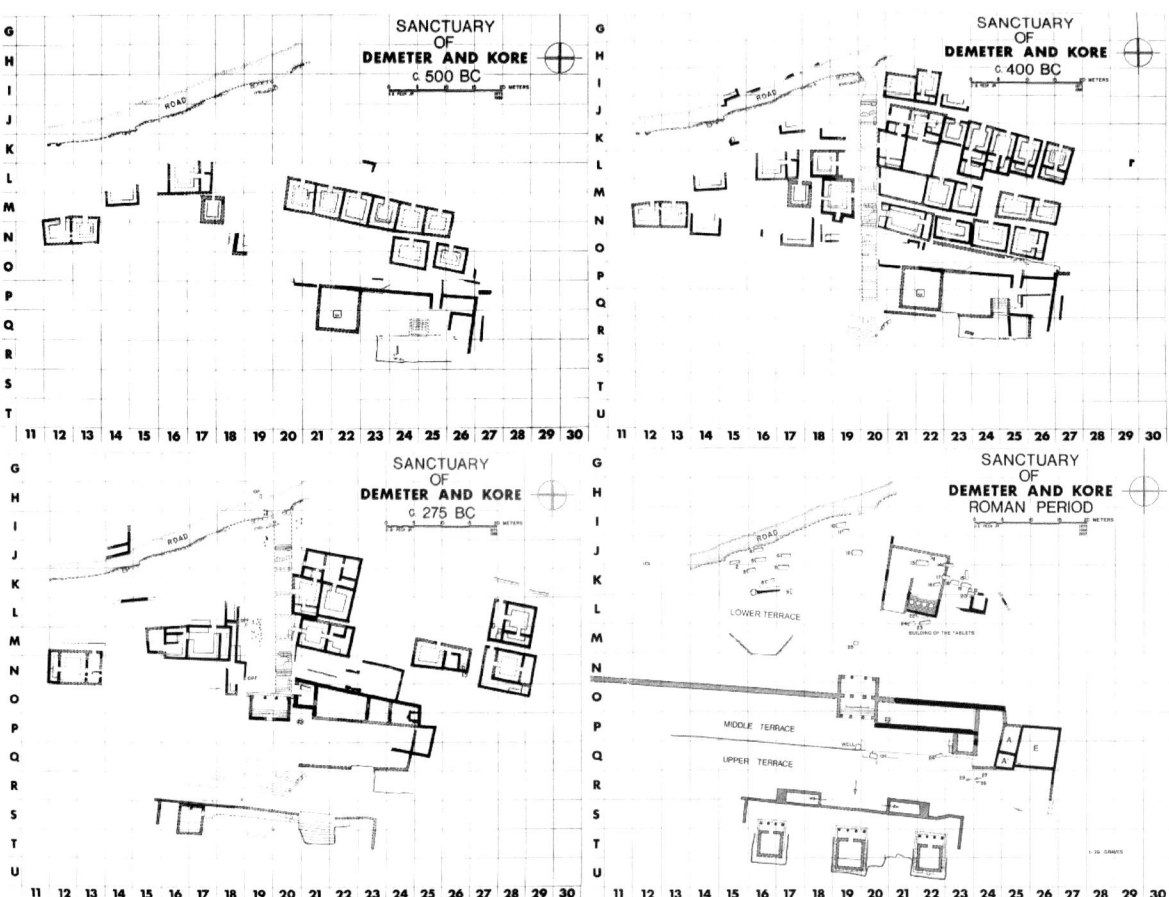

Figure 5.15 The sanctuary of Demeter and Kore from 500 BC to the Roman period (modified after Bookidis and Strout 1997).

---

[821] Bookidis and Strout 1997, 434.
[822] Gilman Romano 2003, 296.
[823] Bookidis and Strout 1997, 436.
[824] Bookidis and Strout 1997, 436.
[825] Bookidis 1998; Bookidis and Strout 1997, 434-5.

The Heruli that invaded Corinth in 267 AD left little traces of their passage on the sanctuary and religious activities seems to continue until the end of the 4th century AD, which corresponds to the end of the sanctuary's use.[826] An exact date cannot be established and the circumstances are still a matter of debate.[827] An earthquake, perhaps the one that occurred in 375 AD, could have marked the beginning of the sanctuary's demise. However, three statue heads torn off their bodies and thrown into a well has led scholars to suggest that its final phases were related to a violent episode, perhaps contextual to Alaric's invasion in 395 AD. In an increasingly Christianised society, with numerous anti-pagan Imperial edicts that were issued over those years, the destroyed sanctuary was then never rebuilt and was subsequently used as a quarry for building materials.[828] A cemetery was then installed in part of the area during the 5th and early 6th centuries, but it is impossible to ascertain if they were pagan or Christian tombs for the lack of tombstones and scarcity of grave goods that were found. Diverse explanations have been put forward for the choice to install a cemetery on this area: either for the still perceived sacred nature of the site,[829] or on the contrary, as a way to obliterate the memory of the place, or, more practically, because it offered an already levelled ground on the steep slope.[830]

In searching for examples that allow us to investigate how the Romans interpreted existing cults, we may turn to the sanctuary of Artemis Orthia in Sparta that was located, as usual for the goddess, close to a water source, on the right marshy bank of the Eurotas River.[831] The sanctuary was most famous for the *rite de passage* of the *diamastigosis*, during which the Spartan youths were whipped near Artemis' altar. According to Xenophon, the ritual was part of Lycurgus' youth education program, for which the *ephebi* had to steal as many cheeses as possible from the altar while enduring the pain of being scourged by others that were meant to prevent them to take the cheese.[832] In later sources the ritual assumes different characteristics and, although maintaining its role as a *rite de passage*, loses its initial connotations to become a bloody competition in which who could sustain the whips the longest won.[833] Epigraphic material that was documented on site testifies to the continuation of the dedications by the winners at least until the 3rd century AD.[834]

The evolution of the ritual can be followed in the modifications that took place in the architectural arrangement of the sanctuary. Remains of burnt animal bones, pottery and small bronzes are the first indications of the cult, which were dated to the end of the 8th century BC.[835] The area underwent several modifications from the Geometric to the Archaic period, starting with the creation of a *temenos* wall that enclosed the area, then with the addition of an altar, and finally with the erection of a temple. A new altar and a new temple were built in the 6th century BC on raised ground, probably as a consequence of a flooding of the river that had destroyed the previous structures.[836] The altar was rebuilt several times,

---

[826] Bookidis and Strout 1997, 437.
[827] See Warner Slane 2008, 466-7.
[828] Bookidis and Strout 1997, 438-9. For an overview of Corinth in Late Antiquity, see Rothaus 2000; Slane and Sanders 2005; Robertson Brown 2008.
[829] This interpretation has been put forward given the higher amount of women and children's tombs which could relate to the passed-on memory of the sacred nature of the site for female cult (Bookidis and Strout 1997, 440).
[830] Warner Slane 2008, 466.
[831] The sanctuary was excavated in the early 1900s and was published in 1929 by R. M. Dawkins (*The Sanctuary of Artemis Orthia at Sparta*, London: MacMillan and Co.) where all the yearly reports of the excavations that had appeared in the Annual of the British School at Athens were revised and organized in a systematic presentation. Dawkins' chronology was then revised by J. Boardman (1963) and by P. Cartledge in his work on Lakonian regional history (Cartledge 2002, 308-12).
[832] Xen. *Const. Lac.* 2.9.
[833] For a discussion on the literary sources that account for this ritual see Baudini 2010.
[834] Cartledge and Spawforth 2002, 187; Brulotte 1994, 224, which presents an overview of the inscriptions and votive offerings found at the site (189-217).
[835] Boardman 1963, 3.
[836] Dawkins 1929, 16; Cartledge 2002, 310.

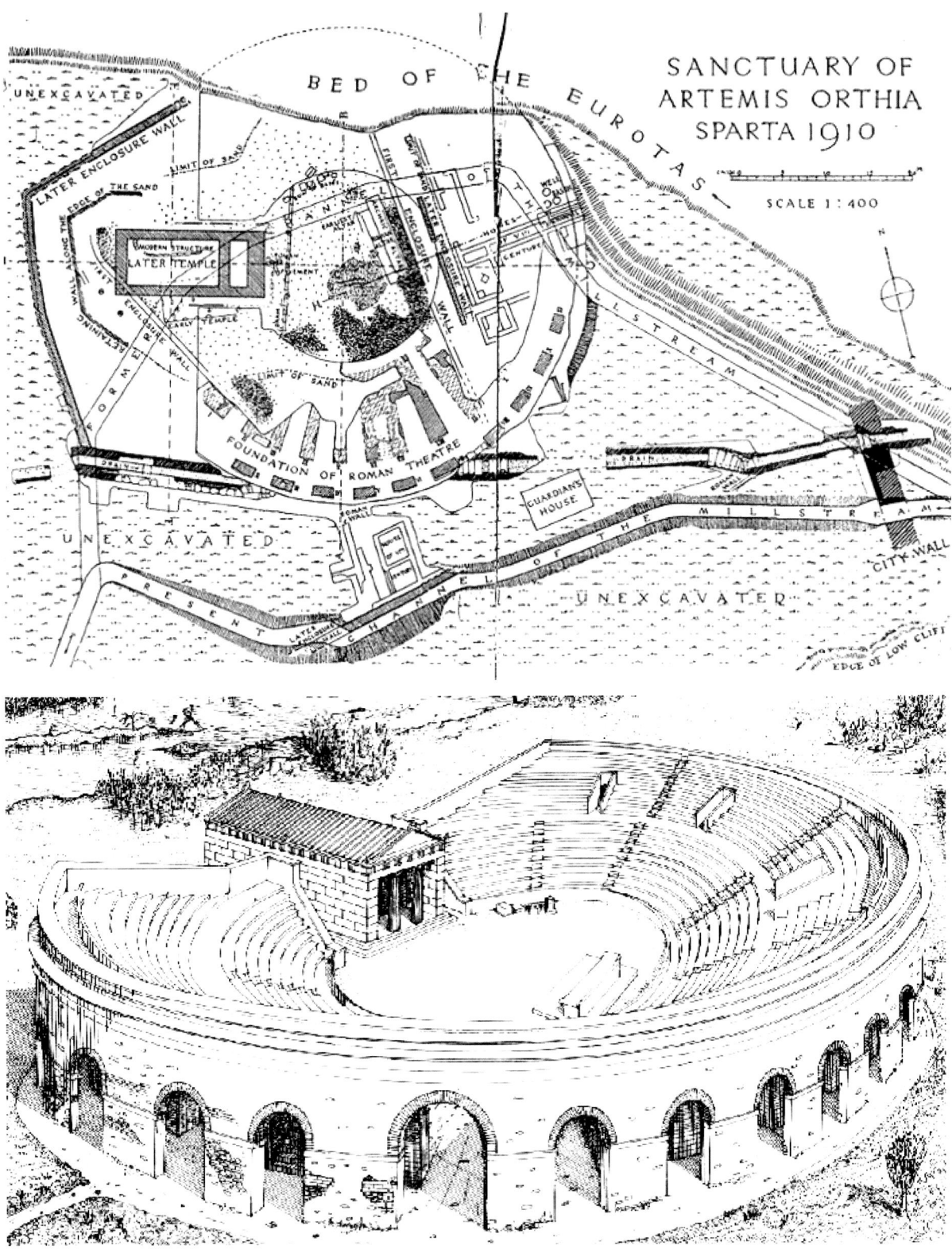

Figure 5.16 Top: Plan of the sanctuary of Artemis Orthia in Sparta at the end of the excavations in 1910 where the excavated temples, the altars and the Roman theatre are visible (Dawkins 1929, pl. 1); bottom: Reconstruction drawing of the Roman theatre (from Pausanias Project at http://www.pausanias-footsteps.nl/english/sparta-eng.html).

and some inscribed roof tiles dated to the Hellenistic period suggest also the temple was rebuilt, or at least re-roofed, during this period.[837]

It is during the Roman period that a major modification took place with the construction of a sort of theatre that enclosed the area around the altar and had the temple in the place usually occupied by the *skene* building (Figure 5.16). The structure was built in the 3rd century AD re-using materials from previous phases. Among the construction materials a marble bench dated to the 1st century BC was found that was dedicated by a member of the Gerousia.[838] This finding is the evidence of the presence of seating facilities for the spectators of the ritual before the construction of the Roman theatre.

The disproportion between the large arena and the relatively small temple, as noted by Baudini, points towards the transformation of the *diamastigosis* into a spectacle which, judging by the accounts of the ancient sources, kept the bloodiest aspects of the *agon* and attracted numerous visitors who needed to be accommodated. The developments at the sanctuary goes in line with the spectacularization of rituals that Mylonopoulos has observed already for the Hellenistic period.[839] The original meaning of the competition was now lost, but the role of *rite de passage* was maintained and became a form of auto-representation of the Graeco-Roman aristocracy.[840] As testified by the names of the winners that are recorded in the inscriptions dedicated to the goddess, the participating youth belonged in fact to the aristocratic families that ruled the city in Roman times. The festival must have enjoyed continuous popularity since a small amphitheatre was added to the theatrical area of the sanctuary in Late Antiquity,[841] and the sophist Libanius of Antioch visited the city in about 336 AD to see the 'festival of the whips'.[842]

5.3.2 Agora

The agora constituted an essential focal point in the urban layout of a Greek town, where political, religious and commercial activities were all represented. The creation and the transformations of this open area go hand in hand with the process of formation and growth of the *polis*. Ancient sources testify that the laying out of the agora was one of the first acts in a newly founded city, often directed directly by the ruler, as in the case of Alexandria where the location and layout of the agora was decided by Alexander the Great himself according to Arrian.[843] The architectural development of the agora reflected the need of the community to formalize a space for the worship of gods and for hosting public functions. The presence of altars and temples[844] testifies to the religious character of the agora,[845] which is especially evident in early agorai, while during the Hellenistic period the religious function seems to be more detached from the political sphere.[846]

The buildings that were present on the agora were deeply connected with the history and the political organization of each community. Monuments, statues and dedications celebrating the city founder,[847]

---

[837] Brulotte 1994, 224.
[838] Dawkins 1929, 294-5; Baudini 2010, 30.
[839] See above, p. 166.
[840] Baudini 2010, 32.
[841] Cartledge and Spawforth 2002, 112.
[842] Cartledge and Spawforth 2002, 113.
[843] Arrian, *Anabasis* 3.1.1.
[844] See for example the presence of temples dedicated to Zeus Agoraios in several agoras (Greco 2006), e.g. at Hyettos (Etienne and Knoepfler 1976) and Thasos (Figure 5.19, 34).
[845] Hölscher 2012, 174.
[846] Dickenson 2012, 128 taking as example the agorai at Pella and Kassope.
[847] Before the Roman period, when elites could be honoured by intramural burial, the city founder was the only one who could have a tomb in the agora. This was the case of Battus, the founder of Cyrene whose tomb at the edge of the agora, mentioned by Pindar (*Pyth.* 5), has been excavated (see Longo 2014, 230-33, which discusses also other possible identifications of founders'

important citizens or benefactors and events were displayed in the agora, and regulations were established to control their locations and costs.[848] The agora, however, was not only the place for civic display and for distinguished activities related to politics and religion, but also a space for commercial enterprises. We should image the hustle and bustle of the market place, with traders' stalls scattered around the square, where the lower social classes, including peasants selling their produce and slaves, could mix with higher status citizens, with much disapproval of the latter, as we read from ancient sources.[849]

The occurrence of debated identifications of agorai, even in extensively excavated sites such as at Olynthos[850] and Corinth, proves that the physical appearance of the agora could greatly vary in different sites and that there are no standardized types of buildings or fixed elements that can lead to a certain identification.[851] The available archaeological data on Greek agorai are in fact unevenly distributed in terms of quantity and quality.[852] Confusing is also the use of the term 'agora' in ancient sources as it is used to identify either an assembly, or the physical space in which people gathered, or (in late texts) the 'place for commercial activities', the terminology that corresponds to its modern use.[853] It has to be noted, moreover, that commercial activities could be carried out also in other spaces, such as at the crossing of important roads or outside the city gate, often in a temporary manner and without leaving recognisable archaeological traces.[854]

In towns that had to cope with an uneven terrain, the agora was preferably located on open flat ground at the crossing point of the main streets.[855] The shape of the agora could therefore greatly vary depending on the layout of the town. Organic layout resulted in irregular agorai, whereas in orthogonally arranged cities agorai were square or rectangular in shape and occupied the area of several housing blocks.[856] During the Iron Age and the early Archaic time, archaeological evidence and textual sources, albeit limited, point towards the existence of multiple agorai, each of them acting as meeting points of the

---

tombs in Magna Graecia). For a discussion of the agora of Cyrene, see Scott 2012, 14-44, esp. 18 and 21. For sites in Asia Minor where city founder's tombs are attested see Schörner 2013.

[848] Hölscher 2012, citing Vitruvius who reprehended the citizens of Alabanda, in Asia Minor for having displayed images of athletes in the agora and of lawyers in the gymnasium.

[849] Plato and Aristotle sustained a more strict division of function where the market should be held in a different area than the civic and religious activities. See Osborne 2000, 49-50.

[850] At Olynthos, the space South of block A iv has been identified by Cahill as the agora, preferring this identification over the suggestion by Robinson and Graham that this space was used for military manoeuvres and the claim by Hoepfner and Schwandner that it was a sanctuary which is unsupported by archaeological evidence (Cahill 2002, 32 and 265). In the northern part (the Southern row of block A iv) a stoa-like building was excavated which was flanked at its north-east corner by another stoa-like building that was identified as the *bouleuterion*. However, a re-examination of the large amount of coins found inside led Cahill to assign to this building a more commercial purpose. Next to this building, the only one known fountain house of the city has been found (Cahill 2002, 265).

[851] Stelai with inscribed the term *horos* were used to demarcate the sacred area of temples and sanctuaries. In Athens and elsewhere in Attica (e.g. Pireus and Sunion) *horoi* are attested as bordering also the agora, marking this area as a sacred space. This practice, however, finds little evidence outside this region and therefore cannot be considered as a typical element of the Greek agora as often has been sustained (Dickenson 2012, 15).

[852] Roland Martin has dedicated a work on the Greek agora: Martin 1951. Recently C. Dickenson has re-examined the available material focussing especially on Hellenistic and Roman Greece (Dickenson 2012).

[853] In the *Iliad* the term agora usually indicates the gathering of people (an exception is Hom. *Il.* 18, 497-508), while in the *Odyssey* the term is more often used to indicate the physical space where the assembly met. For some scholars this change of meaning mirrors an actual transition that took place from the 8th to the 7th century BC (Martin 1951; Greco 2010, 22). From the Classical period onwards, the term agora is used to indicate the market place, although the meaning as assembly can be still found in Classical and Hellenistic sources, see Longo 2010, 203-4. See at this respect also Dickenson 2012, *passim*, Greco 2006, 328 and Martin 1951, 19ff.

[854] For the Roman period, see de Ligt 1993.

[855] See the examples of Athens, Megara and Cyrene discussed by Hölscher 2012, 175.

[856] Dickenson 2012, 87.

aristocratic clans of the *polis* that constituted these early nucleated settlements.[857] In the Archaic period, a hierarchy and specialization of these places is established leading towards the predominance of one agora that becomes the place where the various competing groups met and negotiated power in the *polis*.[858]

As a general trend, the agora gained progressively a more architecturally defined appearance and a more monumental character over the centuries. Although difficult to prove archaeologically, it is traditionally accepted that early agorai were open spaces that were intentionally left unbuilt to host the citizens' assembly,[859] and to gather the troops for military exercises. Archaeological evidence for possible structures that were built in early agorai is scanty as they were probably built in perishable materials such as wood as attested to by ancient writers.[860] Early examples of monumentalized agorai are rare but can be found, especially in Magna Graecia, such as at Megara Hyblaea where a stoa bordering the agora was erected as early as the 7th century BC.[861]

In searching for clues about the architectural appearance of early agorai, archaeologists and historians have relied on textual sources, such as the passage from the *Iliad* in which the depictions on the shield of Achilles are presented (*Il*. 18, 497-508). In one of the scenes representing a law case that was held in the agora, the elders are described as seated on flat stones arranged in a 'sacred circle' (*hieros kyklos*).[862] Archaeological evidence of flights of steps in several sites have been interpreted to match the description of this Homeric agora, such as at the Cretan sites of Lato, Amnisos and Dreros. A re-examination of the existing evidence and the continuation of the archaeological investigations have however proved that these structures belong to later periods,[863] leaving therefore unattested the arrangement described in the *Iliad*.

Buildings hosting political and administrative services, and citizens' assemblies were usually located in or in proximity of the agora. One of the most important buildings was the *prytaneion*, which derives its name from the *prytaneis*, the magistrates chosen within the Boule to cover several administrative services, including social security programmes for the *poleis*.[864] The importance of this building is related to the presence of the sacred hearth of Hestia, which was kept there as a symbol of the life of the *polis* itself. In this place banquets were offered to honour eminent citizens or guests of the *polis* and evidence from some sites suggests that the *prytaneion* was also an archive and a sort of museum where memories of important past events, or statues of relevant historical figures for the *polis* were kept and displayed.[865] According to Miller the *prytaneion*'s functions are visible in its architectural form, which usually included a courtyard with an adjacent hall for dining, the hearth room and a storage space.[866] Notwithstanding its importance, archaeological evidence from the Archaic and Classical period depicts the image of a modest building, while monumental *prytaneia* are more attested during the Hellenistic

---

[857] For the several agorai that are attested in Athens, see Longo 2007.
[858] Longo 2007, 122.
[859] Lefebvre 1991 (1974), 237; Greco 2006.
[860] The ancient sources mention for example *ikria*, wooden benches that were set up to accommodate people. Traces of such structures have been archaeologically attested in sites such as Metaponto (see Longo 2010, 204-5) and in the Athenian agora (Hollinshead 2015, 9-15, which presents also vases where such wooden stepped structures are depicted such as the Athenian *dinos* by Sophilos dated to 570 BC).
[861] Gras et al. 2004, 432-5. For a discussion on early monumental agorai see Hölscher 2012, 179-80.
[862] For the interpretations that several scholars have given to this passage see Longo 2010, 201-2.
[863] Longo 2010, 205-10.
[864] For a discussion of the known *prytaneia*, see Miller 1978; for an updated list, see Hansen and Fischer-Hansen 1994, 30-7.
[865] Miller 1978, 17: In Athens the laws of Solon were displayed in the *prytaneion* and in this location statutes of public figures such as Demosthenes, Miltiades and Themistocles were also standing.
[866] Miller 1978, 91. But in regard to Miller's identification of a standard architectural form for the *prytaneion*, see the critical position of Hansen and Fischer-Hansen (1994, 37).

period.[867] The *prytaneion*'s political and administrative functions diminished after the Classical period but the building was maintained during the Roman period for its religious functions and as a sort of 'museum' of the town.[868]

Buildings for the council's assemblies, the *bouleuteria*, were also a constant presence in the urban topography of Greek *poleis*.[869] The typical feature of *bouleuteria* is the presence of either wooden benches or stone flights around its sides to accommodate the chosen members, and a space for the speaker in the centre. In this case also, as it has been noticed for *prytaneia*, the few archaeologically known structures that are dated to the Archaic and Classical periods look rather inconspicuous in comparison to the monumental character of Hellenistic *bouleuteria*.[870] The meetings of all male citizens, known as the *ekklesia*, on the other hand, are more difficult to situate since the archaeological traces and literary sources are scarce.[871] It is usually believed that they were held in the agora, but other meeting places could be chosen, such as the theatre, which was used as a multipurpose space and seems the most favourable place for assemblies during the Hellenistic period.[872]

It is common that administrative offices were clustered along one side of the square, as shown in the Athenian agora where the Tholos, the Bouleuterion and the Metroon were at the south end of its west side, and at Thasos where they were hosted in the north-east corner of the agora.[873] Often, moreover, the buildings that were meant for political functions were close to the temple(s) that were present in the agora, so as to guarantee godly protection to the decisions that were taken during the meetings. As previously mentioned, the location of political assemblies was not rigidly bound to a specific place during the Archaic and Classical periods, as assemblies could be held in temples[874] or theatres, and a single building could be used for a variety of purposes. The multifunctional character of these buildings and the lack of a standardized architectural appearance make their identification during excavation challenging.

The agora was not only occupied by architecture, but trees could be planted in the agora to embellish the square and create a pleasant shady space, as attested by the already mentioned decision of the Athenian *strategos* Cimon.[875] The presence of fountains in the agora, which seems dictated by practical needs, is attested by only a few examples from the Archaic and Classical period.[876] According to Dickenson a fountain should therefore be seen as a luxury, as the domestic water supply was guaranteed by cisterns or *pithoi* that could collect rain water in houses. In Olynthos, however, one of the two known fountain houses that were found during the excavation was located in the agora,[877] notwithstanding the evidence of *pithoi* in the courtyards that were used to store rain water.[878] A more conspicuous presence of

---

[867] Such as at Kassope, Ephesos and Magnesia on the Maeander (Hansen and Fischer-Hansen 1994, 36).
[868] Miller 1978, 23-4.
[869] For a list of known *bouleuteria*, see Hansen and Fischer-Hansen 1994, 37-44.
[870] *Bouleuteria* of the Classical period are attested among other at Akragas, Argos, Athens, Delos, Delphi, Olympia, Olynthos and Orchomenos (Hansen and Fischer-Hansen 1994, 43-4). For a discussion of the Hellenistic bouleuteria at Sikyon, Mantineia and Thasos, see Dickenson 2012, 116.
[871] Dickenson observes that the majority of epigraphic and literary evidence for *ekklesiasteria* is related to Delos (Dickenson 2012, 131 and note 502).
[872] Dickenson 2012, 132; Hansen and Fischer-Hansen 1994, 50-1.
[873] Camp 2003, 14-6; Grandjean and Salviat 2000, 68.
[874] See e.g. Xenophon's passage (*Hell.* 5.2.29) where he tells that the Theban boule had to gather in a stoa in the agora, instead of in their usual place, the temple of Demeter on the Kadmeia since the latter was used by the women for a festival (cited by Dickenson 2012, 115).
[875] Plu., *Cim.* 13.8.
[876] Dickenson (2012, 118) cites Athens and Eretria.
[877] Cahill 2002, 33. The other fountain house was built near the road at the southeast edge of the South Hill.
[878] Cahill 2002, 79.

fountains is attested in Roman times. In this period, with baths becoming a standard feature in cities,[879] and nymphaea being also introduced[880], more substantial infrastructures were needed to sustain water demand, such as aqueducts that were often financed by Imperial euergetism.

Especially from the Hellenistic periods onwards, an increased attention to the visual impact of the agora,[881] and a higher building density is observed.[882] The power display of Hellenistic rulers found its expression in the construction of honorific monuments inside the open area,[883] and multifunctional stoas bordering the square became a common feature.[884] The construction of such an expensive building implied a great financial effort by the community and was therefore often funded when war booties were available. It is not surprising therefore that financing the construction of stoas was a popular gift from wealthy citizens or Hellenistic rulers, who could mark their presence in the city through the erection of such imposing structures that were placed in a prominent, central location and were therefore visible to every passer-by.[885] In Thasos, an epigraph dated to the 1st century BC which was engraved on the architrave of the north-east portico testifies to the generosity of a citizen, whose name is lost, who donated the building to the community (Figure 5.19, 15).[886] In some cases a controlled access to the square was achieved by means of (monumental) gates, which are nevertheless still rare during the Hellenistic period.[887] At Pella, at both sides of the eastern larger entrance to the agora two rooms were excavated which have been interpreted as guardrooms, where the goods that were sold in the agora could be inspected.[888] Cities with multiple agorai are also more often attested than in the Classical period.[889]

The agora of Kastro Kallithea shows a progressive monumentalization of the open space during Classical and Hellenistic times (Figure 5.17). It occupied the area of about four *insulae* and was divided into two areas by two narrow streets: a square area on the south-west corner that was occupied by the complex of Building 5 and 6, and the remaining open space that was surrounded by Buildings 1 to 4. Building 5, oriented towards the east and with an altar in front of its entrance, has been interpreted as a small temple. Building 6 was in association with Building 5, with which it shares a retaining wall, and consisted of at least thirteen rooms and a courtyard with an underground cistern. A high number of finds was recorded in this complex formed by Buildings 5 and 6, in contrast to the paucity of finds yielded from the northern part of the agora.[890] The excavators interpreted these structures as public buildings with

---

[879] For baths in Roman towns and a comparison between Greek and Roman bathing facilities see Foxhall 2013, 130-1.
[880] Nymphaea arrived in Greece in the 2nd century AD, after being introduced in Asia Minor during the 1st (Dickenson 2012, 299 citing Levick 2000, 630).
[881] In this respect, see the discussion and comparison by Winter of the agorai of Morgantina, Assos, Aigai in Aiolis, Alinda, Magnesia, Priene and Miletos (Winter 2006, 36-40).
[882] For a study on Hellenistic agorai see Sielhorst 2015.
[883] Dickenson 2013.
[884] Although stoas are typically associated with Hellenistic agorai, stoas were present in the agora also in much earlier contexts. The earliest example is attested at Megara Hyblaea (Gras *et al.* 2004, 432-5). Dickenson underlines an association between the construction of stoas and war booties that were used to finance such an expensive undertaking (Dickenson 2012, 523). An interesting example of the variety of activities that were carried out in stoas comes from Pella, where the finds that were recovered in one area are related to pottery production, selling of perfumes, meat, metal objects and lamps, while the northern part was dedicated to administrative duties (Dickenson 2012, 93). For the architectural development of stoas see Coulton 1976.
[885] For a discussion on stoas as gifts from Hellenistic rulers, see Dickenson 2013.
[886] Grandjean and Salviat 2000, 68.
[887] Dickenson 2012, 112-3.
[888] Dickenson 2013.
[889] Dickenson 2012, 88 and 499 with the examples of Athens, Thasos and Messene. It must be noted moreover, that spaces that were used with the functions that we attribute to the agora could exist also outside the 'proper' agora, for example at the crossing point of large streets (see Dickenson 2012, 18, citing Aelius Aristides on Smyrna).
[890] Haagsma *et al.* 2014, 204-6.

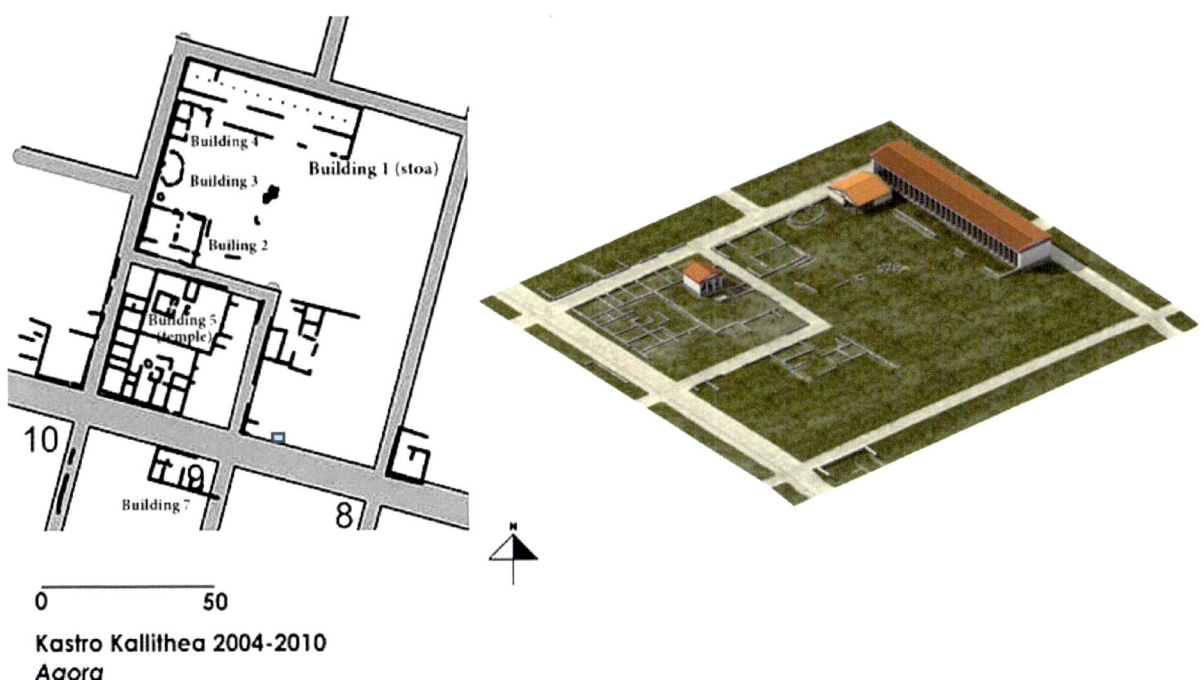

Figure 5.17 Plan of the agora of Kastro Kallithea and 3D reconstructions of the excavated buildings: Building 1 (stoa), Building 4 and Building 5 (Temple) (Haagsma et al. 2014, figs. 2 and 9; 3D modelling by R. C. Lee).

a religious character where a non identified deity was worshipped and dining took place in connection with ritual practices.[891]

On the north edge of the agora a stoa (Building 1) was built and it was constructed around Building 4 (a two room structure with a hall that opened onto the agora). The foundations of building 4 (made by small unworked limestone blocks) are similar to those of Building 3, a circular structure that finds a parallel in Thasos where a similar structure has been interpreted as a heroon.[892] Building 2 consisted of three rooms and was accessed from the north. Although it has not been fully excavated, its heavy foundations and its location pointed towards an interpretation as a public building, perhaps a *prytaneion*.[893] Approximately at the centre of the open area in the Northern sector of the agora, a number of large slabs were found which were interpreted as an altar or a *bema* for public speeches.[894] The buildings on the agora of Kastro Kallithea belong to various phases. Buildings 3 and 4, and perhaps Buildings 5 and 6, seem to be constructed earlier than the more monumental Buildings 1 and 2. This agora is therefore representative of the typical development of this public area towards monumentality that at Kastro Kallithea was reached during the 3rd century BC.[895]

In Roman times, the agora remains the fulcrum of urban life. The Greek sophist Philostratus describing the life of Dionysos of Miletus informs us that he was buried in the most conspicuous part of Ephesos, the market place, which was the most important place in Ephesos.[896] New construction techniques (e.g. *opus caementicium*) and building materials (e.g. marble) started to be introduced and progressively

---

[891] Haagsma *et al.* 2014, 201-4 and 206.
[892] Haagsma *et al.* 2014, 200.
[893] Haagsma *et al.* 2014, 199.
[894] Haagsma *et al.* 2014, 199.
[895] Haagsma *et al.* 2014, 206.
[896] Philostratus, *Lives of the Sophists*, 1.526.

employed, especially from the 1st century AD, and led to the creation of new building types.[897] Among the new buildings that were introduced in Greek urban centres during the Roman period, *odeia*, such as the imposing Odeion of Agrippa in the Athenian agora, basilicas and libraries are the most characteristic. Baths, often built in close proximity to the agora, were also a typical infrastructure that was introduced in Roman times.[898] In new Roman colonies, temples became more prominent in the agora in comparison with Greek traditions.[899]

In this period, it is more frequent to find two agorai, a specialized area with a commercial function and another fulfilling civic and administrative purposes.[900] Often the commercial activities took place in specific buildings, which were dedicated to sell a type of good, as shown by the presence of a meat-vegetable market at Thera,[901] of a fish market in Corinth and of a meat market in Messene that was hosted in a different building than the 'pantopolis stoa' where every type of good was sold.[902]

Contrary to the Hellenistic period, when a relation can be established between the size of the agora and the power and wealth of the city, during the Roman period agorai tend generally to be smaller than in previous eras regardless of the status of the city. According to Dickenson this can be explained by a change in aesthetic values towards a preference for fuller looking space, an effect that could better be achieved in smaller areas.[903] The change in fashion can be perceived by the descriptions that Pausanias left of the agorai at Pharae and at Elis: the former is 'of wide extent after the ancient fashion',[904] and the latter is 'built in the old manner', having two porticoes separated from each other in contrast to the more densely built up agorai that were common in Ionia and in the Greek cities near Ionia.[905] A decrease in size could be also related to the lost function of gathering soldiers for military preparation, which was not necessary anymore,[906] and to the reduced public role in politics.

A change in aesthetics led also to an increased attention to the embellishment of the square, including the provision of marble facades to the overlooking buildings and the substitution of cobbles with marble or limestone floors.[907] A general distinction can be made between newly founded Roman colonies and older cities.[908] In the former, new buildings were constructed to host the imperial cult, while in old cities existing buildings were reused for such purposes, as shown by the house of the Hellenistic tyrant Kleon in Sikyon which was turned into a temple of the imperial cult.[909] Moreover, some buildings, such as council houses, were maintained although their functions were downscaled from state to local affairs.[910] Dickenson observes that the modifications that were made to these buildings during the Roman period were probably meant to improve their appearance, which suggests that reverence was paid to the history of the city.[911] In Corinth, important buildings of the former Greek city were maintained when the new Roman Forum was planned, such as the Archaic Temple of Apollo situated on the Temple

---

[897] Evangelidis 2014.
[898] Evangelidis 2014.
[899] Dickenson 2012, 244.
[900] Evangelidis 2014; Dickenson 2012, 252.
[901] Evangelidis 2014.
[902] Dickenson 2012, 230-1.
[903] Dickenson 2012, 559.
[904] Paus. 7.22.2.
[905] Paus. 6.24.2. For a discussion of this passage and the interpretations that various scholars have put forward (e.g. the distinction between the horseshoe or Ionian agora and the peristyle agora), see Dickenson 2012, 500-4. The open character of the agora in Elis has been confirmed by excavations (Heiden 2006).
[906] Dickenson 2012, 499.
[907] See e.g. Thasos and Corinth (Dickenson 2012, 258-9; Gilman Romano 2005, 31).
[908] Evangelidis 2014.
[909] Evangelidis 2014.
[910] For examples of reused (e.g. Elis) or newly constructed buildings (e.g. Thasos), see Dickenson 2012, 249-52.
[911] Dickenson 2012, 254.

Hill, and the 4th century 164m long South Stoa. The orientation of most of the new buildings in the Roman forum followed the orientation of the pre-existing buildings in the Greek city: some of them were constructed aligned to the Temple of Apollo and the South Stoa, others according to a Hellenistic race course.[912]

The agora of Kos represents well the progressive embellishment and monumentalization of the market place that occurred during Hellenistic and Roman times, maintaining at the same time the buildings which belonged to the construction phase dated to the late 4th BC. The L-shaped elongated square, 350 m long, is one of the largest that is documented for Greek *poleis* and occupied 10 blocks of the urban grid. An artificial terrace was needed to compensate for the different elevation of the areas that it connected, namely the harbour and the southern, higher, districts of the city. The construction of the agora probably started with setting up an area near the harbour that was then progressively enlarged in line with the expansion of the city towards the south. The agora was bordered by a Doric portico along its western side and a series of (store)rooms preceded by a Doric portico along the eastern side. A renovation encompassing the town's public buildings at the beginning of the 2nd century BC led to the rebuilding and remodelling of the porticoes with local white marble.[913] During this phase, a large building was constructed starting from the corner that the western stoa made turning towards the west (Figure 5.18).

During the Roman period, Kos suffered two earthquakes. The first one under Augustus did not cause much damage and only a few reparations to the square were needed, while the second one in 142AD caused more substantial destruction. In relation to this event (and perhaps following earthquakes which are not known epigraphically), a reorganization of the area was carried out which included the insertion of a new monumental propylon to the north of the square (Figure 5.18, bottom right).[914] This gate was reached by a large marble staircase whose core was built with reused blocks from the Hellenistic stoa that was replaced by the new construction.[915] The propylon had a central building that could be interpreted as related to the imperial cult, and which was visible to travellers coming from the sea as acting as a representation of imperial munificence to the city.[916] Within this reorganization programme, a tholos on a podium was constructed in the agora, which has been tentatively identified as dedicated to Fortuna or Tyche.[917]

It is common that buildings or other elements dedicated to the Imperial cult were added inside the square of Greek cities in Roman times. For example, in the agora of Thasos a centrally located monument was dedicated to Lucius Caesar (Figure 5.19, 30) and statues of his brother Gaius and of Augustus himself were also present. The good state of preservation of a statue head of one of the two brothers that was found in the vicinity hint at the presence of a canopy that protected the monument.[918] On some occasions solutions were found to set up monuments in a cost effective way. This is the case of the Temple of Ares, located in the middle of the Athenian agora, which is an example of a so called 'wandering temple'. The foundations date to the early Roman period and the superstructure showing 5th century BC marbles led the excavator to suggest that the temple was taken from one of the deserted demes of Attica and brought to Athens to be rebuilt as a less costly monument to worship the Roman Emperors.[919]

---

[912] Not all the Roman buildings were however constructed following the orientation of the Temple of Apollo and of the South Stoa, see at this respect Gilman Romano 2005, 25-59.
[913] Rocco and Livadiotti 2011, 396.
[914] Rocco and Livadiotti 2011, 401.
[915] Rocco and Livadiotti 2011, 401.
[916] Rocco and Livadiotti 2011, 405-16.
[917] Rocco and Livadiotti 2011, 420.
[918] Grandjean and Salviat 2000, 73.
[919] Camp 2003, 38; McAllister 1959; Dinsmoor 1940.

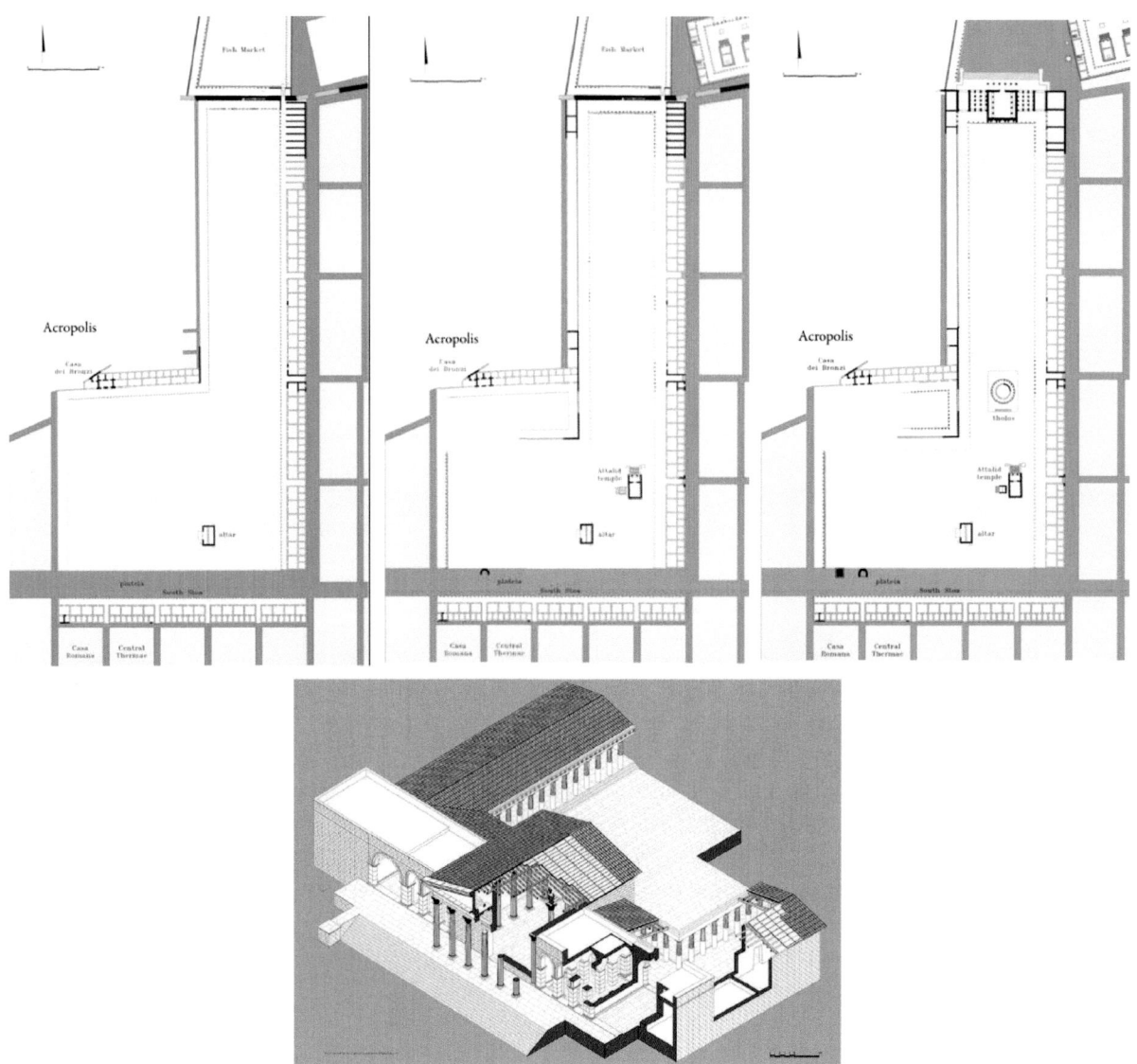

Figure 5.18 Top, left: The agora of Kos during the 4th century BC; Top, centre: The modifications of the 2nd century BC; Top, right: The substantial changes during the 2nd century AD including the creation of a monumental access to the square (Rocco and Livadiotti 2011, 387; 397; 407); Bottom: Reconstruction drawing of the monumental access to the square by arch. G. Campanile, G. Carella, E. Cappilli, D. D'Oria, M. Fumarola, S. Valentini, based on the study of G. Rocco and M. Livadiotti (Rocco and Livadiotti 2011, 404).

Contrasting with the long held belief that generally agorai fell out of use as early as the 4th century AD,[920] restorations of existing buildings and insertion of new constructions on the agora are also attested in the Mediterranean.[921] The extent of the modifications, albeit generally not comparable to the much more imposing interventions of Hellenistic and Roman times, attested in some sites provides evidence of localized continuity of the focus of the urban centre well into the 6th century AD, and even into the early 7th.[922] The agora was still used to host law courts, public ceremonies and punishments,[923]

---

[920] Potter 1995. This booklet aiming at contextualizing Iol Caesarea with parallels from Africa and Italy has become the reference work to sustain that agorai went out of use as early as the 4th century AD.
[921] For an overview of Late Antique agorai/forai in the Mediterranean, see Lavan 2006.
[922] Lavan 2006, 196 and 2013, 298.
[923] Lavan 2006, 213-5.

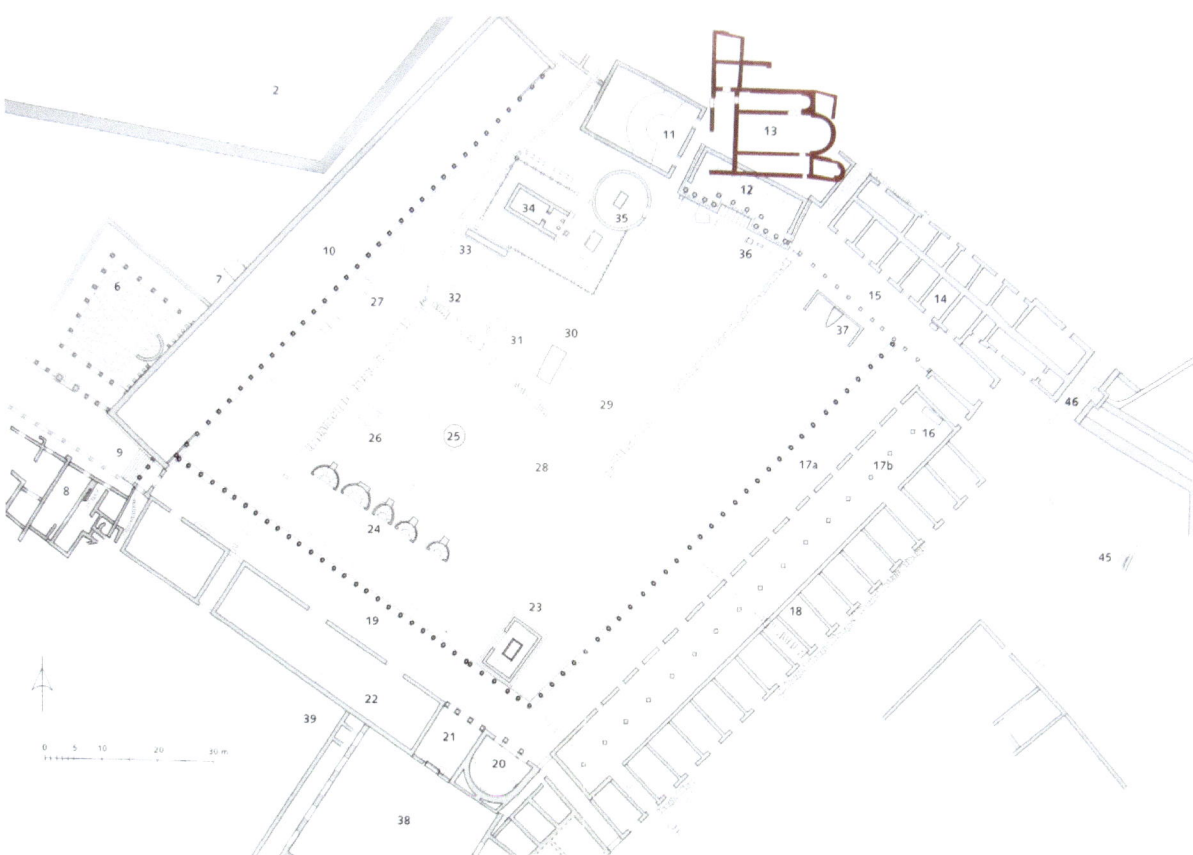

Figure 5.19 The agora of Thasos (Grandjean and Salviat 2000, Figure 21).

but also as a place for social relationships and as a not to be missed destination in the inhabitants' daily routine.[924] In Greece, reparations are widely attested, especially to porticoes, arches and nymphaea.[925] Statue dedications of the early Imperial period were generally maintained and new dedications were made.[926] The more limited resources of the late Empire could not sustain the presence of the often duplicated public spaces that had been created in previous centuries. As such, in some sites, one of the agorai was destined to another use or abandoned (e.g. at Thessaloniki),[927] and temples, basilicas or stoas were repurposed to accommodate other needs and transformed into other buildings, most notably churches.[928] The latter, however, were more commonly built at the edges of the city and close to their city walls than within the agora.[929] At Corinth, inscriptions suggest that major reparation works were made in the forum during the reign of Valens and Valentinian, but this would be left out (together with other central areas of the Classical town) from the Justinian city wall circuit (see Figure 5.8); at Athens the Classical agora was left out from the Late Antique city wall circuit, and in the first half of the 5th century, a large complex, possibly a villa or an official residence also perhaps unfinished, occupied most of the square space, including the area previously covered by the Odeion of Agrippa.[930]

---

[924] Lavan 2006, 215-8.
[925] Lavan 2006, 204.
[926] Lavan 2006, 205.
[927] Bintliff 2012, 361.
[928] Such as at Philippi, Pergamon and Knidos among others (see Lavan 2013, 298-9).
[929] Lavan 2006, 233-4.
[930] Camp 2001, 230-2. For a discussion on Late Antique agorai see Bintliff 2012, 361 and Lavan 2006, 203 and 245 with related bibliography.

The agora is therefore the urban space that represents better than any other the reflection of social and political changes which affected both the community and the overarching political system. A high degree of continuity, although with exceptions and architectural modifications, can be traced in the development of the agora across centuries. This continuity, however, was lost when the functions that were concentrated in the agora in Antiquity will be assigned to different places (political in the palace and religious in dedicated buildings), and the space still nowadays called 'agora' will be used only for commercial purposes.[931]

5.3.3 *Theatres*

Among public buildings, theatres had an important role as places for the self-representation of the *polis* and of its citizens. In the theatre, people of different social classes met to attend the performances, which at first were organised in the context of some religious festival and then assumed a progressively secularized character. The function of theatres was however not confined to the hosting of spectacles, but political assemblies and law courts were also held in this convenient location to accommodate a large number of people.[932] The need of a theatre and its construction has been related to the increased importance that dramatic performances assumed in the Classical period, but other factors, such as population size, financial possibility and desire of status display of each *polis*, played a role in their appearance and distribution across Greece.[933]

Just over 250 theatres are archaeologically attested in Greece;[934] but less than a third of them have survived to such an extent as to allow a systematic study of the evidence.[935] In its canonical form, which was reached in the late Classical and Hellenistic time, the theatre was a complex composed of the *koilon* (the 'hollow') where the spectators sat, the *orchestra* where the chorus sang and danced, and the *skene* that served as the backdrop of the performance and as changing rooms for the actors.[936] Interestingly, theatres reached their more monumental shape during Hellenistic times when the religious character of performances was perceived as less essential, and the entertainment aspect grew instead in importance. Theatre architecture developed in fact towards the design of a comfortable place for the spectators and the creation of a more pleasing experience in terms of acoustics and setting.[937] This intention is even better perceived in Roman theatres in which the cavea and the scene building are adjoined, thus creating a unified complex, secluded from the outside by surrounding high walls.

The location for the theatre within the ancient *polis* was chosen based on the morphology of the terrain. Natural depressions and sloping grounds offered convenient locations to accommodate a large audience. Not always, however, was the simpler solution of exploiting the landscape followed. A notable exception is the theatre at Eretria which was built near the West Gate and within the sanctuary of Dionysos. Instead of building the theatre on the slope of the acropolis, the Eretrians invested great

---

[931] Ananiadou-Tzimopoulou *et al.* 2007.
[932] Frederiksen 2002, 80.
[933] Frederiksen 2002, 87-8.
[934] See the catalogue compiled by Frederiksen (2002) which lists 251 remains of buildings 'which can be securely identified as a monumental Greek theatre at a given place at any time in the Greek period or down to the second century AD in the Hellenic world' (Frederiksen 2002, 67). For a discussion on the use of the word θέατρον in ancient sources, see Frederiksen 2002, 71-6. Erroneous labelling of theatres, *odeia*, *bouleuteria* and *ekklesisteria* can occur in poorly preserved examples since they all share a similar theatre-like shape (although with different characteristics), see Dickenson 2012, 131-3.
[935] Frederiksen 2000, 137.
[936] Frederiksen 2000, 135. For a regional overview of the known theatres in Greece before the Imperial period based on recent bibliography, see Moretti 2014a. For a discussion on the (again problematic) terminology that is used to define the elements that composed the ancient theatre and the adoption of Greek, Roman or modern terms, see Bressan 2009, 11-23. The book by Izenour treats the subject of roofing in ancient theatres: Izenour 1992.
[937] Winter 2006, 96-7.

	North (315-44°)	East (45-134°)	South (135-224°)	West (225-314°)	Total
Mainland Greece	18% (9)	24% (12)	43% (21)	14% (7)	49
Anatolia	15% (7)	21% (10)	48% (23)	17% (8)	48
Greek islands	8% (1)	42% (5)	25% (3)	25% (3)	12
Magna Graecia	14% (2)	29% (4)	50% (7)	7% (1)	14
Total	15% (19)	25% (31)	44% (54)	15% (19)	123

Table 1 Audience orientation in a sample of 123 preserved theatres across the Greek world (after Ashby 1999, 104).

resources in the construction of the theatre by excavating the area to make space for the *orchestra* and creating an artificial mound for the *koilon*. This choice was therefore not by chance and it has been suggested that the construction of the theatre was part of a larger building programme, initiated in the second half of the 4th century BC when the *polis* enjoyed sufficient financial resources, which included the creation of the temple and of the nearby *gymnasion*.[938]

As already observed for the theatre at Eretria, many theatres were built within or near the *temenos* of a sanctuary (most commonly, but not exclusively, of Dionysos). Other examples include Athens (within the sanctuary of Dionysos Elutherios), Delphi (in the sanctuary of Apollo), Elis (nearby the sanctuary of Dionysos), and Megalopolis (close to the sanctuary of Dionysos).[939] A connection between the theatre and the agora is also widely attested, as *agorai* are often found near theatres (such as at Argos, Messene, Megalopolis and Aigai, which were built during the Late Classical period; or at Hellenistic Kassope and Mantineia) or within a short walking distance (e.g. at Eretria and Thasos).[940] The proximity of the theatre to prominent sacred and civic areas testifies to its importance both as a religious and political venue.

As necessary for the study of every aspect of the *poleis*' urban development, only a combined critical analysis of both textual and archaeological evidence can provide a complete picture of the appearance and role of the ancient theatre in the architectural development and the life of an ancient Greek city. Vitruvius has been traditionally taken as the reference point to reconstruct the architectural components of theatre buildings in Greece. However, as already observed for Greek house architecture, recent scholarship warns against taking his descriptions as dogmatic.[941] The most striking example of the difference between Vitruvius' suggestions and the archaeological evidence regards the orientation of theatres. According to Vitruvius a southern exposure was the unhealthiest and had to be avoided;[942] the archaeological evidence analysed by Ashby returned however a very different picture as the majority of the surveyed theatres was in fact oriented towards the south (Table 1).

Early theatres were not necessarily permanent buildings, but could be set up and taken apart when needed. In Archaic and early Classical times, the *orchestra* was generally rectilinear, being created out of levelled ground along a terrace where people could stand or sit to watch.[943] The *skene* (no more than a tent at the beginning) was then added for the actors to change their costumes during the performance and for a space to hide some of the actions that could not be represented in public (e.g. the murder

---

[938] Ducrey 2004, 188-9; Isler 2007.
[939] Frederiksen 2002, 85.
[940] Dickenson 2012, 128-9.
[941] Ashby 1999, 10-1.
[942] Vitr. *De Arch.* 5.3.
[943] See Winter 2006, 97-8 for the evidence from Athens and Attica. In some rare cases, the rectilinear orchestra was maintained up to early Hellenistic times as demonstrated by the excavation of a deme theatre at Trachones, south of Athens (Winter 2006, 97).

of Agamemnon).⁹⁴⁴ As Moretti observed, the word *skene* was used in fact not only in the context of theatrical performances but also to indicate other temporary installations such as market stands.⁹⁴⁵ The temporary theatre was then substituted for by wooden *koila* and *skenai*.⁹⁴⁶ For the lack of early Classical archaeological evidence, the appearance of the *skene* of this period is derived from the surviving plays that were performed in the 5th century.⁹⁴⁷ Movements and positions of actors suggest for example the presence of a roof where the actor could stand and at least one door where he could come into the scene. In some sites, traces of the early wooden theatre have been unearthed. At Hephaisteia in Lemnos, for example, three stairways (*klimakes*) have been found under the 4th century stone *koilon*, which belonged to an earlier wooden theatre with *ikria* that was constructed between the 5th and the beginning of the 4th century BC.⁹⁴⁸

Assigning a secure dating to theatres is quite complex since they were often remodelled and later buildings were built upon earlier foundations.⁹⁴⁹ Despite this difficulty, the second half of the 4th century BC has been recognised as a turning point for the increase in the number of new constructions in the Greek world,⁹⁵⁰ possibly in relation with the new style and requirements of the New Comedy.⁹⁵¹ This growth is observed especially in Attica, the Peloponnese and Sicily, while in the Cyclades and Asia Minor the number of new and monumentalized theatres rises later, in the 3rd and 2nd century BC.⁹⁵² The use of stone and the monumentalization of theatres that was increasingly adopted during the late Classical and Hellenistic periods (in line with what we already previously observed for *gymnasia*) accounts for the greater number of surviving theatres of these periods in comparison to the fewer early Classical examples.⁹⁵³ Despite the fact that stone was now used more commonly, wooden *koila* and *skenai* were still erected, as attested among others at Corinth, Eretria, Megalopolis and Philippi.⁹⁵⁴

Among the theatres that were constructed in the late 4th century, for the theatre of Delos it has been possible to clarify the chronology of its various building phases.⁹⁵⁵ The first theatre, built at the end of the 4th century BC, had a wooden *skene* with a *proskenion* and a *koilon* created from the naturally sloping ground, where some marble thrones were added to provide seating for prominent citizens. The construction of a stone theatre in substitution for the wooden antecedent started at the beginning of the 3rd century BC. The first element that was changed was the *skene* which was completed in 279 BC. After that, a retaining wall was created to support the *koilon*, where flights of steps and the dividing *klimakes* and *diazoma* (the passage that separated the lower and the upper rows of seats) were progressively added. Two ramps were added, one on the north side of the theatre at the level of the *diazoma*, the other one at the top of the *koilon*. During the works to build the stone *koilon*, further modifications were made to the *skene*: a porch was added on its sides and back, and two entrances were built to bridge the

---

⁹⁴⁴ Devices (e.g. the *ekkyklema* and the *mechane*) were used to bring to the view of the spectators the results of actions that were performed backstage (see e.g. Winter 2006, 99).
⁹⁴⁵ Moretti 2014b, 107.
⁹⁴⁶ Moretti 2014b, 108-9. Notable exceptions are the stone cut theatres at Argos, Chaironeia and Syrakousai which probably date to the 5th century BC and are nevertheless not monumental constructions (Frederiksen 2000, 139).
⁹⁴⁷ Moretti 2014b, 112.
⁹⁴⁸ Greco and Voza 2010. Greco and Voza disagree on the dating around the end of the 6th century suggested by the excavator Aglaia Archontidou who had hinted at a continuity between the wooden theatre and the Archaic sanctuary on which site the theatre was constructed (Archontidou and Kokkinophorou 2004).
⁹⁴⁹ Ashby 1999, 105.
⁹⁵⁰ Moretti 2014b, 109-11.
⁹⁵¹ Winter 2006, 101.
⁹⁵² Moretti 2014b, 111.
⁹⁵³ Frederiksen 2000, 139.
⁹⁵⁴ Moretti 2014b, 113-5.
⁹⁵⁵ Fraisse and Moretti 2007.

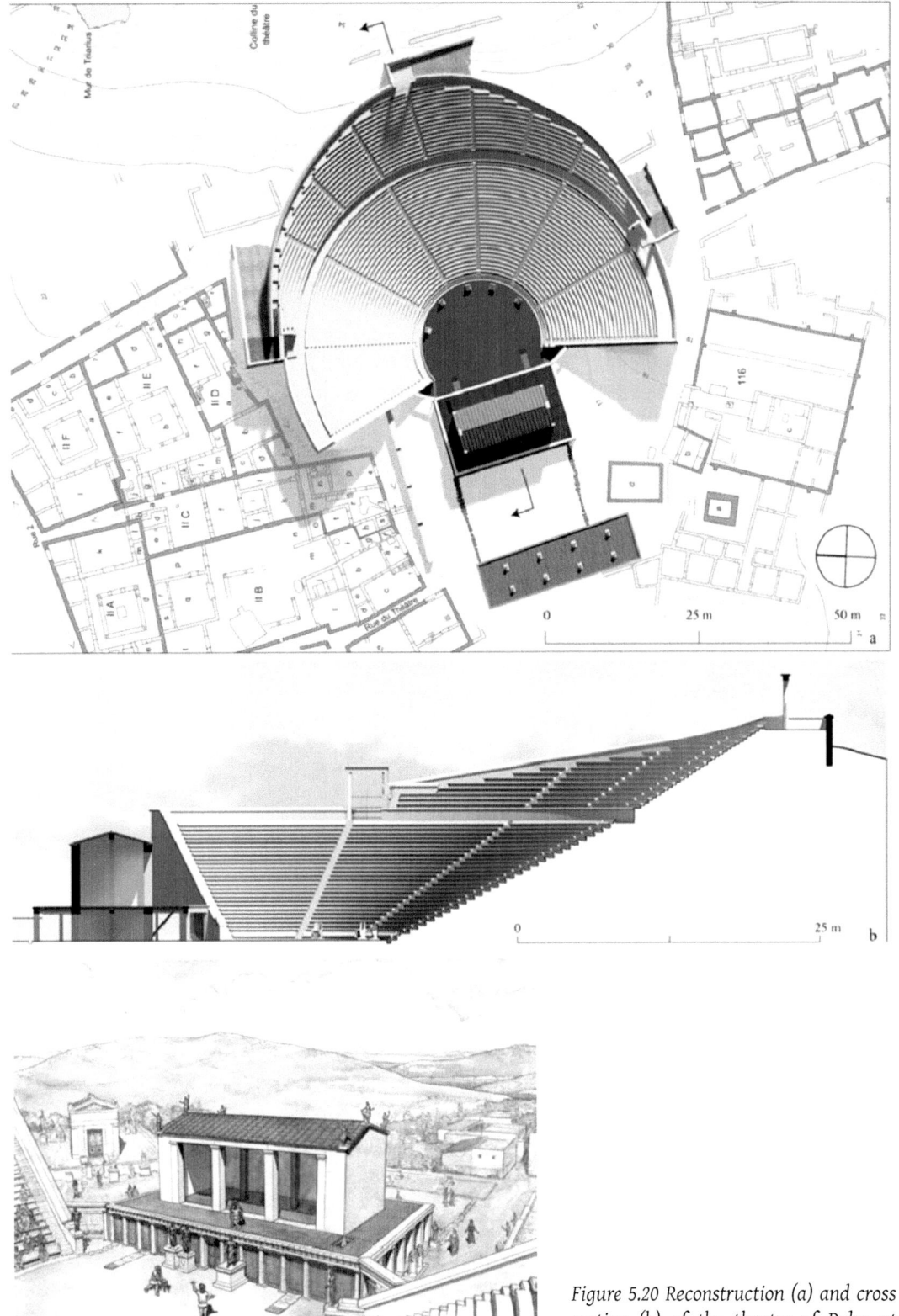

Figure 5.20 Reconstruction (a) and cross section (b) of the theatre of Delos at the beginning of the second half of the third century BC (Moretti 2014b, 122); c) Detail of the last phase of the skene in an aquarelle by Th. Fournet (Fraisse and Moretti 2007, Figure 425).

proskenion with the new *koilon*. In the last building phase, between 250 and 240 BC, a flight of steps was added above the *diazoma* and a third ramp was constructed to its south side (Figure 5.20).[956]

Theatre architecture offers an interesting point of view to observe and analyse the ways in which Roman elements were received and incorporated into the Greek built environment. The adaptations are partly explained by the introduction of typically Roman contests such as the *ludi gladiatorum* and the *venationes*.[957] In Roman Greece, performances in theatres had lost their religious connotation and covered a wide range of spectacles from the traditional comedies and tragedies to mime and pantomime.[958] The introduction of new spectacles and competitions is paired with the revival of some traditional performances, such as the singing of dithyrambs and the recitation of rhapsodies, which seem to enjoy a renewed popularity.[959]

The modifications that theatres underwent are however part of a larger and more profound cultural interaction between Greeks and Romans. A study conducted by Bressan on theatres in Attica and Peloponnese points towards different degrees of reception of Roman elements in Greek theatres, mainly influenced by the status of the city under the Romans (colony or free city) and by the pre-existence of a Greek urban centre to the newly established colony. The theatres of Corinth, Patras and Sparta offer three telling examples. The architecture of the large theatre at Corinth that was originally built in the 4th century BC was heavily modified at the end of the Augustan period. The cavea was restructured and the circular orchestra was then cut by and adjoined to a longer new scene building, which gave the orchestra the semi-circular shape typical of Roman theatres.[960] Under the Flavians, a smaller, typical Roman theatre was built at the back of the large one.[961] The cavea of the new theatre was self-sustained and formed a unified complex with the scene building to which it was attached.[962] The high walls of the cavea and of the scene contributed to the seclusion of the inner space and obstructed views from the outside. Similar to this was the theatre constructed in the 2nd century AD in the colony of Patras.[963]

A different development is followed instead by the theatre at Sparta. The first phase of the theatre in the Roman period was financed by the local aristocrat C. Iulius Eurykles in the last decades of the 1st century BC. The structure followed the Greek tradition of exploiting the sloping ground for the cavea and was probably constructed over a pre-existing Classical-Hellenistic theatre, which is attested only by indirect archaeological traces and passages in ancient sources.[964] The theatre was moreover equipped with a movable scene with tracks that allowed it to be rolled in and out of a building adjoined to the west wing of the cavea. This solution is quite exceptional for Greece and it is known to have been adopted elsewhere only in the 4th century BC theatres of Megalopolis and (perhaps) Phlius in the Peloponnese.[965] The architectural choices that were made in the construction show that the intention of the aristocratic euergetes to donate a theatre to Sparta during the Augustan period was realized in line with the Greek tradition. A different result was instead achieved during the second phase of the theatre, which is dated to the reign of Vespasian and was financed by the Emperor himself. Among numerous modifications, the major change regarded the movable scene building that was substituted by a stable

---

[956] Moretti 2014a, 215.
[957] Aneziri 2014, 426.
[958] Di Napoli 2005, 510. Pantomime was included in the late 2nd century AD, with mime in the 3rd century AD and only in contests where an amount of money was awarded to the winner, see Aneziri 2014, 425.
[959] The rhapsody, appearing regularly in the victors' list of the festivals in Boeotia in the 2nd and 1st century BC, is attested again in the second half of the 2nd century AD, see Aneziri 2014, 427.
[960] Bressan and Bonini 2010, 14-5. For a detailed analysis of the various modifications of the theatre, see Bressan 2009, 158-79.
[961] Bressan and Bonini 2010, 15.
[962] Bressan and Bonini 2010, 15 and 16, Figure 2
[963] Bressan 2009, 214-18.
[964] See at this respect Bressan 2009, 234.
[965] Bressan and Bonini 2010, 19. For a hypothetical reconstruction of the theatre at Megalopolis, see Bressan 2009, 191.

one joined to the cavea. The theatre assumed therefore some typical Roman elements though preserving characteristics usually found in Greek theatres, such as the steep cavea built on sloping ground and that was visible from the outside.[966]

Besides modifications to existing theatres or new constructions, in the early Empire numerous *odeia* were built within or nearby agorai, in such number that these buildings become a constant presence in Greek townscapes.[967] This situation mirrors a similar tendency in Roman Italy, where the construction of new theatres became a popular sign of euergetism during the early Empire.[968] The increase in the number of new theatres has been related to the implications of the *Lex Julia Theatralis*, that was promulgated under Augustus (in 19 or 22 BC) and that set a firmer system than that already existing for the *discrimina ordinum*, by assigning specific sectors and seats in the theatre to the different social groups in the city.[969] In this way Augustus wanted to organize and display the social hierarchy of the city in the place in which it was most visible. In Greece the privilege of *prohedria*, front seat, was granted to distinguished citizens, most notably priests, and in numerous theatres stone thrones around the orchestra testify to this practise.

The role that the theatre played in Greek urban life up to Rome decreases in Late Antiquity. Starting from the 4th century AD, theatres receive increasingly less attention and by the end of the century they lay abandoned or used for very different purposes than what they originally were intended for. Disastrous events such as the strong earthquakes that devastated Greece during the 4th century AD and barbaric raids can be held only partially responsible for the abandonment of theatres. More importantly, the cultural change in the society was the main factor that led to theatres not being recognized anymore as the place where the city's cultural values were expressed. The demise of theatres has been in fact related to the Christianization of the Empire which was ratified officially in the early 4th century AD with Constantine's Edict.

Theatres were part of the buildings that, having lost their original functions or having become too large for the now smaller community, were either used as a quarry for building materials or repurposed. Their structures were used to sustain other buildings that were constructed against them, such as at Tegea and Messene,[970] or occupied by a necropolis as attested for the theatre of Megalopolis. This theatre, one of the largest in Greece, was occupied in Byzantine times by a necropolis and part of its marble was destroyed in a lime kiln of the Ottoman period. The theatre of the Pythion in Gortyna is an example of a public building that was reused in the 3rd (or beginning 4th) AD as a stable and a workshop for the processing of marble before being abandoned after an earthquake in the 4th century AD. The relatively early falling into disuse of the theatre is likely to correlate with the imperial decrees that prohibited sacrifices and pagan cults, and closed all the pagan buildings. The theatre was in fact connected with the sanctuary of Apollo and therefore possibly abandoned at the same time as the sanctuary in relation with these imperial decisions, although recent studies have highlighted the presence of alluvial deposit in the theatre which could offer an alternative, more practical, explanation for its early change in use.[971]

---

[966] Bressan and Bonini 2010, 19-20, Figs. 8a and 8b.
[967] Dickenson (2012, 239) sustains that 'an odeion in the civic centre seems to have become an amenity which no Greek polis should be without'.
[968] Lomas and Cornell 2003, 36.
[969] This subject that here is only touched over for the limited space available has been extensively treated in Rawson 1987.
[970] Bressan 2009, 345.
[971] Bonetto *et al.* 2010.

5.3.4 Houses

Domestic architecture informs us about the socio-political situation, the economy and the technological level of a society. Social complexity, privacy, gender division, wealth, production and storage capacity are reflected in architectural aspects such as room organization and access, materials and construction techniques, and in the type of furniture and artefacts that are used within them. Inferring this type of information from the study of the archaeologically known examples of Greek houses is however for many aspects problematic and there are a number of considerations that must be taken into account before approaching their study.[972]

A relatively small number of houses have been completely excavated and the number decreases if we consider only the contexts in which finds belonging to the houses were recorded and collected allowing for contextual analysis.[973] Some periods have been investigated more thoroughly than others; specifically, the number of Classical and Hellenistic housing quarters for which this kind of data is available is higher than e.g. the Archaic ones. For the latter we lack extensive excavations that would allow us to compose a clearer picture of the forms of social differentiation in domestic context.[974]

Moreover, sites in which housing quarters have been investigated through careful excavation and that allow a diachronic analysis of the development of housing architecture and way of living through centuries are exceptional. The creation of categorizations and typologies for Greek houses have been the main focus of traditional studies and only recently has this approach been questioned. Differences in fact exist both at a regional level and within each site,[975] although, as Jameson pointed out, the technological level and the environmental context create constraints on the types of house that can be built on a site.[976]

As already noted for the ancient Greek city in general, literary sources and painted pottery, mostly Athenian, have been widely used to integrate the missing information for other sites.[977] In literary sources, however, domestic dwellings and the activities that took place inside the privacy of the house are often overlooked or mentioned only incidentally, and when this is the case they often carry an ideological bias. A passage in Lysias (1.9) in which Euphiletos describes his house and how the upper and lower space was used to respond to the necessity of his wife and his new born child, has been traditionally taken as representative of the strict division between male and female quarters in a typical Greek house. The archaeological record, and even other textual sources, provide however a more complex picture, which does not show female seclusion but rather a control on the interaction between female members of the household and male visitors.[978] Moreover, Euphiletos' description reflects an ideal situation and it is functional to Lysias' intention to present him as a good and honest citizen to the law court that has to judge him for murder.[979] Similarly, everyday scenes that are depicted on pottery are the result of a process of selection and interpretation of motives, many taken from mythology, that were familiar to the viewers and could be difficult to be understood correctly by the modern scholar.[980]

---

[972] See in this respect Lang 2005, 12-3; Westgate 2015, 47-95, esp. 50-1.
[973] Examples in which this has been done include Crete (Glowacki and Vogeikoff-Brogan 2011); Halos, Thessaly (Haagsma 2010); Leukas, Acarnania (Fiedler 2005); Olynthos, Chalkidiki (Cahill 2002); Lydian Archaic and Classical houses at Sardis (Cahill 2005); Halieis, Argolis (Ault 1994; Ault 2005); Hellenistic houses at Morgantina (Tzakirgis forthcoming).
[974] Bintliff 2012, 262.
[975] See Haagsma 2010, chapter 1, *passim*.
[976] Jameson 1990, 109.
[977] See in this respect Morgan 2010, 6-12.
[978] Nevett 1994; Nevett 1995a; Bintliff 2010, 24-25. Differences in social statues likely affected social behaviour and women's movements, with less restrictions for lower classes for practical reasons (Bintliff 2012, 300-1).
[979] Morgan 1982; Morgan 2010, 6.
[980] Nevett 1999a, 12.

The ancient source that has been most widely used for gaining information about the architecture and organization of space of Greek houses is chapter 7 of Vitruvius' *De Architectura*. Last century's excavators took many terms and definitions from Vitruvius to label the archaeological remains that they were unearthing, such as the term *prostas* to name the vestibule before the *oikos* that was found in the houses at Priene, and the term *pastas* to call the sheltered portico found in most of the houses at Olynthos. As rightly pointed out by Tzakirgis, however, these terms have come to identify two different elements of the Greek house, even though Vitruvius does not specify any architectural difference and even uses them as synonyms.[981]

Rooms within the Greek house have been labelled not only with Vitruvius' definitions, but also with modern terms such as 'kitchen' or 'sleeping room', thus constraining the use of space to a specific activity. Based on artefact analysis, scholars have come to the conclusion that rooms in the Greek house were instead multifunctional and different activities could take place in the same space according to the time of the day and the season.[982] The *andron*, for example, is traditionally seen as the room of the house where male guests gathered for the symposium. However, a practical and efficient management of space makes it unlikely that this room was used only for this purpose and only by men. Scholars have suggested that it was used during the day for other types of activities that were carried out by women and children,[983] and also on special occasions such as for hosting overnight guests, or for laying out the body of a deceased family member for the *prosthesis*.[984]

A passage from Aeschines' *Timarchus* (123-4) shows the impact of human action on the definition of space: 'For it is neither the dwelling places nor the houses, which give their names to those living in them, but it is the inhabitants who give to the places the names of their own practices.'[985] That the main agents in defining the use of space within a house are the inhabitants is true both for ancient and modern times. A study conducted on the habitation history of a family from Rotterdam in the 1940s recorded nineteen major changes in the house arrangement over a period of twenty six years. This study showed, moreover, a variable degree of specialization of the rooms whose range of functions changed over time. The living room, for example, was used as a bedroom during the war and for a number of other activities, such as bathing children, which would not belong to its expected original use.[986]

These observations show how difficult it is to draw conclusions on the ancient use of space and living habits from the archaeological record. Domestic dwellings of the lower social classes are less represented in the excavated samples and other practices might have left only faint traces that are difficult to retrieve archaeologically. Separation between areas of different use might have been created by using perishable material such as curtains or plants, creating more private spaces than can be identified by the remains left.[987] Cult practices are often attested by the presence of altars or votive offerings, but, as

---

[981] Tzakirgis 1989. Vitr. *De Archit*. 6.7.1: 'This peristyle has colonnades on three sides, and on the side facing the south it has two antae, a considerable distance apart, carrying an architrave, with a recess for a distance one third less than the space between the antae. This space is called by some writers 'prostas' by others 'pastas'".
[982] Nevett 1999a, 71; Trümper 2011. In Olynthos, which was destroyed by Philip in late summer, the archaeological record reflects the distribution of activities in that period of the year (Cahill 2002, 160; see Cahill 2002, 48-61 for the circumstances of the abandonment, looting and subsequent re-occupation of some areas of the site).
[983] Nevett 1999a, 71.
[984] Antonaccio 2000, 527.
[985] See in this respect Morgan (2007, 117-8), who proposes a relational table explaining the words that are found in ancient texts and their contexts of use.
[986] Priemus 1980, 3-6, cited by Haagsma 2010, 14-5.
[987] Kassel and Austin 1984, n. 266, 116.

Morgan pointed out, the act itself, such as burning incense, dancing and singing, was more important than the location where it took place.[988]

It is with these observations in mind that we approach the discussion of the ancient Greek house in the following overview.

Archaic period

The Archaic period marks a series of changes in the Greek political and social sphere that are reflected in modifications in domestic architecture. Notwithstanding regional differences, a change in the organization of space within houses is visible in passing from the Early Iron Age to the Archaic period. Early Iron Age houses were generally linear with one or two rooms, while in Archaic times houses with a radial structure, where more rooms were added and generally did not communicate one with the other, are increasingly attested (for a sample of Archaic house' plans see Figure 5.21, left).[989] A transitional space was moreover included to provide access to the rooms. This space, namely a hall or a courtyard, will remain the characteristic element of Greek houses for centuries. This addition implies also a more pronounced separation between the members of the household and outsiders, as the activities that were previously carried out outside were now performed in the seclusion of the courtyard. These changes reflect a change in Greek society that valued a more marked sense of privacy and increased the separation between the private and public sphere.[990]

The addition of rooms in Archaic times is mirrored by a general increase in size in respect to the houses of previous centuries. This change was assisted by technological developments that allowed new construction techniques to be applied, such as the introduction of stone foundations and clay tiles.[991] Moreover, the Iron Age wattle and daub technique, in which wands were woven around wooden stakes and then plastered over,[992] was progressively abandoned in favour of mud brick. The implementation of these new techniques is visible, among others, at the multi-period site at Karabournaki where the excavated Archaic houses were constructed with stone foundations and walls of sun dried mud bricks.[993]

The new masonry techniques that were introduced in this period allowed the construction of thicker walls that could sustain an upper floor.[994] Evidence for the existence of an upper floor has been found for example in House A at Argilos. In the first occupation phase (mid-6th century BC), a house with a single room was constructed, which was then destroyed and rebuilt according to a different arrangement of space during the late 6th – early 5th century BC. Two storage rooms facing onto a closed courtyard were created, and an upper floor was constructed where the inhabitants lived. On the western side of the house, two other rooms were added (one has been interpreted as a blacksmith's workshop, the other as a storage place) as annexes to the house.[995]

An insight into the domestic economy of the Archaic period has been provided by the recent excavation of an Archaic house at Hephaisteia in Lemnos (Figure 5.21, right). The careful excavation and the

---

[988] Morgan 2007, 113-129, citing for example Euripides' Alcestis where the choir searches for the signs of the ongoing rituals such as the lock of hair hung at the door and the grieving songs (p. 124).
[989] Lang 2005, 26. The linear arrangement is still found in later periods but it is usually related to sacred architecture. Examples of linear houses include those found in Dorian Crete (see below), a 5th century house at the North foot of the Areopagos in Athens and the 4th century BC house at Siphai (Nevett 1999a, 86-8).
[990] See Lang 2005, 29.
[991] See these elements discussed in Lang 2005, 27-8.
[992] See Bowyer 1973, 49.
[993] Tsiafakis 2010, 382.
[994] Lang 2005, 28.
[995] See http://www.argilos.net/fouille-en/ (last accessed Sept. 2016).

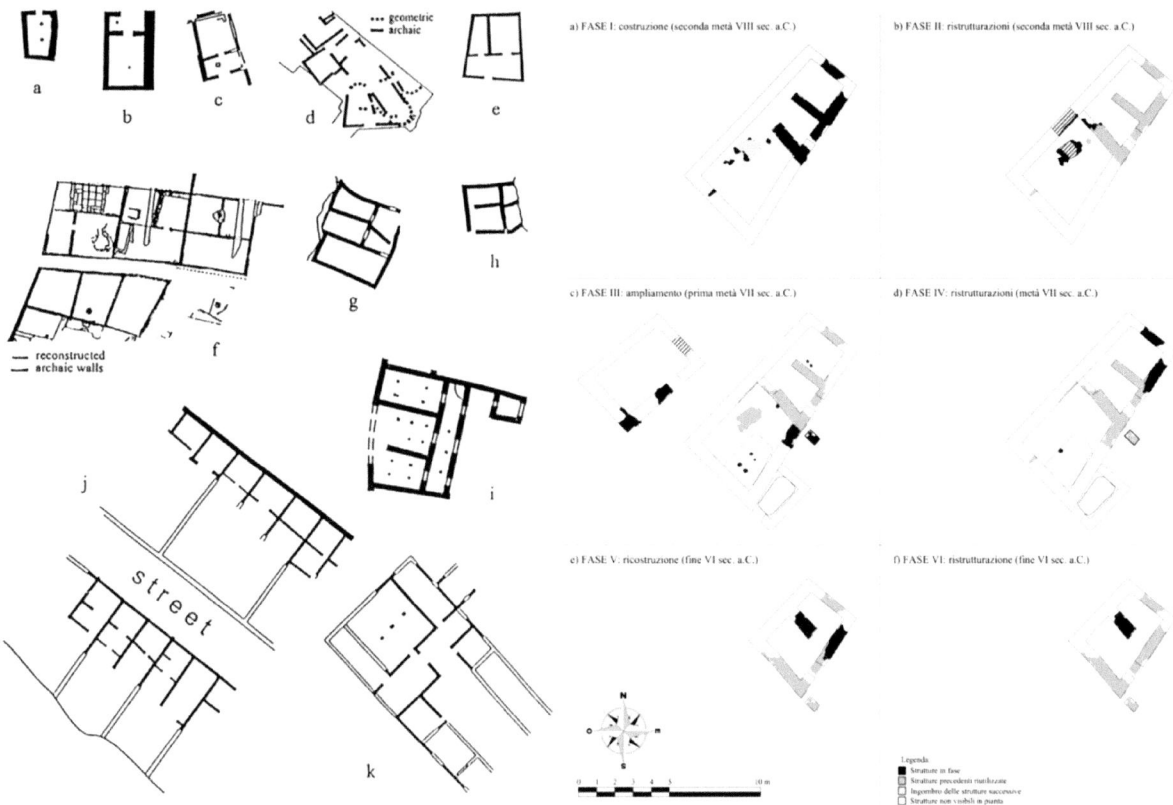

Figure 5.21 Left: Examples of Archaic house plans (a-b) Emporios, Chios; c) Thorikos, Attica; d) Eretria, Euboea; e) Aigina; f) Limenas, Thasos; g) Dreros, Crete; h) Koukounaries, Paros; i) Onythe, Crete; j) Vroulia, Rhodes; k) Kopanaki, Messenia, from Lang 2005, 16. Right: Phases of the Archaic house in Lemnos (Caruso 2011, 190).

contextual study of the material culture allowed the excavators to draw some conclusions on the building techniques, organization of space and domestic economy of the site during the Archaic period. The house, built of dry stone walls, had an irregular and elongated shape and was articulated in three rooms. The central entrance-room led on one side to a space that has been interpreted as a kitchen-bedroom (probably with a mezzanine that served as sleeping area),[996] and on the other side to a storage space.[997] The floor was made of beaten earth. Several pits were excavated outside the house to serve as storage places for the household.[998] In some of them, fragments of *pithoi* have been found. Although archaeometric analysis has not yet been conducted on the *pithoi*, their large dimensions suggest that they were possibly water containers.[999] During the 7th century BC, the house was provided with an external storage room, and with a semi-underground annexe to the main building that was destined for the production of wine. This structure was built on the southern side of the house, so that it was protected from the northern winds. A pit was excavated which could have hosted a *pithos* for the fermentation of wine.[1000] Burnt traces led to the conclusion that a hearth was kept to maintain a constant temperature during the period of wine making in September-October.[1001]

---

[996] Caruso 2011, 191.
[997] For a detailed overview of the habitation phases of the house, see Camporeale *et al.* 2010.
[998] Camporeale *et al.* 2010, 114.
[999] Caruso 2011, 115.
[1000] Camporeale *et al.* 2010, 116-7.
[1001] Caruso 2011, 132-3.

Classical period

Although the specificity of each site and the needs of each owner certainly created variations in the appearance and size of houses, there are some recurrent features that characterize Classical Greek houses, of which Olynthos provides the largest dataset with more than 100 excavated houses (Figure 5.22). Private dwellings were inward looking and specific architectural choices were made to preserve the privacy of the household. As the excavated examples from Ammotopos show, windows to the streets were present but were small and preferably located higher than eye level to prevent passers-by to be able to look inside.[1002] At Lato, where some of the houses are conserved up to two meters high, the walls had no window, suggesting that, if they were present, they must have been located higher than the preserved extent.[1003]

The courtyard that started to appear in Archaic times became a constant element in Greek domestic architecture. This area had multiple functions, acting as a transitional space that connected the outside world and the inside of the house and as a multifunctional place were household activities took place.[1004] Not surprisingly, as Ault noted for Halieis, the court is usually the largest unit of the house, taking up to twenty-five percent or more of the total house size.[1005] In the majority of the excavated examples of Greek houses, the court was centrally located providing access and commanding the view to the rest of the rooms.[1006] The court was often connected to a porch sustained by a row of columns that provided a sheltered area where activities such as cooking and weaving took place. This shaded space adjacent to the courtyard, traditionally called *pastas* (such as at Olynthos) or *prostas* (such as at Priene) based on the configuration of the rooms, was a convenient location to dig cisterns. The presence of altars in the archaeological record from Olynthos suggests that it was also used for cult practices. Storage vessels and other types of pottery such as loom weights and tableware that were found in the Olynthian *pastas* confirm that this area was used also as a storage place.[1007]

The courtyard and its role to organize the pattern of movement within the house have been used by scholars to suggest recurrent types that are identifiable in the archaeological record. Nevett's 'single entrance, courtyard' model encompasses the majority of the excavated examples of houses of this period,[1008] while a smaller sample is represented by the houses defined as the 'Herdraum type' by Hoepfner and Schwandner on the basis of the excavated examples at Kassope in Epiros.[1009] In this type, the court was rather small in comparison with the above mentioned examples and was not crucial for movement around the house. The main area was instead an inner room, called *oikos* by the excavators, which had a hearth and was probably the place where household activities were concentrated. A similar organization of space is visible in the house excavated in the same region at Ammotopos and conserved to an exceptional extent by its stone walls.[1010]

Another type of house arrangement, which is attested especially from the 4th century onwards, is represented by the 'double courtyard house'. The two courtyards identify two different areas of the house, one related to domestic activities and accessible only to the members of the household, the

---

[1002] For Ammotopos/Orraon, see e.g. S. Dakaris 1986.
[1003] Picard and Ducrey 1996, 751.
[1004] For Athens, see e.g. Morgan 2007, 114; for Halieis, see Ault 1994, 60ff (esp. 61 for an overview of rooms's and courts' sizes at Halieis). Westgate (2007) discusses the pratical and ideological factors that are likely to have encouraged the adoption of the courtyard.
[1005] Ault 1994, 60.
[1006] Exceptions are attested, such as some of the houses at the Cretan sites, which show a linear arrangement (see below).
[1007] Nevett 1999a, 69.
[1008] Nevett 1995b, 94.
[1009] Hoepfner and Schwandner 1994, 146-50.
[1010] Dakaris 1986.

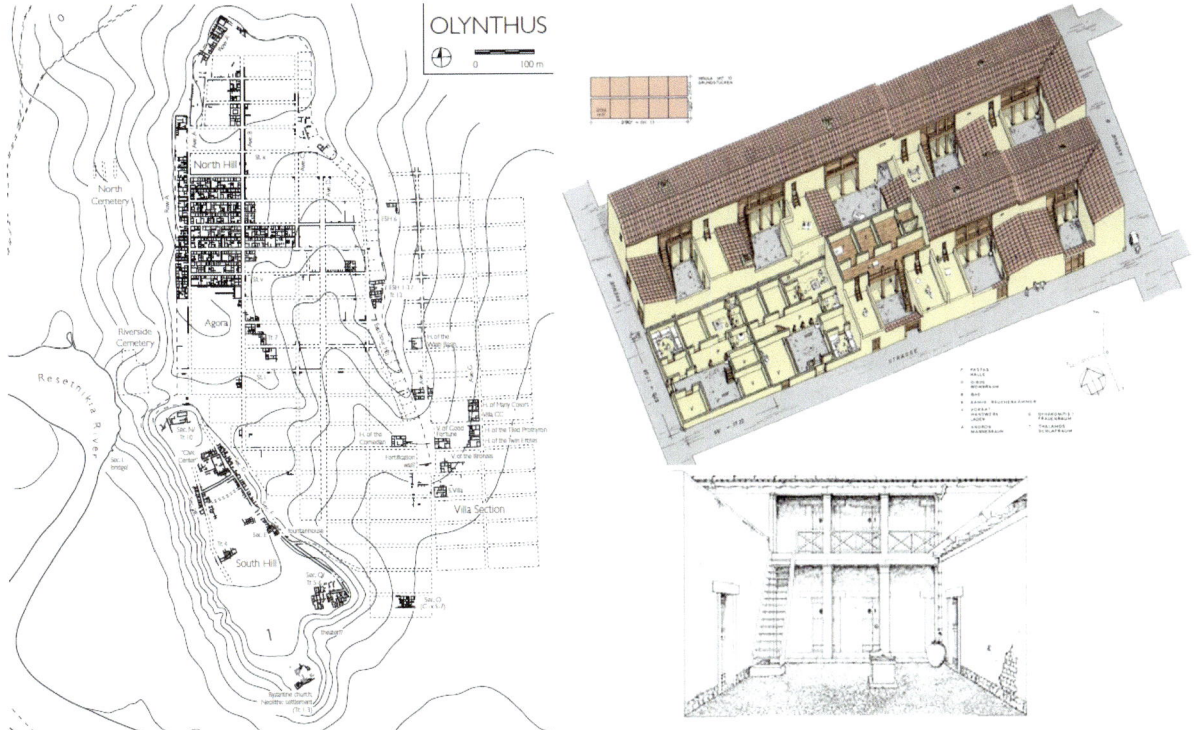

Figure 5.22 Olynthos. Left: Plan of the town (Cahill 2002, 26); Right, top: reconstruction drawing of a domestic insula (Carroll-Spillecke 1989, Figure 3, p. 18); Rigth, bottom: reconstruction drawing of a house's courtyard and pastas (in Hoepfner 2009, 176).

other suggesting a more public connotation. The courtyard of the public area was in fact more richly decorated with pebbled or tessellated mosaics and led to the representational rooms of the house, such as the *andron*. Such organization of space is more frequent than the Herdraum type and, as one would expect, usually corresponds to an increased size of the house plot. It is also seen in relation to a greater display of wealth,[1011] which will become more marked in the Hellenistic period. This arrangement is visible for example in a 4th century house excavated at Maroneia in Thrace and in a sample of houses at Eretria, such as the large house of the mosaics built in the early 4th century.[1012]

More studies at a regional level are needed to contextualize houses, living habits and social organization on the local level. Analysis of Cretan houses of the Classical and Hellenistic periods for example have shown a very different organization of space in respect to the above mentioned types. The houses that have been excavated at Lato, dated from the 4th to the 2nd century BC, present a linear structure similar to the characteristics of some of the houses of the Archaic period and lack a closed courtyard.[1013] They are quite small, their ground floor area being between 40 and 150 m2, and the number of rooms range between two and a maximum of six.[1014] House Δ (Figure 5.23), built against the slope, is representative of the spatial organization of houses at Lato. The dwelling was divided into a large room, which was entered directly from the house and was provided with a central hearth, and a smaller room at the back. A cistern was placed near the entrance on its southern short side, indicating the existence of a semi-private open space in front of the house. The positioning of the door of the back room in line with the entrance suggests a lower concern for privacy than what is visible in courtyard houses. This arrangement

---

[1011] Nevett 1999b, 105.
[1012] See Nevett 1999b, 107-114 for a discussion of these houses.
[1013] Westgate 2007. Courtyard houses have been excavated at other sites in Crete, such as at Phaistos, therefore this type is not completely absent from the island (Westgate 2007, 441).
[1014] Westgate 2007, 427.

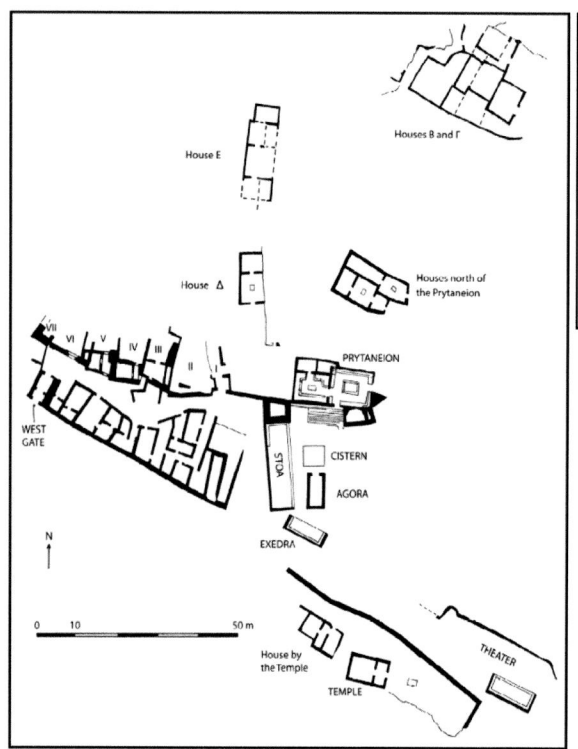
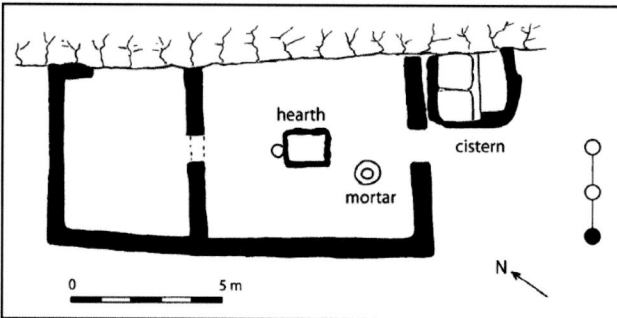

Figure 5.23 Left: Plan of the excavated houses around the agora in Lato; right: Detailed plan of House Δ (Westgate 2007, 429-30).

was not merely resulting from the constraints imposed by the terrain morphology, but represents the expression of a communal social system, in which food and education were shared by male citizens in centralized public buildings. The Archaic or Iron Age tradition fossilized in conservative Dorian Crete, which differentiated some Cretan settlements from other regions of Greece and prevented the development of autonomous and self-sufficient **households represented by the courtyard house.**[1015]

The size and the small number of rooms of the houses at Lato were not exceptional. Some of the houses at the north foot of the Areopagus measured about 50 and 70 m², and at Ano Siphai there are remains of houses that were composed of a courtyard and two rooms.[1016] Variations in size were common within the same town, even when the urban layout was organized in a roughly regular grid. In Halieis, for example, House 7 occupied about 250 m² (to which number an upper floor should probably be added, see Figure 5.24), while House A occupied 120 m² (to which a *pyrgos* should probably be added).[1017] In Olynthos the house that Walter Graham chose as typical (A vii 4) measured about 17 x 17 m, resulting in an average ground floor living space of about 230 m²,[1018] but in the eastern part of the city, the Villa section, houses were larger and more elaborate. Roughly of the same size as the Olynthian dwellings was House I at the site of Ammotopos in Epiros, a settlement that was laid out in a regular grid and inhabited probably from the late 4th to early 3rd century. Houses much larger than these are also attested. In Eretria, for example, the House of the Mosaics extended for about 625 m² and House II in the Western Quarter (Figure 5.25) occupied an area of 1,200 m². The size of the house is given by the organization of the living units around two courtyards: 'n' was a peristyle court giving access to the representational and public rooms (e.g. the *andron* 'f'), while 'l' was the private courtyard that was used exclusively by the members

---

[1015] See it this respect Westgate 2007, 448-53; Bintliff 2010, 22; Bintliff 2012, 303; Bintliff 2014.
[1016] Discussed by Nevett 1999a, 87-8.
[1017] For the houses at Halieis see Ault 2005.
[1018] Nevett 1999a, 76; Cahill 2002 82. See Cahill 200282-4 for a critical discussion on the abstract concept of the 'typical' Olynthian house.

5. The Graeco-Roman town as a physical entity

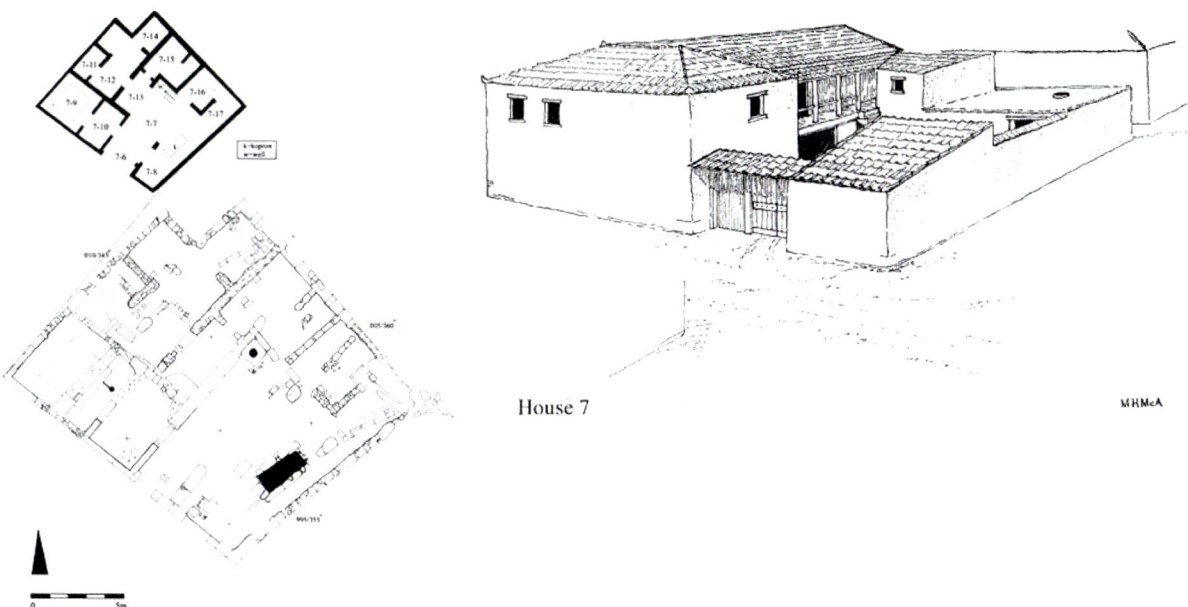

Figure 5.24 Plan (left) and reconstruction (right) of House 7 at Halieis. The entrance is characterized by a roofed vestibule (prothyron) (Ault 2005, Figure 7 and 9).

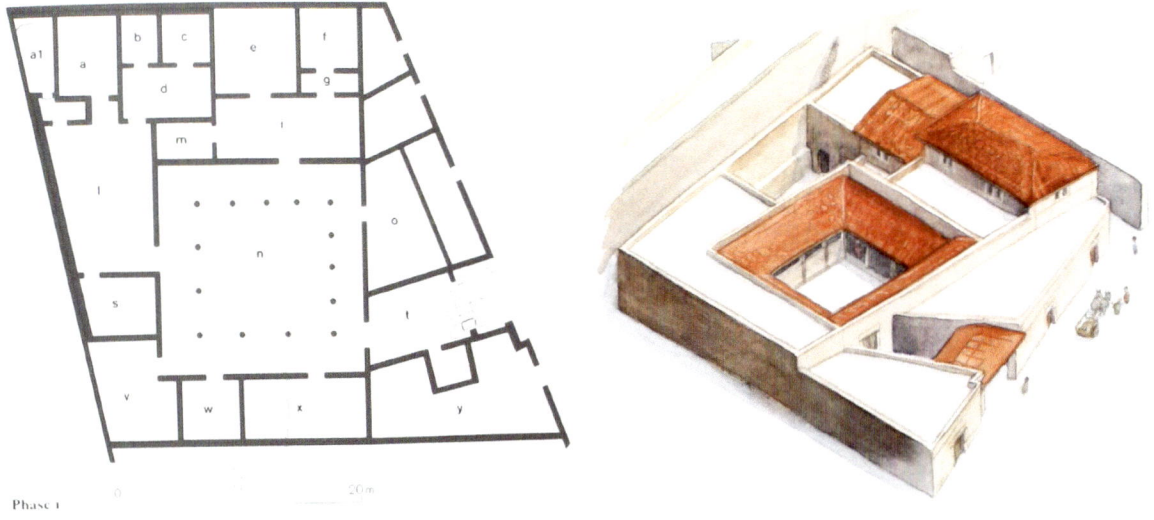

Figure 5.25 Plan and reconstruction of House II at Eretria (Ducrey 2004, 161 and 163).

of the household.[1019] Such organization reflects the social change towards the use of the house as a more representational space which will become more marked in the Hellenistic period.[1020]

The plan that was laid out at the construction phase could be later modified following the needs of the owners. The Olynthian archaeological record shows that adjacent houses could be merged into one when more space was needed (such as in the cases of houses A vii 3 and 5, and houses A v 6 and 8), and parts of the house were abandoned or destined to animals' shelter when the number of occupants decreased.[1021] Similarly to Olynthos' North Hill, redevelopments within the original house blocks are

---

[1019] Reber 2007.
[1020] Bintliff 2010, 28-9.
[1021] Nevett 1999a, 74.

visible also at the new city that was founded at Plataiai after the battle of Chaironeia. The grid was planned in 149 rectangular *insulae* measuring 40-43 m wide and 97-99 m long, with exceptions on the acropolis and on the north side of the space dedicated to Dionysos in front of the theatre.[1022] As Konecny reports, originally the *insulae* were divided in 10 plots of similar size, but their development differed: in some cases each of these plots was occupied by houses, others were merged to create villas, while in other locations they were left unbuilt.

The discovery of staircase bases in some of the archaeologically known houses has led scholars to conclude that in many cases they were provided with a second floor. At Olynthos, flights of stairs measured between 0.80-1.10m in width and 2.50-3.50m in length,[1023] and in Halieis, stair bases of similar size as the Olynthian ones were identified in most of the excavated houses and were preferably located on the north side of the court or in the *pastas*.[1024] The houses at Ammotopos, preserved to an exceptional extent, allowed the excavators to establish the presence of an upper storey both from the remains of the stone staircase and from the holes in the stone walls that were made for the wooden beams sustaining the floor. In other contexts, such as at late Classical - early Hellenistic Halos, no conclusive evidence for the presence of an upper floor was found.[1025] Whether the upper floor used to cover the entire area of the first floor or was limited only to the back of the house cannot however be established with certainty.[1026] According to Nevett, the great amount of tiles recovered from Olynthos and Thasos points towards the presence of pitched roofs.[1027] However, as Ault pointed out, flat roofs could be used along with tiled roofs to add more space for household activities.[1028]

As testified by the presence of wooden beams trespassing between each individual property in Olynthos, an agreement must have been made among the owners of a row of houses about the height of the common roof, although differences in the building techniques show that the houses were not built by the same team of men.[1029] An inscription from Korkyra Melaina, on the island Lumbarda off the coast of Croatia, gives some insight into the system of allotting the land and was used by Cahill to explain the evidence from Olynthos. According to the regulations established by the document, the land was distributed by randomly selecting the names of the citizens and then allowing them to choose their plot.[1030] In this way related citizens sharing common ties such as origin or a similar profession would choose to live close to each other, thus explaining the distribution of different kinds of houses across the site.[1031] Sales inscriptions from Olynthos reporting the prices of properties show that houses nearby the agora were the most expensive (and were sold more frequently), indicating that proximity to the market was valued more than the larger and more decorated houses in the Villa section.[1032]

[1022] Konecny *et al.* 2013, 188.
[1023] Hoepfner and Schwandner 1994, 107.
[1024] Ault 2005, 73.
[1025] Haagsma 2010, 38-9.
[1026] For a discussion on the presence of a second storey in the Olynthian houses, see Nevett 1999a, 75. Excavations at the Hellenistic site of Petres of Florina shed clearer light on the presence of the upper storey, which was made of lighter material for static reasons (Adam-Veleni 2000, 59, see below).
[1027] Nevett 1999a, 56 and 92 citing Grandjean 1988, 387 for Thasos.
[1028] Ault 2005, 73. The restoration of the slope of the roof is problematic. Evidence for temple roofs is available in the cuttings that were realized in the upper sections of stone walls, but as Kraynak pointed out, evidence for buildings with a mudbrick upper structure is scanty. In some cases, vernacular architecture has been used to reconstruct the appearance of house roofs, see Haagsma 2010 for Halos and Robinson for Olynthos (Olynthus VIII, 236). The latter established a slope of approximately 18°. Kraynak suggested a slope of 11°-12° for the Xenon at Nemea, based on the ridge cover tiles (Kraynak 1992, 125).
[1029] Cahill 2002, 203.
[1030] Cahill 2002, 221.
[1031] Cahill 2002, 221.
[1032] Cahill 2002, 278-81.

The access from the street to the house was always limited and controlled. Often, entrances were angled or screened in order to prevent a direct view onto the inner part of the house.[1033] In most cases one entrance was present, although there are examples where possibly two adjacent entrances existed, one for wheeled vehicles and the other one for pedestrians.[1034] The entrance from the street to the court was often characterized by a roofed vestibule entrance (*prothyron*) as recognized in numerous sites such Olynthos, Halieis,[1035] and Halos.[1036] At Athens, the houses on the north slope of the Aeropagus were entered directly from the street (in some of them evidence of post holes suggests that there was a simple shed-roofed portico), while in other areas of the city a vestibule was present (e.g. in House C and D of the industrial district).[1037] Archaeological evidence and depictions on pottery vases show that doors were double-winged. Herms, altars and plants could be placed at the entrance door of the house to ensure protection to the household.[1038]

The construction techniques, internal decorations and furniture of the house vary, depending on several factors, such as the financial possibilities of the owners, the function of each room and the available materials. The outside walls usually had a stone socle as a basis, while the elevation was made of mudbricks and then plastered over. At Olynthos, courts and *pastas* were decorated with coloured plastered walls, while the rest of the house was left with no decoration apart from the *andron*, a room where guests were hosted and the symposium took place. Floor were generally of beaten earth or clay,[1039] with some exceptions for the paving of the courtyard, the *andron* and the kitchen.[1040]

Houses were not only the places for residence, but the members of the household could be involved to a varying degree in industrial and commercial activities, or the owner could rent out parts of the block. Shops and workshops were usually installed in convenient locations for the business, namely within highly populated areas, close or facing into agorai and busy roads, often at crossroads. Some Classical houses have in fact returned clear evidence of the existence of workshops and shops within or adjacent to the living areas. Some houses close to the Athenian Agora offer an insight into the wide range of activities that were carried out in houses.[1041] A large number of iron nails and bone eyelets were found spread on the floor of the so called House of Simon, located at the southern edge of the Athenian agora and partially excavated in the 1950s. These finds, which were present both on the courtyard's and on the excavated rooms' floors, have been interpreted as the working materials of a cobbler.[1042] In the nearby House of Mikion and Menon, the floor was covered by marble chips and some tools were found suggesting that the house was also used as a sculptor's workshop.[1043]

Other sites have returned evidence for industrial activities within residential areas with varying degrees of separation between working and living spaces, such as a potter's kiln within a house at Kassope and olive presses in a house at Rachi.[1044] A wide variety of small scale industrial activities have been found in the Olynthian houses, besides the processing of agricultural produce, such as sculpting,

---

[1033] Nevett 1995b, 94-5.
[1034] Ault 2005, 60.
[1035] Ault 2005, 59 (which provides also a table with the measurements of *prothyra* found in Halieis).
[1036] Haagsma 2010, 34-5.
[1037] Tsakirgis 2005, 69.
[1038] Morgan 2007, 114.
[1039] At Lato, for example, the floor of one excavated house was made of beaten earth, clay and shell fragments (Hadjimichali 1971, 215).
[1040] An overview of building materials used in 5th and 4th century houses is given in Jamenson 1990, 97.
[1041] These houses are discussed in Tsakirgis 2005.
[1042] Tsakirgis 2005, 71-4.
[1043] Tsakirgis 2005, 72-5.
[1044] Tsakirgis 2005, 78.

stone cutting, manufacturing of textiles, terracotta figurines and stone bullets.[1045] In some cases the difference between a production for necessity within the household and a commercial activity is less pronounced. In individual houses at Olynthos, for example, finds related to domestic activities such as weaving or food processing are present in such a great number as to make the excavators wonder whether they were meant for internal consumption or as a trade good.[1046]

Hellenistic period

The political situation under the Hellenistic rulers brought about changes in the social structure that now promoted the display of individual wealth without the moderation that was praised during the Classical period.[1047] These changes are reflected in the spatial arrangement of the houses, at least of the middle and upper social strata. The former closed familial unit is equipped with spaces for networking, prestige and display, anticipating and doubtless inspiring the developed Roman domus and villa.[1048] Hellenistic houses are generally characterized by an average increase in size but a greater range of sizes, and an elaboration in the number of rooms and decoration in respect to the houses of the Classical period. This holds true especially for the houses of the upper level of society, peaking with the palace complexes at Vergina and Pella, which covered respectively 9,450 m^2 and an astonishing 60,000 m^2.[1049]

Variations within the same city, in fact, were great, as can be seen in Delos, which offers one of the most conspicuous datasets of Hellenistic domestic architecture. In this harbour town, which was transformed into a commercial hub and cosmopolitan society after becoming an Athenian cleruchy in 167 BC, 91 houses have been completely excavated.[1050] Areas of the city show different organizations of space which suggest different degrees of planning of the urban layout. The irregularity of the house plots, street width and the general organization of the Theatre Quarter, for example, suggest a piecemeal development for this area, where houses were built where space was available. The northern sectors of the city, instead, are much more regular, and the buildings follow a north-south orientation.[1051]

The Delian dataset shows great variety in the domestic organization of space, with ground floor areas ranging from 53 to 866 m^2.[1052] Some common features are however always present, such as a courtyard, while others occur frequently such as latrines and cisterns or wells to guarantee the water supply.[1053] Upper storeys are present in the vast majority of the houses and they were not necessarily inhabited by the same family as the ground floor, but could be accessed by independent entrances from the street. The domestic units were interwoven with shops and workshops that were strategically placed along main streets and at corners.

The most numerous houses (43%) have a rectangular plan and range between 65 to 200 m^2, thus smaller than the typical Olynthian house, giving shape to *insulae* occupied by two to six houses.[1054] These

---

[1045] Cahill 2002, 238-58. For a discussion on the domestic evidence of industrial activities in Greece and Anatolia, see Cahill 2005.
[1046] Cahill 2002, 238.
[1047] In the *Oration for the State* (ca. 340 BC), Demosthenes, in order to present the uncorrupted and glorious past of Athens, cited as example the houses of great Athenian leaders such as Themistocles, Cimon, Aristides and Miltiades that were indistinguishable from the others, as a contrast to the luxury residences of the elite of his generation. For the political and economic framework of this period, see Bintliff 2012, 329.
[1048] Bintliff 2010, 26-30.
[1049] Winter 2006, 160; Steward 2014, 211. Other large villas and palace complexes have been found e.g. in Samos and Pergamon (see Winter 2006, 165ff).
[1050] Trümper 2003.
[1051] Bruneau 1968, 667-8.
[1052] Tang 2005, 33. Tang notes that the largest houses (e.g. DelN19 with 866 m2) may have been used for other purposes (e.g. clubhouses) besides being habitation.
[1053] Trümper 2003, 24.
[1054] Trümper 2003, 23.

elongated houses were arranged around a courtyard, flanked by one or two service rooms, which gave access to a large room (*oecus maior*)[1055] that, in turn, led to one or two rooms in the back (*oeci minores*, see Figure 5.26). The other two most recurrent types that Trümper identified in the Delian houses are the 'enlarged normal house' and the 'peristyle house'. In the first group, ranging from 120 to 360 m², decorated rooms were added on one side of the courtyard, likely to accommodate guests.[1056] The other group includes the largest houses, which were usually provided with peristyles surrounded by the most lavishly decorated rooms. The negotiation between architecture and terrain is most visible in the latter group of houses where a large area needed to be laid out on several floors according to the terraced landscape. The area of more than 1,500 m² of the House of the Hermes, for example, was spread on four levels that were built against the hill slope.[1057]

Despite the cosmopolitan character of the city, houses show a consistent pattern in decorative motifs, with a few exceptions which hint to the origin of the owner.[1058] The most popular ornamental repertoire was present in the wealthiest houses and was then imitated by less well-to-do owners with less sophisticated techniques or cheaper materials.[1059] Tessellated mosaics, albeit of lower quality than those from Pergamon and Samos, were particularly appreciated in Delos, as evidenced by the fact that here the highest number of mosaics of any Hellenistic site was found.[1060] Wealth was not necessarily proportional to size, as some of the largest houses have no peristyle,[1061] while smaller houses were richly decorated. Interestingly, no spatial division between wealthy and poor is noticeable in the excavated quarters; the houses are in fact diversified as shown in Figure 5.27. This spatial proximity reflected the business relationship between the poor and lower middle classes that were clients of the rich owners of insulae and domus. Shops and workshops were also mixed with houses and, as already observed for the Classical houses on the Athenian Agora, opened up onto important streets (such as that leading to the theatre) and at crossroads.

As already seen in other sites such as Olynthos and Plataiai, redevelopments of the original house plan have been identified also in several of the excavated houses in Delos. The modifications were usually directed towards a segmentation of the larger rooms into smaller units and towards the creation of shops or workshops. Such interventions are visible for example in Houses IC and ID in the Stadium quarter (Figure 5.28). The previous entrance of House IC was closed and room 'a' was turned into a workshop which opened directly onto the courtyard. In House ID, the large rooms 'j' and 'n' are remodelled into smaller rooms used as storage places.[1062] These changes reflect the needs of the owner for more storage, probably in the context of a growing Delian market as testified also elsewhere such as by the addition of shelves and mezzanines in the shops of the Quartier du Théâtre.[1063]

Among the redevelopments that can be observed in domestic architecture between Classical and Hellenistic times, an increased number of spaces devoted to the processing of agricultural produce is attested in a number of sites, such as the installations of olive presses at Halieis[1064] and Eretria. At the latter site, transformations are visible in particular in the West Quarter which was not redeveloped in Roman times, and thus provides an undisturbed example of Classical-Hellenistic domestic architecture at the site. Some of the living units that composed this quarter, which is close to the western city

---

[1055] These terms were first adopted for the Delian houses by Chamonard 1922–1924.
[1056] Trümper 2003, 23.
[1057] Winter 2006, 172-
[1058] Trümper 2003, 32; see also Zarmakoupi 2013, 9.
[1059] See Westgate 2010.
[1060] Westgate 2010, 511 and 516.
[1061] Trümper 2003, 24.
[1062] Zarmakoupi 2014, 559-63.
[1063] Karvonis and Malmary 2009.
[1064] Ault 1999.

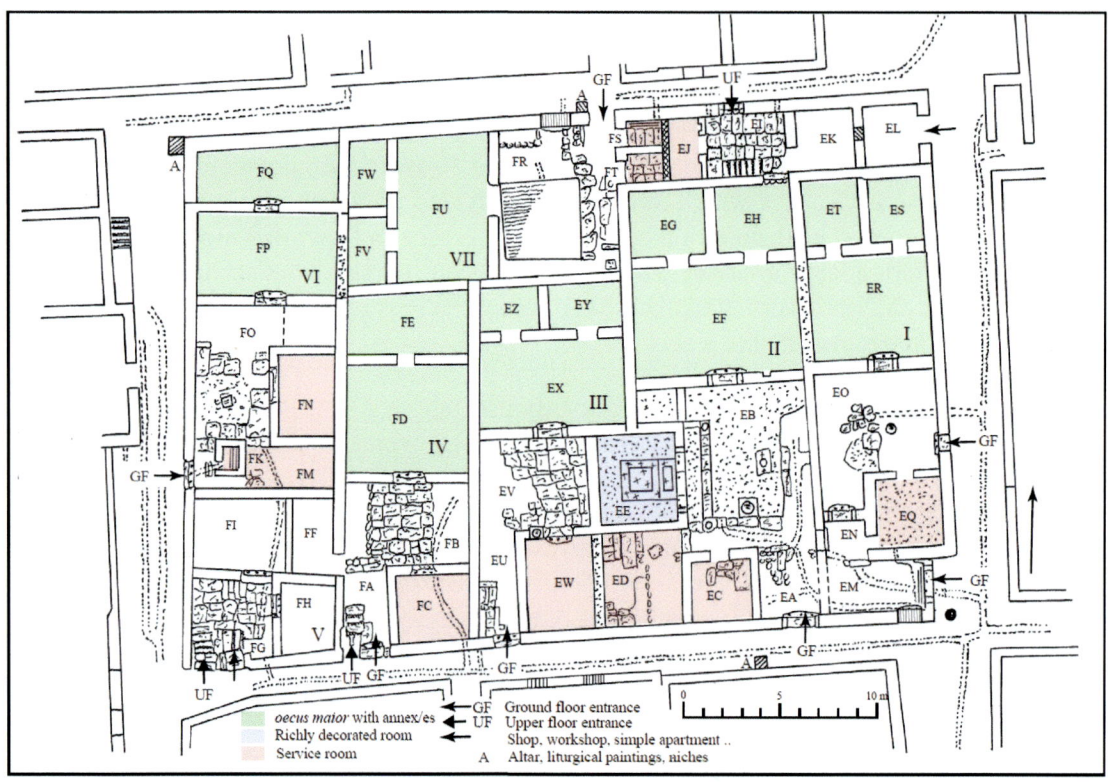

Figure 5.27 Delos: Plan of the excavated quarters near the theatre with the distribution of houses, shops and workshops (Trümper 2003, plate 4).

Figure 5.26 Plan of an insula of 'normal houses' in Delos (Trümper 2003, plate 1).

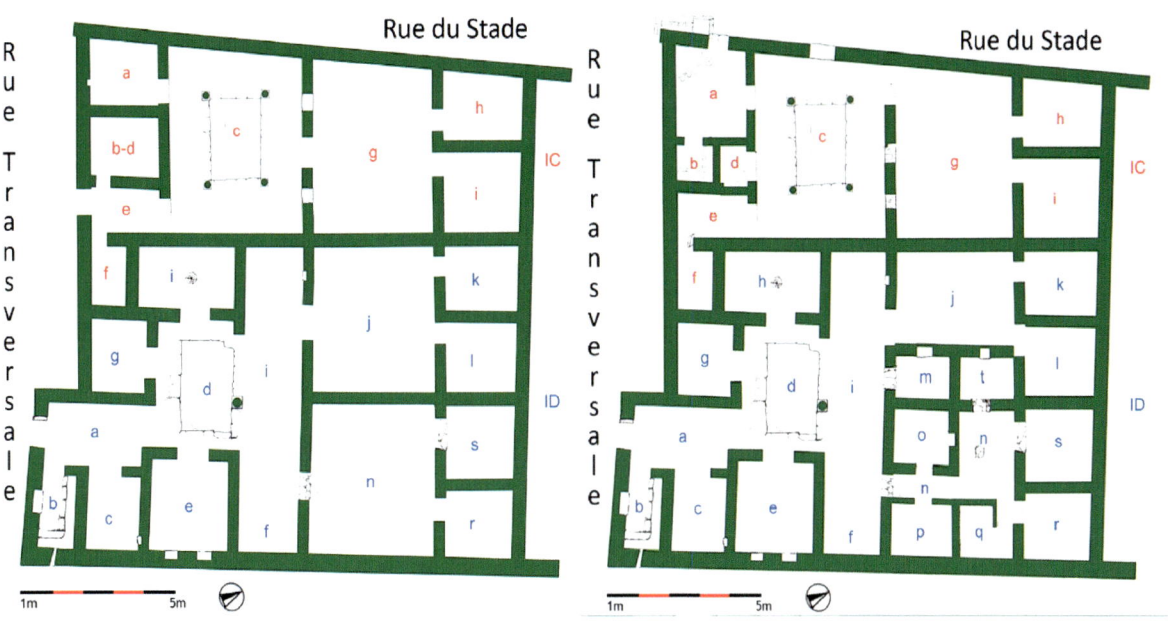

Figure 5.28 Delos: Architectural development of Houses IC and ID (Zarmakoupi 2014, 562).

Figure 5.29 Left: Reconstruction drawing of three houses at Petres with hagiati-like roofed open area (Adam-Veleni 2000, 57); Right: Characteristic hagiati in a house at Livadeia, Boeotia (Sigalos 2004, Figure 97, p. 282).

gate, were turned into industrial complexes, among which grape and olive presses were installed. It is often difficult to find the reason that triggered redevelopments in house design, as this can be related to a variety of factors such as a change in ownership, historical events or transformations in the economic organization of the household. In this case, the decrease of farmsteads in the countryside that has been observed for the Hellenistic and Early Roman periods in several regions of Greece[1065] and the concentration of the landscape use around large villas[1066] can have triggered the need to include production units directly into town houses.

[1065] Alcock 1993a, 48-9. See e.g. the data from the Boeotia project (Bintliff and Snodgrass 1985, 145) and from the survey at the Attic deme Atene (Lohmann 1993, 248).
[1066] Bintliff 2012, 318-9.

Figure 5.30 Examples of masonry techniques for stone socles in Late Classical and Hellenistic domestic architecture: (Right) Eretria (Ducrey 2004, 160) and (left) Knidos (Love 1970, Figure 11).

Other sites where houses of the Hellenistic period have been excavated include Petres of Florina,[1067] Kos,[1068] Leukas,[1069] and Knidos.[1070] At Petres, the excavated houses had a floor area of about 180-200 m² and an upper floor constructed with lighter materials for static reasons. Houses show different room arrangements: besides the classical radial configuration around an open central courtyard, in others the courtyard was on the front side, while in the southern platform two main types were excavated, a short-frontage type and an L-shaped type with a longer front.[1071] The one-and-a-half storey house type was adapted to the steep slopes resulting in houses constructed with one-storey on one side, facing the street, and two-storey on the other. In these cases, the archaeological evidence led the excavators to interpret the room facing the street as the *andron* and the room on the second-storey on the other side as the women's apartment which was provided by a roofed semi-open area to the front, similar to the typical hagiati house found in the Aegean up to the 19th century (Figure 5.29).[1072] The good preservation of some of the walls shows that the walls were made of a mortared rubble masonry up to about 1 meter high, and then of unfired bricks.[1073] The *andron* was often decorated with high quality plaster in proto-Pompeian style, imitating marble.[1074] At Knidos, some of the houses, which were preserved up to more than 2 meters, reveal their construction technique based on a stone socle and mudbrick walls that were painted over (Figure 5.30) and internal decorations including architectural stuccos, painted plasters, wall paintings and mosaics.[1075]

Roman period

The dataset of completely excavated Roman houses in the Aegean is limited. The number of wealthy houses, moreover, heavily outbalances the others, since traditionally only the most decorated examples, where undisputed Roman elements such as *impluvia* were present, have caught the interest of scholars.[1076] Roman houses of the less well-to-do social strata might not have been recognized as such for the absence of what are considered the typical features of Roman dwellings and shortage of

---

[1067] Adam-Veleni 2000.
[1068] Livadiotti 2010, 23-42 (see p. 26 for the reconstruction of a Hellenistic insula at Kos).
[1069] Fiedler 2005.
[1070] Love 1970.
[1071] Adam-Veleni 2000, 57-61.
[1072] For housing architecture in Medieval and Post-Medieval Greece see Sigalos 2004; a review of housing architecture in Late Medieval and Ottoman Boeotia is given in Piccoli and Vionis 2011, for the recording of Greek vernacular architecture, see Piccoli 2012.
[1073] Adam-Veleni 2000, 57.
[1074] Adam-Veleni 2000, 59.
[1075] Love 1970, 152-3 and Figure 11 (pl. 39).
[1076] Nevett 1999a, 101.

contextual finds. It has therefore to be taken into account that the following observations regarding the Roman house in Greece could apply only to the higher classes of Roman immigrants, whose houses probably represent the majority of the excavated examples.

The excavated houses give us some indications about the preferred locations of the properties in the city. Based on the 64 Roman houses in Greece that he has examined, Bonini suggests that the proximity to the agora was not valued as much as during the Classical period as attested by the Olynthian sale inscriptions.[1077] Areas close to the theatre were also not aimed for, while the space around sanctuaries seems to have encountered more favour, as proved by the peristyle house that was erected during the 1st century AD to the east of the sanctuary of Apollo,[1078] and the luxurious house constructed during the 2nd century AD against the acropolis wall at Eleusis.[1079] The excavations in Delos, Patra and Kos show that there was no sharp distinction between wealthy houses and more modest dwellings as they were mixed in the same neighbourhoods.[1080]

In the majority of Roman houses in Greece studied by Bonini, the entrance was not as monumental as in other areas of the Empire, and followed instead the Classical-Hellenistic tradition. In medium-size houses, thresholds were generally between 0,5 and 1,5 m, but could exceed 2 m in larger mansions.[1081] Doors opened towards the inside, according to the Roman habit, and not towards the outside as common during the Classical period.[1082] Contrary to the evidence for other parts of the Empire, in Greece the entrance room was usually a transitional space and was not equipped with benches to accommodate visitors or *clientes* who came to salute their patron.[1083] Among the most important changes in the configuration and use of space, the disappearance of the *andron*, which was quickly substituted for by the typically Roman triclinium,[1084] and the changed role of the courtyard are particularly significant.

As shown by the houses in Delos, the spatial arrangement with a central courtyard or peristyle surrounded by rooms was kept on the island under the Roman rule. The same pattern has been documented in other contexts, such as at Pergamon and Ephesos.[1085] In continuity with the changes which occurred in the Hellenistic period, when (one of the) courtyards turned into a semi-public display zone, the courtyards in Roman houses became more of a decorative feature as they were often occupied by a pool, a basin or a garden (*viridarium*), which are elements foreign to the Classical and Hellenistic tradition.[1086] As shown previously, courtyards were central features of Greek houses, commanding the movement paths along the house, and covering an important role as a multifunctional space where household activities were carried out. These changes led to a different organization of access where rooms were more interconnected between each other and not only accessible from the courtyard as previously attested.[1087]

[1077] Bonini 2006, 44.
[1078] Bonini 2006, 45.
[1079] Papangeli and Chlepa 2011, 52-5.
[1080] Bonini 2006, 46. Cf. the studies on the distribution of elites throughout the city of Pompeii, e.g. Laurence 2007, 166.
[1081] Bonini 2006, 52.
[1082] Bonini 2006, 51.
[1083] Bonini 2006, 55. Bonini (2006, 56) observes that possibly the *clientes* were received elsewhere, perhaps in the courtyard, as hinted in a passage of Plutarch's *Moralia* (814E).
[1084] Bonini 2006, 203.
[1085] Trümper 2003, 40.
[1086] In the dataset of Roman houses in Greece analysed by Paolo Bonini, about half of the courtyards with gardens comes from the Roman colony of Patras, testifying that the introduction of the garden is a typical Roman feature (Bonini 2006, 62). In a Roman house on the north-west slope of the Aeropagus, a large two-apse basin was placed in the centre of the peristyle and was surrounded by a garden (see Bressan and Bonini 2010, 22; the plan of the house is published in *Hesperia* 37 (1968), 71, Figure 12 and is accessible here http://agora.ascsa.net/id/agora/image/2012.58.1185)
[1087] Nevett 1999b, 105-7.

The social implications of the changed role of courtyards are far reaching, but difficult to sustain without a larger dataset to analyse. As Nevett argued, there could be a correlation between this different configuration of space and an increased freedom of movements of the female members of the household. The available dataset representing the wealthier families, however, can create a bias in the interpretation as we might be looking at houses of elite Roman immigrants and not at houses of the local Greek population.[1088] Moreover, the transformation of the courtyard into a decorative space implies that household activities, such as food preparation and weaving, were carried out inside the house instead of in the court, unless there was a second private courtyard that offered this opportunity. Nevett has suggested that this could relate to a decrease of engagement of the women of the household in this type of tasks, which were instead taken over by slaves or servants.[1089]

A large and lavishly decorated example of a Roman house in Greece is a villa in Kos, which was completely excavated and restored during the 1930s.[1090] The house, extending on an area of about 2,400 m², was erected in the second half of the 2nd century AD (and renewed in the 3rd) on an insula that was previously occupied by one or more Hellenistic houses. The rooms were arranged around three courtyards, the largest of which (Figure 5.31, coloured in blue) was a peristyle court occupied by a garden (Figure 5.32). All of the courtyards gave access to richly decorated representational spaces. Mosaics, floors in *opus sectile*, frescos and marble decorations testify to the wealth of the owners and their preferences.[1091] The choice of materials is typically Roman, the iconographic motifs are common elsewhere in Kos, while the selection of Late Hellenistic statuettes and a mosaic *emblema* of the same period among the decorations of the house reveal the owner's antiquarian taste.[1092]

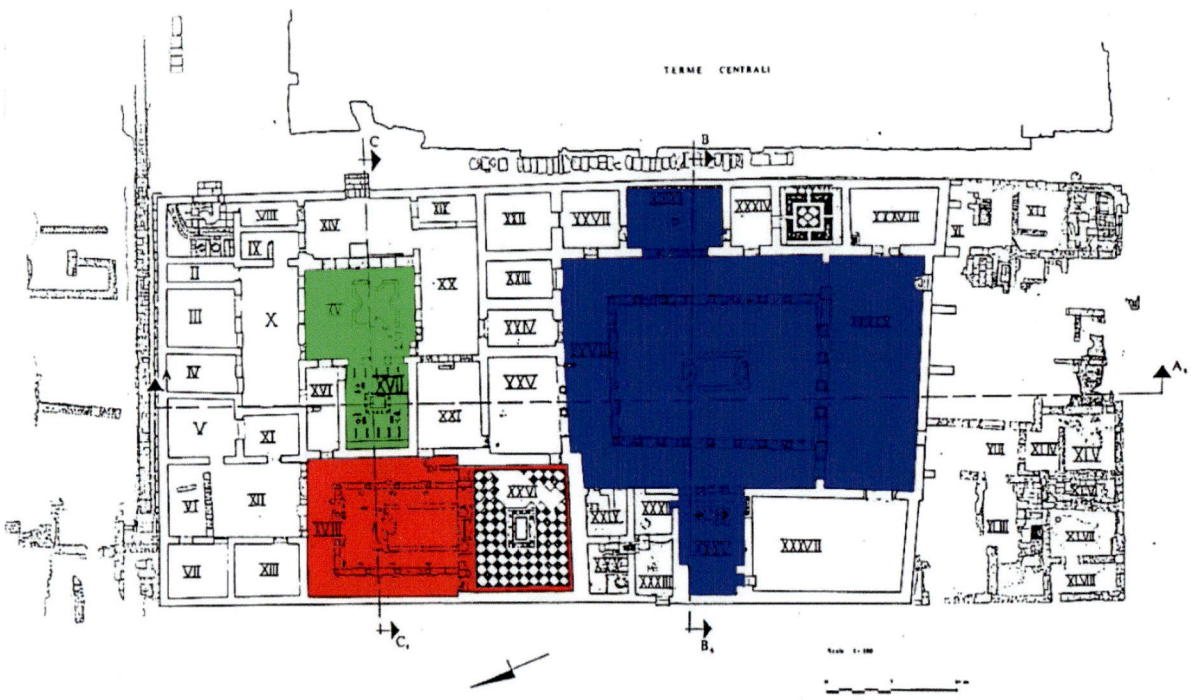

Figure 5.31 Plan of the Roman house at Kos with the three representational spaces in color (Albertocchi 2010, 41).

[1088] Nevett 1999b, 108.
[1089] Nevett 1999b, 107-8.
[1090] Recent restorations have been made on the basis of the 1930s interventions to reconstruct the house (Sideris 2015).
[1091] Albertocchi 2010.
[1092] Albertocchi 2010, 50.

Figure 5.32 Reconstructed court and peristyle of the Roman house at Kos after recent restoration (Sideris 2015, 80-1).

It is reasonable that the various degrees of assimilation of Roman elements within Greek houses related to the status of the city under Roman rule. In Colonies, which were inherently Roman towns, such as Corinth or Patras, the domestic architecture shows more closely typical Roman elements that were introduced by the colonists. In free Greek cities, the role of the upper classes was crucial for the local reinterpretation of Roman domestic architecture. A strong local aristocracy, wishing to maintain its political supremacy, would have adopted (and adapted) the Roman way of living as a way to legitimate their power.[1093] The Roman elites, on the other hand, had already assimilated elements of Hellenistic public architecture, e.g. the columns from *stoas* and the peristyle from the Gymnasium, thus transforming the traditional atrium house in Italy into the characteristic peristyle house.[1094]

Late antiquity

The dataset of Late Antique houses is more numerous than that of Roman houses, especially thanks to relatively recent works that have dedicated more attention to this topic. The majority of the known Late Antique houses are however still the result of accidental discoveries, and belong to wealthy social strata.[1095] General conclusions on Late Antique housing are therefore still difficult to draw from the limited data that are available. A notable exception is the state of the knowledge on Late Antique Crete, where excavations on several sites such as at Gortyn and Knossos are providing a regional perspective on the subject.[1096]

Taking the peristyle as the feature of the typical Roman house, Ellis argued that no new peristyle houses were built completely anew after the mid-6th century AD.[1097] The latest complete attested example was in fact the House of the Falconer at Argos, which was built around 530-550 AD, while the latest incomplete specimen is the House from Hermione in the Peloponnese built at the end of the 6th century.[1098] Transformations in domestic architecture reflect the social-political changes that led to a concentration of wealth in a smaller group of people and to a more formalized relationship between the patron and his *clientes*.[1099] Some of the peristyle houses still surviving, or those built anew, were

---

[1093] Bressan and Bonini 2010, 24-5. See also Bonini 2006, 28-9.
[1094] Cf. Wallace-Hadrill 1994, 20-1.
[1095] See Uytterhoeven 2007 for an overview of the state of the knowledge on Late Antique houses and related bibliography.
[1096] On Late Roman Crete, see Livadiotti and Simiakaki 2004, in particular the contribution by G. W. M. Harrison in the same volume (Harrison 2004). On Gortyn see Di Vita 2000, and the more recent publications of the excavations conducted by the University of Siena and the Italian School of Athens in the neighbourhood between the Pythion and the Praetorium (e.g. Zanini et al. 2009). For Knossos, see Sweetman 2004.
[1097] Ellis 1988.
[1098] Ellis 1988, 565.
[1099] Ellis 1988, 575-6.

provided with more luxurious and ceremonial receptions, such as the apsidal triclinium, to serve for receiving the *clientes*, and by more elaborate private facilities.[1100]

On the other end of the social spectrum, some of the surviving peristyle houses were subdivided into smaller living units to house the lower social classes.[1101] As mentioned earlier in the section on Late Antique town planning,[1102] it is in fact common that the overall extension of city blocks and individual houses was not changed, but modifications were made internally, such as the addition of subdivisions in the peristyle court or of extra porticoes, as attested at the House on the Via Egnatia in Philippi.[1103] In many sites, luxurious Late Antique houses seem not to be concentrated in specific areas of the city, but were instead interspersed with more modest dwellings.[1104] While in some cities, concentrations of upper class houses are attested, such as at Athens near the Greek agora and on the North Slope of the Aeropagus and at Thessalonika around Galerius' palace.[1105]

An example of the less conspicuous and underrepresented Late Antique houses is a house-shop dated to the 5th century AD which has been recently excavated in Hephaisteia, Lemnos as part of the ongoing investigations on the general topography of the site.[1106] The house-shop, composed of three adjacent rooms, was constructed maintaining the same orientation as the Classical-Hellenistic town grid and by re-arranging the northern part of a pre-existing peristyle house that was entered from the south (Figure 5.33). The first, larger room was entered directly from the street as evidenced by a 1.2 m long threshold which bears the pivot holes of a door opening towards the inside. This room had a beaten earth floor where a stone block was positioned probably as a basis for a wooden beam that sustained the roof. The second room was provided with a floor of stone slabs while amphorae lids were found especially concentrated on one side of the room.

From the 5th century, houses that were abandoned were turned into workshops. This phenomenon, which is attested in numerous cases, especially at Delphi and Philippi is contextualized in the process of ruralisation of cities that is typical of Late Antiquity.[1107] With the withdrawal of elites to the larger town and ecclesiastical mansions, public spaces and their former urban homes were taken over by the middle and lower classes.[1108] In Philippi, the excavated *insulae* of the city show a range of production activities that were carried out in buildings that were previously used as residences, such as a glass making workshop.[1109]

In a period of prevailing Christianised society, excavations of house assemblages give us a glimpse of the deities that were still worshipped within the household. A possible domestic shrine of pagan deities was excavated in the Panagia Domus to the south-east of Corinth's Roman forum.[1110] A room of the house, which remained in use until its destruction, possibly due to an earthquake, in the second half of the 4th century AD, contained an assemblage including miniature polychrome statues of Artemis, Asklepios, Roma, Dionysos, Herakles, Pan and possibly Europa. This assemblage is not an isolated case since other statuette groups were found in Corinth and in other contexts such as at Athens and Messene.[1111]

[1100] Ellis 1988, 573; Uytterhoeven 2007, 50.
[1101] Ellis 1988, 573; see also Uytterhoeven 2007, 45-6 with related bibliography.
[1102] § 5.2.5.
[1103] Baldini Lippolis 2007, 216.
[1104] Bonini 2006, 47.
[1105] Bonini 2006, 47.
[1106] Camporeale *et al.* 2008, 204.
[1107] Sodini 2007, 327.
[1108] Bintliff 2012, 360.
[1109] Sodini 2007, 327, citing Gounaris and Velenis 1997.
[1110] Stirling 2008, 89-161.
[1111] Stirling 2008, 132-6.

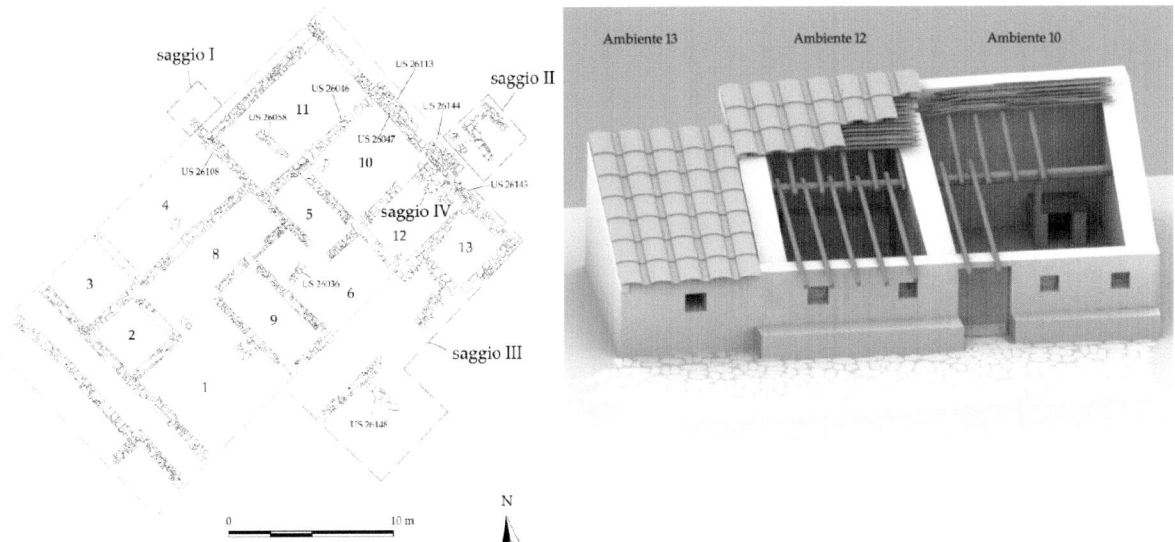

Figure 5.33 Left: Plan of the excavated house at Hephaisteia, Lemnos (Papi et al. 2008, Figure 44, p. 982); rooms 10, 12 and 13 correspond to the Late Antique house-shop; Right: Reconstruction hypothesis of the house-shop (Piccoli 2008, 244).

5.3.5 Training spaces

Training in ancient Greece was an important aspect of the male citizens' education and was deeply connected with the *polis*' identity and military power. It is difficult to identify the spaces that were dedicated to athletic preparation in the early phases of the *polis* as they were usually open multifunctional areas that have disappeared, being covered by the following centuries of city life. An open area on the edge of the town or outside the city walls with water sources in the vicinity and trees to ensure some shadow, perhaps bordered on one side by a portico with changing rooms, would have been enough to create a suitable space.[1112] While the city outskirts were the most convenient locations for training spaces, some evidence of race tracks have been uncovered also in agorai, such as at Athens (Figure 5.34), Corinth and Argos. In the last-named city, the starting line of a race track dated to the 1st century AD has been found, which probably followed an earlier track as it shares its orientation with a triangular basin dated to the late Classical period.[1113]

During the middle 4th – early 3rd century BC the spaces for training become more architecturally defined,[1114] and were called *palaistrai* or *gymnasia*.[1115] These terms identified two different areas of the training facilities that were often, but not always, part of the same complex yet they are usually used as synonyms in ancient texts.[1116] The *palaistra* means literally the wrestling school (*palaíeien* = to wrestle) and was usually a rectangular yard bordered by stoas with rooms for changing, rubbing on oil and bathing. The *gymnasion* (*gymnós* = naked; *gymnázo* = to train naked) consisted of two tracks, one covered by a roof (*xystos*) and one in the open air (*paradromis*). The architectural development, extent and magnificence of the complex could greatly vary, based on the terrain conditions and the financial possibility of the city or of the private sponsor. Fountains, bathing facilities, temples and libraries could be added to the basic components.[1117]

[1112] Foxhall 2013, 127.
[1113] Dickenson 2012, 240-1.
[1114] Owens 2009, 186; Foxhall 2013, 125-9.
[1115] See Foxhall 2013, 125-9.
[1116] See Miller 2004, 179.
[1117] Owens 2009, 186.

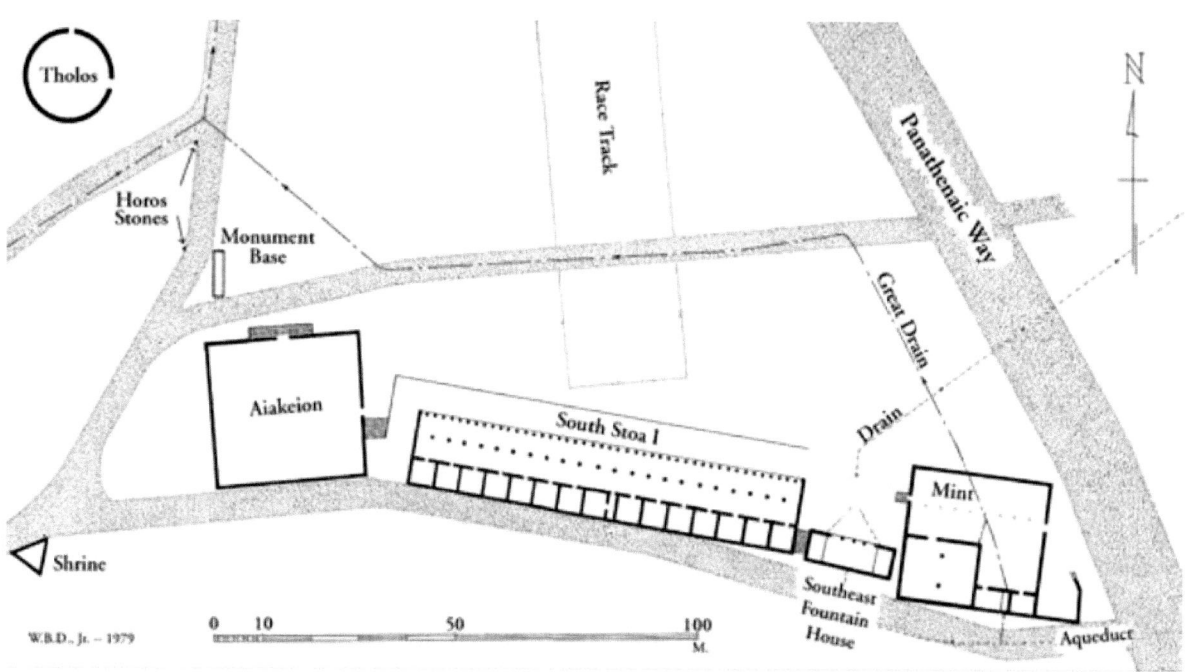

Figure 5.34 Plan of the south side of the Athenian agora in ca. 400 BC with the area occupied by the race track (Camp 2003, 24).

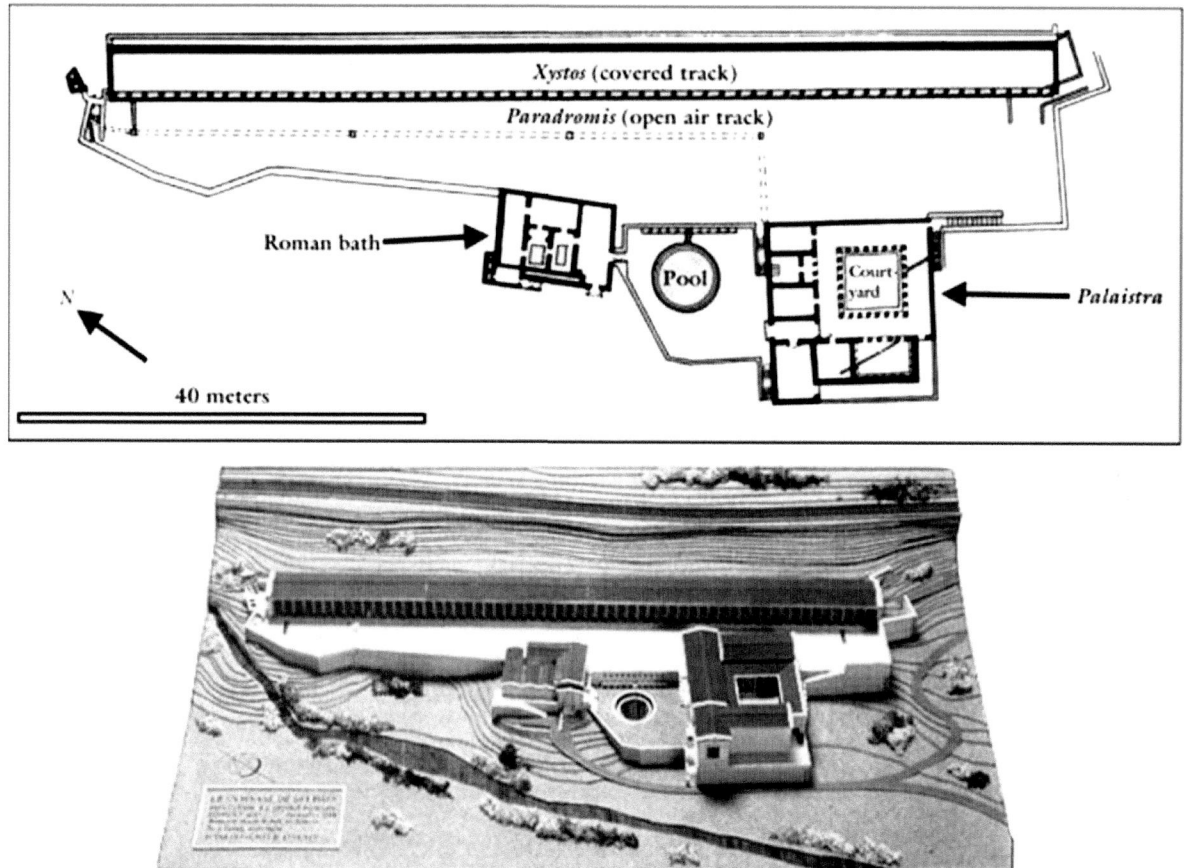

Figure 5.35 Plan and reconstruction model of the palaistra-gymnasion complex at Delphi (ca. 330 BC) (plan: Scott 2013, Map 19.1; picture from http://davidgilmanromano.org/courses/ancient-athletics/lecture-images/24).

The oldest know example of an architecturally defined *gymnasion-palaistra* is the one at Delphi. This complex was built around the middle of the 4th century on the cliffs of Mt. Parnassus close to the Castalia spring which ensured enough water for the bathing facilities.[1118] The traveller coming from Athens would have encountered it after the sanctuary of Athena Pronoia (at Marmaria) and before reaching the sanctuary of Apollo, which was visible from the *gymnasion*. The sloping terrain made it necessary to create earth embankments sustained by walls to obtain two terraces where the buildings were constructed. On the upper terrace the *xystos* (184.43 x 7.5 m) and the *paradromis* were laid out, while the lower terrace was occupied by a pool (*loutron*) receiving water from the Castalia spring, and by the *palaistra* (Figure 5.35). The latter was referred to in the inscriptions as the 'lower *gymnasion*', confirming again the blurred distinction between the two words in ancient texts.[1119] Close to the pool, a bath complex was added in Roman times.

Since the Archaic period, physical training was coupled with singing poetry and dancing as part of the *paideia* of the male youths,[1120] and the role of the *gymnasion-palaistra* as an integral part of the *polis* educational program became even more marked in Classical and especially in Hellenistic times. In the Hellenistic period, moreover, the *palaistrai* became multifunctional spaces and it was not uncommon that one of their rooms was equipped with benches to serve as a classroom.[1121] As an indication of the increased importance of this institution, not only as an athletic facility, but as an educational space, this complex was moved closer to the centre of the *polis*. The increase in the number and importance of *palaistrai* built adjacent to agorai during the Hellenistic periods, especially in newly founded cities,[1122] has been explained as a response to compensate for the lost political freedom under the Hellenistic rulers, with a reinforcement of local cultural identity, which was expressed and transmitted only to the young male elite through the athletics and educational activities that took place in these buildings.[1123] For the changed socio-political scene, these places became elite clubs and therefore acted more as a class divider than as a unifier.

During the Roman period, the importance of the *gymnasion* as part of citizen training and youth education decreased. Training spaces were maintained, but they were now intended for leisure and were used in combination with the bathing facilities that became more elaborate, functional (with the adoption of the Roman heating system) and monumental.[1124] The fact that a number of *palaistrai* were paved, instead of keeping the beaten earth ground that was most suitable for training, is a sign that this aspect was now of smaller concern.[1125] These spaces conserved the multifunctional character that they started to assume in the Hellenistic period and hosted music performances and lectures. An example is provided by an epigraph from Delphi dated from the late 1st century BC, which records the honours that the city gave to an astronomer that had given a series of lectures in its *gymnasion*.[1126]

The end of the traditional use of *gymnasia* is usually placed during the early 4th century AD.[1127] The term 'gymnasium' is still attested in late sources, but it is translated as 'baths' in texts that are later than the 4th century. In the 10th century AD Lexicon Suda, *aleipteria* (rooms where olive oil was distributed), *balaneia* or *loutra* (baths) are indeed used as synonyms for gymnasia.[1128] To the end of the 4th century is

---

[1118] For a description of the architectural complex, see Jannoray and Ducoux 1953; Jannoray 1937.
[1119] Roux 1980, 128.
[1120] Troncoso 2009, 72.
[1121] Scott 2013.
[1122] Dickenson 2012, 130.
[1123] Bearzot 2009, 104; Kousser 2005.
[1124] Remijsen 2015, 259-60.
[1125] Remijsen 2015, 261.
[1126] König 2005, 50-1.
[1127] Remijsen 2015, 259.
[1128] *Suidae Lexicon*, I, Γυμνάσια: ἀλειπτήρια ἢ βαλανεία ἢ λουτρά, 501.

Figure 5.36 Pottery factory in Messenia in the 1940s (Stillwell 1948, pl. 4b).

dated the final use of the *gymnasion* in Delphi that was afterwards occupied by a pottery workshop.[1129] The *gymnasion* offered a suitable location for the workshop as it laid abandoned outside the Late Antique town, and had the flat ground that used to serve as a racing track. The Castalia spring that had provided the necessary water for the training facilities up to Roman times was now a convenient water supplier for the processing of clay.

5.3.6 Industrial spaces

The study of the industrial areas of Graeco-Roman towns, which would shed light on important aspects on local economies, the organization of labour and of the distribution of goods, has traditionally received little attention in literature.[1130] Since the stigma that Finley attached to the ancient economy in the 1970s, scholars dealing with this subject have often interpreted the available evidence under preconceived ideas about the socio-economic characteristics of the ancient world, polarizing their views between 'primitivists' and 'modernists'. In recent years, the increase in archaeological data and the re-examination of old evidence are shedding light on previously overlooked or unknown aspects of the ancient economy, rendering the picture of a complex system that was far from being 'primitive'.[1131]

As far as pottery is concerned, recent studies have started to look beyond its modern artistic value to consider the whole production and distribution chain of these artefacts and the people who manufactured, sold, used and finally disposed of them.[1132] To this end, ethnographical studies are often relied upon to reconstruct the organization and use of space in workshops (Figure 5.36),[1133] and

---

[1129] Petridis 1998.
[1130] Bintliff 2008a, 17-8.
[1131] Bintliff 2008b, 41.
[1132] See in this respect Stissi 2002, 2-4.
[1133] See e.g. Hasaki 2011, 12–24, in particular p. 17 for a review of ethnographic studies in Greece and Cyprus.

mineralogical, petrographic and archaeometrical analysis are being increasingly used in order to shed light on the clay composition, provenance and suggest a dating for artefacts.[1134]

As discussed in section 5.3.4, manufacturing and selling goods was often part, to a varying degree, of the tasks that were carried out within, or close to houses. Rooms for workshops or shops were often open on the side of the house that was facing the street and could be run by the owner of the house or rented out. In the latter case, the leaser could live in his own shop by creating a mezzanine that would make space for a sleeping area. Agricultural produce installations such as olive and grape presses were most conveniently placed near the farms where this produce was harvested, as transport of the processed product into the city would have been easier.[1135] But as previously discussed for Olynthos and Halieis, such installations could be also present in houses within towns, albeit on a smaller scale.

In this section, the focus is specifically on the industrial installations that were clustered on the edges of urban areas. For the limited space available here, I will concentrate mainly on pottery workshops although other types of crafts commonly existed in towns. As Hasaki observed, it is not rare that workshops manufacturing different kinds of goods (such as pottery, sculpture, bronze casts, glass) were often close to each other in the same area of the city. The use of terracotta mould and clay models by bronze smiths and sculptors on the one hand, and the need of lead ties to bind together broken pots by potters on the other hand are in fact just a few examples of the types of exchange in technical expertise, skills and materials among artisans of different crafts which were greatly facilitated by the proximity of their workshops.[1136]

An average of four to six potters working full time on two kilns seems the most plausible reconstruction of the working force of a typical workshop.[1137] Potters usually preferred to build their premises just inside or outside the urban fortifications, preferably in well-connected places along the roads linking the town with nearby centres as in the Keramikos at Athens, or near the harbour as in Piraeus. The choice of these locations removed from the core of the town was mainly due to practical factors, not least to limit the inconveniences and discomforts related to the production process, such as stink, smoke and danger of fire. Not uncommonly, in fact, workshops and cemeteries are often found close to each other for their shared risk of contamination.[1138] A relatively high number of metal workshops are instead attested within sanctuaries. Terracotta cult objects, (miniature) vases and figurines could be in fact produced elsewhere and transported with low risk, while metal votives for their weight and costs were more conveniently manufactured *in loco*.[1139]

Although it seems logical that potters would choose to build their workshop close to the supply of their raw materials, it is not clear, in view of the currently available evidence, how much the proximity of natural resources was crucial for the location of industrial premises.[1140] It seems in fact that closeness of clay supply was not the main determiner to the location of a workshop, unless the latter was bound to specific clays for the types of pottery that it produced.[1141] As Stissi observed, the presence of nearby water should also not be overestimated. This indispensable element would have been anyway in reach,

---

[1134] See e.g. the archaeometric analysis of the Hellenistic-Early Roman kilns at Katerini (Pieria), Olympiada (Chalkididki), Polymylos (Kozani) and Paros by Kondopoulou *et al.* 2014.
[1135] Cahill 2002, 238.
[1136] Hasaki 2002, 287-8.
[1137] See Hasaki 2002, 312-4 with reference to previous studies on the scale of pottery workshops.
[1138] Stissi 2002, 38 but see *contra* Hasaki who concludes that the long held association between cemeteries and workshops was biased by the archaeological excavations that had investigated a larger number of cemeteries in respect to e.g. residential quarters (Hasaki 2002, 292-3).
[1139] Hasaki 2002, 290-1.
[1140] See Stissi 2002, 43-4.
[1141] Stissi 2002, 44-5.

as urban centres grew usually in locations that were conveniently close to streams and rivers.[1142] Finally, accessibility to wood supply was also not crucial as less expensive materials could be used to fuel the kilns. It is obvious, however, that potters would have taken all these elements into account to find the best compromise given the local circumstances when choosing in which side(s) of their town their workshops should be built.

If several studies have dealt with the locations of pottery workshops and their production, less attention has been given to how the space was used and organized within the workshop.[1143] Ethnographic comparisons can be of help in complementing the knowledge on pottery factories in ancient Greece. A recent study by Hasaki on Tunisian pottery workshops has yielded a range of interesting observations. Hasaki's dataset (41 workshops in Kalalet, the potters' quarter in Moknine) shows that in the prevalent layout the rooms do not communicate between each other, but the courtyard is usually used as the connecting space.[1144] Workshops specialized in vessels of a specific height range (and not on shapes) and the height of the manufactured pots relate to the area that the workshop occupied.[1145] An additional area outside the workshop was seasonally and temporarily employed for the initial drying period of the products. Large vessels and tiles would have required a much larger open space than pots of smaller size. Wooden or stone shelves and benches inside the rooms are also present to stack the manufactured vessels to allow them the necessary drying time in the shade before firing.[1146]

Kilns, which have been found in great number in Greece (more than 450 on about 250 sites),[1147] are considered the best marker for the location of a workshop, while the presence of other elements such as pottery dumps, moulds and working tools give circumstantial evidence of its possible nearby existence.[1148] Greeks used a vertical two-chamber kiln. The upper firing chamber was divided from the lower stoking chamber by a perforated floor sustained by a central pillar which allowed the propagation of heat. For their structure kilns were most conveniently dug into sloping ground, occasionally reaching the bedrock, in order to ensure a better insulation and decrease the risk of misfired pots.[1149] In some occasions, walls were constructed around the kiln. According to Hasaki this measure was not aimed to sustain the kiln, but more probably to further protect its content, the walls that are often found around kilns being used to protect the content of the kiln and not to sustain it.[1150]

Kilns for different types of functions such as firing pottery, melting metal or rocks to produce lime shared similar features, which makes it difficult for archaeologists to distinguish them, especially if only partially preserved. This can lead to the erroneous attribution of all circular kilns to the production of pottery, and of rectangular kilns exclusively to the firing of bricks and tiles.[1151] Among the characteristics to look for to identify its purpose, the presence of a perforated floor can be considered a distinctive marker of ceramic kilns and the existence of two stoking channels is common in lime kilns.[1152]

If the technology behind how kilns were constructed and operated remained quite similar throughout antiquity, some peculiar characteristics of how workshops functioned in each period can be identified.

[1142] Stissi 2002, 45-6.
[1143] Hasaki 2011, 17.
[1144] Hasaki 2011, 22.
[1145] Workshops for pots up to 0,15 m had an average extension of 120 m2, for pots between 0,16 and 0,40 the area was 350 m2 and for pots more than 0,40 750 m2 (Hasaki 2011, 20-1).
[1146] Hasaki 2011, 21-2.
[1147] I refer to the catalogue in Hasaki 2002.
[1148] See Hasaki 2011, 15, Table 1, and Hasaki 2002, 257-64 for the criteria used to identify a pottery workshop.
[1149] Hasaki 2002, 73-4.
[1150] Hasaki 2002, 73-4.
[1151] See Hasaki 2002, 302-3. See *ibidem*, 112-38 for an overview of the main characteristics of different kilns.
[1152] Hasaki 2002, 302.

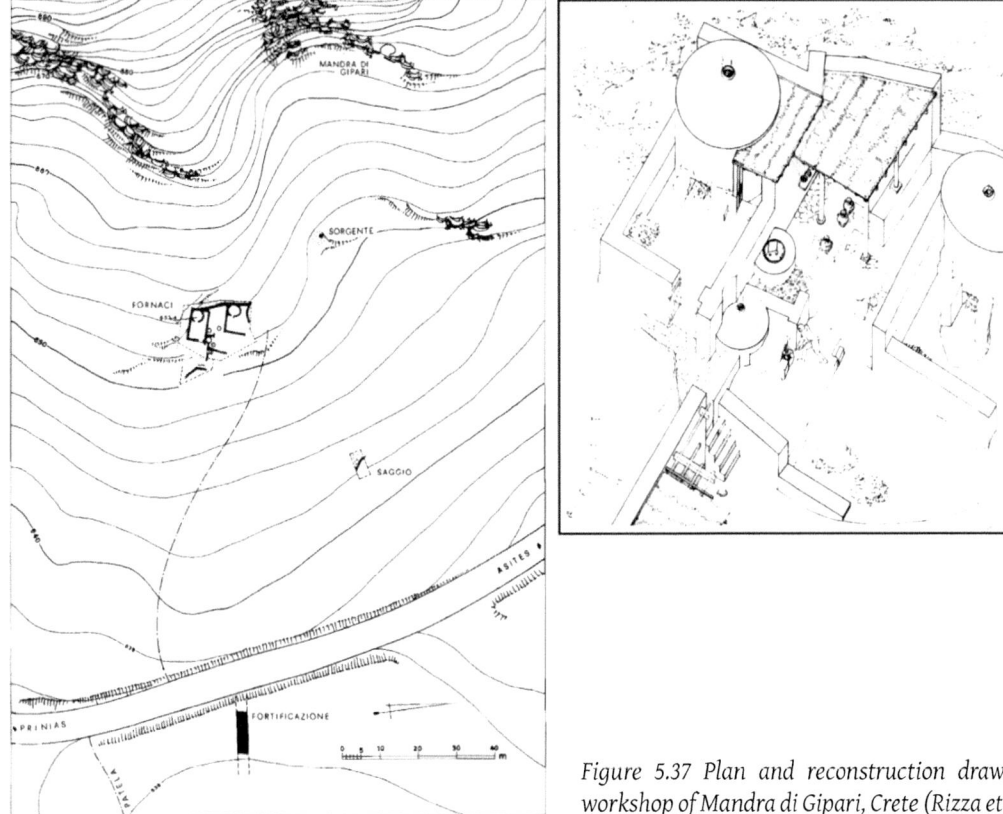

Figure 5.37 Plan and reconstruction drawing of the Archaic workshop of Mandra di Gipari, Crete (Rizza et al. 1992, 17 and 155).

Pottery production increased in Archaic times in comparison to the previous Geometric period, leading to the presence of more than one kiln (possibly functioning simultaneously) in a single workshop.[1153] Of the twenty-two kilns known for the Archaic period,[1154] the highest number is concentrated at the workshop of Mandra di Gipari which is also one of the most completely preserved examples of pottery workshops ever excavated in Greece. The site is located on a series of artificial terraces on the slope west of the urban centre on the Patela hill at Prinias, Crete (Figure 5.37).[1155] The workshop was in use between the second half of the 7th and the beginning of the 6th century BC in an area that seems to be occupied by a craft quarter.[1156] The excavated complex consists of three spaces divided by dry stone walls. The southern one was excavated onto the clay deposits of the slope and was paved with stone slabs. It housed a circular kiln (inner diameter of about 2.5 m) that was partially constructed directly on the bedrock and built against the walls bordering the space. In the central space four smaller ovens were excavated, while the northern space was occupied by an ellipsoidal kiln (3.14 x 2.35 m) built again against the walls and recessed into the excavated bedrock for 0.80 m. Also here evidence of slabs points towards the existence of a paved floor. Four piles of large bricks that were used to sustain the load in the kiln in the southern space have led the excavators to infer that this was used to fire large pithoi, and to interpret the kiln in the northern space as more convenient for pottery of small and medium size, since the perforated floor was not equally firmly supported.[1157]

[1153] Hasaki has catalogued 22 Archaic kilns found in 11 sites (2002, 226).
[1154] The figures I used are taken from the study by Hasaki (2002, 225-9).
[1155] Rizza *et al.* 1992, 29.
[1156] Rizza *et al.* 1992, 29.
[1157] Rizza *et al.* 1992, 40.

Pottery production further increased in Classical Greece, as testified by the higher number of kilns that is known for this period (57 in 32 sites).[1158] Attica and Athens have returned the majority of the evidence, most notably from the Kerameikos, one of the Athenian potters' quarters. Noteworthy for this period is that, besides circular and ellipsoidal kilns of various sizes,[1159] rectangular kilns start to be attested in higher numbers especially from the Late Classical period onwards. At Hellenistic Pella, the available evidence of workshops close to the agora has been further increased by recent excavations, that have uncovered another pottery workshop in the north-west edge of a city block near the neighbourhood of the public baths.[1160] A room was reserved for two kilns and the others around the courtyard for clay processing, pottery storage and working debris.

In the Roman period, centres like Athens and Patras stand out for the high concentration of kilns that have been found, some being in good state of preservation.[1161] For example, in one of the four kilns excavated in Karaiskaki and Kalamogdarti Street at Patras, the armature of the vault that covered the kiln has been uncovered.[1162] In this period rectangular kilns (averaging 2 x 2 m) are more attested than circular. This figure should not per se taken as an indication of a preference towards rectangular kilns, but it can be due to their easily recognisable shape during archaeological excavations.[1163] It has to be noted that isolated rectangular kilns might have been set up close to the site where buildings requiring a large amount of tiles or bricks were constructed.

Due to the contraction of urban areas that has been observed in Late Antiquity, industrial installations were built within the boundaries of the previous Graeco-Roman town. Workshops were installed in buildings in ruin or that had gone out of use, as testified by the artisanal quarters that have been excavated in Delphi, which been dated to the second half of the 6th century AD and the beginning of the 7th.[1164] In a first phase, a pottery workshop was built within the *gymnasion*, and comprised a securely identified kiln with two adjacent basins that were possibly used to sediment the clay.[1165] A later workshop (dated to the end of the 6th century AD) was installed to the south of the sanctuary of Apollo, in an abandoned domestic area of the town.[1166]

5.3.7 Urban fortifications

Urban fortifications became a typical feature of the Greek *polis* starting from the late 6th century. Previously, Geometric settlements remained unwalled, or when walls were present, they were usually confined to the acropolis (e.g. at Emborio on Chios) and only rarely encompassed the whole settlement such as at Zagora.[1167] According to Cooper, and contrary to the traditional view on the policies governing the construction of Greek fortifications, such undertakings were not the result of a planned series of actions, but developed out of the need of defence without a coherent strategy - with the exception of Boeotia under Epaminondas.[1168]

[1158] Hasaki 2002, 230-4.
[1159] Hasaki 2002, 232 identifies three groups based on the diameter: small (smaller than 1 m); average (1-1,59) and large (1,60-3).
[1160] The workshop is published in Lilimbaki-Akamati and Akamatis 2008. For previous knowledge on the Pella workshops, see Akamatis 1996. For the public baths see Lilimbaki-Akamati and Akamatis 2007.
[1161] Hasaki 2002, 238-43.
[1162] Huber and Varalis 1995, 888 (figs. 29-30).
[1163] Hasaki 2002, 242-3.
[1164] Petridis 1998.
[1165] Cf. p. 212; Petridis 1998, 704.
[1166] Petridis 1998, 705.
[1167] Lang 2007, 185. See Lang 1996, 51, Figure 18 for an overview of the chronological distribution of city walls.
[1168] Cooper 2000, 156.

Several factors interplayed in defining the best course of the city wall circuit. The right balance needed in fact to be struck between the needed amount of space within the enclosure and the costs and duration of their construction. In some cases, a larger area than was actually needed to accommodate the population was enclosed. One of the most important factors to trace the path of the circuit was the terrain morphology. Where possible the terrain's natural features such as rock outcrops were exploited.[1169] This strategy had several advantages including the possibility to save materials, create a more solid construction and to build a strong foundation that was impossible to mine.[1170] Areas that could have offered an advantageous position for the enemy to attack the city, such as higher ground in proximity of the circuit, were preferably included.

Usually city walls were made of mud bricks that were laid down on a basis of stone blocks. Walls that were built entirely with stones are attested, but they are more related to fortresses such as Siphai[1171] in Boeotia and Goritza in Thessaly. Winter indicates an average height between 7 and 9.5 meters for the walls in the Classical period, citing as examples Phyle (ca. 8.5-9.5m) and Messene (7-9m).[1172] On the upper part there was the *parodos*, a pavement made of wooden planks or stone labs that allowed one to walk around the circuit and protected the mud bricks, thus preventing the structure from deterioration. Especially from Hellenistic times, the *parodos* could be roofed (*katastegasma*) to protect the artillery and to create a sheltered passage for the defenders.[1173]

Towers were distributed along the perimeter, usually flanking gateways and placed on the locations that needed more protection such as at angles, or where the wall traversed a stretch of level ground, or stood on a gentle slope.[1174] The shape of the towers could vary and would be decided according to the position in which they were constructed. Pentagonal towers are regarded by Philo as those offering most security, but are rarely found in the archaeological record. Round towers were also advisable especially where sections of the circuit met forming a sharp angle. Rectangular towers, on the contrary, would have left the flat surface more exposed to the enemy's attack.[1175] In Halieis in the Argolid, at least 18 towers were present, those near the gates being often round as in the case of the towers protecting the harbour gate, the Hermione and the South-East gate. The 4 km long fortification wall at Eretria was interspersed with 60 towers.[1176] The city walls constructed at Plataiai after Chaironeia had a similar length counting more than 40 towers and at least six gates.

Gates were placed on the most useful locations along the circuit, in order to connect with the pre-existing roads coming from neighbouring towns and to allow farmers to reach their fields with ease. Depending on their position and their rank they could be constructed in several ways. The most common types were the so called courtyard or forecourt gates, which became typical in the Hellenistic period (see Figure 5.38, a). Overlapping or tangential gates were also widely used and were preferred by Vitruvius for the security that they guaranteed.[1177] There were then lower rank smaller gates, so called posterns, which could be located at the end of streets, such as at Kastro Kallithea.[1178] In some Greek towns such as Miletos, Knidos, Priene and Goritza, city walls were intentionally not connected with the urban street network, resulting in a de-synchronization between gates and streets. In this way, a less direct access to

---
[1169] Winter 1971, 170-1.
[1170] As Winter reports, mining was one of the most successful techniques to make an opening into the enemies' fortification (Winter 1971, 133-4).
[1171] Schwandner 1977.
[1172] Winter 1971, 134, footnote 32.
[1173] Winter 1971, 141
[1174] Winter 1971, 154.
[1175] Winter 1971, 199-201.
[1176] Ducrey 2004, 177.
[1177] McNicoll 1997, 6.
[1178] Surtees *et al.* 2014, 438; for postern gates aligned to streets, see also Lawrence 1979, 338.

Figure 5.38 Examples of (top, left) courtyard gate; (top, right) overlapping gate and (bottom) postern gate with overlooking tower at Kastro Kallithea (created by R.C. Lee, source: http://people.tamu.edu/~ryanlee/kallithea.html).

the city centre was created, thus increasing the difficulty of penetrating the urban centre for attacking enemies.[1179]

The evolution of city walls progressed along with the development of siege techniques that improved dramatically especially during the Peloponnesian War.[1180] Their level of sophistication increased during this period with the addition of towers, stone battlements and parapets. According to Winter, the earliest preserved examples of stone battlements are found in the Attic fortress of

---

[1179] Winter 1971, 209.
[1180] Winter 1971, 154-160.

Phyle and can be dated to the end of the 5th or beginning of the 4th century BC.[1181] The inventions of the catapult, dated around 400 BC, and of the torsion engine around 350 BC, were the major modifications that triggered new developments in the ways in which city walls were constructed, such as the reinforcement of towers that could be damaged by such devices.[1182] Although they could be easily broken by siege craft, walls of mudbrick were still being constructed.[1183] Winter notes an increased interest for visually appealing fortifications, with the insertion of arched gates and ornaments on towers.[1184]

One of the most important ancient sources of information about siege craft and fortifications of the Hellenistic period is the book *poliorketikà*, which is part of a treatise on mechanics written by the 3rd century BC Greek engineer Philon of Byzantium.[1185] In this book Philon provided advice on the best ways to construct fortifications, and although it represents an extremely useful source of information, his suggestions do not always find confirmation in the archaeological data. For example, his recommendations of a hexagonal tower as the best shape to protect a gateway and his measurements for the ideal size of wall (no less than 10 cubits/4.43m thick and 20 cubits 8.87m high) are implemented in only a few sites.[1186] McNicoll suggests that he describes recent developments,[1187] but one cannot exclude that Philon's text presents ideal solutions that were then adapted to local circumstances and limited by economic factors.

After the battle of Pydna (168 BC), the urban fortifications of the *poleis* that had sided with Perseus of Macedon against the Romans were demolished. New walls were allowed to be constructed around the acropolis, but not to protect the lower town. An epigraph known as the *Senatus Consultum Thisbaeum*,[1188] dated to 170 BC, reports the decisions of the senate regarding the Boeotian town of Thisbe that had been taken by the praetor C. Lucretius Gallus. As can be read in the document, the Romans' greater concern was to take care of the members of the pro-Roman faction that had been exiled. By this decree they were in fact granted the right to rule for 10 years and settle on the acropolis which could be fortified.[1189] As discussed in chapter 4, a similar document, unfortunately only partially preserved, describes similar measures taken for Koroneia.[1190]

During the relative peace resulting from the *Pax Romana*, the need for fortifications decreased. City walls remain more a sign of the symbolic limit of the urban centre than a practical defensive measure. In Asia Minor, gates received much attention during the Imperial period and were often remodelled and embellished, sometimes thanks to the euergetism of some wealthy citizen. Moreover, in some cities the main gate was linked to the market place by a colonnaded street, such as at Perge and Side.[1191] For Greece, however, it seems that most towns had let their walls fall apart, a fact noted already by Cicero for Thessalonika.[1192]

A new impetus for the construction of fortifications is connected with the unstable and eventful 3rd century AD, most notably with the Herulian incursions in Greece and their sack of Athens in 267 AD,

---

[1181] Winter 1971, 139.
[1182] McNicoll 1997, 4.
[1183] McNicoll 1997, 6.
[1184] Winter 2006, 34-5.
[1185] The book *poliorketikà* is edited by Garland (1974).
[1186] McNicoll 1997, 8 and 12.
[1187] McNicoll 1997, 12.
[1188] *Ephem. Epigr.*, i. 1872, 278-83.
[1189] *Ephem. Epigr.*, i. 1872, lines 27-31; see comments in Sherk 1969, 26-31 and Bagnall and Derow 2004, 83-4.
[1190] See p. 93.
[1191] Nossov 2009, 47.
[1192] Bintliff 2012, 326.

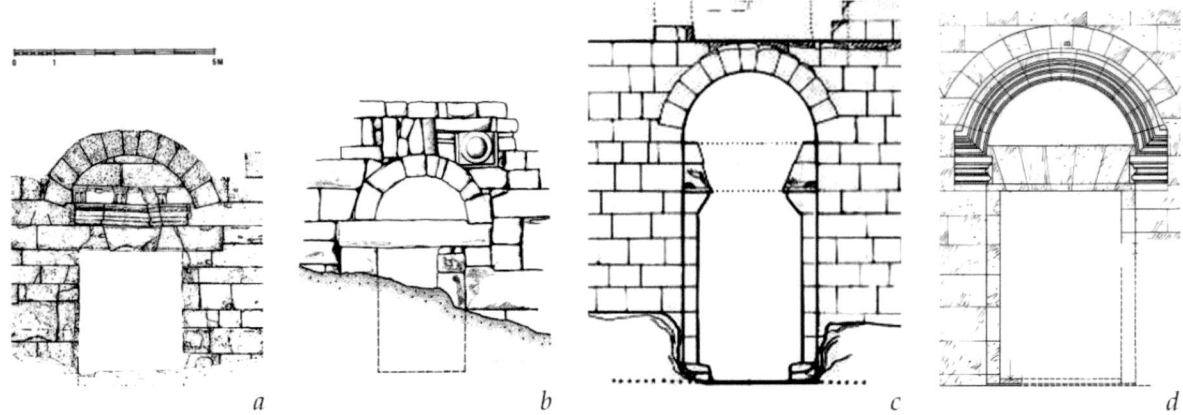

Figure 5.39 Typical Late Antique gates in the Roman East: a) the North Gate of Blaundos; b) a smaller gate at Selge; c) the North Gate of Zenobia and d) the East Gate of Resafa (drawings by I. Jacobs, in Jacobs 2009, 199).

and the raids of the Goths led by Alaric at the end of the 4th century. Fortifications that were erected in Late Antiquity protected a smaller extent than the actual populated urban area, or towns show a reduced urban area such as at Tanagra, as previously discussed. The choice of constructing a shorter circuit can be explained by the need for a city wall that could be efficiently defended by the citizens.[1193] Among the new fortifications that can be perhaps related to the Herulian threat are the walls around the acropolis of Plataiai, which were constructed using blocks from buildings that were at the time in disuse, taken, among others, probably also from the theatre.[1194] Interestingly, this new circuit did not encompass large parts of the lower town, including the agora, which had therefore to be given up in case of attack. Moreover, in the south of the town the existing buildings were demolished to create an open space that the defenders could use to repel the attackers with fire.[1195]

Gates in late Antiquity often assumed or restored the Hellenistic courtyard type flanked by two towers, which was useful for channelling the traffic. Gates had a typical shape with a semi-circular tympanum bounded by a lintel and an arch. The space between these two elements was filled (see Figure 5.39, a) and this is how the gates should be reconstructed even if for later modifications or disturbances the infill between the lintel and the arch was lost.[1196]

5.3.8 Trees, groves and gardens

Since the environmental movement in the 1970s, more attention has been paid to the interaction between people and the environment in antiquity. It is now common practise during an archaeological excavation to collect ground samples to study the archaeobotanical species that were cultivated and planted in the site.[1197] These relatively recent studies are shedding new light on the presence of trees, cultivated plants and flowers in sanctuaries, public spaces, houses and graves, which previously was mainly confined to the information gathered from historical sources, inscriptions recording property transactions, and vase paintings. Plants were used in ancient Greece both for utilitarian reasons and in religious settings. Sanctuaries, temples and altars were usually surrounded by sacred groves (*álsos*). In some sites, it has been possible to identify the species that were planted and that were considered sacred

---

[1193] Kirilov 2007.
[1194] Konecny *et al.* 2013, 46.
[1195] Konecny *et al.* 2013, 46.
[1196] Jacobs 2009, 199.
[1197] See e.g. Valamoti and Bittman 2015; Voutsaki and Valamoti 2013.

to a divinity, such as the *lygos* tree (*Vitex agnus-castus*) sacred to Hera and that was kept in her sanctuary on Samos,[1198] or the pomegranate that was sacred to Hera and Demeter as attested by iconography and archaeological finds.[1199]

For the Archaic period the sources are limited and are mainly restricted to ancient texts and depictions on pottery. Utilitarian gardens are attested in the Homeric poems in the form of kitchen gardens and fruit and vegetable orchards.[1200] Common are also the literary references to sacred trees or groves close to altars and sanctuaries. A palm tree is said to be growing near the altar of Apollo in Delos in the *Odyssey* (6.162), and Sappho (fr. 2) describes an idyllic scenery where altars with burning incense in honour of Aphrodite are surrounded by an apple grove, roses, a meadow of flowers and cool water.[1201] Trees were also planted around graves as a sign of respect for the dead, as attested by the passage of the *Iliad* (6.419) describing the nymphs who planted a grove of elms around the grave of Eetion, the king of the Cilicians, who had been killed by Achilles.

The evidence for the Classical and Hellenistic period is more abundant. The majority of gardens were located at the outskirts of the city or outside the city walls, close to springs and rivers that guaranteed the necessary sources of irrigation.[1202] Such gardens belonged to farms, sanctuaries, *gymnasia* and tombs. Intra urban sanctuaries were also surrounded by sacred (fruit) groves that could be rented out to finance the sanctuary expenditure.[1203] The excavations at the Hephaistèion, at the western edge of the Athenian agora, uncovered rows of rectangular cuttings that were carved during the late Hellenistic period directly into the bedrock around the temple to host the sacred grove (Figure 5.40, left). In some of the cuttings, flower pots were found with a diameter of about 20 cm. These pots were probably used for layering plants to ensure their rapid growth in accordance to ancient gardening prescriptions.[1204] The excavators, based on literary sources and observations on the fragments of carbonized roots, reconstructed the sacred *alsos* as composed by some fruit trees (perhaps pomegranate) and shrubs such as laurel, to which vines and ivy were added during the Roman period.[1205]

In addition to sanctuaries, vegetation could be planted to provide shade and enhance the urban decor of public spaces. Plutarch reported that Cimon was the first to embellish Athens by having plane trees planted in the agora and by turning the Academy into a 'well-watered grove'.[1206] Similarly, trees were planted in the market place at Anthedon, as accounted by the 3rd century BC traveller Herakleides Kritikos in his description of Greek cities.[1207] The buildings on the acropolis could be also interspersed with vegetation. For example, the acropolis of Rhodes, was 'full of fields and groves' according to the 2nd century AD Aelius Aristides (*Or.* 25.6).

In some cities gardens could be an important feature in the urban layout. Thebes in particular seems to have been quite exceptional since, according to Herakleides, it had more gardens than any other city in Greece, which accounts for its enormous size, 320 ha, more than 1.5 the size of Athens.[1208] Generally, however, in densely built-up domestic areas within cities there was no space left for gardens. Courtyards were relatively small, usually paved and, being the major source of light for the

---

[1198] Burkert 1985, 85.
[1199] Martinelli 2012, 85.
[1200] Littlewood 2006, 311.
[1201] Carroll-Spillecke 1992.
[1202] Carroll-Spillecke 1992, 91.
[1203] Carroll-Spillecke 1992, 89-90.
[1204] Burr Thompson 1937.
[1205] Burr Thompson 1937, 425.
[1206] Plut. *Cim.* 13.8.
[1207] *FHG*, II, fr. 23, p. 259.
[1208] *FHG*, II, fr. 12, p. 258.

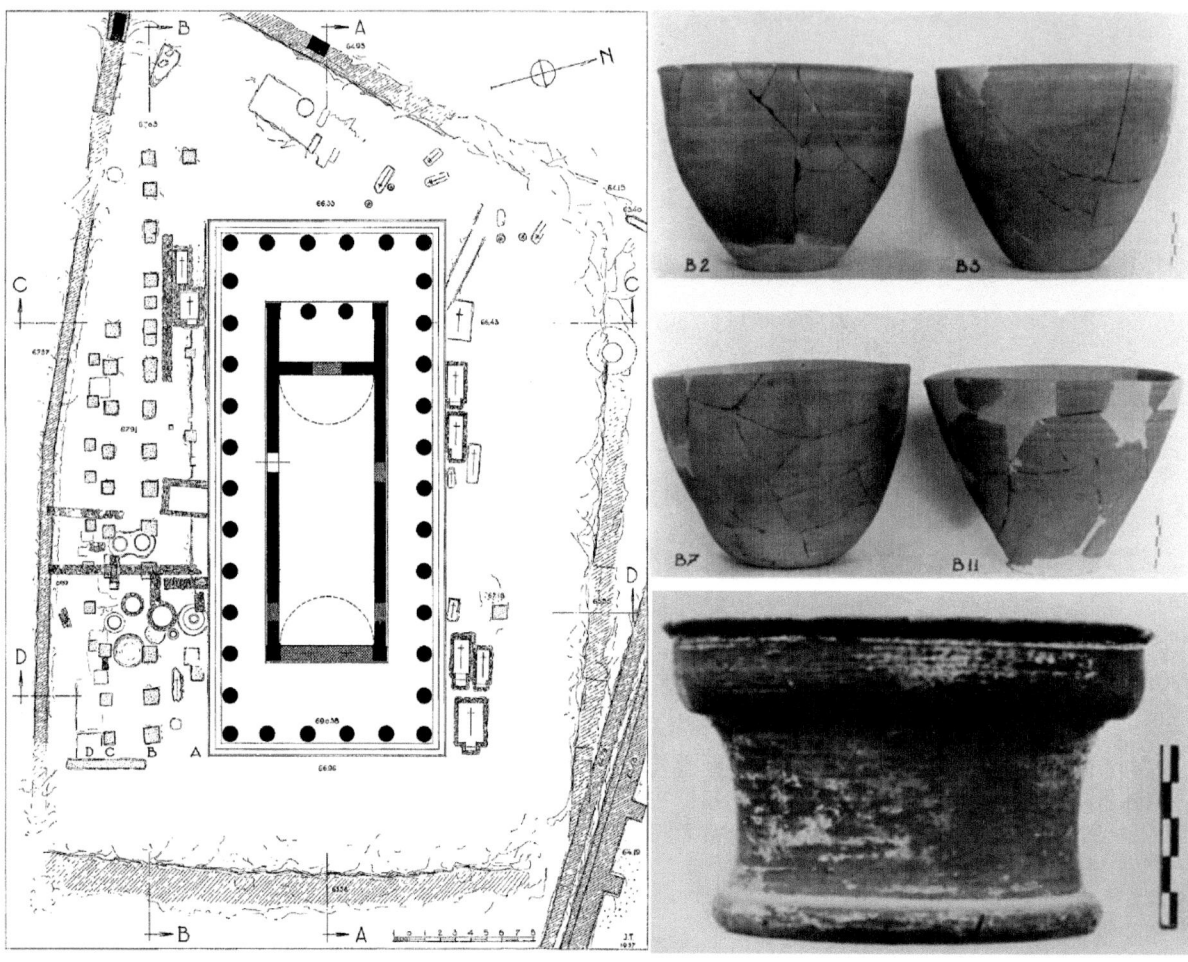

Figure 5.40 Left: Plan of the Hephaisteion; on the left, the rows of cutting in the bedrock to host trees and flower pots; Right: Flower pots from Olynthos (Burr Thompson 1937, 399; 406; 409).

surrounding rooms, were an ill-suited place to plant trees. There were moreover specific concerns about the stability of mudbrick walls which could be damaged by the roots of trees or shrubs. In this regard, an inscription from Pergamon testifies that in this city measures were officially taken to prohibit vegetation to be planted near the walls of houses.[1209] Potted plants, probably herbs, were present in courtyards, as shown by the flower pots that have been found in excavations (in Figure 5.40, right an example from Olynthos).[1210] It is possible that in more loosely built-up neighbourhoods, such as at Olynthos' Villa section, gardens were interspersed with houses, but there is no archaeological evidence that proves it with certainty.[1211] In rockier or hillier sites, however, the built-up area would have been interspersed with zones not suitable for building, which would most likely be covered by plants and trees.

The presence of gardens within houses is foreign to Classical domestic architecture. For the Hellenistic period, gardens are attested in the luxurious royal palace complexes, but the courtyards of more modest houses were usually paved.[1212] As already observed, it is with the Romans that gardens become more

---

[1209] *SEG* XIII, 521, II, 158-61, cited by Carroll-Spillecke 1992, 86.
[1210] Carroll-Spillecke 1992, 86.
[1211] Cahill 2002, 236.
[1212] Nielsen 2001; Carroll-Spillecke 1992, 91-4.

closely and widely associated with domestic architecture in Greece. The peristyle was adapted to create a garden that was further embellished with fountains, pools and statues.[1213] The possibility to bring the garden into the house was opened up by the more sophisticated system of water supply that the Romans had created for public and private buildings. Previously, houses were provided with cisterns or wells, which were enough for the needs of the household, but not sufficient for the irrigation of gardens that were therefore settled close to natural water sources that ensured an adequate water supply.

5.4 Discussion

This chapter has sketched the developments of cities in Greece from the Archaic to the Late Antique period, focussing on specific areas of the urban environment and considering their evolution across the centuries. This overview was meant to assist in the interpretation of the data from Koroneia, by offering comparisons with other sites. Obviously this chapter has only scratched the surface of such a complex and vast subject; the main aim being to present the ancient city as an ever-changing but unified system that should not be artificially divided into disciplinary or chronological compartments.

The different configurations of Graeco-Roman towns that have been discussed in the first part of the chapter are the result of numerous interplaying factors related to the specific historical and geomorphological conditions of each urban centre. New foundations on empty lands offered more favourable ground for experimenting with efficient town planning, namely a regularly spaced distribution of *insulae*; while cities with a longer history are more likely to have grown into an organic or haphazard arrangement of space. In these cases, interventions resulting in considerable changes of the spatial configuration are usually related only to rebuilding after destructions caused by natural phenomena or wars.

Archaeological evidence pointing towards an orthogonal layout should not always be seen as related to a planned action, since a piecemeal development can also generate a regular overall appearance, given by the practical solution of leaning newly constructed houses against previous ones. From the 4th century BC onwards, it is possible to identify a preference for an orthogonal grid, which would be used even more commonly for new foundations during the Hellenistic period. Even in this case, however, several exceptions exist. In some sites, such as at Priene, the regular appearance of the city seems to have been preferred over a more practical arrangement that would have followed more closely the geomorphology of the site, while in other Hellenistic centres, such as at Petres of Florina, a previously gridded layout was given up for a more organic distribution of buildings on the hill's slopes.

Despite the fragmentary and often limited data that are available for some of the types of buildings and of the periods taken into consideration, this overview on the topography of Graeco-Roman towns has shown some general trends in the organization of space that are typical for each age. For example, the organization of the houses around a courtyard is a recurrent feature of domestic architecture from the Classical period onwards; the tendency towards monumentality in public architecture becomes more marked under Hellenistic rules as is the doubling up of the courtyard – one being turned into a decorative space, the other a smaller and peripheral retaining its Classical function; the phenomenon of subdivision is typically encountered in public buildings and houses during Late Antiquity.

These general trends should however not overshadow local variations, which can diverge substantially from what is considered typical for that period. This is the case of the Classical-Hellenistic houses at Lato whose rooms are arranged in a row contrary to the most common radial organization that is found in contemporary houses elsewhere, reflects the peculiar conservatism of Doric serf society

---

[1213] Carroll-Spillecke 1992, 94.

based on shared male citizen activity.[1214] Besides encouraging more studies on a regional level, this kind of evidence shows that there is still much to understand about the social and political processes underlying the city's formation and its development through time.

Recent lines of research investigate the human use of space,[1215] by retracing movement patterns connected to processions or rituals, or other leisure activities such as gaming, which are less visible in the archaeological record as not being architecturally defined. The emergence of sensory studies on ancient urban life is shedding light on how the ancient city was experienced and perceived at the human scale.[1216] Only a holistic study of the ancient city, which combines information from architectural remains, artefacts, literary and epigraphic sources, can succeed in gaining an as much as complete and vivid possible picture of urban life in antiquity, with the ultimate goal to bring individual narratives back into focus within the long term perspective of urban history.

[1214] Bintliff 2010; Bintliff 2012, 303.
[1215] See e.g. the works adopting Space Syntax theory to investigate the spatial organization of houses and its social meaning (for the Greek world see Lang 2005, Westgate 2007, and Bintliff 2014; for the Roman world, see e.g. Stöger 2011).
[1216] See e.g. Hamilakis 2013, the Routledge series on senses in antiquity, of which the first volume was published in 2015 (Bradley 2015), and Betts 2017.

6. Enhancing Koroneia's GIS survey data with the third dimension: A procedural modelling approach

'The Virtual-models are there to be worked with and on rather than consumed, and can and must be negotiated, modified and engaged in the exploration of connections and context inherent in the twin processes of collage and montage that Shanks sees as central to a developing mode of archaeological practice.' (Gillings 1999, 253).

6.1 Introduction

This chapter presents the methodology that I have adopted to create a GIS-based 3D visualization of the ancient town of Koroneia. The implementation of an intellectually transparent 3D visualization is particularly important in this study since comparative materials from other sites have been used (see previous chapter), and educated guesses play a major role in the reconstruction process. As discussed in chapter 4, there are, in fact, still many unknowns in Koroneia's urban layout both because the processing of the data collected during fieldwork is still in progress, and because some areas of the town are not accessible for survey due to overgrown vegetation and property's restrictions.

As highlighted in chapter 3, which reviewed current approaches to the use of 3D modelling in archaeology, the creation of intellectually transparent 3D models has been the target of only a handful of researchers, despite recent initiatives related to the issuing of guidelines on best practices and the launch of field specific journals that address these topics.[1217] Even more underrepresented are the applications focusing on the creation of a research-driven 3D visualization acting also as a heuristic and analytical tool. At Koroneia, the purpose of the 3D visualization was to enhance our understanding of the survey data and to use it as a tool to visualize and test different reconstruction hypotheses of the town layout. We assume in fact that the morphology of the terrain must have greatly influenced urban planning, posing constraints and offering opportunities for the laying out of the townscape. The adopted methodology required therefore to include the terrain morphology in the model in order to reconstruct the built environment – which heavily depends on the slope of the terrain. Such visualization would make it possible to investigate how buildings were constructed over the sloping ground and how many would fit within the estimated city wall circuit to formulate hypotheses regarding the town's population size.

The workflow to reach this result had therefore to be segmented across several software packages, that needed however to guarantee an optimal level of interoperability to avoid data loss in the export and import phases. Specifically, the 3D modelling software had to be able to handle the survey data that are stored in GIS file formats, to create a scene that could be exported in a format compatible with a game engine for the creation of the interactive navigation, and at the same time to be suitable for the efficient modelling and updating of a large built environment. In choosing the most suitable software packages, preference was given to a software that is supported by a large community and that for this reason has the highest probability of being maintained and preserved. At an early stage of this research, Autodesk 3D Studio Max (3DS) was used to create the first conceptual 3D models of Koroneia, in which different possible layouts of the ancient city were tested based on the preliminary results of pottery and architectural survey data combined. The choice fell on 3DS as this is one of the most used Computer Graphics (CG) software together with others such as Maya, Cinema 4D and the open source

---

[1217] See chapter 3, § 3.4.

Blender and it offers a variety of modelling tools and techniques that satisfy the needs of a wide range of applications for 3D models.

In our case, however, this manual modelling approach proved to be not ideal for several reasons. First of all, CG software generally do not support the handling of GIS based data (i.e. the correct retention of their spatial reference system),[1218] which was instead an important requirement for the Koroneia case study, both as we needed to replicate the import of GIS data several times and because we wanted to maintain a visual relationship between original data and 3D reconstruction. Secondly, the 3D visualisation of an entire city – and not just of a single building – poses additional challenges. Besides an efficient modelling of the environment in which a good balance is struck between polygons count and desirable level of detail, there is also the need to create realistic looking variations in the urban fabric. To this end, in 3DS I initially created a set of houses slightly different from one another in regard to the building arrangement and the textures used. For texturing, I made two different images for the houses' facades and four different images for the roofs and I assigned them to the houses. I then combined these slightly different houses in an *insula*-like arrangement, and manually positioned them on the terrain matching the available survey results.

This process was however quite time consuming and it did not provide satisfactory results in terms of realistic variations. Moreover, it would have been very inefficient on the long term, as a great amount of manual intervention is needed to change the 3D visualization in a CG software when new archaeological data become available, especially if considerable modifications are expected over the years as in the case of Koroneia where the study of the material is still in progress. Besides becoming clear that a more automatic approach was best suited for our case study, another requirement for our project was to work

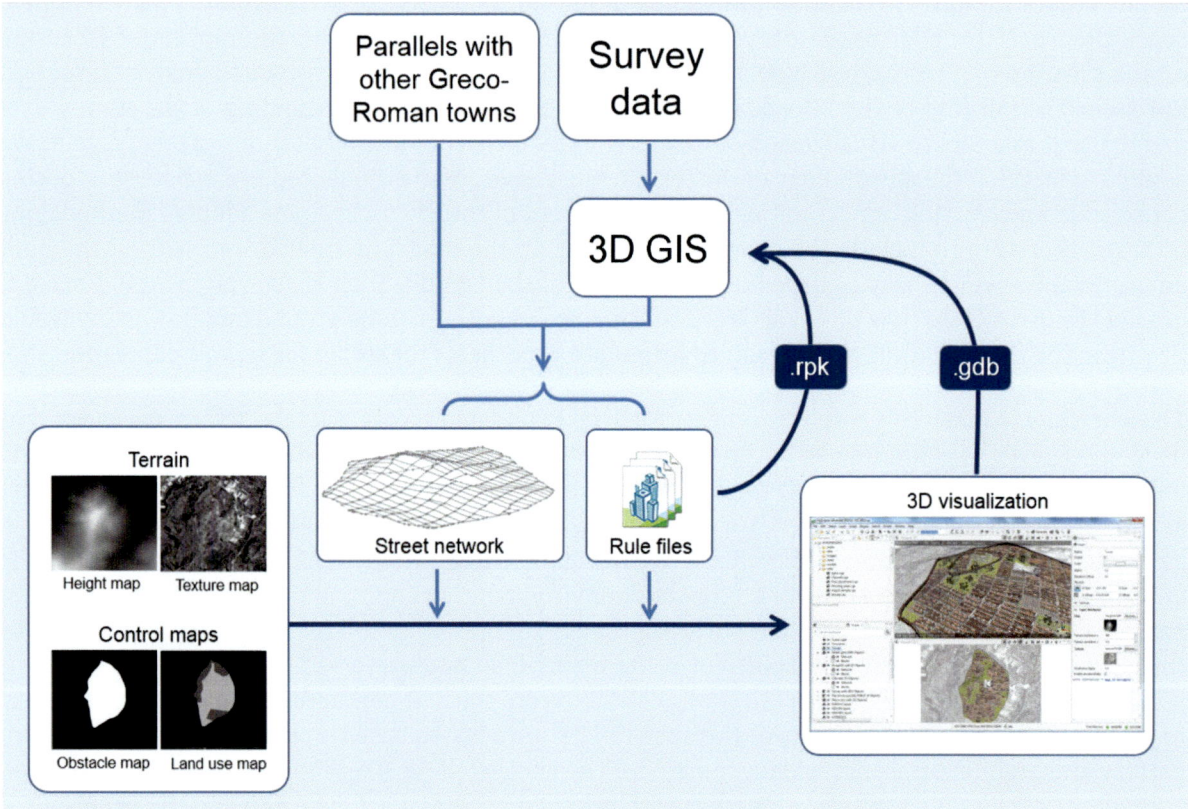

Figure 6.1 The workflow for the creation of Koroneia's 3D visualization.

[1218] In Blender, the interoperability with GIS has been addressed by the add-on BlenderGIS which enables users to import and, with some limitations, export geospatial data (https://github.com/domlysz/BlenderGIS).

in an environment that we could use more as a 'laboratory' to formulate hypotheses instead of only as a visualization of existing knowledge. While CG software packages are suitable for simulations, such as on the use of light and the perception of space as previously discussed, they were less appropriate in our case, where we wanted to combine several layers of information that could function as a tool to enable a more analytical approach towards the built environment.

To fulfil these requirements, we employed advanced techniques based on GIS and procedural modelling that are employed in geo-design and modern urban planning, and that allow a high degree of automation in the process of transforming 2D data into a 3D environment. This chapter presents the workflow that I have developed, which consists of three phases: 1) 3D mapping of the finds onto the Digital Elevation Model of the hill to visualize their distribution and characteristics as recorded during fieldwork; 2) reconstruction of the ancient terrain and the possible layout of the *polis* in the 4th century BC, which corresponds to a moment of possible disruption in the urban life resulting from the *andrapodismos* that the Koroneians suffered in 346 BC;[1219] 3) experimentation with setting up an interactive first-person walk-through to allow a more experiential navigation in the virtual environment and with implementing a platform to communicate our interpretation in the future. Additional elements will be discussed, such as the contribution of this methodology towards the implementation of intellectually transparent and reusable 3D reconstructions. The chapter closes with a discussion on the advantages and disadvantages of using the suggested approach and some possible future applications for Koroneia's 3D environment.[1220]

6.2 Workflow

The approach that I have adopted to deal with the data of this complex urban site is based on the exploitation of GIS in combination with procedural modelling techniques. CityEngine, whose characteristics have been already presented in chapter 3, has been chosen as the procedural modelling software because of its modelling capabilities and its interoperability with ArcGIS. While CityEngine has been already used for the reconstruction of several archaeological sites,[1221] the methodology here presented exploits to the fullest the connection between CityEngine and ArcGIS in order to create a 3D GIS that comprises both the original survey data and the reconstruction hypotheses of the ancient urban layout.

The adopted workflow is summarized in figure 6.1. Comparisons with other Graeco-Roman towns in the Boeotia region and elsewhere in Greece created the framework for the interpretation of the survey data of the Boeotia project, many of which were already stored in a GIS environment.[1222] As will be described in more detail in the following paragraphs, I have written *ad hoc* procedural rules that I have applied 1) as a procedural symbology layer in ArcGIS, which exposes the properties of the architectural dataset (i.e. dimensions and stone type) in an automatic and more customizable way than standard 3D symbology; and 2) to the reconstructed terrain and street network to create a 3D reconstruction hypothesis of the ancient *polis*.

Importantly, each of the components that is included in this methodology and in the chart displayed in figure 6.1 can be modified in isolation from the others, thus enabling an efficient workflow given that data are still being collected in our study. Moreover, the same rule can be applied to an updated dataset, making it possible to iteratively change the 3D scene when new data are available or new hypotheses have to be visualized.

[1219] See chapter 4, p. 92
[1220] The ongoing results of this project have been published in Piccoli 2014 and Piccoli 2016.
[1221] See chapter 3, p. 58.
[1222] By Bart Noordervliet and Janneke van Zwienen.

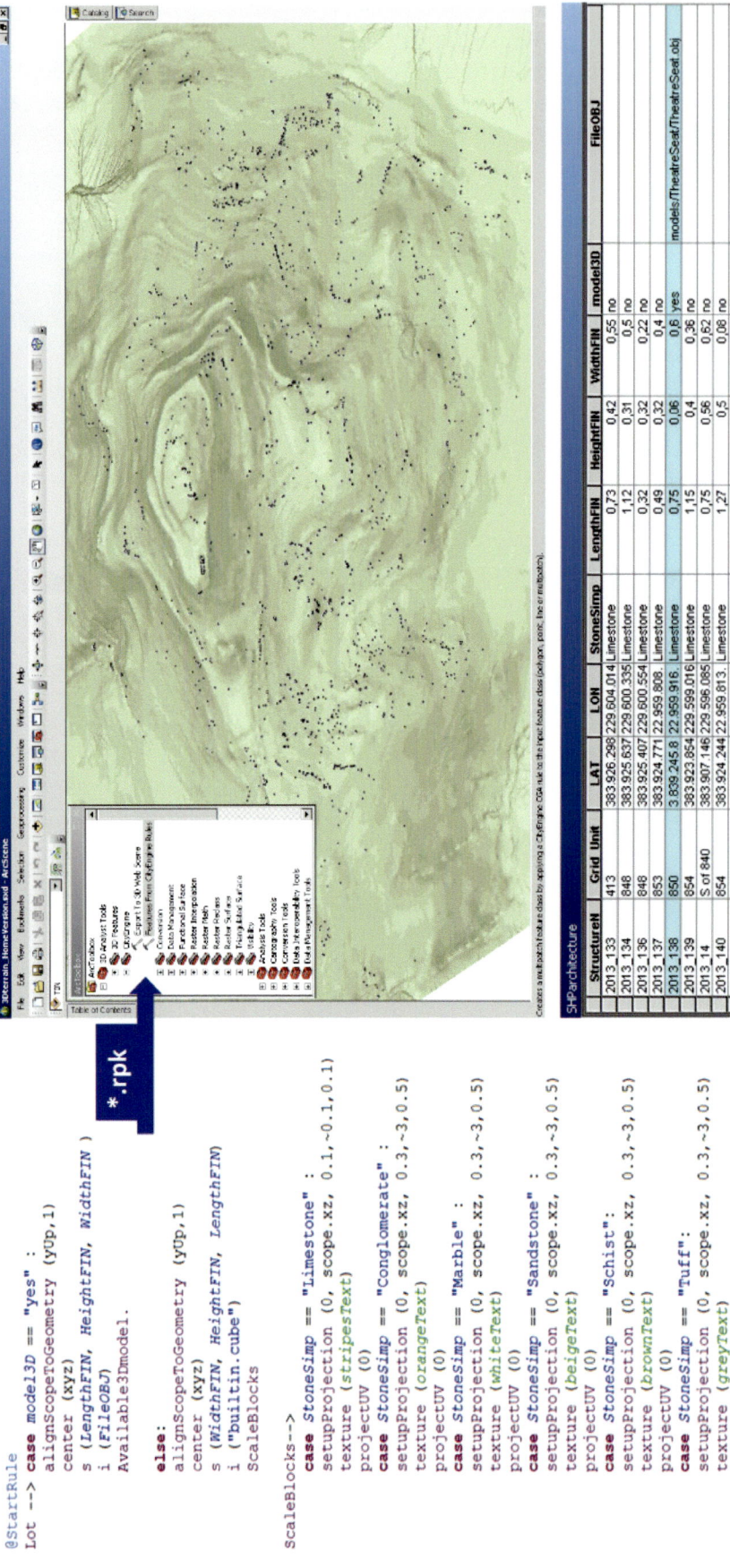

Figure 6.2 Left: Part of the procedural rule written in CityEngine which evaluates the information contained in the specified columns in the architectural pieces' shapefile (e.g. LengthFIN, HeightFIN sand WidthFIN) to modulate size and appearance of the architectural finds based on their characteristics as recorded in the field.

6. Enhancing Koroneia's GIS survey data with the third dimension

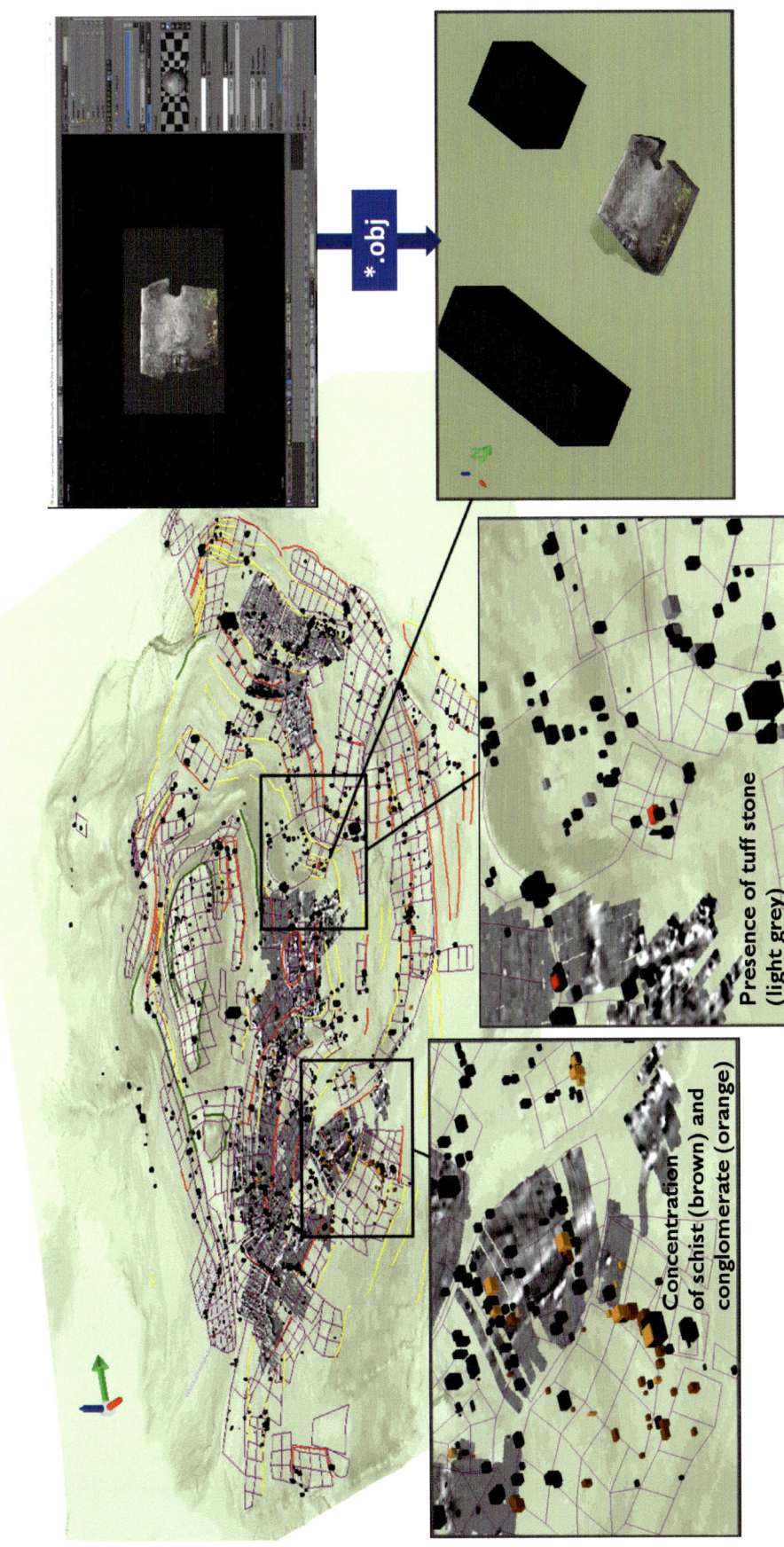

Figure 6.3 An example of some data layers of Koroneia's 3D GIS: the DEM with overlaid grid of the areas that were accessible during the survey, the terraces mapped during the geomorphological survey, the provisional results of the ongoing geophysical prospections, and the architectural finds. The latter are scaled according to their dimensions (here multiplied by a factor of 10 for visualization purposes) as recorded in the field, and categorized per stone type with a procedural rule that was written in CityEngine and imported in ArcGIS. In this way, clusters of stones, the relationship between the dimension of the blocks and the stone type, and special finds (of which 3D models are automatically imported as OBJ files) become immediately apparent.

6.2.1 A rule-based 3D GIS of architectural survey data

The aim of the first phase of this work was the creation of a 3D GIS of the survey data that are currently available, which enables us to have an intuitive overview of the relationships between various data layers, such as terrain morphology, terraces and concentration of finds. To this end, I wrote an *ad hoc* procedural rule in CityEngine (see Figure 6.2), which interrogates the attribute table of the shapefile containing the architectural elements, substitutes the latter with blocks that are scaled according to the real dimensions of the finds as recorded in the field (i.e. length, width and height), and associates different textures to the blocks based on the types of stone they are made of. The rule is exported from CityEngine in *.rpk (rule package) format, which compresses the rule and related assets (e.g. textures), and is applied to the selected 2D features using the CityEngine toolbox that has been introduced in ArcGIS 10.2 among the 3D Analyst tools (see Figure 6.2).

Specifically, the shapefile of the architectural pieces contains information on their dimensions (in columns LengthFIN, HeightFIN, and WidthFIN) and on their stone type (column StoneType). Moreover, I have added an additional column (FileOBJ) that contains the relative path to a more detailed (manually modelled) 3D model of the architectural piece in case this is available (see Figure 6.2, bottom). Besides modulating size and appearance of the architectural blocks, the rule includes the possibility to automatically substitute 3D models of special finds to their corresponding position on the DEM of the hill. For this purpose, I modified the attribute table of the shapefile containing the architectural blocks' coordinates and description by adding two columns, one storing the Boolean values 'yes' or 'no', which indicates the availability of a 3D model, and the other containing the relative path of the 3D model's file (see Figure 6.2). The pictures that were available of the finds were not suitable for a photogrammetry-based 3D model; therefore, I manually modelled some of the architectural finds in Blender using the pictures and the measurements taken on site as reference. This is the case for example of the carved limestone block (catalogue nr. 2013_138) that was found in the vicinity of the location of Koroneia's theatre, now lost, and initially identified as a possible theatre seat. The 3D model of the piece was then saved in OBJ format and automatically imported in ArcScene with the above mentioned rule file.

This workflow therefore extends the current possibilities offered by ArcGIS 3D symbology, which allows the user only to automatically stretch a flat 2D shape according to a predefined height (i.e. to vertically extrude lines and polygons) and to categorize the finds with different textures. The procedural rule, instead, allows the automatic scaling of the initial 2D shape according to all three dimensions (width, depth and height), and the automatic import of pre-made 3D models of finds on their correct location. This results in a more realistic visualization of the surveyed pieces, and thus in a more intuitive interpretation of the finds.

Interpretative visualization for intuitive insights into data clusters

By applying in ArcScene the procedural rule that interrogates the attribute table of the shapefile containing the architectural elements, and modulates their size and appearance according to their dimension as recorded in the field, concentrations of smaller or bigger blocks, clusters of specific types of stone or special finds become immediately visible. In addition, possible correlations between the dimensions of blocks and their stone type can be easily spotted by zooming into the 3D scene (Figure 6.3). Among the visible clusters that clearly stand out after applying the above mentioned rule, there is a concentration of schist and large conglomerate blocks, which emerges from the predominant limestone (textured in black) to the south-east, close to the city wall circuit. Assuming that larger blocks were used for more impressive architecture, such as buildings with a public character, this concentration may point towards the presence of a relatively large building, perhaps a church or

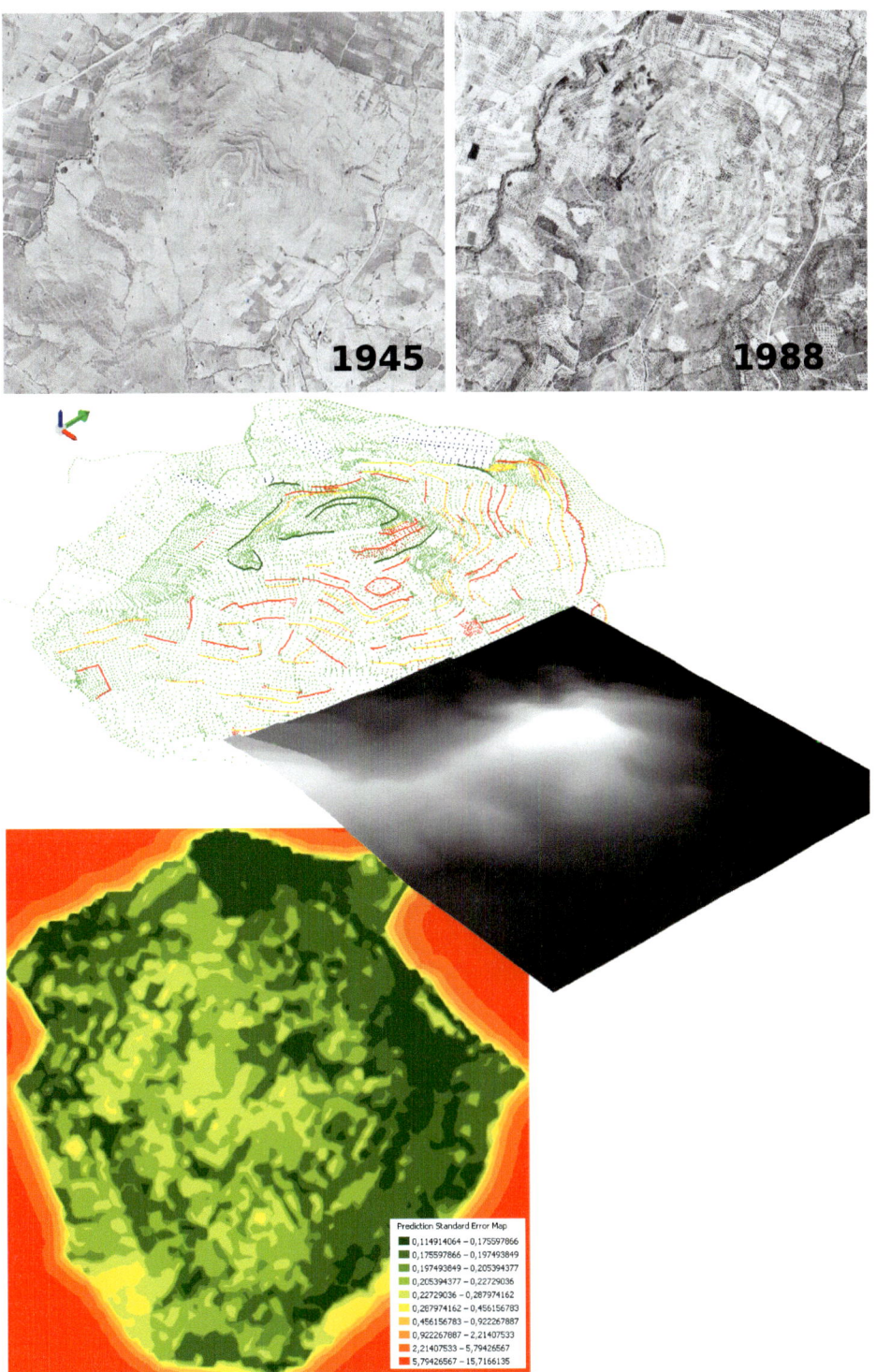

Figure 6.4 Top: Examples of historical aerial imagery that was used together with the terraces mapped by age (overlaid on the DGPS points representing the current terrain morphology) as guides to create a reconstruction hypothesis of the terrain in antiquity. Green lines represent ancient terraces, red lines modern terraces, yellow lines terraces of uncertain age. Points were added to (represented in blue) or subtracted from those originally recorded on the hill during the microtopographic survey. As a result, a new DEM was created by interpolating the points in ArcGIS using a Kriging interpolation method (see prediction error map). This DEM was then stylized as a grey scale image and exported in TIFF format to be used as a terrain heightmap in CityEngine.

a villa.[1223] Moreover, a high number of blocks made of tuff, a relatively soft stone that lends itself to carving and moulding, is visible on the plateau where the agora was located and on the nearby hollow which was occupied by the theatre.

This rule allows, moreover, the automatic placement of the textured 3D models of architectural finds directly on their findspot. This solution is particularly useful for including 3D models of special architectural elements, such as decorated or uncommon pieces, that can therefore be easily spotted by navigating the DEM in the 3D GIS environment. As visible in Figure 6.3, the 3D model of a carved block that I have created in Blender from pictures and measurements taken *in situ* has been automatically loaded onto the position of the piece as was recorded by the GPS during fieldwork.

6.2.2 Reconstruction of the ancient terrain morphology and urban layout

The second phase of the workflow comprised the modelling of a reconstruction hypothesis both for the ancient terrain and for the ancient town. The main sources for the creation of the ancient terrain were the results of the geomorphological survey conducted by Keith Wilkinson[1224] and historical aerial imagery which I have used as a comparison to trace back the modifications that the hill underwent. Specifically, images from 1945, 1960 and 1988 acquired by the project from the Ministry of Agriculture show the progressive agricultural intake of the hill by farmers and the creation of paths to navigate around the hill (see Figure 6.4). The points that were recorded in the field with a DGPS were deleted and new ones were added in ArcScene where modern modifications needed to be smoothed off or filled. In order to facilitate the interpolation of the new DEM, for example, I added points to fill in the large quarry that was opened on the north-western side of the hill in modern times and the two gullies that were caused by rainwater washing away the slopes made of unstable low grade geology (Figure 6.4).

It must be noted that the goal of this process was to reach a plausible hypothesis of the shape of the terrain before the beginning of the agricultural work, one of the main causes of change in the hill morphology. While at this stage it is impossible to 'reconstruct' with certainty the terrain morphology as it used to be in antiquity, it is however possible that the continuation of the archaeological investigation and the geomorphological survey will offer additional data to reconstruct the level of the ancient terrain at least in some parts of the town, e.g. based on the depth of the buried archaeological finds in case of excavation. For this reason, I

Figure 6.5 A TIFF image of the geophysical results and the in situ walls (in red) is imported as map layer in CityEngine, thus allowing the retention of the visual and spatial relationship between the original data and the reconstructed street network.

[1223] See chapter 4, p. 126.
[1224] See chapter 4, p. 106.

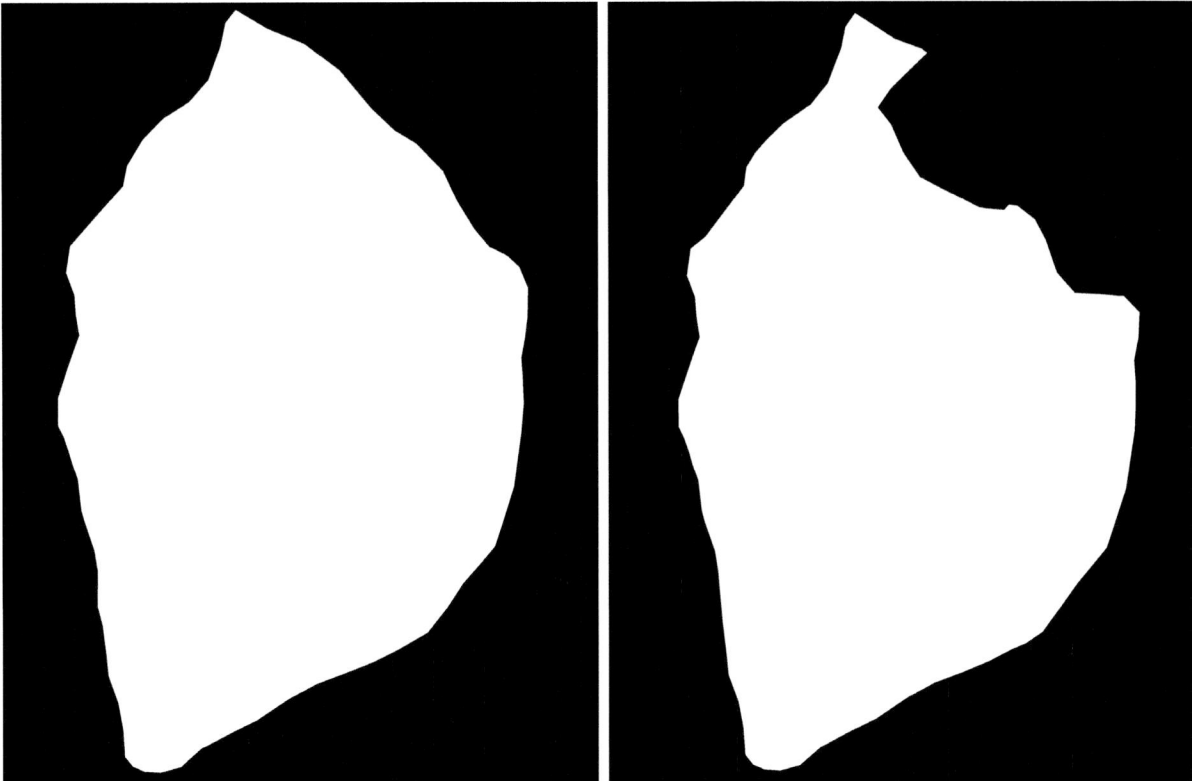

Figure 6.6 The two obstacle maps that limit the generation of the 3D environment only within the white area. Left: the obstacle map covers the largest town extent with the northern stretch at the foot of the slope according to the surveyed architectural remains; right: obstacle map covering the town extent when the geophysical features are considered (for the discussion of the available archaeological evidence, see chapter 4).

have documented all the steps I took in creating the new DEM. Specifically, I have stored all the points that I have deleted or added in separate shapefiles in order to keep the record of the operations that I have performed to change the DEM. After some experimentation and comparison between models created with different interpolation methods, a terrain model resulting from a Kriging interpolation method was used.[1225] The output raster was subsequently stylized as a grey scale image (stretch type: Minimum-Maximum) and exported in TIFF format to be used as a height map for the terrain generation in CityEngine (Figure 6.4).

Map layers

CityEngine offers several so called map layers for the customization of the 3D environment; specifically these are the terrain, texture, obstacle, mapping, and function layers.[1226] The use of map layers is very advantageous to control the city generation, especially in our case when new data can modify our

---

[1225] Ordinary Kriging, model type: Gaussian; Prediction Errors (samples 18547 of 18547):
Mean: -0,013356726893272162
Root-Mean-Square: 0,4033660270359244
Mean Standardized: -0,020829271931495624
Root-Mean-Square Standardized: 0,7823976642156636
Average Standard Error: 0,5374845926168181. The data evaluation and models comparison were carried out following these resources: https://www.azavea.com/blog/2016/09/12/kriging-spatial-interpolation-desktop-gis/; http://desktop.arcgis.com/en/arcmap/latest/extensions/geostatistical-analyst/comparing-models.htm (accessed Sept. 2016).
[1226] For an overview of map layers and their usage, see the CityEngine user manual at http://cehelp.esri.com/help/index.jsp?topic=/com.procedural.cityengine.help/html/manual/al/edit_al_f.html (accessed Sept. 2016).

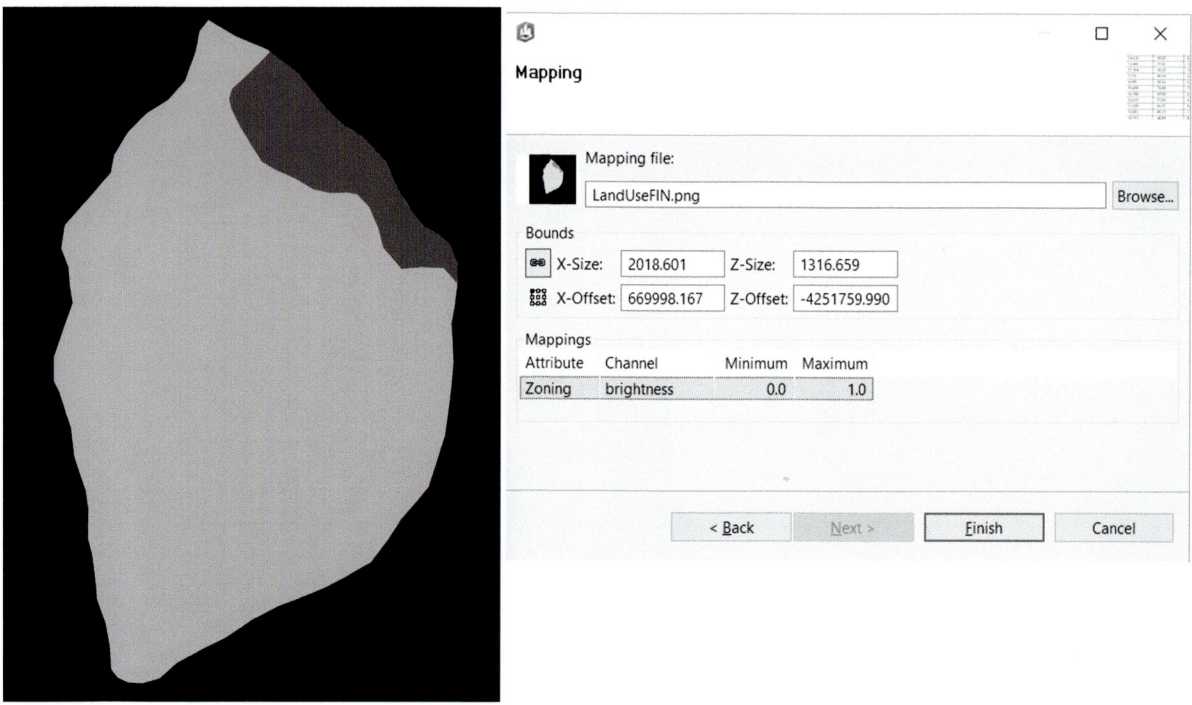

Figure 6.7 Left: TIFF image loaded as attribute layer in CityEngine to guide the creation of different land uses; Right: Window menu that allows the creation of an attribute (i.e. 'Zoning') associated with the land use map.

```
import rule : "Individual_houses_slope.cga"

attr Zoning = 0
attr red   = "#FF0000"
attr green = "#00FF00"
attr blue  = "#0000FF"
attr white = "#FFFFFF"

@StartRule
LandUseType =     case Zoning > 0.5 && Zoning < 1 :
                      "buildingLot"
          else : "vegetation"

Lot --> case LandUseType == "buildingLot" :
              rule.Lot
        case LandUseType == "vegetation" :
              report("Area.Greenspace",geometry.area) rule.LotVegetation
     else : NIL

Garden --> report("Area.Greenspace",geometry.area) rule.Garden
```

Figure 6.8 Rule file that guides the mapping of different land uses according to the input image represented in Figure 6.7.

knowledge about the ancient morphology or the urban layout. Each of the images that represent a layer can in fact be updated and the visualization will adapt accordingly to the new input data. By using map layers, it is moreover possible to easily generate different reconstruction hypotheses in a time efficient manner. To my knowledge, this possibility has never been exploited before in other archaeological projects that have used CityEngine as their main software environment.

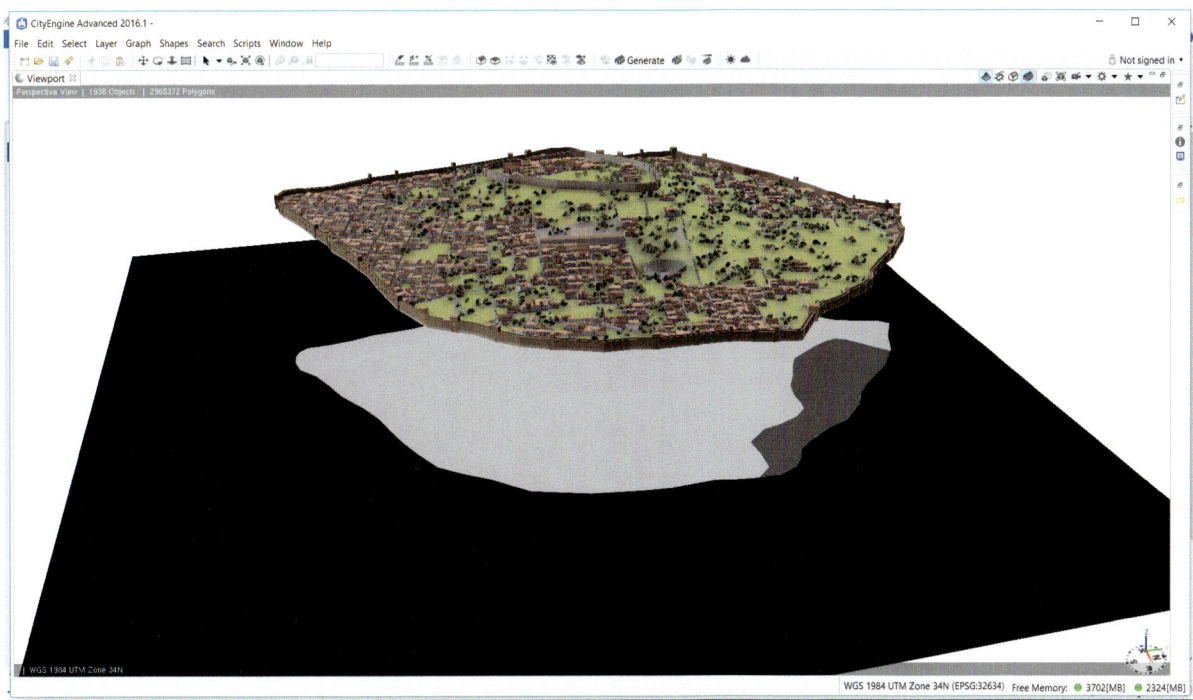

Figure 6.9 Screenshot from the CityEngine viewport showing the results of the application of the attribute map (visualized as the black and grey image underneath the reconstructed town). This map assigns the rule for the creation of buildings to the light grey area and the rule for the generation of vegetation to the darker grey area. In this way, it is possible to quickly create two reconstruction hypotheses that show the northern area of the town as either sparely or more densely built up.

The terrain layer is created by importing a heightmap and a texture and by defining the minimum and maximum elevation values to which the greyscale image corresponds. Since the heightmap for Koroneia was created by modifying the georeferenced DEM of the hill, the TIFF file already contained the correct spatial reference which was then automatically recognized by CityEngine upon import. Additionally, I have created a TIFF image containing the geophysical results and the *in situ* walls in ArcGIS and imported this as an additional map layer. In this way, I was able to keep the reference with the geophysical data while creating the reconstruction hypotheses for the urban layout (Figure 6.5).

Another map layer that I used for Koroneia's case study is the 'obstacle map', a black and white image that defines a Boolean attribute used to limit the generation of the 3D scene within its white areas. I have created such images in GIS by drawing a polygon over the supposed perimeter of the city wall (see chapter 4, Figure 4.32), which was assigned a white colour, and by stylizing the underlying DEM with a black colour (see Figure 6.6). Since parts of Koroneia's perimeter are uncertain, I created two separate obstacle maps. One obstacle map represents the largest projected circuit on the northern slope (the orange line in Figure 4.32) which projects the line of the city wall stretch identified during the architectural survey at the north-western foot of the hill. The other obstacle map stops instead at the features identified by the geophysical survey on the northern slope as a possible city wall stretch and reconnects with the line of the city wall identified during the architectural survey (Figure 6.6, right following the yellow line in Figure 4.32).

Finally, I have used the so called 'mapping attribute layer' to distinguish between buildings and open spaces in the creation of Koroneia's 3D scene. In general, this layer makes it possible to assign different rule files to a lot, depending on its location. It is possible to use a RGB image or a greyscale image as a mapping attribute layer. The different colours or grey intensities are then used in CityEngine to map different land uses. In Koroneia's case, I have created a greyscale image in ArcMap to map

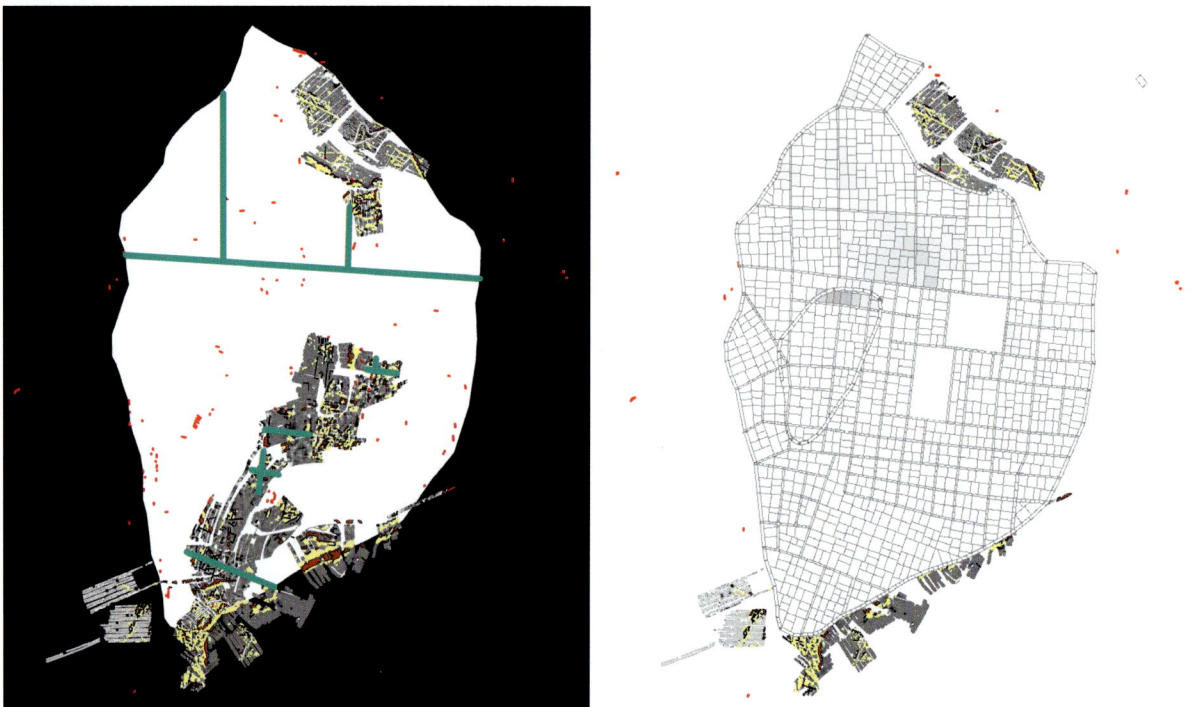

Figure 6.10 Left: Screenshot from ArcMap's workspace displaying the geophysical results and the in situ wall stretches which have informed the reconstruction of the street network (in blue, the lines that were stored in a shapefile and imported as input data into CityEngine); Right: The reconstructed urban grid adapted to the terrain in one of the proposed hypotheses.

two hypotheses regarding the northern slope of the town by modifying one of the obstacle maps. In more detail, I assigned a light grey shade to the intra-mural area and manually mapped the area that appears to be empty of buildings in the northern part of the town with a darker shade of grey (Figure 6.7, left). Upon import of the map layer into CityEngine, I have set an attribute ('Zoning') and specified what kind of channel had to be used to interpret the image (in this case, brightness) and the minimum and maximum values within the channel (from 0.0 t0 1.0) (see Figure 6.7, right). I have then written a rule file which relates a land use to a specific range of values (Figure 6.8). Specifically, the rule containing the formal description of domestic architecture and the agora was assigned to the areas mapped with the lighter shade of grey, while the rule that creates green spaces was associated with the areas mapped in darker grey. Upon generation of the environment, the rule evaluates the parameters in the image and creates the geometry which corresponds to the assigned values (see Figure 6.9).

For the moment, this map facilitated the creation of a reconstruction hypothesis of the larger town extent showing sparse habitation on the lower norther slope. This scenario visualizes the results of the geophysical survey which has yielded only faint traces of occupation on the northern sector of the town. In the future, however, when the results of the pottery data will be available, this mapping will be useful to further refine the creation of different areas within the town – e.g. discerning putative residential and public areas – and map the expansion and contraction of the town through the centuries.

Street network

After importing the obstacle maps, I have created a reconstruction hypothesis of the street network based on the available survey results. I have used the streets that were identified during the geophysical

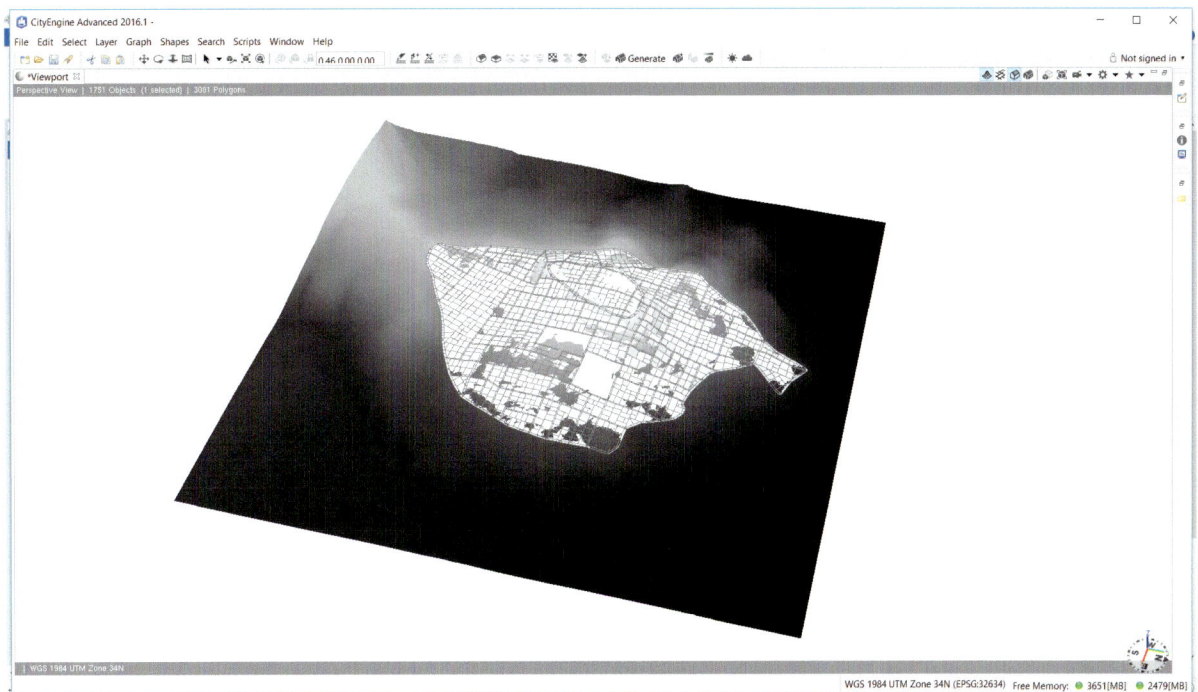

Figure 6.11 Screenshot from CityEngine showing the overlap between the terrain heightmap and the layer with streets and blocks.

survey as the starting point for the generation of the entire street system. Our working hypothesis is that the regular grid that appears both in the geophysical prospections and in the surveyed *in situ* wall lines is part of the same network and can be dated to the 4th century BC. As discussed in chapters 4 and 5, this assumption is based on comparisons with other sites where a (roughly) orthogonal grid started to be used in this century and was maintained until Late Antiquity.[1227] I have digitized the few streets that have been recognised in the geophysical survey in GIS, added and extended the orientation of the surveyed *in situ* wall stretches, imported into CityEngine the shapefile containing the graph and used this as input for street generation (Figure 6.10). To avoid having to manually set the streets' width, I have stored in the attribute table the width of the known streets as these values are recognized by CityEngine and are automatically used to model the correct width. I have then selected these few streets and launched the 'grow street' operation, which offers several parameters to guide the street creation. These include the possibility to set the number of streets, to decide the pattern of major and minor streets (either organic, radial or raster), and to use the environment as a constraint. Specifically, a maximum-allowed street slope can be set and the terrain and obstacle map can be given as parameters.

Each street in CityEngine is typically composed of a series of segments (major or minor edges) connected by nodes, both having as features a number of shapes which represent the surfaces creating the proper street and the adjoining sidewalks. Since the first input consisted of only a few streets, it was necessary to repeat the operation several times and include some manually drawn streets to cover the entire urban area. By running the 'align graph to terrain' tool, the nodes of the graph network have been then automatically aligned with the heightmap representing the terrain.

After creating the graph representing the street network, the software automatically filled in the spaces between streets' segments and created so called 'lots', namely adjacent polygons that are the starting point for rule based modelling. In fact, CGA rules can only be applied to surfaces. Once again, a set of parameters governs the appearance of such lots, such as the way in which they are subdivided and their

---

[1227] See esp. pp. 141 and 155.

```
// ATTRIBUTES
@Group ("LEVEL OF DETAIL")
@Range (Low = 0, High = 1)
attr LOD       = 0 //controls vegetation's detail
attr HighLOD   = true //controls buildings' detail

@Group ("VEGETATION")
attr TreesNumber = 2
attr TreeHeightMin = 5
attr TreeHeightMax = 10

@Group ("HOUSES DIMENSIONS")
attr RoofShedSlope = 10
attr wall = 0.6
attr DoorOpeningRange = rand (1.2, 1.6) // cf. Halos, Haagsma 2003, 43.
attr WingHeightTotal = groundfloorHeight +0.4
attr groundfloorHeight = 2.2
attr firstfloorHeight = 2
```

Figure 6.12 Example of the parameters that I have set as attributes in the rule for domestic architecture. Note the addition of explanatory comments preceded in this case by a double slash (//) to exclude them from the parsed code.

```
// CATEGORIZATION OF HOUSES' FOOTPRINT SIZE
footprintSize(geometry_area) =
/* Classical houses greatly varied in size:
 A database of more than 300 hundred examples of houses in the Aegean from 800 to 300 BC
shows a progressive increase in house size (Morris 2005, 108). In Athens some of the houses
in the 5th c. BC residential block on the north foot of the Areopagus were as small as 50-
70 m2 (Nevett 1999, 86), while Houses C and D near the Great Drain were 130 and 225 m2
respectively (Nevett 1999, 88). Evidence from Athens, Attica and Leucas shows that an
average sized 5th and 4th c. BC dwelling covered around 130 m2 (Konecny 2013, Fiedler 2005,
Nevett 2005, Tsakirgis 2005).
 The 'typical' 4th c. BC Olynthian house of the North Hill covered around 294 m2, while the
houses on Row A were on average 350 m2 (Ault 2005, 66).
 Exceptionally larger houses are also attested as the House of the Mosaics at Eretria with
an area of 625 m2 (Bintliff 2012, 300).
 */
    case geometry_area <= 50: "empty"
    case geometry_area >50 && geometry_area<= 70: "VerySmall"
    case geometry_area >70 && geometry_area<= 130: "Small"
    case geometry_area > 130 && geometry_area <= 300: "Medium"
    case geometry_area > 300 && geometry_area <= 400: "Large"
    else : "VeryLarge"
```

Figure 6.13 Lines from the rule of domestic architecture which categorize the houses according to their size. Note the insertion of comments, which explain the modelling choices that are recorded in the rule files. In this case the multi-line explanation is excluded by the processed script by adding / and */ at its beginning and end (cf. other scripting languages such as C).*

dimensions, how they are aligned over the terrain and whether each of them should have access to the street or not. The minimum and maximum size of the blocks can be set either manually under 'Block parameters' in the inspector, or automatically by using the 'function' map layer. I chose for the latter approach as I wanted to reduce the amount of manual work that was needed to create Koroneia's 3D environment and its following updates as much as possible. The allowed lot sizes range between 50 and 400 square meters, thus giving a representative sample of the variations in house sizes that have been observed in Classical – Hellenistic sites in Greece.[1228]

[1228] See chapter 5, p. 196, and the rule file for domestic architecture, agora area and vegetation (also in Figure 6.13) for a comparison of house plots across sites in mainland Greece.

Figure 6.14 Examples of the procedurally modelled house shapes: Type 2 (top, left); Type 3 (top, right); Type 4, in this instance with closed ground floor (bottom, left), and type 5 (bottom, right). Scan the QR code to view a 3D model of one of the houses on SketchFab.

```
attr porch = 70% : true
          else : false
```

Figure 6.15 Example of how an attribute (in this case 'porch') is used to guide the random, yet controlled generation of 3D geometry. In this case, 70% of the instances will be created with a porch, while the rest will be assigned a closed ground floor.

By comparing the actual appearance of the terrain and the obtained surface created by streets and lots, one notices that the latter does not follow exactly the former, but it approximates it to a degree that depends on several factors, mainly on the amount of nodes that have been introduced in each street and on the size of each lot. It is therefore necessary to create streets that contain several nodes in order to facilitate the alignment between the terrain and the reconstructed environment. It must be noted, however, that in case of hilly sites a certain degree of approximation will be introduced in any case between the original terrain data and the streets/lot layer (see Figure 6.11); it is therefore important to realize this when running analyses and simulations such as those that will be discussed later on in this chapter, as the results will be affected by it.[1229]

6.2.3 Rule based modelling of Koroneia's 3D reconstruction

The core of the methodology discussed in this chapter consists of writing a set of CGA rules for the creation of domestic architecture and vegetation, streets and city walls with towers that are used to populate Koroneia's 3D reconstruction. A sample of the rules is available at https://github.com/cpiccoli/rules. In the next paragraphs, I will discuss their main characteristics.

[1229] One has to remember in fact that CityEngine's primary application is geodesign, to create several different development scenarios in 3D to communicate with other parties and involve communities in the decision making process, see in this respect the tutorials developed by Geodan and VU University Amsterdam at http://wiki.bk.tudelft.nl/toi-pedia/CityEngine_Open_Course (last accessed March 2017).

Figure 6.16 Top: Examples of the images that I have created for texturing and bump mapping (texture/ bump image for doors; texture for the outer walls). Bottom: Example of rendering (in e-on VUE Infinite 2015 PLE) of the procedurally modelled town with textures applied.

Domestic architecture

The overview of excavated houses that I have presented in chapter 5[1230] has informed the parametric description of domestic architecture in the rule files that I have written for Koroneia's 3D visualization. I have created a series of attributes and constants which precedes the starting point of the rule, by which I controlled the houses' dimensions and the vegetation density (Figures. 6.12 and 6.13). Declaring the attributes at the beginning of the rule allows an easy overview of the available parameters and the quick modification of the numerical values or relationships between attributes, that are then passed down wherever the attribute is mentioned in the rule file. The rule gives moreover the possibility to choose between different configurations of space based on the size of the initial lot, e.g. in regards to the presence and dimension of the courtyard, the extension and appearance of an upper floor (covering the whole surface of the house, only the back, or either side of the courtyard).

I have adopted different modelling strategies to create some variations in the configuration of space and position of the courtyard. In Greek architecture, in fact, the peristyle was introduced towards the transition with the Hellenistic period. I have therefore created an option where the peristyle is present,

---

[1230] See pp. 194-200.

6. Enhancing Koroneia's GIS survey data with the third dimension

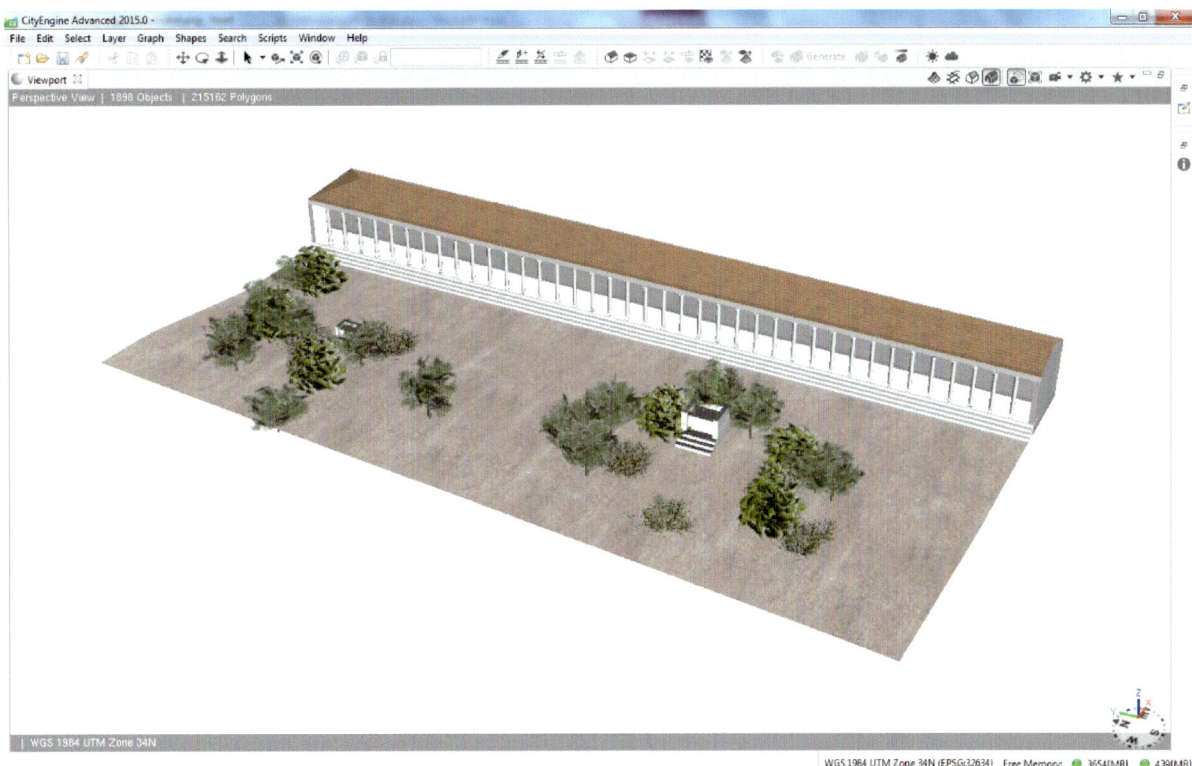

Figure 6.17 The procedurally modelled agora area which is occupied by a long stoa on the eastern side and scattered trees and altars on the open space.

but I had to model also other house types, typically with the courtyard having a porch on some of its sides but not all four of them. The resulting house types have been modelled in 5 different ways (see Figure 6.14):

1. A house without courtyard (by extruding the initial lot in its entirety according to different heights).
2. A two-storey house with in front a courtyard surrounded by one or two wings (by splitting the initial lot in two and modelling each part separately).
3. An L-shaped two-storey house with two sides overlooking the courtyard (using the built-in 'shapeL' operation).
4. A U-shaped two-storey house that surrounds the central courtyard (using the built-in 'shapeU' operation).
5. An O-shaped two-storey house that surrounds the central courtyard (using the built-in 'shapeO' operation).

The different options are generated according to the size of the initial lots: for example, in small lots option 1 is created, while option 4 is assigned to lots that occupy a large area. To further increase the variability among house types, I have included two different possibilities for the ground floor, one which creates a porch (which results in a house similar to the Olynthian standard house, typically House A vii 4) and the other which creates a closed wall and an entrance door. The two options function through the attribute 'porch' which sets the percentage of its presence (Figure 6.15).

The textures that are used to visualize the external appearance of walls, wooden and stone elements, and roofs, were either created in GIMP or re-used from training projects (e.g. the courtyard textures are

Figure 6.18 The 3D model of the theatre (in OBJ format) that I have created in Blender and imported into the CityEngine using an ad hoc rule. To create some vegetation around the theatre, I have used a scatter operation which randomly places on the surface a set number of 3D models of trees according to a Gaussian distribution. Left: The original 3D model of the theatre as modelled in Blender; right: screenshot from the CityEngine viewport showing the result of the application of the CGA rule file (with vegetation displayed with a high LoD).

taken from the medieval town project, which is part of CityEngine's training materials)[1231]. For buildings, I have created different images for both texture and bump mapping (which simulates irregularities on the surface) of walls, doors and windows (see Figure 6.16).

Agora

The CGA code that guides the modelling of the agora is included in the rule for domestic architecture and can be initiated from the so called inspector panel using the tag 'Agora'. The provisional results of the geophysical prospections seem to show an elongated building bordering the eastern side of the agora, while the rest of the area seems to have been left empty.[1232] Currently I have adopted the interpretation that this long building was indeed a *stoa* and I have therefore modelled the agora with a long *stoa* on its eastern side, leaving the rest as an unbuilt space where some trees and altars are scattered (Figure 6.17). The inclusion of the altars is at the moment based only on Pausanias' account, which describes the agora in his own times, but confirms the reasonable assumption that there were probably some altars on Koroneia's agora also in the 4th century BC. Since no archaeobotanical investigations have been carried out on Koroneia's hill, for the moment I have used 3D models of generic trees, for example plane trees in the agora as they are attested in

```
attr amphiprostyle = true
Temple  --> BaseRoof
          Podium t(0,podiumH,0) color( TempleColor )
          TempleTypes

TempleTypes--> case amphiprostyle == true :
             split (x) { 3 : BackTemple
                       | ~1 : cella
                       | 3 : FrontTemple }
       else :    split (x) { ~1 : cella
                           | 2 : FrontTemple }
```

Figure 6.19 Lines added in the rule file for temple architecture to be able to visualize two possible reconstruction hypotheses of the supposed Itonion.

[1231] Available at http://www.arcgis.com/home/item.html?id=2ac365326981411783b1fa6f0d5e9714 (last accessed March 2017).
[1232] Cf. chapter 4, p. 130.

6. Enhancing Koroneia's GIS survey data with the third dimension

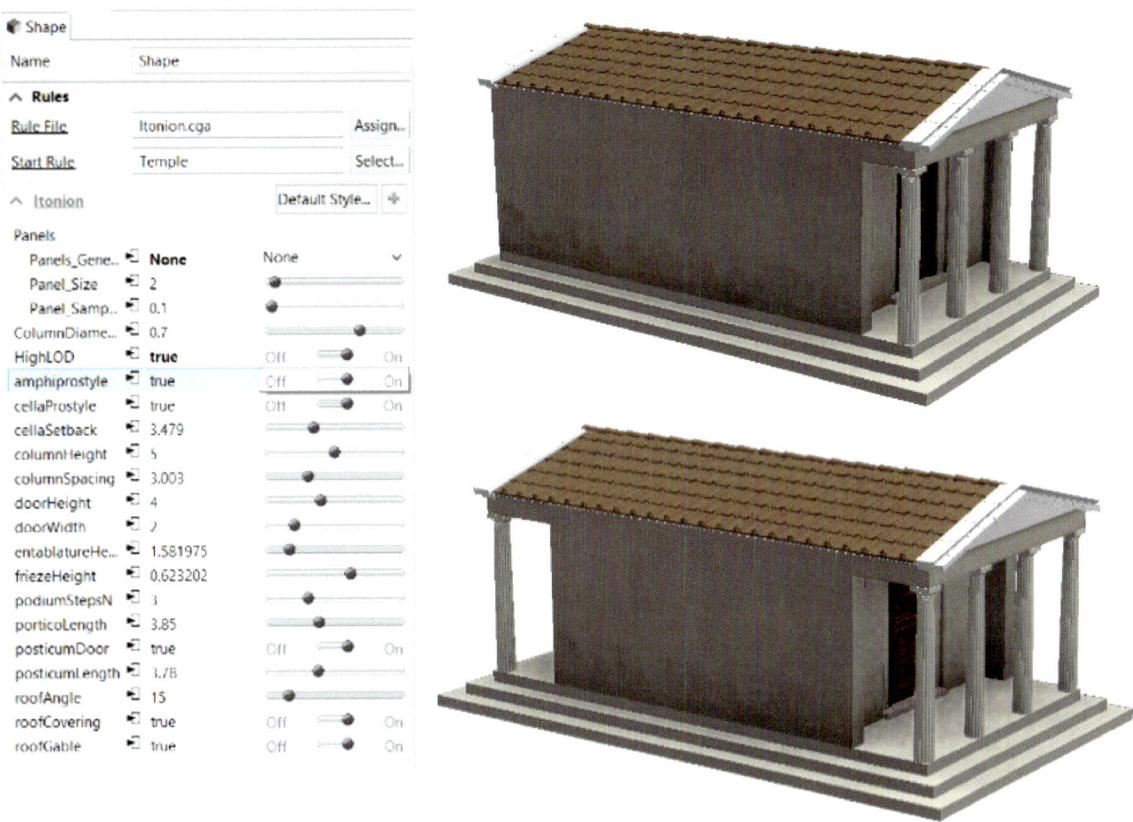

Figure 6.20 Left: Screenshot from the CE inspector with highlighted the Boolean attribute 'amphiprostyle' defining whether columns are only at the front or also at the back of the temple. Right: Visualization of the two reconstruction hypotheses that can be swopped in real time by switching the attribute 'amphiprostyle' on or off.

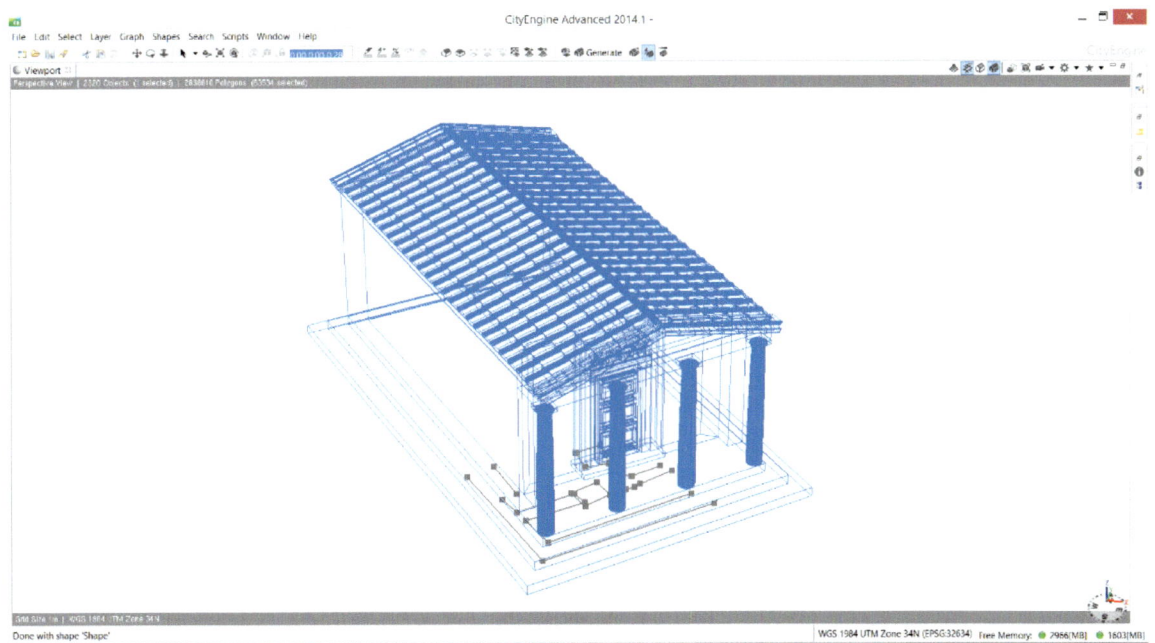

Figure 6.21 The shapefile containing the remains of the temple as recorded in the field (grey lines) is imported into CityEngine and the procedurally generated 3D reconstruction of the temple (here in wireframe mode) is created on top of it, thus making clear the spatial relation between the original data and the reconstruction.

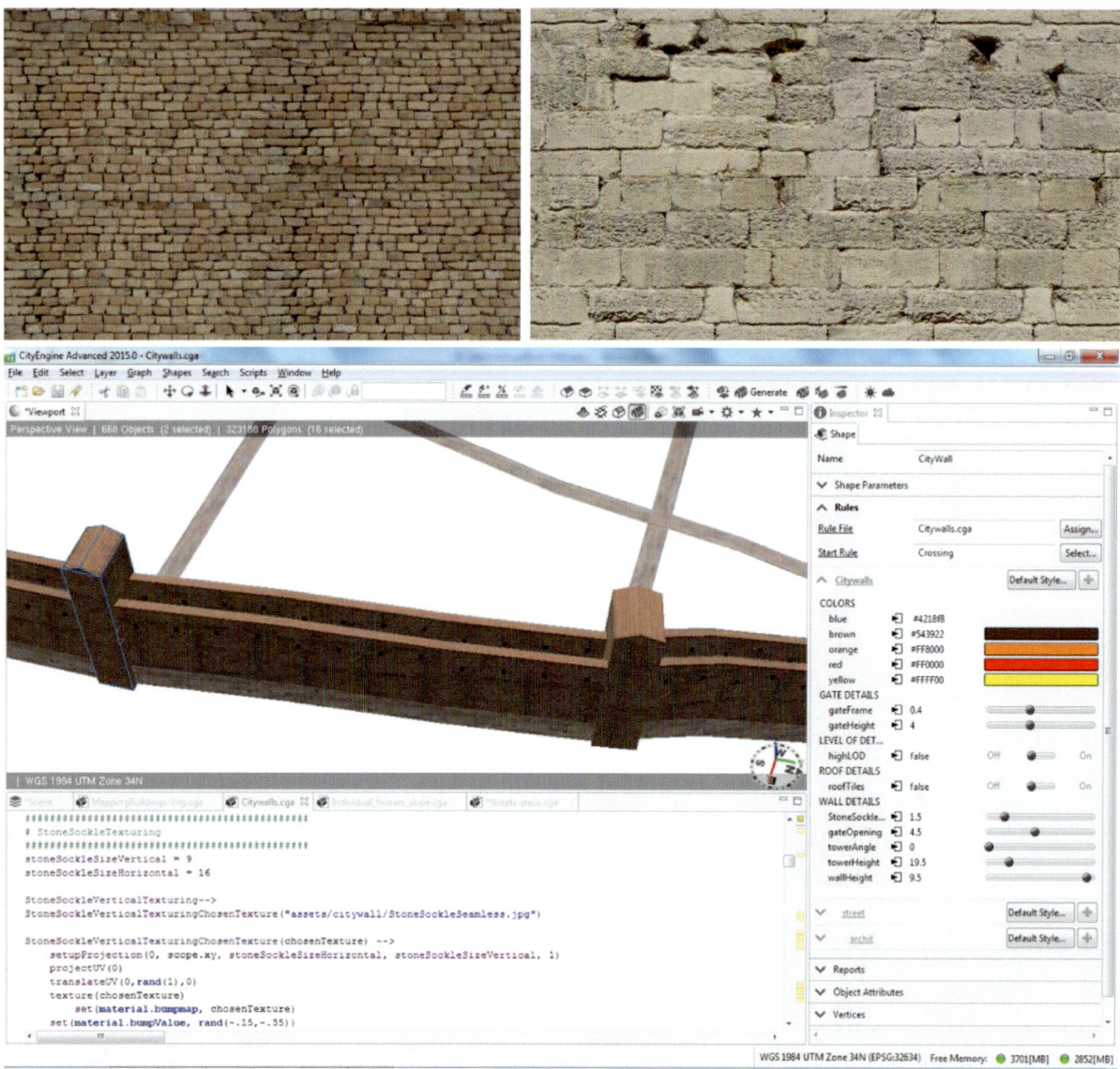

Figure 6.22 Textures of the city wall circuit of the lower town and screenshot from the CityEngine workspace displaying a rule based modelled stretch of the walls. The rule allows the creation of towers at crossing points with streets by inserting 'Crossing' in the inspector's field 'Start Rule'.

ancient sources,[1233] which have been made freely available as part of the Esri/LumenRT vegetation library.[1234] In the future, if more data will be available, these generic trees can be easily substituted by modifying the file path of the current 3D models in the rule file, with the file name of the updated 3D trees displaying a more specific type of vegetation. For the modelling of the altars, I have relied on a manual modelling approach using SketchUp as the time spent for modelling such elements with the CGA shape grammar would not have been justified given the fact that they were individual objects.

[1233] See chapter 5, p. 221.
[1234] The library is available at https://www.arcgis.com/home/item.html?id=0fd3bbe496c14844968011332f9f39b7 (last accessed Oct. 2016).

Theatre

The theatre was manually modelled using the open source software Blender. As there is no archaeological evidence hinting at the overall appearance of the theatre, I chose to model a simple construction with a stone *skene* whose dimensions fit the depression it left on the hill.[1235] The insertion of the theatre posed the additional challenge of finding the best solution to place the 3D model of the theatre despite the uneven morphology of the terrain. This would have caused in fact either the initial lot to intrude in the volume of the theatre or the theatre floating on the lot's surface. To overcome this problem, I modelled both the theatre and its surrounding terrain directly in Blender and substituted the resulting 3D model to the lot corresponding to the theatre's position. Since this strategy required a very precise fitting between the edges of the 3D model and the surrounding streets, I have exported the four streets that surrounded the theatre lot from CityEngine in DAE Collada format and imported them in Blender in order to model the terrain according to its precise shape. I then exported the thus obtained 3D model as an OBJ file and inserted it in the CGA rule file for the theatre. I have moreover included some vegetation around the theatre by using some of the 3D models of the free Esri/LumenRT vegetation library (Figure 6.18).

Temple architecture

The rule file for temple architecture is a modification of the rule file 'parthenon.cga', which was written by Pascal Müller and it is available as learning material for the CityEngine software.[1236] I have maintained the overall structure of the original rule and reused the assets that were included in it (e.g. 3D models of columns, capitals, roof tiles), but I modified some parts and added some lines of code to display alternative reconstruction hypotheses for the temple architecture. Specifically, I have defined the attribute 'amphiprostyle', which can be switched on or off to display either a temple with the portico only on the front (*prostyle*), or an *amphiprostyle* temple, with a portico both on the front and on the back (Figures 6.19 and 6.20). I have applied this rule to suggest two alternative reconstruction hypotheses of the temple located in the plain just north-east of the hill and partially excavated in the 1970s by Spyropoulos.[1237] The front portion of the temple which was unearthed during the excavations does not reveal the characteristics of the back, hence the idea to include the attribute 'amphiprostyle' in the rule file. I have imported in CityEngine the shapefile containing the outline of the excavated remains as recorded in the field in 2012 in order to create the 3D reconstruction of the temple on top of the GIS data. The aim of this approach was to provide an intellectually transparent visualization with a clear distinction between original data and interpretation (Figure 6.21).

City walls

I have created the city walls using the same tool that creates the street network, which allows the editing in real time of their position by dragging the nodes that compose the graph. In this way the circuit can easily be adapted to the terrain and can be modified if new data would alter our hypothesis regarding its path. To create the rules for the city walls I have taken as the starting point the rule for the city walls in the CityEngine show-case project 'Medieval town' which I have modified to suit our purposes. The rule is constructed in such a way that towers are created at crossing points of the city wall circuit, which is a convenient strategy to introduce new towers at the target location. As discussed in chapter 4, so far, in fact, the architectural survey at Koroneia has only yielded evidence for two

---

[1235] See chapter 4, 132 and chapter 5, § 5.3.3 for comparisons.
[1236] The rule is part of the Tutorial 09 Advanced Shape Grammar: Parthenon available at https://www.arcgis.com/home/item.html?id=47c0cc67406641298c10b720415c1fa5 (last accessed Oct. 2016).
[1237] See chapter 4, 103-5.

```
// Functions to determine orientation, slope
y_angle = convert(y, pivot, world, orient,0,0,0)

setpivot_index_uncorrected = floor((y_angle+45)/90)
setpivot_index0 = setpivot_index_uncorrected+0 - floor((setpivot_index_uncorrected+0)/4)*4
setpivot_index1 = setpivot_index_uncorrected+1 - floor((setpivot_index_uncorrected+1)/4)*4
setpivot_index2 = setpivot_index_uncorrected+2 - floor((setpivot_index_uncorrected+2)/4)*4
setpivot_index3 = setpivot_index_uncorrected+3 - floor((setpivot_index_uncorrected+3)/4)*4

slopeDegrees(sx,sy,sz) = geometry.angle(maxSlope)

// START RULE
@StartRule

LotInner --> Lot

Lot --> alignScopeToAxes (y)
        Lot1

/*
From "The Neighborhood Model: Building Block for the Development Areas", p. 106:
On slopes 0 - 10% (0 - 5.74°): most building can occur easily without major regrading
On slopes 10 - 15% (5.74° - ca. 9°): moderate grading may be needed to support development
On slopes 15 - 25% (ca. 9° - ca. 14°): more care with grading is needed so that extremely
steep slopes are not created by regrading
On slopes 25% and greater: extreme care should be taken when building on slopes of 25% so
slopes that are even steeper than 25% are not created. Note however that archaeological
evidence shows that hilly terrain were exploited for construction up to very steep slopes
such as at Ephesus, where the preferred slope was up to 30° of gradient (Groh 2012, 68).
[at Petres of Florinas the hill's gradient was 30-45% (ca. 17° - 24°; see P. Adam-Veleni
2000, Petres of Florinas, 35 - the maximum gradient for construction on slope however is
not given].
*/

Lot1 -->
    case   slopeDegrees(scope.sx,scope.sy,scope.sz) > 13 :
        report("Area.Greenspace",geometry.area)
        LotVegetation

    else:
        alignScopeToAxes(y)
        innerRectangle(edge)
        {shape:
            t(0,-2,0)
            extrude(world.up,2)
            comp(f)
            {top:
                alignScopeToGeometry(yUp,0)
                alignScopeToAxes(y)
                setPivot (xyz, setpivot_index1)
                // in this case I chose the N-E corner of the shape's scope as target pivot
                BuildingArea
            |side:
                alignScopeToGeometry(yUp,0)
                TextureAgora
            }
        |remainder:
            TextureAgora
        }
```

Figure 6.23 Beginning of the annotated rule file for the modelling of Koroneia's houses, showing the lines that allow setting the pivot of the initial shape to a defined location (see section 6.2.3 for a more detailed explanation of this work-around). In this case I chose the north-east corner of the shape's scope as target pivot to be able to orient the courtyards towards south and east. The rule includes moreover the function to calculate the slope, which informs the generation of the 3D environment and has been used to calculate the number of houses in relation to different slope input values (see below, § 6.3.2).

```
/*
Cf. streets's width in 4th century BC sites:
BOEOTIA:
Plataia= street connecting West and East tower (main street): 6.5m; acropolis area: 4.20-
6.70m; South of acropolis: 4.50m-5.50m; East of acropolis: 4.90m-5.80 (Konency 2013, 123-
125)
Tanagra= running NE-SW: ca. 3m (10ft); running SE-NW: ca. 5m (15ft) (Slapsak 2012, 56)
THESSALY:
Halos='Main avenue': 9.11m; Avenues A,B,C,D = 6.5-7.5m; others: 5.5m Reinders 1988, 208)
Goritsa= width varies along the street: major streets: average 4.95m; others: 3.25m (see
Bakhuizen 1992, 171-245)
CHALKIDIKI:
Olynthos= Hoepfner and Schwandner 1994, 77: 5.05m; From Cahill 2002, ill. p. 28: ca. 5m and
ca. 7.35m
PELOPONNESE:
Argolis/Halieis= Avenue A (underwater); Avenue B: 3.55-4.20m; Avenue C: 4.50-5.05m;
crossing roads: 2.60-2.80m (Boyd-Rudolph 1978, 339-345)
Messenia/Messene= various width: from 2m to 12.6m (Müth 2007, 245-256 and table p. 274)
Arkadia/Kyparissia= six parallel streets: 4.60m; plateiai not found (traces seem to
indicate a width of 8m)(Karapanagiotou 2005, 333)
EPIRUS:
Kassope= main street: 6m; 19 narrower streets: 4.50m (Schwandner in Isanger 2001, 109)
ASIA MINOR:
Ionia/Priene= 'Quellenthorstrasse': 5.60-6.18m; 'Athenastrasse': 3.64-4.35m;
'Westthorstrasse': 7-7.35; other streets: 3.10-5.60m (Wiegand and Schrader 1904, 48)
Ionia/Ephesos (3rd BC)= processional way: 8m; plateiai (E-W): 5m; stenopoi (N-W): 3m (Groh
2012, 69)
*/

@StartRule
Street --> alignScopeToAxes ()
          Lot2
Lot2-->   case convert(y, scope, world, pos, 0,1,0) - convert(y, scope, world, pos, 0,0,0)
          < 0 : reverseNormals
          print (slopeValueDegreesStreet)
          LotNormalUp
          else: print (slopeValueDegreesStreet)
          LotNormalUp

slopeValueDegreesStreet = atan (scope.sy / ( scope.sx * float(scope.sx > scope.sz) +
scope.sz * float(scope.sx <= scope.sz) ))

LotNormalUp -->
          case slopeValueDegreesStreet > 11 && slopeValueDegreesStreet < 14: Steps(0.30)
          case slopeValueDegreesStreet > 14 && slopeValueDegreesStreet < 18: Steps(0.25)
          case slopeValueDegreesStreet > 18 && slopeValueDegreesStreet < 27: Steps(0.20)
          case slopeValueDegreesStreet > 27 : NIL
          else: setPivot (xyz,1)Street1
          print (slopeValueDegreesStreet)
          /*
          From "Foothpats and Tracks. A Field Manual for their Construction and Improvement",
          2002, p. 3-26:
          Desiderable maximum gradient:
          For animal drawn carts: 8% (4.6°);
          For pedestrians and packed animals: 12% (6.8°);
          as slope approaches 25% (14°) walking becomes difficult and steps are needed:
          Shallow steps required: 25%
          Moderate steps required: 33% (18.3°)
          Steep steps required: 50% (26.6°)
              */
```

Figure 6.24 Beginning lines of the CGA rule file that is applied to streets. The file starts with commented out references to the dimensions of streets in other 4th century BC sites that have been excavated or surveyed in Boeotia and elsewhere. The proper rule starts at @StartRule and includes the formula to calculate the slope degrees and the conditional rule (case ... else) that guides the creation of a street or different types of steps within the set range of slope degrees. For reference, I have included as a comment the indications from modern construction guidelines.

Visualizing cityscapes of Classical antiquity

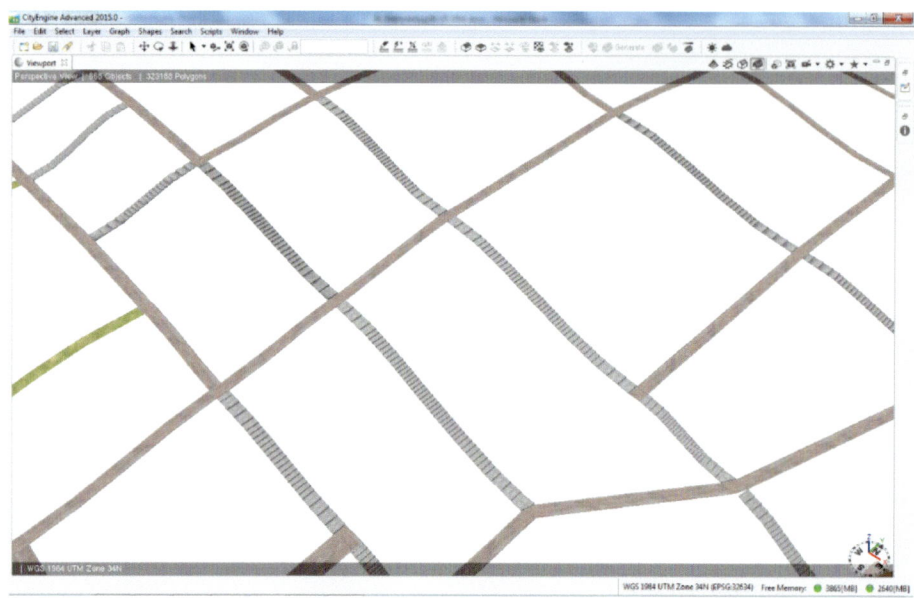

Figure 6.25 Screenshot from the CityEngine workspace where only the street network is selected, to show the dynamic rendering of streets and steps according to the slope degree by applying the rule file written for this project.

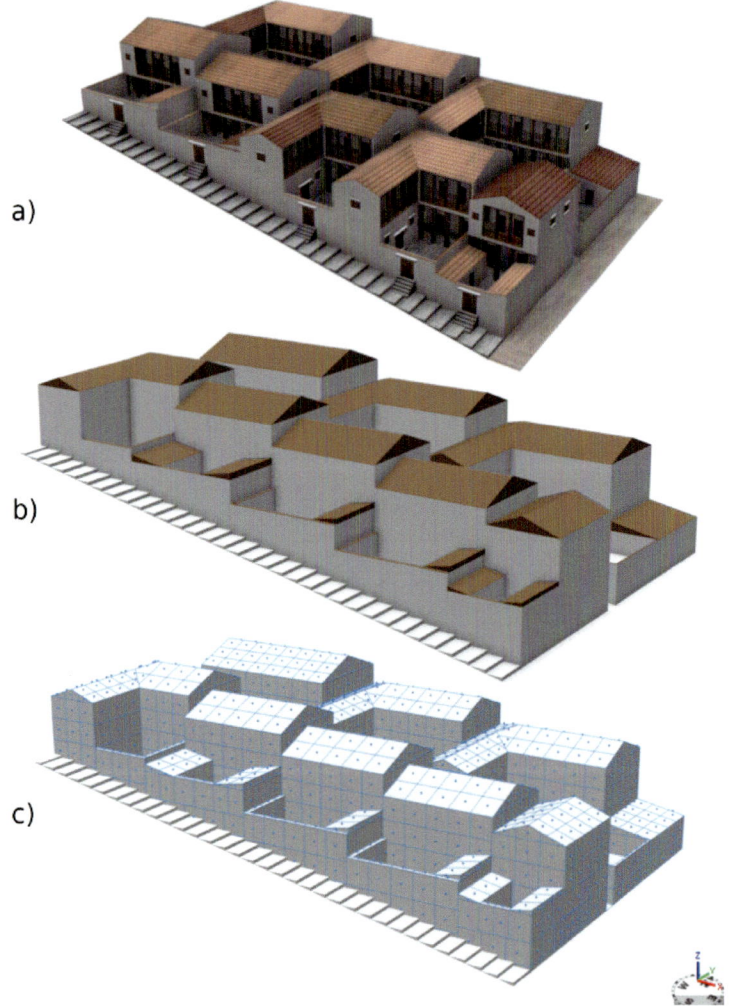

a)

b)

c)

Figure 6.26 A city block generated by the procedural rule for domestic architecture; in a) one of the possible different configurations of space that are encoded in the rule file are represented (HighLOD = true); b) displays the low Level of Detail scene, which generates geometries as coloured volumes (HighLOD = false); c) shows the panels and points that can be exported and used to perform visibility analysis in ArcGIS, as shown in Figure 6.29.

towers on the western slope but it is likely that geophysical prospections will provide further indication for the position of other towers.

The rule generates a polygonal masonry for the acropolis walls, as attested by the stretches that were found during the survey at Koroneia, and a regular, rectangular stone foundation with its higher elevation in mudbrick for the lower circuit wall, as this is the most common construction technique for Classical walls. The various building techniques are visualized by using different textures which I have created in the open source image editor GIMP. These textures originate from images available on the web which I have modified to make them seamless, which avoids the creation of a noticeable edge when the texture is repeated several times to cover the entire surface (see Figure 6.22).

Slope dependency

In the case of Koroneia, the hill's morphology must have conditioned the building choices, as is emerging from the currently available survey results and comparisons with other Boeotian sites.[1238] For this reason, the slope variable needed to be included in the 3D visualization, to be able to create different scenarios by interactively changing the value set as maximum slope degree allowed for building. To this end, I have inserted three possibilities in the rule file for domestic architecture: the calculation of the slope degrees of the initial shape at the beginning of the rules, the definition of a threshold for the maximum slope allowed for construction, and the report on entity count that allows the automatic calculation of the generated number of houses (Figure 6.23). In this case study, one of the biggest challenges was the modelling of buildings with an open courtyard on hilly terrain, which made it necessary to compensate for the sloping ground and avoid that the terrain would protrude through the courtyard (see section 'rule-based modelling: challenges and workarounds' for additional information).

Similar to the rule for domestic architecture, also the rule that I wrote to texture the street network includes the calculation of the slope. The rule works in such a way that steps are created instead of a street when the slope becomes too steep to ascend (see Figures 6.24 and 6.25). Differently than for

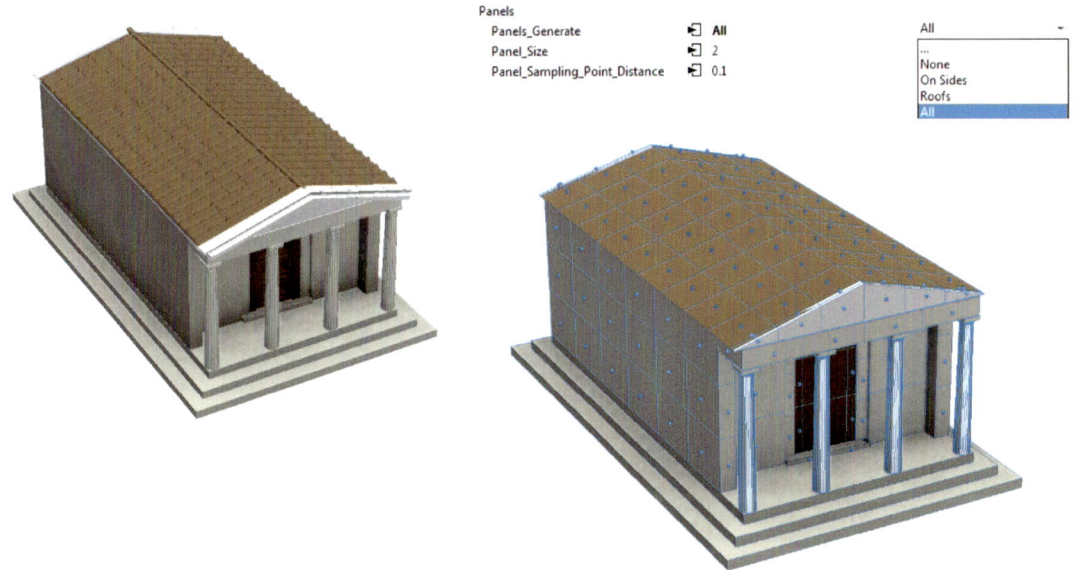

Figure 6.27 The procedure of sampling points and panels on the building's walls and roofs is triggered by switching between the options of the attribute Panels-Generate in the inspector.

[1238] E.g. Hyettos and Haliartos, see p. 132.

the domestic architecture, the slope of the street segment is calculated with the arctangent function using the longest side of the lot as adjacent side, since this corresponds to the direction in which the street will be traversed and, hence, to which the slope applies. The largest value of two variables A and B was determined by the function: A*float(A>B) + B*float(A<=B). Regarding the values that I have used as threshold, comparisons with the Roman world show that roads built by the Romans never exceed 15%, which corresponds to 8.5°.[1239] This value generally agrees with modern construction guidelines, where the desirable maximum gradient for animal drawn carts is given at 8% (4.6°), for pedestrians and packed animals is 12% (6.8°), while as slope approaches 25% (14.0°) walking becomes difficult and steps of different depths are needed (25%: shallow steps required; 33% (18.3°): moderate steps required; 50% (26.6°): steep steps required.[1240] The rule includes moreover some comments on the dimensions of streets that have been excavated or surveyed in 4th century Greek sites and the indications from modern construction guidelines as a comparisons for the values that I have inserted as thresholds (see Figure 6.24). The insertion of these indications contribute to the development of an intellectually transparent 3D visualization.

Level of Detail

Two attributes ('LOD' and 'HighLOD') allow the control of the Level of Detail of vegetation and buildings respectively. The choice of having two different attributes to control the LoD, which can be operated independently, is justified by the easiness to create a different mix of details in the scene that can be changed rapidly when needed (e.g. high LoD for buildings and low LoD for vegetation). By setting the HighLOD attribute as 'true', detailed geometries are created, but roofs are kept as textures to save on the polygon count. When the HighLOD attribute is 'false', instead, the geometries are created with low detail as schematic coloured volumes (Figure 6.26 a, b). I have inserted this second option to keep the

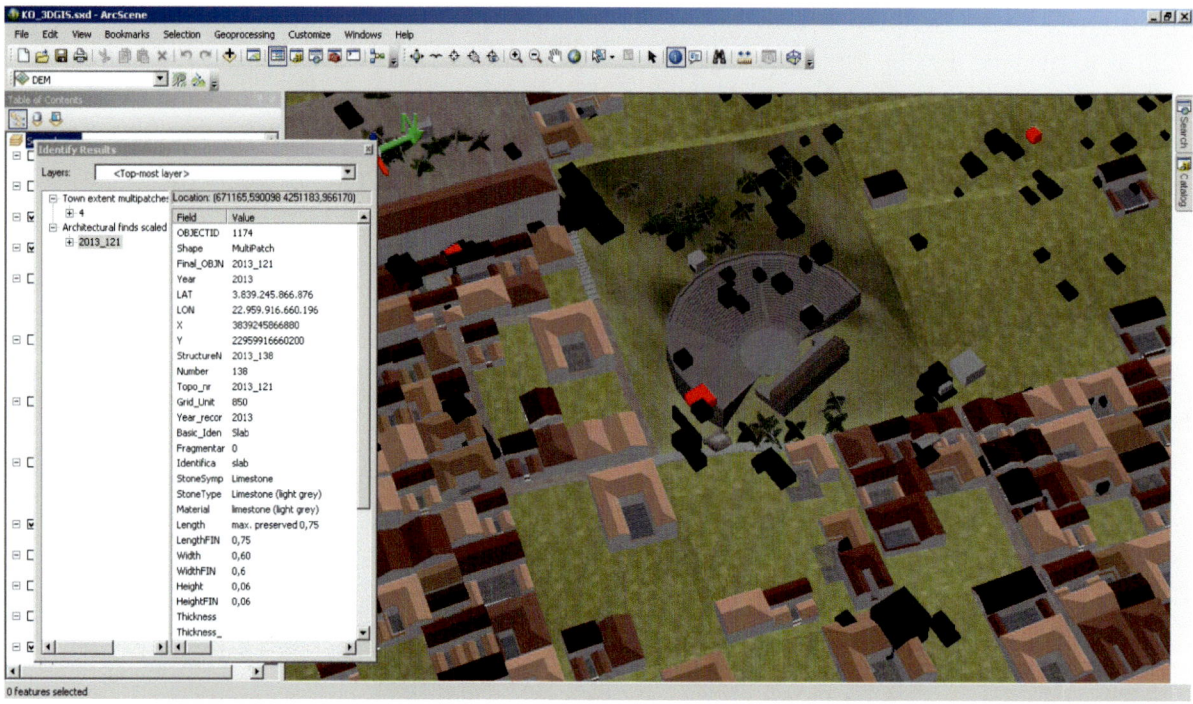

Figure 6.28 Screenshot from ArcScene workspace showing the overlay between the architectural data displayed using the procedural rule described above and the procedurally modelled reconstruction hypothesis (in low LoD) imported as gdb.

[1239] Verhagen *et al.* 2014, 80 citing Hucker 2009 and Quilici 1995.
[1240] I.T. TRANSPORT Ltd. 2002, 3-26.

polygon count at a minimum for exporting the whole scene to another software when only the volumetric information is needed (e.g. for analytical purposes in ArcGIS or for setting up the scene in a CG software). Two different levels of detail have been created also for vegetation, from the LoD of architecture. A low LoD creates trees as a cross-billboard, which consist of two crossing images displaying the tree with a transparent background, and a more detailed version that can be used for a more realistic visualization.

Sampling points on buildings' surfaces

In the rules for domestic and public architecture I have included the possibility to sample points and create panels on the buildings' surfaces. By inserting at the right locations the lines of codes within the rule file, and initiating the corresponding attribute in the inspector (in this case *panels: on*), it is in fact possible to divide the building's facades in equal squares and to create a point at each square's centroid (see Figure 6.26, c and 6.27).[1241] This workflow has been recently introduced for the spatial and visual impact analysis of modern cities,[1242] and it is based on the possibility to export each of the so called leaf-shapes that are generated by a rule as individual GIS features, so that they can be used to perform visibility analysis on the built environment in ArcGIS. Points are used to run a Line of Sight analysis and panels can be used to map the frequency count in order to visualize the visibility of the portion of the building defined by each panel (see below, section 6.3.1).

6.3. Results

The methodology described above has allowed us to create a 3D GIS of the architectural survey data which exposes in an intuitive way some characteristics of the dataset (see section 6.2.1), and to create alternative reconstruction hypotheses of Koroneia's town layout which reflect the current state of our data. The combination of these two layers of information in a 3D GIS allows a visual and spatial overlap between the survey data and the reconstruction hypothesis, thus allowing the possibility to store and compare data and interpretation within the same platform (Figure 6.28).

As will be discussed in this section, the procedurally modelled 3D reconstructions can then be used for a variety of analytical purposes, such as to compute the degree of integration of the street network, to run a visibility analysis in ArcScene, and to estimate population figures according to different input parameters.

6.3.1 Visibility analysis in a 3D GIS

Traditionally, visibility analysis on 3D models in GIS has been problematic. In 1997, Esri developed the multipatch geometry type to define the exterior shell of 3D objects in GIS. Besides the volumetric properties of the object, this format can also store texture information.[1243] Although the implementation of this geometry type pushed considerably forward the capabilities of GIS to handle 3D models, the problem remained that each planar surface that composed the 3D geometry could not be subdivided in smaller subsets. This limited considerably the possibilities for visibility analysis on the built environment, as a building could be either seen in its entirety or not seen at all.[1244] To perform a visibility analysis of the built environment in a 3D GIS, four main elements need in fact to be specified: a terrain layer, an observer, a target, and an obstacle. In the first phase, sightlines are created between the observer point(s) and the target point(s) using the 'construct sight lines' tool in the 3D Analyst toolbox. Next, the line of sight is calculated including the terrain layer and the obstacle layer (e.g. other buildings that

---

[1241] The sample rule files can be downloaded from http://www.arcgis.com/home/item.html?id=b7142081948b4cd9ac1c852d8790c9c9
[1242] Van Maren 2014.
[1243] See 'The Multipatch Geometry Type. An Esri White Paper – December 2008', Esri 2008 available at http://support.esri.com/en/knowledgebase/whitepapers/download/fileid/5111.
[1244] For a thorough discussion on visibility analysis in the fields of urban and landscape research see Paliou 2013.

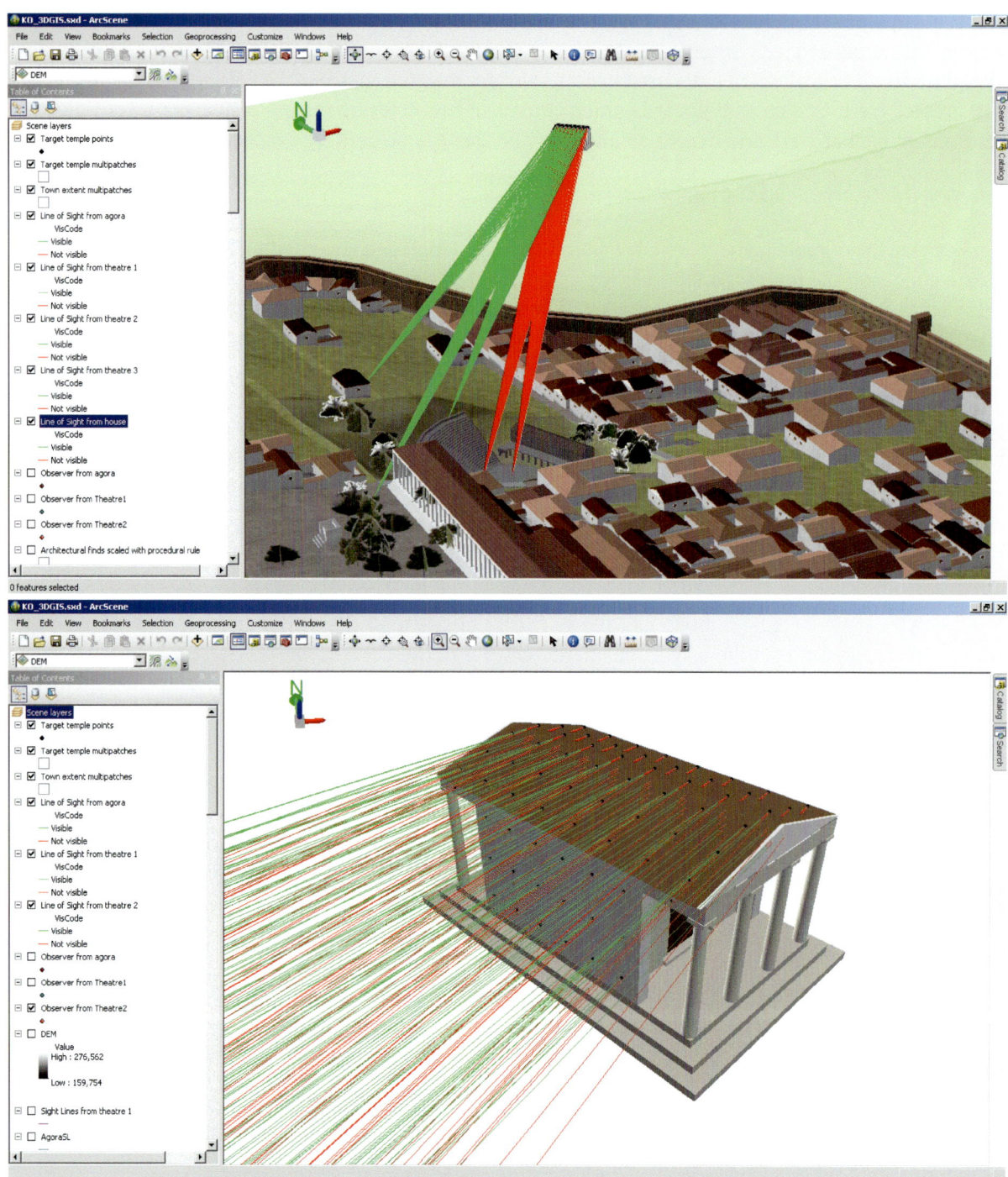

Figure 6.29 The application of the possibility to sample points on the buildings' facades. Top: the results of the Line of Sight analysis that was run in ArcScene on a portion of the procedurally modelled environment in CityEngine to map which parts of the temple are visible from the observer points that were located on the agora, on the theatre and in other parts of the lower town. Bottom: A close-up of the temple which shows the sight lines coded according to the target points' visibility from the observers.

might obstruct the line of sight between observer and target) using the 'Line of Sight' tool in the 3D Analyst toolbox to distinguish between the sight lines which hit the target and those that were instead blocked by the elements in the obstacle layer.

The method that is adopted here allows the automatic sampling of points over the building's planar surfaces and their subdivision into panels and has been developed by ESRI as part of the workflow for the analysis of the 3D modern city.[1245] As discussed above, I have in fact included in the rule file for Koroneia's project the possibility to sample points and panels on the buildings' facades (see Figure 6.26 and 6.27). This integration makes it possible to switch between three different visualization modalities (photorealistic, volumetric and panels/points) within the same rule file. The geometry thus created is exported from CityEngine as a geodatabase by choosing as the feature mapping mode the 'one feature per leaf shape' option in the export dialog. In this way, the points are saved as a point feature class, while the panels are stored as a multipatch feature class and can be therefore used for analysis in ArcGIS. (A portion of) the thus obtained points can be used as observer or target in the intervisibility analysis, while the panels can be used to map the frequency count in order to visualize the visibility of the portion of the building defined by each panel. For Koroneia, we use this workflow to evaluate the visual prominence of the temple partially excavated by Spyropoulos north-east of the hill. As discussed in chapter 4, finds on this area show that the temple was part of a larger sanctuary which was in used from the Archaic to the Late Roman period. It must therefore have been an important cult centre, which some scholars have identified with the regional sanctuary of Athena Itonia (but see chapter 4 for this debated interpretation). Based on the currently available data and with the citywall reconstructed as 8 meters high (an average within the range indicated by Winter for Classical city walls),[1246] the temple would have been visible from some parts of the agora and the upper town, but not visible from most seats in the theatre (Figure 6.29). This method can be taken further in case additional geophysical prospections performed in the area of the sanctuary and of the theatre will clarify the extension of the former and identify the location of the *skene* of the latter, thus giving a more precise indication of its orientation. For example, it would be interesting to create different hypotheses about the height of the city walls and see what impact they would have had on the visibility of the sanctuary in the plain from the town's centre.

The creation of a grid of points overlaid on a wall or facade allows parts of the buildings to be considered as individual entities, thus opening up the possibility to use the 3D visualization as an analytical tool to investigate the spatial relationships within and between buildings in a quantitative way.[1247] By using this method, a building can be analysed in its context, to evaluate its presence in relation to its surroundings, while its visibility can be determined from different locations. The ESRI rule that has been included in our rule set allows an easier creation of such a grid; moreover, the use of this method coupled with the parametric modelling of different hypotheses can offer a way to evaluate and analyse alternative scenarios (for example, which height a building should have reached in order to be seen from a given location). As already stressed, in fact, this modelling strategy allows the quick creation of different reconstruction hypotheses simply by changing the defined numerical parameters (e.g. the height of a building), which can be then exported into ArcGIS to test the most plausible reconstruction hypothesis. It must be noted, however, that the export of the 3D scene to the geodatabase may result in very large files. For instance, Koroneia's scene was about 13 GB when exported with a low LoD. This not only results in long export and import sessions, but also in computationally heavy analyses. It is therefore advisable to subdivide the 3D scene in portions and export and import each of the sub-sections individually.

6.3.2 *Estimating number of houses and population figures*

As discussed above, we were moreover interested in developing an analytical visualization that exploited the hill slope as a threshold for the generation of 3D geometry. In this way, we were able to produce different reconstruction hypotheses where we could see how much the number of houses that could fit

---

[1245] Available here: http://www.arcgis.com/home/item.html?id=84a432d1b26d4fbfac3b0feb3359fa12 (last accessed Dec. 2016).
[1246] See chapter 5, 217.
[1247] See Landeschi *et al.* 2016 for an application of visual analysis in the 3D GIS of the house of Caecilius Iucundus in Pompeii.

within the city wall circuit would vary, when using the slope threshold as a variable. The final aim of this experiment was to formulate some hypotheses on Koroneia's population size.

The calculation of the inhabitants of ancient Greek *poleis* has triggered the interest of many scholars, starting with Julius Beloch's *Die Bevölkerung der griechisch-römischen Welt* published in 1886, as the amount of population within a territory has far reaching implications for understanding economic strategies and can explain conflicts between neighbouring city states under the pressure of finding new resources. In the following paragraphs, I will discuss some of the traditional methods that have been employed to calculate population figures on an individual *polis* and apply them to Koroneia, to allow a comparison with the numbers that resulted from our 3D visualization.[1248]

Surviving evidence on army figures has been extensively used to infer population size on the assumption that the number of troops sent to fight was proportional to the number of citizens.[1249] For the beginning of the 4th century, we have in fact information about the military organization of the Boeotian League from a fragment of papyrus found at Oxyrhynchus. The surviving lines inform us that in 395 BC, Boeotia was divided in 11 districts, each one contributing a federal magistrate (Boeotarch), and military forces corresponding to 1,000 hoplites (heavy infantry) and 100 cavalry (*Hell. Oxy.* 16.4 [Bartoletti]). Among the Boeotian cities, Thebes for example supplied four Boeotarchs, Orchomenos and Thespiai two, Tanagra one, while Haliartos, Lebadeia and Koroneia supplied one in turn.

Using this method to infer the total population presents however a series of problems. If it is certainly true that larger towns must have contributed more than smaller ones to the army, it is not clear what the correct ratio between the two would have been. We must also consider that the amount of light-armed troops and seamen are unknown as they are not included in the papyrus' figures, and that not all men must have served in the army, as some must have stayed to carry the *polis*' administrative tasks.[1250] One has to note, moreover, that it is not certain that the figures that are reported in ancient sources correspond to the real ones, as literary evidence points towards the use of inflated figures.[1251] In his calculation to estimate the population of ancient Boeotia, Bintliff uses these numbers (corrected to include light-armed troops and seamen), and multiplies them by 5 obtaining a total of 165,500 people, including slaves.[1252] If we would apply this method to Koroneia, knowing that this *polis* contributed 1/33 of the total armed forces of the region according to the papyrus' fragment, we would reach a total population of some 5,015 people. In this case, this number would represent both the intramural population and the people in rural sites within Koroneia's *chora*.

An alternative method uses the physical remains of a walled city multiplying the hectares per average number of persons per domestic hectare. For his calculations on the population of some individual Boeotian *poleis* and of ancient Boeotia in general, Bintliff relies on the assumption that about 56% of towns was occupied by domestic units, while the rest was destined to public, commercial and religious functions; he then takes the estimation of 225 people per domestic hectare, which Jameson advanced

---

[1248] For the various approaches that have been used for calculating population figures in Greece, see the overview in Hansen 2006, 1-34.
[1249] Beloch 1886; see also Bintliff's estimation based on the army figures of the Boeotian Confederacy contained in the Oxyrhynchus papyrus (Bintliff 1985, 141-2, updated and revised in Bintliff 1997).
[1250] For the calculation of the army forces that are not included in the papyrus' figures, see Bintliff 1985, 141-2; for the problems related to the use of army figures, see Hansen 2006, 5-6.
[1251] In this regard, P. Hunt cites the words that according to Thucydides Alcibiades pronounced on the eve of the Sicilian expedition (Thuc. 6.17.5): 'As for their hoplites, they have not got so many as they boast of: it is the same with them as with the rest of the Hellenes; the number never came up to the estimate made by each state of its own power; in fact the falsification was a very big one.' (Hunt 2007). On the other hand, however, it is equally possible that this speech could have been aimed at playing down the enemy forces.
[1252] Bintliff 1985, 141-2.

for Argolis,[1253] and multiplies by the amount of domestic hectares that he had calculated for Boeotia to reach an estimation of the total urban population of the region of 131,985 people and applies this method also to individual towns.[1254] Based on these figures, Koroneia's extent of about 34 (yellow line in Figure 4.32) and 37 (orange line in Figure 4.32) hectares would lead to 19 - 20.7 domestic hectares which multiplied by 225 gives a population of between 4,275 and 4,660 within the walled city. However, it must be noted that the 56% of Greek towns being domestic is derived from the situation at Athens, as described by Travlos in his 1960s publication,[1255] but the proportion between the area within the city walls and the area for housing greatly varies among Greek *poleis*,[1256] the terrain morphology playing a major role in defining the zones suitable for building.

In his 'shotgun method', Hansen adopts different percentages based on the size of the *polis*: for very small *poleis* (of up to 10 ha), he assumes that the habitation area took up around two-thirds of the intramural space, for medium *poleis* (10-150 ha) this area would be about half of the entire intramural space and for large *poleis* only one third.[1257] He then takes an average of 30-33 houses per hectare,[1258] and a minimum average household size of 5.5 people (including slaves),[1259] taking into account the many problematic aspects when estimating the occupants of a house, as e.g. many variations may occur over its lifecycle,

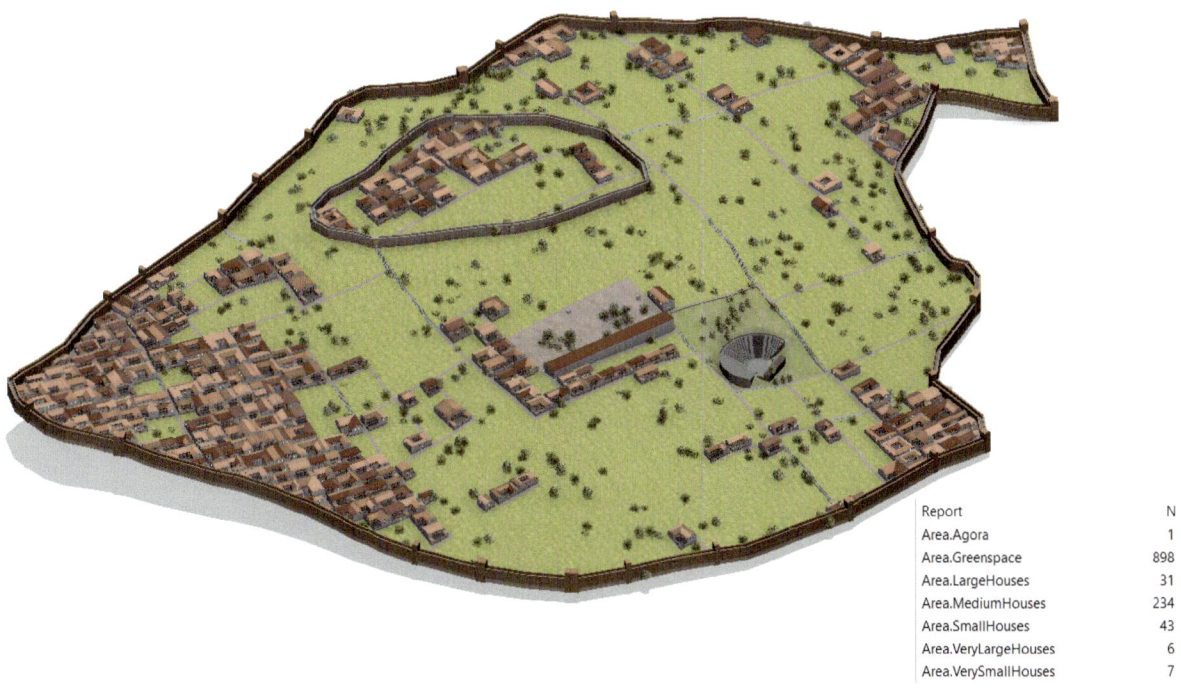

Figure 6.30 Hypothesis 1: The threshold for the terrain suitable for buildings is up to 9°. This scenario returns a total amount of 321 houses (automatically calculated by including the report operation in the rule).

[1253] For other numbers adopted to estimate population figures see also Cahill 2002, note 43.
[1254] Bintliff 1997.
[1255] Travlos 1960, 71; Kolb 1984.
[1256] Hansen 2006, 37-47.
[1257] Hansen 2006, 46-7.
[1258] Among the sites that he lists in table 2.3, the number of houses per ha varies between 26 and 50, but most had 30 to 33 houses per ha (Hansen 2006, 51).
[1259] Hansen 2008, 280; Bintliff reaches a similar figure of 5 people per household, assuming an equal number of men and women, two children per family and a slave (Bintliff 1985, 142).

VISUALIZING CITYSCAPES OF CLASSICAL ANTIQUITY

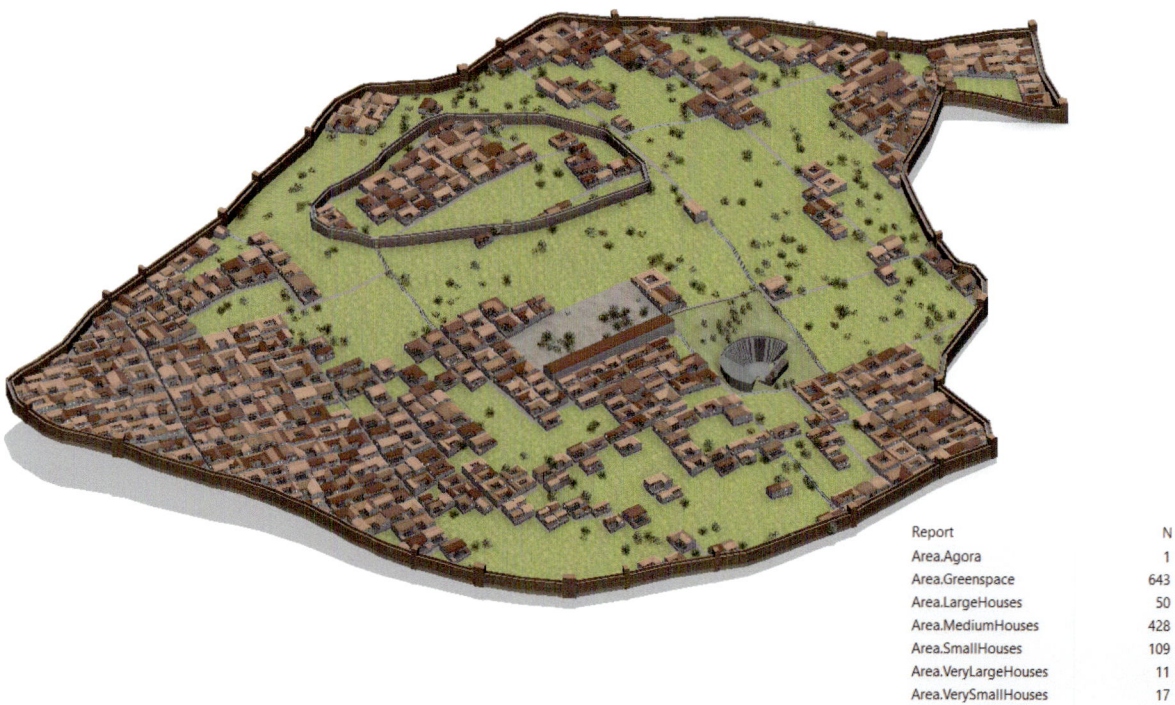

Figure 6.31 Hypothesis 2: The threshold for the terrain suitable for buildings is up to 12°. This scenario returns a total amount of 615 houses.

Figure 6.32 Hypothesis 3: The threshold for the terrain suitable for buildings is up to 13°. In this case, the total amount of houses is 765.

6. Enhancing Koroneia's GIS survey data with the third dimension

Figure 6.33 Hypothesis 4: The threshold for the terrain suitable for buildings is up to 14°, which allows 965 houses.

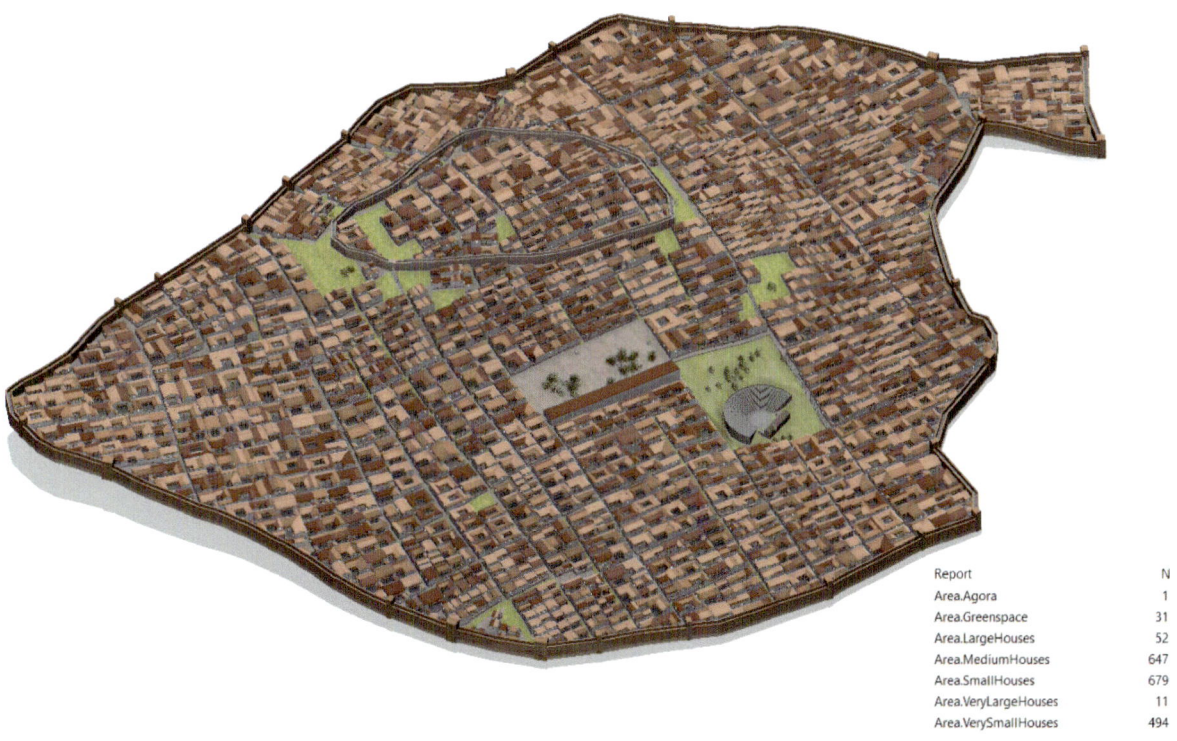

Figure 6.34 Hypothesis 5: The threshold for the terrain suitable for buildings is up to 24°, which allows 1883 houses.

more households could share the same house, the number of slaves is difficult to assess.[1260] By using these figures, about half of Koroneia's intramural space would have been occupied by houses, which would make up a total of ca. 510-561 houses corresponding to about 2,800 and 3,080 people (yellow line in Figure 4.32) and 555-610 houses corresponding to about 3,050 to 3,360 people (orange line in Figure 4.32).

At Koroneia, *in situ* stretches of walls have been recorded up to around 24° of gradient. The evidence we have, however, is too limited to establish whether these walls (sometimes just 3 or 4 adjacent blocks) used to belong to houses or more ephemeral types of buildings. It is possible that the continuation of the survey and the integration of geophysical results with the pottery data will lead to more refined conclusions on the use of the hill in antiquity, which are not possible to draw at this stage of research. Modern construction guidelines and comparison from archaeological sites differ in relation to the maximum slope suitable for construction. In modern guidelines, in fact, it is stated that most building can occur easily without major regrading on slopes between 0 and 10% (0 - 5.71°), moderate grading may be needed to support development on slopes 10 - 15% (5.71° - 8.53°), more care with grading is needed so that extremely steep slopes are not created by regrading on slopes 15 - 25% (8.53° - 14.04°), and extreme care should be taken when building on slopes of 25% and greater so slopes that are even steeper than 25% are not created.[1261] Although only a few papers report clearly the maximum slope that was used for construction at archaeological sites, when this piece of information is present it is clear that in many cases hilly terrains were exploited for construction up to very steep slopes. At Ephesus, for example, Groh reports that the preferred slope was up to 30° of gradient,[1262] while at Petres of Florinas, although the maximum gradient for construction on slope is not given, the overall hill's gradient was between 30 and 45% (16.70° - 24.23°).[1263]

For our purposes, I have created alternative reconstruction hypotheses taking as threshold a slope of 9°, 12°, 13°, 14°, and 24° (maximum slope of *in situ* blocks recorded at Koroneia). The insertion in the rule file of the possibility to automatically report on entities' count and areas makes it easy to calculate the number of houses that were allowed within the given space and the areas that domestic architecture would occupy in percentage. The results are shown in figs. 6.30 - 6.34.

Calculating the number of houses allowed within the city walls gives a starting point for the formulation of population figures for 4th century Koroneia. Our method, in comparison to the approaches briefly mentioned above, allows for the iterative formulation of different hypotheses, by permitting us to change both the parameters of house sizes and the slope's critical threshold, so as to visualize different scenarios, and maintaining at the same time an intellectually transparent approach when it comes to clearly establish the parameters for the calculations. The simulation which takes 9° as the critical slope value generates 321 houses, which would house about 1,760 people if we take the minimum average of 5.5 people per household suggested by Hansen. This value, however, leaves large parts of the town unbuilt where the survey has instead indicated the presence of houses. Despite the fact that currently these walls cannot be dated with certainty, as we lack contextual information (e.g. stratigraphical control), we can assume that this threshold is a too conservative value, resulting in the limited exploitation of the suitable terrain for building.

[1260] Census data for Hellenistic and Roman Egypt depict in fact a complex picture of the inhabitants of houses, see Hansen 2008, 259-86, esp. 276-80, citing Clarysse and Thompson 2006.
[1261] Torti Gallas and Partners-CHK, Inc. and Dodson Associates, 'The Neighborhood Model: Building Blocks for the Development Areas' (March 22, 2000), 106.
[1262] Groh 2012, 68.
[1263] Adam Veleni 2000, 35.

Also the value of 12° degrees leaves unbuilt a part of the town in the north-eastern sector where some structures where identified during the geophysical survey. At the other end of the spectrum we considered, if we take the value of 24° as threshold for building construction and settle for the minimum average of 5.5 people per household, the 1,883 houses allowed within the walled town would have housed more than 10,000 people, which, despite the problems related with the use of army figures as discussed above, seems to be too high a number for a medium sized town such as Koroneia – even more so since the army figures include also the population of Koroneia's *chora*, while our calculation takes into account only the people inside the city walls. The numbers of houses estimated by using slope values above 12° and below 14°, which returns about 3,380 and 5,300 people respectively, correspond to the advised slope values in modern construction guidelines and result in numbers closer to the calculations based on historical sources. This leads us to suggest that the laying out of the town on the hill was made by attempting to find a good balance between maximizing the exploitation of the available terrain for construction and minimizing the effort needed for building on a slope.

Given the fact that the rules report the number of houses by size, our method would allow us to set a different number of inhabitants per house in relation to their dimensions. We could suppose for example that smaller households would have had fewer slaves, while larger houses could house more people (we know that size should not be taken as an indication for wealth, but it is likely that a large house could be shared by more households and allowed lodgers as well), and construct a more refined model of population figures at Koroneia. Obviously we cannot claim that with our method we have reached more accurate figures than with the previously mentioned approaches, but we believe that we have created a model which is explicit in its assumptions and can be interactively used to formulate site-specific hypotheses.

6.3.4 Exporting procedurally modelled Koroneia

As I have argued in the previous chapter, 3D reconstructions are traditionally associated with public outreach, both positively connoted as an approachable means of communication of otherwise difficult to comprehend archaeological evidence, but also, unfortunately still nowadays, negatively connoted as ways to show case technical advances in visualization techniques with little archaeological value. In our view, 3D reconstructions are a very well suited environment to reconcile rigorous research and communication. In the first stage of its development, in fact, the 3D visualisation is deployed as a tool to test different possible hypotheses and the initially schematic and conceptual 3D models can be used as a platform for discussion across the team of experts working on the site. When the 3D model (or a first draft) has passed the phase of revisions and discussion, it can be then used as a platform to communicate the archaeological hypotheses to a broader public.

The previous sections of the chapter focused in particular on the modelling strategy I have adopted for the creation of Koroneia's 3D reconstruction and on the analytical opportunities that this approach opens up, both within CityEngine itself with the possibility of creating different reconstruction hypotheses of the urban layout and within a 3D GIS, especially in relation to visibility analysis. This section is instead dedicated to the exploration of some of the currently existing possibilities to make the 3D reconstruction of Koroneia available to a larger public. As will be discussed below, the 3D reconstruction described in this chapter is currently available online. I have experimented moreover with the game engine Unity3D to set up a prototype navigation in the virtual environment and a VR experience using a cardboard viewer. This application could be further developed when the study of the surveyed material will be completed and the 3D reconstruction updated accordingly.

Figure 6.35 Koroneia's 3D visualization exported in the *.3ws format and viewed in the CityEngine Web Viewer: a) Alternative scenarios can be compared using the swipe view; b) buildings can be tagged so that they are easily searchable, and as shown in c) the lighting conditions can be changed to see their impact on the 3D scene.

Online publication

There are many factors that have to be taken into account when searching for options to guarantee a wide accessibility for a 3D visualisation. Traditionally, 3D models that were available on the internet could be viewed only by downloading a plug-in (e.g. Cortona 3D viewer), which was not an ideal solution for a variety of reasons. The plug-in may in fact be incompatible with the operating system that runs on the computer, and users in public institutions usually do not have the administrator privileges that are required to install the plug-in. The awareness that this procedure precludes the accessibility of 3D content led to alternative solutions.[1264] Recently, the development of the Javascript API Web Graphics Library (WebGL) enables us to see and navigate through virtual scenes without having to download plug-ins. WebGL exploits in fact the graphic card of the computer and makes the 3D visualisation run directly on the hardware, which greatly speeds up navigation and rendering capabilities.

Based on WebGL technologies is the CityEngine Web Viewer, which is made available by ESRI and it is optimized for the handling of 3D scenes that are created in CityEngine (Figure 6.35).[1265] This web app was created to provide urban planners with a tool to be able to share and discuss their development scenarios with people that did not have CityEngine. During the modelling process in CE, the 3D models within the scene can be tagged and the various components of the scene can be organised in layers, and then exported directly to the Web Viewer, where it is possible to navigate through the previously set layers and swipe through different development scenarios, and to query the 3D visualisation in order to find specific buildings according to the tags that were assigned. This online platform allows moreover the user to interactively change lights in the scene, in order to see in real time the effect of sunlight and shadows on buildings and to add comments. These features have been exploited for Koroneia's 3D reconstruction: the two hypotheses displaying the two possible reconstructions of the northern part of the site can be inspected and compared using the swipe view (Figure 6.35, top); a selection of buildings has been tagged, which allows the user to search for and highlight them within the 3D scene (Figure 6.35, middle); different lighting conditions can be set to see the impact of sunlight on the town's built environment (Figure 6.35, bottom).

Interactive navigation and Virtual Reality

The scene created in CityEngine can then be used to create an interactive experience that allows the user to navigate through the virtual world, by relying on game engines. I have experimented with Unity3D,[1266] which offers the basic version of the software for free, it is able to apply the rules of physics, thus creating a realistic interaction with the virtual environment, and it is customisable by adding scripts in e.g. JavaScript and C#. Moreover, it permits the publication of the 3D content on several platforms (among others iOS, Android, Flash Player, Xbox360, Oculus Rift and Google

---

[1264] The European project CARARE identified Adobe PDF as the most widespread software, since it is installed in 85% of computers. Although the possibility of embedding 3D models into PDF's is not widely known, the technical support exists for years now and this format seems to be by far the best choice for exchanging and publishing 3D models in a stable and widely accessible form (see CARARE's deliverable: Pletinckx and Haskiya 2011). 3D models embedded into a PDF can be rotated, zoomed in and measured. Moreover, it makes it possible to change the light and its direction, in order to appreciate features that may be visible only under certain lighting conditions. Also, one can link the text of the PDF to parts of the 3D model, so that when the text is activated by a mouse click, the 3D model rotates to show the part that was linked to the text. Examples of 3DPDF's can be found at http://pro.carare.eu/doku.php?id=training-materials:3d (last accessed March 2017).

[1265] The 3D scene can be accessed via this page: https://www.universiteitleiden.nl/en/staffmembers/chiara-piccoli#tab-1; whether or not WebGL is supported/enabled in the browser and instructions to enable it can be found on https://get.webgl.org/ (last accessed March 2017).

[1266] http://unity3d.com/unity/

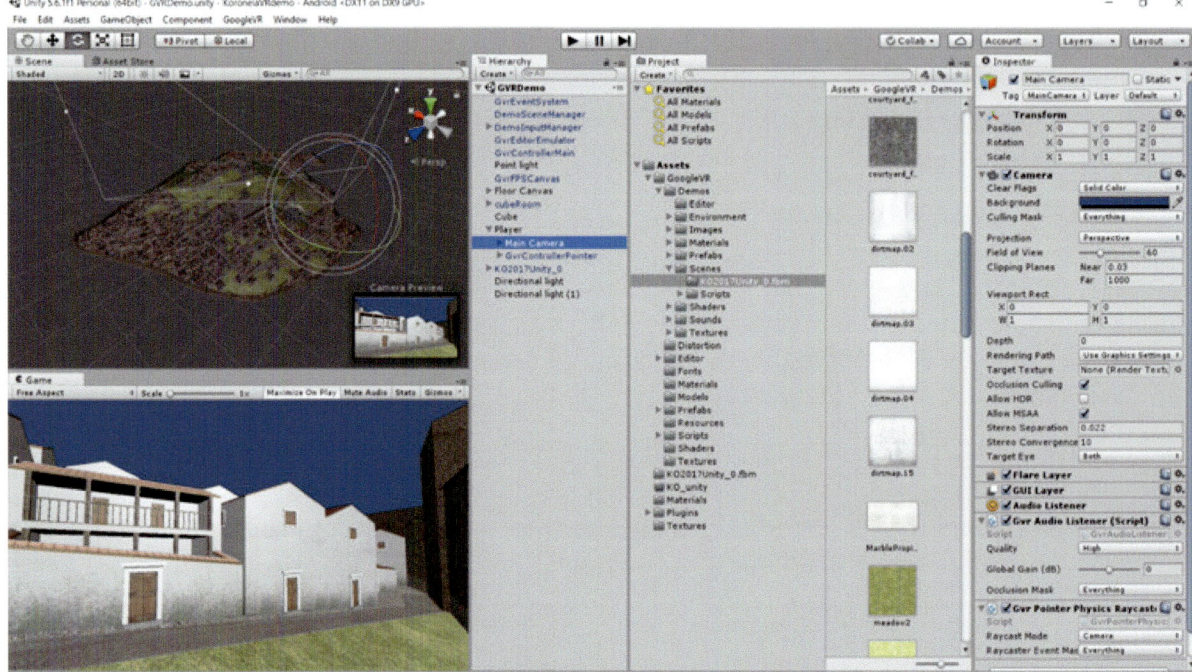

Figure 6.36 Screenshot from Unity3D showing the 3D reconstruction of Koroneia both from a bird-eye view and as it would appear as a first person navigation.

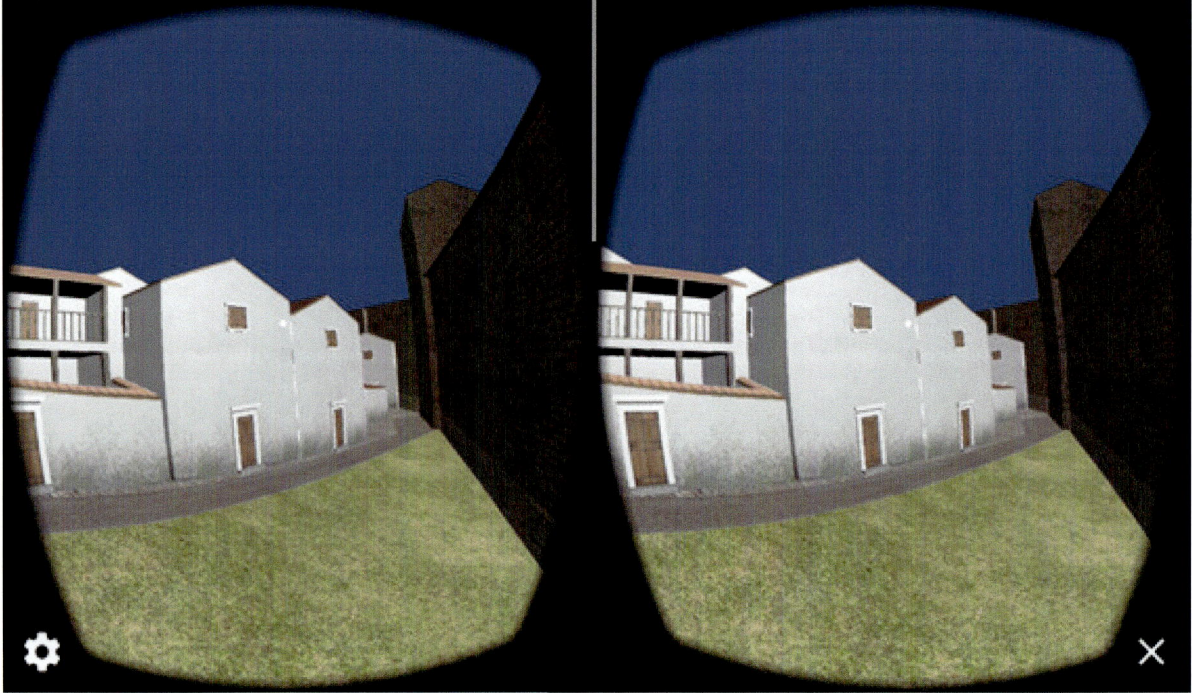

Figure 6.37 A screenshot of the VR experience with a smartphone and a cardboard VR viewer.

Cardboard) in a quite straightforward way, thus enabling an easy re-purpose of the 3D visualisation. The import of the scene created in CityEngine to Unity3D is straightforward using the Autodesk proprietary format FBX, which maintains geometry and textures with no loss of information.

I implemented a walk through the virtual environment of Koroneia, based on a first person controller navigation which allows the user to experience the urban fabric from a pedestrian's point of view (Figure 6.36). From Unity, it was possible moreover to create a prototype VR experience by using a smartphone and an inexpensive cardboard VR viewer which allows the user to stand in a location of the virtual environment and look around (Figure 6.37). Apart from the goal of engaging a public of non-specialists in the exploration of archaeological evidence, from a cognitive point of view, the navigation in the virtual world is useful to enable observations or raise questions that may have not been triggered by merely looking at the picture displaying the final rendering of a 3D visualisation. Observations on how the space is experienced and perceived can be made during the exploration of the virtual environment from within. It is possible to see, for example, what is visible from a certain place and how a change in lighting conditions affects the perception of space. In the case of Koroneia, for example, walking through the virtual environment allows the user to experience how narrow some of the streets were and shows the visual connection between focal points in the urban layout, such as the agora and the acropolis, from the pedestrian point of view.

For the time being, this prototype is used for research purposes only. In the future, however, when the processing of the survey data will be completed, this application can be further developed for heritage purposes. Notwithstanding the wealth of pottery sherds scattered across the site, an occasional visitor or an inhabitant of the nearby villages would struggle to understand the archaeological and cultural value of these apparently unstructured archaeological remains. This fact has unfortunately a major repercussion on the preservation of this ancient city that, as for nearly 80% of Greek sites, is in poor condition and is at risk to disappear. An app that allows the exploration of Koroneia's reconstructed 3D environment could be created as an educational tool, with the involvement of local communities.[1267]

It must be noted, however, the development of such a virtual tour is far from trivial. In fact, a great deal of criticism has been directed at virtual heritage applications that have been developed in the last years, concerning the lack of meaningful content, engagement, and the sense of place, and also the use of expensive technologies that require additional high costs and specialized personnel to guarantee their long term maintenance.[1268] Many factors play a role in how to devise such an interactive tour in order to make it a pleasant and learning experience. The definition of the target group of users is one of the most important aspects to calibrate the storytelling, the type of information that can be accessed and the type of interface that users can find most comfortable to interact with. Ideally, therefore, the application development should include an evaluation phase to monitor the user experience to assess usability, engagement and effectiveness in terms of knowledge acquired, to be able to address any issues.[1269] The time and effort spent for the development of such a virtual visit should also ensure the long term accessibility and maintenance of the applications, in order to avoid that an update in the operating system of the device causes the application to be incompatible with the new OS, thus rendering it useless. These elements will have to be taken into consideration in case of a future implementation of the above mentioned app.

[1267] See Bintliff 2013b.
[1268] A comprehensive review of critical remarks about virtual heritage is given in Tan and Rahaman 2009; see also Pujol and Economou 2009.
[1269] Gockel *et al.* 2013.

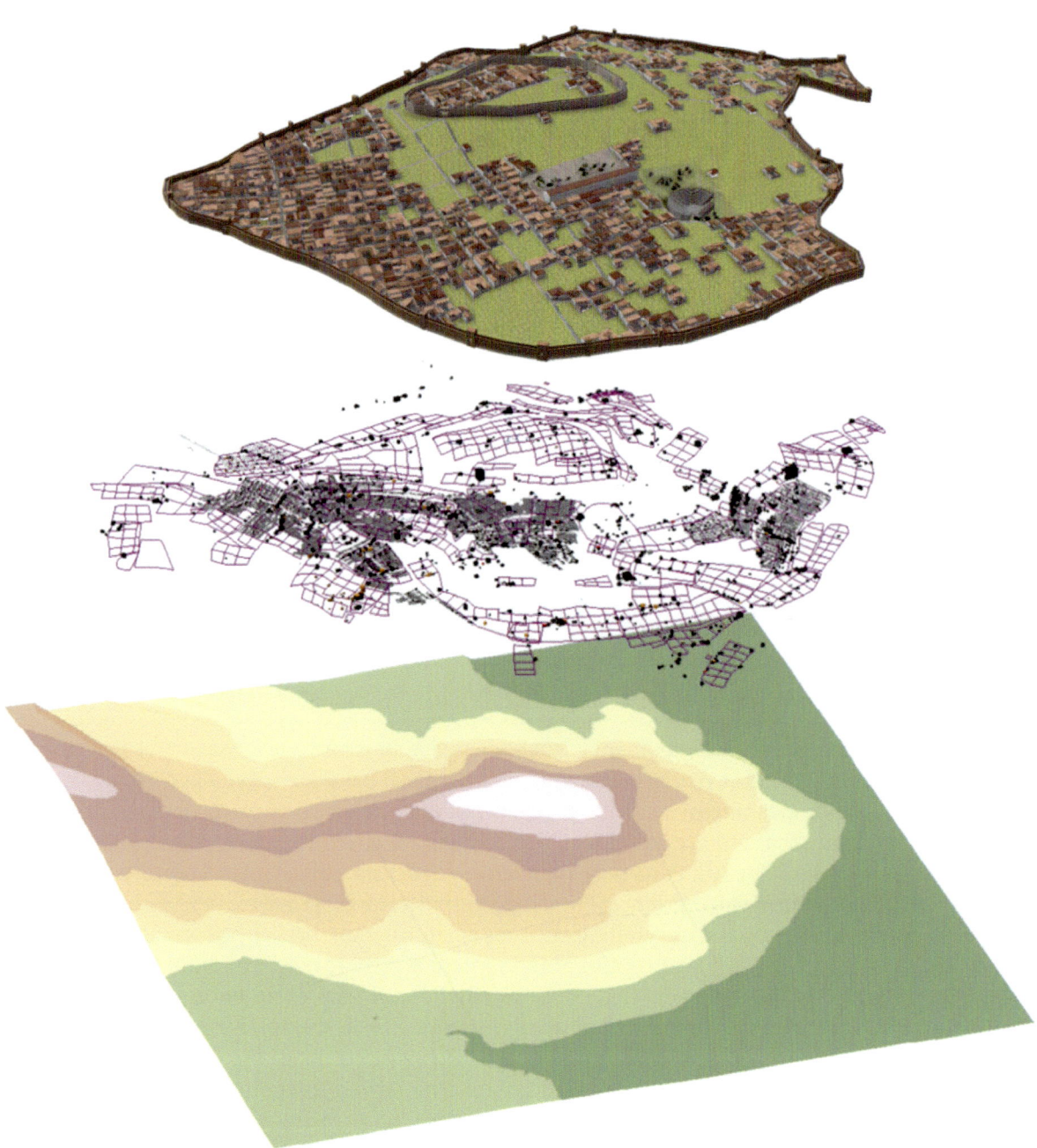

Figure 6.38 The main layers that compose Koroneia's 3D GIS environment. Bottom: terrain layer; middle: survey data (for the moment limited to architecture and geophysical prospections) and survey grids; top: one of Koroneia's procedurally modelled reconstruction hypotheses based on the current state of the data.

6.4. Discussion

6.4.1. Koroneia's 3D reconstruction: Intellectual transparency and reusability

One of the main aims of this study was to develop Koroneia's 3D visualisation taking on board and implementing the London Charter and Seville principles guidelines. As the developers of CE have argued in one of their first papers dealing with the application of this software to historical sites, a procedural modelling approach allows the creation of intellectually transparent and London Charter-compliant 3D models.[1270] In fact, as previously demonstrated, the use of procedural modelling techniques can help us to create multiple hypotheses in a more time efficient way that can then be presented as alternatives, thus conveying the degree of certainty of each element in the reconstruction. The features that are archaeologically documented would remain in fact constant in all the 3D models, while the uncertain parts would be displayed differently according to the range of possibilities that the archaeologists consider as plausible. Moreover, the presentation of multiple reconstructions allows the 3D modeller to avoid choosing a 'peremptory single reconstruction', which is, as already mentioned, one of the problematic aspects of 3D visualisations in archaeology.[1271] While the creation of a 3D model for each possible hypothesis is a very time consuming task in a CG software (and for this reason this solution is rarely adopted), procedural modelling allows the display of multiple reconstructions by changing some parameters' values, as previously shown in the case of Koroneia.

Moreover, procedural modelling allows the insertion of comments in between the lines of the rule files that can, in this way, be enriched with references to all the sources that were used as the basis for the reconstruction and with comments regarding the modelling choices that have been made. The CGA shape grammar being a scripting language, such information can be marked as comments by using a double slash (//) or a hashtag (#) in case of one line comments, or by opening a multi-line comment with /* and closing it with */ (as shown in Figures 6.13, 6.23 and 6.24). This type of information was included in the rule files for Koroneia, which turned out to be useful for two reasons. On the one hand, these comments provide a quick reference to remember the choices made in the modelling process and the data used as comparison. On the other hand, this material allows the rule files to become self-standing sources of information that can be shared as such. In this way, it becomes more accessible and understandable how the 3D reconstruction was developed and according to which data or comparisons the model came into being, which is more difficult to achieve when modelling in a CG software.

Also the exploitation of the interoperability between CityEngine and ArcGIS was geared towards the creation of an intellectually transparent visualization. Since the procedurally modelled 3D reconstruction is created on top of the georeferenced terrain, the former shares the same coordinate system as the original data. In doing so, it can be exported to ArcScene to check the correspondence between the reconstruction and the GIS layers (Figures 6.28 and 6.38).

Besides providing the tools to create an intellectually transparent 3D visualization, procedural modelling also allows an easier re-usability of 3D models. This topic is of particular importance as re-usability goes hand in hand with sustainability and cost/time effectiveness. One of the criticisms raised against archaeological 3D models is in fact that they are quite time consuming to make, and that they are rarely re-used in other projects. With procedural modelling, rule files can be easily shared, and lines of the scripts can be re-used in other rules. It must be noted, however, that the CGA shape grammar can be interpreted by CityEngine only, which limits the reusability of the rule files to this specific software. Nevertheless, all the variations that are procedurally generated can be exported (for example in OBJ or Collada DAE formats), thus allowing wide compatibility with other software packages. In this way, libraries of objects can be easily created that can be combined to create more complex virtual representations. Niccolucci has sustained that, for this reason, 'this methodology will ultimately free users from the need to use skilled craftsmen laboriously to build the 3D models from scratch'.[1272]

[1270] Haegler *et al.* 2009; see chapter 3, 58.
[1271] Forte 2000.
[1272] Niccolucci 2012, 29.

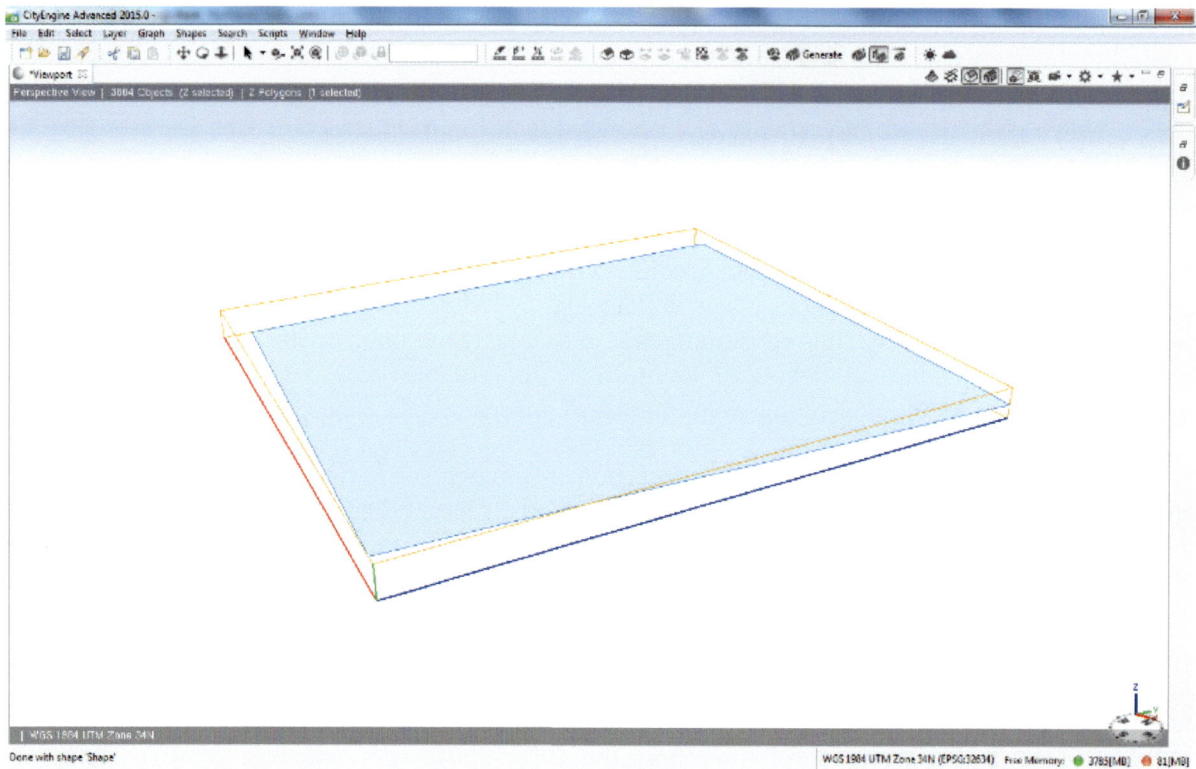

Figure 6.39 A screenshot from CityEngine showing the reference system of the initial lot, which consists of an oriented bounding box ('scope') governing all the operations that are performed on the shape.

6.4.2. Rule-based modelling: challenges and work-arounds

The approach based on procedural modelling, although not devoid of complexity and challenges, proved to be suitable for the display of alternative reconstruction hypotheses of Koroneia in a (semi) automatic way. Moreover, the chosen software CityEngine provides a seamless interaction between the procedurally modelled scene and GIS, as GIS data can be directly imported in CE maintaining their spatial information and their attributes, and CE 3D scenes can be exported to ArcScene in gdb format. In this way, analysis on the built environment is enabled and original data and reconstruction hypotheses overlap, which fosters an intellectually transparent approach to 3D visualizations, further developed by the rule based modelling approach. Besides GIS, this software interfaces well with other environments such as e-on VUE (or Pixar RenderMan) for realistic renderings and Unity3D for interactive virtual tours. The methodology that we have adopted allows us to use the 3D environment as a tool to work with, in order to discover associations between data and evaluate different hypotheses, in line with Gillings' statement that opens this chapter.

Despite the high level of customization that can be reached with the CityEngine's CGA grammar, I have encountered some limitations that required *ad hoc* work-arounds when modelling an archaeologically correct ancient Greek architecture. One of the earliest obstacles I have faced during the creation of this rule set was setting the constraints for the orientation of buildings that could be meaningful in antiquity and the consistent indexing of each shape's axes. In our case, I wanted the houses' courtyards to face a constant direction (towards south or east), as these are the preferable orientations to ensure the best sun exposure. CityEngine's shape grammar includes the possibility to align each shape's scope to the world coordinates, thus allowing control of the geometry's generation. However, in complex geometries this measure reveals shortcomings in the consistent treatment of the scope's alignment across the numerous instances that populate Koroneia's urban environment.

```
y_angle = convert(y, pivot, world, orient,0,0,0)

setpivot_index_uncorrected = floor((y_angle+45)/90)
setpivot_index0 = setpivot_index_uncorrected+0 - floor((setpivot_index_uncorrected+0)/4)*4
setpivot_index1 = setpivot_index_uncorrected+1 - floor((setpivot_index_uncorrected+1)/4)*4
setpivot_index2 = setpivot_index_uncorrected+2 - floor((setpivot_index_uncorrected+2)/4)*4
setpivot_index3 = setpivot_index_uncorrected+3 - floor((setpivot_index_uncorrected+3)/4)*4

//slopeDegrees(sx,sy,sz) = atan (sy / ( (sx + sz)/2 )) This function was used in an earlier
version, CE has now an in-built function to calculate the slope:
slopeDegrees(sx,sy,sz) = geometry.angle(maxSlope)

@StartRule
Lot --> alignScopeToAxes (y)
            //print (slopeDegrees)
            Lot1
Lot1 -->
      case   slopeDegrees(scope.sx,scope.sy,scope.sz) > 13 :
             report("Area.Greenspace",geometry.area)
             LotVegetation

      else:
             alignScopeToAxes(y)
             innerRectangle(edge)
             {shape:
                   t(0,-2,0)
                   extrude(world.up,2)
                   comp(f)
                   {top:
                          alignScopeToGeometry(yUp,0)
                          alignScopeToAxes(y)
                          setPivot (xyz, setpivot_index1)
                          // in this case I chose the N-E corner of the shape's scope
                          as target pivot
                          BuildingArea
                   |side:
                          alignScopeToGeometry(yUp,0)
                          TextureFoundation
                   }
             |remainder: TextureFoundation
             }
```

Figure 6.40 Lines of the CGA rule for domestic architecture which allows a more robust control on the reference system of the initial lot.

To better understand this problem, some clarifications are needed on how CityEngine handles the shape generation. Each shape that is created by the software (from lots to geometry created via procedural rules) has a set of locally interrelated coordinate systems – the object, pivot and scope coordinate systems – upon which all the geometric operations are based (e.g. rotation, translation, scale, split and component split).[1273] According to the CityEngine's guidelines, in the object coordinate system, the origin is placed at the first point of the initial shape's *first edge* (which is identified as the edge facing a street and therefore the 'front'), and the axes are oriented such that the x-axis is along the first edge, the y-axis is along the first face's normal and the z-axis is perpendicular to the former two.[1274] The pivot is located at the origin of the shape and when a component split is performed, it is placed at the first point of the first edge of the component, with x along the first edge of the face and z along the face's normal. The scope coordinate system relates to the pivot's orientation and it is composed by an oriented bounding box, specifying the length and orientation of its x, y and z axes (Figure 6.39). When a split or a component split (which allows one to divide a shape

---

[1273] See CityEngine's help for further information (http://cehelp.esri.com/help/index.jsp?topic=/com.procedural.cityengine.help/html/manual/is/create/block_params.html)
[1274] See CityEngine's help for further information (http://cehelp.esri.com/help/index.jsp?topic=/com.procedural.cityengine.help/html/manual/cga/shape_operations/cga_so_trans_coordinatesystems.html)

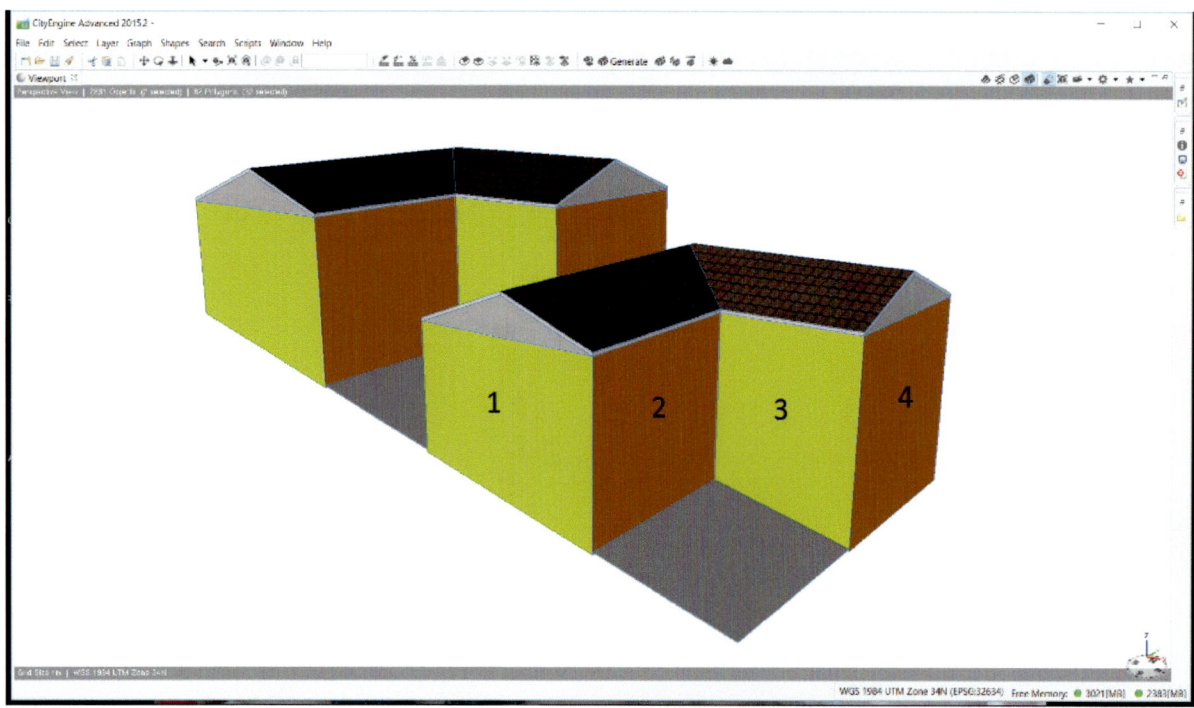

Figure 6.41 The problematic treatment of building facades in default L-shapes: using CityEngine's standard syntax faces 1 and 3 cannot be distinguished and neither can 2 and 4, which makes it challenging to assign a different texture to facades facing the courtyard with respect to those that face the street. The adopted solution is given below.

```
LshapedHouseFacades_i(dx,y1,dy,dz,sx,sz)=
    LshapedHouseFacades_i2((sin(y1)*dx+cos(y1)*dz)/sx, 2+ (dy+45)/90, -(cos(y1)*dx-
    sin(y1)*dz)/sz)

LshapedHouseFacades_i2(xt,yt,zt)=
    LshapedHouseFacades_i3(1*float((xt>0.1)&&(xt<=0.9)) + 2*float(xt>0.9), floor(yt)-
    floor(yt/4)*4, 1*float((zt>0.1)&&(zt<=0.9)) + 2*float(zt>0.9))

LshapedHouseFacades_i3(xt,yt,zt)=
    3*float((yt==0)&&(zt==1)) +         // east side, court
    4*float((yt==3)&&(xt==1)) +         // south side, court
    5*float((yt==0)&&(zt==0)) +         // east side, street right
    6*float((yt==1)&&(xt==0)) +         // north side, street
    7*float((yt==2)) +                  // west side, street
    8*float((yt==3)&&(xt==2))           // south side, street
```

Figure 6.42 Lines of rule that allow a consistent indexing of the L-shaped building's facades.

into its geometric components, such as faces, edges and vertices) is performed, a new coordinate system has to be assigned to the newly created children shapes, which usually take on the coordinate system of the predecessor.

In our case, the problem lies in the identification of the first edge of the initial shape (which is then passed on to the shape's successors) as the edge facing the street. Our lots are randomly distributed within each block and therefore their first edge will not have a consistent position across the various shapes. However, such consistent orientation was needed to create houses that had their courtyards facing a specific, pre-determined direction, in such a way that the appearance of each procedurally modelled facade and roof could be controlled. CityEngine allows the user to manually select the first edge, however this procedure would have been unfeasible for the high number of shapes that needed to be manually checked. In fact, Dobraja specifies that in the case of 1795 buildings that composed her 3D scene of Bavarian rural buildings, it took about 5 hours to manually change the first edge of each shape to the desired location.[1275]

As I wanted to ensure the maximum automatization of the town creation – especially given that the scene would be expected to be remodelled several times due to the ongoing nature of the survey – I have included a different approach within the rules that allows a more robust treatment of the pivot of the initial shape. Instead of taking the street position as reference point, a series of mathematical functions compares the current pivot's position with that of the target pivot (for example, the farthest NE corner of the shape to obtain a courtyard oriented towards S or SE) and determines how many steps the pivot has to shift to create the same angle with the world axes as the target pivot. This work-around concatenates several attributes whose values are calculated on the fly and are assigned as input value to the next one (the corresponding lines are shown in Figure 6.40).[1276] Specifically, the attribute y_angle calculates the orientation of the y-axis of the shape's pivot in relation to the world axes, using the convert function. Next, the attribute setpivot_index_uncorrected uses the floor function[1277] to assign the input value of *y-angle* to a quadrant (i.e. if *y_angle* is comprised between -45 and +45°, then *setpivot_index_uncorrected* = 0; if *y_angle* is comprised between 45° and 135° then *setpivot_index_uncorrected* = 1, etc.). Finally, a set of attributes setpivot_indexN determine the amount of steps that have to be taken to arrive at the target pivot from the initial pivot. Since the situation can occur that the results give values that are outside the 0-3 range (e.g. -1, -2 or 4, 5, etc. in case the angle is calculated cyclically), multiples of 4 have to be subtracted to obtain a number within the 0-3 range as a final result. Each of the setpivot_indexN attributes can then be used as parameter of the setPivot function when control is needed on the orientation of the shapes' pivot, assuming that the shape has 4 vertices. Specifically, in our case, these attributes have been crucial to select the starting pivot that guides the creation of the roof shade so as to guarantee the correct orientation of the slanted roof towards the courtyard.

Another challenging aspect of modelling using the CGA grammar instead of a manual modelling approach regarded the creation of a roofed court. The majority of the other archaeological projects that have used CityEngine have focused on Roman architecture. In a typical Roman house, the courtyard is surrounded by a peristyle, which can be modelled easily in CityEngine by generating an offset to an initial rectangular or square lot, extruding the resulting shape to the desired height, and assigning a sloping roof to the top faces.[1278] In our case, in contrast, the majority of the houses had a roofed porch or a wing around some, but not all, of the courtyard's sides. As a result, each of the facades had to be treated in a different way. The standard functions of CityEngine, however, did not give enough control over individual facades after performing component splits, especially when using the built-in shapeL and shapeU (see Figure 6.41), which is why a function was needed that consistently indexed the facades of a building. Briefly, a hierarchy of functions was developed that calculated the coordinates and orientation of each facade relative to the original shape's bounding box, and then converted these values into an integer range (1 to 8 for U-shaped buildings; 3 to 8 for L-shaped buildings) indicating each individual facade in a consistent way. For more detail, see Figure 6.42 for the rules for indexing the facades of L-shaped buildings.[1279]

[1275] Dobraja 2015, 31.
[1276] I thank J. B. van Klinken for his suggestions on how to deal with this aspect, and for his advice on using the floor function to evaluate and convert the pivot position to the target orientation.
[1277] The floor function gives the *greatest* integer less than or equal to x (e.g. the floor of 2.4 is 2). The opposite to the floor function is the ceiling function which returns the *smallest* integer that is greater than or equal to x (in the example, the ceiling of 2.4 is 3).
[1278] A similar shape can be obtained with the CityEngine in-built OShape, but due to how this in-built shape handles the top face, it would not be possible to create the inward sloping roof typical of peristyles.
[1279] I thank J.B. van Klinken for suggesting to me this way to formalize the indexing of the buildings' facades consistently.

Finally, a challenging issue was to create houses with open courtyards and/or open porches that are situated on a hilly terrain. The easiest solution to ensure that the initial slanted 2D shape would not protrude through the courtyard was to create a foundation beneath the house that would elevate the house to the highest point on the lot. This solution, however, gave irrealistically high foundations for houses on steep slopes, so I chose to compensate the slope only partly by introducing a foundation. For this reason, I used a component split that allowed me to transform this initial 2D shape in the groundfloor of the building (by extrusion). For steep terrains the problem remained that the terrain would intersect the courtyard facades on the ground floor, leaving holes in the facades' geometry. In this case, I had to split the courtyard facades along the y axes and subsequently re-scale the upper part that was not intersected by the terrain to the full extent of the ground floor. For details, see the function **PorchGroundFloor1** in the rule file.

6.5. Conclusions and future work

This chapter presented the methodology aiming to automatize both the organization of Koroneia's survey data in a 3D GIS and the 3D visualization of several reconstruction hypotheses of one of the phases of occupation of the hill, corresponding to a moment of possible destruction and rebuilding of the town centre, and limited to the space within the city wall circuit of that period. By writing an *ad hoc* procedural rule, which enables a customization of the visualization that goes beyond the capability of ArcGIS attribute-driven and 3D symbology, I have created a visualization that provides an intuitive insight into the types of blocks that are present on the hill. These rules have been applied to the reconstructed terrain to obtain a series of possible reconstruction hypotheses for the city layout, which can be interactively displayed by changing the parametric values that are expressed in the rule files. To our knowledge, this is the first implementation of a set of procedural rules for (late) Classical Greek architecture.

The workflow implemented in CityEngine and ArcGIS was integrated by the use of Open Source and free software packages such as QuantumGIS for the quick creation of shapefiles of some specific find classes, GIMP for the creation and editing of the textures that I have used for the 3D models, Blender and SketchUp to manually model some of the 3D buildings that were inserted in the scene, and Unity3D for setting up the interactive navigation. In order to make the creation of different reconstruction hypotheses as automatic as possible, I have used attribute maps (obstacle, mapping and function) to easily switch between visualizations that are plausible given the state of the data. The reconstruction of the terrain and of alternative hypotheses for the possible town layout, besides being useful to visualize the uncertainty in our dataset, has allowed me to estimate population figures, by setting constraints (e.g. slope threshold, house's dimensions and land use) which are explicit and easily modifiable when needed.

The approach here presented embeds the 3D reconstruction within the cycle of hypothesis generation and creates opportunities to use 3D visualizations as interpretative and analytical tools at the service of the archaeological research. The approach is particularly suitable for a site, such as Koroneia, where the study and investigations are still in progress, which implies future updates of the resulting 3D visualization. This workflow allowed me therefore to focus on the *process* of 'reconstructing', and on the analytical aspects of such an endeavour, rather than on the end result. Moreover, the chosen procedural modelling approach allowed me to be explicit about my modelling choices and interpretations. This is an important point in any archaeological research and especially in the case of Koroneia where, as discussed in chapter 4, that there are still many open questions given the ongoing study of some finds categories.

The methodology here described entails the initial effort of compiling the rule files in a way that best suits the characteristics of the dataset and the scope of the project. In the long term, however, this

6. Enhancing Koroneia's GIS survey data with the third dimension

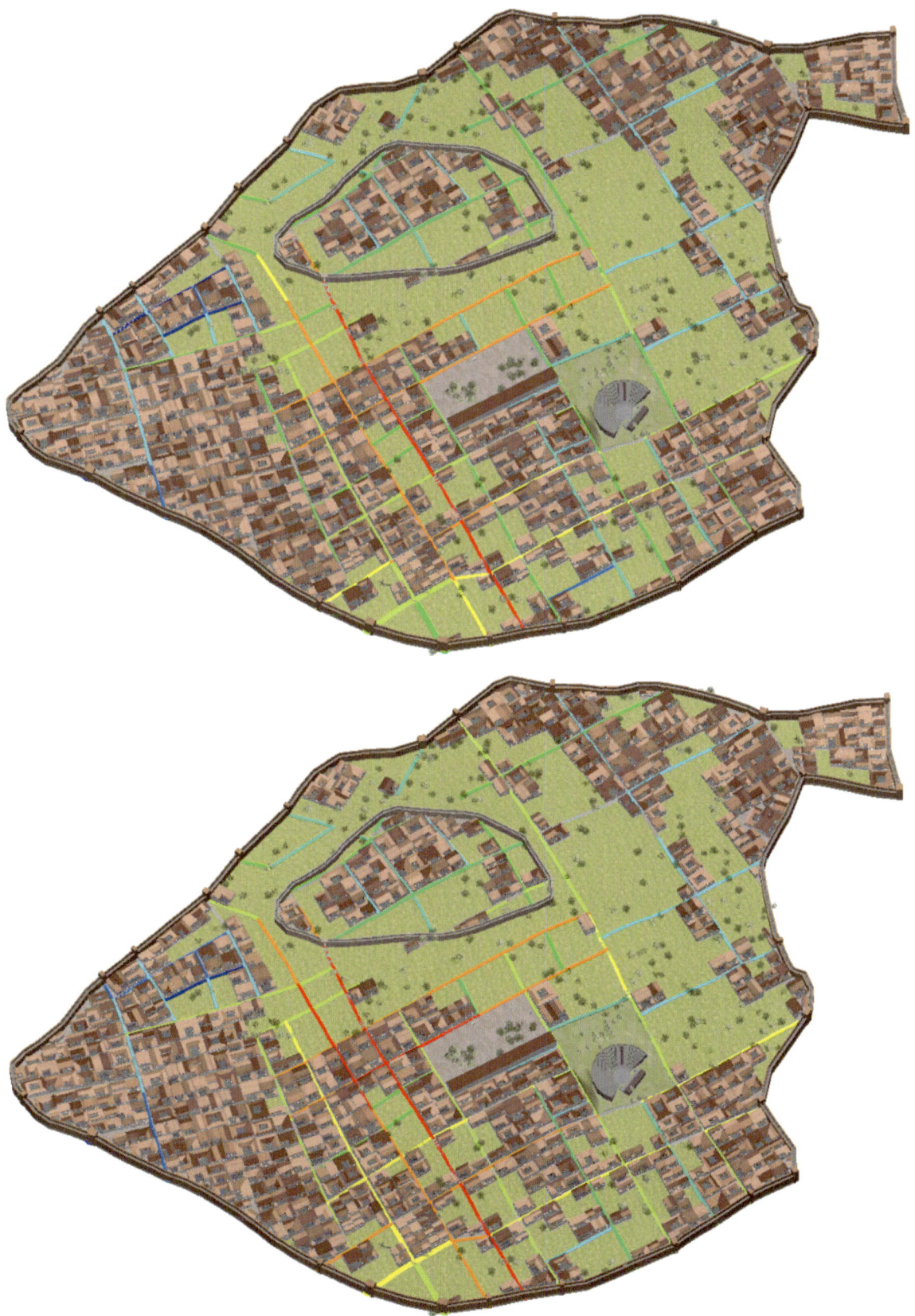

Figure 6.43 Results of the test analysis on global (top) and local (bottom) integration values of Koroneia's reconstructed street network.

approach results in a time efficient data handling, updating and displaying of alternative hypotheses which account for the different interpretations of the available data. This rule-based approach allows the recording of modelling steps to enable the assessment of the work by other scholars and fosters the possibilities of sharing and re-using existing assets for new projects, thus increasing the time and cost efficiency of the approach on the long term. Moreover, the focus on automation and iteration of the modelling process creates the premises to consider the 3D visualization as a tool to work with, instead of a mere representation of already acquired knowledge. To this end, the use of map layers associated with rule files as I show-cased in this chapter represents a time efficient workflow for the modelling of alternative reconstruction hypotheses and in view of the prospective updates needed in the long term.

The drawbacks of using this approach are related to the initial effort spent in learning CityEngine's shape grammar and to the technical aspects of the software installation, which, in its latest releases, requires powerful computers and graphic cards to be able to work.[1280] Moreover, the fact that this software is not backwards compatible and does not allow the user to save the scene in some previous version's format, as is the case in other software such as AutoCAD, heavily impacts the editing and sharing of the 3D scene in CityEngine proprietary format (*.cej) with different users or on different computers. For a study that aims at intellectual transparency, the use of a commercial software for the development of the 3D visualization and of the CityEngine web viewer for its publication may be seen as problematic. However, CityEngine is currently the only software on the market which offers the integration of procedural modelling and GIS and thus fulfils the requirements of Koroneia's 3D visualization project. Moreover, the CityEngine web viewer is optimized for the online publication of 3D scenes that are created in CityEngine and allows the comparison of alternative reconstruction hypotheses by using the swipe view, as shown above.

Future work on this project should include the mapping in a 3D GIS of the settlements in Koroneia's territory (*chora*) and should also extend the 3D reconstruction to include the countryside, to create a holistic view of the functioning of the town within its broader context, as the surrounding territory has always been an integral part of the life of the town. Moreover, the same procedural modelling approach could be extended to other time periods, for example by creating or adapting the libraries of Roman architecture that have been already used in other projects that were mentioned in chapter 3. An additional map layer and related rule file can be created that colour codes the level of reliability of the reconstruction (e.g. green = based on survey data; yellow = inferred from survey data; orange = based on comparisons with other sites; red = conjectural).

Regarding the exploitation of the 3D reconstruction for analysis, there are more possibilities that can be explored – especially when the study of the survey data will be concluded and a more complete overview of Koroneia's urban layout can be offered. One future direction of research that I have started to explore is the analysis of the street network based on the principles of the Space Syntax theory, which relates the spatial configuration of the built environment to the social structure that created it.[1281] For the moment, I have run an analysis which computes the global and local integration values[1282] of Koroneia's street network by using the built-in 'analyse graph' tool in CityEngine. While global integration usually reproduces the patterns of centrality, thus giving predictable results, the local integration index is more suitable to highlight patterns of movements and areas of commercial activities at a local scale.[1283]

[1280] The system requirements for the 2016.1 release include 16 GB or RAM and OpenGL 4.1 or later (the complete list is available here http://desktop.arcgis.com/en/cityengine/latest/get-started/esri-cityengine-system-requirements.htm).
[1281] Hillier and Hanson 1984.
[1282] Global integration computes the closeness of an axial line in the street network to all the other axial lines, while local integration indicates closeness only up to a defined radius of topological distance.
[1283] Cutini 2009, 88; 95.

The analyses of Koroneia's street network show that the most integrated streets both at the global and local level are those bordering the agora on its eastern and western slopes (Figure 6.43). While at this stage it is necessary to be careful in advancing hypotheses based on the analysis of a fragmentary and partially reconstructed street network, it will be interesting to further develop this line of research. The area highlighted in the analysis corresponds indeed to the borders of what the survey has identified as the market place of the town, and to the core of the Roman settlement on the hill.

Besides the further development of a VR experience with a portable headset, another possibility that was discussed at the beginning of this project was the exploitation of Augmented Reality technology to create an on-site navigation where the reconstructed 3D buildings are superimposed on the real world. As already mentioned in chapter 3, AR is a popular technique and holds great promise for the future. The creation of outdoor, on site AR applications is however still challenging. So far, solutions have been offered by commercial companies that sell their development kits with different licensing options or promise to take care of all the process of creation of the AR application.[1284] The market of available platforms is however still fluctuating and the overall impression is that this technology still lacks standards and consistency, a *caveat* that was already voiced by a survey of the state of the art of this field in 2011.[1285] As a consequence, it is at present difficult to create applications that will guarantee to remain functioning in the long term and that work across several operating systems. Developments that are happening at this moment (especially regarding the release of Apple's ARKit and Google's ARCore development kit) however promise to change the situation and will certainly lead in the near future to an increased number of experimentations with this technology which will benefit also the heritage sector.

[1284] Current companies offering such services are e.g. Vuforia (https://developer.vuforia.com/) and Augment (http://www.augment.com/).
[1285] Butchart 2011.

7. Conclusions

This research has focussed on visual reconstructions of historical cities that have been created from the early modern period up to the present day. On a theoretical level, this work aimed at examining how past cityscapes have been visually reconstructed over the centuries, and at reflecting on the current use of digital 3D reconstructions, especially in relation to their applications as means of interpretations and analysis of the archaeological evidence (chapters 2 and 3). On a practical level, these considerations have contributed to the implementation of a workflow for the GIS-based 3D reconstruction of the ancient town of Koroneia, in Boeotia, Central Greece, during the 4th century BC (chapter 6). Moreover, this research has produced a synthesis both of the currently available data for Koroneia and of the urban development of Greek towns from the Archaic period to Late Antiquity (chapters 4 and 5), which can be useful starting points for future research at Koroneia and elsewhere.

The methodology discussed in chapter 6 included the use of tools borrowed from modern urban planning which have been adapted to respond to the requirements of archaeological visualizations, such as intellectual transparency and easy updating. Koroneia's case study is admittedly a difficult one, since the state of preservation of the urban fabric is limited and the use of non-destructive methods for its investigation provides us with a spatially and temporally broad dataset, which lacks however the contextual analysis of stratigraphic sequences. However, as this is a common situation for the majority of urban sites in Greece and elsewhere, Koroneia provided an appropriate dataset to develop and experiment with a workflow that is flexible enough to be applied to other contexts.

The starting point of this research has been the consideration that reconstructions are knowledge representations, thus bound to the specific context of their making.[1286] Their creation and reception depend on the combination of several factors, which include the background of the modeller, the data and technology that are available at the moment of their making, and ultimately also the background of the beholders that will judge the reconstruction according to their own set of previous knowledge and interest.[1287] Following this line of thought, I investigated more closely how the reconstruction of past cityscapes has been approached over the centuries. Chapter 2 therefore analysed a selection of reconstructions of Greek and Roman cities in Europe from the 15th to the 20th century. The works here discussed offered opportunities to reflect on the changing methods, purposes and uses of archaeological reconstruction drawings and three-dimensional physical models over this long period of time. More specifically, some parallel lines of research were examined: When and why did the interest for drawing reconstructions of antiquities arise? Which were the sources and methods used to prepare such reconstructions? When did three-dimensional representations start to be used and which methodological challenges did they pose? To answer these questions, the reconstructions have been contextualized within their historical and cultural framework, as well as the personal background of their creator.

This overview showed how these drawings, far from being neutral representations of a distant past, where instead the expression of specific cultural factors, political and ideological intentions. These reconstructions, however naïve, a-historical and outdated they may appear nowadays to us, provide an insight into the mentality of their time and are valuable sources of information in their own right about the fascinations, interests and political agendas of their creators. This chapter gave moreover a glimpse into the development of a method of scientific inquiry within antiquarian and archaeological studies and aimed to put into historical perspective the work of the present-day researcher, who deals with

---

[1286] Favro 2006, 326.
[1287] Cf. Favro 2006.

reconstructions of archaeological evidence. In fact, as this chapter has demonstrated, many challenges, questions and pitfalls that affected the earlier attempts of reconstructing archaeological evidence are the same that concern scholars nowadays.

Looking at reconstructions of archaeological evidence from a historical perspective evidenced the time-bound and subjective nature of such representations, which brought into focus another aspect, namely the significance of accurately documenting their creation process. The recognition of the transient nature of reconstructions emphasizes in fact the importance of being explicit about the data, the comparative material, and the line of interpretation underlying their creation. These documents will remain in fact as the starting point for future research, even in case of the obsolescence of digital formats and the replacement of current methods with more advanced techniques. This 'intellectual transparency' allows the replicability of the reconstruction process, which presents a double advantage. On the one hand it allows us to iterate its creation and update it when new data are available, on the other hand it allows its long term preservation.

The implementation of intellectually transparent visualizations has received much attention in recent years. In its dawn, the field of 3D digital archaeology had been mainly practice-driven and lacked a more conceptual reflection on methods, purposes, opportunities and pitfalls of this range of techniques. Over the years, not only the technical equipment that archaeologists found at their disposal have expanded, but also the theoretical discussion has converged to provide more conceptual tools to approach this discipline in a critical and mature way. I have dealt with these aspects in chapter 3, which discussed the development of 3D visualisations applied to the archaeological domain, with a particular focus on the built environment. Specifically, the first part of the chapter was dedicated to the presentation of the main methods that are available to create reconstruction hypotheses for buildings and sites that are now (partially) lost. An historical perspective on the applications of Virtual Reality in archaeology was also presented. The second part focused on the solutions that have been adopted so far to make 3D reconstructions more intellectually transparent, by including data, hypotheses, modelling methods and choices that guided the process of their creation. The attention to the philological process behind the creation of 3D reconstructions has represented a great step forward towards their acceptance as valid instruments to communicate scientific knowledge. A tangible risk of deception related to 3D reconstructions in archaeology was in fact recognised since their early applications by practitioners in this field. Providing access to this kind of information has become a crucial prerequisite for the admission of 3D visualizations among the instruments of scholarly communication, as stated in the documents issued in recent years such as the London Charter and the Seville principles. These considerations form the basis onto which I have developed the methodology for the creation of Koroneia's 3D GIS.

In the same chapter, I have moreover elaborated on the assertion that the contribution of 3D visualizations for interpretation and analysis has not been fully exploited yet. While 3D recording techniques have been increasingly adopted as tools for a fast and accurate documentation, 3D reconstructions are in fact usually limited to describe and present knowledge that is already acquired. Through the presentation of published case studies, I have showed how 3D reconstructions can offer instead interpretative and analytical capabilities that allow the formulation of hypotheses on the past use of space and on its social implications. In this regard, I have argued that in order to unlock the analytical potential of 3D visualizations, archaeologists need to have a key role in the creation process, as understanding the technique is a prerequisite to formulate the relevant questions that can be appropriately addressed by using it. To this end, a broader digital literacy among archaeologists is needed to be able to understand the capabilities of these methods in order to assess whether and how the creation of such applications would be beneficial for their research.

The convergence between 3D modelling and GIS and the analytical possibilities that a 3D GIS currently offers is particularly interesting, and the teaching of these techniques should be taken into consideration as part of the academic curriculum. Such applications offer a viable solution for bridging the still existing gap between data collection, analysis and public fruition: the most plausible 3D reconstruction hypothesis, congruent with the dataset and resulting from an iterative modelling process, can in fact be used to communicate the results of the research in a visually appealing way. In this case, an increased digital literacy in this field will constitute a valuable asset to better communicate with technicians in case of the likely scenario that extra technical expertise (e.g. in scripting, game development, animation etc.) needs to be outsourced for the completion of a project.

The introductory chapters 2 and 3, sketching the history of archaeological reconstructions of Greek and Roman architecture before and during the digital age, were followed by three chapters in which the case study and the methodology of this research were presented more in depth. Chapter 4 focused on the ancient town of Koroneia, by presenting its geographical context, historical background and a discussion of the currently available data coming from both the Boeotia survey project and previous investigations at the site. The latter include the accounts of 19th century travellers, the reports of the excavations carried out in the course of the 20th century, and surveys by scholars such as the German topographer Siegfried Lauffer. The combination of old and new data and the interdisciplinary approach that we have taken have allowed the formulation of hypotheses on the function of some of the surveyed structures and areas of the ancient town. The ongoing survey and the consequently continuous flow of incoming data from Koroneia made this site a suitable case study to experiment with the creation of a 3D visualization that is introduced early on in the archaeological investigation and acts as a virtual laboratory where data are merged and compared, and reconstruction hypotheses are generated, tested and refined in the light of incoming new data.

The necessity to study Koroneia's urban life from its beginning during the Archaic period to its abandonment in the late Middle Ages urged us to collect a body of comparisons with other sites that could help in contextualizing Koroneia's urban development in its broader framework. To this end, chapter 5 has outlined general trends and discussed specific case studies that illustrate the development of Greek urban centres, especially from a topographical and architectural point of view, from the Archaic period to Late Antiquity. Specifically, chapter 5 focussed on the elements of continuity and discontinuity in the urban topography of Graeco-Roman towns over the centuries, drawing particular attention to the 'three-dimensionality' of the sites and their relationship with terrain morphology. The first part of the chapter was dedicated to present a brief overview of the range of possible urban layouts that have been documented for Greek urban centres. A selection was made of the sites that share similar characteristics with Koroneia, such as the fact that they are laid out on hilly or irregular terrains, and that have been excavated to such an extent to make it possible to draw conclusions about the relationship between town plan and landscape. The second part of the chapter was dedicated to the buildings that are typically found in a Graeco-Roman town and the transformation they underwent in their architectural development and in the use of space during the centuries taken into consideration. Specific elements and areas of the urban space were discussed, such as sanctuaries, *agorai*, theatres, houses, training spaces, industrial areas and urban fortifications.

Finally, in chapter 6, the methodology for the creation of Koroneia's 3D GIS and the results of this study were presented in more detail. As some areas of Koroneia's hill are not accessible for surveying, or could be only partially investigated due to the presence of overgrown vegetation or a steep slope, a number of questions about the urban structure and its relationship with the hilly terrain arose during the survey, which we aimed to investigate by creating this 3D environment. More specifically, one of the objectives of this research was to formulate a series of hypotheses about the town layout, which preliminary data showed as following two different orientations (a roughly north-south and east-west orientation in the northern part of the town with a shift of about N25°E in the southern part). This in turn led to a series of considerations about the number of houses and hence population estimation, which could be suggested on the basis of explicit assumptions. Interestingly, these estimations independently agree in scale with the results from the calculations based on historical sources. This thesis aimed moreover at exploring the current analytical possibilities of a 3D GIS for the urban environment, which allows the overlay of data and interpretation within the same georeferenced environment, and the evaluation of the buildings' visibility.

In choosing the appropriate methodology to achieve these goals, three requirements needed to be met, which ruled out most of the currently available computer graphics software packages based on manual modelling: the suitability for creating a 3D GIS environment that could store efficiently the survey data and display them on the hilly terrain, the possibility to design a 3D reconstruction that could be easily updated when new data are available, and the ability to model the entire urban fabric in an efficient way, including individual houses. Cities pose in fact methodological challenges in handling data at different resolutions and in integrating the unavoidable missing pieces of such a large environment with comparisons to other sites. In this respect, additional requirements for the resulting 3D reconstruction were moreover the transparency and the replicability of its creation process, which have been considered necessary elements to ensure its assessment and validation by the academic community.

The data from the survey have been visualized and integrated using a novel approach that combines GIS and procedural modelling, which entails the creation of 3D geometries by writing text-based rule files that contain their formal description. The software I used was Esri CityEngine, which is currently targeted to modern urban planners to present different development scenarios to local communities, aiming to foster a form of participatory and interactive urban design. The procedural and parametric modelling that CityEngine affords allows in fact the user to change in real time elements in the 3D scenes, by simply modifying values or lines of script in the rule file. While being developed for satisfying the needs of modern urban planners, this methodology is suitable also for historical towns. Instead of presenting a fixed image of Koroneia, this approach contributes in fact to establish a visual dialogue between the original data and the 3D reconstruction, which can be changed to reflect different hypotheses based on the most updated state of the data. The focus of this project is therefore more on the *process* of creation, and what kind of observations can we gain from it, than on the end result.

The adopted workflow consisted of two phases: 1) mapping of the finds onto the DEM of the hill to visualize their distribution and characteristics as recorded during fieldwork; 2) reconstruction of the ancient terrain and the possible layout of the *polis* in the 4th century BC. As I have discussed in the course of chapter 6, the methodology based on a combination of GIS and procedural modelling met the requirements of the ongoing survey and can be applied to other archaeological contexts with similar characteristics. For Koroneia, I have written a set of rule files, which generate the 3D models of domestic and public architecture, and enables an analytical approach to the built environment. While procedural modelling has already been used for other archaeological sites, this is the first implementation of a set of procedural rules for (late) Classical Greek architecture.

An additional rule was written to be used as a procedural symbology layer in ArcGIS, which exposes the properties of the architectural dataset (i.e. dimensions and stone type) in an automatic and more customizable way in comparison with standard 3D symbology. This provides an immediate overview of concentrations of larger or smaller blocks, and clusters of stone types, which can point to the presence of different types of buildings. Working in a 3D GIS environment has moreover the advantage that it is possible to observe – better than in a 2D GIS – the relationship between the hilly morphology of the terrain and the distribution of finds, such as the locations of the architectural blocks in relation to the terraces' edges. The proposed workflow can be extended to other classes of finds (e.g. pottery sherds), and can be applied to other contexts where stratigraphic information is available to create a 3D GIS of excavated trenches.

The recent acquisition of CityEngine by Esri, moreover, has initiated the assimilation of the software capabilities within the ArcGIS components, resulting in a CityEngine toolbox added to the version 10.2 of ArcGIS among the 3D Analyst tools. This partnership has furthered the creation of a 'true' 3D GIS of cityscapes, and included the possibility of procedurally sampling a grid of points on the 3D geometry's surface that can be used to perform visibility analysis. This workflow, which we included in our rule files, allows the quantitative analysis of which portions of a building are visible from a given location. The application of this workflow in past urban contexts can have a great impact on the understanding of relationships between buildings, and enables the evaluation of different scenarios that are created using the parametric modelling approach that we have adopted.

This methodology addressed also the issue of providing an intellectually transparent 3D visualization. It is in fact impossible to eliminate subjective bias from 3D reconstructions, as these are culturally and historically bound and result from a personal interpretation of the available data. The approach that has been here presented deals with the issue of transparency in several complementary ways. On the one hand, I have created different reconstruction hypotheses that are plausible given our dataset, which is made possible in a time efficient way by the parametric modelling approach that we have adopted. On the other hand, the procedural rules hierarchically record the steps I have taken in modelling the 3D environment and include annotations which clarify the comparative material that I used, thus making the creation process more explicit. In addition, the 3D reconstruction is created on top of the GIS data within the same coordinate system, thus maintaining a spatial and visual relationship between the hypothesis and the original data. Finally, chapters 4 and 5 offer an in-depth textual discussion of the original data and the sources for comparisons that were used for the 3D visualizations, thus providing the starting point for future research. When the study of the survey material will be concluded, additional ways to make available the original data can be explored, such as by adding layers in the CityEngine webviewer, thus allowing users to see for themselves the relationship between data and interpretation.

The multidisciplinary approach that is enabled by using this workflow promotes a holistic approach to the study of past built environments. This process allows a better overview of the available data, helps to trigger new questions that can drive the fieldwork practice, and to generate and evaluate hypotheses. Besides finding the most appropriate workflow for Koroneia, the purpose of this work was also to propose a methodology that could be effectively applied to other urban sites that were investigated with non-destructive methods. The possibility of using 3D reconstructions as an integral part of research is enabled only if these 3D models can be easily modified to visualize and test different hypotheses that emerge from the interpretation of the data, and quickly updated to include new available data. To this end, our rule files can be customized and reused on different configurations of street networks, thus making this approach time-efficient in the long term.

The rule-based approach in combination with GIS mapping has proven to be a viable solution for Koroneia, but it can be applied both to the reconstruction of other historical cities, and to automate (part of) the process of creating or distributing 3D models. Visualizing past cityscapes is a challenging task,[1288] but the application of rule-based modelling helps to tackle some of the issues involved. For early modern cities, or for historical cities in which part of the city layout is preserved, available (cadastral) maps could be digitized and related to a database containing the surviving information about the buildings and their inhabitants. An *ad hoc* rule that interrogates the attributes in the database could

---

[1288] At this regard, see Favro 2006.

then be written to automate the creation of 3D buildings complying with the target characteristics (e.g. roof shape, number of floors and windows etc.), but also to create different visualizations that display additional information on the buildings when available (e.g. census data).

In conclusion, 3D visualizations in archaeology have much more to offer than an artificial image of the past, and the exploration of their potential for the reconstruction of the built environment provides new opportunities to research and to present to the public the complexity of the archaeological record. At the intersection between 3D modelling, GIS and Virtual Reality lies an exciting new field of research that investigates the multisensory experience of the city, which indeed does not only rely on sight but introduces the other senses as co-participants in the exploration.[1289] This approach would encourage the experience of the city from the street level, not only from the bird's eye view that we are accustomed to by the use of 2D plans. Parametric modelling, with its possibility of generating different visualizations based on the encoded numerical values, would allow us to quickly change the characteristics of the reconstructed buildings (e.g. heights) and thus evaluate the impact of these changes on the urban fabric.

The modelling strategy that has been adopted here is instrumental for conveying the 'in progress' nature of our knowledge of a site, and allows the 3D visualization to become a replicable process, which is based on explicit assumptions that can be easily inspected and whose reliability can be assessed. The contribution that this work hopes to have made is indeed in the direction of considering 3D reconstructions not as fixed images of the past, but as laboratories where multiple reconstructions and hypotheses can be visualized, evaluated and discussed.

[1289] Among the advocates of this approach: Favro 2006 and Betts 2011.

Bibliography

Abbreviations

BCH 47 (1923) = *Chronique des fouilles et découvertes archéologiques dans l'Orient hellénique, Bulletin de Correspondance Hellénique*, vol. 47 (1), 498-544.

EPHEM. EPIGR. = *Ephemeris epigraphica, Corporis inscriptionum Latinarum supplementum*, vol. 1, Edita iussu Instituti Archaeologici Romani, 1872.

FHG = *Fragmenta Historicorum Graecorum* edited by Karl Müller, Paris: Ambroise Firmin-Didot, 1848.

Bibliographical references

Abbagnano, N. 1993. *Storia della Filosofia. Volume Quarto. La Filosofia Moderna dei Secoli XVII e XVIII*. Milano: TEA.

Acevedeo, D., E. Vote, D. H. Laidlaw and M. S. Joukowsky 2001. Archaeological Data Visualization in VR: Analysis of Lamp Finds at the Great Temple of Petra, a Case Study. *Proceedings of IEEE Visualization Conference, San Diego, CA*: 493-7.

Adam Veleni, P. 1999. Petres of Florina: A Hypothetical Account of a Foundation and a Destruction, in M. Körner (ed.) *Stadtzerstörung und Wiederaufbau*, vol. II: 147-57. Bern: Verlag Paul Haupt.

Adam Veleni, P. 2000. *Petres of Florina. A Walk Around to a Hellenistic City*. Thessaloniki.

Akamatis, I. M. 1996. Spolium Homericum Pellense. Τεκμήρια 2: 1-7.

Akerstrom-Hougen, G. 1974. *The Calendar and Hunting Mosaics of the Villa of the Falconer in Argos. A Study in Early Byzantine Iconography*. Stockholm: Svenska Institutet i Athen.

Albertocchi, M. 2010. Considerazioni sul Programma Decorativo della 'Casa Romana' di Coo: Modelli dell'Abitare tra Impero e Provincia. *Bollettino di Archeologia Online* 1: 39-52.

Alcock, S. 1993a. *Graecia Capta: The Landscapes of Roman Greece*. Cambridge: Cambridge University Press.

Alcock, S. 1993b. Spaced-out Sanctuaries: The Ritual Landscape of Roman Greece, in E. Scott (ed.), *Theoretical Roman Archaeology. First Conference Proceedings*, Aldershot: 155-65.

Alcock, S. 1995. Pausanias and the *Polis*: Use and Abuse, in M.H. Hansen (ed.) *Sources for the Ancient Greek City State. Acts of the Copenhagen Polis Centre* 2: 326-44.

Allen, D. C., 1949. *The Legend of Noah: Renaissance Rationalism in Art, Science and Letters*. Reprint. Urbana: Univ. of Illinois Press, 1963.

Allison, P. M. 2001. Using the Material and Written Sources: Turn of the Millennium Approaches to Roman Domestic Space, *American Journal of Archaeology* 105: 181–208.

Alroth, B. 1999. Changes in Votive Practice? From Classical to Hellenistic. Some Examples, in R. Hägg (ed.) *Ancient Greek Cult Practice from the Epigraphical Evidence*: 217-28. Stockholm: Paul Aströms Förlag.

Amandry, P. 1978. Bases de trépied à Coronée. *Bulletin de Correspondance Hellénique* 102 (2): 565-9.

Ananiadou-Tzimopoulou, M., A. Yérolympos and A. Vitopoulou 2007. L'espace public et le rôle de la place dans la ville grecque moderne. Évolution historique et enjeux contemporains. *Études balkaniques* 14: 27-52.

Aneziri, S. 2014. Greek Strategies of Adaptation to the Roman World: The Case of the Contests. *Mnemosyne* 67: 423-42.

Antonaccio, C.M. 2000. Architecture and Behavior: Building Gender into Greek Houses. *The Classical World* 93 (5): 517-33.

Archontidou and Kokkinophorou 2004 = Αρχοντίδου, Α., and Μ. Κοκκινοφόρου 2004. *Αρχαίο Θέατρο Ηφαιστίας*. Λήμνος.

Ashby, C. 1999. *Classical Greek Theatre. New Views on an Old Subject*. Yowa City: University of Iowa Press.

Aschwanden, G. D. P. A. 2014. Health and Place: An Analysis of the Built Environment's Impact on Walking Behavior and Health. Unpublished Sc.D. dissertation, ETH Zürich.

Aschwanden, G. D. P. A., S. Haegler, J. Halatsch, R. Jeker, G. Schmitt and L. Van Gool 2009. Evaluation of 3D City Models Using Automatic Placed Urban Agents. *Proceedings 9th International Conference on Construction Applications of Virtual Reality-CONVR 2009, November 5-6, 2009, Sydney, Australia*: 165-76. Sydney: University of Sydney, Faculty of Architecture, Design & Planning.

Ashmole, B. 1959. Cyriac of Ancona. *Proceedings of the British Academy* 45: 25-6.

Auer, M., G. Agugiaro, N. Billen, L. Loos and A. Zipf 2014. Web-based Visualization and Query of Semantically Segmented Multiresolution 3D Models in the Field of Cultural Heritage. *ISPRS Annals of the Photogrammetry, Remote Sensing and Spatial Information Sciences* II-5: 33-9.

Ault, B. A. 1994. Classical Houses and Households: An Architectural and Artifactual Case Study From Halieis, Greece, Unpublished PhD dissertation, Indiana University.

Ault, B. A. 1999. Koprones and Oil Presses at Halieis. Interaction of Town and Country and the Integration of Domestic and Regional Economies. *Hesperia* 68 (4): 549-73.

Ault, B. A. 2005. *The Excavations at Ancient Halieis 2. The Houses. The Organization and Use of Domestic Space*. Bloomington & Indianapolis: Indiana University Press.

Ault, B. A. 2013. Halieis. *The Encyclopedia of Ancient History*: 3043-4.

Aureli, P. V. 2011. *The Possibility of an Absolute Architecture*. Cambridge: MIT Press.

Bagnall, R. S. and P. Derow 2004. *The Hellenistic Period: Historical Sources in Translation*. Blackwell Publishing.

Bajard, S. 1992. Topographie antique sous Paul III (1534-49). Le Mausolée d'Adrien dans les fresques du Château Saint-Ange'. *Mélanges de l'école française de Rome* 104 (2): 549-84.

Bakhuizen, S. C. 1992. *A Greek City of the Fourth Century B.C. by the Gorítsa Team*. Rome: 'L'Erma' di Bretschneider.

Baldini Lippolis, I. 2007. Private Space in Late Antique Cities: Laws and Building Procedures, in L. Lavan, L. Özgenel and S. Sarantis (eds.) *Housing in Late Antiquity from Palaces to Shops*: 197-237. Leiden/Boston: Brill.

Barbanera, M. 2000. Idee per una Storia dell'Archeologia Classica in Italia dalla Fine del Settecento al Dopoguerra, in N. Terrenato (ed.) *Archeologia Teorica. X Ciclo di Lezioni sulla Ricerca Applicata in Archeologia (Certosa di Pontignano 1999)*: 39-57. Firenze: All'Insegna del Giglio.

Barbanera, M. 2010. Dal Testo all'Immagine: Autopsia dell'Antichità nella Cultura Antiquaria del Settecento, in C. Brook and V. Curzi (eds.) *Roma e l'Antico. Realtà e Visione nel '700*: 33-8. Milano: Skira.

Barbier, F. 2010. *Le Rêve Grec de Monsieur de Choiseul: Les Voyages d'un Européen des Lumières*. Paris: Armand Colin.

Barkan, L. 1999. *Unearthing the Past: Archaeology and Aesthetics in the Making of Renaissance Culture*. New Haven and London: Yale University Press.

Bartoletti, V. (ed.) 1959. *Hellenica Oxyrhynchia*. Leipzig: Teubner.

Baudini, A. 2010. I Rituali dell'Orthia a Sparta come Veicolo di Autorappresentazione di un'Élite Civica. *Bollettino di Archeologia Online* 1: 28-33.

Bearzot, C. 2009. *La polis greca*. Bologna: Il Mulino.

Beaumonti, L. A. 2006. Smyrna, in N. Wilson (ed.) *Encyclopedia of Ancient Greece*: 666. New York: Routledge.

Beloch, K. J. 1886. *Die Bevölkerung der griechisch-römischen Welt*. Leipzig: Duncker & Humblot.

Bender, B. 1998. *Stonehenge: Making Space*. Oxford: Berg.

Benson, C. D. 2009. The Dead and the Living: Some Medieval Descriptions of the Ruins and Relics of Rome Known to the English, in Albrecht Classen (eds.) *Urban Space in the Middle Ages and the Early Modern Age*: 147-82. Berlin: de Gruyter.

Bergquist, B. 1998. Feasting of Worshippers or Temple and Sacrifice? The case of Herakleion on Thasos, in R. Hägg (ed.) *Ancient Greek Cult Practice from the Archaeological Evidence*: 57-72. Stockholm: Paul Åström.

Bes, Ph. and M. Van der Enden 2012. Preliminary results of the spring and summer 2010 ceramic studies. Internal report.

Betts, E. 2011. Towards a Multisensory Experience of Movement in the City of Rome, in R. Laurence and D. J. Newsome (eds.) *Rome, Ostia, Pompeii: Movement and Space*: 118-32. Oxford: Oxford University Press.

Betts, E. 2017. *Senses of the Empire. Multisensory Approaches to Roman Urban Space*. Abingdon: Routledge.
Betts, M.W., H.D.G. Maschner, C.D. Schou, R. Schlader, J. Holmes, N. Clement and M. Smuin 2011. Virtual Zooarchaelogy: Building a Web-based Reference collection of Northern Vertebrates for Archaeofaunal Research and Education. *Journal of Archaeological Science* 38: 755-62.
Bigot, P. 1942. *Rome Antique au IV Siècle ap. J.-C.* Paris.
Bintliff, J. 1985. VI. GREECE. The Boeotia Survey, in S. Macready and F. H. Thompson (eds.) *Archaeological Field Survey in Britain and Abroad*: 196-216. London: Society of Antiquaries of London.
Bintliff, J. 1997. Further Considerations on the Population of Ancient Boeotia, in J. Bintliff (ed.) *Recent Developments in the History and Archaeology of Central Greece, Proceedings of the 6th International Boeotian Conference*: 231-52. BAR International Series, Oxford: Archaeopress.
Bintliff, J. 2008a. Considerations on Agricultural Scale-economies in the Greco-Roman World, in R. Alston and O. M. van Nijf (eds.) *Feeding the Ancient Greek City*: 17-31. Leuven: Peeters.
Bintliff, J. 2008b. Recent Developments in the Social and Economic Archaeology of the Mediterranean Region from a Long-term Perspective. *Tijdschrift voor Mediterrane Archeologie* 40: 36-47.
Bintliff, J. 2010. Classical Greek Urbanism: A Social Darwinian View, in R. M. Rosen and I. Sluiter (eds.) *Valuing Others in Classical Antiquity*: 15-41. Leiden: Brill.
Bintliff, J. 2011. Coronea (Antiquity). *Encyclopedia of the Hellenic World, Boeotia*, viewed 02 March 2018, <http://www.ehw.gr/l.aspx?id=12891>.
Bintliff, J. 2012. *The Complete Archaeology of Greece: From Hunter-Gatherers to the 20th Century AD*. Malden, MA; Oxford; Chichester: Wiley-Blackwell.
Bintliff, J. 2013a. Central Greece in Late Antiquity: The Evidence from the Boeotia Project, in L. Lavan, M. Mulryan (eds.) *Field Methods and Post-Excavation Techniques in Late Antique Archaeology* (Late Antique Archaeology 9 – 2012): 189–203. Leiden: Brill.
Bintliff, J. 2013b. Public versus professional perceptions of an invisible heritage: A Greek case study, in E. Niklasson and T. Meyer (eds.) *Appropriate Narratives. Archaeologists, Publics and Stories*: 237-47. Budapest: Archaeolingua.
Bintliff, J. 2014. Spatial analysis of past built environments: Houses and society in the Aegean from the Early Iron Age to the impact of Rome, in E. Paliou, U. Lieberwirth and S. Polla (eds.) *Spatial analysis and social spaces*: 263-76. Berlin: Walter de Gruyter.
Bintliff, J. 2015. Beyond Theoretical Archaeology: A Manifesto for Reconstructing Interpretation in Archaeology, in K. Kristiansen, L. Šmejda and J. Turek (eds.) *Paradigm Found: Archaeological Theory. Present, Past and Future*: 24-35. Oxford and Philadelphia: Oxbow Books.
Bintliff, J. and A. Snodgrass 1985. The Cambridge/Bradford Boeotian Expedition: The First Four Years. *Journal of Field Archaeology* 12: 123-61.
Bintliff J. and P. Howard 2007. *Testing the Hinterland. the work of the Boeotia Survey (1989-1991) in the southern approaches of the city of Thespiai*. Cambridge: MacDonald Institute Monographs.
Bintliff, J., B. Slapšak, B. Noordervliet, J. Van Zwienen and J. Verweij 2009. The Leiden-Ljubljana Ancient Cities of Boeotia Project summer 2007 – spring 2008. *Pharos. Journal of the Netherlands Institute in Athens* 15 (2007): 17-42.
Bintliff, J., B. Slapšak, B. Noordervliet, J. Van Zwienen and R. Shiel 2010. The Leiden-Ljubljana Ancient cities of Boeotia Project 2008 season. *Pharos. Journal of the Netherlands Institute in Athens* 16 (2008): 31-60.
Bintliff, J., B. Noordervliet, J. Van Zwienen, K. Wilkinson, B. Slapšak, V. Stissi, C. Piccoli and A. Vionis 2013. The Leiden-Ljubljana Ancient cities of Boeotia Project 2010-2012 season. *Pharos. Journal of the Netherlands Institute in Athens* 19 (2): 1-34.
Bintliff, J., E. Farinetti, B. Slapšak, A. Snodgrass (eds.) 2017. *Boeotia Project, Volume II: The City of Thespiai: Survey at a Complex Urban Site*. Oxford: Oxbow Books.
Blersch, D., M. Balzani and G. Tampone 2006. The Volumnis' Hypogeum in Perugia, Italy. Application of 3D Survey and Modelling in Archaeological Sites for the Analysis of Deviances and Deformations,

in S. Campana and M. Forte (eds.) *From Space to Place: 2nd International Conference on Remote Sensing in Archaeology, December 4-7 2006, CNR, Rome*: 389-94. Oxford: Archeopress.

Blomfield, R. 1911. *A History of French Architecture*. London: G. Bell and Sons.

Boardman, J. 1963. Artemis Orthia and Chronology. *The Annual of the British School at Athens* 58: 1-7.

Bodnar, E. W. and C. Foss 2003. *Cyriac of Ancona. Later Travels*. Cambridge, MA: Harvard University Press.

Bohrer, F. N. 2011. *Photography and Archaeology*. Chicago: University of Chicago Press.

Bömer, F. 1960. *Untersuchungen über die Religion der Sklaven in Griechenland und Rom. Zweiter Teil: Die sogenannte sakrale Frielassung in Griechenland und die (douloi) ieroi*. Wisbaden: F. Steiner.

Bonanno, M. 2008. Culti Orientali in Beozia: Le Testimonianze Archeologiche, in B. Palma Venetucci (ed.) *Culti orientali tra Scavo e Collezionismo*: 235-47. Roma: Artemide.

Bonetto, J., F. Ghedini, M. Bressan, D. Francisci, G. Falezza, S. Mazzocchin and E. Schindler Kaudelka 2010. *Gortyna* di Creta, Teatro del *Pythion*. Ricerche e Scavi 2007-2010. *Annuario SAIA LXXXVII, Serie III*, 9, vol. 2, 2009: 1087-98.

Bonini, P. 2006. *La Casa nella Grecia Romana. Forme e Funzioni dello Spazio Privato tra I e VI Secolo*. Roma: Quasar.

Boochs, F., A. Hoffman, E. Huxhagen and D. Welter 2006. Digital Reconstruction of Archaeological Objects Using Hybrid Sensing Techniques, in S. Campana and M. Forte (eds.) *From Space to Place: 2nd International Conference on Remote Sensing in Archaeology,* December 4-7 2006, CNR (Rome, 2006): 395-400.

Bookidis, N. 1993. Ritual Dining at Corinth, in N. Marinatos and R. Hägg (eds.) *Greek Sanctuaries. New Approaches*: 45-61. London & New York: Routledge.

Bookidis, N. 1998. Cursing in the Sanctuary of Demeter and Kore at Ancient Corinth, in R. Hägg (ed.) *Ancient Greek Cult Practice from the Archaeological Evidence*: 229-31. Stockholm: Paul Aströms Förlag.

Bookidis, N. and R. S. Stroud 1997. *The Sanctuary of Demeter and Kore. Topography and Architecture*. Princeton, New Jersey: ASCSA.

Bordieu, P. 1984. *The Field of Cultural Production: Essays on Art and Literature*. Columbia University Press.

Boruchoff, D. A. 2012. The Three Greatest Inventions of Modern Times: An Idea and its Public, in K. Hock and G. Mackenthun (eds.) *Entangled Knowledge. Scientific Discourse and Cultural Differences*: 133-64. Münster: Waxmann.

Boswinkel, Y. 2012. Architectural remains at Koroneia, Greece. Research on a group of architectural remains on the acropolis of Koroneia and the methodology of researching ancient urban remains. Unpublished BA dissertation, Faculty of Archaeology, Leiden University.

Boswinkel, Y. 2015. Architecture as an archaeological proxy. The site of Koroneia, Greece as a case-study for researching a multi-period site through architecture and the methodology of studying architecture from a survey context. Unpublished RMA dissertation, Faculty of Archaeology, Leiden University.

Boulaassal, H., T. Landes and P. Grussenmeyer 2011. 3D Modelling of Facade Features on Large Sites Acquired by Vehicle Based Laser Scanning, *Archives of Photogrammetry, Cartography and Remote Sensing* (APCRS) 22: 215-26.

Boutsikas, E. and C. Ruggles 2011. Temples, Stars, and Ritual Landscapes: The Potential for Archaeoastronomy in Ancient Greece. *American Journal of Archaeology* 115 (1): 55-68.

Bowden, W., A. Gutteridge and C. Machado 2006. *Social and Political Life in Late Antiquity*. Leiden: Brill.

Bowen Loftin, R., J. X. Chen and L. Rosenblum 2005. Visualization Using Virtual Reality, in C. D. Hansen and C. R. Johnson (eds.) *The Visualization Handbook*: 479-89. Burlington/Oxford: Elsevier.

Bowyer, J. 1973. *History of Building*. London: Crosby Lockwood Staples.

Bradley, M. (ed.) 2015. *Smell and the Ancient Senses. The Senses in Antiquity*. London; New York: Routledge.

Brasser, J. P. 2013. The City according to the Millstone Assemblage. A complementary approach to the Koroneia urban site survey. Unpublished BA dissertation, Faculty of Archaeology, Leiden University.

Bressan, M. 2009. *Il Teatro in Attica e Peloponneso tra Età Greca ed Età Romana. Morfologie, Politiche Edilizie e Contesti Culturali*. Roma: Edizioni Quasar.

Bressan, M. and P. Bonini 2010, Tradizione e Romanità nella Grecia Imperiale: Convivenza o Integrazione?. *Bollettino di Archeologia Online* 1: 14-26.
Brulotte, E. L. 1994. *The Placing of Votive Offerings and Dedications in the Peloponnesian Sanctuaries of Artemis.* Unpublished PhD dissertation, University of Minnesota.
Brumfield, A. 1997. Cakes in the Liknon. Votives from the Sanctuary of Demeter and Kore on Acrocorinth. *Hesperia* 66 (1): 147-72.
Bruneau, P. 1968. Contribution à l'Histoire Urbaine de Délos. *Bulletin de Correspondance Hellénique* 92 (2): 633-709.
Bruns-Özgan, E. C. 2006. Knidos, in W. Radt (ed.) *Stadtgrabungen und Stadtforschung im Westlichen Kleinasien: Geplantes und Erreichtes. Internationales Symposion 6./7. August 2004 in Bergama (Türkei)*: 167-78. Istanbul: Ege Yayinlari.
Buck, R. J. 1979. *A History of Boeotia*. Edmonton: The University of Alberta Press.
Buckler, J. 1996. The battle of Koroneia and its Historiographical Legacy, in J. Fossey (ed.) *Boeotia Antiqua VI. Proceedings of the 8th International Conference on Boiotian Antiquities (Loyola University of Chicago, 24-26 May 1995)*: 59-72. Amsterdam: Gieben.
Buckler, J. 2003. *Aegean Greece in the Fourth Century BC*. Leiden: Brill.
Buckler, J., and H. Beck 2008. *Central Greece and the Politics of Power in the 4th Century BC*. Cambridge: Cambridge University Press.
Buonarroti, F., 1698. *Osservazioni Istoriche Sopra Alcuni Medaglioni Antichi*. Roma.
Burkert, W. 1985. *Greek Religion*. Harvard: Harvard University Press.
Burrel, B. 2002/3. Temple of Hadrian, not Zeus. *Greek, Roman and Byzantine Studies* 43: 31-50.
Burr Thompson, D. 1937. The Garden of Hephaistos. *Hesperia* 6: 396-425.
Butchart, B. 2011. Augmented Reality for Smartphones. A Guide for Developers and Content Publishers. *JISC Observatory* 48, viewed 02 March 2018, <http://opus.bath.ac.uk/34847/1/AR_Smartphone_final.pdf>.
Caballero López, J.A. 2002. Annio de Viterbo y la Historiografía española del siglo XVI, in J. M. Nieto Ibáñez (ed.) *Humanismo y Tradición Clásica en España y América*: 101-20. León: Ed. Universidad de León.
Cahill, N. 2002. *Household and City Organization at Olynthus*. New Haven & London: Yale University Press.
Cahill, N. 2005. Household Industry in Greece and Anatolia, in B. A. Ault, L. C. Nevett (eds.) *Ancient Greek Houses and Households: Chronological, Regional, and Social Diversity*: 54-66. Philadelphia, PA: University of Pennsylvania Press.
Caliò, L. M. 2012. *Asty: Studi sulla Città Greca*. Rome: Edizioni Quasar.
Callet, P. and S. Dumazet 2010. Natural Lighting, Gilts and Polychromy of Notre-Dame de Paris Cathedral, in A. Artusi, M. Joly-Parvex, G. Lucet, A. Ribes, and D. Pitzalis (eds.) *Conference Proceedings, 11th VAST International Symposium on Virtual Reality, Archaeology and Cultural Heritage*: 63–70.
Camia, F. 2009. Imperatori Romani tra gli Dei Greci: Riflessioni sull'Associazione tra Culto Imperiale e Culti Tradizionali in Grecia a Partire dalla Documentazione Epigrafica, in F. Camia and S. Privitera (eds.) *OBELOI. Contatti, Scambi e Valori nel Mediterraneo Antico. Studi Offerti a Nicola Parise*: 205-22. Paestum-Atene: Pandemos.
Camp, J. M. 2001. *The Archaeology of Athens*. New Haven and London: Yale University Press.
Camp, J. M. 2003. *The Athenian Agora. A Short Guide to the Excavations*. Princeton: ASCSA.
Camporeale, S., D. Caruso and V. Tosti 2010. Le Fasi dei Periodi Arcaico e Classico negli Scavi dell'Area 26 ad Efestia, *ASAtene* 88.3.10: 113-33.
Camporeale, S., G. Carpentiero, F. Martorella, L. Botarelli, D. D'Aco, A. Pecci, E. Bernardoni, V. Bellavia and C. Piccoli 2008. Lo scavo dell'area 26, in E. Greco and E. Papi (eds.) *Hephaestia 2000-2006: ricerche e scavi della Scuola Archeologica Italiana di Atene in collaborazione con il Dipartimento di Archeologia e Storia delle Arti dell'Università di Siena, Paestum, Proceedings of the conference Hephaestia 2000-2006, Siena, 28-29 maggio 2007*: 187-246. Atene: Pandemos.
Capodiferro, A. (ed.) 2006. *Roma Antica Ricostruita nelle Fotografie di Giuseppe Gatteschi*. Rome: American Academy in Rome.

Caraher, W. R. 2003. Church, Society and the Sacred in early Christian Greece. Unpublished PhD dissertation, Ohio State University.
Carroll-Spillecke, M. 1989. *Kepos: der Antike Griechische Garten.* Munich: Deutscher Kunstverlag.
Carroll-Spillecke, M. 1992. The Gardens of Greece from Homeric to Roman Times. *Journal of Garden History* 12 (2): 84-101.
Carter, D. 2013. *Winckelmann. On Art, Architecture, and Archaeology. Translated with an Introduction and Notes by David Carter.* Rochester, NY: Camden House.
Cartledge, P. 2002. *Sparta and Lakonia. A Regional History 1300-362 BC.* New York: Routledge.
Cartledge, P. and A. Spawforth 2002. *Hellenistic and Roman Sparta. A Tale of Two Cities.* London: Routledge.
Caruso, D. 2011. Hephaestia nel Periodo Arcaico. Nuovi Dati di Architettura Domestica dai Recenti Scavi dell'Area Urbana. Unpublished MA dissertation, University of Siena.
Cassanelli, R., M. David, E. de Albentiis and A. Jacques 2002. *Ruins of Ancient Rome. The Drawings of French Architects who won the Prix de Rome 1786-1924.* Los Angeles: Getty Publications.
Catling, C. 2013. Alan Sorrel: An Artist not an Archaeologist. *Current Archaeology* 285 (Dec. 2013): 32-9.
Cecchini, S. 2007. La città e la sua storia: Roma tra restauro filologico e restauro scenografico, in P. D'Alconzo (ed.) *Gli Uomini e le Cose I. Figure di restauratori e casi di restauro in Italia tra il XVIII e XX secolo*: 391-408. Napoli: ClioPress.
Cerato, I. and S. Pescarin 2013. Reconstructing Past Landscapes for Virtual Museums, in C. Corsi, B. Slapsak and F. Vermeulen (eds.) *Good Practice in Archaeological Diagnostics*: 285-95. Berlin: Springer.
Cesarano, M. 2011. L'anfiteatro di Nola in alcune pergamene aragonesi. *Symbolae Antiquariae* 4: 49-82.
Chalmers, A., S. Stoddart, J. Tidmus and R. Miles 1995. INSITE: An Interactive Visualization System for Archaeological Sites, in J. Huggett and N. Ryan (eds.) *Proceedings of the International Conference on Computer Applications and Quantitative Methods in Archaeology, CAA 1994, Glasgow*: 225-8. BAR International Series 600, Oxford: Tempus Reparatum.
Chamberlain, B. 2015. Crash Course or Course Crash: Gaming, VR and Pedagogical Approach, in E. Buhmann, S.M. Ervin, and M. Pietsch (eds.) *Peer Reviewed Proceedings of Digital Landscape Architecture 2015 at Anhalt University of Applied Sciences*: 354-61. Berlin/Offenbach: Herbert Wichmann Verlag.
Chamonard, J. 1922–1924. Le Quartier du Théatre: Étude sur l'Habitation Délienne à l'Époque Hellénistique 1–3. *Délos* 8: 168–76. Paris.
Chapman, G. 1992. Do-it-yourself Reconstruction Modelling, in G. Lock and J. Moffet (eds.) *Computer Applications in Archaeology 1991*: 213-18. Oxford: British Archaeological Reports.
Charalambous, P., H. Iliadou, C. Apostolou and Y. Chrysanthou 2012. Reconstructing Everyday Life in the 19th Century Nicosia, in M. Ioannides, D. Fritsch, J. Leissner, R. Davies, F. Remondino and R. Caffo (eds.) *Progress in Cultural Heritage Preservation. Proceedings of 4th International Conference, EuroMed 2012, Limassol, Cyprus, October 29-November 3, 2012*: 568-77. Berlin/Heidelberg: Springer.
Charitonidis, S., L. Kahil and R. Ginouvès 1970. *La Mosaïque de la Maison du Ménandre à Mytilène*, Berne: Francke Verlag.
Chestnut, J.A. and L.L. Crumpton 1997. Virtual Reality: A Training Tool in the 21st Century for Disabled Persons and Medical Students, in J.D. Bumgardner and A.D. Puckett (eds.) *Proceedings of the 16th Sothern Biomedical Engineering Conference, Biloxi, Mississippi, USA, 4-6 Apr. 1997*: 418-21.
Ciancio-Rossetto, P. 1990. La 'Roma di Coccio' di Giuseppe Marcelliani. *Bollettino dei musei comunali di Roma* 4: 11-5.
Clark, J. T. 2010. The Fallacy of Reconstruction, in M. Forte (ed.) *Cyber-Archaeology*: 63-73. BAR International Series 2177, Oxford: Archaeopress.
Clarke, J. R. 2012. The Villa of Oplontis: A 'Born Digital' Project, in D. Anderson, J. Delve, M. Dobreva, L. Konstantelos (eds.) *The Preservation of Complex Objects (Vol. 1): Visualisations and Simulations*: 54-66. University of Portsmouth.
Clarysse, W., and D. J. Thompson 2006. *Counting the People in Hellenistic Egypt*, 2 vols. Cambridge: Cambridge Classical Studies.

Coffin, D. R. 2004. *Pirro Ligorio: The Renaissance Artist, Architect, and Antiquarian*, University Park, PA: Pennsylvania State University Press.

Cole, S. G. 1994. 'Demeter in the Ancient Greek City and its Countryside', in S. E. Alcock and R. Osborne (eds.), *Placing the Gods: Sanctuaries and Sacred Space in Ancient Greece*, Oxford: Clarendon Press, 199-216.

Cole, S. G. 1998. ' The Uses of Water in Greek Sanctuaries' , in R. Hägg, N. Marinatos and G.C. Nordquist (eds.), *Early Greek Cult Practice*, Stockholm: Göteborg, 161-5.

Cole, S. G. 2004. *Landscapes, Gender, and Ritual Space: The Ancient Greek Experience*, Berkeley: University of California Press.

Cornforth, J., C. Davidson, C. J. Dallas and G. R. Lock 1992. 'Visualizing Ancient Greece: Computer Graphics in the Sacred Way Project', in G. Lock and J. Moffett (eds.), *Computer Applications and Quantitative Methods in Archaeology 1991*, BAR International Series 577, Oxford: Tempus Reparatum, 219-25.

Corsi, C. and F. Vermeulen 2012. *Ammaia I: The Survey. A Romano-Lusitanian townscape revealed*, Ghent: Academia Press.

Connolly, P. and H. Dodge 1998. *The Ancient City. Life in Classical Athens and Rome*, Oxford: Oxford University Press.

Cooper, F. A. 2000. 'The Fortifications of Epaminondas and the Rise of the Monumental Greek City', in J. D. Tracy (ed.), *The Urban Enceinte in Global Perspective*. Cambridge: Cambridge University Press, 155-91.

Corabi, G. 2005. 'Pegio che Babilonia è fatta Roma': gli Scrittori del Gran Sacco, in I. de Michelis (ed.) *Apocalissi e Letteratura*: 81-96. Roma: Bulzoni.

Coulton, J. J. 1975. Towards Understanding Greek Temple Design: General Considerations. *The Annual of the British School at Athens* 70: 59-99.

Coulton, J. J. 1976. *The Architectural Development of the Greek Stoa*. Oxford: Clarendon Press.

Cronk, N. and K. Peeters (eds.) 2004. *Le Comte de Caylus: Les Arts et les Lettres. Actes du Colloque International Université d'Anvers (UFSIA) et Voltaire Foundation Oxford, 26-7 Mai 2000*. Amsterdam-New York: Rodopi.

Cunningham, L., J. Reich and L. Fichner-Rathus 2014. *Culture and Values: A Survey of the Western Humanities*, vol. 1. Stanford: Cengage Learning.

Curran, B. A. 2012. Teaching (and Thinking About) the High Renaissance: With Some Observations on its Relationship to Classical Antiquity, in J. Burke (ed.) *Rethinking the High Renaissance. The Culture of the Visual Arts in Early Sixteenth-Century Rome*: 27-55. Farnham: Ashgate Publishing.

Cutini, V. 2009. The Town at the End of the Town: Integration and Segregation in Suburbia, in B. Murgante, G. Borruso and A. Lapucci (eds.) *Geocomputation and Urban Planning*: 79-97. Berlin: Springer.

Dacos, N. 2004. *Roma Quanta Fuit ou l'Invention du Paysage de Ruines*. Brussel/Paris: Musée de la Maison d'Erasme/Somogy éditions d'art.

Dakaris, S. 1986 = Δάκαρης, Σ. Ι., 1986. Το Όρραον. *Αρχαιολογική Εφημερίς*: 108-46.

Daly Davis, M. (ed.) 2008. *Pirro Ligorio: Libro di M. Pyrrho Ligori Napolitano delle antichità di Roma, nel quale si tratta de' circi, theatri, e anfitheatri, con le Paradosse del medesimo auttore, quai confutano la commune opinione sopra varii luoghi della città di Roma (Venetia 1553)*, herausgegeben und kommentiert von Margaret Daly Davis, Fontes 9, Quellen und Dokumente zur Kunst 1350-1750. Sources and Documents for the History of Art 1350-1750.

Daniel, R. 1997. The Need for the Solid Modelling of Structure in the Archaeology of Buildings. *Internet Archaeology* 2, viewed 02 March 2018, <http://intarch.ac.uk/journal/issue2/daniels_toc.html>.

Daniels-Dwyer, R. 2004. Beyond the Artist's Impression. From Photo-realism to Integrated Reconstruction in Buildings Archaeology, in J.H. Jamenson Jr. (ed.) *The Reconstructed Past: Reconstructions in the Public Interpretation of Archaeology and History*: 261-72. Lanham: Rowman & Littlefield Publisher.

Dawkins, R. M. 1929. *The Sanctuary of Artemis Orthia at Sparta*. London: MacMillan and Co.

De Angelis, F. 2010. Colonies and Colonization, Greek, in M. Gagarin and E. Fantham (eds.) *The Oxford Encyclopedia of Ancient Greece and Rome. Volume 2*: 251-6. Oxford: Oxford University Press.

De Choiseul, G. 1809. *Voyage pittoresque de la Grèce*, vol. 2. Paris.

De Heras Ciechomski, P., B. Ulicny, R. Cetre and Daniel Thalmann 2004. A Case Study of a Virtual Audience in a Reconstruction of an Ancient Roman Odeon in Aphrodisias, in K. Cain, Y. Chrysanthou,

F. Niccolucci, N. Silberman (eds.) *Proceedings of the 5th International Symposium on Virtual Reality, Archaeology and Cultural Heritage VAST*: 9-17.

DeLaine, J. 2008. Between Concept and Reality: Case Studies in the Development of Roman Cities in the Mediterranean, in J. Marcus and J.A. Sabloff (eds.) *The Ancient City: New Perspectives on Urbanism in Old and New Worlds*: 95-116. Santa Fe: School for Advanced Research Press.

De Kleijn, M., R. J. F. de Hond and O. Martinez-Rubi 2016. A 3D GIS Infrastructure for "Mapping the Via Appia". *Digital Applications in Archaeology and Cultural Heritage* 3 (2): 23-32.

De Ligt, L. 1993. *Fairs and Markets in the Roman Empire. Economic and Social Aspects of Periodic Trade in a Pre-Industrial Society*. Leiden: Brill.

Dell'Unto, N., G. Landeschi, A.-M. Leander Touati, M. Dellepiane, M. Callieri and D. Ferdani 2016. Experiencing Ancient Buildings from a 3D GIS Perspective: A Case Drawn from the Swedish Pompeii Project. *Journal of Archaeological Method and Theory* 23 (1): 73-94.

Demetrescu, E. 2015. Archaeological Stratigraphy as a formal language for virtual reconstruction. Theory and practice. *Journal of Archaeological Science* 57: 42-55.

Demetrescu, E. and B. Fanini 2017. A white-box framework to oversee archaeological virtual reconstructions in space and time: Methods and tools. *Journal of Archaeological Science: Reports* 14: 500-14.

Denard, H. 2012. A New Introduction to the London Charter, in A. Bentkowska-Kafel, H. Denard and D. Baker (eds.) *Paradata and Transparency in Virtual Heritage*: 57-71. Farnham: Ashgate.

Del Pesco, D. 1984. Una Fonte per gli Architetti del Barocco Romano: L'*Antiquae Urbis Splendor* di Giacomo Lauro. *Studi di Storia dell'Arte in Memoria di Mario Rotili*, vol. 1, edited by Istituto di Storia dell'Arte dell'Università di Napoli: 413-36. Naples: Banca Sannitica.

De Roy, J. D. 1758. *Les Ruines des plus beaux Monuments de la Grèce*. Paris.

Devlin, K. and A. Chalmers 2001. Realistic Visualization of the Pompeii Frescoes. *AFRIGRAPH '01 Proceedings of the 1st International Conference on Computer Graphics, Virtual Reality and Visualisation*: 43-8. New York: ACM.

Devlin, K., A. Chalmers and D. Brown 2002. Predictive Lighting and Perception in Archaeological Representations. UNESCO World Heritage in the Digital Age 30th Anniversary Digital Congress, viewed 02 March 2018, <http://doc.gold.ac.uk/~mas01kd/publications/unesco_paper.pdf>.

Díaz-Andreu, M. 2007. *A World History of Nineteenth-Century Archaeology. Nationalism, Colonialism and the Past*. Oxford: Oxford University Press.

Di Calisto, L. 2005. Lauro, Giacomo. *Dizionario Biografico degli Italiani* 64. Online edition, viewed 02 March 2018, <http://www.treccani.it/enciclopedia/giacomo-lauro_%28Dizionario-Biografico%29/>.

Di Napoli, V. 2005. The Theatres of Roman Arcadia, Pausanias and the History of the Region, in E. Østby (ed.) *Ancient Arcadia. Papers from the Third International Seminar on Ancient Arcadia, held at the Norwegian Institute at Athens, 7–10 May 2002*: 509-20. Athens: Norwegian Institute at Athens.

Di Vita, A. 2000a. *Gortyn in Crete: Archaeology and History of an Ancient City*. Athens: Lucy Braggiotti Publications.

Di Vita, A. (ed.) 2000b. *Gortina V. Lo Scavo del Pretorio, Monografie SAIA XII*. Padova.

Dixon, S. M. 2005. Illustrating Ancient Rome, or the Ichnographia as Uchronia and Other Time Warps in Piranesi's Il Campo Marzio, in S. Smiles and S. Moser (eds.) *Envisioning the Past. Archaeology and the Image*: 115-32. Malden: Blackwell Publishing.

Dickenson, C. P. 2012. On the Agora. Power and Public Space in Hellenistic and Roman Greece. Unplished PhD dissertation, University of Groningen.

Dickenson, C. P. 2013. Kings, Cities and Marketplaces – Negotiating Power through Public Space in the Hellenistic World, in C. P. Dickenson and O. van Nijf (eds.) *Public Space in the Post-Classical City, Kolloquium Fransum 23, Juli 2007*: 37-75. Leuven: Peeters.

Dinsmoor, W. B. 1940. The Temple of Ares at Athens. *Hesperia*.9: 1-52.

Dobbins, J. and E. Gruber 2013. Modeling Hypotheses in Pompeian Archaeology: The House of the Faun, in F. Contreras, M. Farjas and F.J. Melero (eds.) *CAA 2010 Fusion of Cultures. Proceedings of the 38th Annual*

Conference on Computer Applications and Quantitative Methods in Archaeology, Granada, Spain, April 2010; 77–84. BAR International Series 2494, Oxford: Archaeopress.

Dobraja, I. 2015. Procedural 3D modeling and visualization of geotypical Bavarian rural buildings in Esri CityEngine software. Unpublished MA dissertation, Technische Universität München, Faculty of Civil, Geo and Environmental Engineering, Department of Cartography.

Dovey, M. E. 1994. Virtual Reality: Training in the 21st Century. *Marine Corps Gazette* 78 (7): 23-6.

Dubbini, R. 2002. *Geography of the Gaze: Urban and Rural Vision in Early Modern Europe*. Chicago: The University of Chicago Press, translated from the original *Geografie dello Sguardo: Visione e Paesaggio in Età Moderna*. Milano: Einaudi Editore, 1994.

Duchene, H. 1992. *La Stèle du Port, Fouilles du Port 1. Recherches sur une Nouvelle Inscription Thasienne*. Etudes Thasiennes 14. Paris: De Boccard.

Ducrey, P. 2004. *Eretria: A Guide to the Ancient City*. Fribourg: École Suisse d'Archéologie en Grèce.

Dylla, K., B. Frischer, P. Müller, A. Ulmer and S. Haegler 2010. Rome Reborn 2.0: A Case Study of Virtual City Reconstruction Using Procedural Modeling Techniques, in B. Frischer, J. Webb Crawford and D. Koller (eds.) *Making History Interactive. Proceedings of the 37th Conference in Computer Applications and Quantitative Methods in Archaeology, March 22-26, 2009, Williamsburg, Virginia*: 62-6.

Earl, G. 2005. Texture Viewsheds: Spatial Summaries of Built Archaeological Spaces Derived from Global Light Mapping. *Proceedings of the 11th International Conference on Virtual Systems and Multimedia, Ghent, Belgium, October 2005*: 303–12.

Earl, G. and D. W. Wheatley 2002. Virtual Reconstruction and the Interpretative Process: A Case Study from Avebury, in D. W. Wheatley, G. Earl and S. Poppy (eds.) *Contemporary Themes in Archaeological Computing*: 5-15. Oxford: Oxbow.

Earl, G., V. Porcelli, C. Papadopoulos, G. Beale, M. Harrison, H. Pagi and S. Keay 2013. Formal and Informal Analysis of Rendered Space: The Basilica Portuense, in A. Bevan and M. Lake (eds.), *Computational Approaches to Archaeology*: 265-305. London: UCL Press.

Eisler, J., J. Peiša and K. Preuss 1988. A Digital Model of Archaeological Excavations as the Starting Point of a Database of Primary Information in Egyptology: Method – Procedure – Experience, in S. P. Q. Rahtz (ed.) *Computer Applications in Archaeology 1988*: 109-32. Oxford: British Archaeological Reports.

Ekroth, G. 2001. Altars on Attic Vases: The Identification of *Bomos* and *Eschara*' in C. Scheffer (ed.) *Ceramics in context: Proceedings of the Internordic Colloquium on Ancient Pottery held at Stockholm 13-15 June 1997*: 115-26.

Ellis, S. 1988. The End of the Roman House. *American Journal of Archaeology* 92 (4): 565-76.

Ellis, S. 1994. Lighting in Late Roman Houses, in S. Cottam (ed.) *TRAC 94: Proceedings of the Fourth Annual Theoretical Roman Archaeology Conference, Durham*: 65-72. Oxford: Oxbow.

Ellis, S. 2006. Middle Class Houses in Late Antiquity, in W. Bowden, A. Gutteridge and C. Machado (eds.) *Social and Political Life in Late Antiquity*. Late Antique Archaeology 3.1: 413-37. Leiden: Brill.

Enenkel, K. 2008. Reciprocal Authorisation: The Function of Dedications and Dedicatory Prefaces in the 15th and 16th century 'Artes Antiquitatis, in I. Bossuyt, N. Gabriëls, D. Sacré and D. Verbeke (eds.) *'Cui dono lepidum novum libellum?': Dedicating Latin Works and Motets in the Sixteenth Century*: 35-48. Leuven: Leuven University Press.

Engels, D.W. 1990. *Roman Corinth: An Alternative Model for the Classical City*. Chicago: University of Chicago Press.

Etienne, R. and D. Knoepfler 1976. *Hyettos de Beotie et la chronologie des archontes fédéraux entre 250 et 171 avant J.-C.* Athens: École française d'Athènes.

Evangelidis, V. 2014. Agoras and Fora: Developments in the Central Public Space of the Cities of Greece during the Roman Period. *The Annual of the British School at Athens* 109: 335-56.

Evans, A. 1927. Work of Reconstitution in the Palace of Knossos. *The Antiquaries Journal* 7 (3): 258-67.

Fagan, B. M. 2016. *Brief History of Archaeology: Classical Times to the Twenty-First Century*. Abingdon: Routledge.

Fairbanks, A. 1900. The Chthonic Gods of Greek Religion', *American Journal of Philology* 21 (3): 241-59.

Fanini, B. and D. Ferdani 2012. A New Approach from 3D Modelling and Scanning of Archaeological Data to Realtime Online Exploration, in M. Zhou, I. Romanowska, Z. Wu, P. Xu and P. Verhagen (eds.) *Revive the Past. Proceedings of the 39th Conference on Computer Applications and Quantitative Methods in Archaeology, Beijing, 12-16 April 2011*: 107-15. Amsterdam: Pallas Publications.

Farinetti, E. 2009. Boeotian Landscapes: A GIS-based Study for the Reconstruction and Interpretation of the Archaeological Datasets of Ancient Boeotia. PhD dissertation, Faculty of Archaeology, Leiden University.

Farnetani, A. 2006. Investigations on the Acoustics of Ancient Theatres by Means of Modern Technologies. Unpublished PhD dissertation, Faculty of Engineering, University of Ferrara, Italy.

Favro, D. 1999. Meaning and Experience: Urban History from Antiquity to the Early Modern Period. *Journal of the Society of Architectural Historians* 58 (3): 364-73.

Favro, D. 2006. In the Eyes of the Beholder: Virtual Reality Re-creations and Academia, in L. Haselberger and J. Humphrey (eds.) *Imaging Ancient Rome: Documentation, Visualization, Imagination. Journal of Roman Archaeology Supplementary Series Number 61*: 321-34.

Favro, D. 2013. To Be or Not To Be in Past Spaces: Thoughts on Roman Immersive Reconstructions, in S. Bonde and S. Houston (eds.) *Re-presenting the Past: Archaeology Through Text and Image*. Oxford: Oxbow Books.

Fellini, F. 1978. Preface to *Satyricon*, in P. Bondanella (ed.) *Federico Fellini: Essays in Criticism*: 16-9. New York: Oxford University Press.

Fiedler, M. 2005. Houses at Leukas in Acarnania: A Case Study in Ancient Household Organization, in B. A. Ault, L. C. Nevett (eds.) *Ancient Greek Houses and Households: Chronological, Regional, and Social Diversity*: 99-117. Philadelphia, PA: University of Pennsylvania Press.

Filippi, F. 2007. Introduzione a Italo Gismondi, in F. Filippi (ed.) *Ricostruire l'Antico Prima del Virtuale. Italo Gismondi, un Architetto per l'Archeologia (1887-1974)*: 11-7. Roma: Edizioni Quasar.

Findlay, L. M. 1993. 'We are all Greeks': Shelley's *Hellas* and Romantic Nationalism. *History of European Ideas* 16 (1-3): 281-6.

Fischer-Hansen, T. 1996. The Earliest Town Planning of the Western Greek Colonies, with Special Regard to Sicily, in M.H. Hansen (ed.) *Introduction to an Inventory of Poleis*: 313-73. Copenhagen.

Flensted-Jensen, P. 2004. Knidos, in M. H. Hansen and T. H. Nielsen (eds.) *An inventory of Archaic and Classical poleis*: 1123–5. Oxford: Oxford University Press.

Fletcher, R. 1998. Review of 'Virtual Archaeology: Re-Creating Ancient Worlds'. *Australian Archaeology* 46: 56-7.

Fleury, P. and S. Madeleine 2010. An Interactive Visit to the City of Rome in the Fourth Century A.D., in B. Frischer, J. Webb Crawford and D. Koller (eds.) *Making History Interactive. Computer Applications and Quantitative Methods in Archaeology (CAA). Proceedings of the 37th International Conference, Williamsburg, Virginia, United States of America, March 22-26*: 67-75. Oxford: Archaeopress.

Fleury, P., S. Madeleine and N. Lefèvre 2014. Forum Romanum: A 3D Model for Self-Service Educational Purposes, in F. Giligny, F. Djindjian, L. Costa, P. Moscati and S. Robert (eds.) *CAA 2014. 21st Century Archaeology. Concepts, Methods and Tools. Proceedings of the 42nd Annual Conference on Computer Applications and Quantitative Methods in Archaeology*: 569-74. Oxford: Archaeopress.

Forte, M. 1997. Introduction, in M. Forte and A. Siliotti (eds.) *Virtual Archaeology. Recreating Ancient Worlds*: 9-13. New York: Harry N. Abrams.

Forte, M. 2000. About Virtual Archaeology: Disorders, Cognitive Interactions and Virtuality, in J. A. Barcelo, M. Forte and D. H. Sanders (eds.) *Virtual Reality in Archaeology*, BAR International Series 843: 247-59. Oxford: Archaeopress.

Forte, M. (ed.) 2007. *La villa di Liva. Une percorso di ricerca di archeologia virtuale*. Rome: 'L'Erma' di Bretschneider.

Forte, M. 2010. *Cyber-Archaeology*. Oxford: Archaeopress.

Forte, M. 2015. Cyber-Archaeology: A Post-Virtual Perspective, in P. Svensson and D. T. Goldberg (eds.) *Between Humanities and Digital*: 295-310. Cambridge, MA: The MIT Press.

Forte, M. and A. Siliotti (eds.) 1996. *Archeologia: Percorsi Virtuali nelle Civiltà Scomparse*. Milan: Arnoldo Mondadori Editore.

Forte, M., S. Pescarin and E. Pietroni 2006. Transparency, Interaction, Communication and Open Source in Virtual Archaeology, in M. Forte and S. Campana (eds.) *From Space to Place. 2nd International Conference on Remote Sensing in Archaeology. Proceedings of the 2nd International Workshop, CNR, Rome, Italy, December 4-7, 2006*: 535-9.

Forte, M., S. Pescarin and L. Pujol Tost 2006. VR Applications, New Devices and Museums: Public's Feedback and Learning. A Preliminary Report, in M. Ioannides, D. Arnold, F. Niccolucci, K. Mania (eds.) *The 7th International Symposium on Virtual Reality, Archaeology and Cultural Heritage VAST* (2006): 64-9.

Forte, M., G. Kurillo and T. Matlock 2010. Teleimmersive Archaeology: Simulation and Cognitive Impact, in M. Ioannides, D. Fellner, A. Georgopoulos, D. Hadjimitsis (eds) *Digital Heritage: Third International Euro-Mediterranean Conference, EuroMed 2010, Lemessos, Cyprus, November 2010*: 422-31. Berlin: Springer.

Forte, M. and N. Danelon 2015. Regium@Lepidi 2200 Project. *Archeomatica* 6 (1). 42-8.

Foss, C. 1979. *Ephesus after Antiquity: A Late Antique, Byzantine and Turkish City*. Cambridge: Cambridge University Press.

Fossey, J. M. 1979. The cities of the Kopais in the Roman period. *Aufsteig und Niedergang der Römischen Welt* II.7.1: 549-91. Berlin: Walter de Gruyter.

Fossey, J. M. 1981-82. The City Archive at Koroneia. *Euphrosyne* 11: 44-59.

Fossey, J. M. 1988. *Topography and Population of Ancient Boeotia*. Chicago: Chicago University Press.

Fossey, J. M. 1990. The Cities of the Kopaïs in the Roman Period. *Papers in Boiotian Topography and History*: 220-66. Amsterdam.

Foxhall, L. 2013. *Studying Gender in Classical Antiquity*. Cambridge: Cambridge University Press.

Fraisse, P. and J.-C. Moretti 2007. *Exploration Archéologique de Délos*. Athens: École Française d'Athènes.

Frazer, J. G. (ed.) 1913. *Pausanias's Description of Greece. Volume 5: Commentary on Books IX, X. Addenda*. London: Macmillan.

Frederiksen, R. 2000. Typology of the Greek Theatre Building in Late Classical and Hellenistic Times. *Proceedings of the Danish Institute at Athens*, III: 135-75.

Frederiksen, R. 2002. The Greek Theatre. A Typical Building in the Urban Centre of the *Polis*?, in T. E. Nielsen (ed.) *Even More Studies in the Ancient Greek Polis. Papers from the Copenhagen Polis Centre* 6: 65-124.

Frieman, C. and M. Gillings 2007. Seeing is Perceiving?. *World Archaeology* 39: 4-16.

Frischer, B., F. Niccolucci, N. Ryan and J.A. Barceló 2002. From CVR to CVRO: The Past, Present and Future of Cultural Virtual Reality, in F. Niccolucci (ed.) *Proceedings of VAST 2000*, British Archaeological Reports 834: 7-18.

Frischer, B. and A. Dakouri-Hild (eds.) 2008. *Beyond Illustration: 2D and 3D Digital Tools for Discovery in Archaeology*. BAR International Series 1805, Oxford: Archaeopress.

Frischer, B. and J. Fillwalk 2012. The Digital Hadrian's Villa Project: Virtual World Technology as an Aid to Finding Alignments between Built and Celestial Features. Paper presented at the 40th Conference in Computer Applications and Quantitative Methods in Archaeology CAA2012, Southampton, United Kingdom, 26-30 March 2012.

Fumaroli, M. 2001. Les Abeilles et les Araignées, in A.-M Lecoq (ed.) *La Querelle des Anciens et des Modernes XVIIe-XVIIIe siècles. Précédé de Les Abeilles et les Araignées, essai de Marc Fumaroli de l'Académie française*: 7-220. Paris: Gallimard.

Fumaroli, M. 2007. Arnaldo Momigliano et la Réhabilitation des 'Antiquaires': Le Comte de Caylus et le 'Retour à l'Antique' au XVIIIe Siècle, in P. N. Miller (ed.) *Momigliano and Antiquarianism: Foundations of the Modern Cultural Sciences*: 154-83. Toronto: University of Toronto Press.

Gallo, D. 1999. Per una Storia degli Antiquari Romani del Settecento. *Mélanges de l'Ecole Française de Rome. Italie et Méditerranée* 111 (2): 827-45.

Gallo, F. F. 2007. Il 'Thesaurus Antiquitatum et Historiarum Italiae, Neapolis Siciliae, Sardiniae, Corsicae, Melitae' di Johan Georg Graevius. *Archivio Storico per gli Antichi Studi Guastallesi VII*: 107-21. Guastalla: Associazione Guastallese di Storia Patria.

Garland, Y. 1974. *Recherches de Poliorcétique Grecque*. Athens: Ecole française d'Athènes.

Gatteschi, G. 1897. *Restauro grafico del Monte Capitolino, Foro Romano e monumenti circostanti nell'anno 300 dopo Cr.: conferenza letta al Museo Urbano nell'Orto Botanico l'8 marzo 1897 per invito della comm. archeol. comunale*. Rome.

Gatteschi, G. 1924. *Restauri della Roma Imperiale con gli Stati Attuali e il Testo Spiegativo*. Rome: Bretschneider.

Gebhard, E. R. 1992. The Early Stadium at Isthmia and the Founding of the Olympic Games, in W. Coulson and H. Kyrieleis (eds.) *Proceedings of an International Symposium on the Olympic Games, 5-9 September 1988*: 73-9. Athens: Deutsches Archäologisches Institut Athen.

Gebhard, E. R. 1993. The Evolution of a Pan-Hellenic Sanctuary: From Archaeology towards History at Isthmia, in N. Marinatos and R. Hägg (eds.) *Greek Sanctuaries. New Approaches*: 154-77. London & New York: Routledge.

Gell, W. 1819. *The Itinerary of Greece*. London.

Gell, W. and J.-P. Gandy 1852. *De Pompeiana*. 3rd edition. London: Henry J. Bohn.

Georgiou, R. and S. Hermon 2011. A London Charter's Visualisation of the Ancient Hellenistic-Roman Theatre in Paphos, in M. Dellepiane, F. Niccolucci, S. P. Serna, H. Rushmeier, and L. Van Gool (eds.) *The 12th International Symposium on Virtual Reality, Archaeology and Cultural Heritage (VAST 2011)*: 53-6.

Germani, M. 2012. Ancient theatres in Boeotia. *Encyclopedia of the Hellenic World, Boeotia*, viewed 02 March 2018, <http://www.ehw.gr/l.aspx?id=16727>.

Germani, M. 2015. Boeotian Theatres: An Overview of the Regional Architecture, in R. Frederiksen, E. R. Gebhard and A. Sokolicek (eds.) *The Architecture of Ancient Greek Theatres. Acts of an International Conference at the Danish Institute at Athens 27-30 January 2012*: 351-65. Aarhus: Aarhus Universitetsforlag.

Gibson, J.J. 1986. *The Ecological Approach to Visual Perception*. Hillsdale/London: Lawrence Erlbaum Associates [first edition 1979].

Gillings, M. 1999. Engaging Place: a Framework for the Integration and Realisation of Virtual-Reality Approaches in Archaeology, in L. Dingwall, S. Exon, V. Gaffney, S. Laflin and M. van Leusen (eds.) *Archaeology in the Age of the Internet: Proceedings of the 25th Anniversary Conference of CAA, Birmingham, April 1997*: 247-54. BAR International Series 750. Oxford: Archaeopress.

Gillings, M. 2000. Plans, elevations and virtual worlds: The development of techniques for the routine construction of hyperreal simulations, in J.A. Barceló, M. Forte and D. H. Sanders (eds.) *Virtual Reality in Archaeology*: 59-69. BAR International Series 843. Oxford: Archaeopress.

Gillings, M. 2002. Virtual archaeologies and the hyperreal: or, what does it mean to describe something as virtually-real?, in P. Fisher and D. Unwin (eds.) *Virtual Reality in Geography*: 17-34. London: Taylor & Francis.

Gillings, M. 2005. The Real, the Virtual and the Hyperreal, in S. Smiles and S. Moser (eds.) *Envisioning the Past: Archaeology and the Image*: 223-39. New York: Blackwells.

Gilman Romano, D. 2003. City Planning, Centuriation, and Land Division in Roman Corinth: Colonia Laus Iulia Corinthiensis & Colonia Iulia Flavia Augusta Corinthiensis. *Corinth XX*: 279-301.

Gilman Romano, D. 2005. Urban and Rural Planning in Roman Corinth, in D.N. Schowalter and S.J. Friesen (eds.) *Urban Religion in Roman Corinth*: 25-59. Harvard Theological Studies.

Giuliani, C. F. 2007. Piani di Lavoro per il Plastico di Roma, in F. Filippi (ed.) *Ricostruire l'Antico Prima del Virtuale. Italo Gismondi, un Architetto per l'Archeologia (1887-1974)*: 261-65. Rome: Edizioni Quasar.

Giuliano, A. 1965. Priene. *Enciclopedia dell'Arte Antica Classica e Orientale, VI*. Rome.

Glowacki, K. T. and N. Vogeikoff-Brogan (eds.) 2011. *STEGA: The Archaeology of Houses and Households in Ancient Crete*. Hesperia Supplement 44. Princeton: ASCSA.

Goldhill, S. 2011. *Victorian Culture and Classical Antiquity: Art, Opera, Fiction, and the Proclamation of Modernity*. Princeton, NJ: Princeton University Press.

Golzio, V. 1936. *Raffaello. Nei Documenti, nelle Testimonianze dei suoi Contemporanei e nella Letteratura del suo Secolo*. Città del Vaticano: Pontificia Insigne Accademia Artistica dei Virtuosi and Pantheon.

Goodchild, M. F. 1995. Geographic Information Systems and Geographic Research, in J. Pickels (ed.) *Ground Truth*: 31-50. New York: The Guilford Press.

Gockel B., H. Graf, A. Pagano, S. Pescarin and J. Eriksson 2013. VMUXE An Approach to User Experience Evaluation for Virtual Museums, in A. Marcus (ed.) *Design, User Experience, and Usability: Design Philosophy, Methods and Tools, Part 1*: 262-72. Heidelberg: Springer.

Gordin, D. N. 1997. Scientific Visualization as Expressive Medium for Project Science Inquiry. Unpublished PhD dissertation, Northwestern University, Evanston, Illinois.

Gordin, D. N., D. C. Edison and L. M. Gomez 1996. Scientific Visualization as an Interpretive and Expressive Medium, in C. Edelson and E. A. Domeshek (eds.) *Proceedings of the Second International Conference on the Learning Sciences*, July 1996, Evanston, IL: 409-14. Charlottesville, VA: AACE.

Gounaris and Velenis 1997 = Γούναρη, Γ. and Γ. Βελένης 1997. Πανεπιστημιακή Ανασκαφή Φιλίππων 1988 – 1996. *ΑΕΜΘ* 10Β: 719–33. Thessaloniki.

Gran-Aymerich, È. 2001. *El Nascimiento de l'Arqueologia Moderna, 1798-1945*. Zaragoza: Prensas Universitarias de Zaragoza (original edition: È. Gran-Aymerich 1998. *Naissance de l'archéologie moderne, 1798-1945*. París: CNRS Éditions).

Grandjean, Y. 1988. *Recherches sur l'habitat thasien à l'époque grecque*. École Française d'Athènes. Paris: de Boccard.

Grandjean, Y. and F. Salviat 2000. *Guide de Thasos*. École Française d'Athène. Paris: De Boccard.

Graninger, D. 2011. *Cult and Koinon in Hellenistic Thessaly*. Leiden/Boston: Brill.

Gras, M. and H. Tréziny 1999. Megara Iblea, in E. Greco (ed.), *La Città Greca Antica. Istituzioni, Società e Forme Urbane*: 251-67. Rome: Donzelli.

Gras, M., H. Tréziny and H. Briose (eds.) 2004. *Mégara Hyblaea 5. La ville archaïque*. Rome: École française de Rome.

Greco, E. 1997. Definizione dello Spazio Urbano: Architettura e Spazio Pubblico, in S. Settis (ed.), *I Greci. Storia, Cultura, Arte, Società. Una Storia Greca. Definizione (VI-IV secolo a. C.)*, 2.2: 619-52.

Greco, E. 1999. Turi, in E. Greco (ed.) *La Città Greca Antica. Istituzioni, Società e Forme Urbane*: 413-30. Rome: Donzelli Editore.

Greco, E. 2006. Agora e Zeus Agoraios, in D. Morandi Bonacossi, E. Rova, F. Veronese and P. Zanovello (eds.) *Tra Oriente e Occidente: Studi in Onore di Elena Di Filippo Balestrazzi*: 327-35. Sargon: Padova.

Greco, E. 2010. Sulla Topografia di Atene: Un'Introduzione ai Problemi. *Topografia di Atene: Sviluppo Urbano e Monumenti dalle Origini al III secolo d.C.*, Tomo I: 19-43. Atene: Pandemos.

Greco, E. and O. Voza 2010. Osservazioni sulle Fasi Cronologiche del Teatro di Efestia. *SAIA Annuario LXXXVIII*, Serie III, vol. 10: 169-74.

Groh, S. 2006. Neue Forschungen zur Stadtplanung in Ephesos. *Jahreshefte des Österreichischen Archäologischen Institutes in Wien*, Band 75/2006: 47-116.

Groh, S. 2012. Strategies and results of the urban survey in the Upper City of Ephesus, in F. Vermeulen, G.-J. Burgers, S. Keay and C. Corsi (eds.) *Urban Landscape Survey in Italy and the Mediterranean*: 62-71. Oxford: Oxbow Books.

Grosman, D. 2009. *Aerial Prospection in Boeotia. Report on the 2009 Field Season*. Ljubljana.

Gruber, M., 1999. Managing Large 3D Urban Databases, in D. Fritsch and R. Spiller (eds.) *Photogrammetric Week '99*: 341-9. Heidelberg: Wichmann Verlag.

Gruber, E. and J. Dobbins 2013. Illuminating Historical Architecture. The House of the Drinking Contest at Antioch, in F. Contreras, Francisco, M. Farjas and F. Javier Melero (eds.) *Fusion of Cultures. Proceedings of the 38th Annual Conference on Computer Applications and Quantitative Methods in Archaeology, Granada, Spain, April 2010*: 71-6. BAR International Series 2494. Oxford: Archaeopress.

Grün, A., F. Remondino and L. Zhang 2004. Photogrammetric Reconstruction of the Great Buddha of Bamiyan, Afghanistan. *The Photogrammetric Record* 19 (107): 177-99.

Grupico, T. M. 2008. *The Influence of Urban Planning on Temple Design in West Greece*. Unpublished PhD dissertation, Rutgers, State University of New Jersey.

Gualdo, R. 1993. Fabio Calvo, Marco, in M. Caravale, F. Bartoccini (eds.) *Dizionario Biografico degli Italiani* 43: 723-7.

Günther, H. 1997. L'idea di Roma Antica nella 'Roma instaurata' di Flavio Biondo, in S. Rossi and S. Valeri (eds.) *Le due Rome del Quattrocento*: 380-93. Rome: Lithos.

Gutierrez, D., B. Frischer and F. Seron 2005. The Flavian Amphitheater (Colosseum) in Rome: An Excellent People-Mover?, in A. Figueiredo and G. Leite Velho (eds.) *The World is in Your Eyes. Computer Applications and Quantitative Methods in Archaeology CAA 2005. Proceedings of the 33rd Conference, Tomar, March 2005*: 55-60.

Gutierrez, D., B. Frischer, E. Cerezo, A. Gomez and E. Sobreviela 2005. Virtual Crowds in a Digital Colosseum, in R. Vergnieux and C. Delevoie (eds.) *Actes du Colloque Virtual Retrospect 2005, Archéovision 2*: 140-5. Bordeaux: Editions Ausonius.

Gutierrez, D., B. Frischer, E. Cerezo, A. Gomez and F. Seron 2006. AI and Virtual Crowds: Populating the Colosseum. *Journal of Cultural Heritage* 8 (2): 176-85.

Gutierrez, D., V. Sundstedt, F. Gomez and A. Chalmers 2008. Modeling Light Scattering for Virtual Heritage. *Journal on Computing and Cultural Heritage* 1 (2): 1–15.

Haagsma, M. J. 2010. Domestic Economy and Social Organization in New Halos. Unpublished PhD dissertation, University of Groningen.

Haagsma, M. J., S. Karapanou, T. Harvey and L. Surtees 2014. An Ancient City and its Agora. Results of the Archaeological Project at the Kastro of Kallithea, Greece, in Giannikouri, E. (ed.) *The Agora in the Mediterranean: from Homeric to Roman times, International Conference, Kos, 14-17 April 2011*: 197-208. Athens: Hellenic Ministry of Culture and Tourism, Archaeological Institute of Aegean Studies.

Habicht, C. 1998. *Pausanias' Guide to Ancient Greece*. Berkeley & Los Angeles: University of California Press.

Hadjimichali, V. 1971. Recherches à Latô. III. Maisons. *Bulletin de Correspondance Hellénique* 95: 167-222.

Haegler, S., P. Müller and L. van Gool 2009. Procedural Modeling for Digital Cultural Heritage. *EURASIP Journal on Image and Video Processing 2009*, viewed 02 March 2018, <http://jivp.eurasipjournals.springeropen.com/articles/10.1155/2009/852392>.

Halbertsma, R. B. 2003. *Scholars, travellers and trade. The pioneer years of the National Museum of Antiquities in Leiden, 1818-1840*. London: Routledge.

Hall, J. M. 2008. Foundation Stories, in G. R. Tsetskhladze (ed.) *Greek Colonisation: An Account of Greek Colonies and Other Settlements Overseas* 2: 383-426. Leiden and Boston: Brill.

Hamilakis, Y. 2013. *Archaeology and the Senses: Human Experience, Memory, and Affect*. Cambridge: Cambridge University Press.

Hamilakis, Y. 2016. Some Debts can Never be Repaired: The Archaeo-politics of the Crisis. *Journal of Modern Greek Studies* 34 (2): 227-64.

Hamilakis, Y. and E. Yialouri 1996. Antiquities as Symbolic Capital in Modern Greek Society. *Antiquity* 70: 117-29.

Hansen, M. H. 1996. An inventory of Boiotian *Poleis* in the Archaic and Classical periods, in M. H. Hansen (ed.) *Introduction to an Inventory of Poleis. Acts of the Copenhagen Polis Centre*, vol. 3: 73-116. Copenhagen.

Hansen, M. H. (ed.) 1997. *The Polis as an Urban Centre and as a Political Community, Acts of the Copenhagen Polis Centre*, vol. 4. Copenhagen.

Hansen, M. H. (ed.) 2000. *A Comparative Study of Thirty City-State Cultures: An Investigation Conducted by the Copenhagen Polis Centre*. Copenhagen: C.A. Reitzels Forlag.

Hansen, M. H. 2006. *The Shotgun Method: the Demography of the Ancient Greek City-State Culture*. Columbia, Missouri: University of Missouri Press.

Hansen, M. H. 2008. An Update on the Shotgun Method. *Greek, Roman, and Byzantine Studies* 48: 259-86.

Hansen, M. H. and T. Fischer-Hansen 1994. Monumental Political Architecture in Archaic and Classical Greek *Poleis*. Evidence and Historical Significance, in D. Whitehead (ed.) *From Political Architecture to Stephanus Byzantius: Sources for the Ancient Greek Polis*: 23-90. Stuttgart: Franz Steiner Verlag.

Hansen, M. H. and T. H. Nielsen (eds) 2004. *An Inventory of Archaic and Classical Poleis*. Oxford: Oxford University Press.

Happa, J., A. Artusi, P. Dubla, T. Bashford-Rogers, K. Debattista, V. Hulusic and A. Chalmers 2009. The Virtual Reconstruction and Daylight Illumination of the Panagia Angeloktisti, in C. Perlingieri and D.

Pitzalis (eds.) *The 10th International Symposium on Virtual Reality, Archaeology and Cultural Heritage VAST 2009*: 49-56.

Härkänen, L., S. Helle, L. Järvenpää and T. Lehtonen 2015. Novel Interaction Techniques for Mobile Augmented Reality applications. A Systematic Literature Review. University of Turku Technical Reports, No. 9 — August 2015, viewed 02 March 2018, <https://www.doria.fi/bitstream/handle/10024/113117/Novel_Interaction_Techniques_For_Mobile_Augmented_Reality.pdf?sequence=2>.

Harrison, G. W. M. 2004. Organization of Dwelling Space in Roman Crete: The *Disiecta Membra* of Cities, in M. Livadiotti and I. Simiakaki (eds.) *Creta Romana e Protobizantina: Atti del Congresso Internazionale (Iraklion, 23-30 settembre 2000)*: 751-7. Padova: Bottega d'Erasmo.

Harrison, M., S. Keay and G. Earl 2013. Grammar Modelling and the Visualization of an Uncertain Past: The Case of Building V at Portus, in G. Earl, T. Sly, A. Chrysanthi, P. Murrieta-Flores, C. Papadopoulos, I. Romanowska and D. Wheatley (eds.) *Archaeology in the Digital Era. Proceedings of the 40th Computer Applications and Quantitative Methods in Archaeology Conference (CAA 2012). Southampton, UK*: 895-909. Amsterdam: Amsterdam University Press.

Hart, V. and P. Hicks (eds.) 2006. *Palladio's Rome. A Translation of Andrea Palladio's Two Guidebooks to Rome*. New Haven and London: Yale University Press.

Hasaki, E. 2002. Ceramic Kilns in Ancient Greece: Technology and Organization of Ceramic Workshops. Unpublished PhD dissertation, University of Cincinnati.

Hasaki, E. 2011. Crafting Spaces: Archaeological, Ethnographic and Ethnoarchaeological Studies of Spatial Organization in Pottery Worshops in Greece and Tunisia, in M. Lawall and J. Lund (eds.) *Pottery in the Archaeological Record: Greece and Beyond*: 12–24. Aarhus: Aarhus University Press.

Heiden, J. 2006. Die Agorai von Elis und Olimpia, in W. Hoepfner and L. Lehmann (eds.) *Die Griechische Agora – Bericht über ein Kolloquium am 16 März 2003 in Berlin*: 53-8. Mainz am Rhein: Philipp von Zabern.

Hellmann, M.-Ch. 1992. *Recherches sur le Vocabulaire de l'Architecture Grecque d'après les Inscriptions de Délos*. École française d'Athènes: Athens, Paris.

Hermon, S. 2008. Reasoning in 3D: a Critical Appraisal of the Role of 3D Modelling and Virtual Reconstructions in Archaeology, in B. Frischer and A. Dakouri-Hild (eds.) *Beyond Illustration: 2D and 3D Technologies as Tools for Discovery in Archaeology*: 36-45. BAR International Series 1805. Oxford: Archaeopress.

Hermon, S. and J. Nikodem 2008. 3D Modelling as a Scientific Research Tool in Archaeology, in A. Posluschny, K. Lambers and I. Herzog (eds.) *Layers of Perception. Proceedings of the 35th International Conference on Computer Applications and Quantitative Methods in Archaeology (CAA), Berlin, Germany, April 2-6, 2007 (Kolloquien zur Vor- und Frühgeschichte, Vol. 10)*: 140-6. Bonn: Dr. Rudolf Habelt GmbH.

Hiatt, A. 2004. *The Making of Medieval Forgeries: False Documents in Fifteenth-century England*. The British Library Studies in Medieval Culture. Toronto: University of Toronto Press.

Higgins, R. 1986. *Tanagra and the Figurines*. Princeton: Princeton University Press.

Hillier B. and J. Hanson 1984. *The Social Logic of Space*. Cambridge: Cambridge University Press.

Hodgson, J. 2004. Archaeological Reconstruction Illustrations. An Analysis of the History, Development, Motivations and Current Practice of Reconstruction Illustration, with Recommendation for its Future Development. Unpublished PhD dissertation, Bournemouth University.

Hoepfner, W. 2009. Urban Planning in the Classical Period, in A. Ph. Lagopoulos (ed.) *A History of the Greek City*: 169-82. BAR International Series 2050. Oxford: Archaeopress.

Hoepfner, W. and E.-L. Schwandner (eds.) 1994. *Haus und Stadt im klassischen Griechenland. Wohnen in der klassischen Polis*, 2nd ed.. Munich: Deutscher Kunstverlag.

Hollinshead, M. B. 2015. *Shaping Ceremony. Monumental Steps and Greek Architecture*. Madison; London: University of Wisconsin Press.

Hölscher, T. 2012. Urban Spaces and Central Places: The Greek World, in S.E. Alcock and R. Osborne (eds.) *Classical Archaeology*: 170-86. Oxford: Wiley-Blackwell.

Huber, S. and Y. Varalis 1995. Chronique des fouilles et découvertes archéologiques en Grèce en 1994, *Bulletin de Correspondance Hellénique* 119 (3): 845-1057.

Hucker, R. A. 2009. How Did the Romans Achieve Straight Roads?. Paper presented at FIG Working Week 2009: Surveyors Key Role in Accelerated Development, Eilat 3-8 May.

Hülsen, C. 1907. *La Roma Antica di Ciriaco d'Ancona: Disegni Inediti del Secolo XV*. Rome: Ermanno Loescher & Co.

Hunt, P. 2007. Review of Mogens Herman Hansen, The Shotgun Method: The Demography of the Ancient Greek City-State Culture. *Bryn Mawr Classical Review* 2007.04.58, viewed 02 March 2018, <http://bmcr.brynmawr.edu/2007/2007-04-58.html>.

Hupperetz, W., R. Carlani, D. Pletinckx and E. Pietroni 2012. Etruscanning 3D project. The 3D reconstruction of the Regolini Galassi Tomb as a Research tool and a new Approach in Storytelling. *Virtual Archaeology Review* 3 (7): 92-6.

Isler, H. P. 2007. *Eretria XVIII. Das Theater*. Lausanne: Ecole Suisse d'Archéologie en Grèce Infolio editions.

I.T. Transport Ltd., Consultants in Transport for Rural Development 2002. *Foothpats and Tracks. A Field Manual for their Construction and Improvement*.

Izenour, G. C. 1992. *Roofed Theaters of Classical Antiquity*. New Haven: Yale University Press.

Jacks, P. J. 1990. The Simulachrum of Fabio Calvo: A View of Roman Architecture all'Antica in 1527. *The Art Bulletin* 72 (3): 453-81.

Jacobs, I. 2009. Gates in Late Antiquity. The Eastern Mediterranean. *BABESCH* 84: 197-213.

Jacobs, I. 2013. *Aesthetic Maintenance of Civic Space. The 'Classical' City from the 4th to the 7th c. AD*. Leuven: Peeters Publishers.

Jameson, M. H. 1990. Domestic space in the Greek city-state, in S. Kent (ed.) *Domestic Architecture and the Use of Space*: 92-113. Cambridge: Cambridge University Press.

Jannoray, J. 1937. Le 'Gymnase du Bas' a Delphes. *Bulletin de Correspondance Hellénique* 61: 53-6.

Jannoray, J. and H. Ducoux 1953. *Fouilles de Delphes. Tome 2: Topographie et Architecture. Le Gymnase*. Athens: École Française d'Athènes.

Kalliontzis, Y. 2014. Digging in Storerooms for Inscriptions: An Unpublished Casualty List from Plataia in the Museum of Thebes and the Memory of War in Boeotia, in N. Papazarkadas (ed.) *The Epigraphy and History of Boeotia: New Finds, New Prospects*: 332-72. Leiden: Brill.

Kalliontzis, Y. and N. Papazarkadas 2014. New Boeotian inscriptions from Akraiphia and Koroneia, in W. Eck and P. Funke (eds.) *Öffentlichkeit - Monument - Text. XIV Congressus Internationalis Epigraphiae Graecae et Latinae, Akten*: 550-2. Berlin: Walter de Gruyter.

Kalpaxis, A. 1999. Le città cretesi, in E. Greco (ed.) *La Città Greca Antica. Istituzioni, Società e Forme Urbane*: 111-28. Rome: Donzelli Editore.

Kamermans, H., W. De Neef, C. Piccoli, A. Posluschny and R. Scopigno (eds.) 2016. *The Three Dimensions of Archaeology. Proceedings of the UISPP conference* (Burgos, 1-7 September 2014). Oxford: Archaeopress.

Karasik, A. 2008. Applications of 3D Technology as a Research Tool in Archaeological Ceramic Analysis, in B. Frischer and A. Dakouri-Hild (eds.) *Beyond Illustration: 2D and 3D Digital Tools for Discovery in Archaeology*: 103-16. BAR International Series 1805. Oxford: Archaeopress.

Kardaras, G. 2011. Church of Boeotia in the Byzantine period. *Encyclopedia of the Hellenic World, Boeotia*, viewed 02 March 2018, <http://www.ehw.gr/l.aspx?id=12705>.

Karvonis, P. and J.-J. Malmary 2009. Étude Architecturale de Quatre Pièces Polyvalantes du Quartier du Théâtre à Délos. *Bulletin de Correspondance Hellénique* 133: 195-226.

Kassel, R. and C. Austin 1984. *Poetae Comici Graeci*, vol III.2. Berlin: de Gruyter.

Kékulé von Stradonitz, R. 1878. *Griechische Tonfiguren aus Tanagra*. Stuttgart: Spemann.

Kensek, K. M., L. Swartz Dodd and N. Cipolla 2004. Fantastic Reconstructions or Reconstructions of the Fantastic? Tracking and Presenting Ambiguity, Alternatives, and Documentation in the Virtual Worlds. *Automation in Construction* 13: 175-86.

Kirilov, C. 2007. The Reduction of the Fortified Area in Late Antiquity, in J. Henning (ed.) *Post-Roman Towns, Trade and Settlement in Europe and Byzantium*, vol. 2: 3-24. Berlin: de Gruyter.

Kockel, V. 2005. 'Il palazzo per tutti'. La scoperta ad Ostia dell'antica casa di affitto e la sua influenza sull'architettura della Roma fascista. *Confronto. Studi e ricerche di storia dell'arte europea* 5: 54-73. Naples.

Koehl, M. and F. Roussel 2015. Procedural Modelling for Reconstruction of Historic Monuments. *ISPRS Annals of the Photogrammetry, Remote Sensing and Spatial Information Sciences, Volume II-5/W3. 25th International CIPA Symposium 2015, 31 August – 04 September 2015, Taipei, Taiwan*: 137-44.

Kolb, C. C. 1997. Review of M. Forte and A. Siliotti (eds.), Virtual Archaeology: Re-creating Ancient Worlds. *H-PCAACA, H-Net Reviews*. August, 1997, viewed 02 March 2018, <http://www.h-net.org/reviews/showrev.php?id=1207>.

Kolb, F. 1984. *Die Stadt im Altertum*, München: C. H. Beck.

Kondopoulou, D., I. Zananiri, C. Rathossi, E. De Marco, V. Spatharas and H. Hasaki 2014. An Archaeometric and Archaeological Approach to Hellenistic-Early Roman Ceramic Workshops in Greece: Contribution to Dating. *Radiocarbon* 56: S27-S38.

Konecny, A., V. Aravantinos and R. T. Marchese (eds.) 2013. *PLATAIAI. Archäologie und Geschichte einer boiotischen Polis, Sonderschriften Band 48*. Wien: Österreichisches Archäologisches Institut.

König, J. 2005. *Athletics and Literature in the Roman Empire*. Cambridge: Cambridge University Press.

Kormann, M., S. Katsarou, D. Katsonopoulou and G. Lock 2016. Structural Integrity Modelling of an Early Bronze Age Corridor House in Helike of Achaea, NW Peloponnese, Greece, in S. Campana, R. Scopigno, G. Carpentiero, M. Cirillo (eds.), *Keep the Revolution Going. Proceedings of the 43rd Annual Conference on Computer Applications and Quantitative Methods in Archaeology*: 825-36. Oxford: Archaeopress.

Kountoura-Galaki 1996 = Κουντούρα-Γαλάκη, Ε., 1996. 'Η 'Εικονοκλαστική' NOTITIA 3 και το λατινικό της πρότυπο', *SYMMEIKTA* 10: 35-73.

Kousser, R. 2005. Creating the Past: The Venus de Milo and the Hellenstic Reception of Classical Greece. *American Journal of Archaeology* 109: 227-50.

Kraynak, L. H. 1992. The Xenon, in S. G. Miller (ed.) *Excavations at Nemea*: 99-187. Berkeley: University of California Press.

Krentz, P. 1989. Athena Itonia and the Battle of Koroneia, in H. Beister and J. Buckler (eds.) *Boiotika*: 313-7, pl. 68-9. Munchen: Editio Maris.

Kubovy, M. 1986. *The Psychology of Perspective and Renaissance Art*. Cambridge: Cambridge University Press.

Lagos, C. 2001. Athena Itonia at Koroneia (Boiotia) and in Cilicia. *The Numismatic Chronicle* 161: 1-10.

Landeschi, G., N. Dell'Unto, D. Ferdani, S. Lindgren and A.-M. Leander Touati 2015. Enhanced 3D-GIS: Documenting Insula V 1 in Pompeii, in F. Giligny, F. Djindjian, L. Costa, P. Moscati and S. Robert (eds.) *Proceedings of the 42nd Annual Conference on Computer Applications and Quantitative Methods in Archaeology (CAA 2014)*: 349-60. Paris.

Landeschi, G., N. Dell'Unto, K. Lundqvist, D. Ferdani, D. M. Campanaro and A.-M. Leander Touati 2016. 3D-GIS as a platform for visual analysis: Investigating a Pompeian house. *Journal of Archaeological Science* 65: 103-13.

Lang, F. 1996. *Archaische Siedlungen in Griechenland: Struktur und Entwicklung*. Berlin: Akademie-Verlag.

Lang, F. 2005. Structural Changes in Archaic Greece, in B. A. Ault and L. C. Nevett (eds.) *Ancient Greek Houses and Households: Chronological Regional, and Social Diversity*: 12-35. Philadelphia: University of Pennsylvania Press.

Lang, F. 2007. House – Community – Settlement: The New Concept of Living in Archaic Greece, in R. Westgate, N. Fisher and J. Whitley (eds.) *Building Communities: House, Settlement and Society in the Aegean and Beyond*. British School at Athens Studies, vol. 15: 183-93. London: British School at Athens.

Lauffer, S. 1986. *KOPAIS. Untersuchungen zur historischen Landeskunde Mittelgriechenlands*. Frankfurt am Main: Verlag Peter Lang.

Laurence, K. A. 2012. Roman Infrastructural Changes to Greek Sanctuaries and Games: Panhellenism in the Roman Empire, Formations of New Identities. Unpublished PhD dissertation, University of Michigan.

Laurence, R. 2007. *Roman Pompeii: Space and Society*. London & New York: Routledge.

Lavan, L. 2006. Forai and Agorai in Mediterranean Cities during the 4th and 5th c. AD, in W. Bowden, A. Gutteridge and C. Machado (eds.) *Social and Political Life in Late Antiquity*. Late Antique Archaeology 3.1: 195-249. Leiden: Brill.

Lavan, L. 2013. The Agorai of Sagalassos in Late Antiquity: An Interpretative Study, in L. Lavan and M. Mulryan (eds.) *Field Methods and Post-Excavation Techniques in Late Antique Archaeology* (Late Antique Archaeology 9 – 2012): 289–353. Leiden: Brill.

Lawrence, A. W. 1979. *Greek Aims in Fortification*. Oxford: Clarendon Press.

Leach, M. 2007. John Howard Marsden (1803–1891) First Disney Professor of Archaeology at the University of Cambridge 1851–1865. *Bulletin of the History of Archaeology* 17 (1): 35-9.

Leake, W. M. 1835. *Travels in Northern Greece. In Four Volumes*, vol. 2. London: J. Rodwell.

Lefebvre, H. 1991 (1974). *The Production of Space* (translated by Donald Nicholson-Smith). Oxford: Blackwell Publisher.

Le Roy, J. D. 1758. *Les ruines des plus beaux monuments de la Grèce*. Paris: Guerin & Delatour.

Leto, K. 2013. Nolli e la Visione della Città. Rigore ed Estetica nella Rappresentazione dello Spazio Urbano, in C. M. Travaglini and K. Lelo (eds.) *Roma nel Settecento. Immagini e Realtà di una Capitale Attraverso la Pianta di G.B. Nolli*, vol. 1: 3-42. Rome: Croma-Edilstampa.

Levick, B. 2000. Greece and Asia Minor, in A. K. Bowman, P. Garnsey and D. Rathbone (eds.) *The Cambridge Ancient History, vol. 11: The High Empire, AD 70-192, 2nd edition*: 604-34. Cambridge: Cambridge University Press.

Lewuillon, S. 2002. Archaeological Illustrations: A New Development in 19th Century Science. *Antiquity* 76: 223-34.

Liebeschuetz, J. H. W. G. 2001. *The Decline and Fall of the Roman City*. Oxford: Oxford University Press.

Lilimbaki-Akamati and Akamatis 2007 = Λιλιμπάκη-Ακαμάτη, Μ. ανd Ν. Ακαμάτης 2007. Το δημόσιο λουτρό της Πέλλας. Ανασκαφική περίοδος 2007. *AEMΘ* 21: 99-108.

Lilimbaki-Akamati and Akamatis 2008 = Λιλιμπάκη-Ακαμάτη, Μ. ανd Ν. Ακαμάτης 2008. Ένα νέο εργαστήριο κεραμικής στην Πέλλα. *Το Αρχαιολογικό Έργο στη Μακεδονία και Θράκη* 22: 147–54. Thessaloniki.

Linders, T. 1994. Sacred Menus on Delos, in R. Hägg (ed.) *Ancient Greek Cult Practice from the Epigraphical Evidence*: 71-9. Stockholm: Paul Åström.

Lippolis, E., C. Giatti and E. Interdonato 2009. Contesti, materiali e cronologia nel quartiere del Pretorio, *LANX* 4: 103-20.

Littlewood, A. R. 2006. Gardens, in N. Wilson (ed.) *Encyclopedia of Ancient Greece*: 310-1.

Livadiotti, M. 2010. Processi di Standardizzazione nel Cantiere Ellenistico: Il Caso di Kos. *Meetings Between Cultures in the Ancient Mediterranean, XVII Congresso Internazionale di Archeologia Classica (AIAC), Roma, 22-26 settembre 2008, Bollettino di Archeologia online* 1: 23-42.

Livadiotti, M. 2013. Lo Hestiatorion dell'Asklepieion di Kos, *Thiasos* 2.2: 39-58.

Livadiotti, M. and I. Simiakaki (eds.) 2004. *Creta Romana e Protobizantina: Atti del Congresso Internazionale (Iraklion, 23-30 settembre 2000)*. Padua: Bottega d'Erasmo.

Llewellyn, S. and R. Sorrell (eds.) 2013. *Alan Sorrell: The Life and Works of an English Neo-romantic Artist*. Bristol: Sansom & Co.

Lock, P. 1986. The Frankish Towers of Central Greece. *The Annual of the British School at Athens* 81: 101-23.

Lohmann, H. 1993. *ATENE. Forschungen zu Siedlungs- und Wirtschaftsstruktur des klassischen Attika*. Cologne: Bohlau Verlag.

Lomas, K. and T. Cornell 2003. *Bread and Circuses: Euergetism and Municipal Patronage in Roman Italy*. London: Routledge.

Longfellow, B. 2009. The Legacy of Hadrian: Roman Monumental Civic Fountains in Greece, in C. Kosso and A. Scott (eds.) *The Nature and Function of Water, Baths, Bathing and Hygiene from Antiquity through the Renaissance*: 211-32. Leiden: Brill.

Longfellow, B. 2012. Roman Fountains in Greek Sanctuaries, *American Journal of Archaeology* 116 (1): 133-55.

Longo, F. 2007. L'Agora del Ceramico dalla 'Nascita' alla Spedizione in Sicilia, in E. Greco and M. Lombardo (eds.) *Atene e l'Occidente, i grandi temi: Le Premesse, i Protagonisti, le Forme della Comunicazione e dell'Interazione, i Modi dell'Intervento Ateniese in Occidente: Atti del Convegno Internazionale, Atene, 25- 27 Maggio 2006*: 117-54. Athens: Scuola Archeologica Italiana di Atene.

Longo, F. 2008. L'Impianto Urbano del Pireo tra Dati Reali e Proiezioni Immaginarie. *Atene e la Magna Grecia dall'Età Arcaica all'Ellenismo. Atti del Quarantasettesimo Convegno di Studi sulla Magna Grecia. Taranto 27-30 Settembre 2007*: 137-55. Taranto: Istituto per la storia e l'archeologia della Magna Grecia.

Longo, F. 2010. L' Αγορή di Omero. Rappresentazione Poetica e Documentazione Archeologica. *AION. Annali dell' Università degli Studi di Napoli 'L'Orientale'* 31: 199-223.

Longo, F. 2014. Fondazioni di Città nel Mondo Greco in Età Arcaica, in C. Rescigno and F. Sirano (eds.) *Immaginando Città. Racconti di Fondazioni Mitiche, Forma e Funzioni delle Città Campane. Santa Maria Capua Vetere – Paestum*: 230-3. Naples: Soprintendenza per i beni archeologici di Salerno, Avellino, Benevento e Caserta.

Lo Sardo, P. 1999. Verso il Canone della *Polis*, in E. Greco (ed.) *La Città Greca Antica: Istituzioni, Società e Forme Urbane*: 83-97. Rome: Donzelli.

Love, I. C. 1970. A Preliminary Report of the Excavations at Knidos, 1969, *American Journal of Archaeology* 74 (2): 149-55.

Love, I. C. 1973. A Preliminary Report of the Excavations at Knidos, *American Journal of Archaeology* 77 (4): 413-24.

Lowenthal, D. 1985. *The Past is a Foreign Country*. Cambridge: Cambridge University Press.

Lucas, G. 2001. *Critical Approaches to Fieldwork: Contemporary and Historical Archaeological Practise*. London and New York: Routledge.

Lulof, P. S. 2011. The Art of Reconstruction. De Wetenschappelijke Waarde van 3D-simulaties bij de Analyse van Pre-Romeinse Tempels en Daken. *TMA: Tijdschrift voor Mediterrane Archeologie* 23 (46): 14-24.

Lulof, P. S., L. Opgenhaffen and M.H. Sepers 2013. The Art of Reconstruction. Documenting the Process of 3D Modelling; Some Preliminary Results. *Proceedings of the 2013 Digital Heritage International Congress (DigitalHeritage), Volume 1, Marseille, Oct. 28 2013-Nov. 1 2013*: 333-7. Piscataway, NJ: IEEE.

Ma, J. 2013. *Statues and Cities: Honorific Portraits and Civic Identity in the Hellenistic World. Oxford Studies in Ancient Culture and Representation*. Oxford/New York: Oxford University Press.

Mackil, E. and P. van Alfen 2006. Cooperative coinage, in P. van Alfen (ed.) *Agoranomia: Studies in Money and Exchange Presented to John H. Kroll*: 201-47. New York: American Numismatic Society.

Madonna, M. L. 1991. La 'Rometta' di Pirro Ligorio in Villa d'Este a Tivoli: Un Incunabolo Tridimensionale, in M. Fagiolo (ed.), *Roma Antica (L'Immagine delle Grandi Città Italiane/ 1)*: 15-21. Lecce: Capone Editore.

Magnani, L. and N. Nersessian (eds.) 2002. *Model-Based Reasoning. Science, Technology, Values*. New York: Kluwer Academic/Plenum Publishers.

Magnani, L., N. Nersessian and C. Pizzi (eds.) 2002. *Logical and Computational Aspects of Model-Based Reasoning*. Dordrecht: Kluwer Academic Publishers.

Maier, F. G. 1959. *Griechische Mauerbauinschriften*, vol. 1. Heidelberg: Quelle & Meyer.

Marchand, S. 2007. From Antiquarian to Archaeologist? Adolf Furtwängler and the Problem of 'Modern' Classical Archaeology, in P. N. Miller (ed.) *Momigliano and Antiquarianism: Foundations of the Modern Cultural Sciences*: 248-85. Toronto: University of Toronto Press.

Marcus, J. and J. A. Sabloff (eds.) 2008. *The Ancient City. New Perspectives on Urbanism in the Old and New World*. Santa Fe: School for Advanced Research Press.

Marinatos, N. 1993. What Were Greek Sanctuaries?, in N. Marinatos and R. Hägg (eds.) *Greek Sanctuaries. New Approaches*: 228-33. London & New York: Routledge.

Martin, R. 1951. *Recherches sur l'Agora Grecque. Études d'histoire et d'architecture urbaines*, Bibliothèque des Écoles Françaises d'Athenes. Paris: E. de Boccard.

Martin, R. 1956. *L'urbanisme dans la Grèce antique*. Paris: A. et J. Picard.

Martin, L. H. 1987. *Hellenistic Religion: An Introduction*. Oxford: Oxford University Press.

Martinelli, M. 2012. *Il Giardino nel Mediterraneo Antico: Egitto, Vicino Oriente e Mondo Ellenico*. Florence: A. Pontecorboli.

Massau, D. 2004. Caylus, Diderot et les Philosphes, in N. Cronk and K. Peeters (eds.) *Le comte de Caylus: Les Arts et les Lettres. Actes du Colloque International Université d'Anvers (UFSIA) et Voltaire Foundation Oxford, 26-7 Mai 2000*: 45-57. Amsterdam-New York: Rodopi.

Mazarakis-Ainian, A. 1997. *From Rulers' Dwellings to Temples. Architecture, Religion and Society in Early Iron Age Greece (1100-700 B.C.)*. Jonsered: Astrom.
McAllister, M. H. 1959. The Temple of Ares at Athens. A Review of the Evidence. *Hesperia* 28: 1-64.
McCahill, E. M. 2009. Rewriting Vergil, Rereading Rome: Maffeo Vegio, Poggio Bracciolini, Flavio Biondo and Early Quattrocento Antiquarianism. *Memoirs of the American Academy* 54: 165-99.
McNicoll, A. W. 1997. *Hellenistic Fortifications. From the Aegean to the Euphrates*. Oxford: Oxford University Press.
Meens, A. 2011. Textile implements from Koroneia, producing textile in the ancient city. Unpublished BA dissertation, Leiden University, Faculty of Archaeology.
Meier, L. 2013. Priests and Funding of Public Buildings on Cos and Elsewhere, in M. Horster and A. Klöckner (eds.) *Cities and Priests: Cult Personnel in Asia Minor and the Aegean Islands from the Hellenistic to the Imperial Period*: 41-8. Berlin: De Gruyter.
Merlo, S. 2004. The 'Contemporary Mind'. 3D GIS as a Challenge in Excavation Practice, in K.F. Ausserer, W. Brner, M. Goriany and L. Karlhuber-Vckl (eds.) 2004. *Enter the Past. The E-way into the four Dimensions of Cultural Heritage. CAA 2003, Computer Applications and Quantitative Methods in Archaeology*: 276-9. BAR International Series 1227. Oxford: Archaeopress.
Mertens, D. 2006. *Città e Monumenti dei Greci d'Occidente*. Rome: 'L'Erma' di Bretschneider. Translated from the original *Städte und Bauten der Westgriechen*. Munich: Hirmer, 2006.
Meyer, C. and D. Pilz 2015. Magnetic survey in Koroneia. The Ancient Cities of Boeotia Project (Boeotia, Greece). Internal report.
Meyer, C. and D. Pilz 2016. Magnetic survey in Koroneia. The Ancient Cities of Boeotia Project (Boeotia, Greece). Internal report.
Meyer, C., R. Kniess and L. Goossens 2017. Geophysical prospection in the ancient city of Tanagra (Boeotia, Central Greece, Greece). Internal report.
Meyer, H., S. Hinz and U. Stilla 2008. Automated Extraction of Roads, Buildings and Vegetation from Multi-source Data, in Z. Li, J. Chen, E. Baltsavias (eds.) *Advances in Photogrammetry, Remote Sensing and Spatial Information Sciences: 2008 ISPRS Congress Book*: 213-26. Boca Raton: CRC Press/Taylor&Francis.
Meyer, L. 2012. *Die Finanzierung öffentlicher Bauten in der hellenistischen Polis*. Mainz: Verlag Antike.
Mikalson, J. D. 2010. *Ancient Greek Religion*. Oxford: Blackwell Publishing.
Miglio, M. 2000. Niccolo V. *Enciclopedia dei Papi*, II: 644-58. Rome.
Miller, P. N. (ed.) 2007. *Momigliano and Antiquarianism: Foundations of the Modern Cultural Sciences*. Toronto: University of Toronto Press.
Miller, P. and J.D. Richards 1995. The good, the bad, and the downright misleading: archaeological adoption of computer visualisation, in J. Huggett and N. Ryan (eds.) *Computer Applications and Quantitative Methods in Archaeology, CAA1994*: 249-54. Oxford: Tempvs Reparatvm.
Miller, S. G. 1978. *The Prytaneion: Its Function and Architectural Form*. Berkeley: University of California Press.
Miller, S. G. (ed.) 1990. *Nemea: A Guide to the Site and Museum*. Berkeley: University of California Press.
Miller, S. G. 2004. *Ancient Greek Athletics*. New Haven: Yale University Press.
Mitchell, C. 1960. Archaeology and Romance in Renaissance Italy, in E.F. Jacob (ed.) *Italian Renaissance Studies. A Tribute to the Late Cecilia M. Ady*: London: 455-83. Faber and Faber.
Mitchell, L. G. and P. J. Rhodes (eds.) 1997. *The Development of the Polis in Archaic Greece*. London: Routledge.
Moggi, M. and M. Osanna (eds.) 2010. *Pausania. Guida della Grecia.Libro IX. La Beozia*. Milano: Arnoldo Mondadori Editore.
Momigliano, A. 1954. Gibbon's Contribution to Historical Method. *Historia: Zeitschrift für Alte Geschichte* 2 (4): 450-63.
Moretti, J. C. 2014a. L'Architecture des Théâtres en Grèce Antique avant l'Époque impériale: Un Point de Vue sur les Études Publiées Entre 1994 et 2014. *Perspective* 2: 195-223.
Moretti, J. C. 2014b. The Evolution of Theatre Architecture Outside Athens in the Fourth Century, in E. Csapo, H. Rupprecht Goette, J. R. Green and P. Wilson (eds.), *Greek Theatre in the Fourth Century BC*: 107-37. Berlin/Boston: De Gruyter.

Moretti, J. C., L. Fadini, M. Fincker and V. Picard 2015. *Atlas. Exploration archéologique de Délos*, vol. 43. Athens: École française d'Athènes.

Morgan, C. 1993. The Origins of Pan-Hellenism, in N. Marinatos and R. Hägg (eds.) *Greek Sanctuaries. New Approaches*: 18-44. London & New York: Routledge.

Morgan, C. and J. J. Coulton 1997. The Polis as a Physical Entity, in M. H. Hansen (ed.) *The Polis as an Urban Centre and as a Political Community*: 87-143. Copenhagen.

Morgan, G. 1982. Euphiletos' House: Lysias I. *Transactions of the American Philological Association* 112: 115-23.

Morgan, J. E. 2007. Space and the Notion of Final Frontier. Searching for Ritual Boundaries in the Classical Athenian Home. *Kernos* 20: 113-29.

Morgan, J. E. 2010. *The Classical Greek House*. Exeter: Bristol Phoenix Press.

Morris, I. 2006. Classical Archaeology, in J. Bintliff (ed.) *A Companion to Archaeology*: 288-90. Malden, MA: Blackwell Publishing.

Mortier, R. 1982. *L'Originalité: une Nouvelle Catégorie Esthétique au Siècle des Lumières*. Genève: Droz.

Moser, S. 1992. The Visual Language of Archaeology: A Case Study of the Neanderthals. *Antiquity* 66: 831–44.

Moser, S. 1998. *Ancestral Images: The Iconography of Human Origins*. Cornell University Press.

Moser, S. 2001. Archaeological Representation: The Visual Conventions for Constructing Knowledge about the Past, in I. Hodder (ed.) *Archaeological Theory Today*: 262–83. Cambridge: Polity.

Moser, S. 2012. Archaeological Visualisation: Early Artefact Illustration and the Birth of the Archaeological Image, in I. Hodder (ed.) *Archaeological Theory Today* (revised edition): 292–322. Cambridge: Polity.

Moser, S. 2014. Making Expert Knowledge Through the Image: Antiquarian Images and Early Modern Scientific Illustration. *Isis*: 105 (1): 58–99.

Moser, S. 2015. Reconstructing Ancient Worlds: Reception Studies, Archaeological Representation and the Interpretation of Ancient Egypt. *Journal of Archaeological Method and Theory* 22 (4): 1263–1308.

Muentz, E. 1880. Raphaël archéologue et historien. *Gazzette des Beaux-arts* 22: 307-18.

Mulder, E. 2012. Boeotia, Land of the Kantharos. Explanations for the high number of kantharoi present in the Archaic and Classical period in Boeotia. Unpublished BA dissertation, Faculty of Archaeology, Leiden University.

Müller, C. 2014. A Koinon after 146? Reflections about the Political and Institutional Situation of Boeotia in the Late Hellenistic Period, in N. Papazarkadas (ed.) *The Epigraphy and History of Boeotia: New Finds, New Prospects*: 119-46. Leiden: Brill.

Müller, K. (ed.) 1848. *Fragmenta Historicorum Graecorum*, vol. II. Paris: Editore Ambrosio Firmin Didot.

Müller, P., T. Vereenooghe, A. Ulmer and L. Van gool 2006. Automatic Reconstruction of Roman Housing Architecture, in E. Baltsavias, A. Gruen, L. van Gool and M. Pateraki (eds.) *Proceedings of the International Workshop on Recording, Modelling and Visualization of Cultural Heritage, Ascona, 23-27 May*: 287-97.

Müller, P., T. Vereenooghe, P. Wonka, I. Paap and L. van Gool 2006. Procedural 3D Reconstruction of Puuc Buildings in Xkipché, in M. Ioannides, D. Arnold, F. Niccolucci and K. Mania (eds.) *The 7th International Symposium on Virtual Reality, Archaeology and Cultural Heritage VAST (2006)*: 139-46.

Münster, S. 2013. Workflows and the Role of Images for a Virtual 3D Reconstruction of no Longer Extant Historic Objects. *ISPRS Annals of the Photogrammetry, Remote Sensing and Spatial Information Sciences, Volume II-5/W1, 2013 XXIV International CIPA Symposium, 2-6 September 2013, Strasbourg, France*: 197-202.

Murray, T. 2002. Epilogue: Why the History of Archaeology Matters?. *Antiquity* 76: 234-8.

Murray, T. 2007. Rethinking Antiquarianism. *Bulletin of the History of Archaeology* 17 (2): 14-21.

Murray, T. 2014. *From Antiquarian to Archaeologist: The History and Philosophy of Archaeology*. Barnsley: Pen & Sword Books.

Musialski, P., P. Wonka, D. G. Aliaga, M. Wimmer, L. van Gool and W. Purgathofer 2013. A Survey of Urban Reconstruction. *Computer Graphics Forum* 32 (6): 146-77.

Müth, S. 2007. *Eigene Wege. Topographie und Stadtplan von. Messene in spätklassisch-hellenistischer Zeit*. Rahden, Westf.: Verlag Marie Leidorf GmbH.

Mylonopoulos, J. 2008. The Dynamics of Ritual Space in the Hellenistic and Roman East. *Kernos* 21: 49-79.

Mylonopoulos, J. 2013. Commemorating Pious Service. Images in Honour of Male and Female Priestly Officers in Asia Minor and the Eastern Aegean in the Hellenistic and Roman times, in M. Horster and A. Klöckner (eds.) *Cities and Priests: Cult Personnel in Asia Minor and the Aegean Islands from the Hellenistic to the Imperial Period*: 121-54. Berlin: De Gruyter.

Nevett, L. 1994. Separation or Seclusion? Towards an archaeological approach to investigating women in the Greek household in the fifth to the third centuries BC, in M. Parker Pearson and C. Richards (eds.) *Architecture and Order: Approaches to Social Space*: 98-112. New York: Routledge.

Nevett, L. 1995a. Gender Relations in the Classical Greek Household: The Archaeological Evidence. *The Annual of the British School at Athens* 90: 363-81.

Nevett, L. 1995b. The Organisation of Space in Classical and Hellenistic Houses from mainland Greece and the Western Colonies, in N. Spencer (ed.) *Time, Tradition and Society in Greek Archaeology: Bridging the 'Great Divide'*: 89-108. London: Routledge.

Nevett, L. 1999a. *House and Society in the Ancient Greek World*. Cambridge: Cambridge University Press.

Nevett, L. 1999b. Greek Households Under Roman Hegemony: The Archaeological Evidence, in A. Leslie (ed.) *Theoretical Roman Archaeology and Architecture: The Third Conference Proceedings*: 99-110. Glasgow: Cruithne Press.

Niccolucci, F. 2002. XML and the Future of Humanities Computing. *ACM SIGAPP Applied Computing Review* 10 (1): 43-7.

Niccolucci, F. 2012. Setting Standards for 3D Visualisation of Cultural Heritage in Europe and Beyond, in R. Beacham, H. Denard (eds.) *Paradata and Transparency in Virtual Heritage*: 23-36. London: Ashgate.

Niccolucci, F., A. D'Andrea and M. Crescioli 2001. Archaeological Applications of Fuzzy Databases, in Z. Stancic and T. Veljanovski (eds.) *Proceedings of the 28th CAA conference, Ljubljana, Slovenia,18-21 April 2000 BAR International Series 931*: 107-16. Oxford: Archaeopress.

Niccolucci, F. and S. Hermon 2010. A Fuzzy Logic Approach to Reliability in Archaeological Virtual Reconstruction, in F. Niccolucci, S. Hermon (eds.) *Beyond the Artifact. Digital Interpretation of the Past, CAA2004*: 26-33. Budapest: Archaeolingua.

Nielsen, I. 2001. The Gardens of the Hellenistic Palaces, in I. Nielsen (ed.) *The Royal Palace Institution in the First Millennium BC. Regional development and Cultural Interchange between East and West.* Monographs of the Danish Institute at Athens 4: 165-85. Aarhus: Aarhus University Press.

Nixon, S.M. 2002. .The Source and Fortune of Piranesi's Archaeological Illustrations. *Art History* 25 (4): 469-87.

Noghani, J., E. F. Anderson and F. Liarokapis 2012. Towards a Vitruvian Shape Grammar for Procedurally Generating Classical Roman Architecture, in D. Arnold, J. Kaminski, F. Niccolucci and A. Stork (eds.) *Short & Project Papers Proceedings of the 13th International Symposium on Virtual Reality, Archaeology and Cultural Heritage VAST (2012)*: 41-4.

Nossov, K. 2009. *Greek Fortifications of Asia Minor 500-130 BC: From the Persian Wars to the Roman Conquest*. Oxford: Osprey Publishing.

Ochoa, G. 1998. An Introduction to Lindenmayer Systems, viewed 02 March 2018, <http://ldc.usb.ve/~gabro/lsys/lsys.html>.

Ogleby, C. L. 1999. How real is your reality? Verisimilitude issues and metadata standards for the visualisation of Cultural Heritage. *Proceedings of the 17th CIPA International Symposium, Olinda, Brazil*.

Ogleby, C. L. 2007. The 'truthlikeness' of virtual reality reconstructions of architectural heritage: Concepts and metadata, in F. Remondino and S. El-Hakim (eds.) *3D-ARCH 2007: 3D Virtual Reconstruction and Visualization of Complex Architectures. Proceedings of the 2nd ISPRS International Workshop 3D-ARCH 2007: 3D Virtual Reconstruction and Visualization of Complex Architectures*, vol. XXXVI-5/W47.

Olson, B., R. J. M. Gordon, C. Runnels, and S. Chomyszak, 2014. Experimental Three-Dimensional Printing of a Lower Paleolithic Handaxe: An Assessment of the Technology and Analytical Value. *Lithic Technology* 39 (3): 162-72.

Orengo, H. A. and I. Fiz 2008. The Application of 3D Reconstruction Techniques in the Analysis of Ancient Tarraco's Urban Topography, in A. Posluschny, K. Lambers and I. Herzog (eds.) *Layers of Perception. Proceedings of the 35th International Conference on Computer Applications and Quantitative Methods in Archaeology (CAA 2007). Berlin, Germany, April 2-6, 2007. Kolloquien zur Vor- und Frühgeschichte, Vol. 10.* Bonn: Dr. Rudolf Habelt GmbH.

Osborne, R. 1987. *Classical Landscape with Figures: The Ancient Greek City and Its Countryside*. London: George Philip.

Osborne, R. 2000. *Classical Greece, 500-323 BC, Short Oxford History of Europe*. Oxford: Oxford University Press.

Ostenfeld, E. N. (ed.) 2002. *Greek Romans and Roman Greeks*. Aarhus: Aarhus University Press.

Owens, E. J. 1991. *The City in the Greek and Roman World*. London and New York: Routledge.

Owens, E. J. 2009. The Hellenistic City, in A. Ph. Lagopoulos (ed.) *A History of the Greek City*: 183-90. Oxford: Archaeopress.

Owen, S. 2009. The 'Thracian' Landscape of Archaic Thasos, in S. Owen and L. Preston (eds.) *Inside the City in the Greek World. Studies on Urbanism from the Bronze Age to the Hellenistic Period*: 84-98. Oxford: Oxbow Books.

Özgan, R. 1994. Cnido. *Enciclopedia dell' Arte Antica, Suppl. 2. 2*: 183-5.

Pade, M. 2007. *The Reception of Plutarch's Lives in Fifteenth-century Italy*, vol. 1. Copenhagen: Museum Tusculanum Press.

Pagano, M. 1997. *I Diari di Scavo di Pompei, Ercolano e Stabia di Francesco e Pietro La Vega (1764-1810). Raccolta e Studio di Documenti Inediti*. Rome: 'L'Erma' di Bretschneider.

Paliou, E. 2013. Reconsidering the Concept of Visualscapes: Recent Advances in Three-dimensional Visibility Analysis, in A. Bevan, A. and M. Lake (eds.) *Computational Approaches to Archaeological Spaces*: 243-63. Walnut Creek: Left Coast Press.

Paliou, E. 2014. Visibility analysis in 3D built spaces: a new dimension to the understanding of social space, in E. Paliou, U. Lieberwirth and S. Polla (eds.) *Spatial analysis and social spaces. Interdisciplinary approaches to the interpretation of prehistoric and historic built environments*: 91–114. Berlin, Boston: De Gruyter.

Paliou, E. and D. Wheatley 2007. Integrating spatial analysis and 3D modelling approaches to the study of visual space: Late Bronze Age Akrotiri, in A. Figueiredo and G. Leite Velho (eds.) *The world is in your eyes: Proceedings of the Annual Conference of Computer Applications and Quantitative Methods in Archaeology, CAA 2005, Tomar, March 2005*: 307-12.

Paliou, E. D. Wheatley, G. Earl 2011. Three-dimensional Visibility Analysis of architectural spaces: iconography and visibility of the wall paintings of Xeste 3 (Late Bronze Age Akrotiri). *Journal of Archaeological Science* 38: 375-86.

Paliou, E. and D. J. Knight 2013. Mapping the Senses: Perceptual and Social aspects of Late Antique Liturgy in San Vitale, Ravenna, in F. Contreras, M. Farjas, and F.J. Melero (eds.) *Fusion of Cultures: Proceedings of the 38th Annual Conference on Computer Applications and Quantitative Methods in Archaeology, CAA 2010, Granada, Spain, April 2010*: 229-36. BAR International Series 2494. Oxford: Archaeopress.

Panofsky, E. 1939. *Studies in Iconology. Humanistic Themes in the Art of the Renaissance*. Oxford: Oxford University Press.

Papangeli, K. and E.-A. Chlepa (eds.) 2011. *Transformations of the Eleusinian Landscape. Antiquities and the Modern City*. Athens.

Pappadakis 1916 = Παππαδάκις, Ν., 1916. Περὶ τὸ Χαρόπειον τῆς Κορωνείας, Ἀρχαιολογικόν Δελτίον 2: 217-60.

Pappadakis 1919 = Παππαδάκις, Ν. 1919. Ἀνασκαφαί 1917-19, Ἀρχαιολογικόν Δελτίον 5, Παράρτημα: 25-34.

Papadopoulos, C. and G. Earl 2014. Formal Three-dimensional Computational Analyses of Archaeological Spaces, in E. Paliou, U. Lieberwirth, S. Polla (eds.) *Spatial Analysis and Social Spaces: Interdisciplinary Approaches to the Interpretation of Prehistoric and Historic Built Environments*: 135-65. Berlin/Boston: De Gruyter.

Papadopoulos, J. K. 1997. Knossos, in M. de la Torre (ed.) *The Conservation of Archaeological Sites in the Mediterranean Region*: 93-125. Los Angeles: Getty Conservation Institute.

Papadopoulos, J. K. 2007. *The Art of Antiquity: Piet de Jong and the Athenian Agora*. Athens: The American School of Classical Studies at Athens.

Papagiannaki, A. 2010. Aphrodite in Late Antique and Medieval Byzantium, in A. C. Smith and S. Pickup (eds.) *Brill's Companion to Aphrodite*: 321-46. Leiden: Brill.

Papalexandrou, N. 2008. Boiotian Tripods. The Tenacity of a Panhellenic Symbol in a Regional Context. *Hesperia* 77: 251-82.

Papi, E., L. Botarelli, L. Cerri, D. D'Aco, E. Mariotti and F. Martorella, 2008. Hephaestia: Ricerche e Scavi nell'Area della Città – Scavi nel Terreno Alateras. *ASAtene* 83/2 (2005): 968-76.

Papy, J. 2004. An Antiquarian Scholar between Text and Image? Justus Lipsius, Humanist Education, and the Visualization of Ancient Rome. *The Sixteenth Century Journal* 35 (1): 97-131.

Pasqualini, A. 2006. L'Antiquaria di Gesso: Passato e Futuro del Museo della Civiltà Romana all'Eur. *Mediterraneo Antico* 9 (2): 631-46.

Pedley, J. 2005. *Sanctuaries and the Sacred in the Ancient Greek World*: Cambridge: Cambridge University Press.

Pellegrino, A. 2007. Il Plastico di Ostia Antica, in F. Filippi (ed.) *Ricostruire l'Antico Prima del Virtuale. Italo Gismondi, un Architetto per l'Archeologia (1887-1974)*: 275-6. Roma: Edizioni Quasar.

Perry, S. E. 2009a. Sights of Invention: Deconstructing Depictions of the Earliest Colonisations of Australia and Oceania in the Academic Archaeological Literature. *Archaeological Review from Cambridge* 24 (1): 109-30.

Perry, S. E. 2009b. Fractured Media: Challenging the Dimensions of Archaeology's Typical Visual Modes of Engagement. *Archaeologies: Journal of the World Archaeological Congress* 5 (3): 389-415.

Perry, S. E. 2013. Archaeological visualisation and the manifestation of the discipline: model-making at the Institute of Archaeology, London, in B. Alberti, A.M. Jones and J. Pollard (eds.) *Archaeology after Interpretation: Returning Materials to Archaeological Theory*: 281-303. Walnut, US: Left Coast Press.

Perry, S. E. and M. Johnson 2014. Reconstruction Art and Disciplinary Practice: Alan Sorrell and the Negotiation of the Archaeological Record. *The Antiquaries Journal* 94: 1-30.

Pescarin, S., E. Pietroni and D. Ferdani 2010. A Procedural Approach to the Modeling of Urban Historical Contexts, in F. Contreras, M. Farjas and F.J. Melero (eds) *Proceedings of the 38th Annual Conference on Computer Applications and Quantitative Methods in Archaeology, CAA2010*: 63-70.

Petridis, P. 1998. Les Ateliers de Potiers à Delphes à l'Époque Paléochrétienne. *Topoi* 8: 703-10.

Petridis, P. 2009. A New Approach to an Old Archaeological Site: The Case of Delphi, in J. Bintliff and H. Stöger (eds.) *Medieval and Post-Medieval Greece. The Corfu Papers*: 101-5. BAR International Series 2023. Oxford: Archaeopress.

Petridis, P. 2014. Late Roman/Early Byzantine Archaeology in Greece: A 'Gateway' to the Period of Transformation, in J. Bintliff (ed.) *Recent Developments in the Long-Term Archaeology of Greece, Pharos Journal of the Netherlands Institute in Athens* 20 (1): 269-90.

Picard, O. and P. Ducrey 1996. Recherches à Latô. VII. La Rue Ouest, Habitations et Défense. *Bulletin de Correspondance Hellénique* 120 (2): 721-54.

Piccoli, C. 2008. La Ricostruzione Tridimensionale dell'Unità Commerciale e Abitativa, in E. Greco and E. Papi (eds.) *Hephaestia 2000-2006: ricerche e scavi della Scuola Archeologica Italiana di Atene in collaborazione con il Dipartimento di Archeologia e Storia delle Arti dell'Università di Siena, Paestum, Proceedings of the conference Hephaestia 2000-2006, Siena, 28-29 maggio 2007*: 243-6. Atene: Pandemos.

Piccoli, C. 2012. The recording of Greek Vernacular Architecture. *Pharos. Journal of the Netherlands Institute in Athens* 17 (2): 50-6.

Piccoli, C. 2013. Publishing in the Republic of Letters: Behind the Scenes of Pieter van der Aa's *Thesaurus Antiquitatum et Historiarum Italiae* (Leiden, 1704-25). *Quaerendo* 43: 61-82.

Piccoli, C. 2014. 3D Reconstruction Techniques as Research Tools in Archaeology: The case Study of Koroneia, Greece. *Tijdschrift voor Mediterrane Archeologie* 52: 1-6.

Piccoli, C. 2016. Enhancing GIS urban data with the 3rd dimension: A procedural modelling approach, in S. Campana, R. Scopigno, G. Carpentiero and M. Cirillo (eds.) *Keep the Revolution Going. Proceedings of 43rd Computer Applications and Quantitative Methods in Archaeology Conference (Siena, 30 March – 3 April 2015)*: 35-44. Oxford: Archeopress.

Piccoli, C. 2017. Visualizing antiquity before the digital age: Early and late modern reconstructions of Greek and Roman cityscapes, in H. Kamermans and C.C. Bakels (eds.) *Excerpta Archaeologica Leidensia II, Analecta Praehistorica Leidensia* 47: 225-57.

Piccoli, C. and A. Vionis 2011. Housing architecture in late Medieval and Ottoman Boeotia. *Encyclopedia of the Hellenic World, Boeotia*, viewed 02 Marc 2018 <http://www.ehw.gr/l.aspx?id=12699>.

Piccoli, C., P. Aparajeya, G. Th. Papadopoulos, J. Bintliff, F.F. Leymarie, P. Bes, M. van der Enden, J. Poblome and P. Daras 2015. Towards the Automatic Classification of Pottery Sherds: Two Complementary Approaches, in A. Traviglia (ed.) *Across Space and Time. Selected Papers from the 41st Computer Applications and Quantitative Methods in Archaeology Conference (Perth, WA, 25-28 March 2013)*: 463-74.

Pierdicca, R., E. Frontoni, P. Zingaretti, E. S. Malinverni, F. Colosi and R. Orazi 2015. Making Visible the Invisible. Augmented Reality Visualization for 3D Reconstructions of Archaeological Sites, in L. T. de Paolis and A. Mongelli (eds.) *Augmented and Virtual Reality*: 25-37. Berlin/Heidelberg: Springer.

Piggott, S. 1965. Archaeological draughtsmanship: Principles and practice. *Antiquity* 39: 165-76.

Piggott, S. 1976. *Ruins in a Landscape: Essays in Antiquarianis*. Edinburgh: Edinburgh University Press.

Piggott, S. 1978. *Antiquity Depicted: Aspects of Archaeological Illustrations*. London: Thames & Hudson.

Pletinckx, D. 2007. Interpretation Management. How to Make Sustainable Visualisations of the Past, in H. Gottlieb (ed.) *Know How Books*. Stockholm: The Interactive Institute AB.

Pletinckx, D. and D. Haskiya 2011. D5.1 Functional Specifications of Requirements for Preparing 3D/VR for Europeana, viewed 02 March 2018, <http://pro.carare.eu/lib/exe/fetch.php?media=support:d5_1_functional_specification_3dvr_final.pdf>.

Pletinckx, D. 2012a. How to Make Sustainable Visualisations of the Past: an EPOCH Common Infrastructure Tool for Interpretation Management, in R. Beacham, H. Denard (eds.) *Paradata and Transparency in Virtual Heritage*: 203-33. London: Ashgate.

Pletinckx, D. 2012b. Preservation of Complex Cultural Heritage Objects – a Practical Implementation, in D. Anderson, J. Delve, M. Dobreva, L. Konstantelos (eds.) *The Preservation of Complex Objects (Vol. 1): Visualisations and Simulations*. University of Portsmouth.

Potter, T. W. 1995. *Towns in Late Antiquity: Iol Caesarea and its Context*. Sheffield: Ian Sanders Memorial Committee, Department of Archaeology and Prehistory, University of Sheffield.

Pretzler, M. 2007. *Pausanias. Travel Writing in Ancient Greece*. London: Bloomsbury.

Price, S. 1984. *Rituals and Power. The Roman Imperial Cult in Asia Minor*. Cambridge: Cambridge University Press.

Price, S. 1999. *Religions of the Ancient Greeks*. Cambridge: Cambridge University Press.

Priemus, H. 1980. Wonen: Kreativiteit en Aanpassing: Onderzoek naar Voorwaarden voor Optimale Aanpassingsmogelijkheden in de Woningbouw. Den Haag: Mouton.

Pritchett, W. K. 1969. *Studies in Ancient Greek Topography (Battlefields)*, vol. 2. Berkeley: University of California Press.

Prusinkiewicz, P., J. Hanan and R. Mech 2000. An L-system-based Plant Modeling Language, in M. Nagl, A. Schuerr and M. Muench (eds.) *Applications of Graph Transformations with Industrial Relevance, Proceedings of the International workshop AGTIVE'99, Kerkrade, The Netherlands, September 1999, Lecture Notes in Computer Science 1779*. Berlin: Springer.

Pujol, L. 2008. Does Virtual Archaeology Exist?, in A. Posluschny, K. Lambers and I. Herzog (eds.) *Layers of Perception. Proceedings of the 35th International Conference on Computer Applications and Quantitative Methods in Archaeology (CAA), Berlin, Germany, April 2-6, 2007 (Kolloquien zur Vor- und Frühgeschichte, Vol. 10)*: 101-7. Bonn: Dr. Rudolf Habelt GmbH.

Pujol, L. and M. Economou 2009. Worth a thousand words? The Usefulness of Immersive Virtual Reality for Learning in Cultural Heritage Settings. *International Journal of Architectural Computing* 7 (1): 157-76.

Quattrini, R., R. Pierdicca, E. Frontoni and R. Barcaglioni 2016. Virtual Reconstruction of Lost Architectures: From the TLS Survey to AR Visualization. *ISPRS - International Archives of the Photogrammetry, Remote Sensing and Spatial Information Sciences*, vol. XLI-B5: 383-90.

Quilici, L. 1995. La Via Salaria da Roma all'alto Velino: La Tecnica Costruttiva dei Manufatti Stradali, in L. Quilici and S. Quilici Gigli (eds.) *Strade Romane: Percorsi e Infrastrutture, Atlante Tematico di Topografia Antica 2*: 85-154. Rome.

Rackham, O. 1983. Observations on the Historical Ecology of Boeotia. *The Annual of the British School at Athens* 78: 291-351.

Ragon, M. 1995. *L'Homme et les Villes*. Paris: Albin Michel.

Raja, R. 2012. *Urban Development and Regional Identity in the Eastern Roman Provinces, 50 BC – AD 250. Aphrodisias, Ephesos, Athens, Gerasa.* Copenhagen: Museum Tusculanum Press.

Ratto, M. 2009. Epistemic Commitments, Virtual Reality, and Archaeological Representation, in A. Figueiredo and H. Kamermans (eds.), *Proceedings of the XV World Congress UISPP (Lisbon, 4-9 September 2006) vol. 37*. BAR International Series 2029. Oxford: Archaeopress.

Rawson, E. 1987. Discrimina Ordinum: The Lex Julia Theatralis. *Papers of the British School at Rome* 55: 83-114.

Ray, C. A. and M. van der Vaart 2013. Contextualizing Collections: Using Virtual Reality in Archaeological Exhibitions. *Exhibitionist*: 73-9.

Reber, K. 2007. Living and Housing in Classical and Hellenistic Eretria, in N. Fisher, J. Whitley, R. Westgate (eds.) *Building Communities: House, Settlement and Society in the Aegean and Beyond*, British School at Athens Studies: 281-8. London: British School at Athens.

Reilly, P. 1991. Towards a Virtual Archaeology, in K. Lockyear and S. Rahtz (eds.) *CAA90: Computer Applications and Quantitative Methods in Archaeology*: 133-9. BAR International Series 565. Oxford: British Archaeological Reports.

Remijsen, S. 2015. *The End of Greek Athletics in Late Antiquity*. Cambridge: Cambridge University Press.

Remondino, F. 2011. Heritage Recording and 3D Modeling with Photogrammetry and 3D Scanning, *Remote Sensing* 3(6): 1104-38.

Remondino, F. and S. El-Hakim 2006. A Critical Overview of Image-Based 3D Modeling, in M. Baltsavias, A. Gruen, L. van Gool and M. Pateraki (eds.) *Recording, Modeling and Visualization of Cultural Heritage*: 299-313. London: Taylor & Francis.

Remondino, F. and A. Rizzi 2010. Reality-based 3D Documentation of Natural and Cultural Heritage Sites—Techniques, Problems, and Examples. *Applied Geomatics* 2 (85): 85-100.

Richardson, A. E. 2001. *Monumental Classical Architecture in Great Britain and Ireland*. Mineola, NY: Dover Publications.

Richardson, R.C. 2004. William Camden and the Rediscovery of England. *Transactions of the Leicestershire Archaeological and Historical Society* 78: 108-23.

Richards-Rissetto, H. and R. Plessing 2015. Procedural modeling for ancient Maya cityscapes: Initial methodological challenges and solutions. *Digital Heritage Conference, Granada, 28th Sept.- 2nd Oct. 2015*: 85-8.

Rindel, J. H. 2011. The ERATO Project and its Contribution to our Understanding of the Acoustics of Ancient Theatres, *The Acoustics of Ancient Theatres Conference, Patras, September 18-21, 2011*, viewed 02 March 2018 <http://www.odeon.dk/pdf/AA2011_18_Rindel.pdf>.

Riva, G., B.K. Wiederhold and E. Molinari 1998. *Virtual Environments in Clinical Psychology and Neuroscience: Methods and Techniques in Advanced Patient-Therapist Interaction*. Amsterdam: IOS Press.

Rizza, G., D. Palermo and F. Tomasello 1992. *Mandra di Gipari: Una Officina Protoarcaica di Vasai nel Territorio di Priniàs. Priniàs 2.* Catania: Istituto di Archeologia, Università di Catania.

Roberts, J. C. and N. Ryan 1997. Alternative Archaeological Representations within Virtual Worlds, in Richard Bowden (ed.) *Proceedings of the 4th UK Virtual Reality Specialist Interest Group Conference, Brunel University*: 179-88. Uxbridge, Middlesex: Brunel University.

Robertson Brown, A. 2006. Hellenistic Heritage and Christian Challenge: Conflict over Panhellenic Sanctuaries in Late Antiquity, in H. A. Drake (ed.) *Violence in Late Antiquity: Perceptions & Practices, Shifting Frontiers in Late Antiquity* 5: 309-20. Aldershot: Ashgate.

Robertson Brown, A. 2008. The City of Corinth and Urbanism in Late Antique Greece. Unpublished PhD dissertation, University of California, Berkeley.

Robinson, D. M. 1932. The Residential Districts and the Cemeteries at Olynthos. *American Journal of Archaeology* 36: 118-38.

Robinson, D. M. and J. W. Graham 1938. *Excavations at Olynthus VIII: The Hellenic House*. Baltimore: Johns Hopkins University Press.

Rocco, G. and M. Livadiotti 2011. The Agora of Kos: The Hellenistic and Roman Phases, in A. Giannikouri (ed.) *The Agora in the Mediterranean from Homeric to Roman Times. Proceedings of an International Conference Held at Kos 14-17 April 2011*: 383-423. Athens.

Roller, D. W. 1974. A New Map of Tanagra. *American Journal of Archaeology* 78: 152–6.

Ross, L. 1851. *Wanderungen in Griechenland im Gefolge des Koenigs Otto der Koeniginn Amalie. Mit besondere Ruecksicht auf Topographie und Geschichte*, vol. 1. Halle: C. A. Schwetschke & Sohn.

Rothaus, R. M. 2000. *Corinth, the First City of Greece: An Urban History of Late Antique Cult and Religion*, Religions in the Graeco-Roman World 139. Leiden: Brill.

Roussos, I. 2003. Image Based Flame Lighting. Unpublished PhD dissertation, University of Bristol.

Roux, G. 1980. À Propos des Gymnases de Delphes et de Délos. Le Site du Damatrion de Delphes et le Sens du Mot Sphairistérion. *Bulletin de Correspondance Hellénique* 104 (1): 127-49.

Royo, M. 1992. Le Temps de l'éternité, Paul Bigot et la Représentation de Rome Antique. *Mélanges de l'Ecole française de Rome. Italie et Méditerranée* 104 (2): 585-610.

Royo, M. 2006. *Rome et l'Architecte. Conception et Esthétique du Plan-relief de Paul Bigot*. Caen: Presses Universitaires de Caen.

Ryan, N. 1996. Computer-based Visualisation of the Past: Technical 'Realism' and Historical Credibility, in P. Main T. Higgins and J. Lang (eds.) *Imaging the Past: Electronic Imaging and Computer Graphics in Museums and Archaeology. British Museum London: Occasional Papers*, vol. 114: 95-108. London: British Museum.

Ryan, N. 2001. Documenting and Validating Virtual Archaeology. *Archeologia e Calcolatori* 12: 245-273.

Saldaña, M. 2015. An Integrated Approach to the Procedural Modeling of Ancient Cities and Buildings. *Digital Scholarship in the Humanities DSH* 30 (suppl. 1): 148-63.

Saldaña, M. and C. Johanson 2013. Procedural Modelling for Rapid-Prototyping of Multiple Building Phases. *International Archives of Photogrammetry, Remote Sensing and Spatial Information Sciences*, vol. XL-5/W1: 205-10.

Salonia, P., S. Scolastico and V. Bellucci 2006. Laser Scanner, Quick Stereo-photogrammetric System, 3D Modelling: New Tools for the Analysis and the Documentation of Cultural Archaeological Heritage, in S. Campana and M. Forte (eds.) *From Space to Place: 2nd International Conference on Remote Sensing in Archaeology, December 4-7 2006, CNR (Rome, 2006)*: 347-52.

Sampaolo, V. 1993. La Realizzazione del Plastico di Pompei. *Il museo* 3: 79-93.

Sánchez Hernández, J. P. 2010. Athenae Batavae, Athenae Atticae. Meursius's Antiquarian Works and 17th Century Athens. *Omslag. Bulletin van de Universiteitsbibliotheek Leiden en het Scaliger Instituut* 2: 9-11.

Sapirstein, P. 2015. Photogrammetry as a Tool for Architectural Analysis: The Digital Architecture Project at Olympia, in C. Papadopoulos, E. Paliou, A. Chrysanthi, E. Kotoula, A. Sarris (eds.) *Archaeological Research in the Digital Age. Proceedings of the 1st CAA GR conference, Computer Applications and Quantitative Methods in Archaeology, Greek chapter (CAA GR 2014), 7-8 March 2014, Institute of Mediterranean Studies, Rethymno, Crete*: 129-39.

Sarris, A. and T. Kalayci 2016. Technical Report. Exploring the Urban Fabric of Haliartos, Boeotia, through Remote Sensing Techniques. Internal Report.

Sassu, R. 2013. *Templi senza Altare,* Thesauroi e Oikoi. *Un'Indagine sugli Aspetti Economici del Santuario Greco.* Unpublished PhD dissertation, Università di Roma La Sapienza.

Saxl, F. 1940-41. The Classical Inscription in Renaissance Art and Politics. Bartholomaeus Fontius: Liber Monumentorum Romanae Urbis et Aliorum Locorum. *Journal of the Warburg and Courtauld Institutes* 4 (1/2): 19-46.

Schachter, A. 1981. *Cults of Boeotia 1, Acheloos to Hera,* (BICS Supplements 38.1). London.

Schachter, A. 1986. *Cults of Boiotia 2, Herakles to Poseidon,* (BICS Supplements 38.2). London.

Schachter, A. 1992. Policy, Cult, and the Placing of Greek Sanctuaries, in A. Schachter (ed.), *Le Sanctuaire Grec*, Fondation Hardt Entretiens 37, Vandoeuvres-Genève: 1-64.

Schachter, A. 2007. Egyptian cults and local elites in Boeotia, in L. Bricault, M. J. Versluys, P.G.P. Meyboom (eds.) *Nile into Tiber: Egypt in the Roman World: Proceedings of the IIIrd International Conference of Isis Studies,* Leiden, May 11-14 2005: 364-91. Leiden: Brill.

Schachter, A. and W. J. Slater 2007. A Proxeny Decree from Koroneia, Boiotia, in Honour of Zotion Son of Zotion, of Ephesos. *Zeitschrift für Papyrologie und Epigraphik* 163: 81-95.

Sherk, R. K. 1969. *Roman Documents from the Greek East: Senatus Consulta and Epistulae to the Age of Augustus.* Baltimore: Johns Hopkins Press.

Schönborn, K.J. and T.R. Anderson 2009. A model of factors determining students' ability to interpret external representations in biochemistry. *International Journal of Science Education* 31 (2): 193–232.

Schönborn, K.J. and T.R. Anderson 2010. Bridging the educational research-teaching practice gap – foundations for assessing and developing biochemistry students' visual literacy, *Biochemistry and Molecular Biology Education* 38 (5): 347–54.

Schörner, H. 2013. The Intra-urban Burial inside Greek *Poleis* in Asia Minor, in O. Henry (ed.) *Le Mort dans la Ville. Pratiques, Contextes et Impacts des Inhumations Intra-muros en Anatolie, du Début de l'Age du Bronze à l'Époque Romaine, Deuxièmes Rencontres d'Archéologie de l'IFEA, Istanbul 14-15 Novembre 2011*: 223-30. Istanbul: IFEA-Ege Yayınları.

Schultz, S. K. 1989. *Constructing Urban Culture: American Cities and Cities Planning, 1800-1920.* Philadelphia: Temple University Press.

Schumacher, R. W. M. 1993. Three Related Sanctuaries of Poseidon: Geraistos, Kalaureia and Tainaron, in N. Marinatos and R. Hägg (eds.) *Greek Sanctuaries. New Approaches*: 62-87. London & New York: Routledge.

Schwandner, E.-L. 1977. Die Bootische Hafenstadt Siphai. *Archäologischen Anzeiger* 92: 513-51.

Scodel, R. and A. Bettenworth, 2009. *Whither Quo Vadis: Sienkiewicz's Novel in Film and Television.* Oxford: Blackwell Publishing.

Scott, M. 2012. *Space and Society in the Greek and Roman Worlds*. Cambridge: Cambridge University Press.

Scott, M. 2013. The Social Life of Greek Athletic Facilities (Other than Stadia), in P. Christesen and D. G. Kyle (eds.) *A Companion to Sport and Spectacle in Greek and Roman Antiquity*: 295-308. Malden, MA; Oxford; Chichester: Wiley-Blackwell.

Scully, V. 1962. *The Earth, the Temple and the Gods.* New Haven & London: Yale University Press.

Sideris, G. 2015. Il Progetto di Conservazione e Risanamento della Restaurata 'Casa Romana' di Kos. *Thiasos* 4: 77-94.

Sielhorst, B. 2015. *Hellenistische Agorai: Gestaltung, Rezeption und Semantik eines Urbanen Raumes.* Berlin: Walter de Gruyter.

Sigalos, E. 2004. *Housing in Medieval and Post-Medieval Greece*. BAR International Series 1291. Oxford: Archaeopress.

Sinn, U. 1993. Greek Sanctuaries as Places of Refuge, in N. Marinatos and R. Hägg (eds.) *Greek Sanctuaries: New Approaches*: 88-109. London: Routledge.

Skwara, E. 2013. Quo Vadis on Film (1912, 1925, 1951, 1985, 2001), the Many Faces of Antiquity. *Classica* 26 (2): 164-74.

Slane, K. W. and G. D. R. Sanders 2005. Corinth: Late Roman Horizons. *Hesperia* 74: 243-97.

Slapšak, B. 2012. Towards Integrated Non-invasive Research on Complex Urban Sites, in F. Vermeulen, G.-J. Burgers, S. Key and C. Corsi (eds.) *Urban Landscape Survey in Italy and in the Mediterranean*: 53-61. Oxford: Oxbow Books.

Slapšak, B., B. Mušič and G. Rutar 2005. Tanagra Urban Survey. Groundtruthing of Geophysical Results and Relational Analysis of Data Layers. Paper presented at the 10th Conference on Cultural Heritage and New Technologies, 7-10 November 2005, Vienna.

Smiles, S. and S. Moser (eds.) 2005. *Envisioning the Past: Archaeology and the Image*. Malden, MA: Wiley-Blackwell.

Smith, A. R. 1984. Plants, Fractals, and Formal Languages. *Computer Graphics* 18 (3), SIGGRAPH '84: 1-10.

Smith, I. 1985. Romans Make a High-Tech Comeback: Sid and Dora's Bath Show Pulls in the Crowd. *Computing* (June 1985): 7-8.

Snodgrass, A. M. 1980. *Archaic Greece. The Age of Experiment*. Berkeley: University of California Press.

Sodini, J.-P. 1984. L'Habitat Urbain en Grèce à la Veille des Invasions, in *Villes et Peuplement dans l'Illyricum Protobyzantin. Actes du Colloque (Rome, 12-14 mai 1982) Collection de l'École française de Rome* 77: 341-97.

Sodini, J.-P. 2007. The Transformation of Cities in Late Antiquity within the Provinces of Macedonia and Epirus, in A. G. Poulter (ed.) *The Transition to Late Antiquity on the Danube and Beyond*: 311–36. Oxford.

Sourvinou-Inwood, C. 1993. Early Sanctuaries, the Eighth Century and Ritual Space. Fragments of a Discourse, in N. Marinatos and R. Hägg (eds.) *Greek Sanctuaries. New Approaches*: 11-7. London & New York: Routledge.

Spyropoulos 1973 = Σπυρόπουλος, Θ., 1973. Ειδήσεις εκ Βοιωτίας. *Αρχαιολογικά Ανάλεκτα εξ Αθηνών* 6 (3): 375-95. Athens: Genike Dieythynsis Archaioteton kai Anasteloseos.

Spyropoulos 1975 = Σπυρόπουλος, Θ., 1975. Ανασκαφή παρα την Κορωνειαν Βοιωτίας. *Πρακτικά της εν Αθήναις Αρχαιολογικής Εταιρείας* 130 (Β): 392-414. Athens: The Archaeological Society of Athens.

Steinhauer, G. 2007. Ο Ιππόδαμος και η διαίρεσις του Πειραιώς, in E. Greco and M. Lombardo (eds.) *Atene e l'Occidente, I grandi temi: Le Premesse, i Protagonisti, le Forme della Comunicazione e dell'Interazione, i Modi dell'Intervento Ateniese in Occidente: Atti del Convegno Internazionale, Atene, 25- 27 maggio 2006*: 191-209.

Stenhouse, W. 2012. Panvinio and the Descriptio: Renditions of History and Antiquity in the Late Renaissance. *Papers of the British School at Rome* 80: 233-56.

Stephens, W. 2004. When Pope Noah Ruled the Etruscans: Annius of Viterbo and his Forged Antiquities. *Modern Language Notes* 119 (1), *Italian Issue Supplement: Studia Humanitatis: Essays in Honor of Salvatore Camporeale*: S201-23.

Stephens, W. 2013. From Berossos to Berosus Chaldæus: The Forgeries of Annius of Viterbo and Their Fortune, in J. Haubold, G. B. Lanfranchi, R. Rollinger and J. Steele (eds.) *The World of Berossos. Proceedings of the 4th International Colloquium on the Ancient Near East between Classical and Ancient Oriental Traditions, Hatfield College, Durham 7th –9th July 2010*: 277-89. Wiesbaden: Harrassowitz Verlag.

Steward, A. 2014. *Art in the Hellenistic World: An Introduction*. Cambridge: Cambridge University Press.

Stewart, D. 2013. 'Most Worth Remembering': Pausanias, Analogy, and Classical Archaeology. *Hesperia* 82: 231-61.

Stiebing, W. H. 1993. *Uncovering the Past: A History of Archaeology*. Oxford: Oxford University Press.

Stillwell, A. N. 1948. *Corinth: Results of Excavations Conducted by the American Schools of Classical Studies at Athens, vol. 15, Pt. 1. The Potters' Quarter*. Princeton, New Jersey: The American School of Classical Studies at Athens.

Stinger, C. L. 1998. *The Renaissance in Rome*. Bloomington: Indiana University Press.

Stirling, L. M. 2008. Pagan Statuettes in Late Antique Corinth. Sculpture from the Panayia Domus, *Hesperia* 77: 89-161.

Stissi, V. V. 2002. Pottery to People. The Production, Distribution and Consumption of Decorated Pottery in the Greek World in the Archaic Period (650-480 BC). Unpublished PhD dissertation, University of Amsterdam (UvA).

Stöger, H. 2011. *Rethinking Ostia: A Spatial Enquiry into the Urban Society of Rome's Imperial Port-town*. Archaeological studies Leiden University, 24. Amsterdam: Leiden University Press.

Stoter, J. and S. Zlatanova 2003. 3D GIS, Where are we Standing?. *ISPRS Joint Workshop on 'Spatial, Temporal and multi-dimensional data modelling and analysis', Québec, October, 2003*, viewed 02 March 2018, <http://www.gdmc.nl/publications/2003/3D_GIS.pdf>.

Stoter, J., G. Vosselman, J. Goos, S. Zlatanova, E. Verbree, R. Klooster and M. Reuvens 2011. Towards a National 3D Spatial Infrastructure: Case of the Netherlands. *PFG Photogrammetrie, Fernerkundung, Geoinformation* 6: 405-20.

Stoter, J., H. Ploeger and P. van Oosterom 2013. 3D Cadastre in the Netherlands: Developments and International Applicability. *Computers, Environment and Urban Systems* 36: 56-67.

Sturgis, R. 1905. *Sturgis' Illustrated Dictionary of Architecture and Building*, vol. 1. New York: The Macmillan Company.

Stylianidis, E. and F. Remondino (eds.) 2016. *3D Recording, Documentation and Management of Cultural Heritage*. Caithness: Whittles Publishing.

Sundstaet, V., A. Chalmers and P. Martinez 2004. High Fidelity Reconstruction of the Ancient Egyptian Temple of Kalabsha, *CM SIGGRAPH: Conference Abstracts and Applications, San Diego, USA. July 2003*: 107-13.

Surtees, L. E. 2012. *On the Surface of a Thessalian City: The Urban Survey of Kastro Kallithea, Greece*. Unpublished PhD dissertation, Bryn Mawr College.

Surtees, L. E., S. Karapanou and M. J. Haagsma 2014. Exploring Kastro Kallithea on the Surface: The Foundation and Occupation of Kastro Kallithea, Thessaly, Greece, in D. W. Rupp and J. E. Tomlinson (eds.) *Meditations on the Diversity of the Built Environment in the Aegean Basin and Beyond, Proceedings of a Colloquium in Memory of Frederick E. Winter, Athens, 22-23 June 2012*: 341-452. Athens: The Canadian Institute in Greece.

Sutherland, I. 1965a. The Ultimate Display, in W.A. Kalenich (ed.), *Proceedings of the International Federation of Information Processing Congress, New York City, May 24-29*: 506-8. London: Macmillan and Co.

Sutherland, I. 1965b. A Head-mounted Three Dimensional Display, *Proceedings of AFIPS 68*: 757-64.

Sweet, R. 2004. *Antiquaries. The Discovery of the Past in Eighteenth-Century Britain*. London: Hambledon and London.

Sweetman, R. J. 2004. Late Antique Knossos. Understanding the City: Evidence of Mosaics and Religious Architecture. *The Annual of the British School at Athens* 99: 315-54.

Sweetman, R. J. 2010. The Christianization of the Peloponnese: The Topography and Function of Late Antique Churches, *Journal of Late Antiquity* 3 (2): 203-61.

Sweetman, R. J. 2012. Memory and Loss in Late Antique Cities of Knossos and Sparta, in N. Christie and A. Augenti (eds.) *Vrbes Extinctae: Archaeologies of Abandoned Classical Towns*: 243-74. Farnham: Ashgate.

Sweetman, R. J. 2015. Memory, Tradition, and Christianization of the Peloponnese. *American Journal of Archaeology* 119 (4): 501-31.

Tan, B.-K. and H. Rahaman 2009. Virtual Heritage: Reality and Criticism, in T. Tidafi and T. Dorta (eds.) *Joining Languages, Cultures and Visions: CAAD Futures 2009*, PUM: 143-56. Montréal: Les Presses de l'Université de Montréal.

Tang, B. 2005. *Delos, Cathage, Ampurias: The Housing of Three Mediterranean Trading Centres*. Rome: 'L'Erma' di Bretschneider.

Ten, A. 2007. I Plastici di Villa Adriana, in F. Filippi (ed.) *Ricostruire l'Antico Prima del Virtuale. Italo Gismondi, un Architetto per l'Archeologia (1887-1974)*: 277-80. Roma: Edizioni Quasar.

Terpstra, D. 2012. *Koroneia's 'Bishop's Palace' Investigating Late Antique architectural remains on the acropolis of ancient Koroneia in Central Greece*. Unpublished BA dissertation, Faculty of Archaeology, Leiden University.

Thomas, S. 2008. *Romanticism and Visuality: Fragments, History, Spectacle*. New York: Routledge.

Thuswaldner, B., S. Flöry, R. Kalasek, M. Hofer, Q. Huang and H. Thür 2007. Digital Anastylosis of the Octagon in Ephesos. *Journal on Computer and Cultural Heritage* 2 (1): 1-27.

Tomlinson, R. A. 1980. Review of The Earth, the Temple and the Gods: Greek Sacred Architecture, by Scully Vincent Tomlinson. *The Antiquaries Journal* 60 (2): 372.

Travlos 1960 = Τραυλός, Ι., 1960. *Πολεοδομική εξέλιξις των Αθηνών. Από των προϊστορικών χρόνων μέχρι των* αρχών του 19ου αιώνος. Athens: Kapon.

Tréziny, H. 2005. Les Colonies Grecques de Méditerranée Occidentale. *Histoire Urbaine, Société française d'histoire urbaine* (SFHU) 13: 51-66.

Trippe, R. 2010. Art of Memory: Recollecting Rome in Giovanni Marcanova's *Collection Antiquitatum*. *Art History* 33 (5): 767-99.

Troncoso, V. A. 2009. The Hellenistic Gymnasion and the Pleasures of Paideia. *Symbolae Philologorum Posnaniensium Graecae et Latinae* 19: 71-84. Poznan: Adam Mickiewicz University Press.

Trümper, M. 2003. Material and Social Environment of Greco-Roman Households in the East: The Case of Hellenistic Delos, in D. L. Balch and C. Osiek (eds.) *Early Christian Families in Context. An Interdisciplinary Dialogue*: 19-43. Grand Rapids: Eerdmans.

Trümper, M. 2011. Space and Social Relationships in the Greek *Oikos* of the Classical and Hellenistic Periods, in B. Rawson (ed.) *A Companion to Families in the Greek and Roman World*: 32-52. Chichester, Malden, MA: Wiley-Blackwell.

Tschudi, V. P. 2012. Plaster Empires: Italo Gismondi's Model of Rome. *Journal of the Society of Architectural Historians* 71 (3), *Special Issue on Architectural Representations 1 (September 2012)*: 386-403.

Tsiafakis, D. 2010. Domestic Architecture in the Northern Aegean: The Evidence from the Ancient Settlement of Karabournaki, in H. Tréziny (ed.) *Grecs et Indigènes de la Catalogne à la Mer Noire: Actes des Rencontres du Programme Européen Ramses2 (2006-2008)*: 379-87. Paris: Édition Errance.

Tzakirgis, B. 1989. The universality of the Prostas house. *American Journal of Archaeology* 93: 278-9.

Tzakirgis, B. 2005. Living and Working Around the Athenian Agora: a Preliminary Case Study of Three Houses, in B.A. Ault and L.C. Nevett (eds.) *Ancient Greek Houses and Households. Chronological, Regional and Social Diversity*: 67-82. Philadelphia: University of Pennsylvania Press.

Tzakirgis, B. forthcoming. *The Domestic Architecture of Morgantina in the Hellenistic and Roman Periods* (Morgantina Studies, vol. 6). Princeton University Press.

Tzifalis, A., M. J. Haagsma, S. Karapanou and S. Gouglas 2006. Scratching the Surface: A Preliminary Report on the 2004 and 2005 Season from the Urban Survey Project at Kastro Kallithea ('Pneuma'), Thessaly. *Mouseion*, Series III, 6: 91-135.

Tzortzaki, D. 2001. Museums and Virtual Reality: Using the CAVE to Simulate the Past. *Digital Creativity* 12 (4): 247-51.

Uytterhoeven, I. 2007. Housing in Late Antiquity: Thematic Perspectives, in L. Lavan, L. Özgenel and A. Sarantis (eds.) *Housing in Late Antiquity. From Palaces to Shops*: 25-66. Leiden: Brill.

Uytterhoeven, I. 2012. Architectural Remains at Koroneia. *Pharos. Journal of the Netherlands Institute in Athens* 17.2 (2009-2010): 13-23.

Uytterhoeven, I. 2014a. Koroneia 2012 – Architectural survey. Internal report.

Uytterhoeven, I. 2014b. Koroneia 2013 – Final architectural survey. Internal report.

Valamoti, S. M. and F. Bittman (eds.) 2015. *Proceedings of the 16th Conference of the International Work Group for Palaeoethnobotany, 16-22 June 2013, Vegetation History and Archaeobotany* 24 (1). Berlin: Springer.

Vanegas, C. A., D. G. Aliaga, P. Wonka, P. Müller, P. Waddell and B. Watson 2010. Modelling the Appearance and Behaviour of Urban Spaces. *Computer Graphics Forum* 29 (1): 25-42.

Van Maren, G. 2014. CityEngine 2014.1 released! Blog ArcGIS resources, viewed 02 March 2018, <http://blogs.esri.com/esri/arcgis/2014/09/15/41619/>.

Van Nijf, O. 2001. Local Heroes: Athletics, Festivals and Elite Self-fashioning in the Roman East, in S. Goldhill (ed.) *Being Greek Under Rome: Cultural Identity, the Second Sophistic, and the Development of Empire*: 306-34. Cambridge: Cambridge University Press.

Van Zwienen, J. 2008. Koroneia. Topographical Research using DGPS. Unpublished MA dissertation, Faculty of Archaeology, Leiden University.

Van Zwienen, J. and B. Noordervliet 2009. Micro-topographical research using DGPS on Koroneia hill. *Pharos. Journal of the Netherlands Institute in Athens* 15: 33-7.

Van Zwienen, J. and B. Noordervliet 2010. GIS and GPS Fieldwork at Koroneia, Summer Season, August 2008. *Pharos. Journal of the Netherlands Institute in Athens* 16: 45-9.

Verdonck, L. 2013. GPR prospection at Askra and Koroneia (Boeotia). Internal report.

Verhagen, P., S. Polla and I. Frommer 2014. Finding Byzantine junctions with Steiner Trees, in P. Verhagen and S. Polla (eds.) *Computational Approaches to the Study of Movement in Archaeology: Theory, Practice and Interpretation of Factors and Effects of Long Term Landscape Formation and Transformation*: 73-98. Berlin: De Gruyter.

Vermeulen, F. forthcoming. Scanning and Visualization of Roman Adriatic Townscapes. *Archaeologia e Calcolatori* 28.

Veyne, P. 1988. *Did the Greeks Believe in Their Myths? An Essay on the Constitutive Imagination*, trans. P. Wissig. Chicago: The University of Chicago Press.

Villani, P. 2011. Viaggio senza Ritorno. Per uno studio su Paestum e sul Racconto del Turismo Archeologico. *Rivista di Scienze del Turismo* 1: 85-98.

Vitti, M. 2011. *Provincia Macedonia*: Materiali e Tecniche Costruttive in Età Romana, in S. Camporeale, H. Dessales and A. Pizzo (eds.) *Arqueología de la Construcción II. Los Procesos Constructivos en el Mundo Romano: Italia y Provincias Orientales*: 327-36. Mérida: Consejo Superior de Investigaciones Científicas, Instituto de Arqueología de Mérida.

Vitti, P. 2011. Regola ed Eccezione nei Cantieri Romani della *Provincia Acaia*, in S. Camporeale, H. Dessales and A. Pizzo (eds.) *Arqueología de la Construcción II. Los Procesos Constructivos en el Mundo Romano: Italia y Provincias Orientales*: 301-26. Mérida: Consejo Superior de Investigaciones Científicas, Instituto de Arqueología de Mérida.

Vlachopoulos, A. 2008. The Wall Paintings from the Xeste 3 Building at Akrotiri: Towards an Interpretation of the Iconographic Programme, in N.J. Brodie, J. Doole, G. Gavalas and C. Renfrew (eds.) *Horizon: A Colloquium on the Prehistory of the Cyclades*: 451-65. Cambridge: McDonald Institute for Archaeological Research.

Von Schwerin, J., H. Richards-Rissetto, F. Remondino, G. Agugiaro and G. Girardi 2013. The MayaArch3D project: A 3D WebGIS for Analyzing Ancient Architecture and Landscapes. *Literary & Linguist Computing* 28 (4): 736-53.

Von Schwerin, J., H. Richards-Rissetto, F. Remondino, M.G. Spera, M. Auer, N. Billen, L. Loos, L. Stelson and M. Reindel 2016. Airborne LiDAR Acquisition, Post-processing and Accuracy-checking for a 3D WebGIS of Copan, Honduras. *Journal of Archaeological Science: Reports* 5: 85–104.

Vote, E.L., D. Acevedo, D. Laidlaw and M. S. Joukowsky 2000. ARCHAVE: A Virtual Environment for Archaeological Research, in Z. Stančič and T. Veljanovski (eds.) *Computing Archaeology for Understanding the Past. Proceedings of the 28th Computer Applications and Quantitative Methods in Archaeology Conference (CAA 2000), Ljubljana, Slovenia, April 2000*: 313-6. Oxford: Archaeopress.

Voutsaki, S. and S. M. Valamoti 2013. *Diet, Economy and Society in the Ancient Greek World: Towards a Better Integration of Archaeology and Science. Pharos Supplement* 1. Leuven: Peeters.

Wace, A. J. B. 1921. Archaeology in Greece, 1919 – 1921. *Journal of Hellenic Studies* 41 (2): 260-76.

Waelkens, M., H. Vanhaverbeke, F. Martens, P. Talloen, J. Poblome, N. Kellens, T. Putzeys, P. Degryse, T. van Thuyne and W. van Neer 2006. The Late Antique to Early Byzantine City in Southwest Anatolia. Sagalassos and its Territory: A Case Study, in J.-U. Krause and C. Witschel (eds.) *Die Stadt in der Spätantike: Niedergang oder Wandel? Akten des Internationalen Kolloquiums, München, 30-31 May 2003*: 199-255. Stuttgart: Steiner.

Wallace-Hadrill, A. 1994. *Houses and society in Pompeii and Herculaneum*. Princeton: Princeton University Press.

Ward Larson, G. and R. Shakespeare 1998. *Rendering with Radiance: The Art and Science of Lighting Visualization*. San Francisco: Morgan Kauffman.

Warin, I. 2011. Le Comte de Caylus et l'érudition antiquaire, in Ch. Prigent and F. Journot (eds.) *Actes de la Journée d'étude organisée le 14 janvier 2011, Histoire de l'archéologie et de l'histoire de l'art des mondes antiques et médiévaux*, viewed 02 March 2018, <http://hicsa.univ-paris1.fr/documents/pdf/MondeRomainMedieval/I%20Warin%20texte.pdf>.

Warner Slane, K. 2008. The End of the Sanctuary of Demeter and Kore at Corinth. *Hesperia* 77: 465-96.

Warwick, R.G. 2016. Viget Certe Viget Adhuc: The Invention of the Eternal City in Flavio Biondo's Roma Instaurata. Senior Projects Spring 2016, viewed 02 March 2018 <http://digitalcommons.bard.edu/senproj_s2016/168>.
Watson, S. and E. Waterton 2010. Reading the Visual: Representation and Narrative in the Construction of Heritage. *Material Culture Review* 71 (Spring 2010) / *Revue de la culture matérielle* 71: 84-97.
Weiss, R. 1969. *The Renaissance Discovery of Classical Antiquities*. Oxford: Basil Blackwell.
Weissenberg, J., H. Riemenschneider, M. Prasad and L. van Gool 2013. Is There a Procedural Logic to Architecture?. *Proceedings of the 26th IEEE Computer Society Conference on Computer Vision and Pattern Recognition - CVPR 2013, 23-28 June 2013, Portland, Oregon, USA*: 185-92.
Weissenberg, J. 2014. Inverse Procedural Modelling and Applications. Unpublished PhD dissertation, ETH Zurich.
Westgate, R. 2007. House and Society in Classical and Hellenistic Crete: A Case Study in Regional Variation. *American Journal of Archaeology* 111 (3): 423-57.
Westgate, R. 2010. Interior Decoration in Hellenistic Houses: Context, Function and Meaning, in S. Ladstätter and V. Scheibelreiter (eds.) *Städtisches Wohnen im Östlichen Mittelmeerraum 4. Jh. v. Chr.-1. Jh. n. Chr. Akten des Internationalen Kolloquiums vom 24.-27. Oktober 2007 an der Österreichischen Akademie der Wissenschaften*: 497-528. Vienna: VÖAW.
Westgate, R. 2015. Space and Social Complexity in Greece from the Early Iron Age to the Classical Period. *Hesperia* 84: 47-95.
Wheler, G. and J. Spon 1689. *A Journey into Greece*. London.
Whitelaw, T., M. Bredaki and A. Vasilakis 2006-7. The Knossos Urban Landscape Project. *Archaeology International* 10: 28-31.
Whitley, J. 2001. *The Archaeology of Ancient Greece*. Cambridge: Cambridge University Press.
Wiegand, T. and H. Schrader 1904. *Priene: Ergebnisse der Ausgrabungen und Untersuchungen in den Jahren 1895-1898*. Berlin: G. Reimer.
Wilkinson, K. 2010, Geoarchaeological fieldwork carried out for the Ancient Cities of Boeotia Project. *Pharos. Journal of the Netherlands Institute in Athens* 16: 50-3.
Williams, H. W. 1829. *Select Views in Greece with Classical Illustrations (vol. 2)*. London: Longman, Rees, Orme, Brown and Green.
Winter, F. E. 1971. *Greek Fortifications*. Toronto: University of Toronto Press.
Winter, F. E. 2006. *Studies in Hellenistic Architecture*. Toronto: University of Toronto Press.
Wittur, J. 2013. *Computer-Generated 3D-Visualisations in Archaeology. Between added value and deception*. BAR International Series 2463. Oxford: Archaeopress.
Wood, C. 1999. *Victorian Painting*. London: Weidenfeld.
Woodward, A. M. 1924. Archaeology in Greece, 1922-24. *The Journal of Hellenic Studies* 44 (2): 254-80.
Woodward, C. 2001. *In Ruins*. London: Chatto and Windus.
Wyke, M. 1997. *Projecting the Past. Ancient Rome, Cinema and History*. New York: Routledge.
Wycherley, R. E. 1945. Priene and Modern Town Planning. *Greece and Rome* 14 (40): 12-6.
Zanini, E., S. Costa, E. Giorgi and E. Triolo 2009. Indagini Archeologiche nell'Area del Quartiere Bizantino del Pythion di Gortyna: Quinta Relazione Preliminare (campagne 2007-2010). *ASAtene* LXXXVII, Serie III, 9 Tomo II: 1099-129.
Zanker, P. 1988. *The Power of Images in the Age of Augustus*. Ann Arbor: The University of Michigan Press.
Zarmakoupi, M. 2013. The Quartier du Stade on Late Hellenistic Delos: A Case Study of Rapid Urbanization (fieldwork seasons 2009-2010). *ISAW Papers* 6, viewed 02 March 2013, <http://dlib.nyu.edu/awdl/isaw/isaw-papers/6/>.
Zarmakoupi, M. 2014. Die Hafenstadt Delos, in S. Ladstätter, F. Pirson and T. Schmidts (eds.) *Häfen und Hafenstädte im Östlichen Mittelmeerraum von der Antike bis in Byzantinische Zeit. Neue Entdeckungen und Aktuelle Forschungsansätze*, BYZAS 19: 553-70. Istanbul.
Zerner, H. 1965. Observations on Dupérac and the Disegni de le Ruine di Roma e Come Anticamente Erono. *The Art Bulletin* 47 (4): 507-12.

Zweig, J. 2013. Procedural Architectural Facade Modelling, viewed 02 March 2018, <https://cs.brown.edu/research/pubs/theses/ugrad/2013/zweig.pdf>.
Zubrow, E.B.W. 2006. Digital Archaeology. A historical context, in T. L. Evans and P. Daly (eds.) *Digital Archaeology: Bridging Method and Theory*: 10-31. London and New York: Routledge.

Online resources

Doerr, M. 2012, New Developments of CIDOC-CRM. Paper presented at the 'CIDOC-CRM seminar' (Istituto Centrale per il Catalogo Unico delle Biblioteche Italiane, Rome, 14 Sept. 2012), viewed 02 March 2018, <http://www.otebac.it/index.php?it/22/archivio-eventi/229/roma-seminario-cidoc-crm>.
ESRI 2008. The Multipatch Geometry Type. An Esri White Paper. December 2008, viewed 02 March 2018, <https://www.esri.com/library/whitepapers/pdfs/multipatch-geometry-type.pdf>.
ESRI 2014. 3D Urban Mapping: From Pretty Pictures to 3D GIS. Esri Whitepaper. December 2014, viewed 02 March 2018, <https://www.esri.com/library/whitepapers/pdfs/3d-urban-mapping.pdf>.
Mandarano, N. 2015. Alla prova dei Google Glass e degli Epson Moverio ai Mercati di Traiano, viewed 02 March 2018, <https://nicolettemandarano.wordpress.com/2015/11/06/alla-prova-dei-google-glass-e-degli-epson-moverio-ai-mercati-di-traiano/>.
Pierce, D. 2015. The Future of Virtual Reality inside your Smartphone. *Wired* 3, viewed 02 March 2018, <http://www.wired.com/2015/03/future-virtual-reality-inside-smartphone/>.
Turi, J. 2014. The Sight and Scents of the Sensorama Simulator, viewed 02 March 2018, <http://www.engadget.com/2014/02/16/morton-heiligs-sensorama-simulator/>.

Literary sources

Alcaeus, edited and translated by D. A. Campbell, in *Greek Lyric, Volume I: Sappho and Alcaeus*, Loeb Classical Library 142. Cambridge, MA: Harvard University Press; London: William Heinemann Ltd. 1982.
Aristotle, *Aristotle in 23 Volumes*, vol. 21 (*Politics*), translated by H. Rackham. Cambridge, MA: Harvard University Press; London: William Heinemann Ltd. 1944.
Arrian, *Anabasis*, edited by A.G. Roos. Leipzig: in aedibus B. G. Teubneri, 1907.
Demosthenes, with an English translation by J. H. Vince. Cambridge, MA: Harvard University Press; London: William Heinemann Ltd. 1930.
Diodorus Siculus, translated by C. H. Oldfather. Cambridge, MA: Harvard University Press; London: William Heinemann, Ltd., 1933–1967.
Homer, *The Iliad*, with an English Translation by A.T. Murray in two volumes. Cambridge, MA: Harvard University Press, 1924.
Livy, *History of Rome,* translated by E. T. Sage. Cambridge, MA: Harvard University Press; London: William Heinemann, Ltd., 1935-8.
Pausanias, with an Italian comment and translation by M. Moggi and M. Osanna (*Pausania. Guida della Grecia. Libro IX. La Beozia*). Milano: Mondadori, 2010.
Philo, *De Opificio Mundi* I, translated by F. H. Colson and G. H. Whitaker, The Loeb Classical Library. Cambridge, MA: Harvard University Press; London: William Heinemann, Ltd, 1981 [1929].
Philostratus, *Lives of the Sophists*, with an English translation by W. Cave Wright. London: William Heinemann; New York: G.P. Putnam's Sons, 1922.
Pindar, *Odes*, translated by D. Arnson Svarlien, 1990, available at Perseus Digital Library.
Plutarch, *Cimon*, in Plutarch's *Lives*, with an English translation by B. Perrin. Cambridge, MA: Harvard University Press; London: William Heinemann Ltd., 1914.
Procopius, *Bell. Goth.*, Procopius in seven volumes with and English translation by H. B. Dewing, vol. v, History of the Wars, books VII (continued) and VIII. London: William Heinemann; Cambridge, MA: Harvard University Press, 1962 [1928].
Strabo, *Geography*, translated by H.C. Hamilton and M.A. Falconer. London: George Bell & Sons, 1903.
Suidae Lexicon Græce & Latine, trans. by Aemilius Portus and edited by Ludolf Küster. Cambridge, 1705.

Thucydides, *The History of the Peloponnesian War*, translated by R. Crawley. London: J. M. Dent & Sons, 1950.

Vitruvius, *De Architectura. The Ten Books on Architecture*, translated by M. Hicky Morgan. Cambridge: Harvard University Press, London: Humphrey Milford/ Oxford University Press, 1914.

Xenophon, *Constitution of the Lacedaimonians*, edited by E. C. Marchant, G. W. Bowersock. Cambridge, MA: Harvard University Press; London: William Heinemann, Ltd., 1925.

Xenophon, *Hellenica*, translated by C. L. Brownson and included in *The works of Xenophon I.* Cambridge, MA: Harvard University Press; London: William Heinemann, Ltd., 1918.